J2EE
Professional Projects

J2EE
Professional Projects

Shadab Siddiqui
Pallavi Jain

WITH

NIIT

Premier
Press

Publisher:
Stacy L. Hiquet

Marketing Manager:
Heather Buzzingham

Managing Editor:
Sandy Doell

Editorial Assistant:
Margaret Bauer

**Book Production
Services:** Argosy

Cover Design:
Mike Tanamachi

Premier
P
Press

Important: Premier Press cannot provide software support. Please contact the appropriate software manufacturer's technical support line or Web site for assistance.

Premier Press and the author have attempted throughout this book to distinguish proprietary trademarks from descriptive terms by following the capitalization style used by the manufacturer.

Information contained in this book has been obtained by Premier Press from sources believed to be reliable. However, because of the possibility of human or mechanical error by our sources, Premier Press, or others, the Publisher does not guarantee the accuracy, adequacy, or completeness of any information and is not responsible for any errors or omissions or the results obtained from use of such information. Readers should be particularly aware of the fact that the Internet is an ever-changing entity. Some facts may have changed since this book went to press.

ISBN: 1-931841-22-5

Library of Congress Catalog Card Number: 2001092619

Printed in the United States of America

02 03 04 05 06 RI 10 9 8 7 6 5 4 3 2 1

About NIIT

NIIT is a global IT solutions corporation with a presence in 38 countries. With its unique business model and technology-creation capabilities, NIIT delivers software and learning solutions to more than 1,000 clients across the world.

The success of NIIT's training solutions lies in its unique approach to education. NIIT's Knowledge Solutions Business conceives, researches, and develops all of its course material. A rigorous instructional design methodology is followed to create engaging and compelling course content.

NIIT trains over 200,000 executives and learners each year in information technology areas using stand-up training, video-aided instruction, computer-based training (CBT), and Internet-based training (IBT). NIIT has been featured in the *Guinness Book of World Records* for the largest number of learners trained in one year!

NIIT has developed over 10,000 hours of instructor-led training (ILT) and over 3,000 hours of Internet-based training and computer-based training. IDC ranked NIIT among the Top 15 IT training providers globally for the year 2000. Through the innovative use of training methods and its commitment to research and development, NIIT has been in the forefront of computer education and training for the past 20 years.

Quality has been the prime focus at NIIT. Most of the processes are ISO-9001 certified. It was the 12th company in the world to be assessed at Level 5 of SEI-CMM. NIIT's Content (Learning Material) Development facility is the first in the world to be assessed at this highest maturity level. NIIT has strategic partnerships with companies such as Computer Associates, IBM, Microsoft, Oracle, and Sun Microsystems.

About the Authors

Shadab Siddiqui is a Sun Certified Java Programmer for Platform 2 (SCJP). He has worked for two years at Knowledge Solutions Division (KSB), NIIT Ltd., as a development executive. During his tenure at NIIT, Shadab has developed learning materials for network administrators and programmers on a wide range of technologies such as Windows 2000, SQL, JSP, and Office XP. These materials were developed on different media such as CBTs, WBTs, and books for various NIIT clients such as Microsoft, netvarsity.com, and Course Technologies, USA.

Pallavi Jain is a Microsoft Certified Software Engineer (MCSE). She is working as a consultant with NIIT Ltd. and has been with the Knowledge Solutions Business (KSB) division of NIIT for the past five years. In the KSB division, Pallavi has worked on various platforms and software packages. Her work involves design, development, testing, reviewing, and implementation of instructor-led training courses. Her primary responsibilities include training development executives, project management, instructional review, technical review, and ensuring ISO compliance.

Contents at a Glance

Contents

Chapter 18 Creating the Welcome Page. 353

Chapter 19 Creating a Registration Page
for Account Holders. 381

Introduction

Goal of This Book

This book provides a hands-on approach to learning Java 2 Platform Enterprise Edition (J2EE). It is aimed at readers who have a basic knowledge of programming.

The book starts with a few overview chapters that cover the key concepts of Java and J2EE. The concepts covered in these chapters include:

◆ Programming in Java

◆ Java Foundation Classes

◆ Applets

◆ Layouts and Event Handling

◆ Exceptional Handling

◆ Threading

◆ Network Programming

◆ RMI and CORBA

◆ Enterprise JavaBeans (EJB)

◆ J2EE

◆ XML

◆ EJB Types: Session Beans and Entity Beans

These chapters act as an information store for programmers who need to brush up their Java knowledge. Next, a major portion of the book revolves around professional projects. These projects enable programmers to learn about various tasks by following a simple-to-complex approach. Each project covers a specific subject area and guides readers by using real-world scenarios. The projects range from a simple project using Java, to complex projects using J2EE. The projects make use of the latest technologies, such as Java Beans, JDBC, Servlets, JSP, and EJB. These projects help programmers accomplish their goals by understanding the practical and real-life application of J2EE. These projects also give programmers an understanding of how to create Web sites.

In addition to the overview chapters and professional projects, the book has a section called a "Beyond the Lab" and an Appendix. The "Beyond the Lab" section serves as both a summary of what the reader has learned and a road map for where the reader can go to expand on this knowledge. This section also covers the future direction of the programming language. The Appendix offers a quick reference for topics related to Java.

How to Use This Book

This book has been organized to facilitate a better grasp of the content. The various conventions used in the book include the following:

- *Analysis.* The book incorporates an analysis of code, explaining what it did and why, line-by-line.
- *Tips.* Tips have been used to provide special advice or unusual shortcuts with the product.
- *Notes.* Notes give additional information that may be of interest to the reader, but which is not essential to performing the task at hand.
- *Cautions.* Cautions are used to warn users of possible disastrous results if they perform a task incorrectly.
- *New Term Definitions.* All new terms have been italicized and then defined as a part of the text.

PART

I

**Introduction to Java
Programming**

Chapter 1

**Programming in
Java**

In this chapter, you will learn about the Java architecture, features of Java, and the procedure for creating an application in Java. You will also learn to use Swing API components in Java applications.

An Introduction to Java

To meet the frequently changing requirements of Information Technology, various languages ranging from BASIC to C and C++ have been developed. An ideal language should be adaptable to the constantly changing environment and programming skills. The syntax and power of a language play a major role in its acceptability. Due to its ability to run on various platforms, Java has quickly gained popularity among programmers. Modeled on C++, Java is popular for its "Write Once, Run Everywhere" feature. This feature enables a Java program written on a platform to be executed on any other platform. Java inherits properties from both C and C++. It takes its syntax from the C language and has many object-oriented features of C++.

Now, I'll present a look at the Java architecture.

Java Architecture

The Java architecture consists of the following four components:

◆ Java programming language
◆ Java class file
◆ Java Application Programming Interface (Java API)
◆ Java Virtual Machine (JVM)

When you write, compile, and execute a Java program, all the above components are used. A program is developed using the Java programming language. When you compile the program, a Java class file is created. The JVM executes the class file. During execution of the class file, the methods available in Java API are used to make function calls. The process of Java program execution is depicted in Figure 1-1.

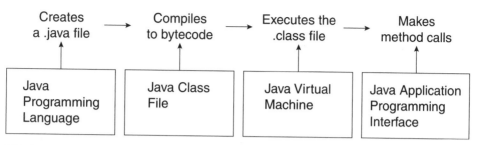

FIGURE 1-1 *The Java program execution process*

The combination of the JVM and Java API forms a platform called *Java Runtime System* or *Java platform*. The Java platform executes Java programs. Now, I'll discuss the advantages of Java.

Advantages of Java

Java is easy to learn, portable, object-oriented, and platform-independent. It can also handle memory management and exceptions. You can learn Java easily because the syntax of the Java language is similar to that of C and C++. Therefore, switching from C or C++ to Java is easy.

Java applications are portable. During compilation, the Java code is converted to an intermediate language called bytecode. The bytecode can be executed on any platform having a JVM. Therefore, only JVM needs to be implemented to run Java applications. The Java architecture provides security to applications as well as the runtime environment.

Next, you'll learn how to write a program in Java.

Programming in Java

You can use Java to create two types of programs:

- ◆ Applications
- ◆ Applets

An *application* is a program that you can execute at the command prompt. Stand-alone applications can either be window-based applications or console applications.

Window-based applications have a graphical user interface (GUI). Such applications use features supported by platforms like Microsoft Windows, Macintosh, Motif, and OS/2.

Console applications are character-based applications lacking a GUI. A stand-alone application uses the resources of a single computer while a network application uses the resources available over a network. Distributed applications can access objects that execute across many computers over a network.

Applications can read and write to the files on a local computer. Applications can also establish network connections, access resources across a network, and launch applications over a network. A stand-alone application is stored on the hard disk of a computer. When you execute the application, it is retrieved from the hard disk into the internal memory and executed.

Applets are Java programs that execute within a Web page. Therefore, unlike applications, applets require a Java-enabled browser like Microsoft Internet Explorer 4.0 or later version. An applet is loaded and executed when a user loads a Web page, which contains the applet, through a Web browser.

You'll learn more about applets in Chapter 2, "Creating Applets."

Now it's time to create and run a simple Java program.

Writing a Simple Java Program

You can use Notepad or any other text editor to write Java source files. These source files contain Java programs.

You'll start with the familiar "Hello World!" program. The code to write the "Hello World!" program is given in Listing 1-1.

Listing 1-1 Hello.java

```
class Hello
{
        public static void main(String args[])
        {
                     System.out.println("Hello World!");
        }
}
```

In the preceding code, the `System.out.println()` method is used to print the arguments, which are passed to it, on the standard output. The `main()` method is the entry point of an application and starts the primary thread of the application. The JVM starts an application by running the `main()` method.

After writing the Java code, you need to save the files with a `.java` extension. To run the above code, you need to save the file as `Hello.java`. It is a requirement of the Java compiler that the file containing a program should be saved as the class name present in the file. For example, if a file contains the source code for the `Animal` class, the file should be saved as `Animal.Java`. Notice that all the code is written within a class definition.

Before you can compile and run the preceding program, you need to set some system variables for the Java runtime environment. Now, take a look at the procedures for setting these variables.

Setting System Variables

You need to set the `PATH` and `CLASSPATH` variables in order to run Java applications on your computer.

Setting the *PATH* Variable

The `PATH` variable is used to identify the location where the Java Development Kit (JDK) is installed. If you have installed JDK version 1.3 in the root of drive C, you'll need to set the environment variable `PATH` to `C:\jdk1.3\bin`. To set the path:

1. Open the Control Panel.
2. Double-click the System icon in the Control Panel dialog box.
3. In the System Properties dialog box, click the Advanced tab.
4. In the Advanced page, click the Environment Variables button.
5. In the Environment Variables dialog box, modify the `PATH` variable to include the `C:\jdk1.3\bin` directory. The bin directory contains all the executables of JDK. Do not remove the previously existing directories in the `PATH`. Directories in the `PATH` variable are separated using semicolons.
6. Save the settings.

You must insert ";." (a semicolon and a period) at the end of the PATH variable. The semicolon is the separator between the entries in the PATH directory and the period is inserted to indicate the current directory. After you have set the PATH variable, you can compile and run Java programs. However, to run the program, you need to be in the same directory that contains the .class file. Sometimes, you may need to run the .class file from a directory different from the directory that contains the class file. To achieve this, you need to set the CLASSPATH variable. Now, take a look at setting the CLASSPATH variable.

Setting the *CLASSPATH* Variable

You can set the CLASSPATH variable to the directory where the .class file is stored. The CLASSPATH variable can be set by using the Control Panel or by using the -classpath option while calling SDK tools such as javac.

CLASSPATH defines the path where the JVM needs to search for class files during execution. For example, say you are working in the root of drive C and you need to run a class file in the C:\Examples directory. To do this, you need to set the CLASSPATH variable to the C:\Examples directory. To set CLASSPATH by using the Control Panel, you need to set the CLASSPATH variable as C:\Examples in the Environment Variables dialog box.

You must insert ";." (a semicolon and a period) at the end of the CLASSPATH variable. The semicolon is the separator between the entries in the CLASSPATH directory and the period is inserted to indicate the current directory. If you do not insert a period at the end, the current directory will not be searched for the .class file during execution. For example, consider that you have set CLASSPATH to C:\Examples without using a period to represent the current directory and you are working in the directory C:\Chapter1. You have compiled the MyFile.java file in the current directory. Therefore, the C:\Chapter1 directory contains both the MyFile.java and MyFile.class files. Now, if you execute the java MyFile command, you will get an error message saying the .class is not found. This happens because the JVM looks for the MyFile.class in the directory C:\Examples.

After setting the system variables, you can compile and run Java programs from any directory.

Compiling and Running a Java Program

You need to compile a program before you can run it. To compile the Java program, type the following command at the command prompt:

```
C:>javac Hello.java
```

The Java compiler, Javac, always searches the current directory for the .java file. When you execute the above command, the Java compiler creates the Hello.class file that contains the bytecode for the above program. Now, to run the program and view the output, you need to use the Java interpreter and pass the class name as the argument. You can execute the program by typing the following command at the command prompt:

```
C:>java Hello
```

 CAUTION

Java is a case-sensitive language. Therefore, you need to be careful while writing Java programs and executing commands at the command prompt. Your code will not run if the casing of the file name is incorrect.

The output of the above code is displayed in Figure 1-2.

FIGURE 1-2 *The figure displays the output of the* Hello *program.*

You've learned to write a simple program in Java. Next, take a look at the data types used in Java.

Data Types

Java provides various data types to work with. The primitive data types of Java are byte, short, int, long, char, float, double, and boolean. These primitive data types can be grouped into four categories. The categories and the data types in each category are listed in Table 1-1.

Table 1-1 Categories of Data Types

Category	Data Types
Integers	byte, short, int, long
Floating-point	float, double
Characters	char
Boolean	boolean

The next section discusses arrays in Java.

Arrays

Arrays are a collection of similar types of variables, objects, or other arrays. The elements in an array are referred to by the same name, the array name, and they can be accessed using indexes.

In C++, an array is a collection of elements. In Java, arrays are real objects because you can allocate memory to an array by using the new operator. In addition, in Java, array accesses are checked to ensure that the indexes are within the range of the array.

You can create an array by:

1. Declaring the array
2. Allocating memory to the array
3. Initializing the array

Consider the following example:

```
int[] var;
var = new int[25];
```

In the previous example, the array var is declared of the type int. Next, an array of 25 elements is created and is referenced by the name var.

You can identify the length of an array by applying the length method to the array.

In the next section, you'll learn about constructs in Java. Java uses constructs to execute statements based on some conditions.

Constructs

Java supports the if…else, while, do…while, and switch constructs. The syntax and use of most constructs are similar to those in C++. The if…else, while, and do…while constructs take expressions that result in a true or false value. In Java, a construct may test more than one expression by using the && operator. If the first expression returns false, the second expression is not evaluated.

You can use the switch construct in Java to execute different code based on the value of an expression. The syntax of the switch construct is similar to that of the switch statement in C++.

You have learned about the fundamentals of data types and constructs you can use in Java programs. You will now learn about the object-oriented features of Java.

Inheritance

Inheritance is one of the key elements of object-oriented programming languages. In Java, a class can be derived from another class. The derived class acquires all features of the base class. In addition, the derived class can add some of its own features. All classes in Java are derived from the Object class. The Object class is the parent class of all classes in Java. Therefore, every class will inherit features of the Object class. To inherit from a class, you use the extends keyword. For example, if you want to derive the TextBook class from the Book class, this is how you will do it:

```
class Textbook extends Book
            {
              //statements
            }
```

Java does not support multiple inheritance. This means that a class in Java cannot inherit from more than one class at a time.

At times, you may need to derive from two or more classes. In such a situation, you can implement an interface. You will learn more about interfaces later in this chapter.

Polymorphism

Polymorphism is implemented by methods in Java in two ways:

◆ Overloading

◆ Overriding

The following sections cover each of these.

Overloading

Using the same method names but with different signatures is known as method *overloading*. Overloaded methods may exist in the same class, or a method in a base class can be overloaded in the subclass. A method is overloaded when another method exists with the same name but with a different signature. A method is said to be overloaded in following scenarios:

◆ The overloading method has the same number of arguments as that of the overloaded method but the sequence and types of arguments vary. For example, the following methods are overloaded:

```
void Method1(int a, long b)
void Method1(String a, long b)
```

◆ The overloading method has a different number of arguments as that of the overloaded method. For example, the following methods are over-loaded:

```
void Method1(int a, long b)
void Method1(int a, long b, long c)
```

Two methods having similar number and types of arguments cannot be overloaded on the basis that they have different return types.

Overriding

To *override* a method, you need to define a method with the same name, identical arguments, and the same return type. The signatures of overridden and overriding methods are the same. As a result, both methods cannot exist in the same class. A method can be overridden only in the subclass of the class containing the overridden method.

You've learned about features, data types, and constructs in Java. Now, I'll discuss packages in Java.

Packages

You use packages to organize related classes. Packages are a collection of classes, and can be used to compartmentalize classes. For example, if you are working on a financial application, you can create an Employee package that will store classes responsible for processing Employee data. Packages also help define accessibility of classes. You can define classes within a package, which will be inaccessible to the classes outside the package. Similarly, you can define classes for interactivity within a package. Packages also avoid class name collisions. You can write programs to access from two different packages the classes that have same name. Packages ensure that two classes in different packages will have a different identity even if their names are same.

Now, take a look at creating a package.

Creating a Package

You can create a package by using the package statement as the first statement in a Java source file. Consider the following example for creating a package:

```
package Chapter1; //package declaration
class Pack
{
public static void main(String args[])
            {
```

```
int abc[];
abc = new int[25];
System.out.println("Length of the array is "+ abc.length);
}
}
```

In the above program, a package called Chapter1 is declared. The package will contain the Pack class. If you want to add more classes to the package Chapter1, you need to simply place the package statement as the first statement in the source file. Remember that the package statement must always be the first statement in a source file. You can compile the above code by using the javac tool in a way similar to the previous examples. However, to run the above code, you need to follow a different approach. Suppose the Pack.class file exists in the folder C:\Examples\Chapter1. You'll need to type the following command at the command prompt:

```
C:\Examples>java Chapter1.Pack
```

CAUTION

To execute the above command, the Pack.class file should exist in the C:\Examples\Chapter1 folder and the CLASSPATH variable should be set to C:\Examples.

Notice that the Java command is executed from the parent directory of the directory that contains the Pack.class file. This is because the package hierarchy reflects the file hierarchy in the Java development system. In the example above, the class Pack.class must be present in a directory called Chapter1.

You can employ Java packages in a program by using the import statement. This is somewhat similar to the C++ include statement. One difference is that a package contains only classes while a header file in C++ can contain independent methods. Another difference is that packages have a hierarchical structure similar to the directory structure on your computer. An example of the import statement is given as follows:

```
package Chapter1; //package declaration
import java.awt.button; //Import single class from a package
```

```
import java.util.*; //Import all the classes from a package
class Length
{
                public static void main(String args[]){
                - - - - - - -// Statements
                }
}
```

In the above example, two import statements are being used. The `import` `java.awt.button` statement will import only one class, button, from the `java.awt` package. The other import statement, `import java.util.*`, will import all the classes in the `java.util` package.

The import statement should follow the package statement in a source file. In case of no package statement, the import statements, if any, will be the first statements in the source file.

There are various packages defined by Java SDK. Some of the packages are:

- `java.lang`
- `java.util`
- `java.io`
- `java.awt`

You'll learn more about each of these classes later in this book.

When you place classes in packages, packages define a boundary for those classes. Modifiers determine the accessibility of classes and data external to and within packages. Modifiers are discussed in the next section.

Modifiers

Modifiers are Java keywords that determine accessibility and other related functionality of code, data, and classes. Modifiers are key for the implementation of encapsulation in Java. Some of the modifiers defined in Java are:

- `public`
- `private`
- `protected`

◆ final

◆ abstract

◆ static

The public, private, and protected modifiers can be categorized as *access modifiers*. When applied to a class, a method, or data, these access modifiers determine the accessibility within and outside a class and a package. Only one access modifier can be applied to a class, a method, or data.

When an access modifier is not explicitly assigned to a feature, the feature is said to have a default access modifier. The default access modifier does not have any standardized name. I'll consider the default access modifier as default.

Now, I'll discuss each of these modifiers.

The *public* Modifier

The public modifier in Java is assigned to variables that are similar to the global variables in C++. Any class, method, or variable declared as public is accessible to all Java classes irrespective of the package.

The *private* Modifier

The private modifier is the most restrictive of all the modifiers in Java. If you declare any feature as private, you have restricted its access outside the class. Anything declared as private can only be accessed by members of the same class. Top-level classes cannot be declared as private.

The *protected* Modifier

The protected access modifier can be applied only to variables and methods. When you declare a variable or a method as protected, you ensure that the feature is available to all the classes in the current package. Additionally, the protected features will be accessible to all the subclasses of the parent class. This access is provided even if the subclass is external to the current package.

A class, a method, or data is said to have a default modifier when you do not explicitly assign any access modifier to it. Classes, methods, and data having the default access modifier are accessible to all the classes in the current package.

NOTE

The default modifier is not an access modifier. I have used default here to indicate the access level that is applied when no access modifier is explicitly specified.

The *final* Modifier

The `final` modifier can be applied to classes, methods, and variables. The `final` features cannot be changed. A `final` class cannot be subclassed. A `final` variable cannot be modified and a `final` method cannot be overridden.

For example, the `java.lang.Math` class is a `final` class. You cannot subclass it. You can access the methods of a `final` class by directly calling the method. For example, you can refer to the `cos()` method defined in the `Math` class as `Math.cos()`.

The *abstract* Modifier

You can apply the `abstract` modifier to classes and methods. You cannot instantiate an `abstract` class. Any class that has an `abstract` method is declared as abstract. To use an `abstract` class, you first need to subclass the `abstract` class and then implement the `abstract` methods declared in the `abstract` class. The syntax to declare an `abstract` method is:

```
abstract <return_type> <method_name>();
```

Notice that the method does not have any body. An `abstract` class can have one or more `abstract` methods. A class is declared as `abstract` in one of the following situations:

- One or more `abstract` methods are present in the class.
- A class inherits an `abstract` class and does not provide implementation for all the classes in the superclass.
- A class implements an interface but does not implement all the methods in the interface.

The *static* Modifier

The `static` modifiers are applied to variables and methods. A `static` method or variable belongs to a class rather than being associated with an individual instance of the class. In the following example, only one x will exist, no matter how many instances of the class Stat_Ex are created.

```
class Stat_Ex
{
static int x;
public static void main(String args[])
            {
            - - - - - - -// Do something here.
            }
}
```

A static method can access only the static features, methods, and variables of its parent class. The static methods do not have this (pointer to the current object). Therefore, such methods cannot access the non-static variables and methods of its parent class.

At times, you may need to design a class and leave the implementation of the methods in it to the subclasses. In such a situation, you can use interfaces. The next section discusses interfaces.

Interfaces

Interfaces are similar to classes but interfaces cannot be instantiated. In addition, the methods in interfaces are declared without any body. Method implementation is deferred to the subclasses that derive from interface. Therefore, interfaces determine the methods to be defined by the subclass but how the method is defined depends on the requirements of each subclass. This is a classic example of polymorphism where a method in an interface will exist in several forms in various subclasses of the interface. The syntax to declare an interface is given here:

```
<modifier> interface <interface_name>
{
<return_type> method1();
<return_type> method2();
<return_type> method3();
}
```

Here, <modifier> can be either public or default. You can also declare variables in an interface. However, the variables can either be final or static. Additionally, the variables should be initialized with a constant value.

Now, you'll learn to implement interfaces. The syntax for a class implementing interfaces is given as follows:

```
<modifier> class <name> [extends <class>] [implements <interface1>, <interface2>]
{
            //class body
}
```

Here, notice that a class can extend from maximum one class while it can implement more than one interface at a time. Another advantage of interfaces is that they provide functionality similar to multiple inheritance in C++.

The methods of an interface should be declared `public` in a class. This requirement is because an interface is either declared as `public` or no explicit access modifier is specified. All methods are implicitly `public` if an interface is `public`. When you implement an interface, you're not sure whether the interface has been declared `public`. The rule of overriding prevents the overriding method from being more `private` than the overridden method, therefore, you should declare the implemented methods as `public`.

You will now learn to create a GUI application by using Java Foundation Classes (JFC).

Java Foundation Classes

So far, you've seen examples for console inputs and outputs. Although Java also contains classes for creating GUI applications, basic aspects of the Java programming language are better understood using console inputs and outputs.

GUI applications provide a graphical interface to users. This interactivity with the users is carried out using GUI components, such as windows, dialog boxes, buttons, and text boxes. These components facilitate user interaction. In addition, a GUI application developer needs to provide functionality to each of these components based on the requirements of the applications. For example, when a user selects an option in a confirmation dialog box, the application should have the functionality to identify the user input and proceed accordingly.

Users find it easier to work with GUI applications. Consequently, the demand for GUI applications has increased. Developers of the Java platform responded to this popular demand by providing a powerful and flexible support for creating GUIs for applications in JDK 1.2.

Starting from JDK 1.2, the Java platform contains APIs to create sophisticated GUI applications. This set of APIs is put under a common package called Java Foundation Classes (JFC). JFC provides you with classes that you can easily use to create components of a GUI application.

JFC consists of the following five APIs:

- Abstract Window Toolkit (AWT)
- Swing
- Java2D
- Accessibility
- Drag-and-Drop

Now, you'll learn about each of these APIs in detail.

The Abstract Window Toolkit (AWT)

The AWT was developed with JDK 1.0. AWT provides a foundation for JFC. AWT is the basis for GUI applications in Java because it supports colors, fonts, events, listeners, layout managers, etc. You can create components by using Swing components. However, you'll need to use layout managers and event listeners defined in AWT. Therefore, AWT is the core of GUI programming.

The Swing API

Swing is a set of components known for being lightweight and pluggable. You'll learn more about Swing API in the section, "Working with Swing API Classes."

The Java2D API

The Java2D API, which is included in JDK 1.2, provides you with a variety of painting styles and features for designing complex shapes and images. Java2D has emerged as an enhancement to the graphics supported by AWT. Java2D was developed to meet the requirement of complex graphics and images due to enhancements in Java applications.

The Accessibility API

The Accessibility API includes assistive technology such as screen readers and screen modifiers. The Accessibility API provides an interface that enables assistive technology to communicate and interact with JFC and AWT components. The Java accessibility APIs are compact, simple, and easy to use.

The Drag-and-Drop API

The Drag-and-Drop API enables you to move data between programs created with the Java programming language. This API provides interoperability between applications developed in various languages.

Now, you'll take a look at the key features of the Swing API classes.

Working with Swing API Classes

The Swing development is based on the Model-View-Controller (MVC) architecture. The MVC architecture allows Swing components to achieve pluggable look and feel feature. This feature enables Java programs to switch the look and feel of JFC components. Java is a platform-independent language that can run on any platform. As a result, the Java program should be capable of acquiring the look and feel of any platform. Apart from the ability to display the native look and feel of platforms, Swing API also enables you to create customized look and feel.

Another advantage of Swing is that its components are lightweight. Starting with JDK 1.1, the AWT supports lightweight GUI components. A lightweight component does not depend on native system classes or peer classes. The Swing API uses this lightweight GUI framework to create a set of GUI components that are independent of the native GUI system. Swing components do not need native support. Consequently, no extra code is needed to handle peer classes.

 NOTE

There's an exception to the fact that all Swing components are lightweight: Some components are heavyweight. Some components, such as the top-level window, need to be heavyweight with a native peer. These windows will contain other lightweight components. The heavyweight Swing components are JApplet, JDialog, JFrame, and JWindow.

The Swing API consists of more than 250 classes and 75 interfaces. These classes and packages are organized into various packages. Some of the packages of Swing API are listed here:

- `javax.swing`
- `javax.swing.border`
- `javax.swing.event`
- `javax.swing.table`
- `javax.swing.text`
- `javax.swing.text.html`

There are two more packages added in JDK 1.2 that store the look and feel of the Motif and Windows operating system. These packages are:

- `com.sun.java.swing.plaf.motif`
- `com.sun.java.swing.plaf.windows`

Components are the core of the Swing API. Next, you'll take a look at how to use Swing components.

Swing Components

All Swing components are derived from the `JComponent` class. `JComponent` is an abstract class that encapsulates the basic features and operations of Swing components.

The `JComponent` class is derived from the `java.awt.Container` class. The hierarchy of the `JComponent` is given in Figure 1-3.

Now, I'll discuss some of the Swing components.

The JApplet *Class*

The `JApplet` class represents Swing applets. It is a heavyweight component that implements the `RootPaneContainer` interface. `JApplet` is an extension of the applet superclass, `java.applet.Applet`. To use the `JApplet` class, you need to create a class that extends the `JApplet` class.

Consider the following example:

```
public class Applet_Exp extends JApplet{ ... }
```

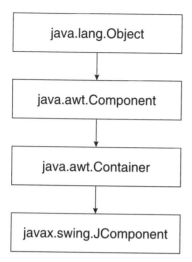

FIGURE 1-3 *Hierarchy of the* JComponent

The JButton *Class*

The JButton class represents Swing buttons. These buttons can contain icons as well as text.

Consider the following example:

```
button1 = new JButton("button label", Icon Path);
```

The JCheckbox *Class*

The JCheckbox class represents check boxes in Swing.

Consider the following example:

```
Check_Box1 = new JCheckBox("Select this check box.");
```

The JComboBox *Class*

The JComboBox class represents a combo box, which is a combination of a drop-down list and a text box. A user can either type text in a text box or select an item from a drop-down list. The JComboBox class is an enhancement over the AWT component called Choice.

Consider the following example:

```
String[] Comp_Parts = {"Monitor", "Mouse", "Keyboard"};
JComboBox Comp_Box = new JComboBox(Comp_Parts);
```

The JDialog *Class*

The JDialog class represents dialog boxes. JDialog is a heavyweight component that implements the RootPaneContainer interface.

Consider the following example:

```
JDialog Dialog = new JDialog(Owner_Frame, "Title");
```

The JFrame *Class*

The JFrame class represents frames where you can add components and menu bars. JFrame is a heavyweight component and it implements the RootPaneContainer interface.

Consider the following example:

```
public class Frame extends JFrame{ ... }
```

The JLabel *Class*

The JLabel class represents a label that can contain text as well as icons.

Consider the following example:

```
JLabel Label = new JLabel("This is a label");
```

The JList *Class*

The JList class represents a list of items in which you can make single or multiple selections. A JList component does not have scroll bars and should be placed in JScrollPane if scroll bars are required.

Consider the following example:

```
String cities[] = {"New York", "San Jose", "Washington"};
JList cList = new JList(cities);
```

The JPanel *Class*

The JPanel class acts as the basic container of other Swing components.

Consider the following example:

```
JPanel panel = new JPanel(new GridLayout(3,3));
```

The JPopupMenu *Class*

The JPopupMenu class represents popup menus.

Consider the following example:

```
JPopupMenu Pop_Menu = new JPopupMenu("Popup Menu");
```

The JRadioButton *Class*

The JRadioButton class represents radio buttons that can either be selected or cleared.

Consider the following example:

```
rButton1 = new JRadioButton("Selected button", true);
```

The JTextArea *Class*

The JTextArea class represents a component for entering and displaying multiple lines of text. A JTextArea component does not have scroll bars and should be placed in ScrollPane if scrollbars are required.

Consider the following example:

```
JTextArea Text_Area = new JTextArea("Initial Text", 6, 30); \\6 rows 30 columns
```

The JTextPane *Class*

The JTextPane class represents graphics editors for text as well as pictures.

Consider the following example:

```
JTextPane Text_Pane = new JTextPane();
```

All the listed components are in the package javax.swing. You'll now look at an example that uses Swing components.

An Example

Take up the familiar "Hello World!" program. The program uses Swing components to display the message. Listing 1-2 contains the code for the "Hello World!" program.

Listing 1-2 HelloWorld.java

```java
import javax.swing.*;
import java.awt.*;
import java.awt.event.*;
public class HelloWorld extends JFrame
{
    public HelloWorld( String titleText )
    {
        super( titleText );
        addWindowListener( new WindowAdapter()
        {
            public void
            windowClosing( WindowEvent e )
            {
                HelloWorld.this.dispose();
                System.exit( 0 );
            }
        });
        JLabel greeting = new JLabel( "Hello World!", JLabel.CENTER );
        getContentPane().add( greeting, BorderLayout.CENTER );
        setSize( 300, 100 );
        setVisible( true );
    }
    public static void main( String[] args )
    {
        new HelloWorld( "Hello World! Sample" );
    }
}
```

The output of the above code is displayed in Figure 1-4.

FIGURE 1-4 *The output of the "Hello World!" program*

This example file (`HelloWorld.java`) is included in the samples folder of this chapter on the Web site that accompanies this book at **www.premierpress-books.com/downloads.asp**.

 NOTE

Frames derive their appearance and behavior from the native operating systems. As a result, the output of the code in Listing 1-1 may vary in different platforms. However, the difference will be minimal. Only the appearance of entities, such as buttons and borders, may change. The functionality will remain the same.

Notice that the class `HelloWorld` is derived from the `JFrame` class. The `JFrame` class represents the Swing frame. A frame acts as a container in programs that use Swing components. Swing frames contain a title and control buttons to minimize, maximize, and close the frame. The `JFrame` class extends the AWT class, `Frame`. The hierarchy of the `JFrame` is displayed in Figure 1-5 on page 28.

Now, take a look at a sample application, `Customer`.

A Sample Program

In this chapter, you've learned the basics of Java and Swing. You'll now look at creating a simple program by using Swing components. In this program, you will create an interface for accepting data from a customer. You will accept information regarding the customer number, name, sex, and age from the user. The code for the program is provided in Listing 1-3 on page 28.

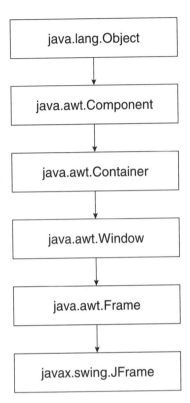

FIGURE 1-5 *Hierarchy of* JFrame

Listing 1-3 Customer.java

```
import javax.swing.*;
import javax.swing.table.*;
import javax.swing.event.*;
import java.awt.*;
import java.awt.event.*;
public class Customer extends JFrame
{
        //Variables of labels
        JLabel    Heading;
        JLabel    labelCustNo;
        JLabel    labelCustName;
        JLabel    labelCustSex;
```

```
JLabel    labelCustAge;
 //Variables for data entry controls
JTextField    textCustNo;
JTextField    textCustName;
JComboBox    comboCustSex;
JTextField    textCustAge;
Customer() {
super("Customer");
Container con;
con = this.getContentPane();
con.setLayout(new FlowLayout());
        labelCustNo = new JLabel("Customer Number");
        labelCustName = new JLabel("Name");
        labelCustSex = new JLabel("Sex");
        labelCustAge = new JLabel("Age");
        //Initializing textfield
        textCustNo = new JTextField(20);
        textCustName = new JTextField(25);
        textCustAge = new JTextField(2);
            String Sex[] = { "Male", "Female"};
            comboCustSex = new JComboBox(Sex);
            //Adding controls for Customer Number
            con.add(labelCustNo);
            con.add(textCustNo);
            //Adding controls for Customer Name
            con.add(labelCustName);
            con.add(textCustName);
            //Adding controls for Customer Sex
            con.add(labelCustSex);
            con.add(comboCustSex);
                        //Adding controls for Customer Age
                        con.add(labelCustAge);
                        con.add(textCustAge);
                        //close the program when the close button is
clicked
                    setDefaultCloseOperation(EXIT_ON_CLOSE);
                    setSize(350,250);
                    show();
```

```
            }

      public static void main(String[] args)
         {
                              Customer cust = new Customer();
}
}
```

The output of the above program is shown in Figure 1-6.

FIGURE 1-6 *The output of the* Customer *program*

This example file (Customer.java) is included in the samples folder of this chapter on the Web site that accompanies this book at **www.premierpressbooks.com/downloads.asp**.

In the preceding listing, a subclass of the frame window is created. The current container is obtained using the getContentPane() method. Next, various components are created and added to the container by using the add() method of the frame. Finally, the window is displayed to the user by using the show() method of the Frame class and resized using the setSize() method.

Summary

In this chapter, you learned the fundamentals of the Java programming language. Java is a platform-independent, object-oriented language. Similar to any other programming language, Java has its own set of data types and constructs. However, most of the data types and constructs are similar to those in C++. Modifiers define accessibility and other related functionality of classes, methods, and variables in Java. You also learned to write a program in Java. To create a GUI application, the Java platform provides you the Swing API in JFC. Swing contains many components that can be displayed in GUI. Finally, you learned to use Swing components to create a simple interface.

Chapter 2

In Chapter 1, "Programming in Java," you learned about the basics of the Java language and how to write a Java application. In this chapter, you will learn to create applets by using applet tags. This chapter will also cover procedures to add images to applets and execute the applets by using the Appletviewer tool.

An Introduction to Applets

Applets are Java programs that are embedded within a Web page. Therefore, unlike applications, applets require a Java-enabled browser, such as Microsoft Internet Explorer 4.0 or later, Netscape Navigator 4.0 or later, or HotJava. These browsers are said to be Java-enabled because they have a built-in Java platform (JVM and Java API).

An applet is loaded and executed when you load a Web page by using a Web browser. When a Web page containing an applet is displayed, you can interact with the applet. You can use applets to add dynamic features, such as animation and sound, to a Web page. You can also use them to make a Web page interactive.

HOTJAVA

HotJava is a browser used to access Web pages with Java special effects. The Java development team at Sun Microsystems created HotJava, which is available for download at the Java Web site. Currently, HotJava is available for Windows 95, Windows NT, and Solaris 2.x platforms.

Now I'll show you some of the unique features of an applet and identify how an applet differs from a Java application. An applet has a graphical user interface and is simple to use because to start an applet, you simply need to access a Web page. On the other hand, to execute an application, you need to download the application to your computer. Applets have fewer security privileges than applications. You can use an applet to access the resources of only the host computer; it cannot access the files on the computer on which it is downloaded.

You use the Applet class instead of the JFrame class to build an applet. Applets do not have a "main" method. Instead, a method known as init() is first called in the applet code. Unlike a Java application, you specify the size of an applet in the HTML code, instead of the Java code.

An applet, in contrast to an application, can be stored on a remote computer. When a local computer needs to execute the applet, the applet is fetched from the remote system into the internal memory of the local computer. After the applet is made available on the local computer, the applet is interpreted, linked to the local resources by the browser, and executed. Applets downloaded to your computer and executed locally reduce the load on the Web server. You can carry out validations and calculations on the computer on which the applet is downloaded.

Now that I've discussed the basic information about applets and how they differ from applications, I'll show you the process of creating applets.

Creating Applets

To create an applet, you use the JApplet class hierarchy. The JApplet class hierarchy enables the applets that you write to use all attributes they need to run off a Web page. Before you write any other statements in your applets, the JApplet class hierarchy can perform certain functions. Some of the functions are interacting with a Web browser, loading and unloading, and responding to changes in the browser window.

The javax.swing package contains the JApplet class, which has over 20 methods that are used to display images, play audio files, and respond when you interact with the applet. You can implement an applet by using certain methods. Now take a look at these methods in detail.

The Life Cycle of an Applet

The Applet class contains four methods that control the creation and execution of an applet on a Web page. These methods are:

- ◆ init()
- ◆ start()
- ◆ stop()
- ◆ destroy()

I'll discuss these methods in detail.

The init() *Method*

The init() method is called when an applet is loaded into the memory of a computer for the first time. The init() method works like a constructor, which means that it is executed automatically by the system. By using the init() method, you can initialize variables and add components such as buttons and check boxes to an applet.

An example of the init() method is given as follows:

```
public class one extends JApplet
{
public void init()
{
    getContentPane().add(new JLabel("Welcome to the world of Applets!"));
}
```

The start() Method

The start() method is called immediately after the init() method is called and is executed each time you visit other pages and return to the page containing the applet. You can use this method when you want to restart a process each time a user visits a page. For example, you can use the start() method in situations where you want to restart an animation sequence or a thread for your applet. If your applet does not execute any statements when a user exits from the current Web page, you need not implement this method.

The stop() Method

The stop() method is called each time an applet loses its focus. For example, when a user exits out of the page on which the applet is loaded, the stop() method is called. You can use this method to reset variables and stop the threads that are running. This method gives you a chance to stop activities that slow down the computer.

 NOTE

You will learn about threads in Chapter 4, "Exception Handling and Threading."

The destroy() Method

The destroy() method is called when you start viewing another Web page. You can use this method to perform clean-up operations, such as closing a file. Java calls the stop() method before calling the destroy() method.

Figure 2-1 summarizes the life cycle of an applet.

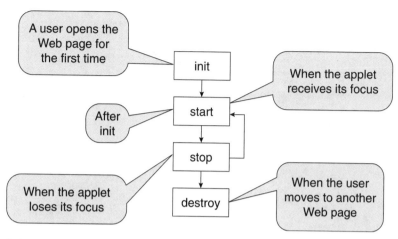

FIGURE 2-1 *Life cycle of an applet*

You may use some, all, or none of the preceding listed methods of an applet. These methods are called automatically by the Java environment, and therefore, must be declared public. A point to note is that none of these methods accept parameters.

In Chapter 1, I discussed the procedure for writing a Java application that you can use to access customer details. Now take a look at converting the same application into an applet to make it Web-enabled.

To convert an application to an applet, you need to perform these tasks:

1. Write the applet code.
2. Place the applet within a Web page by using the APPLET tag.
3. Use the Appletviewer tool to test the applet.

An Example of the Applet Code

Now I'll discuss how to create an applet, as illustrated in Figure 2-2.

 NOTE

You need not bother about the layout of the screen at this point. You will learn to manage the layout of screen components in Chapter 3, "Layout Managers and Handling Events."

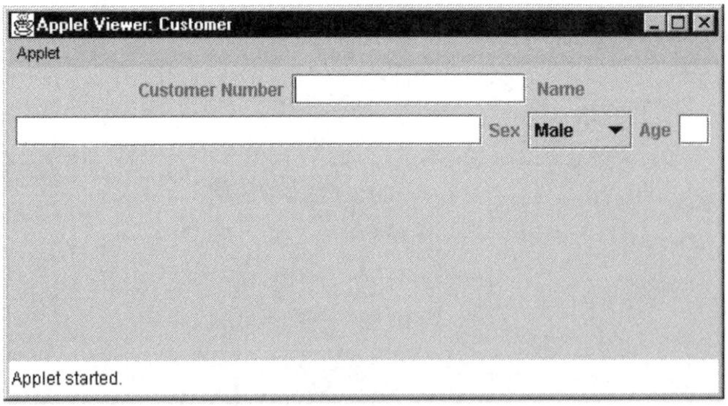

FIGURE 2-2 *The figure displays a* Customer *applet.*

The first step to create an applet is to modify the Customer code to include the init() method. The init() method is used to initialize the controls in a Web-based program. The example code is shown in Listing 2-1.

Listing 2-1 Customer.java

```java
import javax.swing.*;
public class Customer extends JApplet
{
        //Variable for the panel
        JPanel   panelObject;
        //Variables of labels
        JLabel    labelCustNo;
        JLabel    labelCustName;
        JLabel    labelCustSex;
        JLabel    labelCustAge;
         //Variables for data entry controls
        JTextField    textCustNo;
        JTextField    textCustName;
        JComboBox     comboCustSex;
        JTextField    textCustAge;
        public void init()
          {
                // Add appropriate controls to the frame
                //  Create panel
```

```
panelObject = new JPanel();
getContentPane().add(panelObject);
//Create and add the appropriate controls
// Initializing labels
labelCustNo = new JLabel("Customer Number");
labelCustName = new JLabel(" Name");
labelCustSex = new JLabel("Sex");
labelCustAge = new JLabel("Age");
//Initializing textfield
textCustNo = new JTextField(15);
textCustName = new JTextField(30);
textCustAge = new JTextField(2);
String Sex[] = { "Male", "Female"};
comboCustSex = new JComboBox(Sex);
//Adding controls for Customer Number
panelObject.add(labelCustNo);
panelObject.add(textCustNo);
//Adding controls for Customer Name
panelObject.add(labelCustName);
panelObject.add(textCustName);
//Adding controls for Customer Sex
panelObject.add(labelCustSex);
panelObject.add(comboCustSex);
//Adding controls for Customer Age
panelObject.add(labelCustAge);
panelObject.add(textCustAge);
    }
}
```

This example file (Customer.java) is included in the samples folder of this chapter on the Web site that accompanies this book at **www.premierpressbooks.com/downloads.asp**.

 NOTE

Note that the code does not have a main() method.

The Applet Tag

To run the applet I just discussed, you need to embed it in a Web page and view the page by using your Java-enabled Web browser. You use the APPLET tag to place an applet into a Web page. The APPLET tag provides information to the page on how to load and run the applet. The APPLET tag is written within the BODY tag of an HTML document.

The syntax of the APPLET tag is given as follows:

```
<APPLET
CODE= "name of the .class file"
CODEBASE= "path of the .class file"
HEIGHT= "maximum height of the applet, in pixels"
WIDTH = "maximum width of the applet, in pixels"
VSPACE= "vertical space between the applet and the rest of the
HTML, in pixels"
HSPACE= "horizontal space between the applet and the rest of the
HTML, in pixels"
ALIGN = "alignment of the applet with respect to the rest of the
Web page"
ALT = "alternate text to be displayed if the browser does not
support applets"
>
<PARAM NAME= "parameter_name" VALUE= "value_of_parameter">
<PARAM NAME= "parameter_name" VALUE= "value_of_parameter">
</APPLET>
```

The most commonly used attributes of the APPLET tag are CODE, HEIGHT, WIDTH, CODEBASE, and ALT. The PARAM tag is used to pass information to an applet. Next, I'll discuss this tag in a greater detail.

Passing Parameters to Applets

The PARAM tag is specified between <APPLET> and </APPLET> tags. The PARAM tag is used to pass named parameters to an applet. It has two attributes: NAME and VALUE. The NAME attribute is the name of the parameter passed to the applet and the VALUE attribute is the value of the variable that is passed.

You can retrieve the value of an HTML file from the PARAM tag by using the getParameter() method of the Applet class.

The syntax of the `getParameter()` method is given here:

```
String parameterValue = getParameter("parameter_name");
```

The following example illustrates the use of this function:

```
String time = getParameter("StartTime");
```

The next step in creating an applet involves placing the applet in an HTML code.

An Example of the HTML Code

The `APPLET` tag is used to place an applet inside an HTML source.

Listing 2-2 shows the code for the HTML file.

Listing 2-2 Customer.html

```
<HTML>
<APPLET CODE="Customer.class" HEIGHT=500 WIDTH=200>
</APPLET>
</HTML>
```

This example file (`Customer.html`) is included in the samples folder of this chapter on the Web site that accompanies this book at **www.premierpressbooks.com/downloads.asp**.

In this code, the `CODE` parameter identifies the name of the `Applet` class. The `Width` and `Height` parameters specify the space on the Web page to be allocated for the applet. Parameter values are specified in pixels.

 CAUTION

You need to be careful while specifying the name of the .class file in the HTML file. All file names are case-sensitive. The applet will not execute if the file name specified in the HTML file is incorrect.

The last step in creating an applet involves testing the applet.

The Appletviewer Tool

The JDK contains a tool called `Appletviewer`, which is a program that runs applets without the overhead of running a Web browser. This tool provides an easy way to test applets.

To test an applet, you need to type the following command at the command prompt:

```
Appletviewer [options] <URL of the .html file>
```

You can use the –debug option with the `Appletviewer` command to start the applet in the Java Debugger, jdb. This allows you to debug applets in the HTML document. The Appletviewer tool has an applet menu. The options of the applet menu along with their description are listed in Table 2-1.

Table 2-1 Applet Menu Options

Option	Description
Restart	Restarts an applet by using the current settings
Reload	Reloads applets after applying changes in the class file
Stop	Calls the `stop()` method of an applet and terminates the applet
Save	Saves the serialized state of an applet
Start	Starts an applet. This is useful if you select the Stop option on the menu
Clone	Duplicates the current applet to create another AppletViewer instance
Tag	Shows the HTML `<APPLET>` tag that is used to run the current applet
Info	Shows specific information about an applet, which is set within the program of the applet
Print	Causes the PrintGraphics of an applet to be sent to a printer
Properties	Shows the AppletViewer window and terminates an applet
Quit	Closes the AppletViewer window and terminates an applet

To test a customer applet, type the following command at the command prompt:

```
AppletViewer Customer.html
```

An alternative method to test an applet is to insert the APPLET tags in the Java source file as comments, as shown here:

```
// <applet code=Customer width=200 height=100>
// </applet>
```

Next, you can run an applet by typing the following command where Customer is the name of the Java source file:

```
Appletviewer Customer.java
```

The Appletviewer tool picks the <APPLET> tags out of the HTML file and runs the applets without displaying the surrounding HTML text. The advantage of using this method is that you need not create an HTML file for testing the applet.

Now that I've discussed the steps to create an applet, I'll demonstrate painting the applet and drawing graphical images in the applet. You can use the Graphics class for this purpose.

The *Graphics* Class

The Graphics class is an abstract class that represents the display area of an applet. This class is a part of the java.awt package and you use it to draw images within the display area of the applet. The object of the Graphics class is used for painting the applet.

Painting the Applet Method

When you scroll to an applet, you need to refresh the display to view the new content. Windows handles this by marking the area that has to be refreshed. The area is then painted to display the result of scrolling. This is handled by the update() and paint() methods.

The *update()* Method

The update() method takes the Graphics class object as a parameter. When the applet area needs to be redrawn, the Windows system starts the painting process. The update() method is called to clear the screen and it in turn calls the paint() method. The system then updates the screen.

The *paint()* Method

The paint() method draws the graphics of an applet in the drawing area. The method is automatically called when an applet is displayed on the screen for the first time and each time the applet receives focus. The paint() method can be triggered by invoking the repaint() method. The paint() method of an applet takes an object of the Graphics class as a parameter.

The *repaint()* Method

You can call the repaint() method when you want to redraw an applet area. The repaint() method calls the update() method to signal that an applet has to be updated. The default action of the update() method is to clear the applet area and call the paint() method. You can override the update() method if you do not want the applet area to be cleared.

The following code uses the paint() and repaint() methods to check when the init(), start(), and stop() methods of an applet are called.

```java
import javax.swing.*;
import java.awt.*;
public class AppletMethods extends JApplet
{
                int initCounter = 0;
                int startCounter = 0;
                int stopCounter = 0;
                int destroyCounter = 0;
                public void init()
                {
                        initCounter++;
                        repaint();
                }
                public void start()
                {
                        startCounter++;
                        repaint();
                }
                public void stop()
                {
                    stopCounter++;
```

```
                              repaint();
                    }
            public void destroy()
                    {
                            destroyCounter++;
                            repaint();
                    }
public void paint(Graphics g)
{
                g.drawString ("init has been invoked " + String.valueOf
(initCounter) +" time",20,20);
                g.drawString ("start has been invoked " + String.valueOf
(startCounter)+" time",20,35);
                g.drawString ("stop has been invoked " + String.valueOf
(stopCounter)+" times",20,50);
                g.drawString ("destroy has been invoked " + String.valueOf
(destroyCounter)+" times",20,65);
}
}
```

Figure 2-3 illustrates the output of the preceding code.

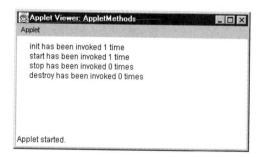

FIGURE 2-3 *The output of the* AppletMethods *code*

The Graphics class provides methods to draw a number of graphical figures.

Drawing Figures

You can use the Graphics class to draw text, lines, circles and ellipses, rectangles and polygons, and images. You cannot create an object of the Graphics class because it is abstract. A few of the Graphics class methods are:

- ◆ drawString()
- ◆ drawRect()
- ◆ fillRect()

I'll discuss these methods in detail.

The *drawString()* Method

You use the drawString() method to write the text provided by the specified string. The text of the string is displayed at position (*x, y*).

The syntax of the drawString() method is given as follows:

```
public abstract void drawString(String str, int x, int y)
```

where:

- ◆ str is the string to be drawn.
- ◆ x is the *x* coordinate.
- ◆ y is the *y* coordinate.

An example of the drawString() method is given here:

```
import javax.swing.*;
import java.awt.*;
public class String extends JApplet
{
public void paint(Graphics g)
{
g.drawString("This is an example",50, 50);
}
}
```

Figure 2-4 illustrates the output of the above code.

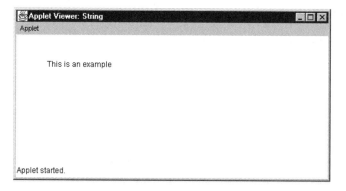

FIGURE 2-4 *An example of the* drawString() *method*

The *drawRect()* Method

You use the drawRect() method to draw the outline of a rectangle.

The syntax of the drawRect() method is given here:

```
public abstract void drawRect (int x1, int y1, int width, int height)
```

where:

- ◆ x1 is the *x* coordinate of the rectangle.
- ◆ y1 is the *y* coordinate of the rectangle.
- ◆ width is the width of the rectangle.
- ◆ height is the height of the rectangle.

An example of the drawRect() method is given here:

```
import javax.swing.*;
import java.awt.*;
public class Rectangle extends JApplet
{
public void paint(Graphics g)
{
g.drawRect(20,40,70,40);
}
}
```

Figure 2-5 illustrates the output of the above code.

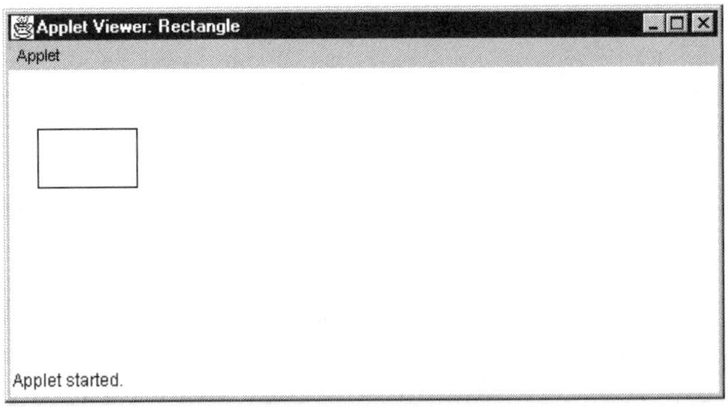

FIGURE 2-5 *An example of the* drawRect() *method*

The *fillRect()* Method

You use the fillRect() method to fill the specified rectangle.

The syntax of the fillRect() method is given here:

```
public abstract void fillRect (int x1, int y1, int width, int height)
```

where:

- ◆ x1 is the *x* coordinate of the rectangle.
- ◆ y1 is the *y* coordinate of the rectangle.
- ◆ width is the width of the rectangle.
- ◆ height is the height of the rectangle.

An example of the fillRect() method is given as follows:

```
import javax.swing.*;
import java.awt.*;
public class FillRectangle extends JApplet
{
public void paint(Graphics g)
{
g.fillRect(20,40,70,40);
}
}
```

Figure 2-6 illustrates the output of the above code.

FIGURE 2-6 *An example of the* `fillRect()` *method*

Next, take a look at changing the text font in an applet.

Changing the Text Font in an Applet

You can change the font of the text displayed in an applet by using the `Font` class. The changes can be made to the font, style, and size of the text.

The following code displays a string in the Times New Roman font in bold and italic style, and a font size of 14 point:

```
import javax.swing.*;
import java.awt.*;
public class FontExample extends JApplet
{
public void paint( Graphics g)
{
Font myFont = new Font("Times New Roman", Font.BOLD + Font.ITALIC, 14);
g.setFont(myFont);
g.drawString("Hello World!!", 20, 20);
}
}
```

Figure 2-7 illustrates the output of the above code.

The preceding code creates an object of the `Font` class and passes the name, style, and size of the font as parameters. You use the `setFont()` method of the `Graphics`

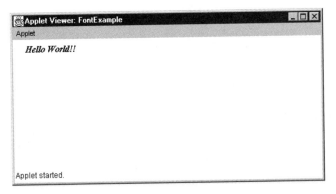

FIGURE 2-7 *An applet with the text font changed*

class to change the text font of the applet. The drawString() method displays the string in the applied font.

Now, I'll show you how to add images to applets.

Adding Images to Applets

An image enhances the communication of ideas and adds aesthetic value to a user interface. It also makes the interface interesting and easy for the user to read. Now I'll teach you about the properties of an image.

The Properties of an Image

An image has certain properties associated with it. These properties include its height, width, format, dimension, and location. An image can be two-dimensional (2-D) or three-dimensional (3-D).

An image can have several types of image formats. The two most commonly used formats are GIF and JPEG. Graphic Interchange Format (GIF) is the standard for images on the Web. This format is used if an image is a line drawing. The GIF format is preferred because it does not adversely impact image quality and helps retain image clarity and originality. Due to these reasons, the GIF format is considered better than the JPEG format. The Joint Photographic Experts Group (JPEG) format is selected for photographic or medical images, and for complex photographic illustrations. JPEG images are inherently full-color images, and therefore, look distorted when viewed on a monitor supporting 256 colors. Java supports both GIF and JPEG image formats.

You can store an image on the local system or on any other computer. In order to access any resource from an applet, such as an image, you need to grant permissions explicitly. Permissions are the rights provided for any system resource such as a file, a network, and AWT. You can grant read, write, execute, and delete permissions to a resource.

To add an image to the applet, you need to create a policy file in Java to set permissions for the image. Subsequently, you write the code to add an image to an applet.

Creating a Policy

In Java, a policy object specifies the permissions, such as read, write, or execute, available on the resources in the application environment. The default policy for a user is stored in the .java.policy file within the user's home directory. The path for the default policy file of a user in Windows NT is:

```
Winnt\Profiles\<Username>\.java.policy
```

Policies can be created using the PolicyTool utility. You can use this utility to set permissions for resources. The steps to create a policy are as follows:

1. Start the Policy Tool
2. Grant the required permission
3. Save the policy file

Starting the Policy Tool

To start the policy tool, type `Policytool` at the command prompt and press Enter. This will display the Policy Tool window, as illustrated in Figure 2-8.

Granting the Required Permission

To grant the required permission, click the Add Policy Entry button to display the Policy Entry window, as illustrated in Figure 2-9. The CodeBase value indicates the source code location. A CodeBase text box without any entry indicates that there is no content in the source code location. The SignedBy value indicates the alias for a stored certificate. The certificate contains a key that is used to verify the digital signature.

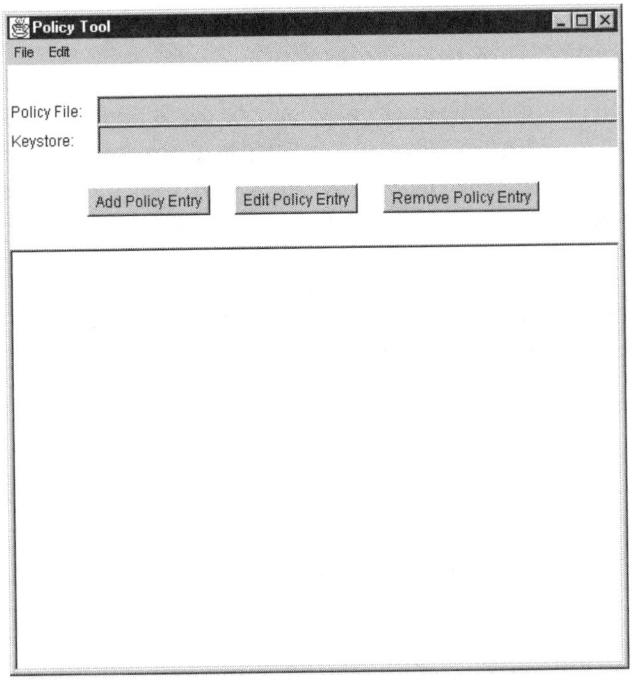

FIGURE 2-8 *The Policy Tool window*

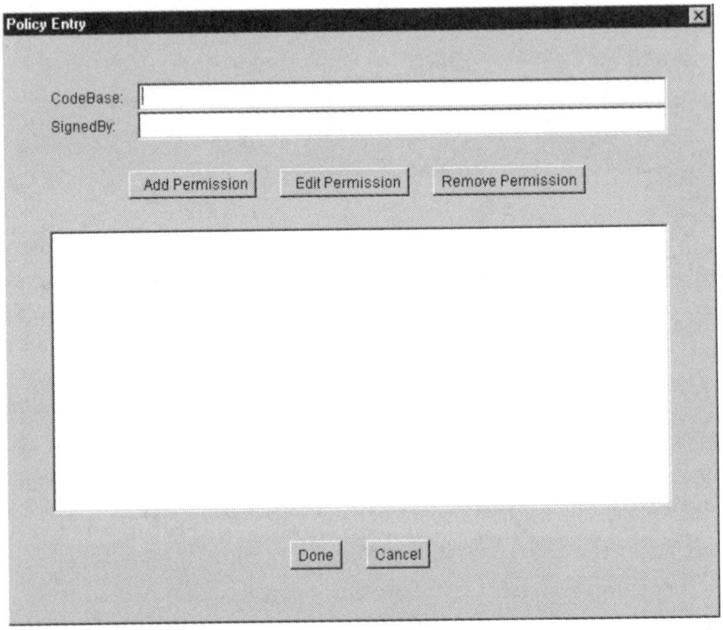

FIGURE 2-9 *The Policy Entry dialog box*

Next, click the Add Permission button to display the Permissions dialog box, as illustrated in Figure 2-10.

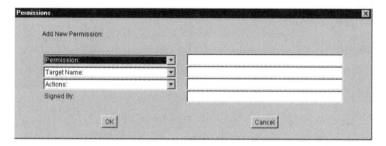

FIGURE 2-10 *The Permissions dialog box*

Select FilePermission from the Permission list box. Next, specify the Target Name entry as the name of the image file and then select read and execute in the Actions list. Finally, click OK to close the Permissions dialog box and click Done to close the Policy Entry dialog box.

Save the Policy File

To save the policy file, choose Save As from the File menu and save the `.java.policy` file in the `Winnt\Profiles\<Username>` directory.

After you have created a policy file and granted the required permission to the image, you need to write the code to add an image to the applet.

Writing the Code to Add an Image to an Applet

To add an image to an applet, you need to create a container control for the image, as shown in the example here:

```
JLabel logoimagePosition;
```

Next, you use the constructor of the `ImageIcon` class to load the image. The `ImageIcon` is a class of the `Icon` interface. This class creates an `ImageIcon` from the specified file, as shown in the following example:

```
Icon logoImage = new
ImageIcon("c:\\Print.gif");
```

Finally, you use the constructor of the container control to display the image into the applet, as shown in this example:

```
logoimagePosition = new JLabel(logoImage);
panelObject.add(logoimagePosition);
```

Now I'll discuss an example code to add an image to an applet.

An Example

You will add an image to the applet as illustrated in Figure 2-11.

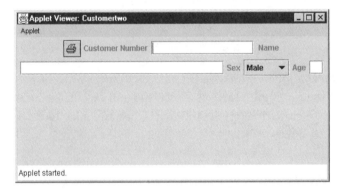

FIGURE 2-11 *The figure displays an image added to an applet.*

The code to add an image to an applet is shown in Listing 2-3.

Listing 2-3 Customertwo.java

```java
import javax.swing.*;
public class Customertwo extends JApplet
{
        //Variable for the panel
        JPanel   panelObject;
        //Variables of labels
        JLabel    labelCustNo;
        JLabel    labelCustName;
        JLabel    labelCustSex;
        JLabel    labelCustAge;
```

```
JLabel logoimagePosition;
//Variables for data entry controls
JTextField    textCustNo;
JTextField    textCustName;
JComboBox     comboCustSex;
JTextField    textCustAge;
public void init()
   {
          // Add appropriate controls to the frame
          //  Create panel
          panelObject = new JPanel();
          getContentPane().add(panelObject);
          //Create and add the appropriate controls
// Initializing labels
          labelCustNo = new JLabel("Customer Number");
          labelCustName = new JLabel(" Name");
          labelCustSex = new JLabel("Sex");
          labelCustAge = new JLabel("Age");
          //Initializing textfield
          textCustNo = new JTextField(15);
          textCustName = new JTextField(30);
          textCustAge = new JTextField(2);
          String Sex[] = { "Male", "Female"};
        comboCustSex = new JComboBox(Sex);
          Icon logoImage = new
          ImageIcon("c:\\Print.gif");
          logoimagePosition = new JLabel(logoImage);
          panelObject.add(logoimagePosition);
          //Adding controls for Customer Number
          panelObject.add(labelCustNo);
          panelObject.add(textCustNo);
          //Adding controls for Customer Name
          panelObject.add(labelCustName);
          panelObject.add(textCustName);
          //Adding controls for customer Sex
          panelObject.add(labelCustSex);
          panelObject.add(comboCustSex);
          //Adding controls for customer Age
```

```
                panelObject.add(labelCustAge);
                panelObject.add(textCustAge);
    }
    }
```

This example file (`Customertwo.java`) is included in the samples folder of this chapter on the Web site that accompanies this book **www.premierpressbooks. com/downloads.asp**.

NOTE

You need to specify the path of the .gif file on your computer to execute the code discussed.

TIP

If you want to avoid creating an HTML file, you can add the APPLET tags as comment entries to the Java code. You then execute the applet by using the `Appletviewer Customertwo.java` command.

The `Applet` class does not have the functionality to change the Web page being displayed by the browser. If you want the applet to interact with the browser, you can use the `AppletContext` interface.

The *AppletContext* Interface

An applet running in a browser can request the browser to fetch an audio file or display a short message on a Web page using the `AppletContext` interface. The browser can carry out the request or reject it. The `AppletContext` is a link to the browser and controls the browser environment in which the applet is displayed. You can use the `getAppletContext()` method to communicate with the browser.

The syntax to use the `getAppletContext()` method is as follows:

```
public AppletContext getAppletContext();
```

You can use the showStatus() method to change the message displayed on the status bar of a browser. The syntax to use the showStatus() method is as follows:

```
public void showStatus();
```

You can use the showDocument() method to display another Web page. The syntax to use the showDocument() method is given here:

```
public void showDocument(URL);
```

The showDocument method can take a second argument that specifies where to display the document. The arguments are listed in Table 2-2.

Table 2-2 The *showDocument()* Method Arguments

Option	Description
_self	Show a document in the current frame that contains the applet.
_parent	Show a document in the parent frame of an applet. If the applet has no parent frame, parent functions in a way similar to _self.
_top	Show a document in the top-level frame of an applet's window. If the applet frame is the top-level frame, top functions in a way similar to _self.
_blank	Show a document in a new, unnamed top-level window that has been assigned a name.
Name of the string	Show a document in the frame or window with the name of the string. If a target name does not already exist, a new top-level window with the specified name is created, where the document is displayed.

The following example shows the document in a new browser window:

```
getAppletContext().showDocument(link,"_blank");
```

The link in the example given above is a string that contains a URL.

The following code illustrates the use of the showStatus() and showDocument() methods:

```
import java.applet.*;
import java.awt.*;
```

```
import java.net.*;
public class ShowDocument extends Applet
{
public void init()
{
getAppletContext().showStatus("Connecting............");
try
{
getAppletContext().showDocument(new URL("http://www.msn.com"));
}
catch (MalformedURLException urlException)
{
getAppletContext().showStatus("Error connecting to URL");
}
}
}
```

To execute the above code, create the HTML file to call the applet and then open the HTML file in the browser. The code displays the www.MSN.com Web page when the applet is loaded. If the URL cannot be accessed, an error message is displayed on the status bar of the browser. The java.net package has been imported because the URL class is used. The URL class is used to specify the address of the Web site. The constructor of the URL class throws an exception if the site is not accessible.

An applet may contain audio and image files. To reduce the download time for an applet, you can download all the applet files together by assembling them into a single .jar file.

Creating Jar Files

A jar file is an archive file similar to a zip file. You can compress and package the applet files into one archive file with the .jar extension. You can use wildcard characters for specifying multiple input files with the jar command. The syntax to use the jar command is given here:

```
jar <options> <filename.jar> <inputfilename(s)>
```

You can use the following option(s) with the jar command.

Option	Function
c	To create a new archive file
t	To display the table of contents
f	To identify files to be created, listed, or extracted
v	To generate verbose output

The following statement displays the use of the jar command:

```
jar cf myarchive.jar *.class
```

Now take a look at how to convert an applet into an application.

Converting Applets to Applications

To convert an applet into an application, you need to add the main() method. This method is used to create, size, and display the window of an application. The main() method enables you to execute a program. The program is no longer run as an applet, therefore, you need to perform some of the start-up tasks that Java automatically performs for applets.

Consider the applet code given here:

```
import java.applet.*;
import java.awt.*;
public class DisplayApplet extends Applet
{
public void paint( Graphics g)
{
Font myFont = new Font("Times New Roman", Font.BOLD + Font.ITALIC, 14);
g.setFont(myFont);
g.drawString("This is displayed by the paint method", 20, 20);
}
}
```

You can modify the above program to convert it into an application. I'll show you how to do this.

```
import java.applet.*;
import java.awt.*;
```

```
public class DisplayApplet extends Applet
{
public void paint( Graphics g)
{
Font myFont = new Font("Times New Roman", Font.BOLD + Font.ITALIC, 14);
g.setFont(myFont);
g.drawString("This is displayed by the paint method", 20, 20);
}
public static void main(String args[])
{
DisplayApplet app = new DisplayApplet();
Frame frame = new Frame();
app.init();
frame.add("Center",app);
frame.setVisible(true);
}
}
```

In the above code, an object of the class and a frame window is created to hold the object. Next, an object of the Applet class is created and started by calling the init() method. The applet object is added to the frame window using the add() method of the frame. Finally, the window is displayed to the user using the setVisible() method of the Frame class and resized using the setSize() method.

Summary

An applet is a program that is embedded inside a Web page and that runs on a browser. An applet offers you a number of advantages when you are building client/server or networked applications. Applets do not have any installation issues. An applet is platform independent, which means that you need not make any changes to your code for different platforms. Applets are automatically installed each time a user loads a Web page. In many client/server systems, it is tedious to build and install a new version of the client software. Security is built into the core Java language and the applet structure so you need not worry about the damage to the system due to the code. These features make Java popular. Applets are automatically integrated with HTML, so that you have a built-in, platform-independent documentation system used to support the applets. However, due to security, applets cannot read or write files on the user's system or communicate with an Internet site other than the one on which they originated.

Chapter 3

In this chapter, you will learn how to organize the components of a user interface by using layout managers. You will also learn about event-driven programming, the event model of Java, and the different ways to handle events.

An Introduction to Layout Managers

Layout managers are special objects that determine how components are organized on a user interface. A layout manager specifies the layout of the components in a *container*. Containers hold components. When you create a container, Java automatically creates and assigns a default layout manager to it. The layout manager determines the placement of the components in the container.

The component class is the superclass for all GUI controls. It includes methods for handling events, colors, images, and fonts. These methods are available to the subclasses of the component class. The container class is derived from the component class and defines the components that can contain other components. For example, the Frame class is a container that can hold other components such as buttons and labels.

Now, I'll discuss how to use layouts.

Using Layouts

You can set different layout managers for different containers in an application. Presented here is a list of the commonly used layout managers in Java:

- ◆ Flow layout
- ◆ Grid layout
- ◆ Border layout
- ◆ Card layout
- ◆ Box layout
- ◆ Grid bag layout

Each layout manager is represented by a class of the same name. These classes are extended from the superclass `Object`. The `Object` class hierarchy is illustrated in Figure 3-1.

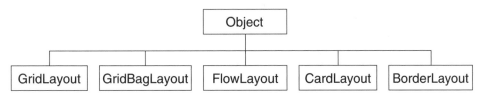

FIGURE 3-1 *The Object class hierarchy*

Next, take a look at these layouts in detail.

The Flow Layout Manager

The flow layout manager is the default layout manager for an applet. You can use the flow layout manager to place controls sequentially in rows in the order in which you add controls to a container. When the layout manager reaches the right border of the applet, it begins placing controls in the next row. In its default state, the flow layout manager centers the controls in each row.

The `FlowLayout` class has the following constructors:

- `public FlowLayout()`
- `public FlowLayout(int align)`
- `public FlowLayout(int align, int hgap, int vgap)`

The `public FlowLayout()` constructor creates a new flow layout manager object with a center alignment and default 5-pixel horizontal and vertical gaps.

The public `FlowLayout(int align)` constructor creates a new flow layout manager with the indicated alignment, and default horizontal and vertical gaps. The alignment argument must be one of the three arguments `FlowLayout.LEFT`, `FlowLayout.RIGHT`, or `FlowLayout.CENTER`.

The public `FlowLayout(int align, int hgap, int vgap)` constructor creates a new flow layout manager object with the specified alignment and horizontal and vertical gaps. The alignment argument must be one of the three arguments `FlowLayout.LEFT`, `FlowLayout.RIGHT`, or `FlowLayout.CENTER`. Here, `align` is the alignment, hgap is the horizontal gap between components, and vgap is the vertical gap between components.

To create a layout manager for a container, you need to create an instance of the appropriate layout class. Next, invoke the setLayout() method for the container to specify the layout to be used to place components. All layout manager classes are available in the java.awt package.

The following code creates a flow layout:

```
import java.awt.*;
import java.applet.*;
import javax.swing.*;
public class SampleLayout extends JApplet
{
                JButton b1,b2,b3;
                FlowLayout f1;
                public void init()
                {
                f1=new FlowLayout(FlowLayout.LEFT);
                    JPanel p1=new JPanel();
                    getContentPane().add(p1);
p1.setLayout(f1);
b1=new JButton("Button 1");
b2=new JButton("Button 2");
b3=new JButton("Button 3");
p1.add(b1);
p1.add(b2);
p1.add(b3);
}
}
{
```

Figure 3-2 displays the output of the preceding code.

The Grid Layout Manager

Although the flow layout manager is the simplest layout manager, you may not be able to use it to create sophisticated frames and applets. When you need greater control on placing components, the grid layout can be used.

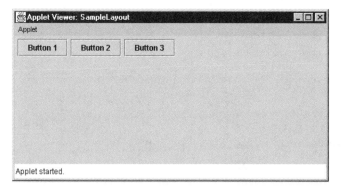

FIGURE 3-2 *The figure displays the flow layout with buttons left aligned.*

The grid layout manager organizes the display into a rectangular grid. The layout manager then places the components you create into each grid beginning from left to right and from top to bottom. The GridLayout class has the following constructors:

♦ public GridLayout(int rows, int cols)

♦ public GridLayout(int rows, int cols, int hgap, int vgap)

The public GridLayout (int rows, int cols) constructor creates a grid layout with the specified number of rows and columns. All the components in the layout are equal and of a specified size. You can place any number of objects in a row or in a column.

The public GridLayout(int rows, int cols, int hgap, int vgap) constructor creates a grid layout with the specified number of rows, columns, and horizontal and vertical gaps.

The following code creates a grid layout:

```
import java.awt.*;
import java.applet.*;
import javax.swing.*;
public class GridLayoutExample extends JApplet
              {
              JButton b1,b2,b3,b4;
          GridLayout g1;
              public void init()
              {
```

```
                g1=new GridLayout(2,2);
                    JPanel p1=new JPanel();
                    getContentPane().add(p1);
p1.setLayout(g1);
b1=new JButton("Button 1");
b2=new JButton("Button 2");
b3=new JButton("Button 3");
b4=new JButton("Button 4");
p1.add(b1);
p1.add(b2);
p1.add(b3);
p1.add(b4);
}
}
```

Figure 3-3 displays the output of the preceding code.

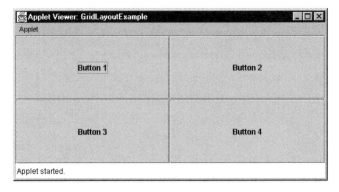

FIGURE 3-3 *The figure displays buttons organized using grid layout.*

The Border Layout Manager

The border layout manager enables you to position components by using the directions: north, south, west, east, and center. The BorderLayout class has the following constructors:

◆ `public BorderLayout()`

◆ `public BorderLayout(int hgap, int vgap)`

The `public BorderLayout()` constructor creates a border layout.

The `public BorderLayout(int hgap, int vgap)` creates a new border layout with the specified horizontal and vertical gaps.

The following code creates a border layout:

```
import java.awt.*;
import java.applet.*;
import javax.swing.*;
public class BorderLayoutExample extends JApplet
{
                JButton b1,b2,b3,b4,b5;
                  BorderLayout bd1;
                 public void init()
                 {
                bd1=new BorderLayout();
                JPanel p1=new JPanel();
                getContentPane().add(p1);
  p1.setLayout(bd1);
  b1=new JButton("Button 1");
  b2=new JButton("Button 2");
  b3=new JButton("Button 3");
  b4=new JButton("Button 4");
  b5=new JButton("Button 5");
  p1.add("North",b1);
  p1.add("South",b2);
  p1.add("West",b3);
  p1.add("East",b4);
  p1.add("Center",b5);
}
}
```

Figure 3-4 displays the output of the preceding code.

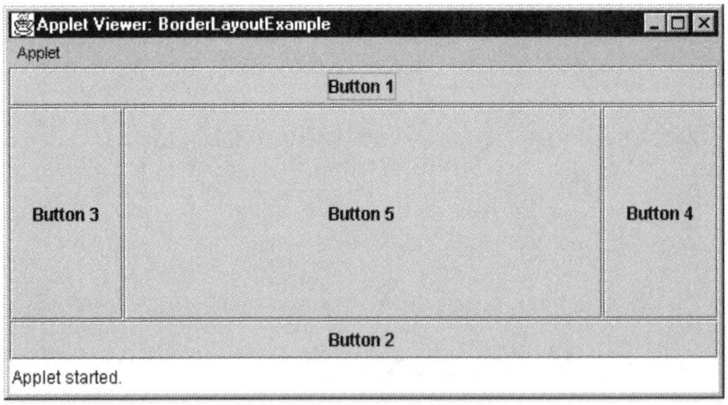

FIGURE 3-4 *The figure displays the buttons organized using a border layout.*

The Card Layout Manager

The card layout manager is one of the most complex layout managers. Using this manager, you can create a stack of layouts like a stack of cards and then flip from one layout to another. An example of this type of display organization is tabbed dialogs in Windows NT.

To create a layout with the card layout manager object, you first create a parent panel to hold the cards. Next, you create an object of the CardLayout class and set the object as the layout manager of the panel. Finally, you add each card to the layout by creating the components and adding them to the panel. The CardLay-out class provides the following constructors:

◆ public CardLayout (int hgap, int vgap)

◆ public CardLayout()

The public CardLayout(int hgap, int vgap) constructor creates a new card layout with the specified horizontal and vertical gaps. The horizontal gaps are placed on the left and right edges. The vertical gaps are placed on the top and bottom edges.

Table 3-1 lists the methods, which are provided by the CardLayout class, to switch between the stack of components placed sequentially in the form of cards.

Table 3-1 The *CardLayout* Class Methods

Method	Function
first(Container parent)	Displays the first card
last(Container parent)	Displays the last card
next(Container parent)	Displays the next card
previous(Container parent)	Displays the previous card
show(Container parent, String name)	Displays the specified card

If you keep the hierarchy of components in mind, you can easily create a card layout. At the bottom of the stack is the applet's display area while the component (usually a panel) that holds the cards is on the top of the stack. The card layout manager is on the top of the parent component. The components you add to the panel are called cards.

The following code creates a card layout:

```
import java.applet.*;
import javax.swing.*;
import java.awt.*
public class SampleLayout extends JApplet
{
JButton button1,button2,button3;
CardLayout c1;
JPanel p1;
public void init()
{
p1 = new JPanel();
c1 = new CardLayout();
p1.setLayout(c1);
getContentPane().add(p1);
button1 = new JButton("Button 1");
button2 = new JButton("Button 2");
button3 = new JButton("Button 3");
p1.add("Button 1", button1);
p1.add("Button 2", button2);
p1.add("Button 3", button3);
}
}
```

Figure 3-5 displays the output of the preceding code.

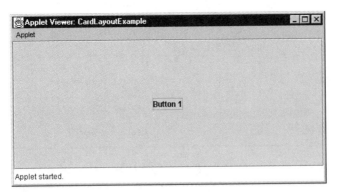

FIGURE 3-5 *The figure displays the button organized using a card layout.*

Each card in the code contains a button. When you execute the code, you see a single button in the display. You need to click the button to switch to the next button in the stack. When you get to the third button and click it, you get back to the first button. You'll learn how to handle button click events later in this chapter.

The Box Layout Manager

As discussed in the previous section, in the case of a card layout, you place components sequentially in a container. By contrast, in the case of a box layout, you can place multiple components side by side arranged vertically or horizontally in a container.

You can use the box layout manager to place components from either left to right or top to bottom. You can do this by specifying its major axis as either the X axis (for left to right component placement) or Y axis (for top to bottom component placement). Components are arranged vertically or horizontally in the same order as you add them to the container. The following example creates vertical and horizontal box layouts:

```
// Vertical and horizontal Box Layouts
import javax.swing.*;
import java.awt.*;
import java.applet.*;
import javax.swing.BoxLayout;
```

```
// <applet code=BoxLayoutExample
// width=450 height=200> </applet>
public class BoxLayoutExample extends JApplet
{
  public void init()
    {
  JPanel jpv = new JPanel();
    jpv.setLayout( new BoxLayout(jpv, BoxLayout.Y_AXIS));
  for(int i = 0; i < 5; i++)
  jpv.add(new JButton("" + i));
  JPanel jph = new JPanel();
    jph.setLayout(new BoxLayout(jph, BoxLayout.X_AXIS));
  for(int i = 0; i < 5; i++)
  jph.add(new JButton("" + i));
  Container cp = getContentPane();
  cp.add(BorderLayout.EAST, jpv);
  cp.add(BorderLayout.SOUTH, jph);
  }
}
```

Figure 3-6 displays the output of the above code.

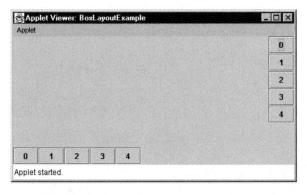

FIGURE 3-6 *The figure displays vertical and horizontal box layouts.*

The Grid Bag Layout Manager

The grid bag layout manager is the most flexible and complex layout manager provided by AWT. Similar to a grid layout, the grid bag layout manager organizes components into a rectangular grid. When using this layout manager, you can place components in any row or column in the grid. This layout manager also allows specific components to span multiple rows or columns.

You can create a grid bag layout by following these steps:

1. Create an object of the `GridBagLayout` class.

2. Set the `GridBagLayout` object to the layout manager for the component.

3. Create an object of `GridBagConstraints`. You can use `GridBagConstraints` to specify constraints such as the size and position of a component.

4. Next, specify the `GridBagConstraints` object with the `setConstraints()` method of the `GridBagLayout` class for associating the constraints with the component.

5. Finally, add the component.

The `GridBagLayout` class has a single constructor that does not take any arguments. Since the position of each component in a layout is controlled by a `GridBagLayout` object and determined by the currently set `GridBagConstraints` object, you need to create the `GridBagConstraints` object before the layout can be built. The object is built by calling the constructor of the class by using the following statement:

```
GridBagConstraints con = new GridBagConstraints();
```

Just like the `GridBagLayout` class, the `GridBagConstraints()` constructor requires no arguments. However, the attributes of the class are initialized to default values, therefore you usually need to change some of these values before adding components to the layout. Next, take a look at the procedure for specifying constraints.

Specifying Constraints

You can reuse a `GridBagConstraints` instance for multiple components, even if the components have different constraints. You can assign the following values to `GridBagConstraints` attributes:

- ◆ `anchor`
- ◆ `fill`
- ◆ `gridwidth`
- ◆ `gridheight`

- ◆ `gridx`
- ◆ `gridy`
- ◆ `insets`
- ◆ `ipadx`
- ◆ `ipady`
- ◆ `weightx`
- ◆ `weighty`

I'll discuss these attributes in detail.

The *anchor* Attribute

The `anchor` attribute is used when a component is smaller than its display area to determine the position of where to place the component within the area. The valid values for the anchor attribute are listed here:

- ◆ `GridBagConstraints.CENTER`
- ◆ `GridBagConstraints.NORTH`
- ◆ `GridBagConstraints.NORTHEAST`
- ◆ `GridBagConstraints.EAST`
- ◆ `GridBagConstraints.SOUTHEAST`
- ◆ `GridBagConstraints.SOUTH`
- ◆ `GridBagConstraints.SOUTHWEST`
- ◆ `GridBagConstraints.WEST`
- ◆ `GridBagConstraints.NORTHWEST`

The *fill* Attribute

The `fill` attribute is used when the display area of a component is larger than the requested size of the component to determine whether to resize the component and the procedure for resizing it. The valid values for the fill attribute are:

- ◆ `GridBagConstraints.NONE`
- ◆ `GridBagConstraints.HORIZONTAL`
- ◆ `GridBagConstraints.VERTICAL`
- ◆ `GridBagConstraints.BOTH`

The *gridwidth* and *gridheight* Attributes

The gridwidth and gridheight attributes specify the number of columns or rows in the display area of a component. The default value for these attributes is 1. The valid values for these attributes are:

- GridBagConstraints.REMAINDER
- GridBagConstraints.RELATIVE

The *gridx* and *gridy* Attributes

The gridx and gridy attributes specify the row and column in the upper left of the component display area. The leftmost column has the address gridx=0 and the topmost cell has the address gridy=0. Use the default value GridBagConstraints.RELATIVE to specify that the component should be placed to the right of (for gridx) or just below (for gridy) the previous component added to the container.

The *insets* Attribute

The insets attribute specifies the external padding of a component, which is the minimum space between the component and the edges of its display area. The value is specified as an Insets object. By default, all components do not have external padding. The default value is insets (0,0,0,0).

The *ipadx* and *ipady* Attributes

The ipadx and ipady attributes specify the internal padding to be added to the minimum size of the component. The default value is 0. The width of the component will be its minimum width plus ipadx*2 pixels (since the padding applies to both sides of the component). Similarly, the height of the component will be its minimum height plus ipady*2 pixels.

The *weightx* and *weighty* Attributes

The weightx and weighty attributes determine whether the components stretch horizontally (weightx) or vertically (weighty) to fill the display area of the applet. The default value for both attributes is 0.

Now I'll discuss how to organize the components of the Customer applet using grid bag layout, as shown in Figure 3-7.

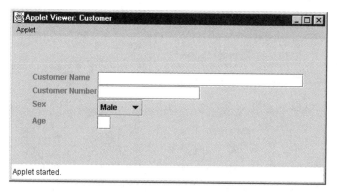

FIGURE 3-7 *The figure displays the customer applet organized using a grid bag layout.*

An Example of a Grid Bag Layout

The code to organize the components of the customer applet by using a grid bag layout is displayed in Listing 3-1.

Listing 3-1   CustomerLayout.java

```java
import javax.swing.*;
import java.awt.*;
// <applet code=Customer width=500 height=200>
// </applet>
public class CustomerLayout extends JApplet
{
                //Variable for the panel
                    JPanel panelObject;
            //variables for labels
                    JLabel labelCustName;
                JLabel labelCustNo;
                  JLabel labelCustSex;
                  JLabel labelCustAge;
                //variables for data entry controls
                      JTextField textCustName;
                  JTextField textCustNo;
                   JComboBox comboCustSex;
                  JTextField textCustAge;
```

```java
//Variables for the layout
GridBagLayout gbObject;
GridBagConstraints gbc;
public void init()
    {
            //Create and add the layout
        gbObject = new GridBagLayout();
        gbc = new GridBagConstraints();
          panelObject = (JPanel)getContentPane();
          panelObject.setLayout(gbObject);
                            //Initialize label con-
trols
                labelCustName = new JLabel("Customer Name");
                labelCustNo = new JLabel("Customer Number");
                  labelCustSex = new JLabel("Sex");
        labelCustAge = new JLabel("Age");
        //Initialize data entry controls
        textCustName = new JTextField(30);
        textCustNo = new JTextField(15);
        textCustAge = new JTextField(2);
    String Sex[] = { "Male", "Female"};
    comboCustSex = new JComboBox(Sex);
    //Add controls for Customer Name
    gbc.anchor = GridBagConstraints.NORTHWEST;
    gbc.gridx = 1;
      gbc.gridy = 5;
    gbObject.setConstraints(labelCustName,gbc);
panelObject.add(labelCustName);
    gbc.anchor = GridBagConstraints.NORTHWEST;
    gbc.gridx = 4;
  gbc.gridy = 5;
      gbObject.setConstraints(textCustName,gbc);
        panelObject.add(textCustName);
        //Add controls for Customer Number
    gbc.anchor = GridBagConstraints.NORTHWEST;
    gbc.gridx = 1;
  gbc.gridy = 8;
```

```
        gbObject.setConstraints(labelCustNo,gbc);
        panelObject.add(labelCustNo);
          gbc.anchor = GridBagConstraints.NORTHWEST;
          gbc.gridx = 4;
           gbc.gridy = 8;
            gbObject.setConstraints(textCustNo,gbc);
            panelObject.add(textCustNo);
           //Add controls for Sex
      gbc.anchor = GridBagConstraints.NORTHWEST;
          gbc.gridx = 1;
          gbc.gridy = 11;
        gbObject.setConstraints(labelCustSex,gbc);
          panelObject.add(labelCustSex);
        gbc.anchor = GridBagConstraints.NORTHWEST;
        gbc.gridx = 4;
        gbc.gridy = 11;
        gbObject.setConstraints(comboCustSex,gbc);
          panelObject.add(comboCustSex);
            //Add controls for Customer Age
              gbc.anchor = GridBagConstraints.NORTHWEST;
            gbc.gridx = 1;
      gbc.gridy = 14;
        gbObject.setConstraints(labelCustAge,gbc);
        panelObject.add(labelCustAge);
        gbc.anchor = GridBagConstraints.NORTHWEST;
        gbc.gridx = 4;
        gbc.gridy = 14;
        gbObject.setConstraints(textCustAge,gbc);
        panelObject.add(textCustAge);
          }
}
```

This example file (`CustomerLayout.java`) is included in the samples folder of this chapter on the Web site that accompanies this book at **www.premierpress-books.com/downloads.asp**.

Now that I've discussed the different types of layout managers, I'll show you how to interact with them by using events.

Events

In Java, *events* represent all the interactions between an application and its user. When a user interacts with a program (say, by clicking on a command button), the system creates an event that represents the action and delegates it to the event-handling code within the program. This code determines how to handle the event so that the user gets an appropriate response.

Event handling is essential for GUI programming. After a user performs an action on the GUI, the action translates to a call to a function that handles the event. This approach is called event-driven programming.

Now, take a look at the components of an event.

The Components of an Event

An event comprises three components:

◆ Event object

◆ Event source

◆ Event handler

When you interact with an application by pressing a key or clicking a mouse button, an event is generated. The operating system traps this event and its associated data. An example of the data associated with an event is the time at which an event occurred and the type of the event (a key press or a mouse click). The operating system then passes on this data to the application to which the event belongs.

An *event object* contains the following information related to the event:

◆ The category of the event, for example, clicking of a mouse, moving of a mouse, or closing a window

◆ The component that generated the event, for example, a button, a frame, or a list

◆ The time when the event occurred

An *event source* is the object that generates an event. For example, if you click a button, it is the source of the event.

An *event handler* is a method that interprets and processes an event. The event-handler method takes an event object as a parameter.

Now I'll discuss the event model.

The Event Model

In an event model, a component can initiate an event. In this model, an event is sent to the component from which it originated. The component registers a *listener* object with the program. The listener object contains appropriate *event-handlers* that receive and process the events. For example, when you click a button, the action to be performed is handled by an object registered to handle the button click event.

A distinct class represents each type of event. Each event listener is an object of a class that implements a particular type of listener interface. Therefore, as a programmer, you only need to create a listener object and register it with the component firing the event. To register the object, you need to call the addXXXListener() method in the event-firing component, in which XXX represents the type of event listened for. You can easily find out the types of events that can be handled by observing the names of the addListener methods. If you try to listen for the incorrect events you'll detect an error during compilation.

Now take a look at an example for attaching an event to a button.

```
// MyFrame.java file
import java.awt.*;
import java.awt.event.*;
import javax.swing.*;
class MyFrame extends JFrame
{
            JButton b1;
    //The main method
                public static void main(String args[])
                    {
                    MyFrame f = new MyFrame();
                    }
    //Constructor
                    public MyFrame()
                    {
                            super("Window Title");
                            b1=new JButton("Click here");
```

```
                    //Place the button object on the frame window
                                     getContentPane().add(b1);
                              //Register the listener for the button
                              ButtonListener blisten= new ButtonListener();
                              b1.addActionListener(blisten);
            //Display the window in a specific size
                                     setSize(200,200);
                                     setVisible(true);
    }
    //The listener class
    class ButtonListener implements ActionListener
    {
        //Definition of the actionPerformed() method
        public void actionPerformed(ActionEvent evt)
        {
                JButton source = (JButton)evt.getSource();
                source.setText("Button clicked");
        }
    }
}
```

When you execute the preceding code, a window with a Click here button is displayed. When you click the button, the label of the button changes to Button clicked.

In the above example, the ButtonListener class has been defined inside the MyFrame class. The ButtonListener class is an *inner class*. You will learn about inner classes in detail later in this chapter.

Now take a look at handling window events.

Handling Window Events

You can handle window-related events by registering the listener object that implements the WindowListener interface. This interface contains a set of methods that are used to handle window events. The events and methods are listed here:

Event	Method
The cross button is clicked	`void windowClosing(WindowEvent e)`
The window is opened	`void windowOpened(WindowEvent e)`
The window is activated	`void windowActivated(WindowEvent e)`
The window is deactivated	`void windowDeactivated(WindowEvent e)`
The window is closed	`void windowClosed(WindowEvent e)`
The window is minimized	`void windowIconified(WindowEvent e)`
The window is maximized	`void windowDeiconified(WindowEvent e)`

Now I will take up an example for handling window events:

```java
// MyFrameWindow.java file
import java.awt.*;
import java.awt.event.*;
import javax.swing.*;
class MyWindowListener implements WindowListener
{
//Event handler for the window closing event
public void windowClosing(WindowEvent w)
{
System.out.println("Window Closing");
System.exit(0);
}
public void windowClosed(WindowEvent w)
{
}
public void windowOpened(WindowEvent w)
{
}
public void windowIconified(WindowEvent w)
{
}
public void windowDeiconified(WindowEvent w)
{
}
public void windowActivated(WindowEvent w)
```

```
{
}
public void windowDeactivated(WindowEvent w)
{
}
}
class MyFrameWindow extends JFrame
{
JButton b1;
            //The main method
                public static void main(String args[])
                        {
                                MyFrameWindow f1 = new MyFrameWindow();
                         }
                //Constructor
                        public MyFrameWindow()
                        {
                              super("Window Title");
                               b1=new JButton("Click Here");
                              //Place the button object on the frame window
                              getContentPane().add(b1);
                              //Register the listener for the button
                              ButtonListener blisten=new ButtonListener();
                               b1.addActionListener(blisten);
                              //Display the window in a specific size
                        setSize(200,200);
                        setVisible(true);
                                //Register the listener for the window
                                        MyWindowListener wListen=new
MyWindowListener();

                                        addWindowListener(wListen);
        }
        //The listener class
        class ButtonListener implements ActionListener
        {
            //Definition of the actionPerformed() method
            public void actionPerformed(ActionEvent evt)
            {
```

```
                JButton source = (JButton)evt.getSource();
                source.setText("Button clicked");
        }
    }
}
```

In the preceding example, the MyFrameWindow class makes a call to the addWindowListener() method, which registers the listener object of the window. This enables the application to handle all window-related events. When you interact with the application window by minimizing or maximizing it or by clicking on the close button, a windowEvent object is created and delegated to the preregistered listener of the window. Subsequently, the designated event-handler is called.

In the above code, the class MyWindowListener has declarations for all methods. This is because when you use interfaces for creating listeners, the listener class has to override all methods declared in the interface. To avoid this, the event package provides *adapter classes*. I'll discuss them in detail.

The Adapter Classes

The Java programming language provides adapter classes that implement the corresponding listener interfaces containing multiple methods. The listener class you define should extend the Adapter class and override the methods you need. The Adapter class used for the WindowListener interface is the WindowAdapter class. The event package provides several Adapter classes.

The MyFrameWindow.java code written earlier is now modified to make use of the WindowAdapter class:

```
import java.awt.*;
import java.awt.event.*;
import javax.swing.*;
class MyWindowListener extends WindowAdapter
{
//Event handler for the window closing event
public void windowClosing(WindowEvent w)
{
System.out.println("Window Closing");
MyFrame f;
f= (MyFrame)w.getSource();
f.dispose();
```

```
System.exit(0);
}
}
class MyFrameWindow extends JFrame
{
               JButton b1;
                  //The main method
                  public static void main(String args[])
                     {
                        MyFrameWindow f1 = new MyFrameWindow();
                     }
                //Constructor
                     public MyFrameWindow()
                     {
                        super("Window Adapter");
                           b1=new JButton("Click Here");
                           //Place the button object on the frame window
                           getContentPane().add(b1);
                        //Register the listener for the button
                       ButtonListener blisten=new ButtonListener();
                       b1.addActionListener(blisten);
                                        //Display the window in a specific
size
                     setSize(200,200);
                   setVisible(true);
                                     //Register the listener for the window
                                     MyWindowListener wListen=new
MyWindowListener();
                                        addWindowListener(wListen);
                                   setVisible(true);
      }
      //The listener class
      class ButtonListener implements ActionListener
      {
         //Definition of the actionPerformed() method
         public void actionPerformed(ActionEvent evt)
         {
               JButton source = (JButton)evt.getSource();
```

```
                    source.setText("Button clicked");
        }
    }
}
```

You can also use *inner classes* to implement an interface when the interface defines only one method. Now take a look at inner classes in detail.

The Inner Classes

Inner classes are declared within other classes and provide additional clarity to programs. Inner classes are also known as nested classes. The scope of an inner class is limited to the class that encloses it. The objects of an inner class can access the members of its outer class. Alternatively, an outer class can access the members of its inner class through an object of the inner class.

The syntax to use inner classes is as follows:

```
<modifiers> class <classname>
{
<modifiers> class <innerclassname>
{
}
//other attributes and methods
}
```

Now that I've discussed the different types of layouts and event handling, I'll give you a look at adding functionality to the customer applet. You will create an applet as shown in Figure 3-8. When you click on the Accept button without entering

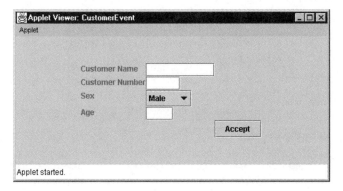

FIGURE 3-8 *The figure displays the customer applet with functionality added to the Accept button.*

the customer number, an error message is displayed on the status bar of the Appletviewer window.

The example code is shown in Listing 3-2.

Listing 3-2 CustomerEvent.java

```java
import javax.swing.*;
import java.awt.*;
import java.awt.event.*;
// <applet code=CustomerEvent width=500 height=200>
// </applet>
public class CustomerEvent extends JApplet
{
                //Variable for the panel
                JPanel panelObject;
                //variables for labels
                JLabel labelCustName;
                JLabel labelCustNo;
                JLabel labelCustSex;
                JLabel labelCustAge;
                JButton buttonAccept;
                //variables for data entry controls
                JTextField textCustName;
                JTextField textCustNo;
                JComboBox comboCustSex;
                JTextField textCustAge;
                //Variables for the layout
                GridBagLayout gbObject;
                GridBagConstraints gbc;
                public void init()
                {
                    //Initialize the layout variables
                    gbObject = new GridBagLayout();
                    gbc = new GridBagConstraints();
                    panelObject = (JPanel)getContentPane();
                    panelObject.setLayout(gbObject);
                    buttonAccept = new JButton("Accept");
```

```java
          //Initialize label controls
     labelCustName = new JLabel("Customer Name");
     labelCustNo = new JLabel("Customer Number");
      labelCustSex = new JLabel("Sex");
              labelCustAge = new JLabel("Age");
      //Initialize data entry controls
              textCustName = new JTextField(10);
       textCustNo = new JTextField(5);
textCustAge = new JTextField(4);
      String Sex[] = { "Male", "Female"};
      comboCustSex = new JComboBox(Sex);
        //Add controls for Customer Name
      gbc.anchor = GridBagConstraints.NORTHWEST;
      gbc.gridx = 1;
      gbc.gridy = 5;
    gbObject.setConstraints(labelCustName,gbc);
      panelObject.add(labelCustName);
gbc.anchor = GridBagConstraints.NORTHWEST;
 gbc.gridx = 4;
      gbc.gridy = 5;
      gbObject.setConstraints(textCustName,gbc);
      panelObject.add(textCustName);
        //Add controls for Customer Number
       gbc.anchor = GridBagConstraints.NORTHWEST;
      gbc.gridx = 1;
     gbc.gridy = 8;
      gbObject.setConstraints(labelCustNo,gbc);
    panelObject.add(labelCustNo);
     gbc.anchor = GridBagConstraints.NORTHWEST;
       gbc.gridx = 4;
        gbc.gridy = 8;
          gbObject.setConstraints(textCustNo,gbc);
         panelObject.add(textCustNo);
         //Add controls for Sex
      gbc.anchor = GridBagConstraints.NORTHWEST;
      gbc.gridx = 1;
      gbc.gridy = 11;
      gbObject.setConstraints(labelCustSex,gbc);
```

```
        panelObject.add(labelCustSex);
    gbc.anchor = GridBagConstraints.NORTHWEST;
    gbc.gridx = 4;
    gbc.gridy = 11;
      gbObject.setConstraints(comboCustSex,gbc);
panelObject.add(comboCustSex);
          //Add controls for Customer Age
    gbc.anchor = GridBagConstraints.NORTHWEST;
  gbc.gridx = 1;
    gbc.gridy = 14;
    gbObject.setConstraints(labelCustAge,gbc);
    panelObject.add(labelCustAge);
    gbc.anchor = GridBagConstraints.NORTHWEST;
  gbc.gridx = 4;
    gbc.gridy = 14;
gbObject.setConstraints(textCustAge,gbc);
panelObject.add(textCustAge);
  gbc.anchor = GridBagConstraints.NORTHEAST;
    gbc.gridx = 5;
      gbc.gridy = 1  7;
    gbObject.setConstraints(buttonAccept,gbc);
    panelObject.add(buttonAccept);
    ValidateAction validateButton = new ValidateAction();
buttonAccept.addActionListener(validateButton);
    }
          class ValidateAction implements ActionListener
    {
  public void actionPerformed(ActionEvent evt)
    {
    //Extracting source of action
    Object obj = evt.getSource();
    if(obj == buttonAccept)
    {
      // Retrieving the Customer ID from the textbox
      String customerNo = textCustNo.getText();
      // Checking whether the user has entered the value
      if(customerNo.length() == 0)
```

```
                    //Displaying the Error message on the StatusBar

getAppletContext().showStatus("Customer Number cannot be empty");
                    return;
                      }
                                    }
              }
                    }
  }
```

This example file (`CustomerEvent.java`) is included in the samples folder of this chapter on the Web site that accompanies this book at **www.premierpress-books.com/downloads.asp**.

Summary

Layout managers are special objects that determine how the components of a container are organized. When you create a container, Java automatically creates and assigns the flow layout manager. You can use different types of layout managers to control the layout of your applets and frames. The different types of layout managers are: flow layout, grid layout, border layout, card layout, box layout, and grid bag layout.

Events enable you to interact with a user-interface. An event comprises three components: event object, event source, and event-handler. In an event model, events are sent to the components from where they originate. The components then delegate the events to the registered listener objects for processing. The `ActionListener` interface contains the `actionPerformed()` method, which is the event-handler for the click event of a button. Listener interfaces and adapters can be used to handle events for different Windows components.

Chapter 4

**Exception
Handling and
Threading**

In Chapter 1, "Programming in Java," Chapter 2, "Creating Applets," and Chapter 3, "Layout Managers and Handling Events," you learned to create applications in Java. In this chapter, you will learn to handle errors thrown by applications using exception classes. You will also learn about user-defined exceptions and threads.

Exceptions

An *exception* is defined as an anomalous event that occurs during program execution and disrupts program functioning. While developing an application, you have to carry out error handling to manage erroneous situations that may occur during program execution. Some unexpected problems that might occur when executing applications are:

◆ Insufficient memory

◆ Resource allocation errors

◆ Problems in network connectivity

◆ Inability to read a file

In case of any of these four situations, a program may stop working or terminate.

Consider a sample Java code:

```
public void example (int num1, int num2)
{
int result;
result = num2/num1;
System.out.println("Result:" + result);
}
```

The preceding code divides two numbers provided as arguments. Now take a situation where you enter 5 and 0 as arguments and execute the program. This leads to a run-time error and the program will terminate.

To handle such abrupt termination of programs, you use exception-handling techniques. Java provides a hierarchy of *exception classes* to manage such errors. I'll discuss the exception classes in detail.

The Exception Classes

Java provides a number of classes that you can use to handle exceptions. The exception hierarchy is displayed in Figure 4-1.

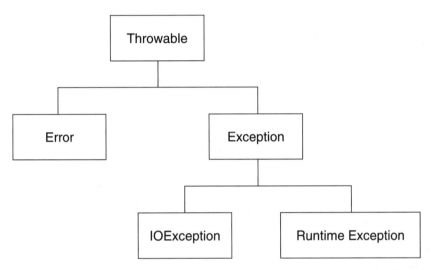

FIGURE 4-1 *The exception hierarchy*

The topmost class in the hierarchy is called Throwable. Two classes are derived from the Throwable class — Error and Exception. The Exception class is used for the erroneous situations that have to be trapped in a program. The Error class describes internal errors that might occur in the Java run-time system. Both these classes are available in the java.lang package.

Java has some predefined exceptions. I'll discuss some of the most common exceptions.

The Common Exceptions

Some of the predefined Java exceptions are:

- ◆ ArithmeticException
- ◆ NullPointerException
- ◆ ArrayIndexOutofBoundsException

Now I'll talk about each of the above exceptions.

The ArithmeticException

The Java run-time environment throws an `ArithmeticException` if an arithmetic condition returns erroneous results. For example, in a calculation, when a number is divided by zero this exception is generated.

The NullPointerException

The Java run-time environment throws a `NullPointerException` if you use an object without allocating memory to it, call methods of a null object, or try to access or modify the attributes of a null object.

The ArrayIndexOutofBoundsException

The Java run-time environment throws an `ArrayOutofBoundsException` if you attempt to access an array element beyond the index of the array. For example, if you try to access the eleventh element of an array that has only ten elements, this exception is thrown.

Some more exceptions are listed in Table 4-1.

Table 4-1 The Predefined Exceptions

Exception Name	Description
`ArrayStoreException`	Thrown when a program tries to store an incorrect data type in an array
`FileNotFoundException`	Thrown when a program tries to access a non-existent file
`IOException`	Thrown in case of I/O failures such as inability to read from a file
`NumberFormatException`	Thrown when strings fail to convert to numbers
`OutofMemoryException`	Thrown when memory to be allocated to a new object is insufficient
`SecurityException`	Thrown when an applet attempts to perform an action, which is not permitted by the security settings of the browser
`StackOverflowException`	Thrown when the stack space of a system is exhausted
`StringIndexOutofBoundsException`	Thrown when a program attempts to access a nonexistent character position in a string

I'll now look at the techniques for handling exceptions.

Exception-Handling Techniques

When an unexpected error occurs in a method, Java creates an object of the exception type. Subsequently, Java sends the object to a program by an action called *throwing* an exception. The exception object contains information about the type of error and the state of the program when the exception occurred. You need to process the exception by using an exception handler. You can implement exception handling in your program by using the following keywords:

- ♦ `try`
- ♦ `catch`
- ♦ `finally`

Now, I'll discuss each of the above techniques.

The try Block

You enclose the statements that may throw an exception in the `try` block. The `try` block determines the statements that are enclosed within it and defines the scope of the exception handlers associated with it. If an exception occurs within the `try` block, the appropriate exception handler that is associated with the `try` block handles the exception. A `try` block must be followed by at least one `catch` block. For example, you can add the `try` and `catch` block as shown here:

```
public void Example(int num1, int num2)
{
int result;
try
{
result=num2/num1;
}
catch()
{
//Statements
}
System.out.println("Result:" + result);
}
```

Now I'll discuss what goes into the `catch` block.

The catch *Block*

You associate an exception handler with the try block by providing one or more catch-handlers immediately after the try block. The catch statement accepts the object of the exception class that refers to the exception caught as a parameter. After the exception is caught, the statements within the catch block are executed. The scope of the catch block is restricted to the statements in the preceding try block only.

Now complete the code in the example I discussed earlier.

```
public void Example(int num1, int num2)
{
int result;
try
{
result=num2/num1;
}
catch(ArithmeticException e)
{
System.out.println("Error…..");
}
System.out.println("Result:" + result);
}
```

In the preceding example, an ArithmeticException is thrown. When writing the catch block, you need to ensure that there are no statements between the try and catch blocks.

Sometimes the try block has statements that might raise different types of exceptions. You can manage this situation by having multiple catch blocks. For example, the following code traps three types of exceptions:

```
public class TryCatch
{
public static void main(String args[])
{
int array[]={0,0};
int num1, num2, result=0;
num1=100;
num2=0;
```

```
try
{
result=num1/num2;
System.out.println(num1/array);
.....
}
catch(ArithmeticException e)
{
System.out.println("Error…..Division by Zero!!");
}
catch(ArrrayIndexOutOfBoundsException e)
{
System.out.println("Error…..Out of Bounds!!");
}
catch(Exception e)
{
System.out.println("Error……..!!");
}
System.out.println("The result is" + result);
}
}
```

In the code given above, the try block has many statements and each of the statements can result in an exception. Three catch blocks follow the try block, one for handling each type of exception. The catch block that has the most specific exception class must be written first. For example, if you write the catch block with the Exception class first, the other catch blocks are not executed. The javac compiler displays an error stating that the particular catch has not been reached. This is because the Exception class, being the base class for all exceptions, handles all the exceptions that are raised.

In the preceding code, the second statement in the try block is not executed. This is because, when an exception is raised, the flow of the program is interrupted and the statements in a particular catch block are executed.

If required, you can have nested try blocks in your code. Nested try blocks are similar to nested constructs. You can have one try/catch block inside another. Similarly, a catch block can contain try/catch blocks. If a lower level try/catch block does not have a matching catch handler, the outer try block is checked for it.

The catch block is followed by the finally block.

The finally *Block*

When an exception is raised, the rest of the statements in the try block are ignored. Sometimes, it is necessary to process certain statements, whether an exception is raised or not. You can use the finally block for this purpose.

Consider the following code:

```
try
{
openFile();
writeFile();
}
catch(…)
{
}
finally
{
closeFile();
}
```

In the preceding code, the file has to be closed regardless of whether an exception is raised or not. You can place the code to close the file in both the try and catch blocks. To avoid rewriting the code, you can place the code in the finally block. The code in the finally block is executed regardless of whether an exception is thrown or not. The finally block follows the catch blocks. You can have only one finally block for an exception handler, but it is not mandatory to have a finally block.

Now consider the example of Listing 4-1.

The code listed in Figure 4-2 is used to display the customer records stored in an array. The try and catch blocks have been added to the code to handle the ArrayIndexOutOfBoundsException. The output of the code is shown in Figure 4-2.

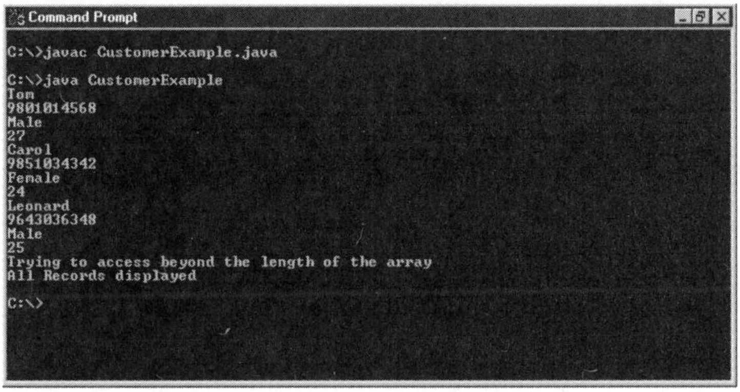

FIGURE 4-2 *The output of the* CustomerExample *code*

Listing 4-1 CustomerExample.java

```java
class Customer
{
 String custName;
 String custNo;
 String custSex;
 int custAge;
  public void displayDetails()
 {
    System.out.println(custName);
    System.out.println(custNo);
    System.out.println(custSex);
    System.out.println(custAge);
 }
 }
 public class CustomerExample
 {
     Customer custObjects[];
     public CustomerExample()
     {
         custObjects = new Customer;
         for(int ctr=0;ctr != 3;ctr++)
         {
             custObjects[ctr] = new Customer();
```

```java
            }
            custObjects[0].custName="Tom";
            custObjects[0].custNo="9801014568";
            custObjects[0].custSex="Male";
            custObjects[0].custAge=27;
            custObjects.custName="Carol";
            custObjects.custNo="9851034342";
            custObjects.custSex="Female";
            custObjects.custAge=24;
            custObjects.custName="Leonard";
            custObjects.custNo="9643036348";
            custObjects.custSex="Male";
            custObjects.custAge=25;
        }
        public void displayCollection()
        {
try
{
for(int ctr=0;ctr!=4; ctr++)
{
  custObjects[ctr].displayDetails();
}
}
catch(ArrayIndexOutOfBoundsException e) //catch block
        {
                System.out.println("Trying to access beyond the length of the
array");
        }
}
        public static void main(String args[])
        {
CustomerExample collectionObj;
collectionObj = new CustomerExample();
collectionObj.displayCollection();
System.out.println("All Records displayed");
        }
}
```

This example file (`CustomerExample.java`) is included in the samples folder of this chapter on the Web site that accompanies this book at **www.premierpress books.com/downloads.asp**.

You looked at predefined exceptions in Java. You can also define user-defined exceptions to address application-specific needs, as the exception classes in Java do not handle them. Now I'll discuss these.

User-Defined Exceptions

In the customer application, you might want to throw an exception if the customer age is less than 20 or greater than 60. You can handle these issues by defining your own exception classes.

You can create exception classes by extending the `Exception` class. The extended class contains constructors, data members, and methods like any other class. The `throw` and `throws` keywords are used while implementing user-defined exceptions.

For example, you can use the `throw` statement to throw an exception when a user enters an incorrect Login ID. The syntax to use the `throw` statement is given here:

```
throw [new] exception [(arguments_of_constructor)];
```

An example is given here:

```
throw new WrongLoginIDException("Login denied');
```

In the above example, an exception is thrown if an incorrect Login ID is entered. The `WrongLoginIDException` class must be defined and made accessible to the class that contains this `throw` statement.

You can place a `throw` statement inside a `try` block. You can also place the `throw` statement in the code of a method. You cannot throw primitive values or arbitrary objects. The thrown object carries information about the error condition.

If a method is capable of raising an exception that it does not handle, it must specify the exception to be handled by the calling method. This is done using the `throws` statement. The `throws` statement is used to specify the list of exceptions that are thrown by the method. The syntax to use the `throws` statement is:

```
[access_specifier>] [<modifier>] <return_type> <method_name> (<arg_list) [throws
<exception_list>]
```

An example is given here:

```
pubic void acceptPassword () throws IllegalAccessException
{
System.out.println("error!!");
throw new IllegalAccessException;
}
```

Now consider an example to use user-defined exceptions. The example code given in Listing 4-2 creates a user-defined exception class called `IllegalAgeException`. The `setAge()` method of the `customer` class checks whether the customer age entered is within the range of 20 and 60.

When you execute the code and enter 15 in the age text field, which is an invalid value, an error message is displayed on the status bar of the applet as shown in Figure 4-3.

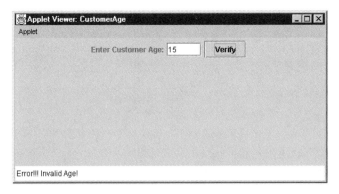

FIGURE 4-3 *The customer applet with the error message*

Listing 4-2 CustomerAge.java

```
import java.awt.*;
import java.awt.event.*;
import javax.swing.*;
// <applet code=CustomerAge width=500 height=200>
// </applet>
class IllegalAgeException extends Exception
{
```

```
        public String getMessage()
        {
            return "Error!!! Invalid Age! ";
}
}
public class CustomerAge extends JApplet
{
 int custAge;
 JPanel panelObject;
 JButton buttonAccept;
 JLabel labelCustAge;
 JTextField textCustAge;
 void setAge(int age) throws IllegalAgeException
 {
    if ((age<20) || (age>60))
           throw new IllegalAgeException();
    custAge=age;
 }
 public void init()
 {
    panelObject=(JPanel)getContentPane();
    panelObject.setLayout(new FlowLayout());
    labelCustAge=new JLabel("Enter Customer Age:");
    textCustAge=new JTextField(5);
    buttonAccept=new JButton("Verify");
    panelObject.add(labelCustAge);
    panelObject.add(textCustAge);
    panelObject.add(buttonAccept);
    ValidateAction validateButton=new ValidateAction();
    buttonAccept.addActionListener(validateButton);
 }
 class ValidateAction implements ActionListener
 {
    public void actionPerformed(ActionEvent evt)
    {
        Object obj=evt.getSource();
        if(obj==buttonAccept)
        {
```

```
            CustomerAge custObj=new CustomerAge();
         int age=Integer.parseInt(textCustAge.getText());
      try
        {
            custObj.setAge(age);
            getAppletContext().showStatus("Valid entry!!");
        }
        catch(IllegalAgeException e)
        {
            getAppletContext().showStatus(e.getMessage());
        }
      }
  }   } }
```

This example file (CustomerAge.java) is included in the samples folder of this chapter on the Web site that accompanies this book at **www.premierpress-books.com/downloads.asp**.

You've learned how to handle user-defined exceptions. Now, I'll discuss threads.

Threads

While working with Microsoft Word you may have noticed that your document is saved automatically after a specific interval of time. Similarly, while playing computer games, you might notice that the score, music, and graphics run simultaneously. Have you ever wondered how all this is possible? This is made possible by *threads*. I'll discuss them in detail.

A thread is similar to a sequential program. A sequential program has a beginning, followed by a sequence of steps to be executed, and an end. However, a thread is not itself a program, but runs within a program. A thread can be defined as the sequential flow of control within a program. Every program has at least one thread that is called the *primary* thread. For example, in every application the main() method is the primary thread. You can create more threads when necessary.

The microprocessor allocates memory to the processes that you execute. Each process occupies its own address space or memory. However, all the threads in a process share the same address space. Therefore, the resources of a program such as its memory, devices, data, and environment are available to all the threads of that program.

A process that comprises only one thread is called a *single-threaded* application. A single-threaded application can perform only one task at a time. In this situation, you wait for one task to be completed so that another can start. A process having more than one thread is called a *multithreaded* application. The multiple threads in the process run at the same time, perform different tasks, and interact with each other. For example, consider a Web browser. Using the browser, you can print a page in the background and scroll the page simultaneously.

Java has built-in support for threads. A major part of the Java architecture is multithreaded. In Java programs, threads are commonly used to allow an applet to accept inputs from a user and simultaneously display animation in another part of the screen. Any application that requires two tasks to be accomplished at the same time can be created using multithreading. I'll discuss how to create multiple threads in a program.

Creating Multithreaded Applications

You can create a multithreaded application by using either of the following two methods:

◆ Subclassing the `Thread` class

◆ Using the `Runnable` interface

I'll discuss these methods.

Subclassing the Thread *Class*

The `java.lang.Thread` class is used to construct and access individual threads in a multithreaded application. It supports many methods that obtain information about the activities of a thread; set and check the properties of a thread; and cause a thread to wait, be interrupted, or be destroyed. You can make your applications and classes run in separate threads by extending the `Thread` class. The syntax is given here:

```
public class <class_name> extends Thread
```

An example is given here:

```
public class MyThread extends Thread
{

}
```

Using the Runnable Interface

Applets extend from the JApplet class. Since Java does not support multiple inheritance, you cannot inherit a class from the JApplet or Thread class. Java provides the Runnable interface to solve this problem. The Runnable interface consists of a single method run(), which is executed when the thread is activated. You can extend from the JApplet class, implement the Runnable interface, and code the run() method. Using applications, you have a choice of extending from the Thread class. In other words, when a program needs to inherit from another class in addition to the Thread class, you need to implement the Runnable interface. The syntax for implementing the Runnable interface is given here:

```
public class <class_name> extends <superclass_name> implements Runnable
```

An example is given as follows:

```
public class MyApplet extends JApplet implements Runnable
{
//Implement the class
}
```

Before working with threads, it is essential for you to know the life cycle of a thread. I'll discuss the life cycle of a thread.

The Life Cycle of a Thread

A thread has four possible states:

- ◆ New thread
- ◆ Runnable
- ◆ Not runnable
- ◆ Dead

Now, I'll discuss each of these.

The new Thread State

When an instance of the Thread class is created, a thread enters the new thread state. The following code illustrates the instantiation of the Thread class:

```
Thread Thread1 = new Thread(this);
```

The `this` keyword signifies that the `run()` method of the current object needs to be invoked.

The above mentioned code creates a thread. Currently, no resources are allocated for it and it is an empty object. You have to invoke the `start()` method to start the thread:

```
Thread1.start();
```

The Runnable *State*

The `start()` method allocates necessary system resources for the thread, schedules the thread to run, and calls the `run()` method of the thread.

When the `start()` method of the thread is invoked, the thread enters the `runnable` state. Since a single processor cannot execute more than one thread at a time, the processor maintains a thread queue. After being started, a thread is queued up for processor time and waits to be executed. Therefore, at any given time, a thread might be waiting for the attention of the processor. That's why the state of the thread is called "`runnable`" and not "running."

Therefore, after the thread starts it enters the `runnable` state. All the activities of a thread occur in the body of the thread — the `run()` method. After a thread is created and initialized, the `run()` method is called, which usually contains a loop.

The Not Runnable *State*

A thread is said to be in the `not runnable` state if it is in any of the following states:

- ◆ Sleeping
- ◆ Waiting
- ◆ Locked by another thread

A thread is placed in the sleeping mode with the `sleep()` method. A sleeping thread enters the `runnable` state after the specified time elapses. Until the specified time elapses, the thread does not execute. The syntax of the `sleep` method is:

```
sleep(long t);
```

In the above syntax, `t` is the number of milliseconds for which the thread is inactive.

The sleep() method is a static method because it operates on the current thread.

The Dead State

A thread can either die naturally or be killed. A thread dies a natural death when the loop in the run() method is completed. For example, if the loop in the run() method has a hundred iterations, the life of the thread equals a hundred iterations of the loop. Assigning null to the thread object kills the thread. The isAlive() method of the Thread class is used to determine whether a thread is started or stopped.

Now consider an example to add the date and time to the customer applet by using threads as shown in Figure 4-4.

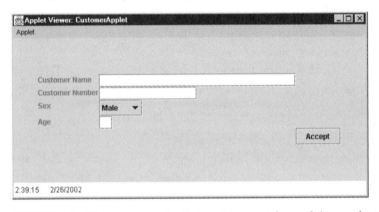

FIGURE 4-4 *The customer applet displays the current date and time on the status bar.*

The code is shown in Listing 4-3.

Listing 4-3 CustomerApplet.java

```java
import java.util.Date;
import java.util.Calendar;
import java.util.GregorianCalendar;
import javax.swing.*;
import java.awt.*;
import java.awt.event.*;
public class CustomerApplet extends JApplet implements Runnable
```

```
{
        //Variable for the panel
      JPanel panelObject;
      Thread datimeThread;
      Date date;
      GregorianCalendar calendar;
      String strDate, strTime, strStatus;
              //variables for labels

                  ............. .
...........//variables for data entry controls

                  .................
      //Variables for the layout

                  ........................ .
              public void init()
              {               // Code to create the layout

                  ............. .

                      ................ .

                      datimeThread = new Thread(this); //Initialize thread
                      datimeThread.start(); //Starting thread
              }
      public void run() // body of the thread
      {        while(datimeThread != null)
        {
              display();
              try
              {
                  datimeThread.sleep(1000);
              }
              catch(InterruptedException e)
              {
                  getAppletContext().showStatus("Thread interrupted");
              }        }        }
      public void display() //displays date and time on the status bar
      {
         date = new Date();
         calendar = new GregorianCalendar();
         calendar.setTime(date);
         strTime =
```

INTRODUCTION TO JAVA PROGRAMMING

```
calendar.get(Calendar.HOUR)+":"+calendar.get(Calendar.MINUTE)+":"+calendar.get(Calen
dar.SECOND);
        strDate =
(calendar.get(Calendar.MONTH)+1)+"/"+calendar.get(Calendar.DATE)+"/"+calendar.get(Ca
lendar.YEAR);
        strStatus=strTime+"        "+strDate;
        getAppletContext().showStatus(strStatus);
            }
    class ValidateAction implements ActionListener
    {
public void actionPerformed(ActionEvent evt)
    {
                // Code to attach event to the button
                ......................... . .

}
    }  }
```

The complete code of CustomerApplet.java is included in the samples folder of this chapter on the Web site that accompanies this book at **www.premierpress-books.com/downloads.asp**.

In the previous code, the customer applet implements the runnable interface. The datimeThread is initialized using the command:

```
datimeThread = new Thread(this);
```

The datimeThread is started using the command:

```
datimeThread.start();
```

The code for the thread is written in the run() method. The display() method in the code is used to display the current date and time on the status bar of the applet.

The Date class is used in the code. The Date class encapsulates the system date and time information. The Calendar class implements the methods that were present in the earlier version of the Date class. It can be extended to incorporate the conversion between different systems. The get() method is used to extract the date, the month, or the year from a given date. It is also used to extract the hour, minute, and seconds from a given time.

The GregorianCalendar class is extended from the Calendar class. You can create an object of this class by using a combination of date, time, and time zones. The setTime() method takes a Date object as an argument. It updates the GregorianCalendar object with the current date. The code also uses the InterruptedException to handle exceptions.

Summary

In this chapter, you learned that exception is defined as an anomalous event that occurs during program execution and disrupts program functioning. Java provides classes for handling exceptions. Exceptions are handled using the keywords try, catch, throw, throws, and finally. Next, you learned that you can create user-defined exceptions by extending the Exception class. You also learned about single-threaded and multithreaded applications, and finally, you learned about the life cycle of a thread.

Chapter 5

In this chapter, you'll look at the Java classes that handle input and output operations and learn how to create a client-server application.

Java Input and Output

Java programs perform I/O operations through streams. Data moves in the form of streams in and out of Java programs. Java provides a set of classes to handle I/O operations. All these classes are stored in a package, `java.io`, which is dedicated to the I/O operations in Java.

The Java Platform defines two types of streams:

- ◆ Byte streams
- ◆ Character streams

I'll now discuss each of these types in detail.

Byte Streams

Byte streams enable you to manage the input and output of bytes. Java defines two different hierarchies of classes for handling the input and output byte streams separately. At the top of the hierarchy are two abstract classes:

- ◆ `InputStream`
- ◆ `OutputStream`

The `InputStream` class creates an input stream and provides methods to read from those input streams. The constructor of the `InputStream` class is:

```
public InputStream()
```

Some of the methods of the `InputStream` class are listed in Table 5-1.

Table 5-1 Methods of the *InputStream* Class

Methods	Description
`int read()`	Reads a byte of data from the input stream
`int read(byte[] <byte>)`	Reads bytes from the input stream to the array `byte`
`int read(byte[] <byte>, int <off>, int <len>)`	Reads the `len` number of bytes into the array `byte` starting from offset, `off`
`long skip(long <n>)`	Skips n number of bytes in the input stream
`void close()`	Closes the file input stream and releases the resources allotted to the input stream

NOTE

To view the complete list of methods in the `InputStream` class and other classes explained in this chapter, please refer to the Sun Java 2 Platform, API specification.

The hierarchy of the `InputStream` is displayed in Figure 5-1 on page 118.

The `OutputStream` class creates an output stream and provides methods for writing to those output streams. The constructor of the `OutputStream` class is:

```
public OutputStream()
```

Some of the methods of the `OutputStream` class are listed in Table 5-2.

Table 5-2 Methods of the *OutputStream* Class

Methods	Description
`void write(int <n>)`	Writes the specified bytes to the file output stream
`void write(byte[] <byte>)`	Writes the elements of the specified array to the file output stream
`void write(byte[] <byte>, int <off>, int <len>)`	Writes the `len` number of elements starting from offset in the specified array to the file output stream
`void close()`	Closes the file output stream and releases the resources associated with the output stream

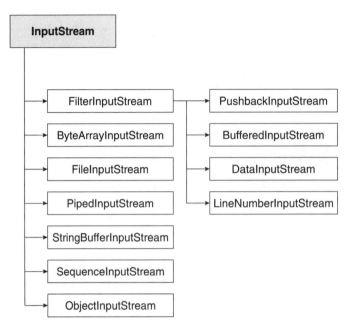

FIGURE 5-1 *Hierarchy of the* InputStream *class*

The hierarchy of the OutputStream is displayed in Figure 5-2.

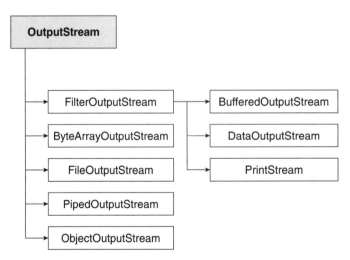

FIGURE 5-2 *Hierarchy of the* OutputStream *class*

Character Streams

Character streams enable you to manage the input and output of characters. Character streams use Unicode. Java defines two different hierarchies of classes for handling the input and output character streams separately. At the top of the hierarchy are two abstract classes:

◆ Reader

◆ Writer

The Reader class creates a character input stream and provides methods to read from those character input streams. The constructor of the Reader class is:

```
protected Reader();
protected Reader(Object <object>);
```

The second constructor creates an input stream that is synchronized on the given object.

Some of the methods of the Reader class are listed in Table 5-3.

Table 5-3 Methods of the *Reader* Class

Methods	Description
int read()	Reads a byte of data from the input stream
int read(byte[] <byte>)	Reads bytes from the input stream to the array byte
int read(byte[] <byte>, int <off>, int <len>)	Reads the len number of bytes into the array byte starting from offset, off
long skip(long <n>)	Skips n number of bytes in the input stream
void close()	Closes the file input stream and releases the resources allotted to the input stream

The Writer class creates a character output stream and provides methods for writing to those character output streams. The constructors of the Writer class are:

```
protected Writer();
protected Writer(Object <object>);
```

The second constructor creates an output stream that is synchronized on the given object.

Some of the methods of the Writer class are given in Table 5-4.

Table 5-4 Methods of the *Writer* Class

Methods	Description
void write(int <n>)	Writes the specified bytes to the output stream
void write(byte[] <byte>)	Writes the elements of the specified array to the output stream
void write(byte[] <byte>, int <off>, int <len>)	Writes the len number of elements starting from offset in the specified array to the output stream
void close()	Closes the output stream and releases the resources associated with the output stream
void write(String <string>)	Writes the specified string to the output stream
void write(String <string>, int <off>, int <len>)	Writes the specified portion of the string to the output stream

The hierarchy of the Reader class is displayed in Figure 5-3.

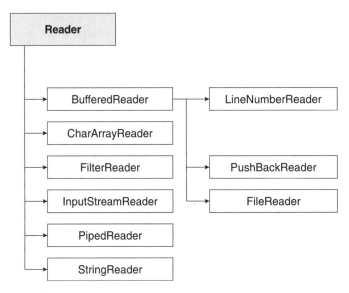

FIGURE 5-3 *Hierarchy of the* Reader *class*

The hierarchy of the Writer class is displayed in Figure 5-4.

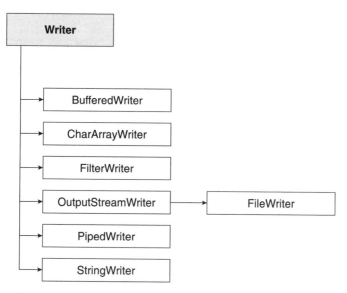

FIGURE 5-4 *Hierarchy of the* Writer *class*

 NOTE

Java 1.0 did not have character stream classes. These classes were included in Java 1.2.

Now I'll create Java programs for I/O by using these streams.

Reading and Writing Console I/O

Using the System class defined in the java.lang package, you can obtain information such as the current time and the other properties of the computer. The System class provides three predefined stream variables:

◆ out

◆ in

◆ err

These variables are declared in the java.lang package. All these variables are defined as static and public. To learn more about the public and static modifiers, refer to Chapter 1, "Programming in Java."

The out variable refers to the standard output stream. The default standard output stream is the console. System.out is an object of the PrintStream class.

The in variable refers to the standard input stream. The default input stream is the keyboard. System.in is an object of the java.io.BufferedInputStream class.

The err variable refers to the standard error stream. The default standard error stream is the console. System.err is an object of the PrintStream class.

All classes contain System.out, System.in, and System.err variables because the java.lang package is imported automatically in every Java class during compilation.

You can use these variables to read and write from the console. Now I'll create Java programs that read and write to the console.

Reading from the Console

In Java 1.0, byte streams were used to perform console inputs. However, since many classes and methods have been deprecated in Java 2.0, using byte stream classes is not recommended. You should use character streams to read inputs.

In Java, System.in is used to read console inputs. System.in is an object of the byte input stream class. Therefore, to receive the character-oriented input from the console, you need to wrap System.in in a BufferedReader object, which supports the buffered input stream. The constructor of the BufferedReader class is:

```
BufferedReader(Reader <Input_Reader>)
```

Here, Input_Reader is the input stream that is wrapped by the BufferedReader class. InputStreamReader, a subclass of the Reader class, converts bytes to characters. The InputStreamReader class reads bytes from byte streams and converts those bytes to characters. The class then writes these characters to character streams. The constructor of InputStreamReader is:

```
InputStreamReader(InputStream <Input_Stream>)
```

The above two code samples can be combined to a single line of code:

```
BufferedReader(new InputStreamReader(InputStream <Input_Stream>))
```

System.in is an object of the type InputStream. Therefore, you can pass System.-in as an argument to the constructor of InputStreamReader.

You can create a BufferedReader input stream by using the following statement:

```
BufferedReader(new InputStreamReader(InputStream <Input_Stream>))
```

Now I'll write a program that accepts inputs from the user. The program then displays the text entered by the user on the console.

The output of the program, readText, is displayed in Figure 5-5.

FIGURE 5-5 *The output of the* readText *program*

The code for the readText program is given in Listing 5-1.

Listing 5-1 readText.java

```java
import java.io.*;
class readText
{
        String[] readL = new String[5];
        readText() throws IOException
        {
                BufferedReader reader = new BufferedReader(new
InputStreamReader(System.in));
                System.out.println("Enter 5 lines--->");
                for(int i = 0;i<5;i++)
```

```
                                readL[i] = reader.readLine();
                                System.out.println("This is what you entered--->");
                                for(int i = 0;i<5;i++)
                                System.out.println(readL[i]);
                }
                public static void main(String[] args)
                {
                                try
                                {
                                                readText rt = new readText();
                                }
                                catch(IOException e)
                                {
                                                System.out.println("IOException
thrown.");
                                }
                }
}
```

In the above code, notice that System.in is passed as an argument to the constructor of InputStreamReader. In addition, an object of InputStreamReader is passed as an argument to the BufferedReader constructor.

Writing to the Console

The println() and print() methods are defined in the PrintStream class. System.out is an object of the PrintStream class. Therefore, you can refer to the standard console output as System.out.println() or System.out.print().

You can also use the PrintWriter class to write to the console. PrintWriter is a character-based class. The advantage of using the PrintWriter class is that it supports internationalization. The constructors of the PrintWriter class are:

```
PrintWriter(OutputStream <outputStream>)
PrintWriter(OutputStream <outputStream>, boolean <flush>)
PrintWriter(Writer <writer>)
PrintWriter(Writer <writer>, boolean <flush>)
```

Here, if flush is true, Java automatically flushes the output stream.

`PrintWriter` supports all the overloaded forms of the `print()` and `println()` methods.

Now, I'll show you how to read and write to files.

Reading and Writing to Files

Java enables you to read and write to files. Files are byte-oriented in Java. Java provides methods to read and write bytes to a file. The two-byte stream classes commonly used for file I/O are:

- ◆ `FileInputStream`
- ◆ `FileOutputStream`

Next, I'll discuss each of these classes in detail.

The *FileInputStream* Class

The `FileInputStream` class is derived from the `InputStream` class, which is the parent class of the byte stream classes. The constructors of the `FileInputStream` are:

```
FileInputStream(File <file_name>)
FileInputStream(String <file_name>)
```

The second form of constructor takes an object of the `File` class as an argument. Before continuing, take a look at the `File` class.

The *File* Class

The `File` class represents the file and directory objects of the host file systems. It uses the file-naming conventions of the host operating system. The constructors of the `File` class are used to create files and directories. The constructors of the `File` class are:

```
File(String <pathname>)
File(String <pathname>, String <filename>)
File(File <file-obj>, String <filename>)
```

Here, `pathname` is the path of the file, `filename` is the name of the file, and `file_obj` is the `File` object.

The constructors accept files and directory names as well as absolute and relative paths as arguments. The methods of the File class allow you to delete and rename files. These methods check for the read and write permissions of the file on the host operating system. You can create, delete, rename, and list directories by using the directory methods of the File class. Some of the methods are listed in Table 5-5.

Table 5-5 Methods of the *File* Class

Methods	Description
boolean canRead()	Returns true only if the file is readable
boolean canWrite()	Returns true only if the Java programs can modify the file
delete()	Deletes the file and returns true only if the file is successfully deleted
boolean exists()	Returns true if the file exists
String getParent()	Returns the pathname of the current file
boolean isDirectory()	Returns true if the File object represents a directory
boolean isFile()	Returns true if the File object represents a file
long length()	Returns the length of the File object
String[] list()	Returns an array of files and directories in the directory represented by the File object
boolean setReadOnly()	Marks the current directory or file represented by the File object as read-only

Now that I've talked about the File class, I'll return to the FileInputStream class.

The FileInputStream class allows you to read a class in the form of a stream. The exception FileNotFoundException is thrown when the file does not exist. Before Java 2, FileInputStream used to throw IOException.

The overloaded constructors of the FileInputStream class are given as follows:

```
FileInputStream(File <filename>)
FileInputStream(FileDescriptor < FileDescriptor>)
FileInputStream(String <name>)
```

Here, <name> represents an actual file on the file system.

The `FileInputStream` class contains methods to read from a file. The `read()` method reads the file and returns -1 on reaching the end of the file. The methods of the `FileInputStream` class are given in Table 5-6.

Table 5-6 Methods of the *FileInputStream* Class

Methods	Description
`int read()`	Reads a byte of data from the input stream
`int read(byte[] <byte>)`	Reads bytes from the input stream to the array `byte`
`int read(byte[] <byte>,` `int <off>, int <len>)`	Reads the `len` number of bytes into the array `byte` starting from offset, `off`
`long skip(long <n>)`	Skips n number of bytes in the input stream
`int available()`	Returns the number of bytes that can read from the file input stream
`void close()`	Closes the file input stream and releases the resources allotted to the input stream

Now, take a look at s an example that uses `FileInputStream` to read from a file. In this example, a file will be read and the content of the file will be displayed on the console. The output is displayed in the Figure 5-6.

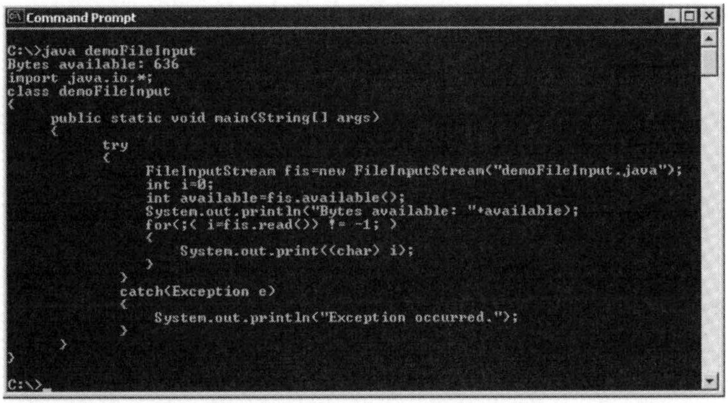

FIGURE 5-6 *The figure displays the file read using the* `FileInputStream` *class.*

The code to generate the above output is given in Listing 5-2.

Listing 5-2 demoFileInput.java

```java
import java.io.*;
class demoFileInput
{
        public static void main(String[] args)
        {
                try
                {
                        FileInputStream fis = new
FileInputStream("demoFileInput.java");
                        int i = 0;
                        int available = fis.available();
                        System.out.println("Bytes available:
"+available);

                        for(;( i = fis.read()) != -1; )
                        {
System.out.print((char) i);
                        }
                }
                catch(Exception e)
                {
                        System.out.println("Exception
occurred.");
                }
        }
}
```

In the above example, a FileInputStream object is created and the name of the file to be read is passed as an argument to the constructor. Next, using the read() method, the content of the file is read until the end of file is reached.

The *FileOutputStream* Class

Java provides you with `FileOutputStream` to write data to a file. The `FileOutputStream` class is derived from the `OutputStream` class, which is the parent class of the byte stream classes. The constructors of the `FileOutputStream` class are:

```
FileOutputStream(File <file_name>)
FileOutputStream(FileDescriptor <FileDescriptor>)
FileOutputStream(String <file_name>)
FileOutputStream(String <file_name>, boolean <append_to_file>)
```

Here, `<file_name>` is the name of the file and `<append_to_file>` assumes true or false values depending on whether the file output stream appends or overwrites the existing content of the file.

Some of the methods provided by the `FileOutputStream` class to write to a file are listed in Table 5-7.

Table 5-7 Methods of the *FileOutputStream* Class

Methods	Description
`void write(int <n>)`	Writes the specified bytes to the file output stream
`void write(byte[] <byte>)`	Writes the elements of the specified array to the file output stream
`void write(byte[] <byte>, int <off>, int <len>)`	Writes the `len` number of elements starting from offset in the specified array to the file output stream
`void close()`	Closes the file output stream and releases the resources associated with the output stream

In Listing 5-3 you'll take a look at an example that uses the `FileOutputStream` class to write to a file.

Listing 5-3 demoFileOutput.java

```java
import java.io.*;
class demoFileOutput
{
          public static void main(String[] args)
          {
```

```
int i = 0;
try
{
FileInputStream fis = new FileInputStream(args[0]);
FileOutputStream fos = new FileOutputStream(args);
for(;(i = fis.read()) ! =  -1;)
{
                fos.write((char) i);
}
}
catch(Exception e)
{
                System.out.println("Please enter cor-
rect file names.");
}
        }
}
```

In the above listing, the file contents are read and written to another file. An error message is displayed when incorrect or nonexistent file names are entered. The file names are entered at the command prompt along with the command to execute the code. For example, to write the content of demoFileOutput.java to the file Test.txt, you run the following command at the command prompt:

```
C:\>java demoFileOutput demoFileOutput.java Test.txt
```

You can also use the RandomAccessFile class to read and write to a file. This class is different from all other file I/O classes. I'll discuss this class to show you its features.

The *RandomAccessFile* Class

The RandomAccessFile is the subclass of the Object class. This class implements the java.io.DataInput and java.io.DataOutput interfaces. You can use the DataInput interface to read from any binary stream and then reconstruct the data in any of the primitive Java data types. The DataOutput interface helps convert primitive Java data types to byte streams and then write those streams to a binary stream.

The RandomAccessFile class implements both DataInput and DataOutput interfaces. Therefore, the class is capable of both reading and writing to a file. In addition, as the name suggests, the RandomAccessFile class can seek any location in a file randomly. First, take a look at the constructors of the class and then the methods of the classes that enable you perform such tasks.

The following are the overloaded forms of the constructors of the RandomAccess-File class:

```
RandomAccessFile( File <file_name>, String <mode>)
RandomAccessFile( String <file_name>, String <mode>)
```

Here, <file_name> represents the file name that needs to be accessed and <mode> is either r (read) or rw (read and write). When the file is opened in the r mode, only read operations can be performed on the file. However, in the files that are opened in the rw mode, you can perform both read and write operations. The security manager in the JVM performs checks to allow read and write operations.

Some of the methods of the RandomAccessFile class are given in Table 5-8.

Table 5-8 Methods of the *RandomAccessFile* Class

Methods	Description
void close()	Closes the I/O streams and releases any resources associated with the streams
long getFilePointer()	Returns the current position of the pointer in the file
long length()	Returns the length of the file
int read()	Reads a byte of data from the file
int read(byte[] <byte>)	Reads bytes into the array byte from the file
int read(byte[] <byte>, int <off>, int <len>)	Reads the len number of bytes from the file into the array byte starting from the offset, off
boolean readBoolean()	Reads a boolean from the file
byte readByte()	Reads signed 8-byte value from the file
char readChar()	Reads a Unicode char from the file
int readInt()	Reads an int value from the file
String readLine()	Reads a line of text from the file

continues

Table 5-8 *(continued)*

Methods	Description
`void seek(long <position>)`	Places the file pointer at the specified position from the beginning of the file
`int skipBytes(int <len>)`	Skips the `len` number of bytes
`void write(byte[] <byte>)`	Writes the bytes in the array `byte` into the file starting from the current position of the file pointer
`void write(int <int>)`	Writes specified bytes to the file
`void writeBoolean (boolean <bool>)`	Writes a boolean to the file as a 1-byte value
`void writeByte(int <byte>)`	Writes a byte to the file as a 1-byte value
`void writeBytes (String <str>)`	Writes a string as a sequence of characters
`void writeChar(int <int>)`	Writes a char as a 2-byte value
`void writeChars (String <str>)`	Writes a string value as a sequence of characters to the file
`void writeInt(int <int>)`	Writes the `int` argument as a 4-byte value

You've looked at the methods of the `RandomAccessFile` class. Now, take a look at an example that uses the `RandomAccessFile` class. In this example, the user is first asked if he wants to enter data in a file. Upon confirmation from the user, the user is prompted to enter the file name. Figure 5-7 displays the output of the example.

FIGURE 5-7 *The figure displays the output of the code to write to a file by using* `RandomAccessFile`.

Now take a look at the code in Listing 5-4 that generates the output in Figure 5-7.

Listing 5-4 demoRAF.java

```java
import java.io.*;
class demoRAF
{
        demoRAF()
        {
                try
                {
                char read;
                System.out.println("Do you want to enter text in a
file? (y/n)--->");
                BufferedReader reader = new BufferedReader(new
InputStreamReader(System.in));
                read = (char)reader.read(); //read the selection made
by the user
                if((read == 'y')||(read == 'Y'))
                openFile();
                else
                System.out.println("Quitting..........");
                }
                catch(Exception e)
                {
                System.out.println("Exception occurred: " + e);
                }
        }
        public static void main(String[] args)
        {
                demoRAF demo = new demoRAF();
        }
        void openFile()
        {
                try
                {
                String fileName;
                String readline;
```

```
                              BufferedReader reader = new BufferedReader(new
InputStreamReader(System.in));
                              System.out.println("Enter file name where you want to
enter text--->");

                              fileName = reader.readLine(); //read the filename
                              long ptr = 0;
                              RandomAccessFile file = new
RandomAccessFile(fileName,"rw"); //access the file
                              System.out.println("Enter text--->");
                              readline = reader.readLine(); //read the text entered
                              ptr = file.length(); //get the length of the file
                              file.seek(ptr); //place the file pointer at the end
of the file

                              file.writeBytes(readline); //write to the file
                              }
                              catch(Exception e)
                              {
                              System.out.println("Exception occurred: " + e);
                              }
                  }
}
```

Here, the `RandomAccessFile` class is used to open the file in the rw mode. Then, using the `length()` and `seek()` methods, the file pointer is placed at the end of the file. The `writeBytes()` method is used to write at the end of file.

There are two more classes that you can use to read and write to files. These are:

- ◆ `FileReader`
- ◆ `FileWriter`

Both these classes are of the character stream type. The `FileReader` class is derived from the `Reader` class, and the `FileWriter` class is derived from the `Writer` class. I'll briefly discuss these classes.

The *FileReader* Class

The `FileReader` class extends `java.io.InputStreamReader`. The `InputStream-Reader` class is the subclass of the `java.io.Reader` class. The `FileReader` class is used to read the contents of a file. The following are the two most commonly used constructors of the class:

```
FileReader(String <file_path>)
FileReader(File <file_obj>)
```

The `FileReader` class does not define any methods of its own. All its methods are inherited from either `InputStreamReader` or the `Reader` classes.

The *FileWriter* Class

The `FileWriter` class extends `java.io.OutputStreamWriter`. The `Output-StreamWriter` class is the subclass of the `java.io.Writer` class.

The `FileWriter` class is used to write to files. The commonly used constructors of the class are shown here:

```
FileWriter(String <file_path>)
FileWriter(File <file_obj>)
FileWriter(String <file_path>, boolean <append>)
```

Like `FileReader`, the `FileWriter` class also does not define any methods of its own. All its methods are inherited from either `OutputStreamWriter` or the `Writer` classes.

You've learned how to perform I/O operations in Java programs. Now I'll show you how to write network applications.

Network Applications

Java support for network applications is provided through `java.net package`. The package contains classes for establishing connections and exchanging data between the computers on a network. Data between computers is usually exchanged through sockets. The sockets are discussed in the next section.

Sockets

Network programs can communicate through sockets. Sockets can be used to transfer the data between processes running either on the same computer or on different computers in a network. A wide range of operating systems supports sockets. The Java platform supports two types of sockets:

- ◆ TCP/IP Sockets
- ◆ Datagram Sockets

Java Platform 2 provides extensive support for these sockets. Take a look at each socket in detail.

TCP/IP Sockets

A TCP/IP socket is connection-oriented. To communicate over TCP, client and server programs establish a connection and bind a socket. Sockets are like the ports that expose your computer to the network. After a communication channel binds the sockets of two computers, data exchange can start through these sockets. The sockets use the I/O streams provided in the Java Platform for I/O.

The Java Platform provides the `java.net.Socket` class to set up client TCP/IP sockets. The `Socket` class is derived from the `Object` class. The constructors of the `Socket` class are given in Table 5-9.

Table 5-9 Constructors of the *Socket* Class

Constructor	Description
`protected Socket()`	Creates an unconnected socket
`Socket(String <host>, int <port_number>)`	Creates a socket and connects it with the specified `port_number` on the specified `host`
`Socket(InetAddress <IP_Address>, int <port_number>)`	Creates a socket and connects it with the specified `port_number` on the specified `IP_Address`

Some of the methods of the `Socket` class are listed in Table 5-10.

Table 5-10 Methods of the *Socket* Class

Methods	Description
`void close()`	Closes the socket
`InetAddress getInetAddress()`	Returns the address of the socket host
`InputStream getInputStream()`	Returns the input socket stream

Methods	Description
`InetAddress getLocalAddress()`	Returns the local address where the socket is bound
`int getLocalPort()`	Returns the local port number to which the socket is bound
`OutputStream getOutputStream()`	Returns the output socket stream
`int getPort()`	Returns the remote port to which the socket is connected
`String toString()`	Converts the stream to a string

Datagram Sockets

Unlike TCP/IP sockets, datagram sockets are not connection-oriented. Datagram sockets send self-contained packets of data. Each packet contains data as well as information about the destination.

In Java, the `java.net.DatagramPacket` class represents datagram packets. The `DatagramPacket` class is derived from the `java.lang.Object` class. The constructors of the `DatagramPacket` class are given in Table 5-11.

Table 5-11 Constructors of the *DatagramPacket* Class

Constructor	Description
`DatagramPacket(byte[] <byte>, int <len>)`	Constructs a datagram packet of length `len`. The array, `byte`, will hold the datagram packet
`DatagramPacket(byte[] <byte>, int <len>)`	Constructs a datagram packet capable of receiving packets of length `len`
`DatagramPacket(byte[] <byte>, int <off>, int <len>, InetAddress <address>, int <port>)`	Constructs a datagram packet, `byte`, to send packets of length `len` with the buff offset `off` to the specified port number on the specified host

Some of the methods of the `DatagramPacket` class are listed in Table 5-12.

Table 5-12 Methods of the *DatagramPacket* Class

Methods	Description
`InetAddress getAddress()`	Returns the IP address of the destination computer
`byte[] getData()`	Returns the data carried by the datagram packet
`int getLength()`	Returns the size of the data being carried by the datagram packet
`int getPort()`	Returns the port number of the source of the datagram packet
`void setAddress(InetAddress <inetaddr>)`	Sets the destination of the datagram packet
`void setData(byte[] <byte>)`	Sets the data for a datagram packet
`void setLength(int <length>)`	Sets the length of the datagram packet, which is the number of bytes that are sent or received (the length must be less than or equal to the length of the packet buffer)
`void setPort(int <iport>)`	Sets the port number of the destination to `iport`

Methods Inherited from the *Object* Class

`protected  Object clone()`	Creates and returns a copy of the object
`boolean equals(Object <object>)`	Returns true if the two objects being compared are equal
`Class getClass()`	Returns the class of an object
`void notify()`	Wakes up a single thread
`void notifyAll()`	Wakes up all the threads
`String toString()`	Returns a string equivalent of the object

In addition to the `Socket` and `DatagramPacket` classes, `java.net  package` contains other classes to facilitate the creation of network applications in Java.

Now I'll create a network server application.

Creating a Network Server Application

Here's how to create a network server and client application. In this example, a client connects to the server and the server sends a message to the client. The communication between the server and the client is carried out over a network. When you run the client application, the user is prompted for the name of the connection. Figure 5-8 displays the output of the client application in Listing 5-6.

FIGURE 5-8 *The figure displays the output of the client application.*

After the client connects to the server and provides the connection name, the name and number of the connection are displayed at the server end. Figure 5-9 displays the server application in Listing 5-5 after two clients have logged in.

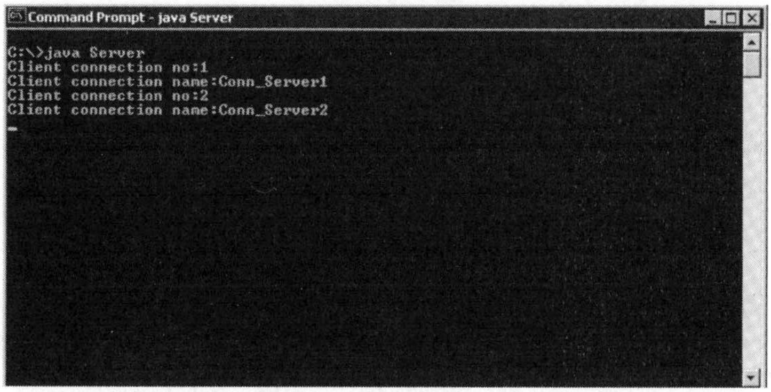

FIGURE 5-9 *The figure displays the output of the server application after two clients log in.*

First, take a look at the network server application in Listing 5-5.

Listing 5-5 Server.java

```java
import java.io.*;
import java.net.*;
public class Server implements Runnable
{
ServerSocket serverSocket;
PrintStream streamToClient;
BufferedReader streamFromClient;
Socket fromClient;
static int count = 0;
Thread thread;
public Server()
{
        try
        {
        serverSocket = new ServerSocket(1001);//create socket
    }
        catch(Exception e)
        {
                System.out.println("Socket could not be created "+e);
        }

        thread = new Thread(this);
    thread.start();
}

public void run()
{
        try
        {
        while (true)
        {
                                fromClient = serverSocket.accept();//accept
connection from client
                count++;
```

```
                                        System.out.println("Client connection
no:"+count);

                                        streamFromClient = new BufferedReader(new
InputStreamReader((fromClient.getInputStream()))));//create an input stream for the
socket

                                        streamToClient = new
PrintStream(fromClient.getOutputStream());//create an output stream for the socket
                                        String str =
streamFromClient.readLine();//read the message sent by client
                                        System.out.println("Client connection name:"
+ str);

                                        streamToClient.println("Welcome
"+str);//message sent message to client
                                }//end of while

                        }
                        catch(Exception e)
                        {
                                        System.out.println("Exception "+e);
                        }
                finally
                        {
                          try
                          {
                                        fromClient.close();
                          }
                          catch(Exception e1)
                           {
                                        System.out.println("Could not close connection
:"+e1);
                           }
                        }
           }
public static void main(String args[])
{
                new Server();
}
}//end of class
```

This example file (`Server.java`) is included in the samples folder of this chapter on the Web site that accompanies this book at **www.premierpressbooks.com/ downloads.asp**.

Here, a server application is created that will accept data from the client and send a message to the client.

```
serverSocket = new ServerSocket(1001);
```

The above statement creates a server socket at the port, 1001. An exception is thrown if the application fails to create a server socket.

The client and the server are the two halves of the client-server architecture. You've looked at the server application. Now take a look at the client application.

Creating a Network Client Application

The client application is listed in Listing 5-6.

Listing 5-6 Client.java

```java
import java.io.*;
import java.net.*;
public class Client
{
            PrintStream streamToServer;
            BufferedReader streamFromServer;
            Socket toServer;
            public Client()
            {
                        connectToServer();
            }
            private void connectToServer()
            {
            try
            {
                        String name;
                        toServer = new Socket("localhost",1001);
                        streamFromServer = new BufferedReader(new
InputStreamReader((toServer.getInputStream()))));
```

```
                                streamToServer = new
PrintStream(toServer.getOutputStream());

                                System.out.print("Enter connection name: ");
                                BufferedReader reader = new BufferedReader(new
InputStreamReader(System.in));

                                name = reader.readLine();
                                streamToServer.println(name);
                                String str = streamFromServer.readLine();
                                System.out.println("The Server says : "+str);
                }
                catch(Exception e)
                {
                                System.out.println("Exception "+e);
                }
                }
                public static void main(String args[])
                {
                                new Client();
                }
}//end of class
```

This example file (`Client.java`) is included in the samples folder of this chapter on the Web site that accompanies this book at **www.premierpressbooks.com/ downloads.asp**.

The output of Listing 5-6 is displayed in Figure 5-8.

Summary

In this chapter, you learned about the complexities of I/O operations in Java applications. In Java, the I/O operations are carried out by either byte or character streams. The Java API provides various classes to help use the I/O streams for reading or writing to a file or console. In addition, Java applications can exchange data. These applications can be on the same computer or on different computers. Some of the classes used for I/O are `InputStream`, `OutputStrean`, `Reader`, `Writer`, `FileInputStream`, `FileOutputStream`, `File`, `RandomAccessFile`, and `Socket`. In this chapter, you looked at all these classes in detail. Examples were provided for I/O operations between the console, the file, and Java applications. You learned to create network server and client applications by using the `Socket` classes.

Chapter 6

In this chapter, you will learn about the architecture of Remote Method Invocation (RMI) and Common Object Request Broker Architecture (CORBA). You will also learn how RMI and CORBA applications work.

An Introduction to RMI

Remote Method Invocation (RMI) is a specification that enables a Java Virtual Machine (JVM) to invoke the methods in an object located on another JVM. The two JVMs can be running on different computers or on the same computer. RMI is implemented in the middle-tier of the three-tier architecture, thereby enabling you to invoke distributed components across a networked environment.

RMI was introduced by Sun Microsystems as an alternative to the complex coding involved in server-socket programming. To use RMI, you need not know socket programming or multi-threading, and you need to concentrate solely on developing the business logic.

A distributed RMI application has two components:

◆ The RMI server
◆ The RMI client

The RMI server contains the objects whose methods you want to invoke remotely. It creates several remote objects and includes a reference to these objects in the *RMI registry*. The RMI registry is a service that runs on the RMI server. The remote objects created by the server are registered by the their unique name in this registry. The RMI client gets the reference of one or more remote objects from the RMI registry by the object name. The client then invokes the methods on the remote object(s) to access the services of the remote object(s). The methods of the remote object(s) are invoked just like the methods of a local object. Figure 6-1 depicts the functioning of an RMI application.

Now, I'll discuss the architecture of RMI.

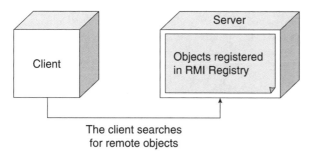

FIGURE 6-1 *Functioning of an RMI application*

The RMI Architecture

The RMI architecture consists of three layers:

◆ The Stub/Skeleton Layer
◆ The Remote Reference Layer
◆ The Transport Layer

I'll now discuss each of the above.

The Stub/Skeleton Layer

The *Stub/Skeleton Layer* is responsible for listening to the remote method calls made by the client and redirecting them to the server. This layer consists of a *stub* and a *skeleton*.

A stub is a client-side proxy representing the remote objects. The stub communicates the method invocations to the remote object through a skeleton that is implemented on the server. The skeleton is a server-side proxy that communicates with the stub. It makes a call to the remote object.

The Remote Reference Layer

The *Remote Reference Layer* (RRL) interprets the references made by the client to the remote object on the server. This layer is present on the client as well as on the server. The RRL on the client-side receives the request for the methods from the stub. The request is then transferred to the RRL on the server-side.

The Transport Layer

The *Transport Layer* is a link between the RRL on the server-side and the RRL on the client-side. It receives a request from the client-side RRL and establishes a connection with the server through a server-side RRL. The architecture of RMI is depicted in Figure 6-2.

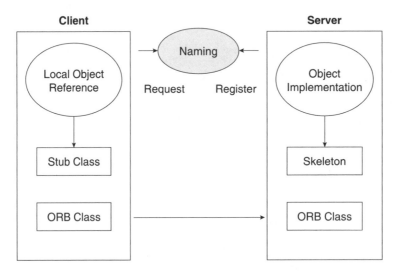

FIGURE 6-2 *Architecture of RMI*

You've learned about the architecture of RMI. Now, I'll discuss how to develop an application in RMI.

Developing an RMI Application

To create an RMI application, you need to create the remote interface class, the server class, and the client class. I'll discuss each of the steps in detail.

Creating the Remote Interface

In the remote interface, you specify the methods that can be invoked remotely by a client. The `java.rmi` package declares the `Remote interface`, `Naming`, and `RMISecurityManager` classes. It also defines a number of exception classes that are used with RMI. The `RemoteException` class is the parent of all exceptions that are generated during RMI. When defining the remote interface, you need to import the `java.rmi` package. Next, you need to declare the remote interface as `public` and extend the `java.rmi.Remote` interface.

Each method must declare `java.rmi.RemoteException` in its `throws` clause to trap network connection and server problems.

A sample code for the remote interface is given as follows:

```
import java.rmi.*;
public interface HelloServer extends Remote
{
String DisplayHello() throws RemoteException;
}
```

Defining the Server Class

The *server class* is a remote object implementation class. In the server class, you need to implement the remote interface and the remote methods. Next, you need to create and install the security manager, create an instance of a remote object, and register a remote object with the RMI registry.

Now, I'll discuss each of the above.

Implementing a Remote Interface

You can implement a remote interface by extending the `UniCastRemoteObject` class. The `UniCastRemoteObject` class extends the `RemoteServer` class and provides the default `RemoteObject` implementation. The classes that implement `RemoteObject` usually subclass the `UnicastRemoteObject` class.

The `java.rmi.server` package implements the interfaces and classes that support both the client and the server of the RMI. The `RemoteObject` class implements the remote interface and provides remote implementation of the `Object` class. All the objects that implement remote objects extend the `RemoteObject` class. The `RemoteServer` class extends the `RemoteObject` class and is a common class subclassed by specific types of remote object implementations.

A sample code to implement a remote interface is as follows:

```
import java.rmi.*;
import java.rmi.server.UnicastRemoteObject;
public class ExampleImpl extends UnicastRemoteObject implements Example
{
}
```

Next, you need to define the constructor for the remote object, as given here:

```
public ExampleImpl() throws RemoteException
{
        super();
}
```

The `super()` method invokes the constructor of the `UnicastRemoteObject` class, which exports the remote object.

Providing Implementation for Remote Methods

The implementation class for a remote object, that is the server class, contains the code that implements the remote method declared in the remote interface. The arguments and return value of the remote method can be of any data type. In RMI, by default, local objects are passed by copy except for static or transient objects. Remote objects are passed by reference. A reference to a remote object is a reference to a stub, which is a client-side proxy for the remote object.

Creating and Installing the Security Manager

A `java.lang.SecurityManager` object protects the system resources from unreliable downloaded code executing within the client JVM. It ensures that the operations performed by downloaded code undergo a security check. This determines whether an operation that a program intends to perform is permitted.

The `main()` method of the server first needs to create and install a security manager using the `RMISecurityManager` class. You use the statement given as follows to create and install the security manager:

```
System.setSecurityManager(new RMISecurityManager());
```

Creating an Instance of the Remote Object

The `main()` method of the server needs to create an instance of the server that implements the remote interface to provide the service. An example is shown here:

```
ExampleImpl instance = new ExampleImpl();
```

Once created, the server object is ready to accept incoming requests.

Registering the Remote Object

The RMI registry is a server-side service that allows remote clients to get the reference of a remote object. You use the `Naming.rebind` method to bind a remote object name to a specified URL of the registry. The `rebind()` method takes two parameters. The first parameter is a URL string that contains the location and name of the remote object. If the port number is not specified, the RMI registry uses the default port 1099. If you need to define the port, you need to change the URL string to `":1234/ServerName"`. The second parameter is a reference to the object implementation.

An example to register the name of a remote object in the RMI registry is given here:

```
Naming.rebind("ServerName",instance);
```

A sample code of the server class is as follows:

```
import java.rmi.*;
import java.rmi.server.UnicastRemoteObject;
public class HelloServerImpl extends UnicastRemoteObject
{
public HelloServerImpl() throws RemoteException
{
super();
}
public String DisplayHello() throws RemoteException
{
return "Hello";
}
public static void main(String args[])
{
```

```
System.setSecurityManager(new RMISecurityManager());
try
{
HelloServerImpl instance = new HelloServerImpl();
Naming.rebind("HelloServer", instance);
System.out.println("Server Registered");
}
catch(Exception e)
{
System.err.println(e);
}
}
}
```

After defining the server class, the next step is to define the client class. Now, take a look at what goes into the client class.

Defining the Client Class

In the client class, you obtain the reference to the remote object implementation and then invoke the remote methods.

The application gets a reference to the remote object implementation from the RMI registry running on the server. You can use the lookup() method in the Naming class to get the reference to the remote server. The lookup() method takes the name that is registered on the server as a parameter. It creates a stub instance to connect to the rmiregistry process running on the server and receives the stub instance and loads the stub class from the codebase property. An example is shown here:

```
ServerName server = (ServerName)Naming.lookup("ServerName");
```

In the preceding statement, ServerName is the name of the server. Next, you need to invoke the remote method on the remote object of the server. A sample code of the client class is given here:

```
import java.rmi.*;
public class Client
{
public static void main(String arg[])
```

```
{
try
{
HelloServer server = (HelloServer) Naming.lookup("HelloServer");
String str = server.DisplayHello();
System.out.println(str);
}
catch(Exception e)
{
System.out.println(e);
}
}
}
```

After defining the server class, the client class, and the remote interface, you need to compile the source files and debug errors, if any.

Now you've learned how to design an RMI application. Next, I'll discuss how to execute an RMI application.

Executing an RMI Application

Before you execute an RMI application across the network, you need to copy the client class file, the interface class file, and the stub class file on the client machine. Next, you need to copy the server class file, the interface class file, and the skeleton class file on the server machine. You also need to give the address of the server in the `Naming.lookup()` method in the client class. An example is shown here:

```
Naming.lookup("rmi://(IP address of the server machine)/MyServer");
```

To execute the RMI application you need to generate the stub and skeleton and create a security policy. Next, you need to start the RMI remote registry, the server, and the client. I'll discuss these.

Generating the Stub and the Skeleton

To generate the stub and the skeleton classes you need to use the `rmic` compiler. The syntax is given here:

```
rmic [option] <fully qualified class name>
```

The rmic options are listed in Table 6-1.

Table 6-1 *rmic* Options

Parameters	Description
-bootclasspath path	The files in the path specified will override the bootstrap class files.
-classpath path	The path specified will override the default or CLASS-PATH environment variable. Semicolons should separate the folders in the path.
-d directory	The stub and skeleton classes will be generated in the directory specified.
-depend	The classes that are referenced are also compiled. By default, only out-of-date and missing classes are compiled.
-extdirs path	The location of installed extensions is overridden.
-g	Line numbers and local variables are generated in the form of a table. This helps in debugging applications.
-J	The options following -J are passed to the java interpreter.
-keep or –keepgenerated	The .java files that are generated for the stub and skeleton classes are retained.
-nowarn	The compiler does not print any warnings.
-vcompat	Creates stubs and skeletons compatible with previous versions of the RMI protocol.
-verbose	Messages are printed as and when classes are compiled or created.
-v<version>	Creates the stubs or skeletons for the previous version as specified.

After you execute the rmic command, the _Skel.class and _Stub.class files are created. The generated stub class implements the same set of remote interfaces as the remote object.

RMI uses the stub class as a proxy in the client machine so that the client can communicate with the remote object. The skeleton class acts as a proxy of the client computer's object that is located on the remote host.

Now, I'll discuss how to create a security policy.

Creating a Security Policy

Java provides protection from viruses through the use of a security manager. Since RMI applications are distributed and execute over the network, the applications need to run under the scrutiny of a security manager. The security manager grants explicit permissions to the applications to access resources.

To obtain permissions to access a resource, you need to create a security policy file. A policy file in Java is an ASCII text file that can be created using a text editor or a graphic policy tool utility.

You need to create a policy file named. `java.policy` under your HOME directory. This file will contain the code to grant permissions to the required objects. To create a security policy file, start the policy tool utility, grant the required permission, and save the policy file.

 NOTE

You learned to work with the policy tool in Chapter 2, "Creating Applets."

Starting the Remote Object Registry

To start the RMI registry on the server, you need to execute the following command at the command prompt:

```
start rmiregistry
```

By default, the registry runs on port 1099. To start the RMI registry on a different port, you need to specify the port number on the command line as given here:

```
start rmiregistry 1234
```

If the registry is running on a port other than 1099, you will have to specify the port number in the URL string specified in the `rebind()` method of the `Naming` class.

The next step is to start the server and the client.

Starting the Server and the Client

To start the server you need to use the Java command, after setting the `codebase` property. The `codebase` property must contain the location of the stub class so that the stub class is automatically downloaded by the client. The next option that you need to specify is the security policy.

The syntax of the java command is given here:

```
java -Djava.rmi.server.codebase=file:///<directory path to the file> -
Djava.security.policy=.java.policy <fully qualified classname>
```

The last step to execute the RMI application is to start the client. The syntax to start the client is given here:

```
java <class name>
```

Now that you are familiar with creating an RMI application, I'll discuss how a CORBA application works.

An Introduction to CORBA

CORBA, or Common Object Request Broker Architecture, provides a standard architecture for distributed and heterogeneous objects to interoperate.

CORBA is defined by the Object Management Group (OMG). Most of the major vendors and developers of the distributed object technology are part of this group. OMG adopted the CORBA standards in 1990. This was followed by many revisions of the CORBA architecture.

Before learning about the architecture of CORBA, I'll compare RMI and CORBA.

RMI and CORBA are both defined for the communication of remote objects in the middle-tier of distributed applications. RMI enables a Java object to remotely communicate with other Java objects. CORBA, on the other hand, provides a solution that is portable across multiple platforms. CORBA provides an environment for the communication of objects regardless of the programming languages they are written in or the operating systems that they are running on. You can use CORBA to enable interaction between legacy systems and new technology applications.

RMI applications are slower than CORBA applications. This is because RMI is based on Java, which is an interpreted language. The execution of an interpreted language has interpretation overheads that are not present in compiled languages. These interpretation overheads include the excess time taken to interpret each line of code as compared to compilation, in which the entire code is compiled in one instance. Therefore, CORBA applications are suitable for real-time systems since their execution time is less than that of RMI.

Another difference between RMI and CORBA is that RMI passes parameters by value whereas CORBA passes parameters by reference. When parameters are passed by value, a copy of the parameter is passed to the calling component. As a result, when an object is passed as a parameter and a method call is made, the method is executed in the calling component. On the other hand, when parameters are passed by reference, instead of a copy of the object, the object reference is passed to the calling component.

Now, I'll discuss the architecture of CORBA.

The Architecture of CORBA

The CORBA architecture consists of the following components:

- ◆ Object Request Broker (ORB)
- ◆ Common Object Services
- ◆ Interface Definition Language (IDL)
- ◆ Internet Inter-ORB Protocol (IIOP)
- ◆ Basic Object Adapter (BOA)

Now, I'll discuss each of the above.

Object Request Broker

The foundation of the CORBA architecture is based on the *Object Request Broker* (ORB). The ORB is a primary mechanism that acts as a middleware between the client and the server. It provides a heterogeneous environment in which a client can remotely communicate with the server irrespective of the hardware, the operating systems, and the software development language used.

The ORB helps establish connection with the remote server. When a client wants to use the services of a server, it first needs reference to the object that is providing the service. Here, the ORB plays its role; the ORB resolves the client's requests for the object reference by locating the object on behalf of the client and thereby enables the client and the server to establish connectivity.

Common Object Services

The Common Object Services help the ORB in enabling objects to interact in a heterogeneous environment. These services are responsible for tasks such as creating objects, and monitoring access control and relocated objects. One of the important object services is the Naming service. This service enables a remote server object to register itself with the ORB so that a client can use its services.

Interface Definition Language (IDL)

CORBA uses the concept of an *Interface Definition Language* (IDL) to implement its services. IDL is a neutral programming language method of defining how a service is implemented. The syntax of this language is independent of any programming language. IDL is used to define an *interface*, which describes the methods that are available and the parameters that are required when a call is made for a remote object.

Internet Inter-ORB Protocol (IIOP)

A protocol, or set of rules, has to be followed for communication over the network. Therefore, distributed architectures must specify the protocol to be followed. The CORBA standard specifies *General Inter-ORB Protocol* (GIOP) as a standard protocol that defines how ORBs communicate with components. GIOP is a generalized protocol and therefore is not used directly. IIOP is a TCP/IP implementation of GIOP. It is a standard protocol for communication between ORBs on TCP/IP based networks.

Vendors can define their own proprietary protocols for their implementation of CORBA. However, they must implement IIOP for their products to be CORBA 2.0/n/ncompliant. This ensures interoperability. When there is more than one protocol, the ORB can negotiate as to which protocol to use.

Since the Internet uses TCP/IP and the IIOP is defined for TCP/IP, a CORBA application can communicate over the Internet.

Basic Object Adapter (BOA)

The ORB also provides services other than those required for object communication. These services are provided by object adapters and can range from user authentication to object activation to object persistence. Object adapters are a part of the ORB. The Basic Object Adapter (BOA) provides the basic functions required for accessing the services of an ORB. If you compare the ORB to a computer, the BOA can be compared to the shell program of the UNIX operating system. You can directly communicate with the operating system using system calls. But certain other services, for example, the C++ compiler, are provided as added services.

One of the most important services provided by the BOA is the server activation policy service. The server activation policies define how a server component should be started and executed. For example, a server might be initialized once and many clients might access the same server object.

Now you are familiar with the components of the CORBA architecture. Next, I'll discuss how a CORBA application works.

The Functioning of CORBA Applications

In a CORBA application, the client application requests the Naming service for a reference to an object. A reference to a CORBA object is returned and passed to the stub. The client invokes the methods through the stub reference. The stub in turn passes requests to the skeleton reference obtained through the Naming service.

The functioning of a CORBA application is illustrated in Figure 6-3.

The first step to design a CORBA application is to create an Interface Definition Language (IDL) file. You specify the functionality of the CORBA application in this file. The IDL file contains the IDL interfaces, which when compiled generate the interface definition files, a server application, the client stub, and the server skeleton.

The IDL language has syntax and keywords only for defining methods and data types. Like Java and C++, IDL has both the primitive and aggregated data types.

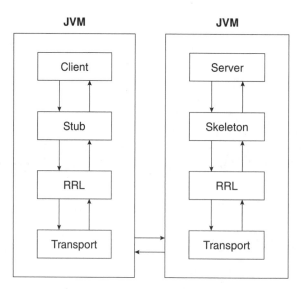

FIGURE 6-3 *Functioning of a CORBA application*

The string type represents a string of characters similar to the string type in Java. This difference is important because IDL is case sensitive. The other constructed data types are described as follows.

The enum *Type*

The enum type defines a set of ordered identifiers, each representing a value. This is similar to the enum type present in C++. Unlike C++, the value of the identifiers need not necessarily be integral.

An example is given here:

```
enum Months
{        Jan,
         Feb,
         March,
         April,
};
```

The struct *Type*

The struct type is similar to the struct type in C++. An example is given here:

```
struct Customer
{    string custname;
     short custage;
     long  custno;
};
```

The union *Type*

The union type contains different variables depending on the value of a variable. The variable, on which the contents of a union depend, is called the discriminator. The union type is similar to a struct with a switch statement. An example is given here:

```
union cust switch(char cust_type)
{
        case 'c':
                string custType;
                long long custId;
                long  balance;
                long minimum_balance;
        case  's':
                 string custType;
                 long long custId;
                 long balance;
        default:
                string errorType;

  };
```

In the above example, cust_type is the discriminator. A value of "c" for cust_type will result in the union cust, with one string and three long types. An example of an interface is given here:

```
module Customer
{
interface Cust
{
```

```
    readonly attribute string CustID;
    readonly attribute string CustName;
    attribute string CustSex;
void Add(in string CustID);
void Modify(in string CustID);
            };
};
```

IDL supports the inheritance of interfaces. You need to use the ":" operator instead of the `extends` keyword of Java to specify inheritance in an IDL file. IDL supports multiple inheritance, the specification of each interface name being separated by a comma. You can also handle exceptions in an IDL file by using the `exception` keyword. The exception type is similar to the `struct` keyword in syntax. You need to save the IDL interfaces with the `.idl` extension

The IDL interfaces are compiled using an IDL compiler. The IDL compilers translate the interface to language-specific source code. For example, a Java IDL compiler will translate the interface to Java source code.

IDL compilers are supplied by CORBA vendors and have different specifications, which are mentioned in the documentation accompanying the product.

Java provides the `idlj` compiler, which compiles an interface to Java source code. The syntax of the `idlj` compiler is:

```
idlj -fserver -fclient  idl_ file_name
```

The IDL compiler generates the stub class, the skeleton class, and a helper class. If there are any attributes defined in the interface, then an operations class will also be generated.

A client stub makes a particular CORBA server interface available to a client. A server skeleton provides a framework on which the server implementation code for a particular interface is built. The helper class provides additional functionality, such as the narrowing of objects. The name of the file has the format:

```
<nameofinterface>Helper.java
```

Now, I'll discuss the CORBA services.

CORBA Services

CORBA provides certain services that can be used by applications. These services support integration and interoperation of distributed objects. The services are defined using IDL interfaces. Therefore, like any other object implementation, they run on the ORB. The way the services are implemented is very similar to coding an IDL interface and then implementing the service. The only difference is that the interfaces and implementation for these services follow the standards specified by OMG. In addition, they come as a part of the vendor-supplied ORB interface. Table 6-2 describes the CORBA services.

Table 6-2 CORBA Services

Service	Description
Life Cycle	This service is used to create, delete, copy, and move CORBA objects. This service also supports the concept of object factory to create CORBA objects.
Naming	This service is used to give names to the CORBA objects. An object has to register itself with the ORB so that a client can use its services. The client will use the name that the object has registered itself.
Event	This service is used to send and receive events. It supports reliable and anonymous delivery of events. In an anonymous delivery, the server and the client are not aware of each other.
Relationship	This service is used to manage the relationship between objects by providing constraint checking and cardinality.
Licensing	This service is used to define policies to control the use of services. There can be three types of licensing policies: time, value mapping, and consumer. As a time policy, a start date or expiry date can be set for the license. In value mapping, the license is specified for units, such as concurrent users and resources used. As a consumer policy, a particular user or machine can be authorized to use a service.
Query	This service is used to query CORBA objects. It supports object indexing and nested queries. The Query service allows queries on objects similar to queries performed on relational databases.

Summary

In this chapter, you learned the architecture of an RMI application. You learned how an RMI application works. Next, you learned to create and execute an RMI application. You learned the differences between an RMI and CORBA application. You also learned about the different components of a CORBA application and how a CORBA application works. Finally, you learned about the CORBA services.

PART II

J2EE Programming

Chapter 7

In this chapter, you'll learn about Java 2 Platform Enterprise Edition (J2EE). I'll discuss the architecture of J2EE and the technologies related to it. In this chapter you'll also learn about J2EE applications, J2EE tools, and J2EE security.

An Introduction to J2EE

You've already learned about multi-tier architectures such as CORBA and have seen their advantages in terms of scalability, performance, and reliability. In a multi-tier architecture, a client does not interact directly with the server. Instead, it first contacts another layer called the *middleware*. The middleware instantiates the server applications and manages the server objects. It returns results to the client. The presence of a middleware layer allows programmers to concentrate on the business logic of an application. The middleware handles low-level services, such as thread handling, security, and transaction management.

Sun Microsystems introduced the J2EE application server and the Enterprise JavaBeans (EJB) specifications as a venture into the multi-tier component architecture. J2EE functions as a middle-tier server in a three-tier architecture. It provides certain specifications that can be used to implement enterprise solutions for catering to all types of business requirements. J2EE also offers cost-effective solutions for business requirements.

J2EE is used for developing, deploying, and executing applications in a distributed environment. The J2EE application server acts as a platform for implementing various server-side technologies such as servlets, Java Server Pages (JSP), and Enterprise JavaBeans. J2EE allows you to focus on business logic in your programs. The business logic is coded in Enterprise JavaBeans, which are reusable components that can be accessed by client programs. Enterprise JavaBeans runs on a J2EE server. I'll discuss EJB in detail in the next chapter, "Creating and Deploying an Enterprise Bean."

In J2EE, security is handled almost entirely by the platform and its administrators. The developers do not have to worry about writing the security logic. I'll discuss the security features in J2EE later in this chapter.

Now I'll show you the architecture of the J2EE SDK.

J2EE Architecture

The J2EE SDK architecture consists of the following components:

◆ The J2EE server
◆ The EJB container
◆ The Web container

The J2EE SDK architecture is depicted in Figure 7-1.

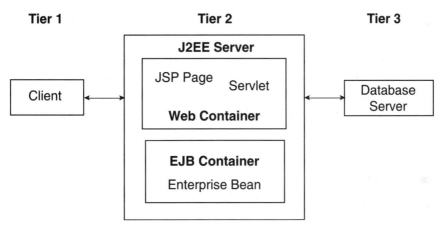

FIGURE 7-1 *The J2EE SDK architecture is displayed here.*

The J2EE server provides the EJB and Web containers. The J2EE server enforces security by authenticating users. The other services provided by the J2EE server are listed here:

◆ It allows clients to interact with enterprise beans.
◆ It enables a Web browser to access servlets and JSP files.
◆ It provides naming and directory services to enable users and various services to locate and search for services and components.

The EJB container manages the execution of enterprise beans for J2EE applications. Enterprise beans and their container run on the J2EE server. EJB is a specification for making server-side components that enable and simplify the task of creating distributed objects. EJB components are server-side components written using Java. They implement only the business logic. You don't need to write code for system-level services, such as managing transactions and security. EJB components provide services such as transaction and security management and can be customized during deployment.

The Web container manages the execution of JSP and servlet components for J2EE applications. Web components and their containers run on the J2EE server. Servlets are Java programs that can be deployed on a Java-enabled Web server to enhance and extend the functionality of the Web server. For example, you can write a servlet to add a messenger service to a Web site. Servlets can also be used to add dynamic content to Web pages. Java Server Pages (JSP) add server-side programming functionality to Java. A Java Server page consists of regular HTML tags representing the static content and the code enclosed within special tags representing the dynamic content. After compilation, a Java Server page generates a servlet and, therefore, incorporates all the servlet functionalities. You'll learn more about these technologies later in this book.

Now that you've learned about the J2EE SDK architecture, I'll discuss J2EE applications.

J2EE Applications

J2EE applications are complex, access data from a variety of sources and cater to a variety of clients. To manage these applications, the business functions are conducted in the middle tier. The J2EE platform acts as a middle tier and provides the necessary environment needed by the applications. The J2EE platform provides "write once, run anywhere" portability and scalability for multi-tier applications. It also minimizes the complexity of building multi-tier applications.

I'll now discuss how to create a J2EE application.

To create a J2EE application, you need to create the following three components:

- ◆ J2EE application clients
- ◆ Enterprise beans
- ◆ Web components

Each of the components is packaged into a file with a specific file format. A J2EE application client is a Java application that runs in an environment that enables it to access the J2EE services. A J2EE application client is packaged into a .jar (Java archive) file. The Web components are packaged into a .war (Web archive) file.

An enterprise bean consists of three files: the EJB class, home, and remote interfaces. The enterprise bean files are bundled into an EJB .jar file. The .jar, .war, and EJB .jar files are assembled into a J2EE application, which is an .ear file. The .ear file is then deployed to the J2EE server. You'll learn about enterprise beans in detail in Chapter 8.

The process of creating a J2EE application is illustrated in Figure 7-2.

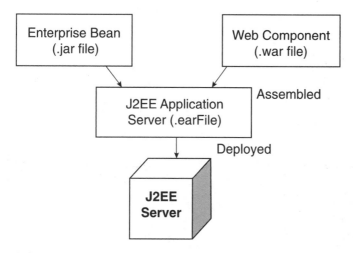

FIGURE 7-2 *The process of creating a J2EE application is depicted in this figure.*

I'll now look at the different J2EE technologies.

J2EE Technologies

J2EE includes many technologies, such as Enterprise JavaBeans (EJB); Remote Method Invocation (RMI); Java Naming and Directory Interface (JNDI); Java Database Connectivity (JDBC); Java Transaction API (JTA) and Java Transaction Service (JTS); Java Messaging Service (JMS); Java servlets and Java Server Pages (JSP); and Extensible Markup Language (XML).

I'll briefly discuss each of these technologies.

◆ **EJB:** Enterprise JavaBeans (EJB) are "write once, run anywhere," middle-tier components consisting of methods that implement the business rule. An enterprise bean encapsulates the business logic. There are two types of enterprise beans, entity beans and session beans. You'll learn about EJB in detail in Chapter 8.

◆ **RMI:** Remote Method Invocation (RMI) is defined for the communication of remote objects in the middle-tier of distributed applications. It enables a Java object to communicate remotely with other Java objects. You learned about RMI in Chapter 6, "RMI and CORBA."

◆ **JNDI:** Java Naming and Directory Interface (JNDI) is an extension to the Java platform and provides multiple naming and directory services. A naming service provides a mechanism for locating distributed objects. A directory service organizes the distributed objects and other resources, such as files, into hierarchical structures. Directory services allow resources to be linked virtually so as to be located in the directory services hierarchy. There are different types of directory services. JNDI allows the different types of directory services to be linked. Thus, clients can use any type of directory service.

◆ **JDBC:** Java Database Connectivity (JDBC) provides a database-programming API for Java programs. A JDBC API contains a set of classes and interfaces that are used to connect to a database built using any DBMS/RDBMS. It also submits SQL queries to a database, and retrieves and processes the results of SQL queries.

◆ **JTA and JTS:** The Java Transaction API (JTA) and Java Transaction Service (JTS) API are transaction APIs. You can use these APIs to demarcate where the transaction starts or ends.

◆ **JMS:** The Java Messaging Service (JMS) is an API that the J2EE platform includes to send mail via the Internet.

◆ **Servlets:** Servlets are used to develop a variety of Web-based applications. They make use of the extensive power of the Java API, such as networking and URL access, multithreading, database connectivity, internationalization, RMI, and object serialization. Java Server Pages (JSP) add server-side programming functionality to Java. Both servlets and JSP allow the creation of database-driven Web applications and have server-side programming capabilities.

◆ **XML:** J2EE uses Extensible Markup Language (XML) as a mark-up language to describe content. The descriptor file created when deploying a J2EE application is an XML file. You'll learn about XML in Chapter 9, "Extensible Markup Language (XML)."

You looked at the various APIs of J2EE. I'll now discuss the J2EE SDK tools.

J2EE SDK Tools

The J2EE SDK includes a number of tools. They're listed here:

◆ The deployment tool
◆ The J2EE server
◆ The Cloudscape server
◆ The cleanup script
◆ The packager tool
◆ The realm tool
◆ The runclient script
◆ The verifier tool

I'll discuss each of the above.

The Deployment Tool

You can use the J2EE SDK deployment tool to deploy J2EE applications. This tool has a number of wizards for configuring the enterprise beans, Web components, and application clients as shown in Table 7-1.

You can start the tool using the following command:

```
Deploytool
```

Table 7-1 The *Deploytool* Command Line Options

Option	Description
-deploy <ApplicationJar> <ServerName> [<ApplicationClientCode.jar]	To deploy the J2EE application on to the J2EE server
-listApps <ServerName>	To list the J2EE applications deployed on the J2EE server
-uninstall <ApplicationName> <ServerName>	To undeploy the J2EE application

continues

Table 7-1 *(continued)*

Option	Description
-help	To display help on using the deploytool
-ui	To run the GUI version

You need to set certain environment variables after you install the tool. These are:

◆ J2EE _HOME: To the path of the J2EE SDK installation
◆ PATH: To the path of the bin directory of the J2EE SDK installation.

The interface of the tool is shown in Figure 7-3.

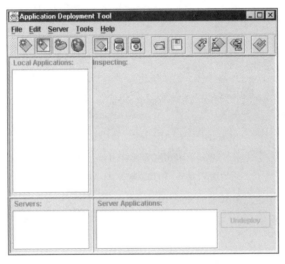

FIGURE 7-3 *The J2EE Server Deployment Tool is illustrated here.*

You'll learn how to use this tool to deploy a J2EE application in Chapter 8.

The J2EE Server

You can start the tool using the command j2ee. You can use the -verbose option with the j2ee command, for debugging. The command is:

```
j2ee -verbose
```

You can stop the J2EE server using the following command:

```
J2ee -stop
```

You can display the version of the J2EE server using the following command:

```
j2ee -version
```

The Cloudscape Server

The J2EE SDK contains a database called the Cloudscape database. Cloudscape DBMS from Informix Software is a Java-based *object relational database management system* (ORDBMS) that implements SQL. An ORDBMS implements object-oriented as well as RDBMS features.

To access the Cloudscape database, you need to start the Cloudscape server using the following command:

```
cloudscape -start
```

To stop the Cloudscape database, type the following at the command prompt:

```
cloudscape -stop
```

The Cloudscape database is named `CloudscapeDB` and is created automatically. The database is present in the Cloudscape directory in which J2EE SDK is installed.

The Cleanup Script

You can remove all the applications deployed on the J2EE server by using the cleanup script. The command to run the cleanup script is given here:

```
cleanup
```

The Packager Tool

Though you can use the deploy tool to package J2EE components, you can also use the command line utility packager tool to package components. You can use the packager tool to create the EJB .jar file package, the Web component .war file package, the application client .jar File package, and the J2EE Application .ear file package.

The syntax to package an EJB .jar file is given here:

```
Packager <RootDirectory> package/Class1.class:package/Class 2.class:pics/me.gif ejb-jar.xml ejb.jar
```

You can package a Web component .war file using the syntax given as follows:

```
Packager -webArchive[ -classpath servlet or jsp bean/classes [classFiles
package/MyClass1.class: package/MyClass2.class] ] <content-root> [-contentFiles
login.jsp:index.html:images/me.gif] web.xml myWebApp.war
```

You can package an application client .jar file using the syntax given here:

```
Packager -applicationClient <RootDirectory>
package/Class1.class:package/Main.Class:pics/me.gif package.Main client.xml
appClient.jar
```

The syntax for packaging a J2EE application .ear file is given here:

```
Packager -enterpriseArchive myWeb.war:myEJB.jar:myOtherApp.ear [-
alternativeDescriptorEntries myWeb/web.xml:myEJB.xml:] [-libraryJArs
ejblib.jar:ejblibl.jar] myAppName myApp.ear
```

The Realm Tool

You can use the realm tool utility to add and remove J2EE users. This utility is run from the command prompt. The syntax to use the realm tool is given here:

```
realmtool <options>
```

The options of the realm tool are listed in Table 7-2.

Table 7-2 The *realmtool* Options

Option	Description
-show	To list the realm names
-list <RealmName>	To list the users in the realm
-add	To add a user to the realm
-addGroup <group>	To add a group to the realm

The Runclient Script

You can run a J2EE application client by executing the runclient script. The syntax is given here:

```
runclient -client <appjarfile> [-name <name>] [<app-arguments>]
```

In the above command, `<appjarfile>` is the J2EE application .ear file, `<name>` is the display name of the J2EE application client component, and `<app-arguments>` are any arguments that are required by the J2EE application.

The Verifier Tool

You can use the verifier tool to check the J2EE component files. You can run the tool from the command prompt using the command given here:

```
Verifier [options] <FileName>
```

In the command, `filename` is the name of a J2EE component file. The options of the command are listed in Table 7-3.

Table 7-3 The *Verifier* Tool Options

Option	Description
-v	To display verbose output
-o <Output File>	To write the result to a file
-u	To run the GUI utility

In the preceding section, I discussed the various J2EE tools. I'll now discuss J2EE security.

J2EE Security

The architecture of J2EE is such that it enforces security in the application. In order to access the J2EE services, a user needs to prove his or her identity. Such users are called J2EE users and the process is called authentication. The J2EE authentication service is different from the security mechanism of the operating system. The users of the operating system and the users of J2EE belong to different *realms*. A realm is a group of users that have the same authentication policy.

The users of J2EE belong to two different realms that are respectively authenticated by certificates and default. J2EE uses certificates to authenticate Web browser clients. In most cases, the J2EE services use the default realm to authenticate a user. J2EE users may also belong to *groups*. A group is a collection of users who have common features. For example, the users belonging to a group may all be software developers coding the same module. Similarly, the Project Managers of the project might belong to a different group.

As discussed in the previous section, "J2EE Tools," you can add users to and remove them from a realm using the realm tool utility.

When you execute a J2EE application client, it requests that you enter the login ID and password. If the combination of both the username and the password is correct, J2EE allows you to access the J2EE services.

The J2EE server also enforces security by a process known as *authorization*. Authorization is a process by which permissions are assigned by the J2EE server to invoke the methods of an enterprise bean. You'll learn about this process in Chapter 8.

Summary

In this chapter, you learned about the function and the architecture of J2EE. Next, I described the components of a J2EE application. You also learned about the related J2EE technologies such as RMI, XML, JTA, JTS, and servlets. I also discussed the J2EE SDK tools such as the deploy tool, the realm tool, the packager tool, and the verifier tool. Finally, you learned about the security features in J2EE.

Chapter 8

**Creating and
Deploying an
Enterprise Bean**

In this chapter, you'll learn what an enterprise bean is, how to create an enterprise bean, the types of enterprise beans, and how to deploy an enterprise bean.

An Introduction to Enterprise Beans

Enterprise JavaBeans (EJB) are server-side components that run on the J2EE server. Some of the features of EJB are:

- ◆ EJB components are written using Java.
- ◆ EJB components implement only the business logic.
- ◆ EJB components provide services such as transaction and security management, and can be customized during deployment.
- ◆ EJB can maintain state information across various method calls.

I'll now discuss the benefits of EJB.

The Advantages of EJB

Some of the advantages of EJB are:

- ◆ Separate roles for application development
- ◆ Transaction management and support
- ◆ Portability and scalability

I'll discuss each of the above.

The Separate Roles for Application Development

In EJB development, separate roles are defined for EJB developers and EJB deployers. EJB developers focus on writing the business logic of the application. The EJB deployers are responsible for installing the EJB classes on the EJB server. An EJB deployer has a good knowledge of the EJB environment. The deployer knows the location of the databases, the schema, and the transactional requirements of the database.

Transaction Management and Support

EJB manages transactions on its own. The developer does not have to bother with starting or terminating transactions. EJB provides distributed transaction support. A transaction can include calls to methods on two different servers.

Portability and Scalability

An enterprise bean is portable and scalable. It can run on any EJB server. The specification of EJB has been written so that it can provide high-performance implementations.

I'll now discuss the architecture of EJB.

The Architecture of EJB

EJB is a layered architecture consisting of:

◆ An EJB server

◆ An EJB container

◆ An enterprise bean

The architecture of EJB is depicted in Figure 8-1.

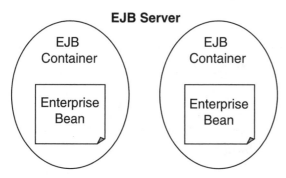

FIGURE 8-1 *The architecture of EJB is illustrated here.*

The EJB Server and Container

An EJB server contains an EJB container. It provides a number of services to the container, such as optimized database access interfaces and CORBA services. The EJB server is also responsible for providing the Java Naming and Directory

Interface (JNDI) service and transaction services. EJB servers may be database servers, application servers, or middleware servers.

An EJB container acts as an interface between an enterprise bean and the clients. It provides a number of services such as security, transaction management, and persistence.

An EJB container provides security by ensuring that only authorized clients access the enterprise bean and its business methods. It uses an *access control list* (ACL) to maintain a list of users who are authorized to access the enterprise bean.

When a client invokes the enterprise bean, the EJB container manages the transactions. The container provides transaction support to the enterprise bean based on the transaction type specified while developing the enterprise bean.

An EJB container provides support for persistence. Persistence is the permanent storage of a state of an object in a data store, such as a database or a file. This allows an object to be accessed at any time, without it being re-created every time it is needed.

An EJB container is also responsible for controlling the life cycle of an enterprise bean. When a client makes a request for an enterprise bean, the container dynamically instantiates, destroys, and reuses the enterprise bean as required. The clients communicate with the enterprise bean through the remote and home interfaces provided by the container. The remote interface defines the business methods available for the enterprise bean. The home interface defines the methods that enable clients to create and find EJB components. You'll learn more about the remote and home interfaces later in this chapter.

Enterprise Beans

Enterprise JavaBeans are middle-tier components that implement the business rule. There are two types of enterprise beans:

◆ Entity beans
◆ Session beans

Entity Beans

Entity beans are enterprise beans that persist across multiple sessions and multiple clients. They have many features such as persistence, shared access, and a primary key.

In an entity bean, persistence is achieved by saving its state in a *data store*. A data store is any database in which data about business entities such as employees, accounts, and products can be stored.

An entity bean can be accessed by multiple clients simultaneously. Entity beans allow transactions to ensure that all data manipulations, such as updating, deleting, and modifications, are concurrent. The primary key is the unique identifier that enables a client to identify an entity bean. For example, an entity bean that represents a business entity, such as an employee, can be identified by the employee code.

There are two types of entity beans based on how they manage transactions and persistence:

♦ Bean-managed persistence

♦ Container-managed persistence

In bean-managed persistence, the programmer has to code for connecting to the database. In this type of transaction, the programmer has to include the programming logic to issue a "begin," "commit," or "abort" statement.

In container-managed persistence, the container takes care of database calls. Container-managed transactions are also called *declarative transactions*. In this type of transaction, it is not necessary for a programmer to specify the "begin," "commit," or "abort" statement. The EJB container manages the transactions. It is easy to develop container-managed transactions.

Session Beans

Session beans perform tasks without having a persistent storage mechanism, such as a database, and can use the shared data. There are two types of session beans:

♦ Stateful session beans

♦ Stateless session beans

A stateful session bean can store information in an instance variable to be used across various method calls. Some applications require information to be stored across various method calls. I'll take an example. You go to a shopping site and use the shopping cart to choose and store the items you want to purchase. After buying the items, you want the bill to be shown to you. How is this done? A stateful session bean has a method that calculates the amount you need to pay and stores it in a variable.

Stateless session beans do not have instance variables to store information. Hence, stateless session beans can be used in situations where information does not need to be used across method calls.

I've discussed what an enterprise bean is, the architecture of an EJB, and the types of enterprise bean. I'll now discuss how to create an Enterprise JavaBean.

 NOTE

You'll learn about the types of enterprise beans in detail in Chapter 10.

Creating an EJB

You need to define the following interfaces and classes to create an EJB:

◆ A remote interface

◆ A home interface

◆ An EJB class

In a remote interface, you define all the business methods of the enterprise bean. The business methods you define in the remote interface are implemented in the EJB class.

To create a remote interface, you need to import the `javax.ejb.EJBObject` and `java.rmi.RemoteException` interfaces. Then, you create a remote interface by extending the `EJBObject` interface. When you create a remote interface, ensure that the access modifier for the remote interface is public, the remote interface name is not a keyword defined by EJB, and the remote interface extends from the `EJBObject` interface. You then define all the business methods that will be implemented in the EJB class.

An example of a remote interface is given here:

```
import javax.ejb.EJBObject;
import java.rmi.RemoteException;
public interface ExampleRemote extends EJBObject
{
    public int Examplemethod(int i) throws RemoteException;
}
```

The Home Interface

You define methods that allow EJB clients to create and find EJB components in the home interface. To write the home interface, you need to import the following interfaces:

◆ `java.io.Serializable`

◆ `java.rmi.RemoteException`

◆ `javax.ejb.CreateException`

◆ `javax.ejb.EJBHome`

You need to extend the `EJBHome` interface to create a home interface. When you create the home interface, ensure that the return type of the `create()` method is the remote interface. The method must also throw the exceptions, `RemoteException` and `CreateException`. `CreateException` indicates to a client that a new EJB object could not be created. The `create()` method can also throw any user-defined exceptions.

Finally, define the `create()` method to create an instance of a particular EJB object. The return type of the `create()` method must be the EJB object's remote interface.

An example of a home interface is given here:

```
import java.io.Serializable;
import java.rmi.RemoteException;
import javax.ejb.CreateException;
import javax.ejb.EJBHome;
public interface ExampleHome extends EJBHome
{
//ExampleRemote is the remote interface
 ExampleRemote create() throws RemoteException, CreateException;
}
```

The EJB Class

The EJB class implements all the business methods declared in a remote interface. To write an EJB class, you need to import the following interfaces:

◆ `java.rmi.RemoteException`

◆ `javax.ejb.SessionBean`

◆ `javax.ejb.SessionContext`

You create the EJB class by implementing the `SessionBean` interface. Then, you implement the business method defined in the remote interface.

Finally, write the `ejbCreate()`, `ejbRemove()`, `ejbActivate()`, `ejbPassivate()`, `setSessionContext()`, and default implementations for the constructor methods.

An example of an EJB class is given here:

```
import java.rmi.RemoteException;
import javax.ejb.SessionBean;
import javax.ejb.SessionContext;
public class ExampleEJBClass implements SessionBean
{
    public ExampleEJBClass() {}
    public int Examplemethod(int i)
    {
        return i+5;
    }
    public void ejbCreate() {}
    public void ejbRemove() {}
    public void ejbActivate() {}
    public void ejbPassivate() {}
    public void setSessionContext(SessionContext sc) {}
}
```

After you have created the remote interface, the home interface, and the EJB class, you need to compile the source files and debug errors, if any.

The next step is to deploy the enterprise bean to a J2EE application.

Deploying an EJB

To deploy an Enterprise JavaBean, you need to perform two steps:

◆ Add the bean to a J2EE application.
◆ Package the enterprise bean.

To add an Enterprise JavaBean to a J2EE application, you need to follow the listed steps:

1. Start the J2EE server using the command, `j2ee -verbose`.
2. Start the deploy tool utility using the command, `deploytool`.

3. Choose File, New application to open the New Application dialog box, as shown in Figure 8-2.

4. Click the Browse button, and select the folder in which you want to place the J2EE application. Enter the file name with an .ear extension.

5. Click the New Application button.

6. Click OK.

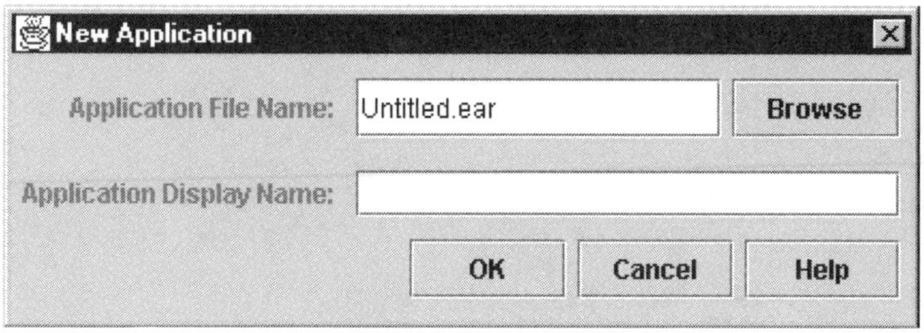

FIGURE 8-2 *The New Application dialog box is shown here.*

I'll now discuss how to package an enterprise bean.

You can package an enterprise bean using the New Enterprise Bean Wizard. The New Enterprise Bean Wizard of the Application Deployment tool creates the *deployment descriptor* file.

A deployment descriptor is an .xml file that contains information about the deployment of an enterprise bean. It enables runtime attributes, such as the security of the server-side component, to be set. It also enables the customizing of some runtime behavior of the enterprise bean without making changes to the EJB class, the home interface, or the remote interface. It also contains the following information: the Access Control List (ACL) of the entities authorized to invoke classes or methods; the name of the EJB class; the home interface; and the remote interface. A list of container-managed fields of the enterprise bean is an entity bean and a value specifying whether the enterprise bean is stateful, or stateless in the case of a session bean.

The Enterprise Bean Wizard packages the files created to define the enterprise bean, the remote interface, the home interface, the EJB class, and the deployment descriptor in a .jar file.

The steps to execute the Enterprise Bean Wizard are listed here:

1. Choose File, New Enterprise Bean, to display the New Enterprise Wizard dialog box as shown in Figure 8-3.

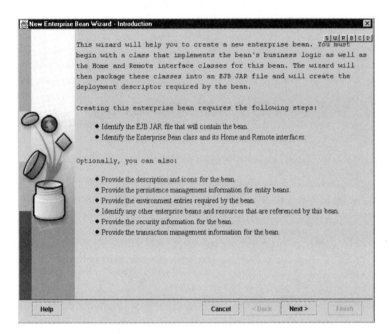

FIGURE 8-3 *The New Enterprise Bean Wizard is shown here.*

2. Click Next. The New Enterprise Bean Wizard — EJB JAR dialog box is displayed.

3. Enter the name of the .jar file in the JAR Display Name text box.

4. Click the Add button in the Contents group box. The Add Files to .JAR dialog box is displayed.

5. Verify if the Root Directory text box displays the directory in which the .class files are stored. Select the .class files, and click the Add button. Add the Home class file and the EJB class file to the Files to be Added text box.

6. Click OK. The New Enterprise Bean Wizard — EJB JAR dialog box displays the .class files that will be added to the enterprise bean.

7. Click Next. The New Enterprise Bean Wizard — General dialog box is displayed.

8. Select the EJB .class file from the Enterprise Bean Class drop-down list, the Home .class file from the Home Interface drop-down list, and the Remote .class file from the Remote Interface drop-down list. Type a name in the Enterprise Bean Display Name text box. Then, select the Stateless option button from the Bean Type group box.

9. Click Next. The New Enterprise Bean Wizard — Environment Entries dialog box is displayed. This dialog box is used to set the environment entries for the enterprise bean.

10. Click Next. The New Enterprise Bean Wizard — Enterprise Bean References dialog box is displayed. This dialog box is used to set references in the deployed enterprise bean to any other enterprise bean.

11. Click Next. The New Enterprise Bean Wizard — Resource References dialog box is displayed. This dialog box is used to list the resources required by the enterprise bean.

12. Click Next. The New Enterprise Bean Wizard — Security dialog box is displayed. This dialog box is used to provide security features for the enterprise bean.

13. Click Next. The New Enterprise Bean Wizard — Transaction Management dialog box is displayed. This dialog box is used to specify the type of entity bean.

14. Click Next. The New Enterprise Bean Wizard — Review Settings dialog box appears. The automatically generated XML deployment descriptor file is displayed.

15. Click Finish. The enterprise bean is added to the J2EE application.

You are now ready to deploy the enterprise bean. The steps to deploy an enterprise bean are:

1. Choose Tools, Deploy Application.

2. Verify if the target server is the localhost, and select the Return Client Jar check box. The target server is the name of the host on which the J2EE server is running. If you select Return Client Jar, a .jar file is created, which is used by the client program to locate the server.

3. Click Next. The Deploy JNDI names dialog box is displayed.

4. Type the JNDI name in the JNDI Name field. The client program will use this JNDI name to locate and search for objects.

5. Click Next.

6. Click Finish.

7. Click OK.

8. Close the Application Deployment tool.

You just learned how to create and deploy an enterprise bean. I'll now discuss how to access an enterprise bean from a client.

Coding the Client

You can access the enterprise bean you created, using a client. I'll now discuss how communication happens between a client and an enterprise bean.

The client invokes a business method on a remote interface. The message is passed to the stub. The stub serializes the arguments into a form that can be transmitted over the network. The arguments are then passed to the skeleton on the remote client. The skeleton deserializes the arguments. The deserialized argument is passed to the EJBObject class, which implements the remote interface. The EJBObject class calls the business method in the enterprise bean. After the business method executes, it returns a value. This value is returned to the EJBObject class, which returns it to the skeleton. The skeleton serializes the return value and sends it back to the stub. The stub deserializes the return value and sends it to the client that invoked the business method. I'll now discuss how to code the client.

Coding the client involves the following steps:

1. Locating the home interface

2. Creating an enterprise bean interface

3. Calling a business method

Locating the Home Interface

To locate a particular home object, the clients make use of JNDI. You can create a JNDI naming context using the InitialContext class as an interface between the EJB client and the JNDI. This class returns an object of the type Context. The Context class provides methods to locate and list objects. An example is given here:

```
Context Example = new InitialContext();
```

After you have created the JNDI naming context, the next step is to locate the JNDI name you specified when deploying the J2EE application. You can use the `lookup()` method for this. When you call this method, an object of the type `Object` is returned. An example is given here:

```
Object obj = Example.lookup("MyJNDI");
```

Next, you need to cast the object returned by the `lookup()` method to the home interface type by using the `PortableRemoteObject.narrow()` method. This method takes two parameters, the object returned by the `lookup()` method and the home interface's .class filename. An example of casting the object to the home interface type is given here:

```
ExampleHome Ex = (ExampleHome) PortableRemoteObject.narrow(obj,myHome.class);
```

Creating an Enterprise Bean Interface

You can create an instance of an enterprise bean by invoking the `create()` method of the home interface. The `create()` method returns a remote interface object.

An example is given here:

```
ExampleRemote Examplebean = h.create();
```

Calling a Business Method

As you are aware, you define the business methods in the remote interface. The client can invoke these methods by using the remote interface object returned by the `create()` method. An example is given here:

```
int var = Examplebean.Examplemethod(20);
```

Executing the Client

After you have written the code for a client, you need to compile it and debug any errors. To run the client, you need the .jar file. The .jar file contains the stub classes that allow communication between the client and the enterprise bean.

In Windows, you can specify the enterprise bean reference by setting the `class-path` to the remote application client .jar file, as shown here:

```
set classpath=%classpath%; .jar file name
```

I'll now discuss how to set security in EJB.

Setting Security

You can define security in EJB by defining the types of users you want to access the enterprise bean. You can do this by creating roles for the application. You can create roles for an enterprise bean using the Application Deployment tool.

To create a role:

1. Select the enterprise bean's EJB .jar file.
2. Select the Roles tab and click Add.
3. Enter the name and description.

After you have created the roles, you can assign permissions to the methods you have defined in the enterprise bean. You can specify permissions to the methods using the Application Deployment tool.

To assign permissions:

1. Select the enterprise bean.
2. Select the Security tab.
3. Select roles in the Method Permissions table.

When developing an enterprise bean, you might not be sure of the roles of users. You can take care of this issue by mapping roles to J2EE users and groups. You can do this by using the Application Deployment tool. To do so:

1. Select the application.
2. Select the Security tabbed pane.
3. Select the role from the Role Name list.
4. Click Add.
5. In the Users dialog box, select the users and groups that belong to the role.

I'll take an example to explain how authentication and authorization happens in J2EE. Suppose a customer wants to update his personal details in a J2EE application. The customer runs the application client and enters his username and password. The authentication service of J2EE validates the username and the password in the realm. To update the personal details, the customer clicks the Modify button, which invokes the modify method of the enterprise bean. The J2EE server grants or denies permission to invoke the modify method of the EJB. The permission is granted based on the settings made in the Application Deployment tool.

The security mechanism in J2EE for access to an EJB is diagrammatically represented in Figure 8-4.

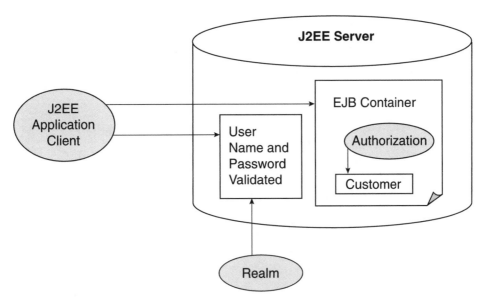

FIGURE 8-4 *This is a diagram of the security mechanism in J2EE.*

Summary

In this chapter, you learned what an enterprise bean is, and the architecture of an enterprise bean. Then, I discussed the advantages of an enterprise bean and the types of enterprise beans. You also learned how to create, package, and deploy an enterprise bean on the J2EE server. I showed you how to code the client to access the enterprise bean. Finally, you learned about setting security options using the Application Deployment tool.

Chapter 9

In Chapter 8, "Creating and Deploying an Enterprise JavaBean," you were introduced to EJB. You are aware that EJB uses Extensible Markup Language (XML) as a document format for deployment descriptors. In this chapter, I will discuss the need for XML, and describe the basic concepts of XML.

An Introduction to XML

As you are aware, the Internet is extensively used for communicating and exchanging information. Since most business today is conducted via the Web, there is a need to share data across different platforms all over the world. It is important for Web applications to present data in a format that is compatible across all platforms. Extensible Markup Language (XML) is one such language that provides a format for describing data.

XML is a markup language defined by the World Wide Web Consortium (W3C). Before I show you the features of this language, I'll discuss the limitations of existing technologies such as Electronic Data Interchange (EDI), Standard Generalized Markup Language (SGML), and HTML.

EDI refers to the process of exchanging documents in a specific format. EDI is based on the use of message standards. A message standard consists of uniform formats that allow electronic transmission of business documents. It also includes security elements and other rules that all the users agree to follow. It uses Virtual Added Networks (VANs) to transmit files. EDI has many limitations, such as high costs. In addition, the EDI standards vary across business units. Thus, EDI does not serve as an effective solution to implement data interchange among heterogeneous systems.

Standard Generalized Markup Language (SGML) is a meta-markup language. It is used to structure, format, and manage large documents. Though this language has been used to deploy applications in the past, it has many limitations. It is a complex language, and developers find it difficult to learn.

Due to the limitations of EDI and SGML, the HTML and XML markup languages evolved. I'll discuss these.

HTML has a set of predefined tags. It is used for presenting data and does not focus on describing the data. Take a look at an example of an HTML code:

```
<HTML>
<HEAD>
<TITLE> Sample Code </TITLE>
</HEAD>
<BODY>
<P>
<B>
        Adam Wilkins <BR>
        1028 <BR>
        $35000 <BR>
</B>
<P>
</BODY>
</HTML>
```

The output of the HTML code example is displayed in Figure 9-1.

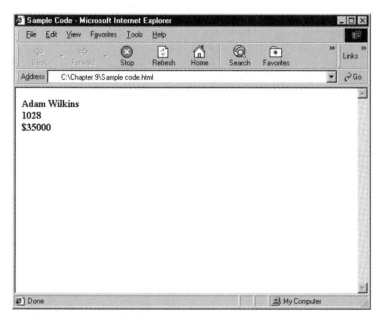

FIGURE 9-1 *Output of the HTML document in the browser*

The preceding figure displays information about the employee name, the employee ID, and the employee salary. Note that the HTML tags do not reveal any information about the content displayed. These tags only specify the format in which you want to display the data. Due to this limitation of HTML, the XML language evolved and became popular. I'll discuss the advantages of XML.

The Advantages of XML

Unlike HTML, which focuses on presenting data, XML focuses on describing data. Using XML, you can represent the information in a format that is easy to understand. XML does not have any predefined tags. It allows you to create your own tags based on your requirement. The other advantages of XML are listed here:

- ◆ XML is easy to use.
- ◆ XML uses a set of standards recommended by the World Wide Web Consortium (W3C). This ensures that data is uniform and independent of vendors.
- ◆ XML stores data in simple text files, which can be easily viewed and edited.
- ◆ XML is the basis for other standards. Sun Microsystems has used XML within its EJB and JSP specifications.
- ◆ XML is supported by the latest technologies such as Microsoft Visual Studio .NET.
- ◆ XML is extensible. You can define your own tags in XML and structure your document the way you like.
- ◆ XML can be used to exchange data.
- ◆ XML enables smart searches.

Now, I'll discuss how XML helps you perform smart searches.

NOTE

World Wide Web Consortium (W3C) helps to standardize the Web. It is responsible for the development of Web specifications that describe the communication protocols and technologies for the Web. Some of the rules of W3C for XML are listed here:

◆ XML must be directly usable over the Internet.

◆ XML must support a wide range of applications.

◆ XML must be compatible with SGML.

◆ XML documents must be concise.

For more information, you can access the World Wide Web Consortium (W3C) Web site at **http://www.w3c.com**.

Smart Searches

Consider an HTML code:

```
The film <b> Harry Potter </b> is doing better business than The Titanic.
```

Suppose you want to perform a search on the Web about the film *Harry Potter*. You enter the text, "Harry Potter," within the tags <b> and </b> as the search criterion. A list of links with references to Harry Potter books, film, and computer games will be displayed. You can store similar data in an XML document, as the format shows here:

```
The film <FILM> Harry Potter </FILM> is doing better business than The Titanic.
```

If you perform a search with the text "Harry Potter" within the tags <FILM> and </FILM>, a list of links on the *Harry Potter* film will be displayed. Thus, XML documents allow you to focus the search, reducing the load on the browser.

Now that you are familiar with why XML is so important, I'll discuss creating an XML document to display content in a meaningful manner.

Creating an XML Document

You begin an XML code by introducing the XML declaration statement:

```
<?xml version="1.0"?>
```

This statement notifies the browser that the document being processed is an XML document and uses version 1.0 of XML. Next, you declare XML elements in the code. An XML element is the basic unit for defining data. An example of an XML element is given here:

```
<NAME> Adam </NAME>
```

As I discussed earlier, in XML you can define your own XML elements. You can create as many tags in an XML document as you want.

Like HTML, XML also supports attributes to provide additional information about the elements. An example is given here:

```
<EMPLOYEE ID="E001">
```

You can create an XML document in Notepad just like an HTML document and save it as an .xml document. The following code is an example of an XML document:

```
<?xml version="1.0"?>
<Employees>
<EmployeeName>
               Adam Wilkins
</EmployeeName>
<EmployeeCode>
               1028
</EmployeeCode>
<EmployeeSalary>
               $35000
</EmployeeSalary>
</Employees>
```

The output of the code for an XML document is displayed in Figure 9-2.

Note that the content in the XML document is structured and easy to understand. The tags are displayed in the form of a tree. You can expand or collapse the tags by clicking the minus sign in the browser.

Like any other language, XML has a set of rules that you should follow when creating an XML document. I'll discuss these rules.

◆ Tag names are case sensitive. Thus, the tag, `<EmployeeName>` is not the same as the tag `<employeename>`.

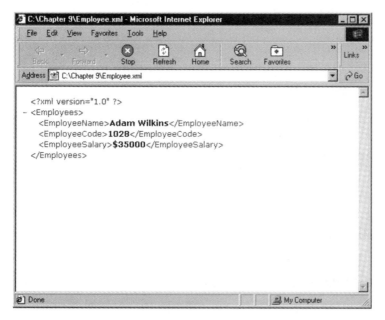

FIGURE 9-2 *Output of the XML document in the browser*

◆ All opening tags should have closing tags. For example, the opening tag, <EmployeeName> must have a closing tag, </EmployeeName>.

◆ All empty tags should be closed by including the "/" character before the closing angular bracket. An example is given here:

```
<Image src = "Picture.pcx" />.
```

◆ All attribute values must be given in double quotation marks. An example is given here:

```
<FONT size="8">
```

◆ All inner tags must be closed before closing the outer tags. For an example, consider the following code:

```
<Employees>
<EmployeeName>
Adam Wilkins
</EmployeeName>
        </Employees>
```

In the preceding code the inner tag `<EmployeeName>` has been closed before the outer tag `<Employees>`.

 CAUTION

When creating XML documents, do not include spaces between the tags you define.

You've learned to create XML documents. Now, I'll teach you about XML-related specifications, i.e., Document Type Definition (DTD), XML namespaces, and XML schemas.

Document Type Definition (DTD)

A DTD specifies the rules to define the structure of XML documents. It allows you to store data in a consistent format. It specifies the elements and attributes that can be present in an XML document. DTD documents have the extension, .dtd. To understand DTD better, you can compare it to the create statements you use in SQL to create tables, databases, etc., in which you define the structure and specify the rules and data types. After defining the DTD for an XML document, you can store data in the XML document. Note that it's not essential to create a DTD for an XML document. However, creating a DTD is good practice. It allows any other user to understand the structure of your XML document. Now take a look at declaring elements in a DTD.

You can declare elements in a DTD using the following syntax:

```
<!Element NameofElement (content-type or content-model)
```

In the above syntax, `NameofElement` is the element name, `content-type` specifies the type of data, and `content-model` specifies what other elements the element will contain.

Consider an example of a DTD file:

```
<!ELEMENT Employee (EmployeeID, FirstName, LastName)>
<!ELEMENT EmployeeID (#PCDATA)>
<!ELEMENT FirstName (#PCDATA)>
<!ELEMENT LastName (#PCDATA)>
```

The above example declares an element named `Employee`. This element can contain three elements, `EmployeeID`, `FirstName`, and `LastName`. The elements named `EmployeeID`, `FirstName`, and `LastName` can contain character data.

You can use Notepad to create the DTD file and save it with a .dtd extension.

 CAUTION

When creating the DTD file, ensure that there is no space between the exclamation mark "!" and ELEMENT. Also ensure that ELEMENT is written in uppercase.

Now, take a look at how to include the DTD in an XML document.

You can include a DTD in an XML document using the syntax given here:

```
<!DOCTYPE RootElement SYSTEM <DTD_ File_Name">
```

In the above syntax, `RootElement` is the name of the first element in a DTD file. `DTD_File_Name` is the name of the DTD file with the .dtd extension.

Consider the following example of an XML document, which includes a DTD file `Employees.dtd`:

```
<?xml version="1.0"?>
<!DOCTYPE Employee SYSTEM "Employees.DTD">
<Employee>
            <EmployeeID> 6668 </EmployeeID>
         <FirstName> Adam </FirstName>
         <LastName> Wilkins </LastName>
</Employee>
```

When you execute the preceding code, the XML document code is checked against the rules specified in the DTD document. If the document matches all the rules specified in the DTD file, it is considered valid, or else an error is reported.

I'll now discuss XML namespaces.

XML Namespaces

XML namespaces are a collection of unique elements. You can use XML to define the elements you have used in your XML documents. XML namespaces help you to avoid declaring two elements with the same name. You can declare XML namespaces using the keyword, xmlns. For example, you can declare an XML namespace for the <ID> element that defines EmployeeID.

```
xmlns: EmployeeID="http://www.Id.com/Id"
```

If you want to refer to the <ID> element of an employee you can refer to it as shown here:

```
<EmployeeID: ID>
```

I'll now talk about XML schemas.

XML Schemas

An XML schema lets you define the structure of the XML document. Microsoft has developed a language called the XML Schema Definition Language (XSD) to define the schema of an XML document. The syntax of XSD is similar to that of XML. Thus, it is easy for you to use XML schemas.

The concept of an XML schema is similar to a DTD, which you looked at in the previous sections of this chapter. However, an XML schema has many advantages over DTD. I'll discuss these advantages.

◆ XSD provides more control of the data that is assigned to elements than DTD.

◆ XSD allows you to create your own data types, unlike DTD, which does not allow you to define your own data types.

◆ XSD allows you to specify restrictions on the data that can be stored in an XML document.

The syntax to declare a simple element in XSD is given here:

```
<xsd: element name="element-name" type="data type"
minOccurs="nonNegativeInteger" maxOccurs="nonNegativeInteger¦unbounded" />
```

In the above syntax, name is the name of the element being declared, type specifies the data type of the element being declared, minOccurs specifies the minimum number of times the element can occur in the document, and maxOccurs specifies the maximum number of times the element can appear.

An example to declare elements in XSD is given here:

```
<xsd:element name="EMPNAME" type="xsd:string"/>
<xsd:element name="EMPCODE" type="xsd:string"/>
```

In the above code, all the elements are associated with the simple data types that are predefined in XSD. You can also associate an element with a user-defined simple data type. Consider the following example:

```
<xsd:simpleType name="EmpZipcode">
            <xsd:restriction base="xsd:string">
                        <xsd:length value="10"/>
                    </xsd:restriction>
</xsd:simpleType>
```

The above code defines a simple data type named `EmpZipCode`. This data type can contain only string values with a maximum length of 10 characters. You can associate an element with the data type `EmpZipCode`, by using the following statement:

```
<xsd:element name="ZipCode" type="EmpZipCode"/>
```

You can integrate the components of XSD using the `schema` element. The sample code of a schema is given here:

```
<xsd: schema xmlns:xsd=http://www.w3.org/XMLSchema>
<xsd:element name="EMPNAME" type="xsd:string"/>
<xsd:element name="EMPCODE" type="xsd:string"/>
<xsd:simpleType name="EmpZipcode">
            <xsd:restriction base="xsd:string">
              <xsd:length value="10"/>
              </xsd:restriction>
</xsd:simpleType>
<xsd:element name="ZipCode" type="EmpZipCode"/>
</xsd:schema>
```

In the above code, the `schema` element uses the `xmlns` attribute to specify the namespace with the element.

You've looked at the basic XML concepts. I'll now talk about how XML is related to other Java technologies such as EJB and JSP.

XML and Other Technologies

EJB uses XML to describe the enterprise beans. All EJB containers have a deployment descriptor file, which is written in XML. A deployment descriptor is a file that defines the following kinds of information:

◆ The EJB name, class, home, and remote interfaces, and the bean type (session or entity)

◆ EJB references and security role references

◆ EJB method permissions, and container transaction attributes

XML is also linked to Java Server Pages (JSP). The structure of the custom tags in JSP is similar to XML tags. JSP supports creation of custom tags that enable the segregation of business complexities from the content presentation. The structure of a custom tag in JSP, like that in XML, contains the start/end tags and a body. The tags are user defined and explicitly render information about the type of data. A JSP file using custom tags consists of the tag handler and the TLD file. The tag handler uses different methods and objects to define the behavior of the tag. The TLD file is an XML file that contains a descriptive list of custom tags.

Summary

In this chapter, you learned the basic concepts of XML. You learned why XML is important and the benefits of using XML to conduct business on the Web. Next, you looked at the limitations of the existing technologies such as EDI, SGML, and HTML. You also learned to create XML documents. You looked at DTDs, XML namespaces, and XML schemas. Finally, you learned the relation of XML to other technologies such as EJB and JSP.

Chapter 10

In this chapter, you will learn about the various types of enterprise beans and how to create each of these types of beans. You will also learn how to connect an entity bean with SQL.

Enterprise Beans

As discussed in Chapter 8, "Creating and Deploying an Enterprise Bean," the two types of enterprise beans are session beans and entity beans. Session beans perform business tasks that access data directly without the use of a persistent storage mechanism such as a database. Although session beans do not represent shared data in a database, they can access shared data. As a result, these beans can be used to read, insert, and update data.

Entity beans, on the other hand, provide object-oriented interfaces to create, modify, and delete data from a database. In other words, entity beans represent shared data in the database that persist across multiple sessions and multiple clients. Due to their persistence, entity beans are cost-effective resource managers. I'll now discuss each of these beans in detail. I'll start with session beans.

Session Beans

Session beans can be categorized into the following two types based on whether a session bean maintains a state between invocations of two consecutive methods. The two types of session beans are:

◆ Stateful session beans
◆ Stateless session beans

A stateful session bean serves as a single client and is associated with one or more instance variables. These variables contain contextual information regarding a client session across method calls. In other words, the state of the application is stored in the instance variable during the client-bean session. The need for session-related information expires with the removal of the bean. As a result, the state disappears at the end of the session triggered by the removal of the associated bean. In Chapter 8, I have already citied an example of an online store that uses a stateful bean to retain information regarding the items added to the shopping cart.

A stateless session bean serves multiple clients and is not associated with any instance variables. However, a stateless session bean may contain client-related contextual information during the period when the client invokes its methods.

Each session bean goes through a life cycle beginning with its initialization and ending with its destruction. I'll now discuss the life cycle of a session bean.

The Life Cycle of a Session Bean

The EJB (Enterprise Java Bean) container manages the life cycle of a session bean. It consists of various stages beginning with the instantiation of the bean and ending with its removal. On removal, a session bean is readied for garbage collection. I'll now discuss the life cycles of both a stateful and stateless session bean. I'll start my discussion with the life cycle of a stateful session bean.

The Life Cycle of a Stateful Session Bean

A stateful session bean goes through the `ready`, `passive` or `active`, and `does not exist` states. Therefore, the life cycle of a stateful session bean includes the following three phases:

- ◆ In the first phase or the `ready` state, the EJB container invokes the `create()`, `setSessionContext()`, and `ejbCreate()` methods.

- ◆ In the second phase the EJB container invokes either the `ejbPassivate()` or `ejbActivate()` methods. Accordingly the beans attain either `passive` or `active` states.

- ◆ In the third phase or the `does not exist` state, the EJB container invokes the `ejbRemove()` method.

The Ready State

The first phase is initiated when the client invokes the `create()` method. Next, the EJB container instantiates the bean and subsequently invokes the `setSessionContext()` and `ejbCreate()` methods. At the end of the first phase the bean is ready for invocation of its business methods.

The *Passive* or *Active* State

The design of a Web application should ensure minimum use of memory resources. Therefore, in the second phase, an idle bean is deactivated or put in passive state by moving it to the secondary storage. The EJB container calls the ejbPassivate() method before placing a bean in passive state.

However, when the client invokes a business method, the EJB container reactivates a passive bean. During this stage, the ejbActivate() method is called and the bean is back to its ready state again.

The Does Not Exist State

The third phase defines the end of the life cycle of a stateful session bean. The client invokes the remove() method that triggers the EJB container into calling the ejbRemove() method. During this phase, the bean is readied for garbage collection.

The phases of the life cycle of a stateful session bean are illustrated in Figure 10-1.

I'll now discuss the life cycle of a stateless session bean.

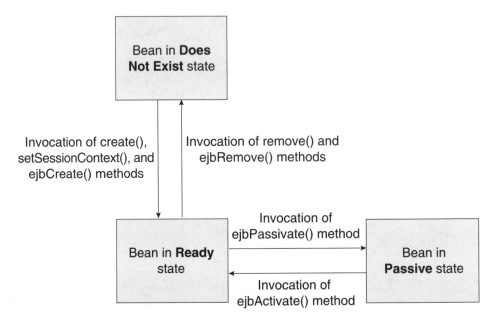

FIGURE 10-1 *The life cycle of a stateful session bean*

The Life Cycle of a Stateless Session Bean

A stateless session bean does not go through a `passive` state. Therefore, the life cycle of a stateless session bean includes the following two phases only:

◆ In the first phase or the `ready` state, the EJB container invokes the `set-SessionContext()` and `ejbCreate()` methods.

◆ In the second phase the EJB container invokes the `ejbRemove()` method and the bean is readied for garbage collection.

The phases of the life cycle of a stateless session bean are illustrated in Figure 10-2.

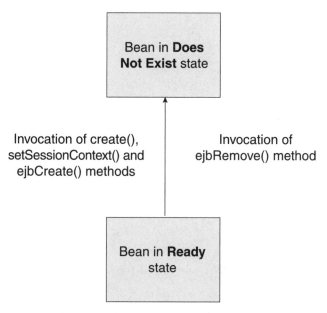

FIGURE 10-2 *The life cycle of a stateless session bean*

Before specifying the deployment descriptor for a session bean, you need to choose between the stateful session bean and the stateless bean management modes. I'll now discuss the modes of managing states in session beans.

The Modes of Managing the States of Session Beans

Bear in mind that a session bean represents a client on the J2EE server. Therefore, most of the time you will prefer to define a stateful session bean for an application.

You can choose to use a stateful session bean if the following conditions are satisfied:

◆ On creation of the bean, the bean's state must be initialized.

◆ The bean needs to contain client-related contextual information across all method calls.

◆ The design of the client application is interactive.

There may, however, be situations that require defining a stateless session bean. You can choose to use a stateful session bean if the following conditions are satisfied:

◆ The bean performs a generic task that is not customized for a particular client.

◆ The bean does not need to contain client-related contextual information across all method calls.

Often, it may happen that two stateful session beans contain the same object identities. In such situations, how will you confirm that the object references used by the two beans are not identical? I'll now discuss concepts that'll help ascertain whether the object references used by the two beans are identical.

Comparing Two Stateful Beans

A client can use the boolean return value of the isIdentical() method to distinguish the identities of two stateful session beans. A return value of true signifies that the two beans have the same object identity. On the contrary, a return value of false signifies that the two beans do not have the same object identity.

In the case of stateless session beans, the isIdentical() method always returns true because stateless session beans have the same object references.

You need to define the following interfaces and classes to create a stateful session bean:

◆ A home interface

◆ A remote interface

◆ A helper class

I'll use the example of an online shopping site to write the code for the home interface, remote interface, and helper class. All online purchases made using

MasterCard or Visa are validated for the credit card information entered by the user. I'll discuss the various classes and interfaces required for creating an application to validate the credit card number by using a stateful session bean. I'll start by identifying the methods included in each of these interfaces.

Coding the Home Interface

The home interface must extend the `javax.ejb.EJBHome` interface that in turn extends the `java.rmi.Remote` interface. The home interface contains the methods that define the various phases of the life cycle of a bean. It includes methods for creating, locating, and removing beans. The EJB container implements the home interface, which declares the following methods:

- The `create()` method
- The `getEJBMetaData()` method
- The `getHomeHandle()` method
- The `remove(Handle handle)` method
- The `remove(java.lang.Object PrimaryKey)` method

I'll now discuss each of these methods.

The create() *Method*

The `create()` method acts as a constructor by initializing the EJB object. Therefore, the EJB container does not need to instantiate a new object for each client reference to the EJB object. The EJB container, however, maintains a pool of the instantiated objects. An application can contain multiple definitions of the `create()` method. This method returns an object of the remote interface type. The `create()` method throws the following two types of exceptions:

- A `CreateException` if the client is unable to create the new EJB object
- A `RemoteException` on system failure

At runtime, the EJB container implements the home interface and calls the corresponding `ejbCreate()` method. The signatures of the `create()` and `ejbCreate()` methods are identical. However, the `create()` method returns an object of the remote interface type while the `ejbCreate()` method returns void.

The getEJBMetaData() Method

The `getEJBMetaData()` method returns the EJBMetaData interface of the bean. The client can access information regarding a bean from this interface. On system failure, this method throws a `RemoteException`.

The getHomeHandle() Method

The `getHomeHandle()` method returns a handle for the home object, which can be used as a reference to the home object. On system failure, this method throws a `RemoteException`.

The remove(Handle handle) Method

The `remove(Handle handle)` method helps to remove the EJB object that is identified by the handle. This method throws the following two types of exceptions:

◆ A `RemoveException` if the client is unable to remove the identified object

◆ A `RemoteException` on system failure

The remove(java.lang.Object PrimaryKey) Method

The `remove(java.lang.Object PrimaryKey)` method removes the EJB object that is identified by the primary key. This method also throws two exceptions similar to the `remove(Handle handle)` method.

The rules for defining the `create()` methods are as follows:

◆ The number and types of the `create()` method arguments declared in the home interface must correspond to those of the corresponding `ejbCreate()` method implemented in the EJB class.

◆ The arguments and return types must match the rules for Remote Method Invocation (RMI).

◆ The object returned must be of the remote interface type.

◆ The `java.rmi.RemoteException` and `javax.ejb.CreateException` must be included in the `throws` clause of the `create()` method.

The home interface that I'll use for the example is `CustomerHome`. The `create()` method of the home interface accepts two parameters of String type and returns an object of the remote interface type. The code for the home interface is given here:

```
import java.io.Serializable;
import java.rmi.RemoteException;
import javax.ejb.CreateException;
import javax.ejb.EJBHome;
public interface CustomerHome extends EJBHome
{
Customer create(String name, String card_no) throws RemoteException,
CreateException;
}
```

Coding the Remote Interface

The remote interface must extend the `javax.ejb.EJBObject` that in turn extends the `java.rmi.Remote` interface. It contains the definitions for all the business methods that can be invoked by the client. The `javax.ejb.EJBObject` declares the following methods:

- ◆ The `getEJBHome()` method
- ◆ The `getHandle()` method
- ◆ The `getPrimaryKey()` method
- ◆ The `isIdentical()` method
- ◆ The `remove()` method

The `getPrimaryKey()` and the `remove()` methods are used for entity beans only. At runtime, the EJB container creates a class to implement the remote interface. This class passes all the method class to the bean class and can be used by the client to:

- ◆ Find a reference to the home interface of the bean by using `getEJB-Home()` method
- ◆ Delete the object by using the `remove()` method

The rules for defining the methods of the remote interface are:

- ◆ The methods in the remote interface and the EJB class must match.
- ◆ The signatures of the methods in the remote interface must be identical to the signatures of the methods in the EJB class.
- ◆ The arguments and return types must match the rules for Remote Method Invocation (RMI).

◆ The arguments and return types need to pass from the client to the server and therefore must be serialized.

◆ The `throws` clause of all business methods must include the `java.rmi.RemoteException` to handle any network problem between the client and the server.

The remote interface that I'll use for the example is `CustomerRemote`. The business method defined to validate the card number is `validate()`. This method also needs to be implemented in the helper class. The `validate()` method accepts the credit card number as parameter and returns a variable of int type. The code for the remote interface is given here:

```
import java.util.*;
import javax.ejb.EJBObject;
import java.rmi.RemoteException;
public interface CustomerRemote extends EJBObject
{
public int validate(String card_no) throws RemoteException;
}
```

Coding the Helper Classes

The method definitions in a helper class must follow these rules:

◆ Each definition of the `create()` method in the home interface must correspond to the `ejbCreate()` method of the helper class.

◆ The `ejbCreate()` method must throw the `CreateException` if the client is unable to create the new EJB object.

◆ A method corresponding to the business methods in the remote interface must be defined in the helper class.

◆ The signatures of the methods in the remote interface must be identical to the signatures of the methods in the helper class.

The helper class that I'll use for the example is `CustomerEJB`, which implements the `SessionBean` interface. The helper EJB class also contains definitions of an `ejbCreate()` method corresponding to the `create()` method in the home interface. The code snippet for the helper class with the definition for the `ejbCreate()` method is given here:

```
import java.util.*;
import javax.ejb.*;
public class CustomerEJB implements SessionBean
{
String cName;
String cNo;
public void ejbCreate(String name, String c_no) throws CreateException
{
if ((name.equals("")) ¦¦ (card_no.equals("")))
{
throw new CreateException("Invalid name, card number not allowed.");
}
}
```

In addition, the EJB class also contains a business method `validate()`, containing the same signature as that of the method in the remote interface. The `validate()` method in turn contains the `ltchar()`, `rtchar()`, and `chtoint()` methods that are user-defined. The code snippet for the helper class with the definition for the business method is given here:

```
public static int chtoint(char ch)
{
if (ch=='0') return(0);
if (ch=='1') return(1);
if (ch=='2') return(2);
if (ch=='3') return(3);
if (ch=='4') return(4);
if (ch=='5') return(5);
if (ch=='6') return(6);
if (ch=='7') return(7);
if (ch=='8') return(8);
if (ch=='9') return(9);
return(0);
}
public static char ltchar(String card_no)
{
return(card_no.charAt(0));
}
public static char rtchar(String card_no)
```

```
{
return(card_no.charAt(CardNo.length()-1));
}
public int validate(String card_no)
{
int i;
int total = 0;
String tempMult = "";
for(i = card_no.length();i >= 2; i -=2)
{
total = total + chtoint(card_no.charAt(i-1));
tempMult = "" + (chtoint(card_no.charAt(i-2)) * 2);
total = total + chtoint(ltchar(tempMult));
if (tempMult.length()>1)
{
total = total + chtoint(rtchar(tempMult));
}
}
if (card_no.length() % 2 == 1)
{
total = total + chtoint(ltchar(card_no));
}
if (total % 10 == 0)
{
return 0;
}
else
{
return 1;
}
}
```

The code snippet for the EJB class with the definitions for the `ejbRemove()`, `set-SessionContext()`, `ejbActivate()`, and `ejbPassivate()` methods is given here:

```
public CardEJB(){}
public void ejbRemove(){}
public void ejbActivate(){}
public void ejbPassivate(){}
```

```
public void setSessionContext(SessionContext sc){}
}
```

You can define a client application with controls to accept the customer name and card number. On execution, the stateful session bean validates the card number and displays a corresponding message. The card number is retained in the form of contextual information as long as the user is logged on to the site. As a result, further purchases made by the user can be easily associated to the retained information.

That completes the discussion on session beans. I'll now move on to discussing the second type of enterprise bean, or the entity bean.

Entity Beans

Entity beans can be categorized into the following two types based on how they manage persistence. *Persistence* can be defined as perseverance, which is a feature of an entity bean that supports its existence even after an application is closed. In an entity bean, persistence is attained by saving its state in a database. The two types of entity beans are:

◆ Bean-managed persistence (BMP)
◆ Container-managed persistence (CMP)

True to its name, persistence that is explicitly managed by the bean itself is called bean-managed persistence. The developer coding for the particular bean writes the code for database manipulation in the case of bean-managed persistence. The created instance of the bean manages the persistence guided by the EJB container that informs the bean when to insert, update, and delete data from a database.

A container-managed persistence entity bean is luckier to have the EJB container automatically manage its persistence. The fields of the bean instance are automatically mapped to those of a database by the EJB container. In addition, the container also takes care of inserting, updating, and deleting data from the database.

Similar to a session bean, an entity bean, too, has a life cycle distinguished by the initialization and destruction stages. I'll now discuss the life cycle of an entity bean.

The Life Cycle of an Entity Bean

The life cycle of an entity bean goes through the does not exist, pooled, and ready states. Therefore, the life cycle of an entity bean includes the following three phases:

◆ The first phase or the does not exist state is represented by the beans that have yet to be instantiated by the EJB container.

◆ The second phase or the pooled state is represented by the beans that have been instantiated by the EJB container.

◆ The third phase or the ready state is represented by the beans that can accept client requests.

I'll now discuss each of these states of the entity bean life cycle. I'll start with a discussion on the does not exist state.

The does not exist *State*

The does not exist state of an entity bean does not contain any instance of the bean. The bean exists in the form of a collection of files containing the deployment descriptor, the remote and home interfaces, the primary key, and all support classes generated during deployment.

The pooled *State*

On server startup, instances of an entity bean are created by calling the newInstance() method. The instantiated beans are placed in a pool. After instantiation, the bean moves to the pooled state and the EJB container then calls the setEntityContext() method. This method links the bean with all environmental information. The bean instances of a pool are used by the container to serve incoming client requests.

The ready *State*

On accepting a request, the client invokes the create() method. The bean now moves to the ready state. The EJB container subsequently calls the ejbCreate() and ejbPostCreate() methods. A bean in ready state is associated with a specific EJB object containing a remote reference to the client. The ejbCreate() method initializes the bean after which a primary key is created. In the case of container-managed persistence the primary key is created automatically. However, in the case of bean-managed persistence, the primary key is populated during the bean instantiation. Next, the ejbPostCreate() method is called to complete any post processing before the bean is made available to the client. After this, the bean instance and the EJB object are both available to serve requests from the client.

An instance of a bean can also be moved to ready state by invoking the ejbActi-
vate() method. On invocation, this method is responsible for allocation of resources
such as sockets to the bean. In addition, invocation of the ejbPassivate()
method results in the change of state of a bean from ready state back to its pooled
state.

When the client calls the remove() method, the EJB container calls the ejbFRe-
move() method, and a bean in ready state moves to the pooled state. During this
time all data from the database that is associated with the bean is deleted.

The life cycle of an entity bean ends with the invocation of the unsetEntityCon-
text() method. This method releases all resources associated with the bean and
readies the bean for garbage collection.

The phases of the life cycle of an entity bean are illustrated in Figure 10-3.

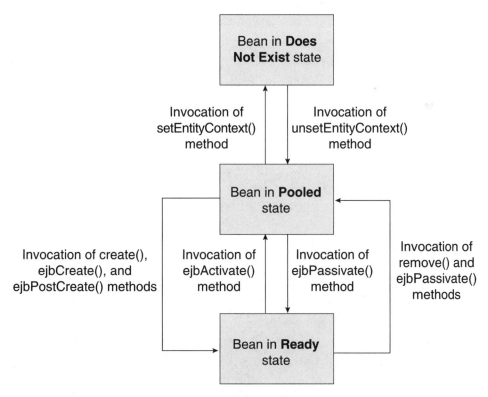

FIGURE 10-3 *The life cycle of an entity bean*

There have been quite a few references to primary key and shared access in the preceding discussions. Beginning with primary key, I'll now discuss the definitions of each of these terms.

The Primary Key

A *primary key* is a unique object that identifies an entity bean. For example, a roll number may be used to identify a student entity bean. The client uses a primary key to identify a particular entity bean.

Shared Access

Multiple clients can reference an entity bean at a given instance. As a result, it is quite possible that two clients may access and update the same data simultaneously. For example, one client may update data in a database while another client attempts to delete the same data at the same time. It is therefore important that entity beans work within transactions to maintain concurrency of all such data manipulations. I'll now discuss transaction, to show you how the EJB container provides transaction management for an entity bean.

The Transaction

A *transaction* can be defined as a series of tasks that together execute as a single operation. In other words, a transaction is an undivided unit of work. A transaction is said to be successful if all its defined tasks execute. The failure in completion of a single task leads to a failed or unsuccessful transaction. For example, consider the following pseudocode that lists the tasks of an online shopping transaction.

    Begin transaction

        Add items to shopping cart

        Enter customer information

        Enter payment details

        Validate card for credit purchase

        Display invoice

    End transaction

In the preceding example, the failure in executing any of the tasks results in the failure of or the cancellation of the transaction. Each transaction is defined within the boundaries of the begin transaction and the end transaction statements. A failed transaction ends in a roll back while a successful transaction ends in a commit. During a roll back, the outcome of the earlier tasks is undone and the transaction is aborted. However, during a commit, the outcome of the transaction and the subsequent data modifications are saved.

Transactions are defined by using the ACID properties. ACID stands for *a*tomicity, *c*onsistency, *i*solation, and *d*urability. Transactional experts have identified these characteristics to ensure perfect execution every time while preserving the integrity of data. I'll now discuss each of these properties. I'll start with a discussion on atomicity.

Atomicity

An atomic transaction is that which executes completely or does not execute at all. As a result, each task of the transaction is executed without any error. In case a task fails, the transaction is rolled back and aborted.

Consistency

Consistency defines the integrity of the data within a transactional system. For example, consistency ensures that the balance at the end of a bank transaction is maintained and not manipulated until the next transaction.

Isolation

Each transaction should execute undeterred by interferences from other transactions. In other words, multiple transactions of multiple clients are isolated from each other.

Durability

Durability ensures that the modifications made to the data during a transaction are written to a physical storage before the completion of a transaction. As a result, all updates performed during a transaction survive contingencies such as system crashes.

Transactions for an entity bean can be either bean-managed or container-managed. Bean-managed transactions are also called programmatic transactions that require explicit inclusions of the programming logic to implement a begin, commit, or abort statement. Container-managed transactions, also called declarative transactions, are managed by the EJB container. As a result, a programmer does not need to explicitly specify a begin, commit, or abort statement.

This concludes the preliminary discussion about entity beans. I'll now discuss the classes and interfaces that need to be included in the application using entity beans for storing data on a Cloudscape database.

 NOTE

The J2EE SDK includes the Cloudscape DBMS from Informix software. Cloudscape is a Java-based object relational database management system (ORDBMS) that uses SQL as the supporting query language. An ORDBMS is a management system that implements the features of an object-oriented, relation-based database management system. To access the Cloudscape database, you first need to start the Cloudscape server. The commands to start and stop the Cloudscape server are more or less similar to the commands used to start and stop the J2EE server. Type the following command at the DOS prompt to start the Cloudscape server:

```
Cloudscape -start
```

The command to stop the Cloudscape server is:

```
Cloudscape -stop
```

Creating an Entity Bean Demonstrating Bean-Managed Persistence

After starting the Cloudscape database, you can access the data in the tables of the database by using SQL commands. I'll now list the interfaces and classes needed to create an entity bean. Similar to the interfaces and classes of a session bean, to create an entity bean you need to define the following interfaces and classes:

◆ A home interface

◆ A remote interface

◆ An enterprise bean class

I'll continue to use the example of an online shopping site to write the code for the home interface, remote interface, and helper class. As discussed in the preceding sections, during a typical online shopping transaction, a customer needs to fill a customer registration form at the end of the purchases. The detail of the customer registrations is stored in a central database so that the data is available for reference at all times.

The state of the entity bean created in this section is stored in the Registration table of a relational database. The following SQL statement is used to create the Registration table:

```
CREATE TABLE Registration (id VARCHAR(5) PRIMARY KEY, cFirst_Name VARCHAR(20),
cLast_Name VARCHAR(10), cAddress VARCHAR(30), cPhone VARCHAR(10);
```

Let us begin by identifying the methods included in each of these interfaces.

Coding the Home Interface

In addition to the create() method, the home interface includes a finder method to help the client locate entity beans in a database. The create() method in the home interface should conform to the following requirements:

◆ The number and types of arguments in the create() method should match those of the ejbCreate() method in the EJB class.

◆ The exceptions included in the throws clauses of the ejbCreate() and ejbPostCreate() methods should match.

◆ The create() method of the home interface should return the remote interface type of the bean.

The finder method in the home interface should conform to the following requirements:

◆ Each finder method in the home interface should correspond to a finder method in the EJB class. However, the naming conventions for the finder methods in the home interface and EJB class are different. The finder method of the home interface starts with find, while the finder method in the EJB class includes the prefix ejb and is written as ejbFind. For example, the findByPrimaryKey() of the home interface has a corresponding ejbFindByPrimaryKey() method in the EJB class that identifies an entity bean by its primary key.

◆ The number and types of arguments in the finder methods of the home interface and the EJB class should match.

◆ The finder methods of the home interface should return the remote interface type of the bean.

◆ The `throws` clauses of finder methods should contain the `javax.ejb.FinderException` and the `javax.ejb.RemoteException` exceptions.

The code for the home interface is:

```
java.util.Collection;
import java.rmi.RemoteException;
import javax.ejb.*;


public interface RegistrationHome extends EJBHome {
   public RegistrationRemote create(String id, String fname, String lname, String
address, String phone) throws RemoteException, CreateException;


public RegistrationRemote findByPrimaryKey(String id) throws FinderException,
RemoteException;
   }
```

Coding the Remote Interface

As discussed earlier, the remote interface contains the definitions for the client invoked business methods. The method definitions of the remote interfaces of a session bean and an entity bean conform to the same requirements. As a result, for the online shopping site example, the remote interface contains only the signatures of the `getFirstName()`, `getLastname()`, `getAddress()`, and `getPhone()` business methods. In addition, all these business methods of the remote interface are implemented in the EJB class and are used in the EJB class to access the data in a database.

The code for the remote interface is:

```
import javax.ejb.EJBObject;
import java.rmi.RemoteException;
public interface RegistrationRemote extends EJBObject
{
```

```
    public String getFirstname() throws RemoteException;
    public String getLastname() throws RemoteException;
    public String getAddress() throws RemoteException;
    public String getLoantype() throws RemoteException;
    public String getPhone() throws RemoteException;
    public double getAnnualincome() throws RemoteException;
    public double getAmount() throws RemoteException;
}
```

Coding the Enterprise Bean Class

The entity bean class extends the EntityBean interface, which in turn extends the `EnterpriseBean` interface. The classes and methods defined in the enterprise bean class fall into the following three categories:

◆ The EntityBean interface

◆ Business methods that are used to access the data in a database.

◆ Call back methods that are used by the EJB container to manage the beans and inform the bean when to insert, update, and delete data from a database.

The EntityBean Interface

An entity bean class must implement the EntityBean interface. This interface extends the `Serializable` interface. The EntityBean interface declares a few methods that must be implemented in the bean class. These methods are `ejbActivate()`, `ejbLoad()`, `ejbPassivate()`, `ejbRemove()`, `ejbStore()`, `setEntityContext()`, and `unsetEntityContext()`.

The Business Methods

The enterprise bean class contains definitions for business methods that are represented by `getter` methods for all the corresponding signatures of the business methods defined in the remote interface.

For the online shopping site example, the business methods are therefore defined as:

```
public String getFirstname()
    {
```

```
        return fname;
  }
public String getLastname()
{
    return lname;
  }
public String getAddress()
{
    return address;
  }
public String getPhone()
{
    return phone;
```

The Call Back Methods

The following call back methods are defined in the enterprise bean class:

◆ The ejbStore() method
◆ The ejbLoad() method
◆ The getEJBObject() method
◆ The getPrimaryKey() method
◆ The ejbRemove() method
◆ The setEntityContext() method
◆ The ejbPostCreate() method
◆ The finder methods

Now take a look at each of these methods in detail.

The *ejbStore()* Method

The ejbStore() and ejbLoad() methods are used to match the instance variables of an entity bean with the corresponding values in the database. The ejbStore() method is used to write a variable value to the database.

In the example for the online shopping site, the ejbStore() method calls the storeRow() method to write the values of the user input in the customer registration form to the database by using an SQL update statement. The ejbStore()

The *unsetEntityContext()* Method

The `unsetEntityContext()` method is used by the container to move an entity bean from the `pooled` state to the `does not exist` state. After the execution of this method, all resources allocated to the entity bean are released and the bean is readied for garbage collection. The code snippet for the `unsetEntityContext()` method is given here:

```
public void unsetEntityContext()
    {
       try {
          con.close();
           }
       catch (SQLException ex)
           {
 throw new EJBException("unsetEntityContext: " + ex.getMessage());
           }
    }
```

The *finder* Methods

The client uses the `finder` methods to locate entity beans. Every `finder` method of a client application must contain a corresponding method in the EJB class prefixed by an `ejbFind`. It is mandatory to define the finder method, `ejbFindByPrimaryKey()`. Defining any other finder method is optional.

The following code snippet is the definition for the `ejbFindByPrimaryKey()` method used in the online shopping site example.

```
    public String ejbFindByPrimaryKey(String primaryKey)
       throws FinderException {

       Id result;
       try
          {
          result = selectByPrimaryKey(primaryKey);
          }
       catch (Exception ex)
          {
             throw new EJBException("ejbFindByPrimaryKey: " +
```

```
ex.getMessage());
    }
if (result)
{
    return primaryKey;
}
else
{
    throw new ObjectNotFoundException
        ("Row for id " + primaryKey + " not found.");
}
}
```

The preceding example included storage and retrieval of data from a database. It is interesting to note that entity beans with bean-managed persistence also connect to other databases such as SQL Server and Oracle. I'll now discuss how to connect an entity bean to an SQL database.

Connecting an Entity Bean to an SQL Database

In Chapter 8, I discussed how the JDBC API is used as a standard for Java programs to access databases. However, to connect to a database other than Cloudscape, you need first to configure the database and then write the code to connect to the database in the EJB class. To configure a database, do the following:

◆ Create a DSN for the database in the SQL server. The DSN contains information about the location of the database server, database name, username, and password to be used to connect to the database server.

◆ Make the following modifications in the `default.properties` file. The `default.properties` file contains the database specifications for the default database, which is Cloudscape. Therefore, before establishing a connection with an SQL database, you need to edit the `default.properties` file.

◆ To edit the `default.properties` file, open the `default.properties` file in the `config` folder of the J2EE installation directory. Edit the files so that the entries for `jdbc.drivers` and `jdbc.datasources` have the following values:

```
jdbc.drivers=COM.cloudscape.core.RmiJdbcDriver:sun.jdbc.odbc.JdbcOdbcDriver
jdbc.datasources=jdbc/sqlServer¦jdbc:odbc:MyDataSource¦jdbc/Cloudscape¦jdbc:
cloudscape:rmi:CloudscapeDB;create=true
```

Alternatively, you can also comment the existing values for the two properties in the `default.properties` file and add the code lines shown above.

The syntax for the `jdbc.drivers` property specifying a list of JDBC driver class names is:

```
jdbc.drivers = <classname>:<classname>:…
```

The syntax for the `jdbc.datasources` property associating the JNDI name of the data source with the URL of a database is:

```
jdbc.datasources=<datasource>¦<URL>¦<datasource>¦<URL>…
```

After editing, save and close the `default.properties` file.

The `default.properties` file contains configuration information about the JDBC driver. The contents of the file can be edited to configure the required drivers for connectivity to different databases. By default, the file is configured for the Cloudscape driver.

Many times, the database that you are connecting to requires you to download certain drivers. In such situations, the .jar files of the drivers have to be copied to the `<system drive>:\<root installation directory of Java Enterprise Edition Folder>\lib\classes` folder. In addition, the values of the environment variable `J2EE_CLASSPATH` has to be modified to reflect the classpath of the driver files.

 NOTE

J2EE accesses a database by means of a JDBC driver. To locate the driver's .jar files, the J2EE server accesses the value of the `J2EE_CLASSPATH`. As a result, you have to edit the `userconfig.bat` file to modify the value of the `J2EE_CLASSPATH`. This file is found in the bin folder in the root directory where J2EE is installed. In the case of SQL Server 2000, it is not necessary to download any drivers. However, the `default.properties` file has to be modified.

After configuring the database, I'll now discuss the steps to connect to a database. The statements for connecting to a database are written in the enterprise bean class. The three steps to connect to a database are:

1. First, you need to specify the name of the logical database. The syntax for this statement is as follows:

```
private String dbName =  "java:comp/env/jdbc/ToyzDB";
```

The `java:comp/env/` prefix is the JNDI context for the component. The `jdbc/ToyzDB` string is the logical database name.

2. Secondly, you need to obtain the value of the `DataSource` that is associated with the logical name. The following statements are used to retrieve the value of the `DataSource`:

```
InitialContext ic = new InitialContext( );
DataSource ds = (DataSource) ic.lookup(dbName);
```

3. Finally, you need to get the `Connection` from the `DataSource` by using the following statement:

```
Connection con =  ds.getConnection();
```

Creating a Container-Managed Entity Bean

In the preceding sections, I have already discussed that in container-managed persistence (CMP), the entity bean is not coded to handle persistence. To the contrary, during deployment, the developer specifies the bean instance variables that map to the database. The container then automatically generates the code and logic for writing the bean's state to the database.

The bean instance variables that are mapped to the database are also known as fields. The container-managed fields are called persistent fields. Persistent fields can be of the following types:

◆ A Java primitive type

◆ A Java `Serializable` class

◆ A reference to home interface

◆ A reference to remote interface

Similar to creating an entity bean demonstrating bean-managed persistence, you need to define the following interfaces and classes to create an entity bean with container-managed persistence:

- A home interface
- A remote interface
- An EJB class

There is not much variation in the definitions for the home interface and remote interface in BMP and CMP. However, the definition of the EJB differs due to the absence of the database calls.

NOTE

CMP is implemented only if the development time is minimal and the database has one table.

I'll now discuss the definitions of each of these interfaces and classes. I'll continue to use the example of the online shopping site and create a bean to search and retrieve data from the `Registration` table of the database by using CMP.

Coding the Home Interface

The home interface must extend the `EJBHome` interface and contain definitions for the `create()` and `find()` methods. The client uses these methods to create and find entity beans.

The rules for defining a method in the home interface of a CMP remain the same as that of an entity bean created using BMP.

NOTE

The number of `find()` methods in the home interface must correspond to the number of `ejbFind()` methods in the bean class.

The code for the home interface `customerHome`, defines three methods: the `create()`, `findByPrimaryKey()`, and `findByfirstname()` methods, which must be implemented in the EJB class. The code for the home interface is as follows:

```
import java.util.Collection;
```

```
import java.rmi.RemoteException;
import javax.ejb.*;

public interface customerHome extends EJBHome
{
public registration create(int Id, String firstname, String lastname, String
address, String phoneno) throws RemoteException, CreateException;

public registration findByPrimaryKey(int Id) throws FinderException,
RemoteException;

public Collection findByfirstname(String firstname) throws FinderException,
RemoteException;

}
```

Coding the Remote Interface

The remote interface must extend the `javax.ejb.EJBObject` interface. The `javax.-ejb.EJBObject` in turn extends the `java.rmi.Remote` interface. The remote interface also contains the definitions for the business methods.

 NOTE

The `throws` clause in the remote interface must include
`java.rmi.RemoteException`.

For the online shopping site example, the remote interface defines the following four business methods:

- The `getFirstname()` method
- The `getLastname()` method
- The `getAddress()` method
- The `getPhoneno()` method

All the preceding methods must be implemented in the EJB class. The code for the remote interface is as follows:

```
import javax.ejb.EJBObject;
import java.rmi.RemoteException;


public interface Customer extends EJBObject
{

public String getFirstname() throws RemoteException;
public String getLastname() throws RemoteException;
public String getAddress() throws RemoteException;
public String getPhoneno() throws RemoteException;
}
```

Coding the Enterprise Bean Class

The entity bean class must implement the EntityBean interface and be defined as `public`. This class must implement all the business methods and the `ejbCreate()` and `ejbPostCreate()` methods. The definition for the EntityBean interface remains the same as that of the interface in BMP.

The other methods implemented in the entity bean class are:

- The `ejbCreate()` method
- The `ejbPostCreate()` method
- The `ejbActivate()` method
- The `ejbLoad()` method
- The `ejbStore()` method
- The `ejbPassivate()` method
- The `ejbRemove()` method
- The `setEntityContext()` method
- The `ejbFindXXX()` method

I'll now discuss each of these methods one by one.

The ejbCreate() *Method*

When the client calls the `create()` method, the container invokes the `ejbCreate()` method. The `create()` method sets the container-managed fields to the values of the input parameters and initializes these fields. You'll recall that in the case of BMP, the `create()` method updates the database with the entity state, initializes the instance variables of the entity bean, and returns the primary key. In the case of CMP, this method typically returns a null value. After the execution of this method, the container inserts the values of the container-managed fields into a database.

The code snippet for the `create()` method is as follows:

```
public String ejbCreate(int Id, String firstname, String lastname, String address,
String phoneno) throws CreateException
{
if (String.valueOf(regnId)) == null)
{
throw new CreateException(" The registration id is required");
}

this.regnId = regnId;
this.firstname = firstname;
this.lastname = lastname;
this.address = address;
this.phoneno = phoneno;
return null;
}
```

The ejbPostCreate() *Method*

Each definition of the `ejbCreate()` method must have a definition for the corresponding `ejbPostCreate()` method. After invoking `ejbCreate()`, the container invokes the `ejbPostCreate()` method. The `ejbPostCreate()` method invokes the `getPrimaryKey()` and `getEJBObject()` methods of the entity context interface.

 NOTE

The number and signatures of `ejbCreate()` and the corresponding `ejbPostCreate()` methods must match in the bean class.

The code snippet for the ejbPostCreate() method is as follows:

```
public void ejbPostCreate(int Id, String firstname, String lastname, String
address, String phoneno) {}
```

The ejbActivate() Method

The container calls the ejbActivate() method when the bean instance moves from the pooled state and is associated with a particular EJB object. The code snippet for the ejbActivate() method is:

```
public void ejbActivate()
{
Object obj = context.getPrimaryKey();
String rid = obj.toString();
regnId = Integer.parseInt(rid);
}
```

The ejbStore() Method

The container calls the ejbStore() method to write or save the entity's bean state to the database. This method retrieves the values from the fields and updates the row in the database with the corresponding values. You'll recall that in the case of BMP, the ejbStore() method saves the instance variable values to the underlying database.

 NOTE

The ejbStore() method is usually not overridden in the bean class.

The ejbLoad() Method

The container uses the ejbLoad() method to refresh an entity bean's state with values from the database. The container selects the specific row from the database, assigns its values to the corresponding container-managed fields, and finally calls the ejbLoad() method. You'll recall that in the case of BMP, the ejbLoad() method typically assigns the specific row values to the instance variables.

NOTE

The `ejbLoad()` method is usually not overridden in the bean class.

The ejbPassivate() *Method*

The container calls the `ejbPassivate()` method before a bean instance is relieved of its association with the EJB object. The bean instance can then be removed or moved to the `pooled` state. The code snippet for the `ejbPassivate()` method is as follows:

```
public void ejbPassivate()
{
Id = 0;
}
```

The ejbRemove() *Method*

When the client invokes the `remove()` method, the container calls the `ejbRe-move()` method. After the execution of this method, the container deletes the row from the database and throws an exception if the container is unable to delete the row. You'll recall that in case of BMP, the `remove()` method deletes the entity's state and the values of the instance variables from the database.

The setEntityContext() *Method*

The container calls the `setEntityContext()` method on the bean instance after creating the bean instance, to associate the bean instance with a specific context. This method takes an `EntityContext` interface as parameter. This `setEntityContext()` method corresponds to the `setSessionContext()` method of session beans. The code snippet for the `setEntityContext()` method is as follows:

```
public void setEntityContext(EntityContext context)
{
this.context = context;
}
```

The unsetEntityContext() *Method*

The container calls the `unsetEntityContext()` method on the bean instance before removing the instance of the bean.

The ejbFindXXX() *Method*

In CMP, the `finder` methods specific to the application are not implemented. The Application Deployment Tool implements the `finder` methods, `findByPrimaryKey()` and `findByfirstname()`. The necessary SQL statement is generated for the `findByPrimaryKey()` method. However, for the `findByfirstname()` method, the partial SQL statement is generated along with the "where" clause.

The container-managed fields for the shopping site example are `Id`, `firstname`, `lastname`, `address`, and `phoneno`. These variables are declared `public` so that the container can access these variables.

The four business methods that are implemented are:

- The `getFirstname()` method returns the `firstname` value of the specific row as a String value.

- The `getLastname()` method returns the `lastname` value of the specific row as a String value.

- The `getAddress()` method returns the `address` value of the specific row as a String value.

- The `getPhoneno()` method returns the `phoneno` value of the specific row as a String value.

The code snippet containing the definitions for the `ejbFindXXX()` methods is:

```
public String getFirstname()
{
return firstname;
}


public String getLastname()
{
return lastname;
}


public String getAddress()
{
return address;
}


public String getPhone()
```

```
{
return phoneno;
}
```

I am sure that by the end of this chapter, you'll be able to create your own application using session and entity beans.

Summary

In this chapter, you learned the differences between session beans and entity beans. You learned about the stateful and stateless session beans. You also learned about the various stages in the life cycle of both a stateless and a stateful session bean. Then, you learned about the classes and interfaces definitions required to create a stateful session bean.

In the later sections of the chapter, you learned about the two types of entity beans that demonstrate bean-managed persistence (BMP) and container-managed persistence (CMP). You also learned about the various stages in the life cycle of an entity bean. Finally, you learned the different class and interface definitions required to create an application using bean-managed persistence and container-managed persistence.

PART III

III

**Professional
Project — 1**

Project 1

Project 1 Overview

A chat application is utility software that enables users to communicate over networks. A chat application can be efficiently used as a medium for various forums. The functionalities provided by chat applications include displaying messages in a chat room, displaying a list of online users, and enabling users to send personal messages to other users. In addition, chat applications enable you to communicate with chat friends.

In this project, I'll discuss how you can build a chat application by using Java concepts. The use of Java, which is a platform-independent language, will enable you to run your chat application on any platform. The concepts that I'll use to build the chat application are:

- ◆ Java Swing API
- ◆ Networking
- ◆ Socket programming
- ◆ I/O concepts
- ◆ Event handling
- ◆ Error and exception handling

Java Swing API classes will be used to create graphical interfaces of the application. A chat application is a network-based application. I'll use networking and socket programming to establish connections between users over a network. In addition, the I/O classes of Java will be used extensively in this application. These classes can be used for sending messages over a network to the input and output streams established using socket programming. Various events, errors, and exceptions will be handled effectively in this application.

Chapter 11

FunSoftware is a software development company with the head office at New York. The company has 300 employees who are spread across branch offices in six cities in the United States. FunSoftware has developed a Web site exclusively for its own use. The Web site acts as an interface between management and employees, and contains information such as the latest announcements and policies, and any changes in the company's organization. In addition, the Web site provides work-related features such as:

- Forms for leave applications
- Forms for the reimbursement of various expenses incurred by the employees
- Payroll and personal information
- Details of the policies and results of the company
- Forum for exchange of opinions between employees and management

The Web site has been in use for the last six months. Suggestions for improvement of the Web site were invited from the users. One of the suggestions was to introduce a chat application on the Web site. The chat application would not only encourage employees to visit the Web site more often but also would help them remain constantly in touch while in the office. In addition, the management could use it for other activities, such as conducting official Net meetings and seminars. Thus, employees and managers, while having the comfort of sitting at their workstations, could interact and discuss official matters.

The suggestion was submitted to the management of FunSoftware. After conducting a poll, which indicated that employees favored having the chat application on the company Web site, the management decided to have a chat application on the Web site. A five-member team of Java application developers was assigned the task of developing a chat application named "FunChat." Thus began the development of another application at FunSoftware.

The members of the FunChat development team, which was named "FunTeam," were:

- Larry Peterson, the Project Manager
- John Wallace

- Henry Forsythe
- Ken Barrett
- Katie Frye

The members of FunTeam met to identify the deadlines and the life cycle of the FunChat project. You, as part of FunTeam, need to develop the chat application. Take a look at the life cycle of the project as identified by FunTeam.

The Project Life Cycle

The development life cycle of a project usually involves three stages:

- Project initiation
- Project execution
- Project completion

In the project initiation stage, a team prepares the project plan and finalizes the outcome of each stage. In this stage, the team also prepares a comprehensive list of tasks involved in this stage, and the project manager assigns responsibilities to the team members, depending on their skills.

In the project execution stage, the team develops the product. In the case of FunTeam, they developed the online chat utility. This stage consists of the following phases:

- Requirements analysis
- High-level design
- Low-level design
- Construction
- Testing
- Acceptance

I'll discuss each of these phases in detail.

Requirements Analysis Phase

During the requirements analysis, FunTeam analyzed the requirements to be fulfilled by the chat utility and identified the probable approach for meeting these requirements. To identify the requirements for FunChat, FunTeam studied the existing chat utilities at various Web sites and conducted extensive interviews with chat application users. In addition, the employees of FunSoftware were free to send FunTeam a list of their requirements for the chat utility.

Finally, the following requirements were identified. The application should:

◆ Enable a first-time user to register by filling in some personal details

◆ Enable a registered user to log on after his/her login details are validated

◆ Allow an online user to view a list of other online users

◆ Allow users to chat in the common chat room

The High-Level Design Phase

In this stage, the team decides how the system should function. The formats for data input and output are finalized in this stage. The functional specifications documentation of the system is presented in a language that can be understood by all. The finished project design is, however, executed only on the project manager's approval. FunTeam designed the following interfaces for FunChat.

The Login Interface

The login interface is the first screen that a user will view. It will accept the username and the password for the chat utility. The user will have the option to cancel the login attempt. First-time users can select the option to register with FunChat.

A sketch of the login interface is depicted in Figure 11-1.

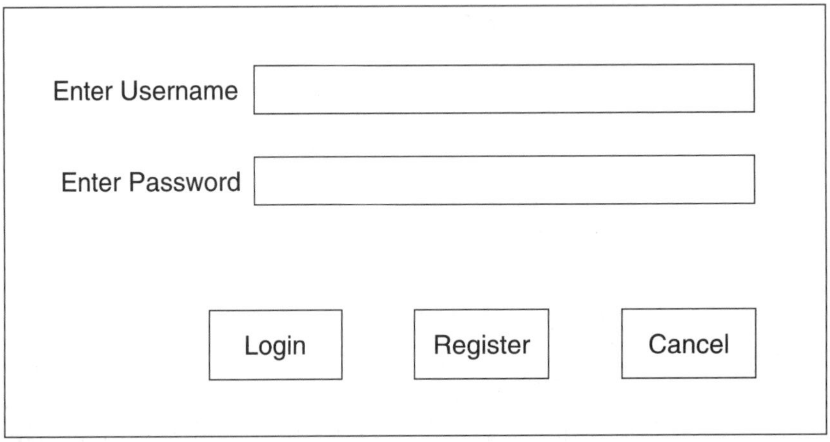

FIGURE 11-1 *Sketch of the login interface*

The Registration Interface

The registration interface enables users to register with FunChat. The interface will enable a user to specify a username and a password. In addition, other personal information about the user is accepted. The registration interface designed by FunTeam after much discussion and consultation is shown in Figure 11-2.

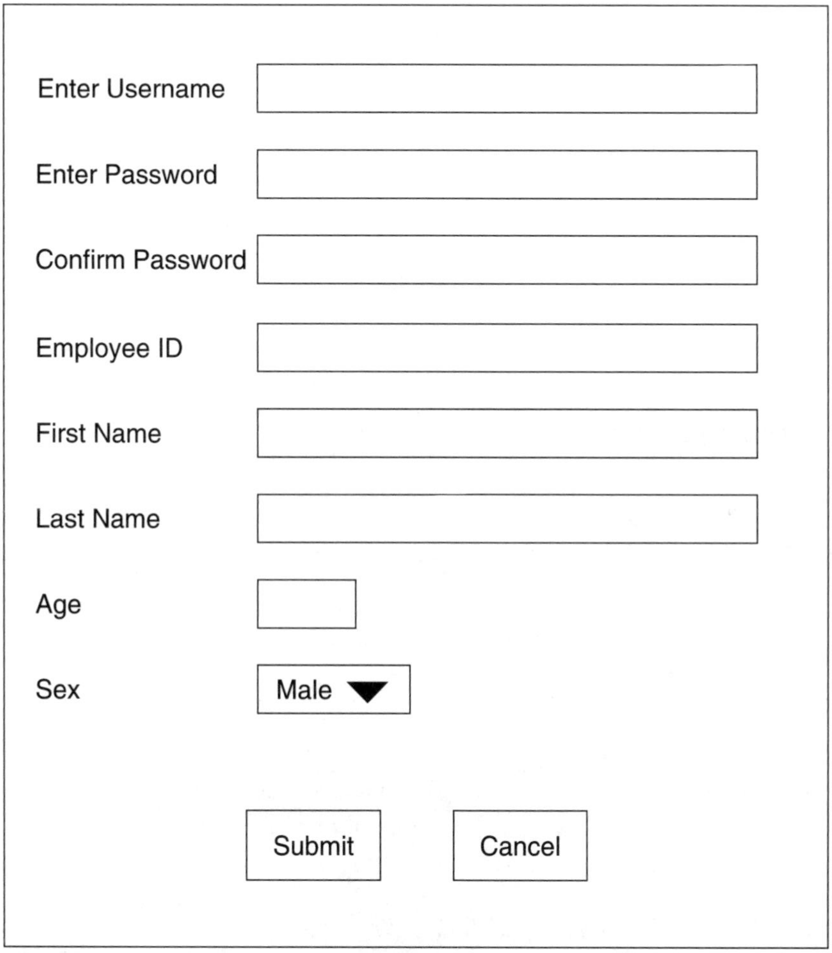

FIGURE 11-2 *Sketch of the registration interface*

The Chat Room Interface

After a registered user is authenticated, he/she will enter the chat room. The chat room, as designed by FunTeam, is illustrated in Figure 11-3.

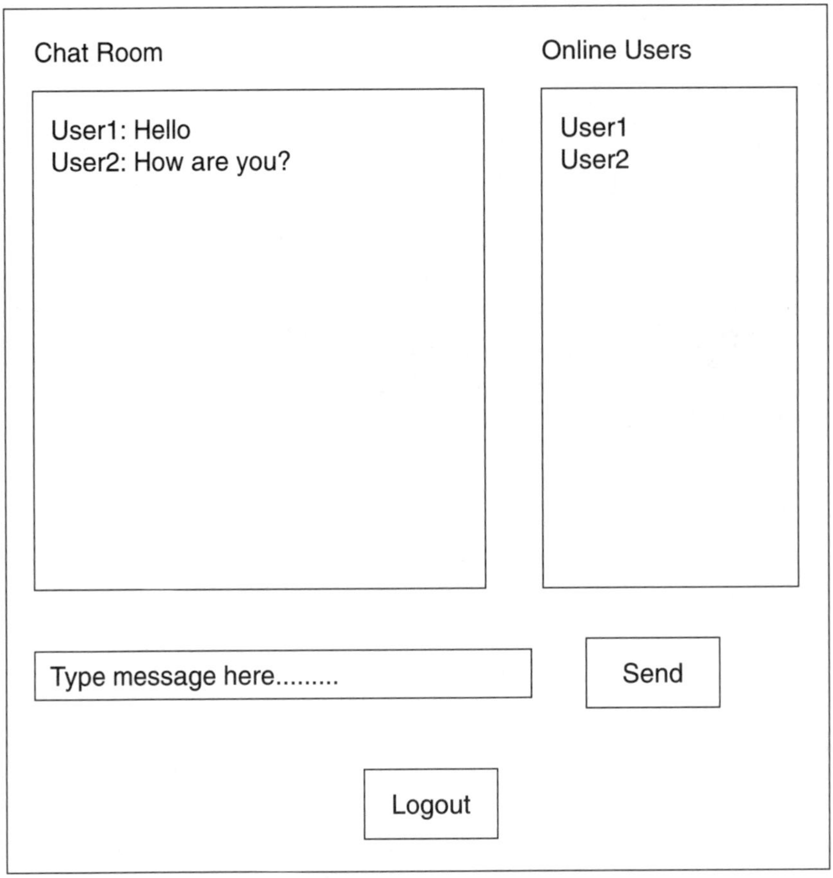

```
┌─────────────────────────────────────────────────────────┐
│  Chat Room                         Online Users          │
│  ┌──────────────────────────┐   ┌──────────────────┐     │
│  │ User1: Hello             │   │ User1            │     │
│  │ User2: How are you?      │   │ User2            │     │
│  │                          │   │                  │     │
│  │                          │   │                  │     │
│  │                          │   │                  │     │
│  │                          │   │                  │     │
│  │                          │   │                  │     │
│  │                          │   │                  │     │
│  └──────────────────────────┘   └──────────────────┘     │
│                                                           │
│  ┌──────────────────────────┐      ┌──────────┐          │
│  │ Type message here.........│      │  Send    │          │
│  └──────────────────────────┘      └──────────┘          │
│                      ┌──────────┐                         │
│                      │  Logout  │                         │
│                      └──────────┘                         │
└─────────────────────────────────────────────────────────┘
```

FIGURE 11-3 *Sketch of the chat room interface*

In the chat room interface, a user can view the messages sent by other online users. In addition, the names of the online users will be visible.

The Low-Level Design Phase

In this phase, a detailed design of the software modules, based on the high-level design, is produced. In addition, the team also lays down specifications for the various software modules of an application. FunTeam decided on a number of Java classes, names of these classes, and other such details for the project.

The functionality of the FunChat application and the interaction between the chat server and various interfaces in the application are illustrated in Figure 11-4.

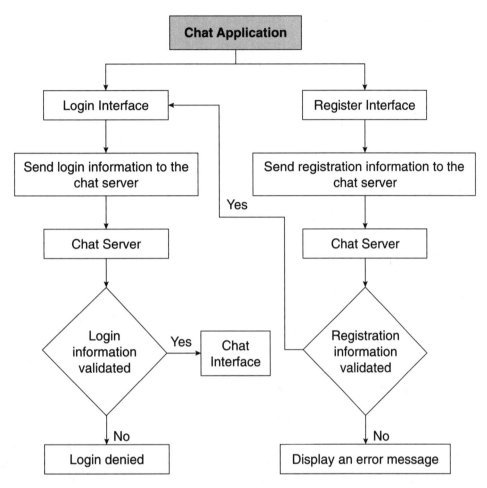

FIGURE 11-4 *Sketch of the registration interface*

The Construction Phase

In the construction phase, the software components are built. This phase uses the output of the low-level design to produce software items. During the construction phase, FunTeam divided the responsibilities among its team members. Some team members were assigned the task of designing the interface, and others took on the job of writing the code to develop FunChat.

The Testing Phase

Software modules are tested for their functionality as per the requirements identified during the requirements analysis phase. To test the functionality of FunChat, a Quality Assurance (QA) team was formed. The requirements identified during the requirements analysis phase were submitted to the QA team. The QA team tested FunChat for these requirements. FunTeam also submitted a test case report to the QA team so that FunChat could be tested in various possible scenarios.

The Acceptance Phase

In this phase, based on the pre-defined acceptance criteria, the marketing team conducts acceptance testing for the client projects. Since FunChat was an internal project, acceptance was obtained from the Quality Assurance team. After the project was developed and the employees started using FunChat, constant support was provided by FunTeam in terms of installation and debugging errors, if any.

In the next few chapters, you'll look at the creation and development of the chat application.

Summary

In this case study, you learned about the development phases in the life cycle of FunChat, a chat application being designed by FunSoftware. A team was assigned to develop the application. The requirements of the application were identified by the team. Based on these requirements, the various interfaces of the application were determined during the high-level and low-level design phases.

In the next few chapters, you'll look at the creation and development of this chat application.

Chapter 12

In this chapter, you'll learn how to create the login interface for accepting login information from a user. The login information provided by users will be verified by the server application. You'll use Swing components to design the login screen based on a layout manager. In addition, you'll learn about the event handling and networking concepts, and you'll use these concepts to handle events and communicate over a network.

Designing the Login Interface

As per the high-level design, the FunChat application at FunSoftware will allow only registered users to log in and chat. The login information generally includes usernames and passwords. Some applications may require users to provide other information such as their name and date of birth. FunTeam has decided to accept only the username and the password from a user.

Since the login interface is a network client application, the user's credentials are validated by the server application of FunChat. The username and the password of the user are sent to the server, which validates the information. Upon successful validation, the user is directed to the chat room.

For unregistered users, the option to register with the FunChat application needs to be provided. In addition, a user can cancel the login attempt. Therefore, the options for registration and cancellation are provided in the login interface.

You looked at the sketch of the login interface in the previous chapter. Figure 12-1 shows the login interface screen as it is displayed in the FunChat application.

These functionalities of the login screen identified during the design phase are listed as follows:

- ◆ When the user clicks the Login button, the login information is passed to the server and the information is verified at the server end.
- ◆ The login screen has an option for enabling first-time users to register with the FunChat application. A user can access the registration screen by clicking the Register button on the login screen.

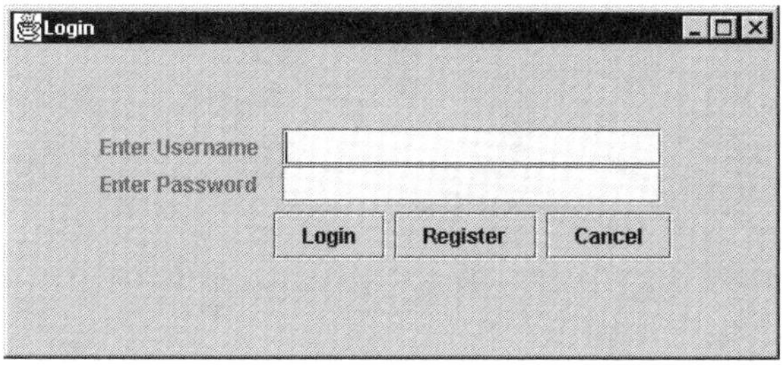

FIGURE 12-1 *The Login screen*

◆ In case a user decides to quit the login attempt, the user can do so by clicking the Cancel button on the login screen.

Now take a look at the concepts that you'll use for creating and adding the functionalities to the login screen. The Java concepts to be used in the login screen are:

◆ Java Swing API components

◆ Layout managers

◆ Event handling

◆ Networking concepts

◆ Exception handling

I'll discuss each of these.

Java Swing API Components

You can use the Swing API components to create graphical components such as text boxes and buttons on the login screen. Various Swing API methods can be used to customize the appearance of these components. The graphical components used for the login screen are:

◆ Labels

◆ Text boxes

◆ Buttons

Now look at how these components can be used in the login screen.

Creating Labels

Labels are used to indicate the component names and other textual information as needed. You can use the JLabel class of Swing API to create labels in GUI applications. The code to create the labels on the login screen is given as follows:

```
JLabel lblUserName = new JLabel("Enter Username ");
JLabel lblUserPwd = new JLabel("Enter Password ");
```

Creating Text Boxes

The other component used is a text box. To create a text box, the JTextArea or JTextField component can be used. The difference between these two components is that JTextArea can have multiple rows. In contrast, JTextField cannot have multiple rows of text. JTextField is most suitable for text boxes that require information in a single row only, for example, the Username text box only accepts the name from the user. To create the Username text box, you'll use the following statement:

```
JTextField txtUsrName = new JTextField(20);
```

The preceding statement will create a text field of 20 columns.

The other information to be accepted from the user is the password. Passwords can be accepted in text fields but this is avoided to preserve privacy. Text fields will display the password information entered by you. You can use the JPasswordField class of Swing API to accept passwords. The JPasswordField class hides the password by displaying characters such as an asterix (*) instead of the text entered by you. To create the password text box, you use the following code:

```
JPasswordField txtUsrPwd = new JPasswordField(20);
```

Creating Buttons

The next graphical component used in the login screen is a button. The three buttons used in the login screen are:

- ◆ The Login button
- ◆ The Register button
- ◆ The Cancel button

These buttons can be created using the `JButton` class of Swing API, as given here:

```
JButton btnLogin = new JButton("Login");
JButton btnRegister = new JButton("Register");
JButton btnCancel = new JButton("Cancel");
```

Now take a look at the layout of components on the login screen.

Layout Managers

Layout managers determine the layout of the components in a container in GUI applications. You can use the various types of layout managers available such as:

◆ `FlowLayout`

◆ `GridLayout`

◆ `BorderLayout`

◆ `CardLayout`

◆ `BoxLayout`

◆ `GridBagLayout`

You must select the layout manager based on the requirements of your application and how you want to place components on interfaces. You'll use the `GridBagLay-out` manager for the login screen because it provides more flexibility for placing components.

The `GridBagLayout` manager works closely with the `GridBagConstraints` class, which determines the placement of components.

The layout managers are covered in detail in Chapter 3, "Layout Managers and Handling Events."

The code to apply the layout on the login screen is given as follows:

```
 JPanel panel = new JPanel();
                panel.setLayout(new GridBagLayout()); //apply the layout to the
panel
                GridBagConstraints gbCons = new GridBagConstraints(); //create an
instance of the GridBagConstraints class

//add the components to the panel based on the settings of the GridBagConstraints
class
```

```
gbCons.gridx = 0;
gbCons.gridy = 0;
lblUserName = new JLabel("Enter Username ");
panel.add(lblUserName, gbCons);
gbCons.gridx = 1;
gbCons.gridy = 0;
txtUsrName = new JTextField(20);
panel.add(txtUsrName, gbCons);

gbCons.gridx = 0;
gbCons.gridy = 1;
lblUserPwd = new JLabel("Enter Password ");
panel.add(lblUserPwd, gbCons);

gbCons.gridx = 1;
gbCons.gridy = 1;
txtUsrPwd = new JPasswordField(20);
panel.add(txtUsrPwd, gbCons);

JPanel btnPanel = new JPanel();
btnLogin = new JButton("Login");
btnPanel.add(btnLogin);
btnRegister = new JButton("Register");
btnPanel.add(btnRegister);
btnCancel = new JButton("Cancel");
btnPanel.add(btnCancel);

gbCons.gridx = 1;
gbCons.gridy = 3;
gbCons.anchor = GridBagConstraints.EAST;
panel.add(btnPanel, gbCons);
```

I have added components to the container. Now, when these components are displayed on the login screen and the user clicks a button, nothing will happen. This is because I have not added any functionality to the button. Java provides various classes for event handling. Now I'll show you the code to handle events generated by the components in the login screen.

Event Handling

An event is generated when a user interacts with the GUI components of an application.

As you have learned in Chapter 3, an event has three components:

◆ The event object
◆ The event source
◆ The event handler

In the login screen, the event that needs to be handled is the clicking of a button. Therefore, the event source is the button and the event is the click of a mouse on the button. You'll need to define separate event handlers for the different buttons on the login screen.

When you click the Login button, the event handler should send the login information to the server for verification. When a user clicks on the Register button, the registration screen needs to be displayed. The login screen should be closed when the Cancel button is clicked.

The code to handle the events associated with the clicking of the buttons on the login screen is given here:

```
JButton btnLogin = new JButton("Login");
btnPanel.add(btnLogin);
btnLogin.addActionListener(this); //add a listener to the Login but-
ton

JButton btnRegister = new JButton("Register");
btnPanel.add(btnRegister);
btnRegister.addActionListener(this); //add a listener to the
Register button

JButton btnCancel = new JButton("Cancel");
btnPanel.add(btnCancel);
btnCancel.addActionListener(this); //add a listener to the Cancel
button
```

In the preceding code, the addActionListener() method is used to attach an event listener object to the button. The this argument indicates that the current class itself is an event listener. Later you'll see that the Login class extends the event listener class, ActionListener. Now, whenever you click the buttons, the actionPerformed() method of the ActionListener class is called. The action-Performed() method, depending on the source button, will perform the necessary action. The actionPerformed() method is defined as:

```
public void actionPerformed(ActionEvent e)
{
                //statements
}
```

When the Login or Register button is clicked, the information entered by the user needs to be sent to the server for verification. In the chat application, the chat server and the login screens will be placed on different computers. Therefore, you need to send this information to the server over a network. Now you'll brush up on the networking concepts.

Networking Concepts

The network setup for a chat application requires that the server and clients should be on different computers. The classes in the java.net package can be used to create network applications. You can use either the Socket class or the Datagram-Socket class to exchange information between the server and the client.

Since the login program is a client application, you'll need to connect to the server of the chat application. The following code enables connection between the client and the server:

```
Socket toServer = new Socket("machine-name",1001);
```

You can specify the server name and the port number of the server as arguments to the constructor of the Socket class. Then, you need to create input and output streams for moving data in and out of the client. For this purpose, you can use the classes in the java.io package. The following statements create input and output streams using the ObjectInputStream and PrintStream classes, respectively.

```
        ObjectInputStream msgFromServer = new
ObjectInputStream(toServer.getInputStream()); //create an input stream to receive
data from the server
        PrintStream streamToServer = new PrintStream(toServer.getOutputStream());
//create an output stream to send data to the server
```

Now, you can read and write to these streams using the methods in the classes of the `java.io` package.

```
streamToServer.println("Send this message to the server");
String msgFromServer = (String)streamFromServer.readObject();
```

You've learned about the networking classes in `java.io` package in Chapter 5, "Storing Data and Creating a Network Application."

The next important step while creating an application is handling exceptions. I'll discuss handling exceptions in detail.

Exception Handling

The server and the clients of the chat application can now interact. However, sometimes exceptions may be raised due to reasons such as a specified port being busy or the server not being found. You can use the `try/catch` blocks to handle such exceptions. The following is an example of `try/catch` block.

```
try
{
        toServer = new Socket("machine-name",1001);
}
catch(UnknownHostException e)
{
            System.out.println("Server not found.");
}
```

 NOTE

To create a socket connection with the chat server, you need to replace `machine-name` in the preceding code with the computer name that will run the chat server.

You learned in detail how to handle exceptions in Chapter 4, "Exception Handling and Threading."

Now that you've seen the concepts used to create and add functionalities to the login screen, take a look at the code of the login screen in Listing 12-1.

Listing 12-1 Login.java

```java
//import classes

import java.io.*;
import java.net.*;
import javax.swing.*;
import java.awt.event.*;
import java.awt.*;
import java.util.*;
import javax.swing.Timer;

public class Login extends JFrame implements ActionListener
{

//declare components

JLabel lblUserName;
JLabel lblUserPwd;
JTextField txtUsrName;
JPasswordField txtUsrPwd;
JButton btnLogin;
JButton btnCancel;
JButton btnRegister;
String UsrName;
char[] UsrPwd;
String strPwd;

Socket toServer;
ObjectInputStream streamFromServer;
PrintStream streamToServer;


  public Login()
  {
              this.setTitle("Login"); //set the title
              JPanel panel = new JPanel();
```

```
panel.setLayout(new GridBagLayout());
GridBagConstraints gbCons = new GridBagConstraints();

//place the components on the frame
gbCons.gridx = 0;
gbCons.gridy = 0;
lblUserName = new JLabel("Enter Username ");
panel.add(lblUserName, gbCons);

gbCons.gridx = 1;
gbCons.gridy = 0;
txtUsrName = new JTextField(20);
panel.add(txtUsrName, gbCons);

gbCons.gridx = 0;
gbCons.gridy = 1;
lblUserPwd = new JLabel("Enter Password ");
panel.add(lblUserPwd, gbCons);

gbCons.gridx = 1;
gbCons.gridy = 1;
txtUsrPwd = new JPasswordField(20);
panel.add(txtUsrPwd, gbCons);

JPanel btnPanel = new JPanel();
btnLogin = new JButton("Login");
btnPanel.add(btnLogin);
btnLogin.addActionListener(this); //add listener to the Login button
btnRegister = new JButton("Register");
btnPanel.add(btnRegister);
btnRegister.addActionListener(this); //add listener to the Register
button
btnCancel = new JButton("Cancel");
btnPanel.add(btnCancel);
btnCancel.addActionListener(this); //add listener to the Cancel but-
ton

gbCons.gridx = 1;
```

```
                    gbCons.gridy = 3;
                    gbCons.anchor = GridBagConstraints.EAST;
                    panel.add(btnPanel, gbCons);

                    getContentPane().add(panel);
                    setVisible(true);
                    setSize(450,200);

                    setDefaultCloseOperation(EXIT_ON_CLOSE);

        }


    //show the error message
    void showdlg()
    {
                    JOptionPane.showMessageDialog(this,"Invalid Password or Login name",
    "Message",

    JOptionPane.ERROR_MESSAGE);
    }

    public void actionPerformed(ActionEvent e1)
    {
                    JButton button = (JButton)e1.getSource(); //get the source of event
                    if(button.equals(btnCancel))
                    {
                                    this.dispose(); //close the current frame
                    }
                    else if(button.equals(btnRegister))
                    {
                                    new Register(); //call Register program
                                    this.dispose();
                    }
                    else
                    {

                    try
                    {
```

```
                        //create socket and input-output socket streams
                        toServer = new Socket("machine-name",1001);
                        streamFromServer = new
ObjectInputStream(toServer.getInputStream());
                        streamToServer = new
PrintStream(toServer.getOutputStream());


                        //send message to server for login
                        streamToServer.println("LoginInfo");
                        UsrName = txtUsrName.getText();
                        UsrPwd = txtUsrPwd.getPassword();
                        strPwd = new String(UsrPwd);


                        //send the username and password to the server
                        streamToServer.println(UsrName+":"+strPwd);


                        //read the message from the server
                        String frmServer =
(String)streamFromServer.readObject();


                        if(frmServer.equals("Welcome"))
                        {
                                new clientInt(UsrName); //start the
chat screen
                                this.dispose();
                        }
                        else
                        {
                                showdlg();//show error message
                        }

        }//end of try
                catch(Exception e)
                {
                        System.out.println("Exception Occurred: "+e);
                }
                }//end of if..else
}//end of actionPerformed
```

```
public static void main(String args[])
{
                new Login();
}
}//end of class Login
```

This example file (Login.java) is included in the samples folder of this chapter on the Web site that accompanies this book at **www.premierpressbooks.com/downloads.asp**.

The interaction between the login interface and the chat server is illustrated in Figure 12-2.

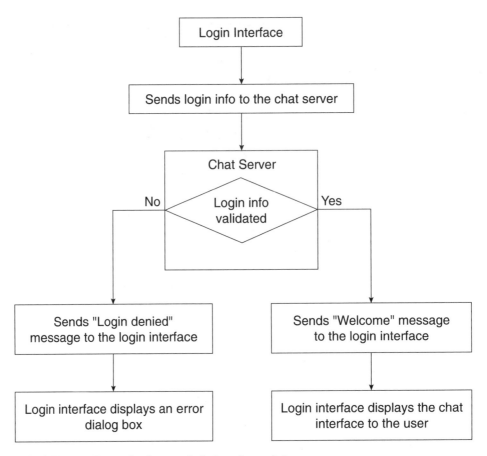

FIGURE 12-2 *Interaction between login interface and chat server*

Now you'll analyze the code. You'll look at the key code snippets of the login program and their explanation.

```
public class Login extends JFrame implements ActionListener
```

The `Login` class extends the `JFrame` class, and it implements the `ActionListener` interface. The `JFrame` class will need to define the `actionPerformed()` method of the `ActionListener` interface.

```
panel.setLayout(new GridBagLayout()); //apply layout
GridBagConstraints gbCons = new GridBagConstraints();s
```

In the above code snippet, the `GridBagLayout` is applied to the container and an instance of the `GridBagConstraints` class is created. This instance will be used to position the components on the login screen.

```
gbCons.gridx = 0;
gbCons.gridy = 0;
lblUserName = new JLabel("Enter Username ");
panel.add(lblUserName, gbCons);
```

For example, in the code given above, the label is placed at column 0 and row 0.

```
btnLogin = new JButton("Login");
btnPanel.add(btnLogin);
btnLogin.addActionListener(this); //attach listener to the Login button
btnRegister = new JButton("Register");
btnPanel.add(btnRegister);
btnRegister.addActionListener(this); //attach listener to the Register button
btnCancel = new JButton("Cancel");
btnPanel.add(btnCancel);
btnCancel.addActionListener(this); //attach listener to the Cancel button
```

Next, three buttons are created and an event listener is added to those buttons. The `this` argument to the `addActionListener()` method indicates that the current class itself is a listener object.

```
setDefaultCloseOperation(EXIT_ON_CLOSE);
```

The preceding statement will cause the current frame to close when you click the Exit button on the title bar.

```
public void actionPerformed(ActionEvent e1)
```

```
{
JButton button = (JButton)e1.getSource();
if(button.equals(btnCancel))
{
                this.dispose();
}
```

The `actionPerformed()` method is invoked whenever any action is performed on any of the three buttons on the login screen. In the above code snippet, the get-Source() method is used to identify the button that invoked the method. If you click the Cancel button, the current frame is closed by using the dispose() method.

```
else if(button.equals(btnRegister))
{
                new Register();
                this.dispose();
}
```

If you click the Register button, the `Register` class is instantiated and the constructor of the `Register` class displays the registration screen to the user. The login screen is disposed of.

```
else
{
     try
{
                            toServer = new Socket("machine-name",1001);
```

If neither the Cancel button nor the Register button has been clicked, then the user has clicked the Login button. Therefore, the login program creates a socket to establish a connection with the server.

```
                streamFromServer = new ObjectInputStream(toServer.getInputStream());
//input stream
                streamToServer = new PrintStream(toServer.getOutputStream()); //out-
put stream
```

Next, an input stream, `ObjectInputStream`, is created to accept input from the server, and an output stream, `PrintStream`, is created to send messages to the server. The `getInputStream()` and `getOutputStream()` methods of the `Socket` class are used to get the input and output streams for the socket.

```
                        streamToServer.println("LoginInfo"); //send a message to
the server

                        UsrName = txtUsrName.getText();
                    UsrPwd = txtUsrPwd.getPassword();
                  strPwd = new String(UsrPwd);
                        streamToServer.println(UsrName+":"+strPwd); //send username &
password to the server
                        String frmServer = (String)streamFromServer.readObject();
```

Here, a message, `"LoginInfo"`, is sent to the sever using the `streamToServer.``println()` method. This message will help the server to identify that a user is logging in. After that, the username and the password are sent to the server. The server verifies the username and the password and sends a message of acceptance back to the client. The client, the login program, reads the message sent by the server by using the `streamFromServer.readObject()` method.

```
                if(frmServer.equals("Welcome"))
                {
                        new clientInt(UsrName);
                        this.dispose();

                }
```

If the message from the server is `"Welcome"`, the `clientInt` program is called. The server sends the `"Welcome"` message if the login information is validated. The `clientInt` program contains the client chat interface. You'll look at the client chat interface in Chapter 14, "Creating the Chat Interface." The current login screen is closed.

```
public static void main(String args[])
{
        new Login();
}
```

In the `main()` method, the constructor of the `Login` program is called. Then, the constructor will display the login screen and the login process will begin.

Summary

In this chapter, you learned how to create a login screen for the FunChat application. The `GridBagLayout` manager has been used to place the Swing GUI components on the login screen. You learned how to attach events with the GUI components and to handle exceptions. Next, you used the classes in the `java.io` package to enable clients and server of the chat application to communicate.

That's all you have to do to create the login screen. The next GUI in FunChat is the registration screen. You'll learn how to create the registration screen in Chapter 13, "Creating the Registration Interface."

Chapter 13

**Creating the
Registration
Interface**

In this chapter, you'll learn how to create the registration screen for accepting registration information from users. You'll use concepts such as Swing API components, layout managers, event handling, networking, and exception handling to create a registration screen.

Designing the Registration Interface

As per the design, the FunChat application should enable new users to register with the application before logging in. The new users will have the freedom to select any username or password of their choice provided the combination of the username and the password does not match exactly with that of an existing user. A separate screen needs to be created, which will accept the user information for registration. The registration screen will be accessible from the login screen. The login screen will have a Register button that will invoke the registration screen.

The interface of the registration screen is displayed in Figure 13-1.

FIGURE 13-1 *The figure displays the registration screen of FunChat.*

The registration screen will accept the following information from the user:

- ◆ Username
- ◆ Password
- ◆ Employee ID
- ◆ First name
- ◆ Last name
- ◆ Age
- ◆ Sex

In the chat application, you'll use a txt file, `UsrPwd.txt`, to store the username and password information of the users. This txt file will be used to validate the user's login attempt.

 NOTE

You can also use databases to store and validate user information. You'll learn to develop Java programs capable of interacting with databases in Chapter 28, "Designing Interfaces and a Database."

You'll use the same concepts of Swing API components, layout managers, event handling, networking, and exception handling as was used in the Chapter 12, "Creating the Login Interface."

The registration process needs to perform some validations on the user inputs before accepting a request for registration. These validations are:

- ◆ The Username, Password, Confirm Password, Employee ID, First Name, and Last Name fields should not be empty.
- ◆ The specified age should be between 21 and 58.
- ◆ The entries in the Password and the Confirm Password text boxes should match exactly.

Now take a look at the code in Listing 13-1, "Register.java," for creating and validating the input on the registration screen.

Listing 13-1 Register.java

```java
//import classes

import java.io.*;
import java.net.*;
import javax.swing.*;
import java.awt.event.*;
import java.awt.*;
import java.util.*;

public class Register extends JFrame implements ActionListener
{

//declare components
JLabel lblHeading;
JLabel lblUserName;
JLabel lblUserPwd;
JLabel lblCnfUserPwd;
JLabel lblFrstName;
JLabel lblLstName;
JLabel lblAge;
JLabel lblEmpId;
JLabel  lblSex;

String usrName;
char[] usrPwd;
char[] cnfPwd;
String frstName;
String lstName;
String age;
String empid;

Socket toServer;
ObjectInputStream streamFromServer;
PrintStream streamToServer;

JComboBox lstSex;
```

```
JTextField txtUserName;
JPasswordField txtUsrPwd;
JPasswordField txtCnfUsrPwd;
JTextField txtFrstName;
JTextField txtLstName;
JTextField txtAge;
JTextField txtEmpId;
Font f;
Color r;
JButton btnSubmit;
JButton btnCancel;

public Register()
{
                this.setTitle("Register");
                JPanel panel = new JPanel();

                //apply the layout
                panel.setLayout(new GridBagLayout());
                GridBagConstraints gbCons = new GridBagConstraints();

                //place the components
                gbCons.gridx = 0;
                gbCons.gridy = 0;
                lblHeading = new JLabel("Registration Info");
                Font f  =  new Font("Monospaced" , Font.BOLD , 24);
                lblHeading.setFont(f);
                Color c = new Color(0,200,0);
                lblHeading.setForeground(new Color(131,25,38));
                lblHeading.setVerticalAlignment(SwingConstants.TOP);
                gbCons.anchor = GridBagConstraints.EAST;
                panel.add(lblHeading, gbCons);

                gbCons.gridx = 0;
                gbCons.gridy = 1;
                lblUserName = new JLabel("Enter Username");
                gbCons.anchor = GridBagConstraints.WEST;
```

```
panel.add(lblUserName, gbCons);

gbCons.gridx = 1;
gbCons.gridy = 1;
txtUserName = new JTextField(15);
panel.add(txtUserName, gbCons);

gbCons.gridx = 0;
gbCons.gridy = 2;
lblUserPwd = new JLabel("Enter Password ");
panel.add(lblUserPwd, gbCons);

gbCons.gridx = 1;
gbCons.gridy = 2;
txtUsrPwd = new JPasswordField(15);
panel.add(txtUsrPwd, gbCons);

gbCons.gridx = 0;
gbCons.gridy = 3;
lblCnfUserPwd = new JLabel("Confirm Password ");

panel.add(lblCnfUserPwd, gbCons);

gbCons.gridx = 1;
gbCons.gridy = 3;
txtCnfUsrPwd = new JPasswordField(15);
panel.add(txtCnfUsrPwd, gbCons);

gbCons.gridx = 0;
gbCons.gridy = 4;
lblEmpId = new JLabel("Employee ID");
panel.add(lblEmpId, gbCons);

gbCons.gridx = 1;
gbCons.gridy = 4;
txtEmpId = new JTextField(15);
panel.add(txtEmpId, gbCons);
```

```
gbCons.gridx = 0;
gbCons.gridy = 5;
lblFrstName = new JLabel("First Name");
panel.add(lblFrstName, gbCons);

gbCons.gridx = 1;
gbCons.gridy = 5;
txtFrstName = new JTextField(15);
panel.add(txtFrstName, gbCons);

gbCons.gridx = 0;
gbCons.gridy = 6;
lblLstName = new JLabel("Last Name");
panel.add(lblLstName, gbCons);

gbCons.gridx = 1;
gbCons.gridy = 6;
txtLstName = new JTextField(15);
panel.add(txtLstName, gbCons);

gbCons.gridx = 0;
gbCons.gridy = 7;
lblAge = new JLabel("Age");
panel.add(lblAge, gbCons);

gbCons.gridx = 1;
gbCons.gridy = 7;
txtAge = new JTextField(3);
panel.add(txtAge, gbCons);

gbCons.gridx = 0;
gbCons.gridy = 8;
lblSex = new JLabel("Sex");
panel.add(lblSex, gbCons);

gbCons.gridx = 1;
gbCons.gridy = 8;
String[]  sex =  {"Male", "Female"};
```

```
                    JComboBox lstSex = new JComboBox(sex);
                    lstSex.setSelectedIndex(0);
                    panel.add(lstSex, gbCons);

                    JPanel btnPanel = new JPanel();

                    btnSubmit = new JButton("Submit");
                    btnPanel.add(btnSubmit);
                    btnSubmit.addActionListener(this); //add listener to the Submit
        button
                    btnCancel = new JButton("Cancel");
                    btnPanel.add(btnCancel);
                    btnCancel.addActionListener(this); //add listener to the Cancel
        button

                    gbCons.gridx = 0;
                    gbCons.gridy = 9;
                    gbCons.anchor = GridBagConstraints.EAST;
                    panel.add(btnPanel, gbCons);

                    getContentPane().add(panel);

                    setDefaultCloseOperation(EXIT_ON_CLOSE);

                    setVisible(true);
                    setSize(450,400);

    }//end or Register()

    public void actionPerformed(ActionEvent e1)
    {

                    JButton button = (JButton)e1.getSource(); //get the source of the
        event
                    if(button.equals(btnCancel))
                    {
                            this.dispose();
                    }
```

```
              else
              {
                            int ver = verify(); //call the verify()
                            if(ver==1)
                            {

                            try
                            {
                                          //establish a socket connection and
create I/O socket streams
                                          toServer = new Socket("machine-
name",1001);
                                          streamFromServer = new
ObjectInputStream(toServer.getInputStream());
                                          streamToServer = new
PrintStream(toServer.getOutputStream());

                                          //send a message to server for
Registration

streamToServer.println("RegisterInfo");
                                          usrName = txtUserName.getText();
                                          usrPwd = txtUsrPwd.getPassword();
                                          String pwd = new String(usrPwd);

                                          //send the username and password to
the server

streamToServer.println(usrName+":"+pwd);

                                          //read the response from the server
                                          String frmServer =
(String)streamFromServer.readObject();

                                          if(frmServer.equals("Registered"))
                                          {
                                                    new Login();
                                                    this.dispose();
                                          }
```

```
                                              else if(frmServer.equals("User
Exists"))
                                              {
                                                      showUsrExists();
//show error message
                                              }

                              }//end of try
                              catch(Exception e)
                              {
                                      System.out.println("Exception "+e);
                              }
                              }//end of if
                  }//end of else
}//end of actionPerformed()

int verify() //test the validity of the user information
{
              int ctr = 0;
              int intAge = 0;
              try
              {
                      usrName = txtUserName.getText();
                      usrPwd = txtUsrPwd.getPassword();
                      cnfPwd = txtCnfUsrPwd.getPassword();
                      frstName = txtFrstName.getText();
                      lstName = txtLstName.getText();
                      age = txtAge.getText();
                      empid = txtEmpId.getText();
                      String strUsrPwd = new String(usrPwd);
                      String strCnfPwd = new String(cnfPwd);
                      try
                      {
                              intAge   =
(int)Integer.parseInt(age.trim());
                      }
                      catch(Exception e)
                      {
```

```
                                             showErrordlgInt();
                        }
if((usrName.length()>0)&&(strUsrPwd.length()>0)&&(strCnfPwd.length()>0)&&(frstName.l
ength()>0)&&(lstName.length()>0)&&(intAge>21)&&(intAge<58)&&(empid.length()>0)&&(str
UsrPwd.equals(strCnfPwd)))
            {
                        ctr = 1;
                        return ctr;
            }
            else
            {
                        showErrordlg();
            }//end of else

            }//end of try
            catch(Exception e)
            {
                        System.out.println("exception thrown "+e);
            }//end of catch
            return ctr;
}//end of verify()


//error msg- User Exists
void showUsrExists()
{
            JOptionPane.showMessageDialog(this,"User exists.", "Message",
JOptionPane.ERROR_MESSAGE);
}


int flg = 0;


//error msg- Incorrect Entry
void showErrordlg()
{
            JOptionPane.showMessageDialog(this,"Incorrect entry.", "Message",
JOptionPane.ERROR_MESSAGE);
}
```

```
//error msg- Incorrect Age entered
void showErrordlgInt()
{
                JOptionPane.showMessageDialog(this,"Age incorrect.", "Message",
JOptionPane.ERROR_MESSAGE);
}

public static void main(String args[])
{
                new Register();
}
}//end of class
```

This example file (`Register.java`) is included in the samples folder of this chapter on the Web site that accompanies this book at **www.premierpressbooks.com/ downloads.asp**.

The interaction between the register interface and the chat server is in Figure 13-2.

Table 13-1 displays the user-defined methods in the registration program.

Table 13-1 User-Defined Methods in the Registration Program

Method	Description
int verify()	This method validates the information entered by the user on the registration screen. It returns a value 1 if the information is validated or else 0 is returned.
void showUsrExists()	This method displays an error message that another username with the same combination of username and password exists.
void showErrordlg()	This method displays an error message when a user doesn't provide all the information required.
void showErrordlgInt()	This method displays an error message if the age entered by the user is not between 21 years and 58 years.

Now you will analyze the code. You'll look at the key code snippets of the registration program.

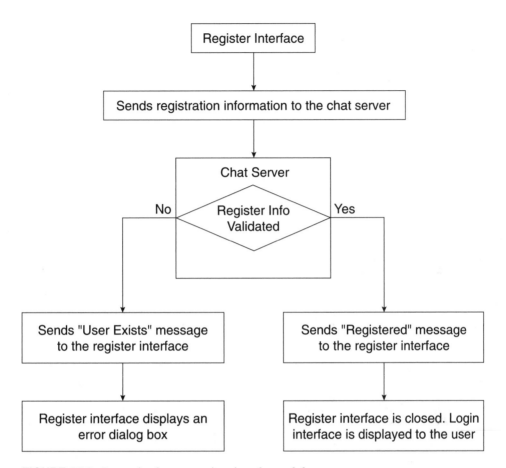

FIGURE 13-2 *Interaction between register interface and chat server*

```
btnSubmit = new JButton("Submit");
btnPanel.add(btnSubmit);
btnSubmit.addActionListener(this);
btnCancel = new JButton("Cancel");
btnPanel.add(btnCancel);
btnCancel.addActionListener(this);
```

In the above code snippet, the Submit and Cancel buttons are created and event listeners are added to these buttons. Since the Register class implements the ActionListener interface and defines the actionPerformed() method, the this argument is passed to the addActionListener(this) method.

```
                public void actionPerformed(ActionEvent e1)
{
                JButton button = (JButton)e1.getSource(); //get the source of the
event
                if(button.equals(btnCancel))
                {
                                this.dispose();
                }
                else
                {
                                int ver = verify(); //call the verify()
                                if(ver==1)
                                {
                                try
                                {
                                                //establish a socket connection and
create I/O socket streams
                                                toServer = new Socket("machine-
name",1001);
                                                streamFromServer = new
ObjectInputStream(toServer.getInputStream());
                                                streamToServer = new
PrintStream(toServer.getOutputStream());
```

In the `actionPerformed()` method, the source of the event is identified using the `getSource()` method. If the source is the `Cancel` button, the `Register` screen is closed. If the source is the `Submit` button, the `verify()` method, which returns an integer value, is called.

If the value returned by the `verify()` method is equal to 1, a socket connection is established with the server at port 1001. Then, an input socket stream and an output socket stream are obtained.

```
                streamToServer.println("RegisterInfo");
                usrName = txtUserName.getText();
                usrPwd = txtUsrPwd.getPassword();
                String pwd = new String(usrPwd);
                streamToServer.println(usrName+":"+pwd);
```

Next, the message "RegisterInfo" is sent to the server to trigger the registration process on the server. Then, the username and the password of the user are also sent to the server.

```
String frmServer = (String)streamFromServer.readObject();
            if(frmServer.equals("Registered"))
            {
                        new Login(); //display the login interface
                        this.dispose();
            }
            else if(frmServer.equals("User Exists"))
            {
                        showUsrExists(); //display an error message
            }
```

The reply from the server is read using the `streamFromServer.readObject()` method. If the reply is "Registered," which implies that the user has been registered by the server, the `Login` program is called and the current frame is disposed of. Now, the user can enter the login information and move to the chat room. However, if the reply from the message is "User Exists," an error message is displayed stating that another user with the same combination of username and password already exists.

Now take a look at the user-defined methods.

The verify() Method

First, you'll look at the code of the verify() method.

```
int verify()
{
            int ctr = 0;
            int intAge = 0;
            try
            {

            usrName = txtUserName.getText();
            usrPwd = txtUsrPwd.getPassword();
            cnfPwd = txtCnfUsrPwd.getPassword();
```

```
frstName = txtFrstName.getText();
lstName = txtLstName.getText();
age = txtAge.getText();
empid = txtEmpId.getText();
String strUsrPwd = new String(usrPwd);
String strCnfPwd = new String(cnfPwd);
try
{
            intAge  = (int)Integer.parseInt(age.trim());
}
```

In the verify() method, the information entered by the user is obtained. This information is stored in various variables. The age is converted into an integer value by using the Integer.parseInt(age.trim()) method.

```
if((usrName.length()>0)&&(strUsrPwd.length()>0)&&(strCnfPwd.length()>0)&&(frstName.l
ength()>0)&&(lstName.length()>0)&&(intAge>21)&&(intAge<58)&&(empid.length()>0)&&(str
UsrPwd.equals(strCnfPwd)))
        {
                    ctr = 1;
                    return ctr;
        }
        else
        {
                    showErrordlg();
        }//end of else
```

Next, the values obtained are validated by using the if...else construct. If any of the conditions set is found to be false, an error dialog box is displayed by calling the showErrordlg() method. If the information entered by the user is found to be valid, a counter variable, ctr, is set to 1 and it is returned to the calling method.

The **showErrordlg()** *Method*

The code for the showErrordlg() method is given as follows:

```
void showErrordlg()
{
        JOptionPane.showMessageDialog(this,"Incorrect entry.", "Message",
```

```
JOptionPane.ERROR_MESSAGE);
}
```

The showErrordlg() method will display the message dialog box by using the static JOptionPane.showMessageDialog(<parent frame>, <message>, <title>, <type>) method. This error message is displayed if a user enters incorrect information on the registration screen.

The showErrordlgInt() *Method*

The showErrordlgInt() method displays an error message when the user enters an age that is not between 21 and 58 years. The code for the showErrordlgInt() method is given as follows:

```
//error msg- Incorrect Age entered
void showErrordlgInt()
{
            JOptionPane.showMessageDialog(this,"Age incorrect.", "Message",
JOptionPane.ERROR_MESSAGE);
}
```

The showUsrExists() *Method*

To register with the FunChat application, a user needs to specify a username and password. If a new user selects a combination of username and password that is the same as that of an existing user, the server sends the message "User Exists" to the client. Then, the client calls the showUsrExists() method, which invokes an error message dialog box.

```
void showUsrExists()
{
            JOptionPane.showMessageDialog(this,"User exists.", "Message",
JOptionPane.ERROR_MESSAGE);
}
```

Summary

In this chapter, you learned how to create the registration interface of the chat application. Users enter their personal information on the registration screen and the chat application accepts and validates the user information. After validation, the username and password information is stored in a txt file. The registration interface uses the Swing API components to display GUI components, based on a selected layout manager. Event and exceptions handlers are attached with these components. Then, using networking concepts, the information is exchanged between the client and the server over a network.

You looked at the code for the registration interface. The next interface after the login and registration screens is the chat screen. Chapter 14, "Creating the Chat Interface," discusses the chat screen.

Chapter 14

In this chapter, you'll learn how to design a chat interface and add the required functionalities to the chat interface. You'll also learn how to use the Timer class to constantly update messages and online users information.

Designing the Chat Interface

After a successful login to the chat application, the user can view the chat screen. Here, the user can chat with other online users. The upper part of the chat screen will show the messages sent by the online users and also a list of online users. A text box will be provided in which the user can type a message and send it by clicking the Send button. The screen will also have a Logout button that will close the chat screen. Therefore, the chat screen will have the following components:

- ◆ A messages box
- ◆ A users list box
- ◆ A send message text box
- ◆ A Send button
- ◆ A Logout button

As per the design, the chat screen will perform the following functions:

- ◆ It will show a list of online users.
- ◆ It will show the messages sent by other users in a common chat room.
- ◆ When the user logs out, by clicking the Logout button or by closing the chat screen, that user will no longer be visible on the chat screen of other users.
- ◆ The chat room and online users box will be updated automatically.

Figure 14-1 displays the layout of the chat screen.

Listing 14-1 contains the code to create the chat screen and add required functionalities to it.

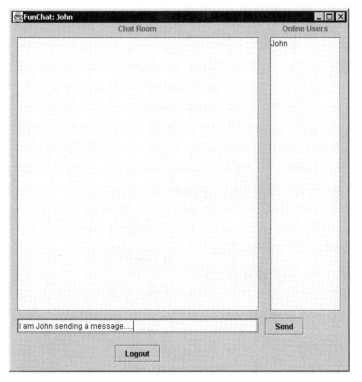

FIGURE 14-1 *A display of the chat screen*

Listing 14-1 clientInt.java

```
import java.io.*;
import java.net.*;
import javax.swing.*;
import java.awt.event.*;
import java.awt.*;
import java.util.*;
import javax.swing.Timer;


public class clientInt extends JFrame implements ActionListener
{
        Timer t = new Timer(5000,new TimerAction());
        String usr_name;
        public String remUser;
```

```
class TimerAction implements ActionListener
{
        Socket toServer;
        ObjectInputStream streamFromServer;
        PrintStream streamToServer;
        public void actionPerformed(ActionEvent e2)
        {

        try
        {
                toServer = new Socket("machine-name",1001);

                streamFromServer = new
ObjectInputStream(toServer.getInputStream());

                streamToServer = new
PrintStream(toServer.getOutputStream());

                message = txtMsg.getText();

                //send a message to the server
                streamToServer.println("From Timer");

                //receive vectors from the server
                Vector vector =
(Vector)streamFromServer.readObject();

                Vector vector1 =
(Vector)streamFromServer.readObject();

                //show the online users
                txtListUsers.setText("");
                for(int j = 1;j<vector1.capacity();j++)

                {

txtListUsers.append((String)vector1.elementAt(j));

txtListUsers.append("\n");
```

```
                                        }

                                        //show the messages
                                        int i = messageCount;
                                        for(;i<vector.capacity();i++)
                                        {


txtMessages.append((String)vector.elementAt(i));


txtMessages.append("\n");

                                        }
                                        messageCount = i;
                        }//end of try

                        catch(Exception e)
                        {
                                        System.out.println("Exception
"+e);
                        }

                }//end of actionPerformed
}//end of TimerListener class

int messageCount = 0;
String name;
PrintStream  streamToServer;
ObjectInputStream streamFromServer;
Socket toServer;

JTextArea txtMessages;
JTextArea txtListUsers;
JTextField txtMsg;
JButton msgSendBtn;
JButton userLoginBtn;
JButton userRegisterBtn;
JButton userLogoutBtn;
```

```java
JLabel lblChatRoom;
JLabel lblUserList;

JScrollPane jspSendMsgPane;
JScrollPane jspTxtMsgPane;
JScrollPane jspUserListPane;

JTextField textWriteMsg;
String message;
int nSend;

public clientInt(String nm)
{
            remUser = nm;
            usr_name = nm;
            this.setTitle("FunChat: "+usr_name); //set the title name
            JPanel panel = new JPanel();
            panel.setLayout(new GridBagLayout());
            GridBagConstraints gbCons = new GridBagConstraints();

            gbCons.gridx = 0;
            gbCons.gridy = 0;
            lblChatRoom = new JLabel("Chat Room", SwingConstants.LEFT);
            panel.add(lblChatRoom, gbCons);

            gbCons.gridx = 1;
            gbCons.gridy = 0;

            lblUserList = new JLabel("Online Users", SwingConstants.LEFT);
            panel.add(lblUserList, gbCons);

            gbCons.gridx = 0;
            gbCons.gridy = 1;
            gbCons.gridwidth = 1;
            gbCons.gridheight = 1;
            gbCons.weightx = 1.0;
            gbCons.weighty = 1.0;
            txtMessages = new JTextArea(25,35);
```

```
                txtMessages.setEditable(false);
                jspTxtMsgPane = new
JScrollPane(txtMessages,JScrollPane.VERTICAL_SCROLLBAR_AS_NEEDED,JScrollPane.HORI-
ZONTAL_SCROLLBAR_AS_NEEDED);
                panel.add(jspTxtMsgPane, gbCons);

                gbCons.gridx = 1;
                gbCons.gridy = 1;
                gbCons.gridwidth = 1;
                gbCons.gridheight = 1;
                gbCons.weightx = 1.0;
                gbCons.weighty = 1.0;
                txtListUsers = new JTextArea(25,10);
                txtListUsers.setEditable(false);
                jspUserListPane = new

JScrollPane(txtListUsers,JScrollPane.VERTICAL_SCROLLBAR_AS_NEEDED,JScrollPane.HORI-
ZONTAL_SCROLLBAR_AS_NEEDED);
                panel.add(jspUserListPane, gbCons);

                gbCons.gridx = 0;
                gbCons.gridy = 2;
                gbCons.gridwidth = 1;
                gbCons.gridheight = 1;
                gbCons.weightx = 1.0;
                gbCons.weighty = 1.0;
                txtMsg = new JTextField(35);

                jspSendMsgPane = new JScrollPane(txtMsg,
JScrollPane.VERTICAL_SCROLLBAR_AS_NEEDED,JScrollPane.HORIZONTAL_SCROLLBAR_AS_NEED-
ED);
                panel.add(jspSendMsgPane, gbCons);

                gbCons.gridx = 1;
                gbCons.gridy = 2;
                gbCons.gridwidth = 1;
                gbCons.gridheight = 1;
                gbCons.weightx = 1.0;
```

```
gbCons.weighty = 1.0;
gbCons.anchor = GridBagConstraints.WEST;
msgSendBtn = new JButton("Send");
panel.add(msgSendBtn, gbCons);

msgSendBtn.addActionListener(this);

JPanel btnPanel = new JPanel();

userLogoutBtn = new JButton("Logout");
userLogoutBtn.addActionListener(this);

//add a listener to the window
this.addWindowListener(
                new WindowAdapter()
                {
                public void windowClosing(WindowEvent e1)
                        {
                        try
                        {
                            Socket toServer;
                            ObjectInputStream
streamFromServer;
                            PrintStream
streamToServer;
                            toServer = new
Socket("machine-name",1001);
                            streamToServer = new
PrintStream(toServer.getOutputStream());
                            streamToServer.print-
ln("User Logout");
streamToServer.println(remUser);
                        }//end of try
                        catch(Exception e2)
                         {
System.out.println("Exception Occured: "+e2);
```

```
                                                  }
                                          }

                          }
                );

                btnPanel.add(userLogoutBtn);

                gbCons.gridx = 0;
                gbCons.gridy = 3;
                gbCons.gridwidth = 1;
                gbCons.gridheight = 1;
                gbCons.weightx = 1.0;
                gbCons.weighty = 1.0;
                gbCons.anchor = GridBagConstraints.EAST;
                gbCons.fill = GridBagConstraints.HORIZONTAL;
                panel.add(btnPanel, gbCons);

                getContentPane().add(panel);

                setDefaultCloseOperation(EXIT_ON_CLOSE);

                setVisible(true);
                setSize(546,567);
                t.start();

}//end of clientInt()
public void actionPerformed(ActionEvent e1)
{
                JButton button = (JButton)e1.getSource();

                //if logout button clicked
                if(button.equals(userLogoutBtn))
                {
                                try
                                {
                                                toServer = new Socket("machine-
name",1001);
```

```
                                        streamToServer = new
PrintStream(toServer.getOutputStream());

                                        //send a msg to server for logging out
                                        streamToServer.println("User Logout");
                                        streamToServer.println(remUser);
                        }
                        catch(Exception e)
                        {
                                System.out.println("Exception Occured:
"+e);

                        }
                        this.dispose();
                }
                //else if Send button is clicked
                else
                {
                        int num1 = 0,num2 = 0,res = 0;
                        String name = "";
                        try
                        {
                                        toServer = new Socket("machine-
name",1001);
                                        streamFromServer = new
ObjectInputStream(toServer.getInputStream());
                                        streamToServer = new
PrintStream(toServer.getOutputStream());

                                        message = txtMsg.getText();
                                        String msg = message;

                                        //send the username and msg typed
to the server

streamToServer.println(usr_name+":"+msg);

                                        txtMsg.setText("");
```

```
                                              //read the reply from the server
                                              Vector vector =
(Vector)streamFromServer.readObject();

                                              int i = messageCount;
                                              for(;i<vector.capacity();i++)
                                              {

txtMessages.append((String)vector.elementAt(i)); //display the messages

txtMessages.append("\n");

                                              }//end of for
                                              messageCount = i;


                    }//end of try
                    catch(Exception e)
                    {
                                              System.out.println("Exception
Occurred: "+e);
                    }
           }//end of else
}//end of actionPerformed()

public static void main(String args[])
{
           String nm = new String();
           clientInt CI = new clientInt(nm);
}

}//end of class
```

This example file (clientInt.java) is included in the samples folder of this chapter on the Web site that accompanies this book at **www.premierpressbooks.com/downloads.asp**.

The interaction between the chat interface and the chat server is illustrated in Figure 14-2.

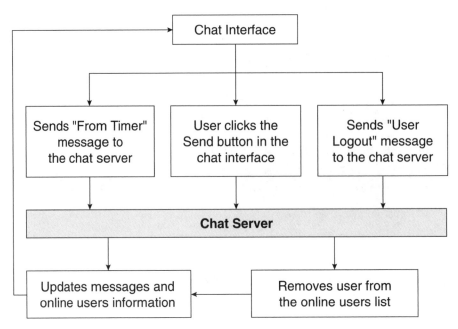

FIGURE 14-2 *Interaction between chat interface and chat server*

Now, analyze the code.

```
public clientInt(String nm)
    {
                remUser = nm;
                usr_name = nm;
                this.setTitle("FunChat: "+usr_name);
                JPanel panel = new JPanel();
                panel.setLayout(new GridBagLayout());

                GridBagConstraints gbCons = new GridBagConstraints();
```

The constructor of the clientInt class accepts a String argument. Notice that in the login program, the clientInt program is called with the username as an argument. This username is passed to the constructor of the clientInt class. In the above code, the title of the current frame is set by using the setTitle() method. Then, the GridBagLayout is applied to the chat screen. The GridBagConstraints class determines the placement of the components on the chat screen.

```
                        jspTxtMsgPane = new JScrollPane(txtMessages,
JScrollPane.VERTICAL_SCROLLBAR_AS_NEEDED,JScrollPane.HORIZONTAL_SCROLLBAR_AS_NEED-
ED);
```

The text area that contains the messages sent by online users is placed inside JScrollPane. Whenever the messages exceed the visible area of the text area, scroll bars will appear. Similarly, JScrollPane is used for displaying the list of online users.

```
userLogoutBtn = new JButton("Logout");
userLogoutBtn.addActionListener(this);
```

The ActionListener interface is added to the Logout button. As you will see later, this is done to ensure that a user will not be visible in the online users list after logging out. Whenever a user logs out of the chat room, the chat screen is closed.

```
this.addWindowListener(
                    new WindowAdapter()
                            {
                            public void windowClosing(WindowEvent e1)
                            {
                                        try
                                        {
                                        Socket toServer;
                                        ObjectInputStream
streamFromServer;
                                        PrintStream streamToServer;
                                        toServer = new Socket("machine-
name",1001);
                                        streamToServer = new
PrintStream(toServer.getOutputStream());
                                        streamToServer.println("User
Logout");
                                        streamToServer.println(remUser);
                                        }
                                        catch(Exception e2)
                                        {
                                                System.out.print-
ln("Exception Occurred" +e2);
```

```
                                                    }

                                          }

                               }

                       );


            btnPanel.add(userLogoutBtn);
```

Users can log out from the chat application either by clicking the Logout button or by closing the chat screen. A listener interface is added to the Logout button. Now, to handle the event of a user closing the chat screen by clicking the Close button on the title bar, you need to add a listener interface to the container frame. This is done by using the `this.addWindowListener()` statement. Notice that an anonymous class of type `WindowAdapter` class is passed as an argument to the `addWindowListener()` method. In the `WindowAdapter` class, the `windowClosing()` method is defined. In this method, the message `"User Logout"` along with the username is passed to the server.

```
public void actionPerformed(ActionEvent e1){
JButton button = (JButton)e1.getSource();
if(button.equals(userLogoutBtn)){
            try{
            toServer = new Socket("machine-name",1001);
            streamToServer = new PrintStream(toServer.getOutputStream());
            streamToServer.println("User Logout");
            streamToServer.println(remUser);
            }
            catch(Exception e)
            {
                      System.out.println("Exception Occurred: " + e);
            }
this.dispose();
}
```

In the `actionPerformed()` method, the source of the event is identified. If the source is the Logout button, a socket connection is established with the server. The message `"User Logout"` and the username and the password are passed to the server.

```
            message = txtMsg.getText();
              String msg = message;
```

```
int ctr1 = 0;
streamToServer.println(usr_name+":"+msg);
txtMsg.setText("");

Vector vector = (Vector)streamFromServer.readObject();
```

The `actionPerformed()` method is also invoked when a user clicks the Send button after typing a message. When the user clicks the Send button, the message written by the user is obtained and sent to the server along with the username. The text box in which the message was typed is cleared. Next, a vector is received from the server. A vector is an object of the `Vector` class. The `Vector` class implements a flexible array of objects. As you'll see in the `AppServer` program, this vector contains the messages entered by online users.

```
int i = messageCount;
for(;i<vector.capacity();i++)
{
                txtMessages.append((String)vector.elementAt(i));
                txtMessages.append("\n");
}//end of for

messageCount = i;
```

Next, the vector is read and the messages are displayed in the text box. The integer variable, `messagecount`, keeps track of the messages that have been already displayed. This ensures that messages are not repeated in the messages text box. Now, come back to the `TimerAction` class.

```
Timer t  =  new Timer(5000,new TimerAction());
```

First, an instance of the `Timer` class is created. The `Timer` class implements the `Serializable` interface, and it causes an event to be repeated after a predefined interval of time. Here, the `Timer` class calls the constructor of the `TimerAction` class after every 5000 milliseconds.

```
t.start();
```

This preceding statement will start the `Timer`, causing it to send the `actionPerformed()` messages to the listeners.

The `TimerAction` class is a user-defined class. Now take a look at the task performed by the `TimerAction` class.

The TimerAction *Class*

The code of the TimerAction class is given here. I'll now discuss the code.

```
class TimerAction implements ActionListener
                {

                                Socket toServer;
                                ObjectInputStream streamFromServer;
                                PrintStream streamToServer;
                                public void actionPerformed(ActionEvent e2)
                                {

                                try
                                {
                                                toServer = new Socket("machine-
name",1001);
                                                streamFromServer = new
ObjectInputStream(toServer.getInputStream());
                                                streamToServer = new
PrintStream(toServer.getOutputStream());

                                                message = txtMsg.getText();

                                                //send a message to the server
                                                streamToServer.println("From
Timer"); //send a message to the server

                                                //receive vectors from the server
                                                Vector vector =
(Vector)streamFromServer.readObject();

                                                Vector vector1 =
(Vector)streamFromServer.readObject();
```

The TimerAction class implements the ActionListener interface. In the action-Performed() method, the message "From Timer" is passed to the server. Then, the client chat interface receives two vectors from the server. One of the vectors contains messages while the other vector contains the names of online users.

```
                                                //show the online users
                                                txtListUsers.setText("");
```

```
                                          for(int j = 1;j<vector1.capaci-
ty();j++)

                                          {


txtListUsers.append((String)vector1.elementAt(j));


txtListUsers.append("\n");

                                          }
```

The list of online users is updated. The vector1, which contains a list of online users, is read, and the names of the users are appended to the online users text box on the screen.

```
                                          //show the updated messages
                                          int i = messageCount;
                                          for(;i<vector.capacity();i++)
                                          {


txtMessages.append((String)vector.elementAt(i));


txtMessages.append("\n");

                                          }
                                          messageCount = i;
                         }//end of try
                   catch(Exception e)
                         {
                                          System.out.println("Exception
"+e);
                         }

              }//end of actionPerformed
}//end of TimerListener class
```

Next, the messages in the chat room are updated.

Summary

In this chapter you learned how to create the chat interface for the FunChat application. The chat interface uses the classes in the java.io package to enable communication between the chat server and the chat interface. In addition, you used the Timer class to constantly update the messages and online users information maintained by the chat server. This information is displayed on the chat interface.

You've now looked at all the three client GUIs of the FunChat application. In Chapter 15, "Creating the Chat Server," you'll look at the chat server application.

Chapter 15

Creating the Chat Server

In this chapter, you'll learn how to create the chat server of the FunChat application. The chat server will run on a computer and will coordinate the exchange of messages between online users. In addition, the server will control the login and registration attempts. It will also keep track of online users.

The FunChat Server

The server of the FunChat application will run from the command prompt and it will not be a GUI. Now, take a look at the mechanism to create the server. The Java components to be used in the server are:

◆ Network programming concepts

◆ Thread handling

◆ Exception handling

The following are the required functions of the chat server. It should:

◆ Maintain a list of online users

◆ Update the messages on each client chat screen

◆ Validate login attempts

◆ Register new users

Listing 15-1 contains the code for achieving the above requirements.

Listing 15-1 AppServer.java

```
//import classes
import java.awt.event.*;
import java.net.*;
import java.io.*;
import java.util.*;
import javax.swing.Timer;


//Code for the AppServer class
```

```
public class AppServer implements Runnable
{

                ServerSocket server;
                Socket fromClient;
                Thread serverThread;

                public AppServer()
                {
                    System.out.print("FunChat server started.........");
                    try
                    {
                                    server = new ServerSocket(1001);
                                    serverThread = new Thread(this);
                                    serverThread.start();
                    }
                    catch(Exception e)
                    {
                                                    System.out.println("Cannot
start the thread: " + e);
                    }
                } //end of AppServer

                public static void main(String args[])
                {
                                new AppServer();
                }

public void run()
{
                try
                {
                                while(true)
                                {
                                                //Listening to the clients
request
                                                fromClient = server.accept();
```

```
                                                            //Creating the connect object
                                                            Connect con = new

              Connect(fromClient);
                                                }
                                }
                                catch(Exception e)
                                {
                                                System.out.println("Cannot listen to the client"
              + e);
                                }
              } //end of run
              } //end of AppServer

              //Code for the connect class
              class Connect
              {
                                ObjectOutputStream streamToClient;
                                int ctr = 0;

                                BufferedReader streamFromClient;
                                static Vector vector;
                                static Vector vctrList;
                                String message = " ";
                                static String str = new String("UsrList");

                                static
                                {
                                                vector = new Vector(1,1);
                                                vctrList = new Vector(1,1);
                                                vctrList.addElement((String)str);
                                }

                                int verify(String mesg)
                                {
                                        try
                                        {
                                        RandomAccessFile RAS = new RandomAccessFile("UsrPwd.txt",
              "r");
```

```
                    int i = 0;
                    String str = "";
                    while((RAS.getFilePointer())!=(RAS.length()))
                    {
                              str = RAS.readLine();
                              if(str.equals(mesg))
                              {
                                        ctr = 1;
                                        break;
                              }
                    } //end of while
                    RAS.close();
                    } //end of try
                    catch(Exception e)
                    {
                              System.out.print("Exception Occurred: "+e);
                    }
            return ctr;

            }//end of verify()


int checkFile(String mesg)
{
            int chk = 1;
            try
            {
            RandomAccessFile RS = new RandomAccessFile("UsrPwd.txt", "r");
            int i = 0;
            String str = "";
            String colon = new String(":");
            int index = ((String)mesg).lastIndexOf(colon);
            String userName = (String)mesg.substring(0,index);
            while((RS.getFilePointer())!=(int)(RS.length()))
            {
                    str = RS.readLine();
                    int index1 = ((String)str).lastIndexOf(colon);
                    String usrName = (String)str.substring(0,index1);
                    if(usrName.equals(userName))
```

```
                                    {
                                            chk = 0;
                                            break;
                                    }
                }//end of while
                RS.close();
                }//end of try
                catch(Exception e)
                {
                            System.out.print("Exception Occurred: "+e);
                }
                return chk;
}//end of chkFile


public Connect(Socket inFromClient)
{
                //Retrieving the clients stream
                String msg = "";
                String mesg = "";
                try
                {
                streamFromClient = new BufferedReader(new
InputStreamReader(inFromClient.getInputStream()));
                streamToClient =   new
ObjectOutputStream(inFromClient.getOutputStream());

                msg = streamFromClient.readLine();
                if((msg.equals("From Timer")))
                {
                            streamToClient.writeObject(vector);
                            streamToClient.writeObject(vctrList);
                }
                else if(msg.equals("LoginInfo"))
                {
                            msg = streamFromClient.readLine();
                            int ver = verify(msg);
                            if(ver==1)
                            {
```

```
                                                 String colon = new String(":");
                                                 int index =
((String)msg).lastIndexOf(colon);
                                                 String userName =
(String)msg.substring(0,index);

                                                 if(!(vctrList.indexOf((String)userName)>0))
                                                 {

streamToClient.writeObject("Welcome");

vctrList.addElement((String)userName);

                                                 }
                                   else
                                   {
                                                 streamToClient.writeObject("Login denied");
                                   }
                     }
                     else if(msg.equals("RegisterInfo"))
                     {
                                   msg = streamFromClient.readLine();
                                   int ret = checkFile(msg);
                                   if(ret==0)
                                   streamToClient.writeObject("User Exists");
                                   if(ret==1)
                                   {
                                                 FileOutputStream out = new
FileOutputStream("UsrPwd.txt",true);
                                                 PrintStream p = new PrintStream( out );
                                                 p.println();
                                                 p.println(msg);
                                                 p.close();
                                                 streamToClient.writeObject("Registered");
                                   }
                     }
                     else if(msg.equals("User Logout"))
                     {
                                   String remUser = streamFromClient.readLine();
```

```
                    boolean b = vctrList.removeElement((String)remUser);
        }
        else
        {
                message = message+msg;
                vector.addElement((String)message);
                streamToClient.writeObject(vector);
        }
        }//end of try
        catch(Exception e)
        {
                System.out.println("Cannot get the client stream connect"
+ e);
        }
        finally
        {
                try
                {
                        inFromClient.close();
                }
                catch(IOException e)
                {
                        System.out.print("Exception Occurred: "+e);
                }
        }
}//end of Connect()
}
```

This example file (AppServer.java) is included in the samples folder of this chapter on the Web site that accompanies this book at **www.premierpress-books.com/downloads.asp**.

The interaction between the chat server and the other client interfaces of the chat application is depicted in Figure 15-1.

Now, analyze the code. First, you'll look at the key code snippets of the AppServer program.

```
public class AppServer implements Runnable
```

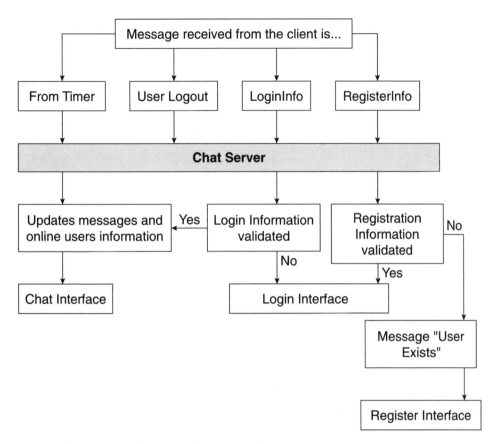

FIGURE 15-1 *Interaction between chat server and interfaces of the application*

The `AppServer` program implements the `Runnable` interface.

```
ServerSocket server;
```

The `ServerSocket` class implements the server socket. The server socket waits for requests from the client and then sends the response back to the client.

```
public AppServer()
{
        try
        {
                server = new ServerSocket(1001);
                serverThread = new Thread(this);
```

```
                                      serverThread.start();

             }
```

In the constructor, the server socket is created at the specified port and the thread is started.

```
public void run()
{
        try
        {
                while(true)
                {
                        //Listening to the clients request
                        fromClient = server.accept();
                        //Creating the connect object
                        Connect con = new Connect(fromClient);
                }
        }
}
```

When you start the thread, the run() method is executed. In the run() method, the accept() method listens for any connection attempt from a client and returns a socket. After the socket is returned, an instance of the Connect class is created and the socket returned by the accept() method is passed as an argument to the constructor. The Connect class contains the code to perform most of the tasks of the chat server. Now, take a look at the code for the Connect class.

The Connect *Class*

```
public Connect(Socket inFromClient)
{
streamFromClient = new BufferedReader(new
InputStreamReader(inFromClient.getInputStream()));
streamToClient =  new ObjectOutputStream(inFromClient.getOutputStream());
msg = streamFromClient.readLine();
```

In the constructor, Connect(), first the input and output socket streams to the client are created. Then, by using the readLine() method, the message from the client is read by the server. There are four types of messages that the chat server can receive from its clients:

◆ The "From Timer" message

◆ The "LoginInfo" message

◆ The "RegisterInfo" message

◆ The "User Logout" message

Now, look at the task performed by the chat server upon receiving each of these messages.

The *"From Timer"* Message

```
if((msg.equals("From Timer")))
{
        streamToClient.writeObject(vector);
        streamToClient.writeObject(vctrList);
}
```

If the message from the client is "From Timer," the server sends two vectors that contain the messages and the user's list to the client. The chat interface sends the "From Timer" message after a time period specified by the Timer object.

The *"LoginInfo"* Message

```
            else if(msg.equals("LoginInfo"))
            {
                    msg = streamFromClient.readLine();
                    int ver = verify(msg);
                    if(ver==1)
                    {
                            String colon = new String(":");
                            int index =
((String)msg).lastIndexOf(colon);
                            String userName =
(String)msg.substring(0,index);
                            if(!(vctrList.indexOf((String)userName)>0))
                            {
streamToClient.writeObject("Welcome");
```

```
vctrList.addElement((String)userName);
                              }
              }
```

When a user attempts to log in to the chat application, the login interface sends the username and password information of the user to the server for validation. Along with the login information, the login interface sends the "LoginInfo" message to indicate that a user is attempting to log in. If the message from the client is "LoginInfo," the chat server calls the verify() method to validate the login information.

If the value returned by the verify() method is 1, the login attempt is validated and the user is allowed to log in. However, there is a possibility that the user might try to log in twice. To avoid this, the username is compared with the contents of vctrList, which contains a list of online users. If the username is not found in vctrList, the "Welcome" message is sent to the client and the username is added to vctrList.

The *"RegisterInfo"* Message

```
              else if(msg.equals("RegisterInfo"))
              {
                              msg = streamFromClient.readLine();
                              int ret = checkFile(msg);
                              if(ret==0)
                              streamToClient.writeObject("User Exists");
                              if(ret==1)
                              {
                                              FileOutputStream out = new
FileOutputStream("UsrPwd.txt",true);

                                              PrintStream p = new PrintStream( out );
                                              p.println();
                                              p.println(msg);
                                              p.close();
                                              streamToClient.writeObject("Registered");
                              }
              }
```

Next, if the message from the client is "RegisterInfo," the server knows that a new user is trying to register. The validation has been performed at the client side by the Register program. Therefore, the server now only needs to add the user to the list of registered users. But, before that, the server needs to ensure that the username and the password of the new user are not the same as any of the existing users. To perform this check, the server calls the checkFile() method.

In the checkFile() method, the UsrPwd.txt file is checked for any existing user with the same username and password. It returns a value accordingly. If the value returned by the checkFile() method is 1, the UsrPwd.txt file is opened in the read-write mode and the new user is added in it. The message "Registered" is sent back to the client to indicate that the user is registered successfully.

The *"User Logout"* Message

```
else if(msg.equals("User Logout"))
{
                String remUser = streamFromClient.readLine();
                boolean b = vctrList.removeElement((String)remUser);
}
```

Next, if the message from the client is "User Logout", it implies that either an online user has logged out or the user has closed the chat screen. In such a situation, the name of the user is read from the socket input stream and the user is deleted from vctrList.

```
message = message+msg;
vector.addElement((String)message);
streamToClient.writeObject(vector);
```

Finally, if there is no message from the client, online users most probably have sent some messages to the chat room. These messages are added to the vector and the vector is sent to the client by using the writeObject() method.

There are two user-defined methods in the code for the chat server. These methods are:

◆ The checkFile() method
◆ The verify() method

Now, take a look at each method in detail.

The checkFile() *Method*

The code for the checkFile() method is given as follows.

```
int checkFile(String mesg)
{
        int chk = 1;
        try
        {
        RandomAccessFile RS = new RandomAccessFile("UsrPwd.txt", "r");
        int i = 0;
        String str = "";
        String colon = new String(":");
        int index = ((String)mesg).lastIndexOf(colon);
       String userName = (String)mesg.substring(0,index); //obtain the user-
name entered by the user
        while((RS.getFilePointer())!=(int)(RS.length()))
        {
                str = RS.readLine(); //read from the file
                int index1 = ((String)str).lastIndexOf(colon);
                String usrName = (String)str.substring(0,index1);
//obtain the username
                if(usrName.equals(userName))
                {
                        chk = 0;
                        break;
                }
        }//end of while
        RS.close();
        }//end of try
        catch(Exception e)
        {
                System.out.print("Exception Occurred: "+e);
        }
        return chk;
}//end of chkFile
```

The checkFile() method is called when the chat server receives the "Register-Info" message from the client. The checkFile() compares the username selected by the new user with those already registered. The registered usernames are stored in the file UsrPwd.txt. If another user with the same username exists, the variable chk is assigned the value 0, otherwise the value of chk is 1. The variable chk is then returned to the calling method.

The verify() *Method*

The code for the verify() method is given as follows.

```
int verify(String mesg)
{
        try
        {
        RandomAccessFile RAS = new RandomAccessFile("UsrPwd.txt",
"r");

        int i = 0;
        String str = "";
        while((RAS.getFilePointer())!=(RAS.length()))
        {
                str = RAS.readLine();
                if(str.equals(mesg))
                {
                        ctr = 1;
                        break;
                }
        } //end of while
        RAS.close();
        } //end of try
        catch(Exception e)
        {
                System.out.print("Exception Occurred: "+e);
        }
    return ctr;

    }//end of verify()
```

The verify() method validates the username and password entered by the user with the registered username and password in the UsrPwd.txt file. If the login information is validated, the `verify()` method assigns value 1 to the variable `ctr` and the variable is returned to the calling method.

Summary

In this chapter, you looked at how the chat server handles various requests from clients. The server receives messages, such as `"LoginInfo"` and `"RegisterInfo,"` and performs various tasks accordingly. The server sends replies to the clients regarding success or failure of the login and registration attempts. In addition, the server also updates the messages and online users information and sends them to the clients.

The three client GUI interfaces and the chat server are now ready. In Chapter 16, "Running the Chat Application," you'll see how the application works.

Chapter 16

In this chapter, you'll learn how to run the chat application that you have developed. To do this, you'll take the hypothetical example of Henry, Julie, and John, who wish to chat using FunChat. But before doing this, you need to compile the files of the FunChat application.

Compiling Files

The FunChat application is divided into server and client applications. First, you need to compile the server application. To compile the server application, execute the following command:

```
C:\>javac AppServer.java
```

When the server application has been compiled, you can start the chat server by executing the following command:

```
C:\>java AppServer
```

Next, you need to compile the three interfaces that you have created. To compile them, execute the following command:

```
C:\>javac Login.Java
C:\>javac Register.Java
C:\>javac clientInt.java
```

Now, the class files for all the three interfaces of the chat application are created. You need to copy all the three class files to another computer and run the chat client application. In order to run the client chat application on a computer, you need to install the JDK on the computer.

To run client applications, you need to execute the following command on the client computer:

```
C:\java Login
```

Login is the first program that you need to run. You can enter the login details in the login screen and start chatting.

Running the FunChat Application

Now, you'll learn how to run the application, using the example of Henry and Julie, who wish to send messages to each other on FunChat. Henry is already online. Julie needs to log on to the chat application before she can chat with Henry. Therefore, Julie needs to enter the following command:

```
C:\java Login
```

The login screen is displayed in Figure 16-1.

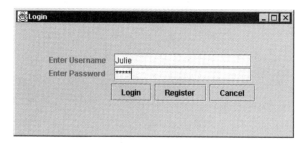

FIGURE 16-1 *The display of the login screen*

After a successful login, Julie can view the chat screen, as displayed in Figure 16-2.

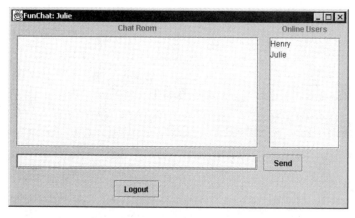

FIGURE 16-2 *The display of Julie's chat screen*

Now, Henry and Julie can chat. Henry sends a message to Julie. Figure 16-3 shows the message that appears on Julie's chat screen.

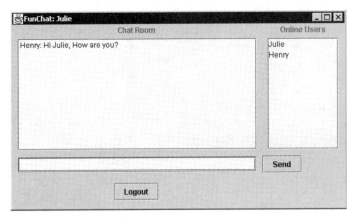

FIGURE 16-3 *The display of Henry's message received by Julie*

Julie sends a reply that appears on Henry's chat screen, as seen in Figure 16-4.

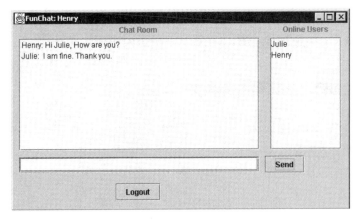

FIGURE 16-4 *The reply from Julie on Henry's chat screen*

Meanwhile, a new user, John, wants to register with FunChat. To do so, he needs to open the registration screen by clicking the Register button on the login screen. John enters the details as requested on the registration screen, depicted in Figure 16-5.

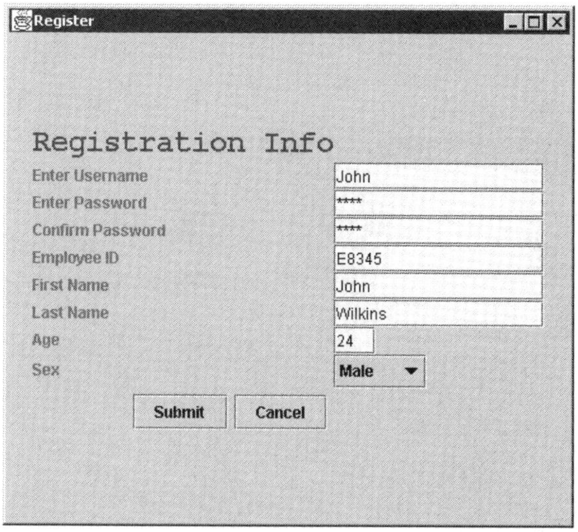

FIGURE 16-5 *The display of the registration screen*

After registering, John logs on to the chat application. John's username appears on the chat screens of both the online users, Henry and Julie, as seen in Figure 16-6.

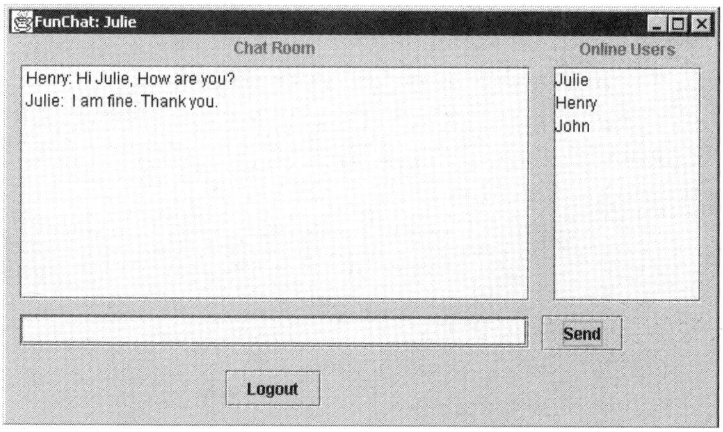

FIGURE 16-6 *The display of John's name on Julie's chat screen*

Now, Julie logs out of the chat application. Julie's name disappears from the screen of the other online users, as shown in Figure 16-7.

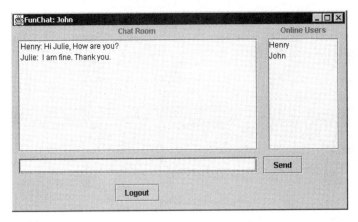

FIGURE 16-7 *Julie's name disappears from the screen of the other online users.*

Summary

In this chapter, first you learned how to compile the application. Then, with the example of three hypothetical users of the FunChat application, you saw how users register, log in, chat, and then exit the application. You saw that as a new user registers to use the application, his username immediately appears on the screens of the other online users. Per one of the stated requirements of the application's design, when a user exits the chat room, his or her name is deleted from the screens of the other online users.

PART IV

Professional Project — 2

Project 2

**Creating an
Online Banking
Application**

Project 2 Overview

A banking application will enable customers to use the Web site of a bank to perform banking transactions online.

The banking application will have the following functionalities:

- The application will enable a user to open an account with the bank.
- The application will enable an account holder of the bank to register to use the application.
- The application will enable registered account holders to log on to the banking Web site after entering their login details. The banking application will enable the account holders to view their account details. The registered user will also be able to modify any personal details such as address or phone number.
- The application will also provide utilities such as an interest calculator and a foreign exchange calculator.
- The application will also display the number of the hits on the banking Web site.

The concepts that I'll use to build the banking application are:

- Servlets and Deploying Servlets
- Servlets API and Handling Requests and Responses in Servlets
- Cookies in Servlets and Creating Counter Servlets
- Servlet API Classes and Interfaces
- Java Database Connectivity (JDBC)
- JDBC API and JDBC Drivers
- Java Server Pages (JSP)
- Requests and Response Cycle of JSP and JSP Tags
- HTML and JavaScript Event Handlers
- Java Beans Component Specifications
- Java Beans Properties and Testing Beans
- Java Beans API

Chapter 17

oney Banks, Inc., has its head office in New York. The branches of the bank are spread out in 30 cities across the United States. With the increase in popularity of the Internet, more and more banks are providing their customers with online banking facilities. To stay in the competition, Money Banks has decided to develop an online banking application.

The new software will enable a customer to register to use the application. Registered customers will not only be able to view the details of their account but also transfer money online.

A team of developers is selected to build the application. The members of the team are:

◆ Larry Peterson, Project Manager

◆ John Wallace, Web Designer

◆ Henry Forsythe, Web Developer

◆ Ken Barrett, Web Developer

◆ Katie Frye, Web Developer

You, as part of the team, need to develop the online banking application. Now, I'll discuss the life cycle of the project as identified by the team.

The Project Life Cycle

The development life cycle of a project usually involves three phases:

◆ Project initiation

◆ Project execution

◆ Project completion

In the project initiation phase, the development team prepares the project plan and finalizes the outcome of each phase. In this phase, the team also prepares a comprehensive list of tasks involved in this phase, and the project manager assigns responsibilities to the team members, depending on their skills.

In the project execution phase, the team develops the product. In the case of the banking application development team, they will develop the online banking application. This phase consists of the following stages:

- Requirements analysis
- High-level design
- Low-level design
- Construction
- Testing
- Acceptance

I'll now discuss each of these stages in detail.

The Requirements Analysis Phase

During the requirements analysis phase, the development team analyzes the requirements to be fulfilled by the online banking application and identifies the probable approach for meeting these requirements. To identify the requirements of the application, the team decides to study the existing bank applications at various bank sites and conduct extensive interviews among the Money Banks customers.

Finally, the team identifies that the banking application should:

- Enable a non-account holder to apply for opening an account with the bank
- Enable an account holder of the bank to register to use the application
- Enable registered account holders to log on after their login details are validated and view their account details
- Provide additional utilities, such as interest calculator and foreign exchange calculator, to the viewers of the application

The High-Level Design Phase

In this phase, the team decides how the application will function. The formats for data input and output are finalized in this stage. The functional specifications documentation of the application is presented in a language that can be understood by all. The finished project design is, however, executed only on the project manager's approval. The development team designs the following interfaces for the application:

◆ The Welcome Page

◆ The Home Page

◆ The Registration Page for Account Holders

◆ The Registration Page for Non-Account Holders

◆ The Login Screen Page

◆ The Account Details Page

◆ The Interest Calculator Page

During this phase the design of the database is also finalized.

I'll now discuss the functionality of each interface.

The Welcome Page

The Welcome page is the first page to be displayed to the viewers. The page will display a welcome message, and, in addition, it will display the number of viewers who have visited the site. This will allow the bank to know the popularity of the site among Web users.

A sketch of the Welcome page is depicted in Figure 17-1.

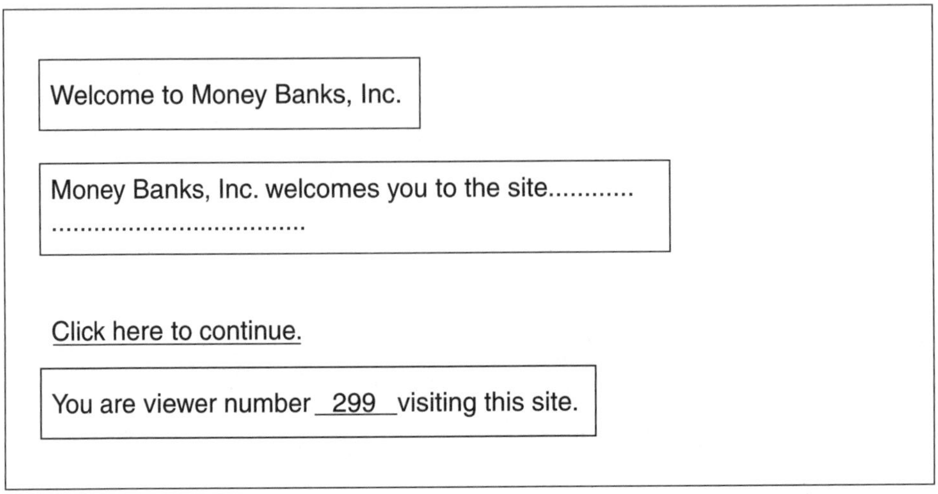

FIGURE 17-1 *The figure displays the design of the Welcome page.*

The Home Page

The Welcome page contains a link to the Home page. When a viewer clicks the link, the Home page of the application is displayed. The Home page provides viewers the options to log on, register with the online banking application, apply to open an account with the bank, and utilities such as the interest calculator. The Home page as designed by the development team is shown in Figure 17-2.

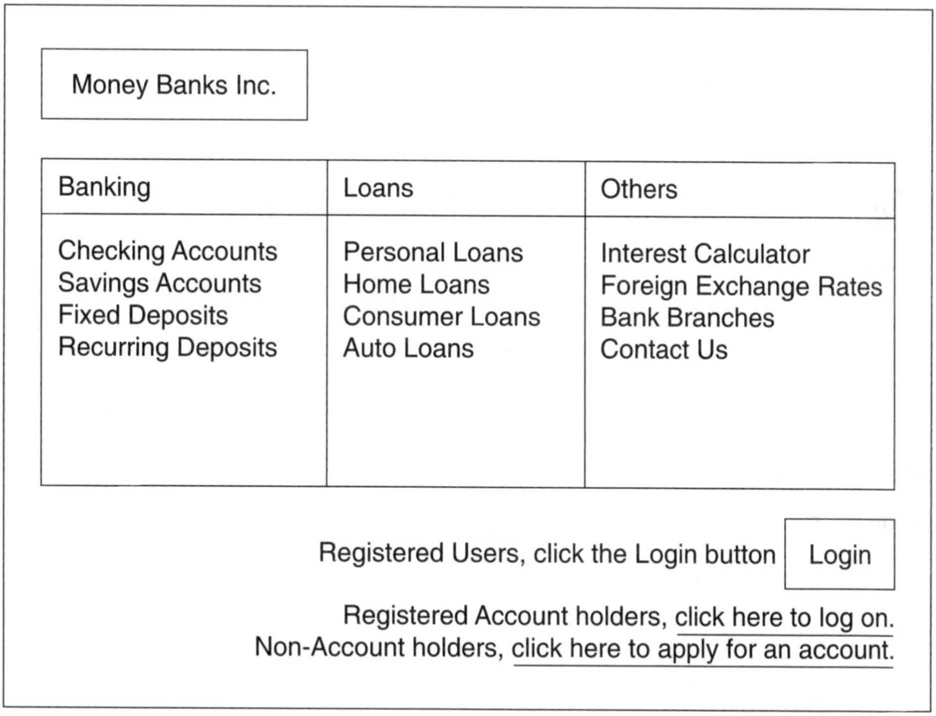

Money Banks Inc.		
Banking	**Loans**	**Others**
Checking Accounts Savings Accounts Fixed Deposits Recurring Deposits	Personal Loans Home Loans Consumer Loans Auto Loans	Interest Calculator Foreign Exchange Rates Bank Branches Contact Us

Registered Users, click the Login button | Login |

Registered Account holders, click here to log on.
Non-Account holders, click here to apply for an account.

FIGURE 17-2 *The figure displays the design of the Home page.*

The Registration Page for Account Holders

The Registration page enables the account holders of Money Banks to register to use the online banking application. The account holders need to provide information, such as the account number and name, for verification purposes. Account holders can select a password of their choosing. A sketch of the Registration page is shown in Figure 17-3.

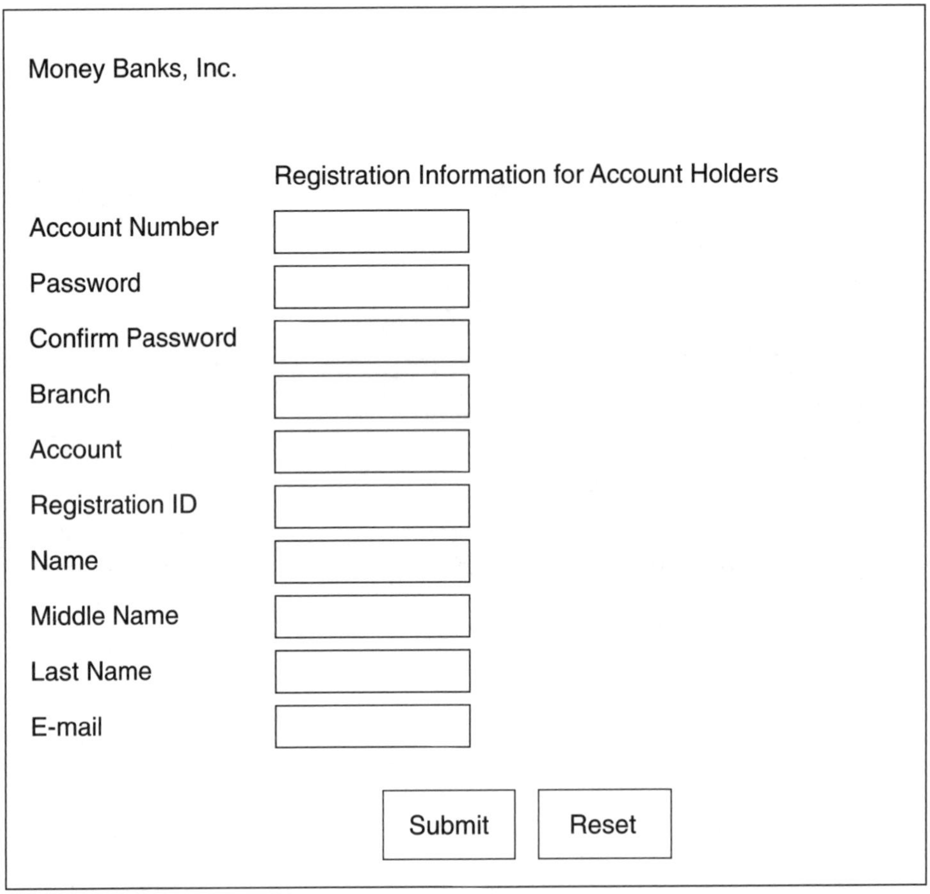

Money Banks, Inc.

Registration Information for Account Holders

Account Number

Password

Confirm Password

Branch

Account

Registration ID

Name

Middle Name

Last Name

E-mail

Submit   Reset

FIGURE 17-3 *The figure displays the design of the Registration page for the Account Holders page.*

The Registration Page for Non-Account Holders

This Registration page enables the non-account holders to apply online to open an account with Money Banks. After validation, the information provided by the user is stored in a database. A confirmation message is then displayed to the user. A sketch of the Registration page for non-account holders is shown in Figure 17-4.

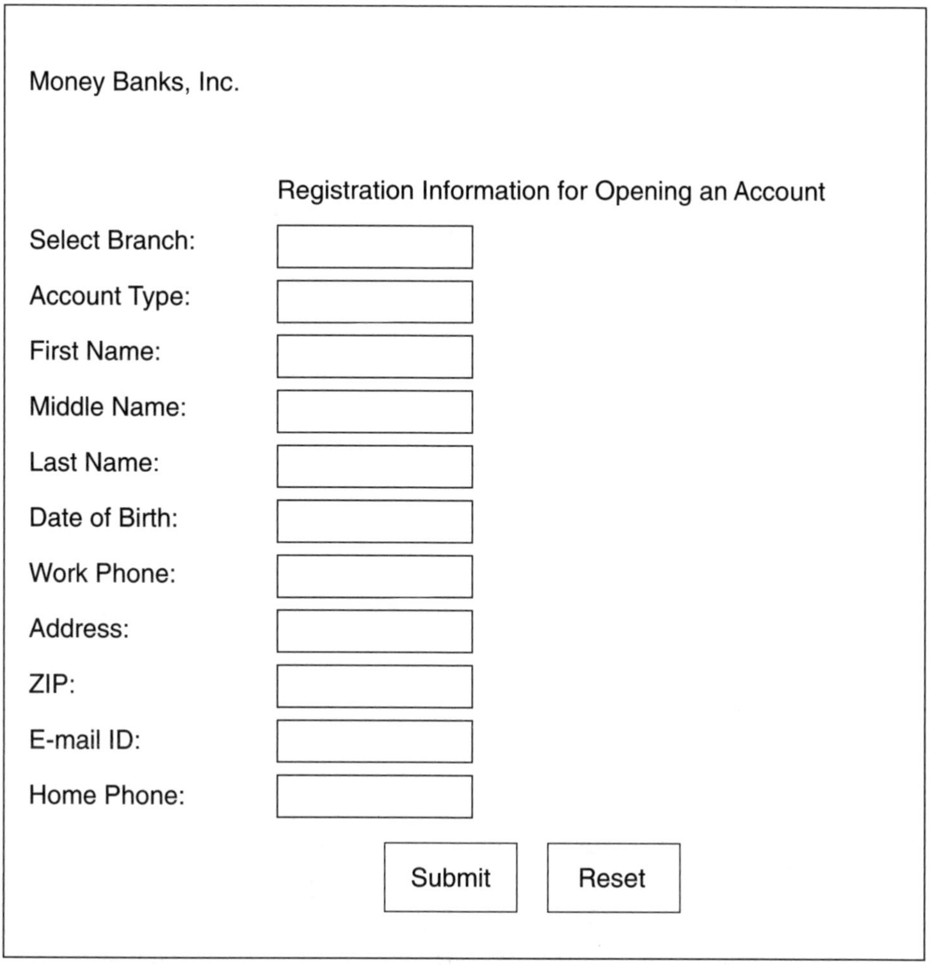

Money Banks, Inc.

Registration Information for Opening an Account

Select Branch: [   ]

Account Type: [   ]

First Name: [   ]

Middle Name: [   ]

Last Name: [   ]

Date of Birth: [   ]

Work Phone: [   ]

Address: [   ]

ZIP: [   ]

E-mail ID: [   ]

Home Phone: [   ]

[Submit]   [Reset]

FIGURE 17-4 *The figure displays the design of the Registration page for the Non-Account Holders page.*

The Login Screen Page

The Login Screen accepts and validates the account number and password of a registered user. After validation, the account details of the user are presented. Since every bank account at Money Banks has a unique account number, the development team decides to accept the combination of account number and password for validation. A sketch of the Login Screen is displayed in Figure 17-5.

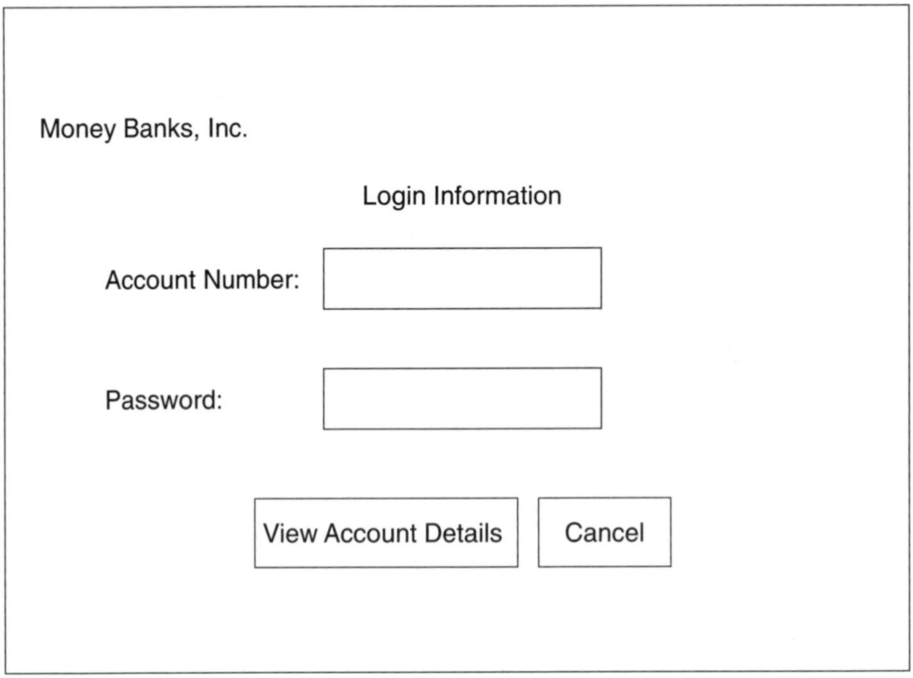

FIGURE 17-5 *The figure displays the design of the Login Screen page.*

The Account Details Page

The Account Details page is displayed to a user after successful login. The page displays the details of all the transactions for the account number used for the specific account number and password given at login. A sketch of the Account Details page is illustrated in Figure 17-6.

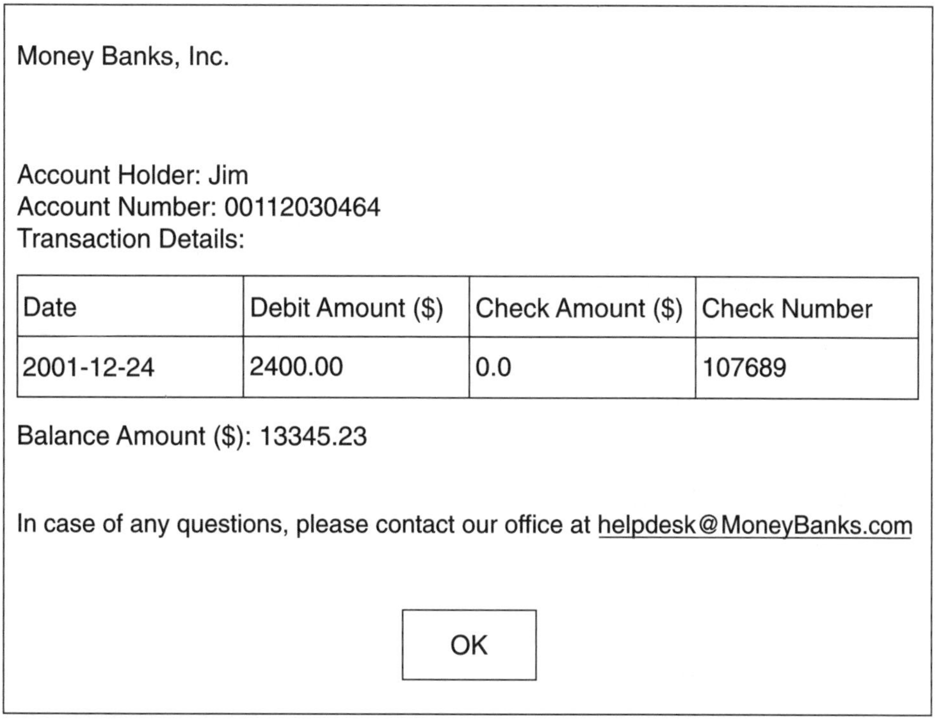

Money Banks, Inc.

Account Holder: Jim
Account Number: 00112030464
Transaction Details:

Date	Debit Amount ($)	Check Amount ($)	Check Number
2001-12-24	2400.00	0.0	107689

Balance Amount ($): 13345.23

In case of any questions, please contact our office at helpdesk@MoneyBanks.com

OK

FIGURE 17-6 *The figure displays the design of the Account Details page.*

The Interest Calculator Page

The Interest Calculator utility provides an interface to the viewers to calculate interest on a specified amount based on a particular rate of interest and period of time. This utility is available to all the viewers. A sketch of the Interest Calculator utility is shown in Figure 17-7, on the next page.

The Bank Database

Next, the database to hold information needs to be designed. The development team designs a database called Bank, which will be created by using Microsoft SQL Server 200. The Bank database will hold the data of the bank application. The tables of the database are explained as follows.

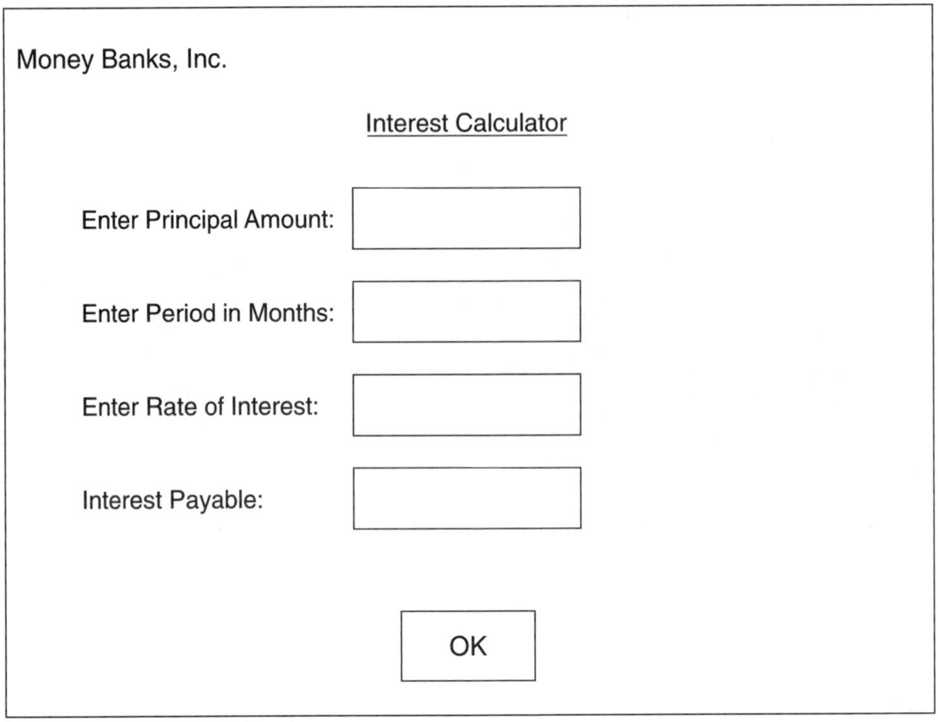

Money Banks, Inc.

<u>Interest Calculator</u>

Enter Principal Amount: [   ]

Enter Period in Months: [   ]

Enter Rate of Interest: [   ]

Interest Payable: [   ]

[OK]

FIGURE 17-7 *The figure displays the design of the Interest Calculator page.*

The *Ac_Requests* Table

The Ac_Requests Table will hold the information of all the requests for opening accounts at Money Banks. The table structure is given in Table 17-1.

Table 17-1 The *Ac_Requests* Table

Column Name	Data Type	Size
Request_ID	char	10
Branch	char	15
Account_Type	char	15
Title	char	4
First_Name	char	15

Column Name	Data Type	Size
Middle_Name	char	15
Last_Name	char	15
Date_of_Birth	char	10
Work_Phone	char	10
Address	char	30
State	char	15
Zip	char	10
E-mail	char	35
Home_Phone	char	10

The *AcHolder_Info* Table

The AcHolder_Info Table will contain information such as account type and branch of the account numbers. The table structure is given in Table 17-2.

Table 17-2 The *AcHolder_Info* Table

Column Name	Data Type	Size
Account_No	char	6
Register_ID	char	6
Balance	money	8
Account_Type	char	25
Branch	varchar	25

The *Login_Info* Table

The Login_Info Table will contain the logon information (such as the password) about the account holders who have registered with the application. The table structure is given in Table 17-3.

Table 17-3 The *Login_Info* Table

Column Name	Data Type	Size
Register_ID	char	10
Account_No	char	10
Password	char	10

The *TransCounter_Info* Table

The TransCounter_Info Table will store the transaction information of an account holder. The table structure is given in Table 17-4.

Table 17-4 The *TransCounter_Info* Table

Column Name	Data Type	Size
Transaction_ID	char	10
Account_No	char	6
Transaction_Date	datetime	8
Debit_Amount	money	8
Credit_Amount	money	8
Check_No	char	10

The *Register_Info* Table

The Register_Info Table will store information such as personal details about account holders of Money Banks. The table structure is given in Table 17-5.

Table 17-5 The *Register_Info* Table

Column Name	Data Type	Size
Request_ID	char	10
Register_ID	char	6
First_Name	varchar	15

Column Name	Data Type	Size
Middle_Name	varchar	15
Last_Name	varchar	15
Date_of_Birth	datetime	8
House_No	int	4
Locality	varchar	15
City	varchar	15
PIN	varchar	6
E-mail_ID	varchar	25
Fax	varchar	15
Phone_Res	char	7
Phone_Office	char	7

The relationship between tables of the Bank database is displayed in Figure 17-8.

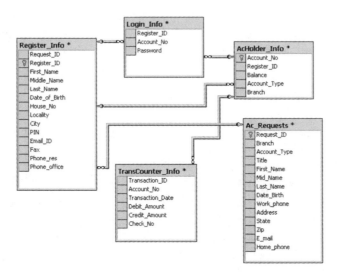

FIGURE 17-8 *A diagram of the Bank database is displayed.*

The Low-Level Design Phase

In this phase, a detailed design of software modules, based on the high-level design, is created. In addition, the team creates specifications for the various software modules of an application.

The functionality of the online banking application and the interaction between the various interfaces in the application is illustrated in Figure 17-9.

The Construction Phase

In the construction phase, the software components are built. This phase uses the output of the low-level design to produce software items. During the construction phase, the development team divides the responsibilities among its team members. Some team members are assigned the task of designing the interface, whereas others take the job of writing the code to develop the application.

The Testing Phase

Software modules are tested for their functionality as per the requirements identified during the requirements analysis phase. To test the functionality of the banking application, a Quality Assurance (QA) team is formed. The requirements identified during the requirements analysis phase are submitted to the QA team. In this phase the QA team tests the application for these requirements. The development team also submits a test case report to the QA team so that the application can be tested in various possible scenarios.

The Acceptance Phase

In this phase, based on the predefined acceptance criteria, the marketing team conducts acceptance testing for client projects. In the case of the online banking application, the acceptance criteria are the fulfillment of all the requirements identified during the requirements analysis phase.

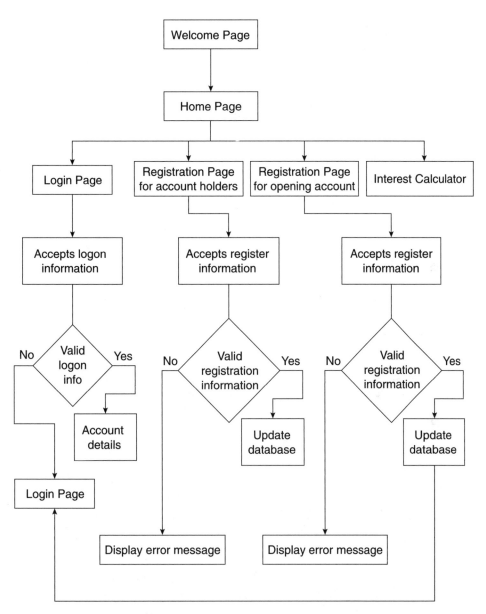

FIGURE 17-9 *The figure illustrates the functionality and interaction of the banking application.*

Summary

In this case study, you learned about the development phases in the life cycle of the banking application. A team was constituted to develop the application. The various interfaces of the application were determined during the design phase. In addition, the database design was finalized during the design phase.

In the next few chapters, you'll look at the creation and development of the banking application.

Chapter 18

In this chapter, you'll learn how to create the Welcome page for the online banking application of Money Banks, Inc.

The Welcome Page

The Welcome page is the first page to be displayed to a user who visits the banking application site of Money Banks. The Welcome page will display a welcome message with the information about the company. The page will also display a counter indicating the number of users who have visited the site. The Welcome page uses servlets to display the number of viewers who have visited the page. Since servlets have been used to create the Welcome page, I'll now discuss servlets before explaining how to create the page.

An Introduction to Servlets

Servlets are Java programs that can be deployed on a Java-enabled Web server to enhance and extend the functionality of the server.

Consider that a stockbroker is buying and selling in shares of stock from his office by using his personal computer. To determine the shares of stock to buy and sell, he needs to know the latest prices of stock in the stock market. To enable the stockbroker to view the latest prices of stock, you can create a Web page that will use servlets to interact with a database and display the latest prices of shares of stock to the user. Thus, servlets can be used to create dynamic Web pages.

In addition to displaying dynamic pages, servlets can be used to process data at the server end. Transaction data can be processed either on the client side or the server side. Client-side processing is performed on client browsers. Consider that you need to ensure that all the mandatory fields on the logon screen displayed to a user are filled. This can be done on the client side by using scripting languages, such as JavaScript. If the user has provided the required information, the logon information will be sent to the server. The verification of the logon information will be done at the server side. You can use server-side programming languages, such as servlets, to perform processing at the server.

On the Web, a client, which is usually a browser, sends a request for a servlet to the server. The request is sent as an HTTP request that contains the URL of the servlet. The servlet on the server runs in response to an HTTP request. The servlet produces an HTML page that is returned to the client.

The interaction between the server and a client is illustrated in Figure 18-1.

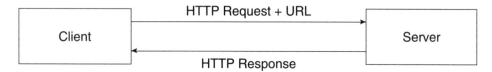

FIGURE 18-1 *The interaction between the server and a client*

The advantages of using servlets are given as follows:

♦ Servlets are loaded in the memory when they are executed for the first time. During subsequent requests, the servlets don't need to be loaded again. This increases the efficiency of the server. In addition, servlets are executed within the address space of the Web server. Therefore, creating separate processes for handling different client requests is not required.

♦ Since servlets are written in Java, they are platform-independent. Several Web servers from different vendors support servlet API. Therefore, servlet programs can run on these servers without requiring recompilation.

♦ Since servlets are written using Java, all the features of Java library classes are available to them. They can use Java API for tasks such as networking and URL access, multithreading, database connectivity, internationalization, remote method invocation (RMI), and object serialization.

I'll discuss the life cycle of a servlet. But first I'll explain about the GET and POST methods, which play an important role in the interaction between server and clients.

The GET and POST Methods

When a client sends a request to the server, the client can also pass additional information with the URL to describe what exactly is required as output from the server by using the GET and POST methods. For example, the `<form method="Get" action="http://www.ExampleURL.com/login.html?username= 'Carol'&passwd='3445H'" >` tag can be used in an HTML page to display the specified URL when the HTML page is submitted.

The request from the client to the server contains the following information:

♦ The protocol to be used for communication

♦ Whether the method GET or POST is to be used

♦ The URL of the requested document

♦ A query string that contains information such as login and registration details

In the specified URL, HTTP is the protocol to be used for sending the request. The request is being sent through the GET method. `www.ExampleURL.com/ login.html` is the URL of the requested document and `username="Carol" &passwd="3445H"` is the query string.

The difference between the GET and POST methods is that the information, if any, sent with the request to the server is visible on the browser while using the GET method. Therefore, sending requests to the server by using the GET method can be risky. For example, when a user enters the logon information on the logon page of a Web site, the login details become visible on the browser. Therefore, using GET may pose security risks.

To overcome this disadvantage, you can use the POST method to send HTTP requests to the server. The POST method sends the data as packets by using a separate socket connection. When data is transferred in the form of data packets, the data is hidden from the viewers. The disadvantage of the POST method is that it is slower than the GET method. Now I'll discuss the life cycle of a servlet.

The Life Cycle of a Servlet

The life cycle of a servlet differs from those of applications and applets. The servlets reside in a Java Virtual Machine (JVM) after they are loaded. They continue to reside in the JVM until the server stops. A few servers enable you to specify the servlets that will be loaded automatically when the server starts and the servlets that will be loaded on demand. You can also explicitly unload a servlet. A few Web servers automatically reload the servlets that are modified.

There are three key methods that control the life cycle of servlets. These methods are:

- `init()`
- `service()`
- `destroy()`

On receiving the request, the Web server maps the request to a particular servlet and the servlet is loaded. After loading the servlet, the server invokes the `init()` method of the servlet. The `init()` method is invoked only after the servlet is loaded.

The next method that is invoked by the server is the `service()` method. The client request is processed in the `service()` method. The `service()` method identifies the type of request and dispatches the request to the `doGet()` or `doPost()` method. The `doGet()` or `doPost()` methods are called by the server depending on the receipt of the request through GET or the POST method, respectively. The processing of the requests received from clients takes place in the `doGet()` and `doPost()` methods. The server also creates an HTTP response to be sent to the client. The `service()` method is called for each client request.

Finally, the `destroy()` method is executed by the server when the servlet is removed from the server. The `destroy()` method performs clean-up tasks, such as releasing resources and saving data to a persistent storage.

The life cycle of a servlet is illustrated in Figure 18-2, on the next page.

The Servlet API provides the support for the servlet. Servlet API is discussed in the next section.

The Servlet API

Two Java packages provide servlet API. These packages are:

- `javax.servlet`
- `javax.servlet.http`

I'll now discuss each of these packages in detail.

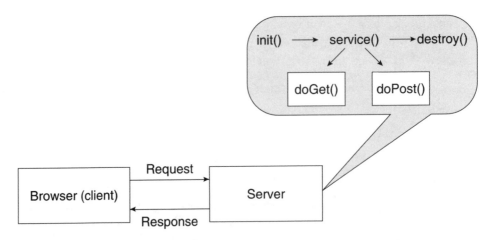

FIGURE 18-2 *The figure displays the life cycle of a servlet.*

The *javax.servlet* Package

The javax.servlet package contains classes and interfaces that provide the framework in which the servlets operate. The interfaces and classes of javax.servlet package are listed in Tables 18-1 and 18-2, respectively.

Table 18-1 The Interfaces of the *javax.servlet* Package

Interface	Description
Servlet	This interface describes the servlet life cycle methods, such as init(), service(), and destroy(). These methods are called during the life cycle of a servlet. The getServletConfig() method is used to obtain initialization parameter.
ServletRequest	This interface is used to read data from client requests. A few methods provided by the ServletRequest interface are getAttribute(), getContentLength(), getParameter(), getProtocol(), and getServerName().
ServletResponse	This interface used to write a response to the client. A few methods of this interface are getCharacterEncoding(), getWriter(), and setContentLength().

Interface	Description
ServletConfig	This interface is implemented by the server. The `ServletConfig` interface allows a servlet to determine the configuration, such as the name of the current servlet instance and value of a named initialization parameter, when the servlet was loaded. The `getServletContext()` method returns the context of the servlet. The other two methods declared in this interface are `getInitParameter()` and `getInitParameterNames()`.
ServletContext	This information provides the methods that enable a servlet to obtain information about the environment. A few methods provided by this interface are `getMimeType()`, `getServletInfo()`, `getServlet()`, and `getServletNames()`.
SingleThreadModel	This interface is used to indicate that only a single thread should execute the `service()` method of a server.

Table 18-2 The Classes of the *javax.servlet* Package

Classes	Description
GenericServlet	This class implements the `Servlet` and `ServletConfig` interfaces. This class provides implementation of the life cycle methods of a servlet.
ServletInputStream	This class extends the `InputStream` class. It provides an input stream that can be used to read data from a client request.
ServletOutputStream	This class provides an output stream to send information to the client. This class extends the `OutputStream` class. This class also defines the `print()` and `println()` method.
ServletException	This class is used to indicate a servlet problem.
UnavailableException	This class extends the `ServletException`. The methods of this class are used to identify whether a servlet is available temporarily or permanently. A servlet becomes permanently unavailable due to reasons such as the servlet might be configured incorrectly or its state may be corrupt. Corrective action by the servlet developer needs to be taken when a servlet is permanently unavailable. A servlet might be temporarily unavailable due to computer-related problems, such as insufficient memory or disk space. The system needs to take corrective actions.

The *javax.servlet.http* Package

The javax.servlet.http package provides classes and interfaces for working with HTTP requests and responses. The interfaces and classes of this package are specified in Tables 18-3 and 18-4, respectively.

Table 18-3 The Interfaces of the *javax.servlet.http* Package

Interface	Description
HttpServletRequest	This interface provides methods to read data from HTTP requests. A few methods of this package are getCookies(), getHeader(), getHeaderNames(), getQueryString(), and getSession().
HttpServletResponse	This interface provides methods to prepare an HTTP response to the client. A few methods of this interface are addCookie(), encodeURL(), setDateHeader(), setHeader(), and setStatus().
HttpSession	This interface enables a servlet to read and write the information associated with an HTTP session. A few methods of this interface are getCreationTime(), getId(), getValue(), and putValue().
HttpSessionBindingListener	This interface is implemented for the objects that are notified when they are bound to or unbound from an HTTP session.
HttpSessionContext	This interface enables a servlet to access the sessions associated with it. The methods of this class are: getIds() and getSession().

Table 18-4 The Classes of the *javax.servlet.http* Package

Classes	Description
Cookie	This class encapsulates a cookie. A cookie is stored on a client computer and stores session information. A cookie can be written to the user's machine by using the addCookie() method of the HttpServletResponse interface. The name, the value, the expiration date, the domain, and the path are stored on the user's computer. A few methods of this class are getMaxAge(), getName(), setMaxAge(), getPath(), and getValue().

Classes	Description
`HttpServlet`	This class is used by the servlets that receive and process HTTP requests. A few methods of `HttpServlet` class are `doDelete()`, `doGet()`, `doPut()`, and `getLastModified()`.
`HttpSessionBindingEvent`	This class extends the `EventObject` class. This class is generated when an event listener is bound or unbound to a source of event in the `HttpSession` object.
`HttpUtils`	This class provides utility methods for servlets. A few methods provided by this class are `getRequestURL()`, `parsePostData()`, and `parseQueryString()`.

I'll now help you write a simple servlet that displays a message to the user.

Writing Your First Servlet

The code for a simple servlet is listed in Listing 18-1.

Listing 18-1   FirstServlet.java

```
import java.io.*;
import javax.servlet.*;
import javax.servlet.http.*;
public class FirstServlet extends HttpServlet
{
    public void doGet( HttpServletRequest request, HttpServletResponse response)
        throws IOException, ServletException
    {
    response.setContentType( "text/HTML" );
    PrintWriter out = response.getWriter();
    out.println( "<HTML>" );
    out.println( "<head>" );
    out.println( "<title>First Servlet</title>" );
    out.println( "</head>" );
    out.println( "<body>" );
    out.println( "Congratulations!!! You have created your first servlet.");
```

```
        out.flush();
        out.println( "</body>" );
        out.println( "</HTML>" );
    }
}
```

After writing the code, you need to compile it by using the following command:

```
C:\>javac FirstServlet.java
```

You'll now deploy the FirstServlet.

Deploying the Servlets

After you write the servlet program, you need to deploy the servlet before it is accessible to the clients. You can deploy a servlet on a Java Web Server (JWS), JRun, Apache, or Java 2 Enterprise Edition (J2EE) server. I'll use a J2EE server to deploy servlets.

 NOTE

Ensure that the following paths are set before you configure the servlet:

```
CLASSPATH:
C:\j2sdkee1.2.1\lib\j2ee.jar;C:\j2sdkee1.2.1\lib\classes;C:\jdk1.3\bin;C:\j
2sdkee1.2.1\bin;.
J2EE_HOME: C:\j2sdkee1.2.1
JAVA_HOME: C:\jdk1.3
Path=%path%;c:\jdk1.3\bin;C:\j2sdkee1.2.1\bin;.;C:\j2sdkee1.2.1\lib\classes
```

The steps to deploy the servlet on a J2EE server are given as follows:

1. Start the J2EE server by typing J2EE -verbose at the command prompt.
2. Open another command prompt and type deploytool to display the Application Deployment Tool dialog box.
3. Select the New Application command from the File new.

4. In the New Application dialog box, click the Browse button to select the directory where the new application will be stored. Specify the name of the application as FirstServlet in the File Name dialog box. Click the New Application button.

5. The New Application dialog box is displayed again. Verify the application name in the Application File Name and Application Display Name text boxes. The New Application dialog box is displayed in Figure 18-3.

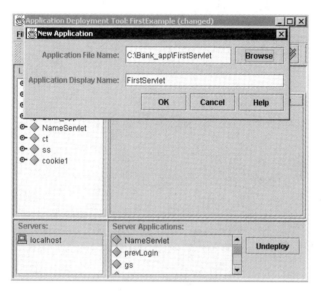

FIGURE 18-3 *The New Application dialog box*

6. Click the OK button to close the New Application dialog box. Notice that the application is displayed in the Local Applications list box.

7. Next, select New Web Component from the File menu.

8. The introduction page of the New Web Component Wizard is displayed. Click the Next button to proceed.

9. The WAR File General Properties page of the wizard is displayed.

10. Click the Add button. The Add Files to .WAR — Add Content Files pane is displayed. In this dialog box, you need to add HTML and JSP files, if any, to the application. HTML or JSP files are required right now. Therefore, you need to click the Next button.

11. The Add Files to .WAR — Add Class Files page is displayed. In this dialog box, you need to select the class files to be added. To add the servlet class file, click the Browse button and select the folder that contains the `FirstServlet.class` file.

12. Click the Choose Root Directory button after selecting the folder. The content of the folder is displayed. Select the `FirstServlet.class` file and then click the Add button.

13. The `FirstServlet.class` file is displayed in the Files to be Added list box. Click the Finish button.

14. The WAR File General Properties page is displayed again. Notice that in Figure 18-4, the `FirstServlet.class` file is displayed in the Contents list box. Click the Next button.

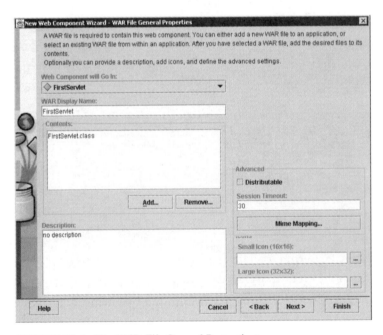

FIGURE 18-4 *The WAR File General Properties page*

15. The Choose Component Type page of the wizard is displayed again. The Servlet component type is selected by default. Click the Next button.

16. The Component General Properties page is displayed. Select `First-Servlet` from the Servlet class drop-down list box.

17. Type `FirstServlet` in the Web Component Display Name text box.

18. Click the Next button. The Component Initialization Parameters page of the wizard is displayed. Click the Next button again.

19. The Component Aliases page is displayed, as illustrated in Figure 18-5. Click the Add button and type `FirstServlet` in the text box that is displayed. Click the Next button.

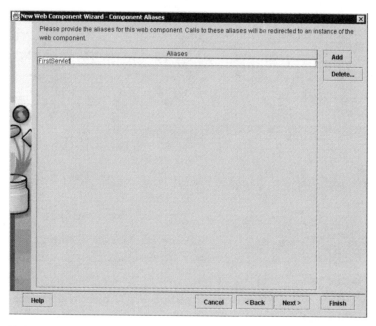

FIGURE 18-5 *The Component Aliases page*

20. Now you need to click the Next button on the subsequent pages of the wizard until you reach the Review Settings page, which is the last page. In the Review Settings page, you need to click the Finish button.

21. The Application Deployment Tool dialog box is displayed again. Notice that the `FirstServlet` component appears in the Local Applications list box.

22. Next, click the Web Context tab on the right pane of the Application Deployment Tool dialog box, as seen in Figure 18-6. To provide a context name to the application, type `FirstServletContext` in the Context Root text box.

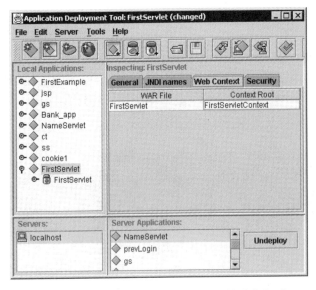

FIGURE 18-6 *The Application Deployment Tool dialog box*

23. Next, select the Deploy Application command from the Tools menu.

24. The Deploy FirstServlet — Introduction page box is displayed. Verify that the Target server is the localhost server. Click the Next button.

25. The Deploy FirstServlet — .WAR Context Root page is displayed. Notice that the context name that you specified earlier is displayed in the Context Root text box. Click the Next button.

26. The Deploy FirstServlet — Review page is displayed, as illustrated in Figure 18-7. Click the Finish button to deploy the application.

27. The Deployment Progress dialog box is displayed as in the Figure 18-8.

28. Click OK to close the dialog box when the deployment is complete. Close the application deployment tool window.

You have now deployed the FirstServlet servlet on the J2EE server. To view the output of the servlet, type http://localhost:8000/FirstServletContext/ FirstServlet in the address bar of the browser. The output of the FirstServlet code is displayed in Figure 18-9.

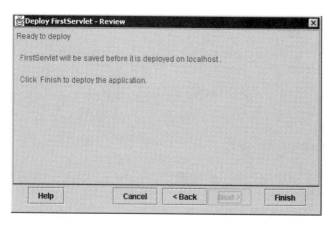

FIGURE 18-7 *The Deploy FirstServlet — Review page*

FIGURE 18-8 *The Deployment Progress dialog box*

FIGURE 18-9 *The output of the FirstServlet code*

I'll now analyze the code of `FirstServlet`.

```
import javax.servlet.*;
import javax.servlet.http.*;
```

These statements are used to import classes of javax.servlet and javax. servlet.http packages. These packages form the core of Servlet API.

```
public class FirstServlet extends HttpServlet
```

Next, the `FirstServlet` is declared. It extends the `HttpServlet` class of the javax.servlet.http package. The `HttpServlet` class provides methods for handling HTTP requests and responses.

```
    public void doGet( HttpServletRequest request, HttpServletResponse response)
throws IOException, ServletException
```

Here, the `doGet()` method of the `HttpServlet` class is overridden. The `doGet()` method is used to generate an HTML page and send the output to the client. The other two important methods of the `HttpServlet` class are the `doPost()` and `service()` methods. The `doPost()` method is generally used when input from an HTML page from the client needs to be accepted. The `service()` method is invoked when an HTTP request arrives for the servlet. A servlet must override at least one of these three methods.

The `doGet()` method accepts `HttpServletRequest` and `HttpServletResponse` objects as arguments. These objects enable the `doGet()` method to access HTTP requests and responses.

```
    {
    response.setContentType( "text/HTML" );
    PrintWriter out = response.getWriter();
    out.println( "<HTML>" );
    out.println( "<head>" );
    out.println( "<title>First Servlet</title>" );
    out.println( "</head>" );
    out.println( "<body>" );
    out.println( "Congratulations!!! You have created your first servlet.");
    out.flush();
    out.println( "</body>" );
    out.println( "</HTML>" );
    }
```

In the previous code, the setContentType() method is used to set the type of the response. The getWriter() method is used to obtain a PrintWriter object that can be used to write character data to the response. Then, using the println() method, the HTML output is written to the response.

Now I'll show you how the responses and requests are handled by servlets.

Handling Requests and Responses in Servlets

In the previous example, you looked at a servlet that simply generated an HTML page as the output. Now take a look at a servlet that generates an HTML page depending on a value entered by the user. First, I'll develop a servlet that handles HTTP GET requests by using the doGet() method.

Using the *doGet()* Method

I'll take an example where an HTML page accepts a username and sends an HTTP request for the servlet to the server. The servlet reads the username that is sent as an HTTP request by the client. After reading the username, the servlet displays a Welcome page for the user. You need two files for this example. An HTML page that will accept the username and a servlet class file that will display the resulting HTML page.

The code for the HTML page is given as follows:

```
<HTML>
<head>
<title>Name Servlet</title>
</head>
<body>
<form action="http://localhost:8000/NameServletContext/NameServlet">
<input type="text" name="name">
<input type="submit" name="submit" value="submit">
</form>
</body>
</HTML>
```

In this HTML page, notice the way in which the action parameter has been specified.

While deploying a servlet, you need to specify a name for the servlet context. A servlet context specifies the directory in which the servlets are deployed in a Web server. When a servlet is deployed, a folder with the same name as the context name is created in the `<system drive>:\<root directory>\<J2EE Folder>\public_html` folder. The WAR file, the class files, and the HTML files are placed in this directory. The server retrieves these files during execution. In this example, I've specified the context name of the servlet as `NameServletContext` and `NameServlet` is the name of the servlet.

The servlet code is listed here:

```java
import java.io.*;
import javax.servlet.*;
import javax.servlet.http.*;


public class NameServlet extends HttpServlet


{
    public void doGet( HttpServletRequest request, HttpServletResponse response)
        throws IOException, ServletException
    {
    response.setContentType( "text/HTML" );
    String name=request.getParameter("name");
    PrintWriter out = response.getWriter();
    out.println( "<HTML>" );
    out.println( "<head>" );
    out.println( "<title>Name Servlet</title>" );
    out.println( "</head>" );
    out.println( "<body>" );
    out.println( "Welcome "+name+"," );
    out.println( "<p>This page has been created by using the doGet() method.");
    out.flush();
    out.println( "</body>" );
    out.println( "</HTML>" );
    }
}
```

Notice that the code is similar to the code of FirstServlet. However, the difference lies in the way the getParameter() method is used. In this example, a user can enter the name in the HTML page. When the user clicks the Submit button, the information is passed to the server. The server loads the NameServlet servlet. The NameServlet servlet obtains the username by using the request.getParameter() method. Notice that the name of the text box in the HTML page is passed as an argument to the getParameter(). After obtaining the username, the servlet displays the welcome message to the user.

The output of the HTML page is displayed in Figure 18-10, and the output of the NameServlet is displayed in Figure 18-11.

FIGURE 18-10 *The output of the HTML page*

FIGURE 18-11 *The output of the* NameServlet

I'll now explain how to use the doPost() method.

Using the *doPost()* Method

I'll take the same example as in the previous section, "Using the doGet() Method." Now, when a client sends the username information to the server by using the POST method, the doPost() method in the servlet needs to be overridden. The HTML page remains the same except for a few minor changes, which I'll show you now.

```
<HTML>
<head>
<title>Name Servlet</title>
</head>
<body>
<form method="post" action="http://localhost:8000/NameServletContext/NameServlet">
<input type="text" name="name">
<input type="submit" name="submit" value="submit">
</form>
</body>
</HTML>
```

Notice the highlighted code. The method in the <form> tag is specified as POST. The code for the servlet class is given as follows:

```
import java.io.*;
import javax.servlet.*;
import javax.servlet.http.*;
public class NameServlet extends HttpServlet
{
    public void doPost( HttpServletRequest request, HttpServletResponse response)
        throws IOException, ServletException
    {
    response.setContentType( "text/HTML" );
    String name=request.getParameter("name");
    PrintWriter out = response.getWriter();
    out.println( "<HTML>" );
    out.println( "<head>" );
    out.println( "<title>Name Servlet</title>" );
    out.println( "</head>" );
    out.println( "<body>" );
    out.println( "Welcome "+name+"," );
```

```
        out.println( "<p>This page has been created by using the doGet() method.");
        out.flush();
        out.println( "</body>" );
        out.println( "</HTML>" );
    }
}
```

Notice that the doPost() method is overridden. In the doPost() method, the request.getParameter() method has been used to obtain the username. Then a Welcome message is displayed to the user.

Now I'll show you how to handle cookies by using servlets.

Handling Cookies in Servlets

A *cookie* is a text file that is stored on a client computer and may contain user information. For example, a cookie on a client computer can store the login information so that the client doesn't have to provide login information during each login attempt. The Cookie class encapsulates cookies in Java.

A servlet can store a cookie on the client computer by using the addCookie() command of the HttpServletResponse interface. The data for the cookie is sent with the HTTP response to the client. The cookie information such as the name, the value, and the expiration date are stored on the client computer.

The Cookie class provides various methods to handle cookies. Some of these methods are mentioned in Table 18-5.

Table 18-5 Methods of the *Cookie* Class

Method	Description
int getMaxAge()	This method returns the maximum age, in seconds, of the cookie.
String getName()	This method returns the name of the cookie.
String getValue()	This method returns the value of the cookie.
void setMaxAge(int secs)	This method sets the maximum age of the cookie in seconds.
void setValue(String val)	This method sets the value of the cookie to val.

I'll create a servlet that displays the time of the user's previous access to the servlet. The servlet will store the information in a cookie. The code for the servlet that stores cookie information is given in Listing 18-1.

Listing 18-1　prevLogin.java

```java
import javax.servlet.*;
import javax.servlet.http.*;
import java.io.*;
import java.util.*;

public class prevLogin extends HttpServlet
{
            public void service(HttpServletRequest req, HttpServletResponse
res) throws IOException
            {
            boolean prevCookie=false;
            Cookie myCookie=null;
            Cookie[] cookies=req.getCookies();
            res.setContentType("text/html");
            PrintWriter pw=res.getWriter();
        pw.println("<HTML>");
        pw.println("<BODY>");
        for (int ctr=0;ctr<cookies.length;ctr++)
        {
                        if (cookies[ctr].getName().equals("PrevLogin"))
                        {
                                    prevCookie=true;
                                    myCookie=cookies[ctr];
                        }
        }
        if (prevCookie)
        {
                        pw.println("You logged previously on");
                        pw.println(myCookie.getValue());
                        Calendar cl=Calendar.getInstance();
```

```
                                Date dt=cl.getTime();
                                String date=dt.toString();
                                myCookie.setValue(date);
                                res.addCookie(myCookie);
                                prevCookie=false;
                }
                else
                {
                                pw.println("This is the first time you have
logged on to the server");

                                Calendar cl=Calendar.getInstance();
                                Date dt=cl.getTime();
                                String date=dt.toString();
                                myCookie=new Cookie("PrevLogin",date);
                                res.addCookie(myCookie);
                }
                pw.println("</BODY>");
                pw.println("</HTML>");
        }
}
```

In the code, the cookie is created using the default constructor of the Cookie class. The constructor assumes the name of the cookie and the value of cookie as arguments. Next, the cookie is attached to the response by using the addCookie() method. I'll now discuss the code in detail.

```
                for (int ctr=0;ctr<cookies.length;ctr++)
                {
                                if (cookies[ctr].getName().equals("PrevLogin"))
                                {
                                                prevCookie=true;
                                                myCookie=cookies[ctr];
                                }
                }
```

The above code snippet looks for a cookie named PrevLogin, among the various cookies available. If the cookie is found, the value of boolean variable, prevCookie, is set to true. The true value indicates that the cookie has been found.

```
if (prevCookie)
                {
                                pw.println("You logged previously on");
                                pw.println(myCookie.getValue());
                                Calendar cl=Calendar.getInstance();
                                Date dt=cl.getTime();
                                String date=dt.toString();
                                myCookie.setValue(date);
                                res.addCookie(myCookie);
                                prevCookie=false;
                }
```

The above statements are executed if the value of prevCookie is true. These statements will print the value of the cookie and then assign a new value to the cookie by using the setValue() method. The value that is assigned is the current date.

```
                {
                                pw.println("This is the first time you have
logged on to the server");
                                Calendar cl=Calendar.getInstance();
                                Date dt=cl.getTime();
                                String date=dt.toString();
                                myCookie=new Cookie("PrevLogin",date);
                                res.addCookie(myCookie);
                }
```

The above statements are executed if the value of prevCookie is false. These statements will display a message that the user has visited for the first time. Next, a cookie is created, assigned value, and added with the response that is sent to the client.

The output of the prevLogin servlet when the user accesses it for the first time is displayed in Figure 18-12.

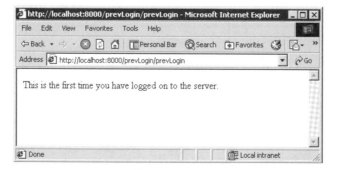

FIGURE 18-12 *The figure displays the output of servlet when visited for the first time.*

The output of the servlet on subsequent visits is displayed in the Figure 18-13.

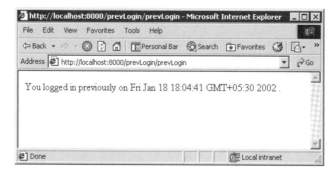

FIGURE 18-13 *The output of the servlet on subsequent visits is displayed.*

You've learned about servlets. I'll now create the Counter servlet.

Creating the Counter Servlet

The first page of the online banking application at Money Banks displays the Welcome message to the viewers. A counter is also displayed indicating the number of viewers of this page.

The code written for the Counter servlet is given in Listing 18-2.

Listing 18-2 Counter.java

```java
import javax.servlet.*;
import javax.servlet.http.*;
import java.io.*;
import java.util.*;
public class Counter extends HttpServlet
{
static int counter;
public void init(ServletConfig config) throws ServletException
{
                super.init(config);
}
public void doGet(HttpServletRequest request, HttpServletResponse response) throws
ServletException, IOException
{
                response.setContentType("text/html");
                PrintWriter out=response.getWriter();
                counter++;
                out.println("<html>");
                out.println("<head><title>Money Banks, Inc. -- Welcome
Page</title></head>");
                out.println("<body bgproperties=\"fixed\" bgcolor=\"#CCCCFF\">");
                out.println("<p><b><font><font size=\"6\">Welcome to Money
Banks, Inc.</font></font></b></p>");
                out.println("Money Banks, Inc. welcomes you to the site. Money
Banks, Inc. is a leading bank dealing and fulfilling the needs of all categories:
financial organizations, hospitals, universities, and individuals. The services
offered by Money Banks, Inc. include bank accounts and loans for all needs. You
will find complete information regarding various schemes of the bank in this site.
In addition, the site enables online banking transactions. You can view your
account details and if not an account holder, you can apply for an account online.
You'll also find various utilities such as interest calculator and foreign exchange
calculator on this site.");
out.println("<p><b><fontsize=\"3\"><a href=\"Home_page.htm\">Click here to contin-
ue.</a></font></b></p>");
                out.println("You are viewer number     " + String.valueOf(counter)+
"  visting our Web site."+ "\n");
```

```
                out.println("</body></html>");
}
public String getServletInfo()
{
                return "BasicServlet Information";
}
}
```

I'll now analyze the code.

```
public void init(ServletConfig config) throws ServletException
{
                super.init(config);
}
```

The `init()` method is called when the servlet is initialized. The initialization parameters can be obtained from the `ServletConfig` object that is passed as an argument to the `init()` method.

If the `Counter` servlet is deployed with the root context name as `Bank~app`, you need to type the following URL in the browser.

```
http://localhost:8000/Bank_app/Counter
```

The output of the `Counter` servlet code is displayed in Figure 18-14.

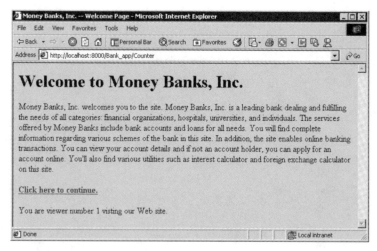

FIGURE 18-14 *The output of* Counter *Servlet*

Summary

In this chapter, you learned about the benefits and life cycle of the servlets. You also looked at the Servlet API and the classes and interfaces within the API. You learned to create and deploy servlets. You also learned how to use cookies to store client-side information. Finally, you learned how to create the counter servlet for the banking application.

Chapter 19

*Creating a
Registration Page
for Account Holders*

In this chapter, you will learn how to create the Registration page that allows account holders of Money Banks, Inc., to register with the online banking application. After registering with the application, the account holders can log on to the application and view their account details and other information.

The Registration Page for Account Holders

Money Banks has many account holders. To enable these existing account holders to register with the online banking application, the development team decides to create a registration page. This registration page will enable the account holders to register after it has accepted and validated details such as account numbers and account types. The technologies used to create the registration page are:

- ◆ Java Database Connectivity (JDBC)
- ◆ Java Server Pages (JSP)

I'll now discuss JDBC and JSP in detail.

Java Database Connectivity (JDBC)

You use databases to store data. In addition to storing data in a structured manner, databases help in easy retrieval and processing of data. However, the maintenance of databases can be arduous for some people. Imagine that a store owner has to maintain data about a large department store on an SQL server. In order to update or query the database, he will need to learn about SQL statements. This can be a tedious task for the store owner. The solution is to build applications that will act as an interface between the store owner and the database. The applications will accept values from the store owner by using user-friendly GUIs, and the application will update or query the database. The Java environment provides you the JDBC API necessary to create Java applications that are capable of interacting with a database.

I'll now discuss the JDBC API.

The JDBC API

The JDBC API is composed of methods defined by a set of classes and interfaces that enable Java applications to communicate with database management systems (DBMS) or relational database management systems (RDBMS). For this to happen, the database should be installed on the computer and the RDBMS should provide a driver. JDBC classes and interfaces defined in the package java.sql constitute the JDBC API.

A Java program interacts with a database. The program invokes the methods of the JDBC API. The JDBC API then calls the JDBC driver and submits the queries to it. The JDBC driver then converts the queries to a form, such as SQL statements, that a database can understand. After the query has been performed, the JDBC driver retrieves the result of the query from the database. The result is converted into the JDBC API classes that can be used by the Java program. Then, the Java program obtains the result of the query.

The interaction between a Java program, the JDBC API, the JDBC driver, and the database is depicted in Figure 19-1.

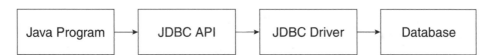

FIGURE 19-1 *The figure illustrates the process of accessing a database.*

The JDBC API enables a Java application to:

◆ Store data in a database

◆ Update, delete, or insert rows in a database

◆ Retrieve the data in a database and present it in a proper format to the user

The JDBC API can be used with both two-tier and three-tier database architectures. In two-tier architecture, Java programs invoke methods of the JDBC API. The JDBC API, in turn, communicates with the database server. Therefore, there is direct interaction between Java programs and databases. In three-tier architecture, a Java program submits queries to a server. The server then uses the JDBC API to interact with the database server.

JDBC drivers are covered in the next section.

JDBC Drivers

Database vendors provide a driver along with the database to enable Java programs to communicate with the database. The availability of database drivers takes care of key issues such as:

◆ The mechanism for communication between Java applications and the databases

◆ The portability of Java applications with different databases. Java applications written to communicate with one kind of database should be able to communicate with other databases, such as SQL Server, Sybase, and Oracle. For example, there should be no modification needed in an application using MS Access to communicate with SQL Server.

These issues are resolved by using the JDBC API. The JDBC API converts the Java command to SQL statements.

The JDBC drivers are provided by database vendors to enable the JDBC API to communicate with the database. The Java programs invoke the methods of the JDBC API. The JDBC API then uses the JDBC driver to communicate with the databases.

There are some databases, such as MS Access, that do not provide a JDBC driver. Instead they provide Open Database Connectivity (ODBC) drivers. You can access such databases by using the ODBC-JDBC bridge. The ODBC-JDBC bridge is a database driver supported by Java platforms. The support for the ODBC-JDBC bridge is provided in the `sun.jdbc.ojbc.JdbcOdbcDriver` package. The ODBC-JDBC bridge is a mixture of Java code and native code.

JDBC drivers are divided into four categories. Each category defines JDBC driver implementation with increasingly higher levels of platform independence, performance, and deployment administration. The four categories of JDBC drivers are:

◆ Type 1: JDBC-ODBC bridge

◆ Type 2: Native-API/partly-Java driver

◆ Type 3: Net-protocol/all-Java driver

◆ Type 4: Native-protocol/all-Java driver

I'll now discuss each of these driver categories in detail.

Type 1: JDBC-ODBC Bridge

The JDBC-ODBC bridge driver converts all JDBC calls into ODBC calls and sends them to the ODBC driver. The ODBC driver then forwards the call to the database server. Figure 19-2 displays a typical JDBC-ODBC ridge environment.

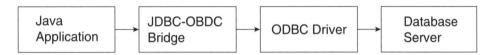

FIGURE 19-2 *The JDBC-ODBC bridge environment is displayed.*

The benefit of using the JDBC-ODBC bridge driver is that it allows access to almost any database. Type 1 drivers are useful in scenarios where ODBC drivers are already installed on the client computers.

The disadvantage of using the JDBC-ODBC bridge is that the performance is slow. This is because the JDBC calls are first converted to ODBC calls. ODBC calls are then converted to native database calls. The same steps are performed in reverse order when the result of the query is obtained. Therefore, Type 1 drivers may not be suitable for large-scale database-based applications.

Type 2: Native-API/partly-Java Driver

The JDBC Type 2 driver, or the native-API/partly-Java driver, communicates directly with the database server. Therefore, the vendor database library needs to be loaded on each client computer. The Type 2 driver converts JDBC calls into database-specific calls for databases such as SQL Server or Sybase. An illustration of the workings of the Type 2 driver is displayed in Figure 19-3.

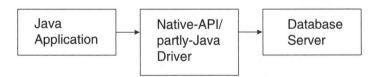

FIGURE 19-3 *The figure shows the workings of the JDBC Type 2 driver.*

The benefit of using Type 2 drivers is that they provide better performance than the JDBC-ODBC bridge. The disadvantage of using Type 2 drivers is that the vendor database library needs to be loaded on each client computer. Therefore, Type 2 drivers are not suitable for distributed applications.

Type 3: Net-protocol/all-Java Driver

The JDBC Type 3 driver, or the net-protocol/all-Java driver, follows a three-tiered approach. In the three-tiered approach, JDBC database requests are passed to a middle-tier server. The middle-tier server then translates the requests to the database-specific native-connectivity interface and forwards the requests to the database server. If the middle-tier server is written in Java, it can use the Type 1 or Type 2 drivers to forward the requests to the database server. The three-tiered approach is illustrated in Figure 19-4.

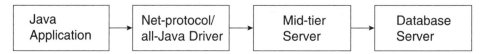

FIGURE 19-4 *The three-tiered approach of the Type 3 driver is displayed.*

Type 3 drivers are used to connect a client application or applet to a database over a TCP/IP connection. The presence of any vendor database library on client computers is not required because the Type 3 JDBC driver is server-based. Type 3 drivers enable you to achieve optimized portability, performance, and scalability. A Type 3 driver typically provides support for features such as caching of connections, query results, load balancing, and advanced system administration such as logging and auditing. The disadvantage of using a Type 3 driver is that it requires database-specific coding to be done in the middle tier. Additionally, traversing the recordset may take longer because the data comes through the backend server.

Type 4: Native-protocol/all-Java Driver

Type 4 drivers, or native-protocol/all-Java drivers, are completely implemented in Java to achieve platform independence. Type 4 JDBC drivers convert JDBC calls into the vendor-specific DBMS protocol. Therefore, client applications can communicate directly with the database server when Type 4 JDBC drivers are used. The functionality of Type 4 JDBC drivers is illustrated in Figure 19-5.

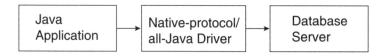

FIGURE 19-5 *The figure displays the functionality of Type 4 drivers.*

The performance of Type 4 JDBC drivers is better than other drivers because Type 4 JDBC drivers do not have to translate database requests to ODBC calls or a native connectivity interface or pass the request on to another server. However, while using Type 4 drivers, a different driver is needed for each database.

Now that I've discussed the JDBC drivers, you'll study the JDBC API.

The java.sql Package

The JDBC API consists of the methods defined by the interfaces and classes in the package java.sql. The interfaces and classes of the java.sql package are listed here:

♦ **Array:** This interface defines the Java mapping for the SQL type ARRAY. The Array interface provides methods for bringing an SQL ARRAY's data to the client as either an array or a ResultSet object. Some of the methods of the Array interface are getArray(), getBaseTypeName(), and getResultSet().

♦ **Blob:** This interface defines the Java mapping for binary large objects or SQL BLOBs. Some of the methods of this interface are getBinary-Stream(), getBytes(), length(), and position().

♦ **CallableStatement:** This interface provides the methods you can use to execute stored procedures. The JDBC API provides a stored procedure SQL escape syntax that allows stored procedures to be called in a standard way for all RDBMSs. Some of the methods of this interface are getArray(), getBlob(), getBoolean(), getByte(), getDate(), get-String(), and getTimeStamp().

♦ **Clob:** This interface defines the Java mapping for character large objects or SQL CLOBs. A SQL CLOB type stores a character large object as a column value in a row of a database table. Some of the methods of this

interface are `getAsciiStream()`, `getSubString()`, `length()`, and posi-
tion().

♦ **Connection:** This interface encapsulates a connection to the database.
SQL statements are executed and results are returned within the context
of a `Connection`. Methods of this interface are `createStatment()`,
`getCatalog()`, `commit()`, `prepareCall()`, `nativeSQL()`, `prepareState-`
`ment()`, `rollback()`, and `setAutoCommit()`.

♦ **DataBaseMetaData:** This interface describes the database as a whole.
Many methods of the `DataBaseMetaData` interface return lists of information in the form of `ResultSet` objects. This interface provides many
methods that represent comprehensive information of the database.

♦ **Driver:** This interface defines the methods that all database vendors
must implement in their JDBC drivers. Each driver should supply a class
that implements the `Driver` interface. The methods of this interface are
`acceptURL()`, `connect()`, `getPropertyInfo()`, and `jdbcCompliant()`.

♦ **PreparedStatement:** This interface represents a precompiled SQL statement. You can create an SQL statement and store it in a `Prepared-`
`Statement` object. This object can then be used to execute the SQL
statement many times. The methods of this interface are `execute()`,
`executeQuery()`, `executeUpdate()`, `getMetaData()`, `setArray()`, and
`Boolean()`.

♦ **Ref:** This interface is used to reference SQL structured types stored in
the database. You can persistently store a `Ref` object and can also derefer-
ence it by passing the object as a parameter to an SQL statement and
executing the statement. The interface defines a single method, `getBase-`
`TypeName()`.

♦ **ResultSet:** This interface represents a table of result data set generated
by executing a statement that queries a database. The methods of the
interface are `getTime()`, `getStatement()`, `isFirst()`, `isLast()`, `next()`,
`previous()`, `rowInserted()`, `rowUpdated()`, `updateBytes()`, and
`updateRow()`.

♦ **ResultSetMetaData:** This interface provides methods for obtaining
information about the types and properties of the columns in a `Result-`
`Set` object. The methods of this interface are `getColumnCount()`, `get-`
`ColumnType()`, `getColumnName()`, `isReadOnly()`, and `isWritable()`.

◆ **SQLData:** This interface allows custom mappings of SQL user-defined types to Java types. Any Java class that is registered in a type mapping must implement this interface. Methods of this interface are getSQL - TypeName(), readSQL(), and writeSQL().

◆ **SQLInput:** This interface represents an input stream containing values that represent an instance of an SQL structured or distinct type. The methods of this interface are readDouble(), readFloat(), readInt(), readLong(), readShort(), readString(), and readArray().

◆ **SQLOutput:** This interface represents an output stream used for writing attributes of a user-defined type to the database. This interface is used by the driver and is never invoked by a programmer. The methods of this interface are writeArray(), writeString(), writeLong(), writeByte(), and writeBoolean().

◆ **Statement:** The objects of this interface are used for executing SQL statements and obtaining the results produced by it. Only one ResultSet object per Statement object is possible. The methods of this interface are execute(), executeBatch(), executeQuery(), executeUpdate(), getCon- nection(), getResultSet(), and getMaxRows().

◆ **Struct:** This interface defines the standard mapping for an SQL struc- tured type. The methods of this interface are getAttributes() and get- SQLTypeName().

The classes of the java.sql package are listed below:

◆ **Date:** This class wraps a millisecond value that enables JDBC to identify the millisecond as an SQL DATE value. A millisecond value represents the number of milliseconds that have passed since January 1, 1970. The methods of this class are getHours(), getMinutes(), getSeconds(), set- Seconds(), and setTime().

◆ **DriverManager:** This class provides access to database drivers. The Dri- verManager class loads driver classes. The methods of this interface are getConnection(), getDrivers(), setLoginTimeout(), and register- Driver().

◆ **DriverPropertyInfo:** This class contains the property information needed by drivers to make a connection. The class defines only one method of its own, which is DriverPropertyInfo().

- ◆ **SQLPermission:** This class represents permission that will be checked by the security manager when the code that is running in an applet calls one of the setLogWriter methods.

- ◆ **Time:** This class wraps a java.util.Date object so that it can be used as an SQL TIME value. The methods of this class are getDate(), get-Day(), getMonth(), setMonth(), setTime(), and setYear().

- ◆ **Timestamp:** This class wraps a java.util.Date object so that the JDBC API can identify it as an SQL TIMESTAMP value. The methods of this class are after(), before(), equals(), getNanos(), toString(), and valueOf().

- ◆ **Types:** This class defines constants that can be used to identify generic SQL types, which are also called JDBC types. Some of the constants defined by this class are ARRAY, BINARY, BLOB, DATE, DECIMAL, FLOAT, INTEGER, NULL, REF, TIME, STRUCT, VARBINARY, and VARCHAR.

In addition to these interfaces and classes, the SQL package defines exceptions that can be thrown by JDBC methods. These exceptions are BatchUpdateException, DataTruncation, SQLException, and SQLWarning. You can use exception handlers to handle these exceptions. You are now ready to create programs to query databases.

Writing a Java Program for Databases

Next you'll take a look at the procedure for creating a Java program that interacts with a database. Take an example. There's an employee database that contains the details of employees in a company. Now attempt to code a program that will display the details of an employee after accepting the employee ID from the user. The steps to write such a program are given here:

1. Create the database and tables
2. Create the DSN
3. Load the driver
4. Establish database connection
5. Execute SQL statements
6. Process the result

I'll now discuss each of these steps in detail.

Creating the Database and Tables

The database that you need will store the details of the employees. Therefore, you'll name the database as Employee. The table that will hold the details will be named as Emp_details table. The design of the table is given here:

- ◆ Emp_Code char(10) not null,
- ◆ Emp_Name varchar(25) not null,
- ◆ Emp_DOJ datetime,
- ◆ Emp_DOB datetime,
- ◆ Emp_Dept varchar(20),
- ◆ Emp_Location varchar(20)

I've created the database and the table in SQL Server 2000 and I'll use this table for database connectivity.

After creating the database, a DSN needs to be created.

Creating a DSN Source

The Data Source Name (DSN) contains information, such as the location of the database server, database name, user name, and password to be used to connect to the database server. The DSN also contains information about the log file name to be used to store lengthy queries and driver statistics.

You can create a DSN source by using the control panel. The steps to create the DSN source are given here:

1. Double-click the Administrative Tools icon in the Control Panel window.
2. In the Administrative Tools window, double-click the Data Sources (ODBC) icon.
3. The User DSN tab page of the ODBC Data Source Administrator dialog box is displayed, as shown in Figure 19-6. Click the Add button to create the DSN source.

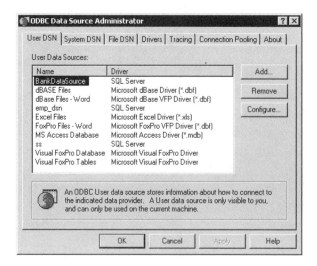

FIGURE 19-6 *The figure displays the User DSN tab page.*

4. The Create New Data Source dialog box is displayed, as shown in Figure 19-7. A list of drivers for which you can create a data source is displayed. Since you'll use the SQL Server, you need to select SQL Server from the list.

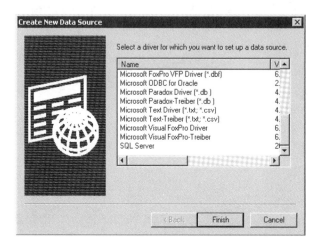

FIGURE 19-7 *The figure displays the Create New Data Source dialog box.*

5. The Create a New Data Source to SQL Server dialog box is displayed, as shown in Figure 19-8. Provide the name as `Emp_DSN`. The server has been selected for you. Click the Next button.

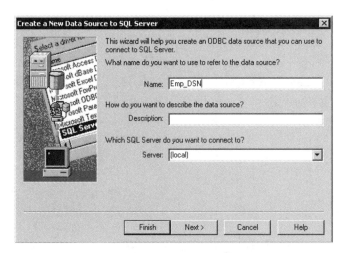

FIGURE 19-8 *The figure displays the Create a New Data Source to the SQL Server dialog box.*

6. To select the default configuration on this page, click the Next button.

7. In this page, check the box to select "Change the default database," and then select the `Employee` database from the drop-down list. Click the Next button and then click the Finish button. The selection of the default database is depicted in Figure 19-9.

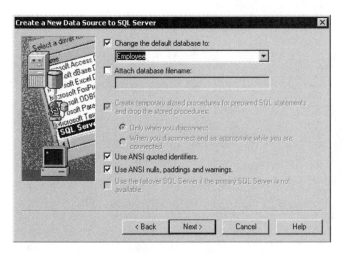

FIGURE 19-9 *This illustrates how to select the default database.*

8. The ODBC Microsoft SQL Server Setup dialog box is displayed, as shown in Figure 19-10. Click the Test Data Source button to test the data source.

FIGURE 19-10 *The figure displays the ODBC Microsoft SQL Server Setup dialog box.*

9. The TESTS COMPLETED SUCCESSFULLY! message is displayed, as shown in Figure 19-11. Click the OK button to close the dialog box.

FIGURE 19-11 *The message is displayed to indicate the successful completion of tests.*

10. Click the OK button.

11. The User DSN page is displayed again, as shown in Figure 19-12. Notice that emp_dSN is displayed in the list. Click the OK button to close the dialog box.

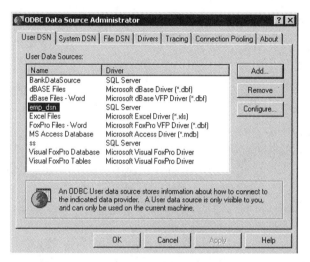

FIGURE 19-12 *The User DSN page is shown with* emp_dSN *in the list.*

Now that you've created the DSN source, you're ready to load the driver. The command to load the driver is written in Java programs.

Loading the Driver

Before you can connect to a database from a Java program, you must load the database driver into the JVM. In a JDBC program, the JDBC driver is loaded by calling the forName() static method of the Class class. The forName() method takes one string parameter, which is the name of the driver along with its package. For JDBC-ODBC bridge, this string is "sun.jdbc.odbc.JdbcOdbcDriver". Therefore, the command will look like this:

```
Class.forName("sun.jdbc.odbc.JdbcOdbcDriver");
```

The statement will load the JDBC-ODBC bridge driver. After loading the driver, you need to establish the database connection.

Establishing the Database Connection

You can establish a connection with a database by using the `Connection` object of the `java.sql.Connection` class. The `Connection` object represents a connection with a database. You can have several `Connection` objects in an application. You can use the `getConnection()` method of the `DriverManager` class to establish a connection with a database. This method attempts to locate the driver that can connect to the database represented by the JDBC URL, which is passed to the `getConection()` method. The JDBC URL is a string that provides a way of identifying a database. A JDBC URL consists of three parts:

```
<protocol>:<subprotocol>:<subname>
```

Here, the `<protocol>` attribute is always `jdbc`. The `<subprotocol>` attribute is the name of the database connectivity mechanism. If the mechanism is the JDBC-ODBC bridge, the `<subprotocol>` must be `odbc`. The `<subname>` identifies the database. The `<subname>` is the DSN, which contains information about the location of database server, database name, username, and password. This information will be used to connect to the database. You can connect to a database by executing the following statement:

```
Connection con=DriverManager.getConnection ("jdbc.odbc.Emp_Dsn","","");
```

Notice that the last two arguments of the `getConnection()` method are blank. These arguments identify the username and the password to provide connectivity to the database. These arguments have been left blank because you have not identified any particular user while creating the DSN source.

The `getConnection()` method is defined in the `DriverManager` class. Several overloaded forms of the `getConnection()` method exist. These overloaded forms are given here:

```
Connection getConnection(String url )
Connection getConnection(String url, Properties info )
Connection getConnection(String url, String user, String password )
```

Now you're ready to create SQL statements for performing queries with the database.

Executing SQL Statements

You can use `Statement` objects to perform queries with the databases. The methods of the `Statement` objects allow you to execute simple queries. These methods are:

1. The `executeQuery()` method that executes a query and returns a `ResultSet` object.

2. The `executeUpdate()` method that executes an SQL INSERT, UPDATE, or a DELETE statement. The `executeUpdate()` method returns an int value specifying the number of rows affected by the query or 0 if the query does not return any value.

The `createStatement()` method of the `Connection` object is used to create a `Statement` object. Consider the following code:

```
Class.forName("sun.jdbc.odbc.JdbcOdbcDriver");
 Connection conn;
 conn=DriverManager.getConnection("jdbc:odbc:Emp_Dsn",  "","");
Statement state=conn.createStatement();
ResultSet result=state.executeQuery("Select * from Emp_Details");
```

In the code, the `forName()` method is used to load the JDBC-ODBC driver. Next, by using the `getConnection()` method of `DriverManager`, you establish a connection with the database through the DSN source. Next, a `Statement` object is created by using the `createStatement()` method. Then, a SQL query is executed by using the `executeQuery()` method of the `Statement` object. The result of the query is stored in a `ResultSet` object, `result`.

Processing the Result

The `ResultSet` object represents a table in the form of rows and columns. The table is returned as a result of the query executed by the `Statement` object. The `ResultSet` object provides methods for navigating through the result data and accesses the data by the name or number of the columns. The `ResultSet` object maintains a cursor pointing to the current row of data. Initially, the cursor is positioned before the first row. You can retrieve data from the `ResultSet` rows by calling the `getXXX(int col_number)` method where XXX refers to a datatype of a column, such as a `String`, an `Integer`, or a `Float` and `col_number` specifies the column number in the result table. Some of the commonly used methods are listed here:

- ◆ `String` getString(int col_number)
- ◆ `int` getInt(int col_number)
- ◆ `float` getFloat(int col_number)
- ◆ `Date` getDate(int col_number)

The overloaded forms of these methods accept the String value containing the names of the columns. For example:

- ◆ String getString("Emp_Name")
- ◆ int getInt("Emp_Age")
- ◆ float getFloat("Emp_Sal")
- ◆ Date getDate("Emp_DOJ")

Consider an example. A database is queried and then the content of two columns in the ResultSet are displayed.

```java
import java.sql.*;
public class Query_app
{
    public static void main(String a[])
    {
      try
        {
          Class.forName("sun.jdbc.odbc.JdbcOdbcDriver");
                Connection conn =
DriverManager.getConnection("jdbc:odbc:Emp_Dsn","","");
          Statement state=con.createStatement();
          Resultant result=stats.executeQuery("Select * from Emp_Details");
                while(result.next())
          {
                System.out.println(result.getString(2));
                    System.out.println(result.getString("Emp_DOJ"));
          }
            }
            catch(Exception e) {
          System.out.println("Exception while executing query" +e);
            }
      }
}
```

In the code given above, the result.next() command is used to move the cursor to the next row of the result data. The next() method will be executed till the cursor reaches the end of the result.

Now consider the examples of performing insertion and deletion of rows in a database by using the JDBC API in Java programs.

Inserting Rows in a Database

You'll create a Java program that'll add a new employee to the Employee database. The code to do this is given as follows:

```
import java.sql.*;
public class Query_app
{
    public static void main(String a[])
    {
     try
      {
            Class.forName("sun.jdbc.odbc.JdbcOdbcDriver");
        Connection conn;
            conn=DriverManager.getConnection("jdbc:odbc:ss","","");
        Statement state=conn.createStatement();
        String query="insert into Emp_Details values( 'E00110' ,'Mark' ,'Stores
Manager')";
        state.executeUpdate(query);
            }
            catch(Exception e) {
         System.out.println("Exception while executing query" +e);
            }
    }
}
```

In the preceding program, the user enters the details of the new employee and then by using the executeUpdate() method, the row is inserted in the database.

Deleting Rows from a Database

Rows can be deleted from a table based on a condition. For example, if an employee leaves an organization, you can delete the employee details based on Emp_Id. The following code accepts Emp_Id from an employee and deletes the corresponding row from the table in the database.

```java
import java.sql.*;
public class Query_app
{
    public static void main(String a[])
    {
      try
       {
          Class.forName("sun.jdbc.odbc.JdbcOdbcDriver");
          Connection conn;
conn=DriverManager.getConnection("jdbc:odbc:ss","","");
          Statement state=conn.createStatement();
          String query="delete from Emp_Details where Emp_code='E00110' ";
          state.executeUpdate(query);
          }
          catch(Exception e) {
          System.out.println("Exception while executing query" +e);
          }
    }
}
```

I've discussed JDBC concepts in details. Using JDBC API, you can now create Java programs to interact with databases. I'll now explain the concepts of JSP.

An Introduction to JSP

Java Server Pages (JSP) is a technology used to create dynamic content on the Web. With the spread of the Internet and increasing number of users registering with Web sites, the static pages developed using HTML have became obsolete. Consider an example. A Web site displays a Welcome message along with the name to the registered user when the user logs on. Imagine that a static HTML page is developed for each user. In this scenario, when a user logs on, the server looks for the HTML page of the user and sends the page back to the client. If there are thousands of users, the server will take considerable amount of time to search for a user's HTML page. Therefore, the disadvantages are delay in sending the response; development time; and the increased probability of error. The solution lies in using a dynamic Web page.

You can use JSP to create dynamic Web pages. Essentially, a JSP page is an HTML document with embedded Java code. A JSP file must be saved with the .jsp extension.

A Web application consists of both presentation and business logic. Presentation represents the elements used to design the structure of a Web page in terms of page layout, color, and text. Business logic involves application of financial and business calculations. JSP technology segregates presentation from the business logic. For example, a Web designer can design HTML pages. At the same time, a Web developer can use JSP to write business logic. Therefore, both Web designers and Web developers can simultaneously work in their areas of specialization, leading to better quality and productivity.

A JSP page is converted to a servlet after compilation. Therefore, a JSP page incorporates all servlet functionalities. Servlets and JSP share common features, such as platform independence, creation of database-driven Web applications, and server-side programming capabilities. However, some differences exist between JSP and servlet. Some of these differences are listed as follows:

◆ Any change required in presentation and business logic necessitates recompilation of servlets. This is because the servlets tie up both an HTML file for the static content and Java code for the dynamic content, to handle presentation and business logic. On the other hand, JSP allows Java code to be embedded directly into an HTML page by using special tags. JSP files are automatically compiled and loaded onto the server. Therefore, any changes made to either presentation or business logic in a JSP is implemented automatically whenever the JSP page is loaded.

◆ Servlet programming requires extensive coding. In addition, there's no scope of division of labor between designers of static content and developers of dynamic content during servlets development or servlet modification. However, a JSP page facilitates both Web developers and the Web designer to work independently since JSP enables separate placement of the static and dynamic content.

I'll now discuss how to create a simple JSP page.

A Simple JSP Page

The following is a simple JSP code that displays the current date and time to the user.

```
<head>
<title>Welcome JSP</title>
</head>
<body>
<%@ page import="java.util.*"%>
Welcome user.
The date today is <%= new Date()%>
</body>
</html>
```

In the code above, the statements in bold are JSP code. Notice that the JSP code snippets are surrounded by <% and %> tags. You'll learn more about JSP tags later in this chapter.

To run this code, you need to save the file with the extension .jsp. Next, you need to copy the file in the c:\j2sdkee1.2.1\public_html folder. The public_html folder is the document root of the HTTP and HTTPS services. All the JSP files need to be stored in the public_html folder. However, you can change the document root by modifying the documentroot entry of the c:\j2sdkee1.2.1\config\web.properties file.

Next, type http://<server_name>:8000\<file_name>.jsp in the address bar of the browser. Ensure that the J2EE server is running. If you type the mentioned address in the browser on the same computer where the J2EE is running, you can type http://localhost:8000\<file_name>.jsp in the address bar of the browser. The output of the code is displayed in Figure 19-13.

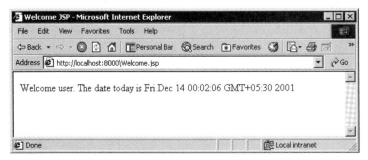

FIGURE 19-13 *The output of the JSP page is displayed and welcomes the user.*

I'll now discuss how JSP files are processed at the server end.

The Life Cycle of JSP

When a client browser sends a request to the server, the server recognizes the request for JSP files by the file extension. The server compiles and converts the JSP page into a servlet class. The server calls a process called *page compile* to convert the JSP page into a servlet. The process creates a servlet class and builds a service() method by extracting contents of the .jsp file. All the HTML tags in the JSP page are wrapped in the print method or the output methods. The Java code snippets between the JSP-specific tags in the .jsp file are copied into the servlet class. The JSP tags are ignored. The elements of the JSP file, HTML, and Java code appear in the servlet in the same order as they are in the JSP file. The servlet is then compiled and run. The servlet creates an HTTP response, which is sent to the client.

Compilation and generation of the .class file of the servlet is required only for the first time the JSP page is invoked by the server. The subsequent request will not go through the translation phase. Instead, the subsequent requests to the server will call the compiled .class file. Therefore, the overhead of the page compilation usually happens at the first call to the server. The life cycle of a JSP page is depicted in Figure 19-14.

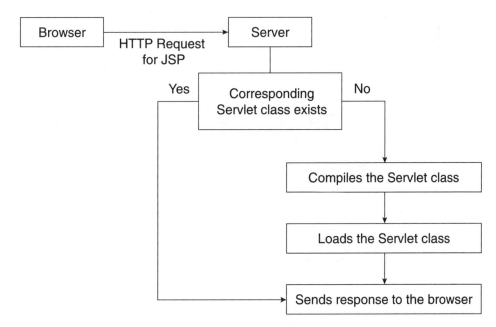

FIGURE 19-14 *The figure displays the life cycle of a JSP page.*

If you make any changes to the source .jsp file, the server recompiles and loads the corresponding servlet class in Java Virtual Machine (JVM). The servlet class remains in JVM until the source is changed again.

The request and response cycle of a JSP page is discussed in the following section.

The Request and Response Cycle of JSP

You're familiar with the request and response cycle of the interaction between a server and clients. The steps involved in the request and response cycle are listed here:

1. The client sends an HTTP request for a JSP page to the server. The request can be sent by using either a GET method or a POST method.

2. The browser identifies the JSP file and compiles and loads the corresponding servlet class if the servlet class is not already present in the JVM. The server calls the service() method. The default service() method often passes the request and response to the doGet() method or doPost() method. The servlet processes the input from the request and prepares an HTML page as a response.

3. The response is sent back to the client browser.

JSP can be used in different application models. These application models are discussed in the next section.

The JSP Application Models

The JSP application model defines how JSPs can interact with each other. The JSP 1.1 specification defines many models that describe how JSPs can interact. Some of these applications are listed here:

- ◆ The Simple Model
- ◆ The n-Tier Model
- ◆ The Loosely Coupled Model
- ◆ The Including Requests Model
- ◆ The Forwarding Requests Model

I'll now discuss each of these models in detail.

The Simple Model

The simple model consists of a single JSP page. In this model, there is one JSP page that accepts requests and generates responses. It interacts with a database or a legacy system to generate responses. For example, you can create a JSP page to determine the account type of a bank account holder. Generally, the account numbers of the same type follow a similar pattern. The JSP page will accept the account number and then, based on the account type, it can display the Home page of that particular account type. The advantage of using this model is that it's simple to develop. The disadvantage of using this model is that it doesn't scale easily when the number of users increases.

The n-Tier Model

In n-tier models, the JSP pages interact with server-side applications such as Enterprise JavaBeans or databases. These server-side applications handle access to the backend resources. For example, a JSP page that accepts logon information validates the logon information against that in the database. The database resides in the server and the JSP page might use EJB to interact with the database. The advantage of this model is scalability because server-side applications manage the resources on the server. These server-side applications can be used by many JSPs.

The Loosely Coupled Model

The loosely coupled model allows JSPs on remote systems to act as peers or have a client and server relationship. The applications can either be on the same intranet, or they can communicate over an extranet or the Internet. The JSP applications communicate over HTTP by using either HTML or XML. For example, an application might be distributed on two servers. A JSP page on a server accepts logon information. After validating the information, the JSP forwards the logon information to another JSP on another server. This JSP extracts the transaction details corresponding to the logon information and displays it to the user.

The Including Requests Model

You can use this model to distribute work among multiple JSPs. In the including requests model, one JSP page can handle requests and responses. This JSP page can use the output of the other JSPs in the model. For example, a theater manager needs a daily report on sales of various categories of seats. You can create a

JSP page for displaying each category of seat and then include the output of each JSP page in the JSP page, which displays the consolidated report. The advantage of using this model is that one JSP page handles all the requests and responses from the client. Other functions, such as interacting with the database and displaying results, are carried out by other JSPs in the application.

The Forwarding Requests Model

Another way of dividing work between JSPs is to use the forwarding requests model. This model is also known as the redirecting requests model. In this model, JSPs are chained by forwarding requests or responses to other JSPs. A JSP page accepts the request and forwards it to another JSP page, which may generate and send a response to the browser or forward the request to another JSP page after performing the required business calculations. For example, two types of users, customers and administrators, exist for an application. Different Home pages have been created for each user by using JSP. Depending on the type of user that has logged on, the Login JSP page of the application forwards the user to the Home page meant for the respective user. The advantage of using this model is the division of work between various JSPs. The disadvantage is the increasing complexity as the number of JSPs involved increases.

Now that you know what a JSP is and how JSPs function, you'll look at the components that make up a JSP.

The Components of JSP

A JSP page consists of the following components:

- ◆ HTML code
- ◆ JSP tags
- ◆ JSP implicit objects

The HTML code component of a JSP page decides the static presentation layout of the page. You can use any HTML tags on the JSP page. The output of the JSP page may vary on different browsers due to the difference in behavior of HTML tags on different browsers.

I'll now discuss JSP tags and implicit objects in detail.

JSP Tags

JSP tags are used to embed programming logic in HTML pages. JSP tags enable you to include Java code snippets in the JSP page. The various categories of JSP tags are:

- ◆ Declaration tags
- ◆ Expression tags
- ◆ Scriptlet tags
- ◆ Directive tags
- ◆ Comment tags
- ◆ Action tags

The Declaration Tags

JSP declaration tags are used to declare variables and methods that are accessible to the rest of the JSP page. For example, in the following code, the variables and methods are declared in JSP code.

```
</head>
<body>
<body bgproperties="fixed" bgcolor="#CCCCFF">
<p>Now declaring variables</p>
<%!
    int ctr=0;
    String name="";
%>
<p>Now declaring methods</p>
<%!
    void methodA(int i)
    {
        ctr=i ;
    }
%>
</body>
</html>
```

In this code, two variables and a method have been declared in JSP. Notice that the statements to declare the variables and the method are enclosed by the <%! tag and the %> tag. These tags are declaration tags. Although the variable ctr and the method methodA() are not declared in the same set of tags, the method is able to access the variable.

The Expression Tags

The expressions are a combination of constants and references to variables and methods. Expressions can exist either inside a JSP scriptlet or in a JSP expression tag. Scriptlets are the Java code embedded in JSPs. When an expression is in a JSP scriptlet, the expression is usually a part of the assignment or method call. In JSP scriptlets, assignments and assignments operators are declared in the same way as in the Java programs. The syntax for declaring a JSP expression tag is:

```
<%= expression %>
```

An example of JSP code that uses the expression tag is given as follows:

```
<head>
<title>Example JSP</title>
</head>
<body>
<body bgproperties="fixed" bgcolor="#CCCCFF">
<%!
    int ctr=10;
    String name="This is a test string.";
%>
<%= name %>
<%! int ctr1=ctr;%>
The value of ctr1 is <%= ctr1%>
</body>
</html>
```

In the code above, two variables, ctr and name, are declared and assigned values. The value of ctr is assigned to the ctr1 using the assignment operator. Next, the values of the variables are displayed by using the expression tags. The output of the code given above is displayed in Figure 19-15.

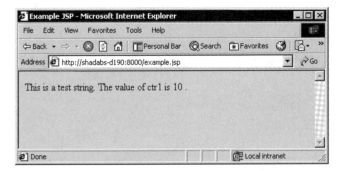

FIGURE 19-15 *The figure displays the output given by using the JSP expression tags.*

The Scriptlet Tags

Scriptlet tags are used to embed Java code in JSP pages. Therefore, using the scriptlet tags, Web developers can use the features of Java programming language in JSPs. A scriptlet provides several flow control structures such as decision and iteration control structures. Decision control structures allow developers to generate dynamic output on the Web pages based on the decision-making criterion. For instance, a JSP page can display a Welcome message to a registered user. If the user is not registered, the JSP page can request the user to register. The following code is an example.

```
<body>
<body bgproperties="fixed" bgcolor="#CCCCFF">
<%! String name="Mark";%>
<%
    if(name.equals("Mark"))
    {
%>
    <h2>Welcome Mark</h2>
<%    }
    else
%>
    <h2>You are not registered. Only registered user is allowed to view this
page.</h2>
</body>
</html>
```

The scriptlet tags consist of the <% tag and the %> tag. Notice that in the code given previously, the if...else statements are declared within the scriptlet tags. Similarly, you can use iteration control statements in JSP pages. The following example displays the use of iteration control statements in JSP scriptlet tags.

```
<html>
<title> Example JSP</title>
</html>
<body>
<body bgproperties="fixed" bgcolor="#CCCCFF">
<%! int ctr=0;%>
<%
    for(;ctr<=5;ctr++)
    {
%>
    <p>The value of ctr is <%=ctr%>
<%
    }
%>
</body>
</html>
```

The output of the preceding code is given in Figure 19-16.

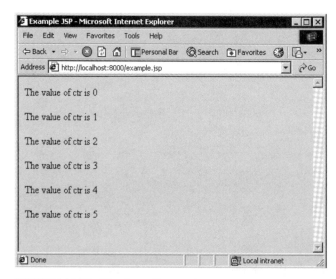

FIGURE 19-16 *The figure displays the output of the iteration statement in JSP.*

The Directive Tags

The next sets of tags that can be declared in JSP are directive tags. Directive tags are used to command JSPs to perform certain steps or behave in a specified way. There are three kinds of JSP directives:

♦ page

♦ include

♦ taglib

The page directives are used to set attributes for the JSP page. A page directive defines attributes that notify the servlet engine about the general settings of a JSP page. The syntax for page directives is given here:

```
<%@ page attribute="value"%>
```

The attributes that can be specified for a page directive are listed in Table 19-1.

Table 19-1 The Attributes of the Page Directive

Attribute	Description
contentType="text/html"	This attribute defines the type of the response.
extends="classname"	This attribute declares the parent class that will be extended by the resulting servlet class.
errorPage="page_url"	This attribute identifies an error page that will handle the exceptions, if any, in the JSP page.
import="file"	This attribute defines the file that will be available for the JSP page. This import directive is the same as the import statements in Java or C++ languages.
language="language"	This directive specifies the scripting language that will be used while compiling the JSP page. The language currently available is Java.
session="boolean(true/false)"	This directive is used to specify the availability of the session data for the JSP page. The default value is true.

At times, you might need to include some pages, such as HTML, in the JSP output. For example, you have created a standard HTML frame to be displayed on top of all the JSP pages of an application. Instead of writing the HTML code in every JSP page, you can create a separate HTML page and then give the command in the JSP page to include the output of the HTML in the JSP output. You can give this command by using the include directive. The include directive is used to specify the names of the files to be inserted during the compilation of the JSP page. Therefore, the content of the files included become part of the JSP page. The include directive can also be used to insert a part of the code that is common to multiple pages.

For example, in the following code, the JSP page includes a header file. This header file contains the name and logo of the organization.

```
<html>
<body bgproperties="fixed" bgcolor="#CCCCFF">
<%@ include file="orgHeader.htm"%>
The above content is of the orgHeader.htm file.
</body>
</html>
```

Notice the syntax of the include directive. The file attribute is used to specify the name of the file to be included. Now the output will display the content of the orgHeader.htm page above the rest of the content of the JSP page.

In the example given above, I have included the content of an HTML page. Similarly, you can include the content of another JSP page. Consider an example. In this example, you'll write a JSP page and then display its output by using the include directive in another JSP page. The first JSP page is given as follows:

```
<html>
<body>
<%! int ctr=0;%>
<%
    for(;ctr<=5;ctr++)
    {
%>
    <p>The value of ctr is <%=ctr%>
<%
    }
%>
</body>
</html>
```

You've saved the JSP given above as `includeJSP.jsp`. The following JSP code includes this file.

```
<html>
<body bgproperties="fixed" bgcolor="#CCCCFF">
<%@ include file="includeJSP.jsp"%>
<p>The above content is generated by another JSP page.
</body>
</html>
```

The output of the above code is given in Figure 19-17.

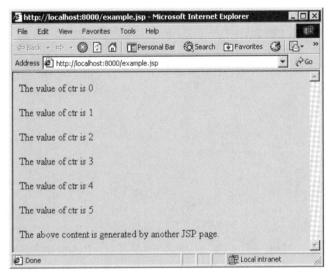

FIGURE 19-17 *The figure displays the output using the* `include` *directive.*

NOTE

The `taglib` directive is used to import a tag library into the JSP. A tag library is a collection of user-defined action tags. The `taglib` directive locates the tag library and assigns a handler to the specified tag library. The syntax of the `taglib` directive is:

```
<%@ taglib uri="tag_library_path" prefix="tag_handler" %>
```

(continues)

NOTE *(continued)*

The uri attribute specifies the location of the tag library, and the prefix attribute specifies the handle to the tag library. If the tag library defines custom actions, you can use the actions by using the syntax given here:

```
<tag_handler: custom_action />
```

You've looked at the directive tags. The next section explains how to insert comments.

The Comments Tags

Comments tags are used to insert comments in JSP code. There are three types of comments:

- ◆ HTML
- ◆ JSP
- ◆ Java

HTML comments are created using the `<!--` tag and the `-->` tag. These comments are added to the response of the JSP pages and the tags appear in HTML code that is sent to the browser as a response. The browser then ignores the comments and displays the output of the JSP page. For example, in the following JSP code, the HTML comments are used.

```
<html>
<body bgproperties="fixed" bgcolor="#CCCCFF">
<%! int ctr=0;%>
<% ctr=1000;%>
<!-- Simple HTML comment -->
<!-- The value of ctr is <%=ctr%> -->
</body>
</html>
```

The code of the resulting HTML page is given as follows:

```
<html>
<body bgproperties="fixed" bgcolor="#CCCCFF">
```

```
<!-- Simple HTML comment -->
<!-- The value of ctr is 1000 -->
</body>
</html>
```

Notice that the JSP expression tags in the first code are replaced by a value in the HTML page.

The JSP comments tags are used to document the JSP code. Unlike HTML tags, the JSP tags are not included in the resulting HTML page that is sent as a response to the browser. The JSP comments are created using the `<%--` tag and the `--%>` tag. The syntax for the JSP comments is given here.

```
<%-- This is an example of JSP comments. --%>
```

The Java comments are used to comment the Java code embedded in a JSP. The syntax for providing Java comments is the same as the syntax you use in Java programs. To comment out a single statement, the statement should be preceded with `//`. If multiple lines of code are to be commented out, use the `/*` and `*/` pair. Java code is always enclosed between scriptlet tags in a JSP page. Therefore, Java comments are also enclosed between scriptlet tags.

The Action Tags

The action tags extend the functionality of JSPs. The action tags allow JSPs to use objects created in Java, include other JSPs, forward requests to other JSPs, and interact with Java plugins. There are six action tags:

- `useBean`
- `setProperty`
- `getProperty`
- `include`
- `forward`
- `plugin`

The `useBean` tag, the `setProperty` tag, and the `getProperty` tag are used to handle JavaBeans. You'll learn more about these tags in Chapter 23, "Creating the Interest Calculator." You have already learned about the `include` action tag.

The `forward` action tag is used by a JSP page that accepts a request from a user and passes the request to another JSP page. Therefore, one JSP page accepts a request while another JSP page is responsible for sending the response back to the user. The syntax of the forward action tag is:

```
<jsp:forward page="JSP_path" />
```

Now look at an example of the forward action tag.

```
<html>
<body bgproperties="fixed" bgcolor="#CCCCFF">
<%! int ctr=0;
. . .
. . .
. . .
%>
<% if(ctr>=101)
    {
%>
    <jsp:forward page="show1.jsp"/>
<%
    }
    else
    {
%>
    <jsp:forward page="show2.jsp"/>
<%
    }
%>
</body>
</html>
```

In this example, the forward action is used to pass the request to another JSP page.

The plugin action tag is used to insert Java applets in the JSP pages. The syntax of the plugin action tag is given here:

```
<jsp:plugin type="bean¦applet" code="objectCode" codebase="URI of class file"
{align="alignment"}
{archive="archiveList"}
{height="height"}
{hspace="hspace"}
```

```
{jreversion="JREversion"}
{name="componentName"}
{vspace="vspace"}
{width="width"}
{nspluginurl="url"}
{iepluginurl="url"}>
<params>
    <param name="name" value="value">
</param>
<fallback>text</fallback>
</jsp:plugin>
```

The description of the highlighted attributes of the `plugin` action tag is given in Table 19-2.

Table 19-2 The Attributes of the Action Tag

Attribute	Description
type	The type of component being inserted in the JSP.
code	The applet class file.
codebase	Base URI for the applet class file.
align	Vertical or horizontal alignment.
archive	Archive list of the class files.
height	Initial height in pixels
hspace	Number of white spaces at the top and bottom of the applet.
jreversion	The version of Java Runtime Environment (JRE) required for the component.
Name	The name of the component of Java object.
vspace	Number of white spaces on the left and right of the applet.
width	Initial width in pixels.
nspluginurl	The URL from where the JRE version can be downloaded for Netscape Navigator.
iepluginurl	The URL from where the JRE version can be downloaded for Internet Explorer.

There can be parameters passed to an applet. JSPs can pass these parameters and values by using param tags. A param tag groups together all other param tags since there can be more than one param tag. The text within the fallback tag is displayed when the user's browser is not Java enabled and the user cannot view the applet.

An example of an applet plugged in a JSP page follows.

```
<html>
<head>
<title>Simple Calculator</title>
</head>
<body bgproperties="fixed" bgcolor="#CCCCFF">
<jsp:plugin type="applet" code="AdderApplet.class" width="200" height="250">
</jsp:plugin>
</body>
</html>
```

In this code, the plugin action tag is used to display the AdderApplet.class applet in the JSP page. The AdderApplet applet displays a simple calculator. The width and height attributes of the plugin action tag are specified. The output of the code given above is displayed in Figure 19-18.

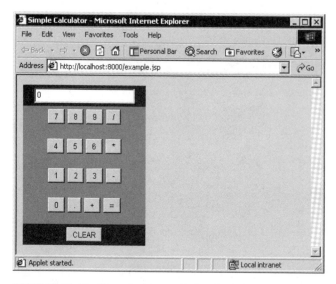

FIGURE 19-18 *The calculator is displayed using an applet in the JSP.*

> **NOTE**
>
> The AdderApplet.class has been downloaded from the **www.javafile.com** site. The site provides various applet classes and other Java programs that you can download at no charge.

You've now looked at JSP tags. The next component of a JSP page is JSP implicit objects. Next, I'll discuss JSP implicit objects.

JSP Implicit Objects

JSP pages have access to various objects, such as variables and instances of classes, that provide functionality to process a request from a browser and then generate a response. Objects in JSPs can be created implicitly or explicitly. Implicit objects are created by using directives, while explicit objects are created by using standard actions. Explicit objects, such as variables, are declared and created within the code of a JSP page. Explicit objects are accessible to the parent JSP page and other JSP pages according to the scope specified. Implicit objects are pre-defined variables that are accessible to all JSP pages. Some of the implicit objects are:

- request
- response
- session
- out
- pagecontext
- application
- page
- config

I'll now discuss each implicit object in detail.

The request *Implicit Object*

JSPs can access the requests from a browser by using request implicit objects. The request object implements the javax.servlet.http.HttpServletRequest interface. The HttpServletRequest interface represents a request from a browser. The interface provides various methods, such as `getParameter()`, that you can use to access user information and the data that is sent along with the request.

For example, consider the following syntax:

```
protocol://host:port_number/path?queryString
```

Here, `protocol` is the underlying mechanism used to transfer information between remote computers. Some of the protocols that can be specified are `http`, `https`, `ftp`, `rmi`, and `corba`. The `host` attribute specifies the machine name or the IP number of the machine to which the request will be forwarded. The `port_number` attribute specifies the port number at which the remote number will listen for the request. The `path` is the location of the JSP page, which will process the request. The `queryString` is a list of name and value pairs, which is passed as a request. An example of a URL is given here:

```
http://serverMachine:8000/sampleRequest.jsp?name=Mark&password=pass
```

The name and value pairs in the `queryString` are separated by an ampersand (&).

You can use the methods in the request objects to extract path and URL information. Some of these methods are given here.

- String `getPathInfo()`
- String `getPathTranslated()`
- String `getContextPath()`
- String `getQueryString()`
- String `getRequestURI()`

A sample program that uses the above methods is given as follows:

```html
<html>
<head>
<title>Usage of request Methods </title>
</head>
<form action="sampleRequest.jsp">
getPathInfo()= <%= request.getPathInfo() %>
getContextPath()= <%= request.getContextPath() %>
getQueryString()= <%= request.getQueryString() %>
getRequestURI()= <%= request.getRequestURI() %>
<input type="submit" name="submit" value="submit">
```

```
</form>
</body>
</html>
```

In this program, various methods of the `request` objects are used to extract information about the request sent by the browser. Notice that the methods of the `request` implicit object can be directly invoked by the JSP page.

The `request` object also provides methods for extracting host and port information about the machine from where the request originated. These methods can be used to implement security policies. Some of the machine-related methods are:

- String `getRemoteAddr()`
- String `getRemoteHost()`
- String `getServerName()`
- int `getServerPort()`
- String `getScheme()`
- String `getProtocol()`
- String `getMethod()`
- String `getCharacterEncoding()`
- boolean `isSecure()`
- int `getContentLength()`
- String `getContentType()`

The request can contain a list of name and value pairs as arguments to the JSP page. Some of the methods that can be used for extracting the parameters and their values from the request are given here:

- String `getParameter(String parameter_name)`
- Enumeration `getParameterNames()`
- String[] `getParameterValues(String parameter_name)`

The following example shown in Listing 19-1 uses request methods to enable you to extract the parameters. In this example, an HTML form has been created. This form will accept some input from the user and forward these inputs to the JSP page. The JSP page displays the request methods to extract these inputs and display the values to the user.

Listing 19-1   requestExample.htm

```
<html>
<body>
<form action="showParam.jsp">
<p>Enter Country: <input type="text" name="country"></p>
<p>Enter Capital: <input type="text" name="capital"></p>
<p>Enter City 1: <input type="text" name="city"></p>
<p>Enter City 2: <input type="text" name="city"></p>
<p>Enter City 3: <input type="text" name="city"></p>
<p>Enter City 4: <input type="text" name="city"></p>
<input type="Submit" name="Submit" value="Submit">
</form>
</body>
</html>
```

In the HTML code given above, the user will provide the inputs and then click the Submit button to submit the values to the JSP page. The code for the JSP page is shown in Listing 19-2.

Listing 19-2 showParam.jsp

```
<html>
<body>
You entered the following values in the HTML page:
<p>Country: <%= request.getParameter("country") %></p>
<% String[] city = request.getParameterValues("city"); %>
<p>Capital: <%= request.getParameter("capital") %></p>
<p>City 1: <%= city[0] %></p>
<p>City 2: <%= city%></p>
<p>City 3: <%= city%></p>
<p>City 4: <%= city%></p>
</body>
</html>
```

This JSP page accesses the parameters of the request by using the getParameter() method. There are multiple city parameters. Therefore, to access the values in the city parameter, the getParameterValues() method is used. The city values are stored in a String array. Figure 19-19 displays the output of the HTML page.

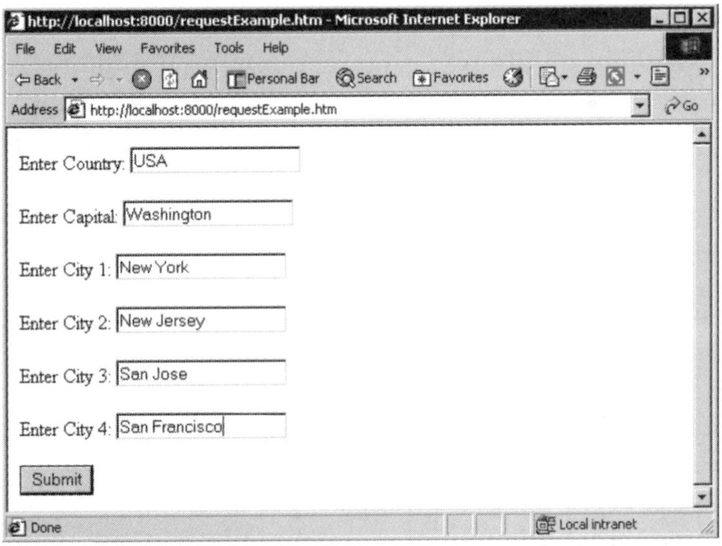

FIGURE 19-19 *The output of the HTML page*

After the form is submitted, the JSP page displays the input from the user. Figure 19-20 displays the JSP page.

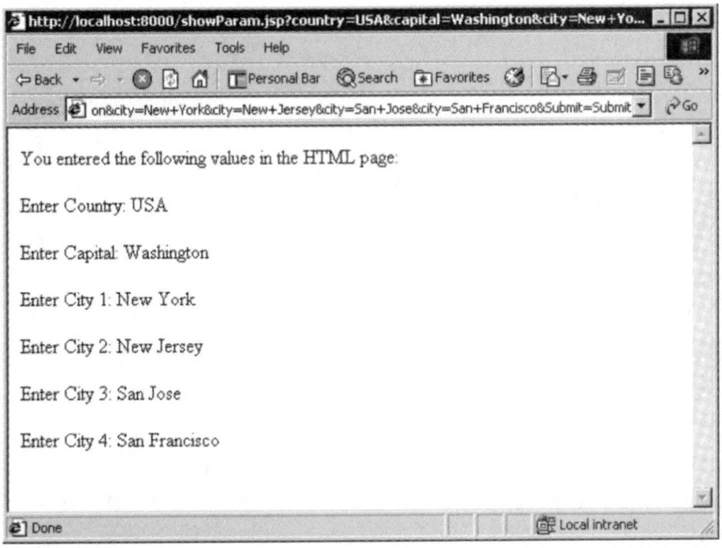

FIGURE 19-20 *The output of the JSP page*

The response *Implicit Object*

JSPs are used for creating dynamic Web pages. These dynamic pages can be created as a result of some conditions or calculations. The dynamic Web pages are sent as a response to the client browser. The output of various JSPs that you've seen in this chapter are the response generated by JSPs.

The session *Implicit Object*

The session implicit object is used to keep track of user information. The session needs to be tracked explicitly if the interaction between the client and the server happens over HTTP. This is because the HTTP protocol is a stateless protocol. The information regarding the communication between two computers is not maintained when you use the HTTP protocol. However, the session object along with the cookies enables a JSP page to keep track of the user information. *Cookies* are the objects that reside in the client's computer and store user information.

The session objects in JSPs are implemented using the HttpSession interface. The HttpSession interface provides JSPs with the functionality to store and share information. The HttpSession interface is accessible through the getSession() method of the HttpServletRequest interface. The methods of the HttpServlet-Request interface relevant to managing sessions are listed here:

- ◆ HttpSession getSession()
- ◆ HttpSession getSession(boolean)
- ◆ String getRequestSessionId()
- ◆ boolean isRequestedSessionIdValid()
- ◆ boolean isRequestedSessionIdFromCookie()
- ◆ boolean isRequestedSessionIdFromURL()

Every user who interacts with a JSP page is associated with a unique session object. This is accomplished by creating a unique ID for every user and then storing the ID as a cookie on the user's computer. The JSP page identifies users with this ID. This ID is also used to identify the session instance associated with the corresponding user. JSPs can store and access data in a session by using the setAttribute() method and the getAttribute() method. The session object is an implementation of the HttpSession interface. The methods of the interface are listed here:

- ◆ `Object getAttribute(String)`
- ◆ `void setAttribute(String, Object)`
- ◆ `void removeAttribute(String)`
- ◆ `Enumeration getAttributeNames()`
- ◆ `long getCreationTime()`
- ◆ `long getLastAccessedTime()`
- ◆ `int getMaxInactiveInterval()`
- ◆ `void setMaxInactiveInterval(int)`
- ◆ `boolean isNew()`
- ◆ `void invalidate()`
- ◆ `String getId()`

The out Implicit *Object*

The out implicit object is an instance of the `javax.servlet.jsp.JspWriter` class. The out object provides methods to generate output to the browser as well as the methods to control the behavior of the output.

The pageContext *Implicit Object*

The pageContext implicit object is an instance of the `javax.servlet.jsp.Page-Context` class. This class allows JSPs to access page attributes and forward or include the request object to or from application components.

The application *Implicit Object*

The application implicit object implements the `javax.servlet.ServletContext` interface. The application object is used for communicating with the servlet container, which manages the life cycle of servlets and maintains information about all servlets.

The page *Implicit Object*

The page implicit object represents the servlet that has been generated by processing the JSP. This is equivalent to Java's this object, which refers to the current object.

The config *Implicit Object*

The config object implements the javax.servlet.ServletConfig interface. The config object enables you to access the configuration data for initializing the JSP page. The methods of the ServletConfig class are listed here:

- String getInitParameter(String paramName)
- Enumeration getInitParameterNames()
- ServletContext getServletContext()
- String getServletName()

Now that I've discussed JSP concepts in detail, I'll use these concepts to create the logon page of the online banking application of Money Banks, Inc.

Writing Code for the Registration Page for Account Holders

Before proceeding to writing the code, you should examine the functionality of the page. Based on the design of the online banking application, the account holder enters the registration information in an HTML page. After the user submits the information, the details are passed on to a JSP page. The JSP page uses the JDBC API to connect to a database and verify the details provided by the account holder. If the details match, the account holder is registered with the application. The illustration in Figure 19-21 depicts this.

The code for the HTML page is listed in Listing 19-3.

Listing 19-3 Registered_usr_page.htm

```
<html>
<head>
<title>Money Banks, Inc. -- Registration Page for Account Holders</title>

  <form name="form" method="POST" action="Registered_User.jsp">
<script Language="JavaScript">
function checkPass()
{
```

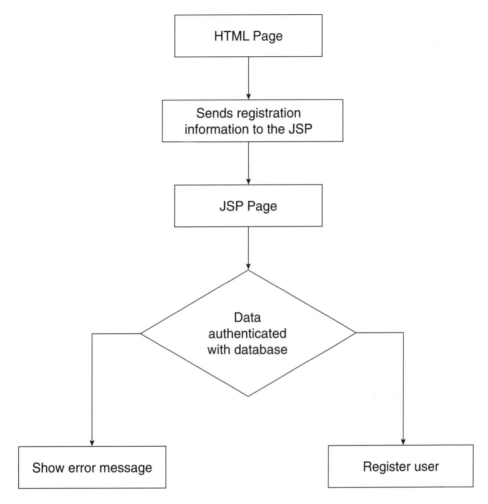

FIGURE 19-21 *The figure displays the flowchart for the registration page.*

```
if(((form.Act_No.value).length==0)||((form.pwd.value)!=(form.cnf_pwd.value))||((form
.pwd.value).length==0)||((form.cnf_pwd.value).length==0)||((form.frstName.value).len
gth==0)||((form.lstName.value).length==0)||((form.email.value).length==0)||((form.cu
st_id.value).length==0))
    {
        alert("Please provide complete and correct information");
    }
    else
```

```
        form.submit();
    }
</script>
</head>
<body bgproperties="fixed" bgcolor="#CCCCFF">
<p></p>
<table border="0" width="100%" height="42">
  <tr>
    <td width="50%" height="36"><b><font size="5" ><i>Money Banks,
Inc.</i></font></b></td>
    <td width="50%" height="36"></td>
  </tr>
</table>
<p align="center"><b><font size="4" >Registration Information for
Account Holders</font></b></p>
<p style="margin-top: 5; margin-bottom: 5"><font >Account
  Number: 
  <input type="text" name="Act_No" size="15"></font>
<p style="margin-top: 5; margin-bottom: 5"><font
>Password:            
<input type="password" name="pwd" size="15"></font>
<p style="margin-top: 5; margin-bottom: 5"><font >Confirm Password:<input
type="password" name="cnf_pwd" size="16">  </font>
<p style="margin-top: 5; margin-bottom: 5"><font
>Branch:            &nbs
p;   
</font><select size="1" name="Branch">
  <option>New York</option>
  <option>Washington</option>
  <option>San Jose</option>
  <option>California</option>
  <option>New Jersey</option>
  <option>Santa Cruz</option>
  </select> 
  <p style="margin-top: 5; margin-bottom: 5">
  <font >Account type:       <select size="1"
name="AC_Type">
  <option>Savings Account</option>
```

```
              <option>Checking Account</option>
              <option>Fixed Deposits</option>
              <option>Recurring Deposits</option>
              <option>Personal Loans</option>
              <option>Home Loans</option>
              <option>Consumer Loans</option>
              <option>Auto Loans</option>
              </select> </font>
      <p style="margin-top: 5; margin-bottom: 5"><font>Registration
      ID:    
      <input type="text" name="cust_id" size="20"></font> </p>
      <font >
      <p style="margin-top: 5; margin-bottom: 5">
      Name:                 
      <input type="text" name="frstName" size="20">
      <p style="margin-top: 5; margin-bottom: 5"> Mid
      Name:          
        <input type="text" name="midName" size="20">
        <p style="margin-top: 5; margin-bottom: 5"> Last
      Name:          
        <input type="text" name="lstName" size="20">
       <p style="margin-top: 5; margin-bottom: 5">E-mail:
                    
        
        <input type="text" name="email"
      size="20">            &n
      bsp;  
      </p>
      </font>
      <p align="center"><input type="button" value="Submit" name="Submit"
      onClick="checkPass()"><input type="reset" value="Reset" name="B2"></p>
      </form>
      <p align="right"><font ><a href="Home_page.htm">Home Page</a></font></p>
      </body>
      </html>
```

The output of this HTML page is displayed in Figure 19-22.

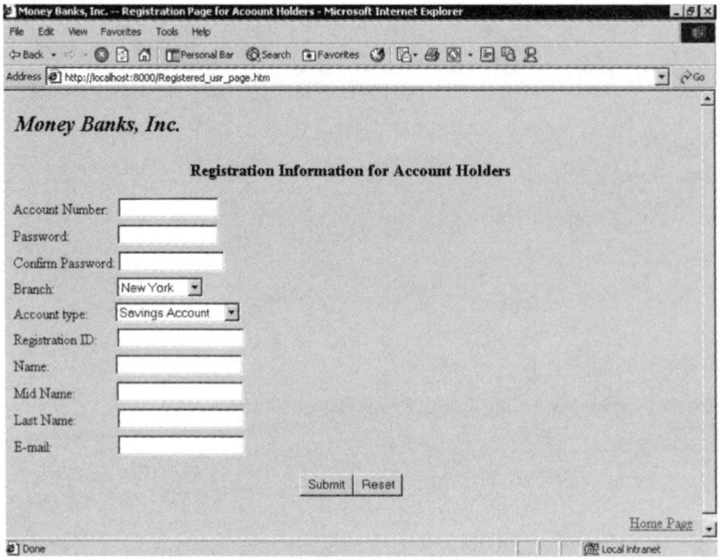

FIGURE 19-22 *This illustrates the output of the HTML page.*

The code for the JSP page is given in Listing 19-4.

Listing 19-4 Registered_User.jsp

```
<html>
<head>
<title>Money Banks, Inc. -- Home Page</title>
</head>
<body bgproperties="fixed" bgcolor="#CCCCFF">
<p></p>
<table border="0" width="100%" height="42">
  <tr>
    <td width="50%" height="36"><b><font size="5"><i>Money Banks,
Inc.</i></font></b></td>
    <td width="50%" height="36"></td>
  </tr>
```

```
</table>
<%! int ctr=0; %>
<%! int flag=0;
int flag1=0;
int flag2=0;
%>
    <%@ page import="java.util.*" %>
    <%@ page import="java.sql.*" %>
    <%@ page import="java.text.*" %>
    <%@ page import="java.sql.Date" %>
    <%@ page language = "java" %>
    <%
    try
    {
    Class.forName("sun.jdbc.odbc.JdbcOdbcDriver");
    Connection connect, connect1;
    connect=DriverManager.getConnection("jdbc:odbc:BankDataSource","","");
    connect1=DriverManager.getConnection("jdbc:odbc:BankDataSource","","");
    Statement state1,state2,state3;
    String str1, str2, str3, str4;
    state1 = connect.createStatement();
    str2=(String)request.getParameter("Act_No");
    String strQuery1 = "select * from Login_Info" ;
    ResultSet result1 = state1.executeQuery(strQuery1);
    while(result1.next())
    {
        str1=(String)result1.getString("Account_No");

        str1=str1.trim();
        str2=str2.trim();
        if(str2.equals(str1))
        {
            flag=1;
            out.println("found");
            break;
        }
    }
    out.println("flag"+flag);
```

```
        state2 = connect1.createStatement();
        str4=request.getParameter("cust_id");
        str4=str4.trim();
        out.println(str4);
        String strQuery2 = "select * from Register_Info where Register_Id='" + str4
+"'";
        String fname,
frstname,lname,lstname,mname,midname,email,e_mail,actype,act_type,branch,
branch_city;
        frstname=request.getParameter("frstName");
        frstname=frstname.trim();
        lname=request.getParameter("lstName");
        lname=lname.trim();
        mname=request.getParameter("midName");
        mname=mname.trim();
        email=request.getParameter("email");
        email=email.trim();
        actype=(String)request.getParameter("AC_Type");
        actype=actype.trim();
        branch=(String)request.getParameter("Branch");
        branch=branch.trim();
        ResultSet result2 = state2.executeQuery(strQuery2);
        while(result2.next())
        {
            fname=result2.getString("First_Name");
            fname=fname.trim();
            midname=result2.getString("Middle_Name");
            midname=midname.trim();
            lstname=result2.getString("Last_Name");
            lstname=lstname.trim();
            e_mail=result2.getString("email_id");
            e_mail=e_mail.trim();

            if((fname.equals(frstname))&&(lname.equals(lstname))&&(mname.equals(mid-
name))&&(email.equals(e_mail)))
            {
                ctr=1;
                flag1=2;
```

```
                break;
        }
        out.println(flag1);


    }
    connect1.close();
    connect1=DriverManager.getConnection("jdbc:odbc:BankDataSource","","");
    state3 = connect1.createStatement();
    String strQuery3 = "select * from AcHolder_Info where Register_Id='" + str4
+"'";
    ResultSet result3 = state3.executeQuery(strQuery3);
    while(result3.next())
    {
        act_type=result3.getString("Account_Type");
        act_type=act_type.trim();
        branch_city=result3.getString("Branch");
        branch_city=branch_city.trim();
        out.println("branch"+branch);
        out.println(branch_city);
        if((actype.equals(act_type))&&(branch.equals(branch_city)))
        {

            ctr=1;
            flag2=3;
            break;
        }
out.println(flag2);

    }
    connect1.close();
    if((flag!=1)&&(flag1==2)&&(flag2==3))
    {

connect1=DriverManager.getConnection("jdbc:odbc:BankDataSource","","");
        String pwd=request.getParameter("pwd");
        PreparedStatement stat4= connect1.prepareStatement("insert into
Login_Info values(?,?,?)");
        stat4.setString(1,str4);
```

```
                    stat4.setString(2,str2);
                    stat4.setString(3,request.getParameter("pwd"));
                    stat4.executeUpdate();
                    out.println("Congratulations!!!! You are now registered online. Click
the login button to login and view your account details.");
            %>
<input type="button" value="Login" name="Login" onClick="login()">
        <%
        }
        else
        {
            out.println("<b>");
            out.println("Sorry, your request for registration is rejected. Either you
are already registered online or the data supplied doesn't match with our data-
base.");
        }
        }
        catch(Exception e)
        {
            out.println("done exception" +e);
        }
        %>
<p>
<%
out.println("<h4>");
%>
</p>
<p><input type="button" value="Back to Register Page" name="Back"
onClick="goBack()">  <input type="button" value="Cancel" name="Login"
onClick="goHome()"></p>

<script Language="JavaScript">
function goBack()
{
    open("Registered_usr_page.htm");
}
function goHome()
{
```

```
    open("Home_page.htm");
}
function login()
{
    open("Login_page.htm");
}
</script>
<p> </p>
</body>
</html>
```

I'll now analyze the code. In this code, the information provided by an account holder in the HTML page is validated with that in the databases. There are three types of information that is being validated. These validations are:

1. The account holder shouldn't be already registered with the banking application.

2. The name and e-mail information matches the information in the database.

3. The account details, such as account type and branch, provided by the account holder is correct.

I'll now look at the code to perform these validations.

Checking for Registration with the Application

The code snippet written to check whether the account number entered by the user is already registered with the application is given as follows:

```
        Class.forName("sun.jdbc.odbc.JdbcOdbcDriver");
Connection connect, connect1;
connect=DriverManager.getConnection("jdbc:odbc:BankDataSource","","");
connect1=DriverManager.getConnection("jdbc:odbc:BankDataSource","","");
Statement state1,state2,state3;
String str1, str2, str3, str4;
state1 = connect.createStatement();
str2=(String)request.getParameter("Act_No"); //JSP code
String strQuery1 = "select * from Login_Info" ;
ResultSet result1 = state1.executeQuery(strQuery1);
```

```
while(result1.next())
{
    str1=(String)result1.getString("Account_No");

    str1=str1.trim();
    str2=str2.trim();
    if(str2.equals(str1))
    {
        flag=1;
        out.println("found");
        break;
    }
}
```

In this code, a connection with the database is established. Next, the account number entered by the user in the HTML page is obtained. Then, an SQL query is executed to select rows from the Login_Info table. The Login_Info table contains account numbers that have been registered with the online banking application. If the account number already exists in the Login_Info table, the variable flag is set to 1.

Validating Personal Information

The personal information is validated to check whether the name and the e-mail address provided by the user matches with existing data in the database. The code to do this is given here:

```
state2 = connect1.createStatement();
str4=request.getParameter("cust_id");
str4=str4.trim();
out.println(str4);
String strQuery2 = "select * from Register_Info where Register_Id='" + str4
+"'";
String fname,
frstname,lname,lstname,mname,midname,email,e_mail,actype,act_type,branch,
branch_city;
frstname=request.getParameter("frstName");
frstname=frstname.trim();
lname=request.getParameter("lstName");
lname=lname.trim();
```

```
mname=request.getParameter("midName");
mname=mname.trim();
email=request.getParameter("email");
email=email.trim();
actype=(String)request.getParameter("AC_Type");
actype=actype.trim();
branch=(String)request.getParameter("Branch");
branch=branch.trim();
ResultSet result2 = state2.executeQuery(strQuery2);
while(result2.next())
{
    fname=result2.getString("First_Name");
    fname=fname.trim();
    midname=result2.getString("Middle_Name");
    midname=midname.trim();
    lstname=result2.getString("Last_Name");
    lstname=lstname.trim();
    e_mail=result2.getString("email_id");
    e_mail=e_mail.trim();

    if((fname.equals(frstname))&&(lname.equals(lstname))&&(mname.equals(mid-
name))&&(email.equals(e_mail)))
    {
        ctr=1;
        flag1=2;
        break;
    }
}
```

In this code, an SQL query is performed to obtain a row from the `Register_Info` table based on the account number provided by the user. The information entered by the user in the HTML page is then obtained. The SQL query is then executed and the information in the database is matched with the information provided by the user. If these pieces of information match, the value of the `flag1` variable is set to 2.

Validating Account Details

The account details, such as account number and account type, provided by the user need to be validated. The code to do this is given here:

```
    state3 = connect1.createStatement();
String strQuery3 = "select * from AcHolder_Info where Register_Id='" + str4
+"'";
    ResultSet result3 = state3.executeQuery(strQuery3);
    while(result3.next())
    {
        act_type=result3.getString("Account_Type");
        act_type=act_type.trim();
        branch_city=result3.getString("Branch");
        branch_city=branch_city.trim();
        out.println("branch"+branch);
        out.println(branch_city);
        if((actype.equals(act_type))&&(branch.equals(branch_city)))
        {

            ctr=1;
            flag2=3;
            break;
        }
    }
```

In this code, the account type and the branch selected by the user in the HTML page is obtained and matched with account type and branch of the corresponding account in the database. If the two match, the value of the flag2 variable is set to 3.

Next, the values of various flag variables are checked to find out the status of the validations. The code for doing this is given here:

```
if((flag!=1)&&(flag1==2)&&(flag2==3))
{
        connect1=DriverManager.getConnection("jdbc:odbc:BankDataSource","","");
        String pwd=request.getParameter("pwd");
        PreparedStatement stat4= connect1.prepareStatement("insert into
Login_Info values(?,?,?)");
        stat4.setString(1,str4);
        stat4.setString(2,str2);
        stat4.setString(3,request.getParameter("pwd"));
        stat4.executeUpdate();
        out.println("Congratulations!!!! You are now registered online. Click
the login button to login and view your account details.");
    %>
```

```
<input type="button" value="Login" name="Login" onClick="login()">
    <%
    }
    else
    {
        out.println("<b>");
        out.println("Sorry, your request for registration is rejected. Either you
are already registered online or the data supplied doesn't match with our data-
base.");
    }
```

In this code snippet, the value of the variables is checked using the `if` statement. If all the variables have values indicating that the registration information is valid, the account number and password is added to the `Login_Info` table. A message regarding successful registration is displayed to the user. However, if the registration attempt fails, an error message is displayed.

I'll now explain the functionality of the code.

Figure 19-23 displays the HTML page with the details entered by the user.

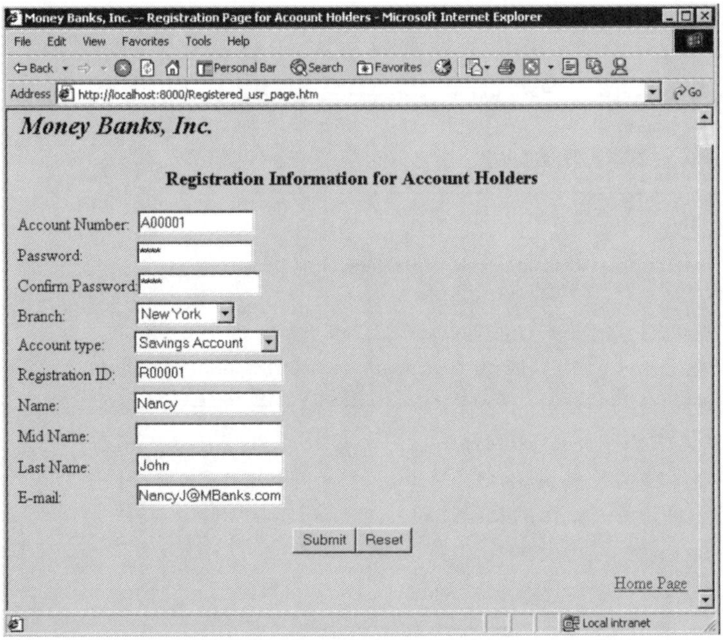

FIGURE 19-23 *This figure displays the HTML page, with details filled in by the user.*

When the user clicks the Submit button the form is submitted to the JSP page and the information is transferred to the JSP page by using the POST method. The JSP page uses the JDBC API to validate the details. On successful registration, the output as shown in Figure 19-24 is displayed.

FIGURE 19-24 *The figure shows the output of the registration page.*

If the information fails the validation test, the JSP page displays an error message as shown in Figure 19-25.

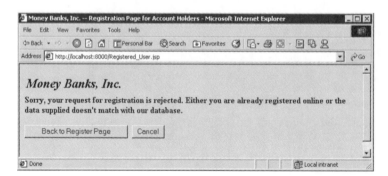

FIGURE 19-25 *A "Reject" message is displayed if the information fails the validation test.*

Summary

In this chapter, you created the Registration page of the online banking application of Money Banks, Inc., by using the concepts of JDBC and JSP. The Registration page validates the information provided by the user before registering the user. These validations are performed comparing the information stored in the databases. You learned to use JDBC to create Java programs capable of interacting with databases. You looked at various database drivers, and advantages and disadvantages of each of these drivers. Next, you studied the classes and interfaces of the JDBC API. The `java.sql` package makes up the JDBC API. You used the JDBC API to query, insert, and delete rows in databases.

In this chapter, you also learned about the JSP concepts in detail. You learned the benefits and advantages of using JSPs and JSPs in relationship with servlets. The role and use of JSP pages in various applications was discussed in this chapter. Various components that make up a JSP page were discussed in detail in this chapter. These components are HTML code, JSP tags, and implicit objects.

Chapter 20

In this chapter, you'll learn how to create the Login page for the online banking application you are developing for Money Banks, Inc.

The Login Page

As the name suggests, the Login page of the online banking application at Money Banks, Inc., will be used to accept and validate logon information from the users. After validation, a user will be allowed to access the application and perform transactions. The logon information generally includes username and password. At Money Banks, the development team decides to use the account number and password as logon information because every account holder has a unique account number. The technologies used to validate logon information are:

◆ JDBC
◆ JSP

You learned about these technologies in detail in the Chapter 19, "Creating the Registration Page for Account Holders." JDBC is required because the details of account numbers and corresponding passwords are stored in a database.

You'll now create the Login page.

Creating the Login Page

The code for the Login page is given in Listing 20-1.

Listing 20-1 Login_page.htm

```
<html>
<head>
<title>Money Banks, Inc. -- Login Page</title>
</head>
<body bgproperties="fixed" bgcolor="#CCCCFF">
<form name="form" method="POST" action="Login_page.jsp">
```

```
<p align="center"></p>
<table border="0" width="100%" height="42">
  <tr>
    <td width="50%" height="36"><b><font size="5" ><i>Money Banks,
Inc.</i></font></b></td>
    <td width="50%" height="36"></td>
  </tr>
</table>
<p align="center"><b><font size="4" >Login Information</font></b></p>
  <p ><font >Account Number:  </font><input type="text" name="txtActNumber"
size="20"></p>
  <p >
<font >
Password:            
  </font><input type="password" name="txtUsrPwd" size="20"> </p>
  <p align="center"><input type="button" value="View Account Details" name="login"
onClick="check()"> <input type="button" value="Cancel" name="cancel"
onClick="home()"></p>
</form>
<p > </p>
<script language="JavaScript">
function check()
{
    if(((((form.txtActNumber.value).length==0)¦¦((form.txtUsrPwd.value).length==0)))
    alert("Please enter both account number and password.");
    else
    form.submit();
}
function home()
{
    open("Home_page.htm");
}
</script>
</body>
</html>
```

The output of the above HTML page is displayed in Figure 20-1.

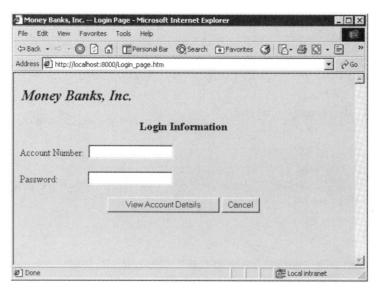

FIGURE 20-1 *The figure displays the output of* `Login_page.htm`, *showing Login Information.*

In this HTML page, two JavaScript methods have been used. These methods are:

- ◆ `check()`
- ◆ `home()`

Before looking at these methods, I'll discuss JavaScript.

JavaScript is a scripting language. These languages make a Web page dynamic. A *script* is a set of instructions that is interpreted by the Web browser. A script allows the developer to capture keystrokes on the client side, without any server interaction.

JavaScript is available in two formats: client-side and server-side. The client-side JavaScript is available to HTML pages and it is displayed in a Web browser. They are used to perform client-side validations on Web pages. The server-side Java-Script is used to perform validations at the server-end, such as communicating with a database to validate the logon information.

The syntax of JavaScript is similar to Java. Some of the characteristics of Java-Script are given as follows:

- ◆ *JavaScript is event-driven.* It can be programmed to respond to user actions through input devices.

◆ *JavaScript is platform-independent.* JavaScript programs run within an HTML document. The browser needs to support the execution of JavaScript.

◆ *JavaScript does not involve time-consuming compilation.* Scripts can be developed in a relatively short time.

◆ *JavaScript is easy to learn.* It does not have a complex syntax and set of rules.

◆ *JavaScript is object-based.* An object-oriented program handles a program as a collection of individual objects that are used for specific tasks, and not as a sequence of statements that perform a specific task.

◆ JavaScript supports constructs such as if...else, switch...case, while, for, and do...while.

◆ Like Java, JavaScript is case-sensitive.

There are various events, such as the click of the Submit button and change of focus from one object to another, that are generated while a user interacts with a Web page. The events are listed in Table 20-1.

Table 20-1 The Events Generated on a Web Page

Event	Description
Click	This event occurs when a user clicks a form element or a link.
Change	This event occurs when a user changes the value of a form field.
Focus	This event occurs when an element in a form gains focus.
Load	This event occurs when a page is loaded into the browser.
MouseOver	This event occurs when a user moves the mouse pointer over a link or an object.
MouseOut	This event occurs when the mouse pointer leaves the link or an object.
Select	This event occurs when a user selects a field in a form.
Blur	This event occurs when the input focus is removed from a field.

JavaScript provides event handlers for each of these events. The event handlers are listed in Table 20-2.

Table 20-2 The Event Handlers

Field	Event Handler
Button	onClick
Reset	onClick
Submit	onClick
Radio	onClick
Checkbox	onClick
Link	onClick, onMouseOver, and onMouseOut
Form	onSubmit and onReset
Text	onChange, onFocus, onBlur, and onSelect
Textarea	onChange, onFocus, onBlur, and onSelect
Select	onChange, onFocus, and onBlur
Image	onAbort and onError
Area	onClick, onMouseOver, and onMouseOut
Window	OnLoad, onUnLoad, and onError

The syntax of an HTML code that uses JavaScript is given as follows:

```
<HTML>
<HEAD> <TITLE> Title </TITLE>
<SCRIPT language="JavaScript">
<!--
---write JavaScript code here---
//-->
</SCRIPT>
</HEAD>
<BODY>
...
<SCRIPT>
<!--
---write JavaScript code here---
// -->
</SCRIPT>
</BODY> </HTML>
```

I'll now write a simple HTML code that uses JavaScript to display a message when the button on the HTML page is clicked.

```html
<html>
<head>
<title>JavaScript Example</title>
</head>
<body>
<script language="JavaScript">
function showMsg()
{
    alert("You have clicked the button.");
}
</script>
<form method="POST">
<p><input type="button" value="Button" name="button" onClick="showMsg()"></p>
</form>
</body>
</html>
```

The code above displays a message when the button is clicked. On the click of the button, the showMsg() method is called. The showMsg() is written in JavaScript, therefore the body of the method is enclosed between <script> and </script> tags. In the method, the alert() method, which is a built-in JavaScript method, displays the message.

I'll now explain the JavaScript methods in Listing 20-1 in detail.

The check() *Method*

The JavaScript code for the check() method is given here:

```javascript
function check()
{
    if((((form.txtActNumber.value).length==0)||((form.txtUsrPwd.value).length==0)))
    alert("Please enter both account number and password.");
    else
    form.submit();
}
```

The check() method is called when the View Account Details button is clicked. This code will check if the user has provided all the required information. If any of the two text boxes, account number and password, is blank, an error message is displayed. If the user has provided all the information, the page is submitted.

The home() *Method*

```
function home()
{
    open("Home_page.htm");
}
```

The home() method is called when the user clicks the Cancel button. This method will open the Home page of the banking application.

After all the fields are entered and the View Account Details button is clicked, the logon information is passed to the Login_page.jsp page where it is validated with the database. The code for the Login_page.jsp page is given in Listing 20-2.

Listing 20-2 Login_page.jsp

```
<html>
<head>
<title>Money Banks, Inc. -- Login Page</title>
</head>
<body bgproperties="fixed" bgcolor="#CCCCFF">
<form name="form" method="POST">
    <%@ page import="java.util.*" %>
    <%@ page import="java.sql.*" %>
    <%@ page import="java.text.*" %>
    <%@ page import="java.sql.Date" %>
    <%@ page language = "java" %>
<%! int flag=0; %>
<%! int ctr=0; %>
    <%
    try
    {
    Class.forName("sun.jdbc.odbc.JdbcOdbcDriver");
```

```
Connection connect;
connect=DriverManager.getConnection("jdbc:odbc:BankDataSource","","");
Statement state;
String actNumber,actNo, password,pwd;
state = connect.createStatement();
actNumber=(String)request.getParameter("txtActNumber");
password=(String)request.getParameter("txtUsrPwd");
password=password.trim();
actNumber=actNumber.trim();
String strQuery1 = "select * from Login_Info where Account_No='" + actNumber
+"'";
ResultSet result1 = state.executeQuery(strQuery1);
while(result1.next())
{
    actNo=(String)result1.getString("Account_No");
    pwd=(String)result1.getString("Password");
    actNo=actNo.trim();
    pwd=pwd.trim();

if((actNo.equals(actNumber))&&(pwd.equals(password))&&(actNo.length()!=0)&&(pwd.leng
th()!=0))
    {
        flag=1;
%>
<jsp:forward page="actDetails.jsp"/>
<%
    }
}
}
catch(Exception e)
{
}
%>
<p align="center"></p>
<table border="0" width="100%" height="42">
  <tr>
    <td width="50%" height="36"><b><font size="5" ><i>Money Banks,
Inc.</i></font></b></td>
```

```html
      <td width="50%" height="36"></td>
   </tr>
</table>
<p align="center"><b><font size="4" >Login Information</font></b></p>
   <p ><font >Account Number:  </font><input type="text" name="txtActNumber"
size="20"></p>
   <p ><font
>Password:           
   </font><input type="password" name="txtUsrPwd" size="20"> </p>
   <p align="center"><input type="submit" value="View Account Details" name="login"
> <input type="button" value="Cancel" name="cancel" onClick="home()"></p>
</form>
<p > </p>
<script language="JavaScript">
function home()
{
    open("Home_page.htm");
}
</script>
</body>
</html>
```

On successful logon, the Login_page.jsp page forwards the request to the acDe-
tails.jsp page. The output of the acDetails.jsp page is displayed in Figure 20-2.

Now I'll analyze the code and examine the logon process in the banking application.

```java
Class.forName("sun.jdbc.odbc.JdbcOdbcDriver");
Connection connect;
connect=DriverManager.getConnection("jdbc:odbc:BankDataSource","","");
Statement state;
String actNumber,actNo, password,pwd;
state = connect.createStatement();
actNumber=(String)request.getParameter("txtActNumber");
password=(String)request.getParameter("txtUsrPwd");
password=password.trim();
actNumber=actNumber.trim();
String strQuery1 = "select * from Login_Info where Account_No='" + actNumber
```

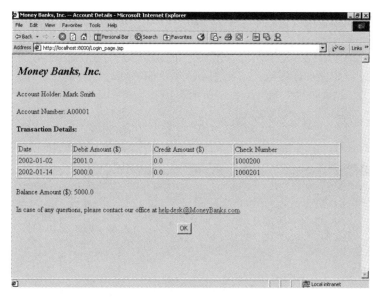

FIGURE 20-2 *The figure displays the output of* Login_page.jsp, *showing Account Details.*

```
+"'";
    ResultSet result1 = state.executeQuery(strQuery1);
```

In Login_page.jsp, the code snippet that is given above establishes a connection with a database. This is done using the JDBC concepts. The Login_Info table that holds the logon information about the registered users is queried to obtain the rows in the table.

```
while(result1.next())
    {
        actNo=(String)result1.getString("Account_No");
        pwd=(String)result1.getString("Password");
        actNo=actNo.trim();
        pwd=pwd.trim();

if((actNo.equals(actNumber))&&(pwd.equals(password))&&(actNo.length()!=0)&&(pwd.leng
th()!=0))
        {
            flag=1;
    %>
    <jsp:forward page="actDetails.jsp"/>
```

If the logon information matches the information in the database, the request is forwarded to another JSP page, which is the actDetails.jsp. If the user provides incorrect information, the JSP page will not be forwarded. Instead, the JSP page will again display the text boxes to accept logon information from the user. The output of the Login_page.jsp page after an unsuccessful logon attempt is displayed in Figure 20-3.

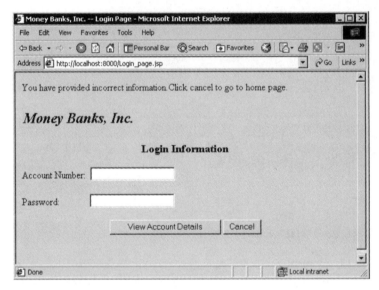

FIGURE 20-3 *The output, after an unsuccessful login attempt, is displayed.*

Summary

In this chapter, you learned how to create the Login page of the online banking application at Money Banks, Inc. You used JDBC and JSP to create the Login page. You learned how the JSP code validates the logon information by using the JDBC concepts to connect to a database. In this chapter, you also learned about the scripting language, JavaScript. JavaScript methods were used in developing the Login page to ensure that a user submits all the required logon information.

Chapter 21

In this chapter, you'll create the Home page of the banking application. The Home page will provide viewers with links to other pages of the application.

The Home Page

Every Web site has a Home page, which is the central location where you can access other pages of the application. Listing 21-1 contains the code for the Home page of the banking application.

Listing 21-1   Home_page.htm

```html
<html>
<head>
<title>Money Banks, Inc. -- Home Page</title>
</head>
<body bgproperties="fixed" bgcolor="#CCCCFF">
<table border="0" width="100%" height="42">
  <tr>
    <td width="50%" height="36"><b><i><font size="5">Money Banks,
Inc.</font></i></b></td>
    <td width="50%" height="36"></td>
  </tr>
</table>
<p> </p>
<table border="1" width="100%">
  <tr>
    <td width="33%"><b><font size="4">Banking </font></b></td>
    <td width="33%"><b><font size="4">Loans</font></b></td>
    <td width="34%"><b><font size="4">Others</font></b></td>
  </tr>
  <tr>
    <td width="33%"><font size="4"><b><font color="#FF0000"> </font></b><font
color="#FF0000"> <b>  </b></font></font><font color="#FF0000" size="4"><b>
```

```
      </b><a href="http:\\localhost:8000\checkingAccounts.htm">Checking
Accounts</a></font></td>
      <td width="33%"><font color="#FF0000" size="4">  <a
href="http:\\localhost:8000\personalLoans.htm">Personal Loans</a></font></td>
      <td width="34%"><font color="#FF0000" size="4">  <a
href="http:\\localhost:8000\Interest_calc.htm">Interest
        Calculator</a></font></td>
  </tr>
  <tr>
      <td width="33%"><font color="#FF0000" size="4">  <a
href="http:\\localhost:8000\savingsAccount.htm">Savings Accounts</a></font></td>
      <td width="33%"><font color="#FF0000" size="4">  <a
href="http:\\localhost:8000\homeLoans.htm">Home Loans</a></font></td>
      <td width="34%"><font color="#FF0000" size="4">  <a
href="http:\\localhost:8000\currExchange.htm">Foreign Exchange
        Rates</a></font></td>
  </tr>
  <tr>
      <td width="33%"><font color="#FF0000" size="4">  <a
href="http:\\localhost:8000\fixedDeposits.htm">Fixed Deposits</a></font></td>
      <td width="33%"><font color="#FF0000" size="4">  <a
href="http:\\localhost:8000\consumerLoans.htm">Consumer Loans</a></font></td>
      <td width="34%"><font color="#FF0000" size="4">  <a
href="http:\\localhost:8000\bankBranches.htm">Bank Branches</a></font></td>
  </tr>
  <tr>
      <td width="33%"><font color="#FF0000" size="4">  <a
href="http:\\localhost:8000\recurringDeposits.htm">Recurring
Deposits</a></font></td>
      <td width="33%"><font color="#FF0000" size="4">  <a
href="http:\\localhost:8000\autoLoans.htm">Auto Loans</a></font></td>
      <td width="34%"><font color="#FF0000" size="4">  <a
href="http:\\localhost:8000\contact.htm">Contact Us</a></font></td>
  </tr>
</table>
<p align="right"><font size="3">Registered users, click the Login button.</font>
<input type="button" value="Login" name="btLogin" onClick="showLoginHtm()"></p>
<p align="right"><font size="3">Registered A/c holders, </font>
```

```
<font size="3" color="#FF0000"> <a
href="http:\\localhost:8000\Registered_usr_page.htm"> click here to register for
online
banking</a>.</font>
<p align="right"><font size="3">Non A/c holders,</font><font size="3"
color="#FF0000"> <a href="http:\\localhost:8000\Register_page.htm"> click here to
apply for an account</a>. </font></p>
<p > </p>
<script language="JavaScript">
function showLoginHtm()
{
            open("Login_page.htm");
}
</script>
</body>
</html>
```

Listing 21-1 is a pure HTML code. A JavaScript method called showLoginHtm() has been declared in the code. This method is invoked when a user clicks the Login button. This method will display the Login page to the user. The output of the above HTML code is displayed in Figure 21-1.

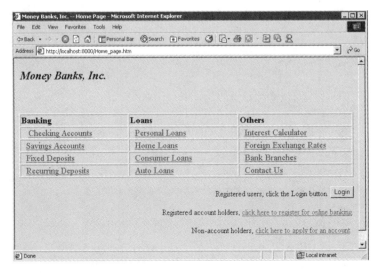

FIGURE 21-1 *The Home page is displayed in the figure.*

Summary

In this chapter, you learned how to create the Home page of the banking application. This page has been created using the HTML code. The Home page provides you with the navigation links for other pages of the application.

Chapter 22

Creating a Registration Page for Non-Account Holders

In this chapter, you'll create the Registration page for non-account holders of Money Banks, Inc. This page will enable a user to send requests for opening a new bank account.

The Registration Page for Non-Account Holders

Based on the design of the banking application, the Registration page for non-account holders will enable the viewers to apply for opening new bank accounts at Money Banks, Inc. The Registration page will accept the following details from the user:

- Branch
- Account Type
- First Name
- Middle Name
- Last Name
- Date of Birth
- Work Phone
- Address
- ZIP
- E-mail ID
- Home Phone

The code for the registration page is given in Listing 22-1.

Listing 22-1 Register_page.htm

```
<html>
<head>
<title>Money Banks, Inc. -- Register Page</title>
```

```
</head>
<body bgproperties="fixed" bgcolor="#CCCCFF">
<form name="form" method="POST" action="http:\\localhost:8000\Register_page.jsp">
<script Language="JavaScript">
function year()
{
            for (i=1900;i<2000;i++)
            {
                                    document.write("<option
value="+i+">"+i+"</option>");
            }
}
function date()
{
            for (i=01;i<=31;i++)
            {
                                    document.write("<option
value="+i+">"+i+"</option>");
            }
}
function verify()
{
            var ctr=0;
            var txtFrstName1=form.txtFrstName.value;
            var txtLastName1=form.txtLastName.value;
            var month1=form.month.value;
            var date1=form.date.value;
            var year1=form.year.value;
            var phone_office1=form.phone_office.value;
            var zip1=form.zip.value;
            var address1=form.address.value;
            var state1=form.state.value;
            var E_mail1=form.E_mail.value;
            if(!((E_mail1.indexOf('@'))>=0))
            {
                    alert("email not proper");
                    ctr=1;
            }
```

```
              var zip1=form.zip.value;
              var ph_res1=form.ph_res.value;
              var branch1=form.branch.selectedIndex;
              var AC_Type1=form.AC_Type.options[form.AC_Type.selectedIndex].value;
              var title1=form.title.selectedIndex;

if((txtFrstName1.length==0)||(txtLastName1.length==0)||(phone_office1.length==0)||(a
ddress1.length==0)||(state1.length==0)||(zip1.length==0)||(ph_res1.length==0))
              {
                           alert("Please enter all the values.");
                           ctr=1;
              }
              if(ctr!=1)
              form.submit();
}


</script>
<p></p>
<table border="0" width="100%" height="42">
  <tr>
    <td width="50%" height="36"><b><font size="5"><i>Money Banks,
Inc.</i></font></b></td>
    <td width="50%" height="36"></td>
  </tr>
</table>
<p align="center"><b><font size="4" >Registration Information for Opening an
Account</font></b></p>
<table border="0" width="95%" height="153">
  <tr>
    <td width="84%" valign="top" height="153">
  <p style="margin-left: -2; margin-right: -2; margin-top: 5; margin-bottom:
5"><font ><b>* </b>Select branch:  <select size="1" name="branch">
  <option selected>New York</option>
  <option>Washington</option>
  <option>California</option>
  <option>San Jose</option>
  <option>New Jersey</option>
  </select>
```

```
</font>
  <p style="margin-left: -2; margin-right: -2; margin-top: 5; margin-bottom:
5"><font ><b>* </b>Account type: 
  <select size="1" name="AC_Type">
  <option>Savings Account</option>
  <option>Checking Account</option>
  <option>Fixed Deposits</option>
  <option>Recurring Deposits</option>
  <option>Personal Loans</option>
  <option>Home Loans</option>
  <option>Consumer Loans</option>
  <option>Auto Loans</option>
  </select> </font></p>
  <p style="margin-left: -2; margin-right: -2; margin-top: 5; margin-bottom:
5"><font >* First Name:    
  <select size="1" name="title">
  <option selected>Mr</option>
  <option>Ms</option>
  <option>Dr</option>
  <option>Prof</option>
  </select>
<input type="text" name="txtFrstName" size="20">
  </font>
  <p style="margin-left: -2; margin-right: -2; margin-top: 5; margin-bottom:
5"><font >Middle Name:   
  <input type="text" name="txtMidName" size="20"></font></p>
  <p style="margin-left: -2; margin-right: -2; margin-top: 5; margin-bottom:
5"><font >* Last Name:     <input type="text" name="txtLastName"
size="20"></font></p>
  <p style="margin-left: -2; margin-right: -2; margin-top: 5; margin-bottom:
5"><font >* Date of Birth:  
<select size="1" name="date">
  <script Language="JavaScript">
                date();
  </script>
  </select>
  <select size="1" name="month">
  <option>January</option>
```

```
<option>February</option>
<option>March</option>
<option>April</option>
<option>May</option>
<option>June</option>
<option>July</option>
<option>August</option>
<option>September</option>
<option>October</option>
<option>November</option>
<option>December</option>
</select>
<select size="1" name="year">
<script Language="JavaScript">
            year();
</script>
</select>
</font>
</p>
<p style="margin-left: -2; margin-right: -2; margin-top: 5; margin-bottom:
5"><font >* Work Phone: 
<input type="text" name="phone_office" size="20"> 
</font></p>
<p style="margin-left: -2; margin-right: -2; margin-top: 5; margin-bottom:
5"><font>* Address:         <input
type="text" name="address" size="20"></font></p>
<p style="margin-left: -2; margin-right: -2; margin-top: 5; margin-bottom:
5"><font >*
State:             
 <input type="text" name="state" size="20"></font></p>
<p style="margin-left: -2; margin-right: -2; margin-top: 5; margin-bottom:
5"><font >*
Zip:         
      <input type="text" name="zip"
size="20"></font></p>
<p style="margin-left: -2; margin-right: -2; margin-top: 5; margin-bottom:
5"><font >* E-mail
ID:       <input type="text" name="E_mail"
```

```
size="20"></font></p>
  <p style="margin-left: -2; margin-right: -2; margin-top: 5; margin-bottom:
5"><font >* Home Phone: 
  <input type="text" name="ph_res" size="20"></font></p>
  </tr>
</table>
  <p align="center" style="margin-top: 2; margin-bottom: 1">
<input type="button" value="Submit" name="Submit" onClick="verify()">
<input type="reset" value="Reset" name="B2">
  <font ><a href="Home_page.htm">Home Page</a>
  </font>
</form>
<p align="left"><font size="2">Fields marked (* ) are mandatory.</font></p>
</body>
</html>
```

`Register_page.htm` is an HTML page that will accept and validate inputs from the user. If the user has provided all the required information, the inputs are forwarded to a JSP page, `Register_page.jsp`.

Now I'll analyze the code of `Register_page.htm`.

In this code, there are three user-defined JavaScript methods. These methods are:

- ◆ `year()`
- ◆ `date()`
- ◆ `verify()`

The year() *Method*

The code for the `year()` method is given as follows:

```
function year()
{
        for (i=1900;i<2000;i++)
        {
                                document.write("<option
value="+i+">"+i+"</option>");
```

```
        }
}
```

The year() method is used to display the years in the list box, which will enable the user to select the year of birth. The method uses the for loop and the document.write() method to display years.

The date() *Method*

The code for the date() method is given as follows:

```
function date()
{
        for (i=01;i<=31;i++)
        {
                                document.write("<option
value="+i+">"+i+"</option>");
        }
}
```

The date() method is used to display the days of a month in the list box, which will enable the user to select the day of birth. The method uses the for loop and the document.write() method to display days of a month.

The verify() *Method*

The code for the verify() method is given as follows:

```
function verify()
{
        var ctr=0;
        var txtFrstName1=form.txtFrstName.value;
        var txtLastName1=form.txtLastName.value;
        var month1=form.month.value;
        var date1=form.date.value;
        var year1=form.year.value;
        var phone_office1=form.phone_office.value;
        var zip1=form.zip.value;
```

```
var address1=form.address.value;
var state1=form.state.value;
var E_mail1=form.E_mail.value;
if(!((E_mail1.indexOf('@'))>=0))
{
            alert("email not proper");
            ctr=1;
}
var zip1=form.zip.value;
var ph_res1=form.ph_res.value;
var branch1=form.branch.selectedIndex;
var AC_Type1=form.AC_Type.options[form.AC_Type.selectedIndex].value;
var title1=form.title.selectedIndex;

if((txtFrstName1.length==0)||(txtLastName1.length==0)||(phone_office1.length==0)||(a
ddress1.length==0)||(state1.length==0)||(zip1.length==0)||(ph_res1.length==0))
        {
                    alert("Please enter all the values.");
                    ctr=1;
        }
        if(ctr!=1)
        form.submit();
}
```

This method is called when the user clicks the Submit button. The `verify()` method checks whether the user has provided all the required values in the page. If any of the required values is missing, an error message is displayed. After validating the inputs from the user, the HTML page forwards the user information to the `Register_page.jsp` page for updating database. The code for `Register_page.jsp` is given in Listing 22-2.

Listing 22-2 Register_page.jsp

```
<html>
<head>
<title>Money Banks, Inc. -- Register Page</title>
</head>
<body bgproperties="fixed" bgcolor="#CCCCFF">
```

```
<form method="POST" action="Home_page.htm">
<script language="JavaScript">
function home()
{
          open("Home_page.htm");
}
</script>
<%! int update=0; %>
          <%@ page import="java.util.*" %>
          <%@ page import="java.sql.*" %>
          <%@ page import="java.text.*" %>
          <%@ page import="java.sql.Date" %>
          <%@ page language = "java" %>
          <%
          try{
          Class.forName("sun.jdbc.odbc.JdbcOdbcDriver");
          Connection connect;
          connect=DriverManager.getConnection("jdbc:odbc:BankDataSource","","");
          Statement state;
          state = connect.createStatement();
          String strQuery1 = "select * from Ac_Requests" ;
          ResultSet result1 = state.executeQuery(strQuery1);
          int ctr1=0;
    while(result1.next())
          {
                    ctr1=ctr1+1;
          }
          String cRegister="R000"+(ctr1+1);
          PreparedStatement stat2= connect.prepareStatement("insert into
Ac_Requests values(?,?,?,?,?,?,?,?,?,?,?,?,?,?)");
          stat2.setString(1,cRegister);
          stat2.setString(2,request.getParameter("branch"));
          stat2.setString(3,request.getParameter("AC_Type"));
          stat2.setString(4,request.getParameter("title"));
          stat2.setString(5,request.getParameter("txtFrstName"));
          stat2.setString(6,request.getParameter("txtMidName"));
          stat2.setString(7,request.getParameter("txtLastName"));
          String strdate=request.getParameter("year")+"-"+"02"+"-
```

```
"+request.getParameter("date");
                Date date;
                date=Date.valueOf(strdate);
                stat2.setString(8,date.toString());
                stat2.setString(9,request.getParameter("phone_office"));
                stat2.setString(10,request.getParameter("address"));
                stat2.setString(11,request.getParameter("state"));
                stat2.setString(12,request.getParameter("zip"));
                stat2.setString(13,request.getParameter("E_mail"));
                stat2.setString(14,request.getParameter("ph_res"));
                          stat2.executeUpdate();
                }
                catch(Exception e){
                out.println("done exception" +e);
                update=2;
                }
                %>
<p></p>
<table border="0" width="100%" height="42">
   <tr>
      <td width="50%" height="36"><b><font size="5" ><i>Money Banks,
Inc.</i></font></b></td>
      <td width="50%" height="36"></td>
   </tr>
</table>
<p><font size="3" >Database has been updated with the following
details. Our representative will soon visit you to complete the legal formalities.
To modify the details, click the <b>Back</b> link.</font></p>
<table border="0" width="635" height="245">
   <tr>
      <td width="96" valign="top" height="239">
   <p style="margin-left: -2; margin-right: -2; margin-top: 5; margin-bottom:
5"><font ><b>Bank branch:</b></font>
   <p style="margin-left: -2; margin-right: -2; margin-top: 5; margin-bottom:
5"><font><b>Account
   Type:</b>
   <p style="margin-left: -2; margin-right: -2; margin-top: 5; margin-bottom: 5">
<b> Name:</b>
```

```
   <p style="margin-left: -2; margin-right: -2; margin-top: 5; margin-bottom:
5"><font ><b>Date of Birth:</b></font>
   </p>
   <p style="margin-left: -2; margin-right: -2; margin-top: 5; margin-bottom:
5"><font ><b>Work Phone:</b>
   </font></p>
   <p style="margin-left: -2; margin-right: -2; margin-top: 5; margin-bottom:
5"><b>Address:</b>
   </p>
   <p style="margin-left: -2; margin-right: -2; margin-top: 5; margin-bottom:
5"><b>State:</b></p>
   <p style="margin-left: -2; margin-right: -2; margin-top: 5; margin-bottom:
5"><b>Zip:</b></p>
   <p style="margin-left: -2; margin-right: -2; margin-top: 5; margin-bottom:
5"><b>E-mail ID:</b></p>
   <p style="margin-left: -2; margin-right: -2; margin-top: 5; margin-bottom:
5"><b>Home Phone:</b></p>
   </font>
   </td>
   <td width="525"><p style="margin-left: -2; margin-right: -2; margin-top: 5; mar-
gin-bottom: 5"><%= request.getParameter("branch") %>
   <p style="margin-left: -2; margin-right: -2; margin-top: 5; margin-bottom: 5"><%=
request.getParameter("AC_Type") %></b>
   <p style="margin-left: -2; margin-right: -2; margin-top: 5; margin-bottom: 5"><%=
request.getParameter("txtFrstName") %>  <%=
request.getParameter("txtMidName") %>  <%=
request.getParameter("txtLastName") %>
   <p style="margin-left: -2; margin-right: -2; margin-top: 5; margin-bottom: 5"><%=
request.getParameter("date") %>  <%= request.getParameter("month")
%>  <%= request.getParameter("year") %>
   </font>
   </p>
   <p style="margin-left: -2; margin-right: -2; margin-top: 5; margin-bottom: 5"><%=
request.getParameter("phone_office") %>
   </p>
   <p style="margin-left: -2; margin-right: -2; margin-top: 5; margin-bottom: 5"><%=
request.getParameter("address") %></p>
   <p style="margin-left: -2; margin-right: -2; margin-top: 5; margin-bottom: 5"><%=
```

```
request.getParameter("state") %></p>
  <p style="margin-left: -2; margin-right: -2; margin-top: 5; margin-bottom: 5"><%=
request.getParameter("zip") %></p>
  <p style="margin-left: -2; margin-right: -2; margin-top: 5; margin-bottom: 5"><%=
request.getParameter("E_mail") %></p>
  <p style="margin-left: -2; margin-right: -2; margin-top: 5; margin-bottom: 5"><%=
request.getParameter("ph_res") %></p>
  </font>
  </td>
  </tr>
</table>
  <p align="center"><input type="button" value="OK " name="Ok" onClick="home()">
  <font ><a href="Register_page.htm">Back</a>
  </font>
</form>
</body>
</html>
```

The JSP code given above will update the Requests table by inserting a row with the user's request information in the table. After updating the Requests table, a message of confirmation is displayed to the user. The code is analyzed in the paragraphs given as follows:

```
function home()
{
        open("Home_page.htm");
}
```

In the statements given above, the home() method written in JavaScript will display the Home page of the banking application. The home() method is invoked when the user clicks the OK button in the JSP page.

```
try{
        Class.forName("sun.jdbc.odbc.JdbcOdbcDriver");
        Connection connect;
        connect=DriverManager.getConnection("jdbc:odbc:BankDataSource","","");
        Statement state;
        state = connect.createStatement();
        String strQuery1 = "select * from Ac_Requests" ;
        ResultSet result1 = state.executeQuery(strQuery1);
```

The previous statements will establish a connection with the database represented by the `BankDataSource` DSN. The statement for selecting rows from the `Ac_Requests` table is executed, and the result is stored in the `ResultSet` object, `result1`.

```
            PreparedStatement stat2= connect.prepareStatement("insert into
Ac_Requests values(?,?,?,?,?,?,?,?,?,?,?,?,?,?)");
            stat2.setString(1,cRegister);
            stat2.setString(2,request.getParameter("branch"));
            stat2.setString(3,request.getParameter("AC_Type"));
            stat2.setString(4,request.getParameter("title"));
            stat2.setString(5,request.getParameter("txtFrstName"));
            stat2.setString(6,request.getParameter("txtMidName"));
            stat2.setString(7,request.getParameter("txtLastName"));
            String strdate=request.getParameter("year")+"-"+"02"+"-
"+request.getParameter("date");
            Date date;
            date=Date.valueOf(strdate);
            stat2.setString(8,date.toString());
            stat2.setString(9,request.getParameter("phone_office"));
            stat2.setString(10,request.getParameter("address"));
            stat2.setString(11,request.getParameter("state"));
            stat2.setString(12,request.getParameter("zip"));
            stat2.setString(13,request.getParameter("E_mail"));
            stat2.setString(14,request.getParameter("ph_res"));
            stat2.executeUpdate();
```

Next, in the statements given above, a row is inserted in the `Ac_Requests` table. The table contains the account opening request information from users. The query to insert a row is executed by using the `prepareStatement()` method and the `executeUpdate()` method.

The rest of the JSP code displays the information entered by the user in the `Register_page.htm` page.

I'll now show you the output of the code in Listing 22-1 and Listing 22-2. The user first enters the information in `Register_page.htm` as displayed in Figure 22-1.

The JSP code receives the information from the HTML page and updates the database. The output of JSP code is displayed in Figure 22-2.

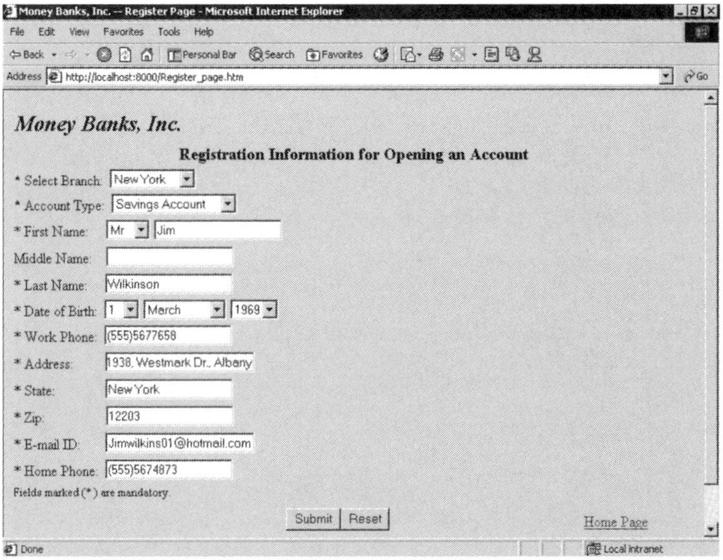

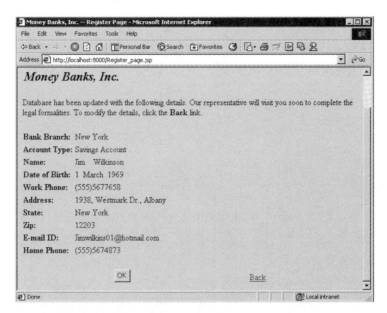

FIGURE 22-1 *The figure displays output of the HTML code for the Registration page to open a new account at Money Banks, Inc.*

FIGURE 22-2 *The figure displays output of the JSP code for the page to verify details to open a new account at Money Banks, Inc.*

Summary

In this chapter, you learned how to create the Registration page for accepting requests for opening bank accounts with Money Banks, Inc. You also learned how to create a page to validate user inputs and update the database after accepting requests.

Chapter 23

**Creating the
Interest
Calculator Page**

In this chapter, you'll create the Interest Calculator page of the Money Banks banking application. The page will be created by using JavaBeans.

The Interest Calculator Page

The Interest Calculator page provides a utility to the users of the banking application to calculate interests payable at a specified rate on a specified amount. The user will need to provide the following values:

◆ Principal amount

◆ Rate of interest

◆ Period in months

Since JavaBeans has been used to create this page, I'll first explain JavaBeans before creating the interest calculator utility.

JavaBeans

Software components are the building blocks of an application. A software component is a reusable object that can be plugged into different software applications on different platforms. Some of the examples of software components that you can create are a spell-check utility, a calculator, and a text editor. The benefits of using software components as building blocks can be understood better by taking an example. To assemble a computer, you need many hardware components such as resistors, capacitors, and integrated chips. These components together make up a computer. Different manufacturers can supply these components. Similarly, different vendors can develop software components. Application developers should be able to understand the benefits and capabilities of these components and use them in applications across various platforms.

A JavaBean is a software component created using Java and takes advantage of all the security and platform-independent features of Java.

The advantages of beans are listed in the following section.

The Advantages of JavaBeans

JavaBeans provides you with the following advantages:

♦ A bean inherits all the benefits of "run-once, run-anywhere" feature of Java.

♦ A bean can be designed to operate in different locales, making it truly global.

♦ The configuration settings of a bean can be saved in a persistent storage and restored at a later time.

♦ A bean can receive and send events to other objects.

Now I'll discuss the requirements for a software program to qualify as a bean.

 NOTE

A JavaBean is different from an Enterprise JavaBean (EJB). JavaBeans runs within a JVM whereas EJB is executed within application servers. Therefore, EJB has the benefits of additional run-time infrastructure services provided by the server.

The JavaBeans Component Specifications

A bean is nothing but a class. You can have several data members in a bean. All the data members of a bean are private and are accessible only through the get and set methods of the class. These methods enable you to assign and obtain values of the member data. The set method enables you to assign a value to a member data. The set methods are also known as mutator methods. The syntax of the set method is given as follows:

```
public void set<member_data>(<data_type> <variable_name>);
```

Here, <member_data> is the name of the member data of the bean that is being assigned a new value. <data_type> is the data type of the value and <variable_name> is the name of the variable that receives the value. This value is assigned to the member data in the body of the method.

The get method is used to obtain the value of a member data. The get methods are also known as accessor methods. The syntax of a get method is given as follows.

```
public <data_type> get<member_data>();
```

Here `<data_type>` is the data type of the value returned by the get method. `<member_data>` represents the member data in the beans whose value is being returned.

 NOTE

If the member data is `propone`, then by convention, the get and set methods should be declared as `getPropone()` and `setPropone()` with the member data name starting with an uppercase in the method name.

As per the JavaBean Component Specification, a simple Java object should have the following features for it to qualify as a bean:

◆ Properties

◆ Introspection

◆ Customization

◆ Events

◆ Persistence

I'll now discuss each of these features in detail.

Properties

Properties are nothing but the member data of a bean and are accessible through the accessor and mutator methods. A bean should have properties that can be customized by the users or manipulated programmatically. Properties can be of three types:

◆ Simple

◆ Boolean

◆ Indexed

A simple property has a single value. A simple property has the following syntax:

```
private type <Name>
public type get<Name>{}
public void set<Name>(<type> <value>){}
```

Here, `<Name>` is the property name, and `<type>` is the property type.

A boolean property has value either `true` or `false`. A boolean property has the following syntax:

```
private boolean <name>;
public boolean is<Name>(){}
public boolean get<Name>(){}
public void set<Name>(boolean <value>){}
```

You can use either the `is<Name>` or the `get<Name>` methods to retrieve the value of a boolean property.

An indexed property consists of multiple values. An indexed property has the following syntax:

```
private type <name>[];
public type get<Name>(int <index>){}
public void set<Name>(int <index>, <type> <value>){}
public type[] get<Name>(){}
public void set<Name>(<type> value[]){}
```

Introspection

Introspection is the process of determining the capabilities of a bean. It enables a software designer to obtain information about a bean. This is an essential feature of beans. Without this feature, the JavaBeans technology cannot operate. There are two ways in which a bean's properties can be exposed. The first way is to use the simple naming convention. For example, the `set` and `get` methods follow a naming convention where you can assign and obtain access to a member's data value if you know the member's data name. The second method is to use the JavaBeans API class, `BeanInfo` class, which explicitly supplies the information.

Customization

Customization is the feature that enables a bean to allow its property to be changed by the user. A bean should enable a user to change all or some of its properties. For example, a user can select whether to display a normal calculator or scientific calculator in an application.

Events

The events feature allows a bean to generate and handle events. Beans use the delegation event model as discussed in Chapter 3, "Layout Managers and Handling Events." Beans can generate events and delegate them to other objects for handling. The syntax for handling events in beans is given as follows:

```
public void add<type>Listener (<type>Listener eventListener);
public void remove<type>Listener(<type>Listener eventListener);
```

The first syntax delegates the event handling to a listener. Whereas the second syntax is used when a developer decides to no longer delegate the event handling to the listener. An example of event handling in a bean is given here.

```
public class eventBean
{
        public eventBean()
        {
                                addMouseListener(new MouseAdapter()
                                {
                                                public void
mousePressed(MouseEvent me)
                                                {

System.out.println("Mouse has been pressed.");
                                                }
                                });
                }
-------Remaining code---------
}
```

Here, the class, eventBean, is a bean. In this bean, the addMouseListener() method has been used to add an event listener to the bean and delegate the mouse-related events to the event listener.

Persistence

Persistence is the feature that enables a bean to save its settings and properties to a disk or any other storage device. The bean can be restored later with the same settings. For example, the state of the text editor bean such as the words you typed the last time and the configuration settings, can be saved to a file.

The three types of beans that you can create are discussed in the next section.

The Types of Beans

The three types of beans that you can create are:

◆ Control beans

◆ Container beans

◆ Invisible runtime beans

Table 23-1 gives a description of these types of beans.

Table 23-1 The Types of Beans

Type of Bean	Description
Control beans	Control beans or User Interface beans are the GUI beans that you can plug into various applications. Control beans are usually created by extending the Swing component classes. A button is an example of a control bean.
Container beans	Container beans, as the name indicates, can be used to hold other beans. Container beans can be created by extending Swing container classes. An explorer is an example of container bean.
Invisible runtime beans	Invisible beans are the beans that perform tasks in the background. They remain invisible during execution. A bean that provides connectivity with data sources is an example of an invisible runtime bean.

There are various tools available that you can use to create and test beans. I'll now discuss how to use these tools.

The Application Builder Tools

A wide variety of application development tools such as Forte for Java, IBM Visual Age, Beans Development Kit (BDK), and Symantec Visual Cafe are available to support the creation, building, and testing of beans. These tools enable you to configure a set of beans, connect them together, and develop an application.

I'll use BDK to explain how to create and use beans. You can download BDK from the **java.sun.com/products/javabeans/software/bdk_download.html** site. You'll now learn how to start BDK. The steps to do so are:

1. Ensure that JDK is configured on your computer.

2. Download and install BDK from the site.

3. Change to the directory `c:\bdk\beanbox`.

4. Execute the batch file called `run.bat`. The BDK will start now and three windows, ToolBox, BeanBox, and Properties, are displayed. These windows are displayed in Figure 23-1, Figure 23-2, and Figure 23-3, respectively.

FIGURE 23-1 *The figure displays the ToolBox window of BDK.*

The ToolBox window of BDK lists all the beans that have been included with the BDK.

FIGURE 23-2 *The figure displays the BeanBox window of BDK.*

The BeanBox window of BDK provides the working area to layout and connect beans selected from the ToolBox window.

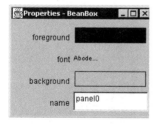

FIGURE 23-3 *The figure displays the Properties window of BDK.*

The Properties window of BDK enables you to configure the bean selected in the BeanBox window.

Using BDK, you'll now learn how to create a simple bean.

Creating a Simple Bean

The bean that I'll create is called `FirstBean`. The `FirstBean` will either appear in rectangle or circle shape. In addition, this bean will be filled with color selected randomly. The color will change randomly each time the bean is clicked. The steps to create and test a bean are listed here:

1. Create and compile the Java source file(s).
2. Create a manifest file.
3. Generate a JAR file.
4. Start the BDK.
5. Test the bean.

I'll now perform each of these steps one-by-one.

Creating and Compiling Java Source Files

A JavaBean consists of one or more class files, gif files, and HTML files. You need to create each of these files separately. I'll now create the class file for the sample bean. You first need to create the Java source file for the bean and store it in the directory `c:\bdk\demo\sunw\demo\FirstBean`. The code for the source is given here.

```
package sunw.demo.FirstBean;
import java.awt.*;
import java.awt.event.*;
public class FirstBean extends Canvas{
transient private Color color;
private boolean circle;
public FirstBean()
{
            addMouseListener(new MouseAdapter()
        {
```

```
                                public void mousePressed(MouseEvent me)
                                {
                                                clr_change();
                                }
                });

circle=false;
setSize(200,100);
clr_change();
}
public boolean getCircle(){
return circle;
}

public void setCircle(boolean flag)
{
                this.circle=flag;
                repaint();
}
public void clr_change()
{
                color=randomColor();
                repaint();
}
private Color randomColor()
{
                int red=(int)(255*Math.random());
                int green=(int)(255*Math.random());
                int blue=(int)(255*Math.random());
                return new Color(red,green,blue);
}
public void paint(Graphics g)
{
                Dimension d=getSize();
                int height=d.height;
                int width=d.width;
                g.setColor(color);
                if(circle)
```

```
                    {
                                g.fillOval(0,0,width-1,height-1);
                    }
                    else
                    {
                                g.fillRect(0,0,width-1,height-1);
                    }
        }
}
```

Next, compile the source code by executing the following command at the command prompt:

```
c:\>javac FirstBean.java
```

Store the `FirstBean.class` file in the `C:\BDK\beans\demo\sunw\demo\FirstBean` folder.

Create the Manifest File

A manifest file is a text file that enables you to specify the JavaBeans components in a JAR file. A manifest file consists of a list of all class files and resource files that are required for implementing bean functionality. A JAR file contains the set of bean classes and associated resources such as sound and image files. An example of a manifest file is given here:

```
Name: sunw\demo\animal\Lion.gif
Name: sunw\demo\animal\Lion.wav
Name: sunw\demo\animal\Cat.gif
Name: sunw\demo\animal\Cat.wav
Name: sunw\demo\animal\Lion.class
Java-Bean: True
Name: sunw\demo\animal\Cat.class
Java-Bean: True
```

You need to remember these points while creating a manifest file:

1. Press Enter after each line, including the last line, in the manifest file.
2. Leave a single blank space after the colon in each line.
3. Specify filename as <bean_name>.mft.

In the previous code, the last two entries, `Lion.class` and `Cat.class`, are beans. Notice that each entry has been followed by the statement `Java-Bean: True`. This is required as per the specification to indicate the beans. The `Java-Bean: True` statement should immediately follow the bean entry.

To create the manifest file for `FirstBean`, switch to the `c:\bdk\beans\demo` directory. The manifest files for the BDK demos are stored here. Now, create a manifest file, `FirstBean.mtf`, and make the following entry in it:

```
Name: sunw\demo\FirstBean\FirstBean.class
Java-Bean: True
```

This entry indicates that there is only one file in the JAR file. The next step is to create a JAR file.

Generating a JAR File

A bean is packaged and distributed as a JAR file. It contains all the class files and resource files that make up a bean. To generate the JAR file for `FirstBean`, switch to the `c:\bdk\beans\demo` folder and execute the following command at the command prompt:

```
c:\>jar cfm ..\jars\FirstBean.jar FirstBean.mtf sunw\demo\FirstBean\*.class
```

The above command will create the JAR file, `FirstBean.jar`, and place it in the directory `c:\bdk\beans\jars`. All the JAR files need to be stored in the `c:\bdk\beans\jars` folder.

Start the BDK

To start the BDK, execute the Run command from the directory `c:\bdk\beanbox`. The three windows of the BDK will be displayed. Figure 23-4 displays the `FirstBean` in the ToolBox window.

FIGURE 23-4 *The figure displays the ToolBox window containing the* `FirstBean`.

Test the Bean

To test the bean, you first need to create the instance of `FirstBean` in the Bean-Box window. You can create the instance by clicking on `FirstBean` in the Tool-Box and then clicking on the blank area of BeanBox. Figure 23-5 displays the instance of `FirstBean` in the BeanBox.

You can now test the bean by clicking the bean. Notice that the color changes immediately. You can change its shape by changing the circle property in the Property window. You have now learned to create, use, and test a simple bean. You'll now learn to connect two beans. You'll create an instance of `OurButton` bean available in the BDK and associate it with the `FirstBean`. The steps to do this are given as follows:

1. Create an instance of `OurButton` in the BeanBox window. The instance is displayed in Figure 23-6.

2. In the Properties window, change the label of the bean to Change Color. Notice that the label of the button is changed.

3. Select Edit → Events → Action → actionPerformed from the menu bar.

4. Place the cursor within the `FirstBean` and click the left mouse button. The EventTargetDialog dialog box is displayed. See Figure 23-7.

FIGURE 23-5 *The* FirstBean *is now in the BeanBox.*

5. The dialog box lists the methods that will be invoked when the button is clicked. Select the clr_change method from the list and click the OK button.

6. The message, "Generating and compiling adaptor class," is displayed briefly.

7. Click the Change Color button. The color of FirstBean has changed. See Figure 23-8.

You've learned to create, connect, and test beans. I'll now discuss the JavaBeans API, which provides interfaces and classes to implement bean functionalities.

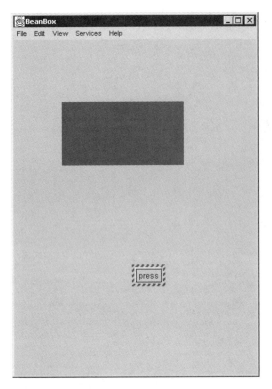

FIGURE 23-6 *The figure displays the BeanBox window of BDK.*

FIGURE 23-7 *The figure displays the EventTargetDialog box.*

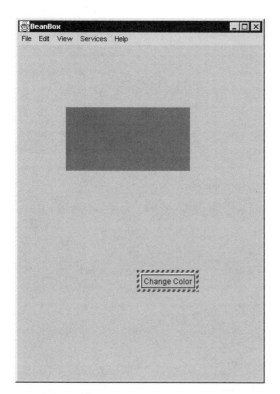

FIGURE 23-8 *The color of the* FirstBean *is now changed.*

The JavaBeans API

The java.beans package contains the interfaces and classes that constitute the JavaBeans API. I'll briefly discuss these interfaces and classes. Table 23-2 contains the description of interfaces of java.beans package.

Table 23-2 The Interfaces of the *java.beans* Package

Interface	Description
AppletInitializer	This interface provides methods to initialize applet beans. The methods of this interface are activate() and initialize().
BeanInfo	This interface provides methods that enable bean developers to specify information about the methods, properties, and

continues

Table 23-2 *(continued)*

Interface	Description
	events of the beans. Some of the methods of this interface are getBeanDescriptor(), getDefaultPropertyIndex(), and getMethoddescriptors().
Customizer	This interface enables a bean developer to provide a GUI through which the bean can be customized. The methods are addPropertyChangeListener(), removeProperty-ChangeListener(), and setObject().
DesignMode	This interface provides methods that identify whether the bean is executing in the design mode. The methods are isDesignTime() and setDesignTime().
PropertyChangeListener	This interface provides a method called propertyChange(), which is invoked when a bound property of a bean is changed.
PropertyEditor	This interface allow users to change and display property values. Methods are getCustomEditor(), getValue(), paintValue(), setAsText(), and setValue().
Visibility	This interface enables a bean to run in environments where a GUI is not available. Methods of this interface are avoidingGui(), dontUseGui(), needsGui(), and okToUseGui().

Table 23-3 contains the description of classes of the java.beans package.

Table 23-3 The Classes of the *java.beans* Package

Class	Description
BeanDescriptor	This class provides global information about a bean such as its Java class and display name. The constructor of this class also enables you to associate a customizer with the bean. The methods of the class are getBeanClass() and getCustomizerClass().
Beans	This class provides some general-purpose bean control methods. Some of the methods of this class are getInstanceOf(), instantiate(), isDesignTime(), isGuiAvailable(), setDesignTime(), and setGuiAvailable().

Class	Description
EventSetDescriptor	This class describes the events that can be generated by a bean. Methods are getListenerMethods(), getListenerMethod-Descriptors(), and getAddListenerMethod().
Introspector	This class provides the tools to learn about the properties, events, and methods supported by a bean. Some of its methods are getBeanInfo() and getBeanInfoSearchPath().
MethodDescriptor	This class describes a method of a bean. Its methods are getMethod() and getParameterDescriptors().
PropertyChangeEvent	This event is generated when the bound or constrained property of a bean changes. Some of its methods are getNewValue(), getPropertyName(), and getPropagationId().
PropertyDescriptor	This class describes a property that a Java Bean exports via a pair of accessor methods. Some of its methods are getPropertyType(), isBound(), isConstrained(), setBound(), setConstrained(), and setProperty-EditorClass().
SimpleBeanInfo	This class provides a facility that can be used while writing BeanInfo classes. Thus, it makes it easier to provide the BeanInfo class. Some of the methods of this class are getAdditionalBeanInfo(), getBeanDescriptor(), getEventSetDescriptors(), and getMethodDescriptors().

You've learned about JavaBeans in detail. Now you'll create the interest calculator utility of the banking application.

Creating the Interest Calculator

To create the interest calculator, I've created three files. These files are:

♦ **Interest_calc.htm** This is an HTML file that'll accept and forward values to a JSP page.

♦ **Interest_calc.jsp** This JSP page will use the bean to calculate interest.

◆ **IntCal.java**   This is the bean source file.

The code for the Interest_calc.htm file is given in Listing 23-4.

Listing 23-4 Interest_calc.htm

```html
<html>
<head>
<title>Money Banks, Inc. -- Interest Calculator</title>
</head>
<body bgproperties="fixed" bgcolor="#CCCCFF">
<p></p>
<table border="0" width="100%" height="42">
  <tr>
    <td width="50%" height="36"><b><i><font size="5">Money Banks,
Inc.</font></i></b></td>
    <td width="50%" height="36"></td>
  </tr>
</table>
<p align="center"><b><font size="4">Interest Calculator</font></b></p>
<form method="POST" action="Interest_calc.jsp">
  <p><font size="4">Enter Principal Amount:</font><font size="4"
color="#FF0000">    
  </font><input type="text" name="amount" size="20"></p>
  <p ><font size="4">Enter Period in Months:</font><font size="4"
color="#FF0000">    
  </font><input type="text" name="period" size="20"></p>
  <p ><font size="4">Enter Rate of Interest:</font><font size="4"
color="#FF0000">      
  </font><input type="text" name="int_rate" size="20"></p>
  <p><font size="4">Interest
  Payable:</font><font size="4"
color="#FF0000">           &n
bsp;
    </font><input type="text" name="int_pay" size="20"></p>
  <p align="center"><input type="submit" value="Submit" name="Submit"><input
type="reset" value="Reset" name="Reset"></p>
</form>
```

```
</body>
</html>
```

The output of the HTML page is given in Figure 23-9.

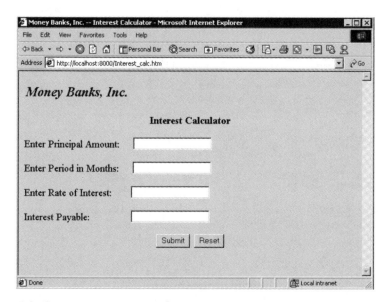

FIGURE 23-9 *The output of the HTML page, showing the Interest Calculator page.*

The code for the Int_Cal.java is given in Listing 23-5.

Listing 23-5 Int_Cal.java

```java
import java.io.*;
import java.sql.*;
import java.util.*;
public class Int_Cal
{
        private String amount;
        private double int_amount;
        private String period;
        private double int_period;
        private double rateInt;
```

```
            private String rate1;
            private double interest;
            public Int_Cal()
            {
            }
            public void setAmount(String amount)
            {
                        this.amount=amount;
                        int_amount=Double.parseDouble(this.amount);
            }
            public String getAmount()
            {
                            return this.amount;
            }
            public void setPeriod(String str_period)
                {
                            period=str_period;
                        int_period=Double.parseDouble(period);
                }
            public String getPeriod()
                {
                            return period;
                }
            public void setRate1(String rt)
                {
rate1=rt;
rateInt=Double.parseDouble(rate1);
System.out.println(rateInt);
                }


            public String getRate1()
                {
                            return rate1;
                }
            public double getInterest()
                {
                            interest=(int_period*int_amount*rateInt)/100;
```

```
                    return interest;
           }


}
```

Notice that properties of this bean have been declared as private. The getter and setter methods have been defined for these properties, period, interest rate, and amount. The getInterest() method in the bean calculates the payable interest and returns it to the caller. You need to store the .class file of the bean in the j2sdkee1.2.1\lib\classes folder.

The third file that has been created for the interest calculator is Interest _calc.jsp. The code for this JSP file is given in Listing 23-6.

Listing 23-6 Interest_calc.jsp

```
<html>
<head>
<title>Money Banks, Inc. -- Interest Calculator</title>
</head>
<%@ page language = "java" %>
<%@ page errorPage="error.jsp"%>
<jsp:useBean id="IntCalc" class="Int_Cal" scope="page" />
<body bgproperties="fixed" bgcolor="#CCCCFF">
<p></p>
<table border="0" width="100%" height="42">
  <tr>
    <td width="50%" height="36"><b><font size="5"><i>Money Banks,
Inc.</i></font></b></td>
    <td width="50%" height="36"></td>
  </tr>
</table>
<p align="center"><b><font size="4">Interest Calculator</font></b></p>
  <p><font size="4">Enter Principal Amount: 
  </font> <%= (String)request.getParameter("amount") %>
        <%! int amnt; %>
<%
    String str1;
```

```
            str1=request.getParameter("amount");
            str1=str1.trim();
       %>
                <jsp:setProperty name="IntCalc" property="amount" value="<%=str1%>"/>
</p>
        <p ><font size="4">Enter Period in Months: </font>
        <%= (String)request.getParameter("period") %>
                <%
                    String prd=request.getParameter("period");
            str1=str1.trim();
                %>
        </p>
                <jsp:setProperty name="IntCalc" property="period" value="<%=prd%>"/>
        <p ><font size="4">Enter Rate of Interest: </font>
          <%= (String)request.getParameter("int_rate") %>
                    <%

            String str2=request.getParameter("int_rate");
            str2=str2.trim();


                %>
        </p>


<jsp:setProperty name="IntCalc" property="rate1" value="<%=str2%>"/>
        <p><font size="4">Interest
        Payable: </font>
        <% double tot_int=IntCalc.getInterest();
                out.println(tot_int);
       %>
        </p>
     <p align="center"><input type="button" value="OK" name="OK"
onClick="show_Home()"></p>
<script language="JavaScript">
function show_Home()
{
        open("Home_page.htm");
}
</script>
```

```
</body>
</html>
```

This code introduces you to three new JSP tags. These tags are:

- The `<jsp:useBean>` tag
- The `<jsp:setProperty>` tag
- The `<jsp:getProperty>` tag

Using these JSP tags enables you to incorporate beans in JSP pages. As a result, the JSP pages will provide the functionality of the beans. I'll discuss each of these tags in detail.

The `<jsp:useBean>` tag enables you to instantiate and use an existing bean in the JSP code. The syntax of the `<jsp:useBean>` tag is given as follows:

```
<jsp:useBean id="bean_instance" class="bean_class" scope="bean_scope"
beanName="bean_reference">
```

The `id` attribute of the bean is used to specify the instance name of the bean. The `class` attribute specifies the name of the bean class. The `scope` of the bean identifies the limit where the instance of the bean will be accessible. The `scope` attribute can have the following values:

- Page
- Session
- Application

The `beanName` attribute specifies a referential name for the bean.

The `<jsp:setProperty>` tag is used to set the value of a property of the specified bean. To set the value of the bean property, either an explicit value is specified or the value is obtained from a request parameter. Corresponding to the specified request property value, the set method in the bean is called with the matching value. The syntax of the `<jsp:setProperty>` tag is given here:

```
<jsp:setProperty name="bean_name" property="property_name" value="property_value"
param="parameter">
```

Here, bean_name is the name of bean. The `property` attribute specifies the property whose value, specified by the `value` attribute, needs to be set. The `param` attribute specifies the name of the request parameter to be used to set the value of the property.

The `<jsp:getProperty>` tag is used to retrieve the value of a bean property. The retrieved value is converted to a String. The syntax of the `<jsp:setProperty>` tag is given here:

```
<jsp:getProperty name="bean_name" property="property_name">
```

The `property` attribute specifies the property of the bean, bean_name, whose value is being retrieved.

Now I'll analyze the code of `Interest_calc.jsp` in detail.

```
<%@ page language = "java" %>
<%@ page errorPage="error.jsp"%>
<jsp:useBean id="IntCalc" class="Int_Cal" scope="page" />
```

The above statements specify the language as Java for the JSP page. The `error.jsp` page will be displayed in case any error or exception is raised. Next, the `<jsp:useBean>` tag is used to instantiate the `Int_Cal` bean. The scope of the bean is limited to the current JSP page.

```
<%
    String str1;
    str1=request.getParameter("amount");
    str1=str1.trim();
%>
<jsp:setProperty name="IntCalc" property="amount" value="<%=str1%>"/>
```

In the above statements the amount entered by the user in the `Interest_calc.htm` page is obtained and stored in a variable. Then by using the `<jsp:setProperty>` tag, the value of the amount property is set. Similarly, the values of other properties have been set in this code.

```
<% double tot_int=IntCalc.getInterest();
              out.println(tot_int);
   %>
```

The interest calculated by the bean is obtained by executing the above statements. Here, notice the `getInterest()` is invoked through the bean instance.

The illustration in Figure 23-10 depicts the interaction between the three files.

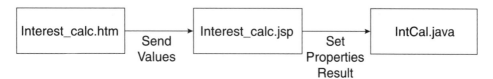

FIGURE 23-10 *The working of interest the calculator is depicted.*

Now see how the interest calculator works. The sample values entered in the HTML page are displayed in Figure 23-11.

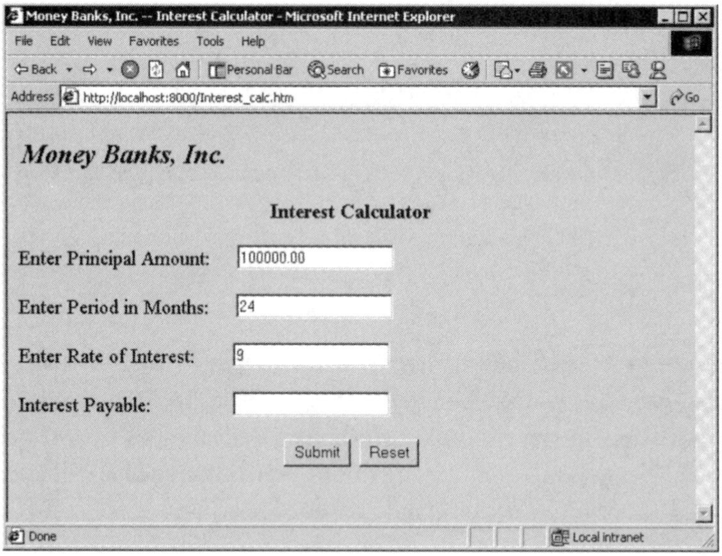

FIGURE 23-11 *These are the sample values entered in the HTML page.*

When the values in the HTML page are submitted, the JSP page calls the bean to calculate the interest and it displays the calculated interest. The calculated interest is displayed in Figure 23-12.

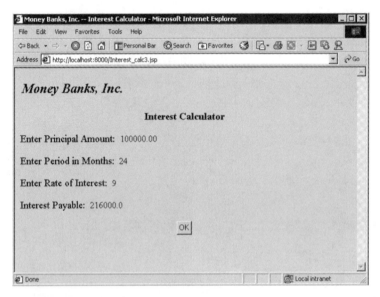

FIGURE 23-12 *The output of the HTML page is displayed, showing the calculated interest.*

Summary

In this chapter, you learned how to create the Interest Calculator page of the banking application. You used JavaBeans to create this utility. You also learned in detail about JavaBeans in the chapter, including the advantages of and necessity for using beans. Next, JavaBeans specifications were discussed in this chapter. Finally, you used BDK to create, use, and connect beans.

Chapter 24

In this chapter, you'll learn how to create the Currency Exchange Calculator page of the banking application at Money Banks, Inc.

The Currency Exchange Calculator

As per the stated design of the application, the Currency Exchange Calculator page will enable a user to determine how much a specified amount of currency would value when converted into a different currency. The JavaBeans technology will be used to create the currency converter bean. You learned about JavaBeans in Chapter 23, "Creating the Interest Calculator Page." The three files that are used to create the exchange rate utility are:

◆ `currExchange.htm`

◆ `currExchangeBean.jsp`

◆ `calc.Java`

The `currExchange.htm` page accepts values for conversion, such as currencies and amounts, from a user. When submitted, the page forwards these values to a JSP page, `currExchangeBean.jsp`. The JSP page calls the `calc.java` bean to calculate the results. The interaction between the three components of the currency exchange utility is displayed in Figure 24-1.

FIGURE 24-1 *The figure shows the interaction between components of the currency exchange calculator.*

Now take a look at the code used in the three files that make up the currency exchange utility.

The *currExchange.htm* Page

The code for the currExchange.htm page is given in Listing 24-1.

Listing 24-1   currExchange.htm

```
<html>
<head>
<title>Money Banks, Inc. -- Currency Exchange</title>
</head>
<body bgproperties="fixed" bgcolor="#CCCCFF">
<form method="POST" action="http:\\localhost:8000\currExchangeBean.jsp">
<p align="center"></p>
<table border="0" width="100%" height="42">
  <tr>
    <td width="50%" height="36"><b><font size="5"><i>Money Banks,
Inc.</i></font></b></td>
    <td width="50%" height="36"></td>
  </tr>
</table>
<p align="center"><b><font size="4">Currency Conversion</font></b></p>
    <p ><font>Convert: <select size="1" name="frmCurr">
    <option>US Dollar</option>
    <option>British Pound</option>
    <option>Canadian Dollar</option>
    <option>Euro</option>
    <option>Australian Dollar</option>
    </select></font>
  <font>to</font> <font><select size="1" name="toCurrency">
    <option>US Dollar</option>
    <option>British Pound</option>
    <option>Canadian Dollar</option>
    <option>Euro</option>
    <option>Australian Dollar</option>
    </select>
    </font> </p>
    <p ><font>Amount: </font><input type="text" name="amount" size="20"><font>
</font></p>
```

```
            <p align="center"><input type="submit" value="OK" name="submit" ></p>
    </form>
    <p > </p>
    </body>
    </html>
```

The output of the code in Listing 24-1 is displayed in Figure 24-2.

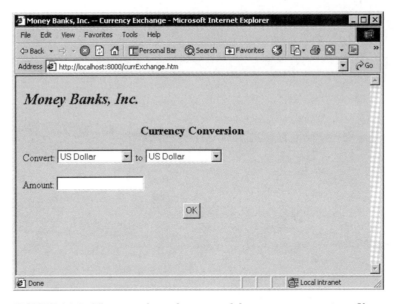

FIGURE 24-2 *The screen shows the output of the* currExchange.htm *file.*

The *currExchangeBean.jsp* File

Listing 24-2 shows you the code for the currExchangeBean.jsp page.

Listing 24-2 currExchangeBean.jsp

```
<html>
<head>
<title>Money Banks, Inc. -- Currency Exchange</title>
</head>
<%@ page language = "java" %>
```

```jsp
<%@ page errorPage="error_curr.jsp"%>
<jsp:useBean id="calc" class="calc" scope="session" />
<%@ page import="java.lang.*" %>
<body bgproperties="fixed" bgcolor="#CCCCFF">
<form action="Home_page.htm">
<p align="center"></p>
<table border="0" width="100%" height="42">
  <tr>
    <td width="50%" height="36"><b><font size="5" ><i>Money Banks,
Inc.</i></font></b></td>
    <td width="50%" height="36"></td>
  </tr>
</table>
<p align="center"><b><font size="4" >Currency Conversion</font></b></p>
    <p ><font >Convert: </font><%= request.getParameter("frmCurr")%>
    <% String frCrr[]={"US Dollar", "British Pound", "Canadian
Dollar","Euro","Australian Dollar"};
            String crr=request.getParameter("frmCurr");
            int ctr=0;
            while(!(crr.equals(frCrr[ctr])))
            ctr++;
    %>
    <jsp:setProperty name="calc" property="fromCurr" value="<%= ctr%>"/>
    <font >to</font>  <%= (String)request.getParameter("toCurrency") %>
<% String toCrr[]={"US Dollar", "British Pound", "Canadian
Dollar","Euro","Australian Dollar"};
            String tocrr=request.getParameter("toCurrency");
            int ctr1=0;
while(!(tocrr.equals(toCrr[ctr1])))
            ctr1++;
    %>
    <jsp:setProperty name="calc" property="toCurr" value="<%= ctr1%>"/>
    <p ><font >Amount: </font>
    <%= (String)request.getParameter("amount") %>
    <% int amnt=0;
     String str1;
     str1=request.getParameter("amount");
     str1=str1.trim();
```

```
        amnt=Integer.parseInt(str1,10);
%>

    <jsp:setProperty name="calc" property="amt" value="<%= amnt%>"/>
  <p ><font >Result: </font>
  <% double res=calc.calculate();
            out.println(res);
            %>
  <p align="center"><input type="submit" value="OK" name="OK"></p>
</form>
<p > </p>
</body>
</html>
```

The above code uses JSP tags to instantiate and use the calc bean. I'll now explain the highlighted code.

```
<jsp:useBean id="calc" class="calc" scope="page" />
```

The above statement instantiates the calc bean. The bean instance will be accessible in the current page only.

```
<jsp:setProperty name="calc" property="fromCurr" value="<%= fromCurr%>"/>
<jsp:setProperty name="calc" property="toCurr" value="<%= toCurr%>"/>
<jsp:setProperty name="calc" property="amt" value="<%= amnt%>"/>
```

The above statements set the values of the properties of the bean. The properties whose values are set are fromCurr, toCurr, and amt.

```
<% double res=calc.calculate();
    out.println(res);
%>
```

The above code invokes the calculate() method of the bean and displays the result.

The *calc.java* File

Listing 24-3 contains the code for the calc.java bean.

Listing 24-3 calc.java

```
import java.util.*;
import java.io.*;
import javax.naming.Context;
import javax.naming.InitialContext;
import javax.rmi.PortableRemoteObject;
public class calc
{
    private String currency="";
    private int fromCurr=0;
    private int toCurr=0;
    private int amt=0;
    private double result;
    private double[][] curr={

{1,1.4365,0.633673,0.8904,0.5148},

{0.696136,1,0.441122,0.619839,0.358371},

{1.5781,2.26694,1,1.40514,0.812406},

{1.12308,1.61331,0.711672,1,0.578167},

{1.9425,2.7904,1.23091,1.7296,1}
                                            };
    public void calc()
    {
    }
public String getCurr()
{
                        return currency;
}
public void setCurr(String str)
```

```java
{
                         currency=str;
}
public void setFromCurr(int frmCurr)
{
        fromCurr=frmCurr;
}
public int getFromCurr()
{
        return fromCurr;
}
public void setToCurr(int toCrr)
{
        toCurr=toCrr;
}
public int getToCurr()
{
        return toCurr;
}
public double calculate()
{
                        result=curr[fromCurr][toCurr]*amt;
                        System.out.println(result);
                        return result;
}
public void setAmt(int amount)
    {
        amt=amount;
    }
public double getAmt()
    {
        return amt;
    }
}
```

In the above code, the properties of the bean have been declared as private. The GET and SET methods have been defined for these properties.

```
public double calculate()
{
                    result=curr[fromCurr][toCurr]*amt;
                    System.out.println(result);
                    return result;
}
```

The `calculate()` method calculates the result and returns the amount to its caller.

Now I'll show you how the currency exchange calculator works.

When the `Foreign Exchange Rates` link is clicked on the Home page, the `currExchange.htm` page is displayed in Figure 24-3. A user can select currencies from the list boxes.

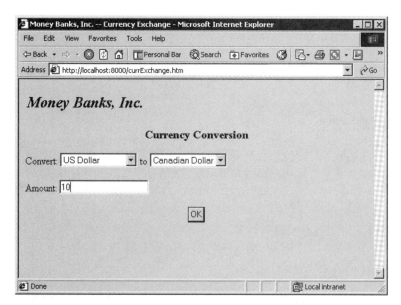

FIGURE 24-3 *The screen shows the output of the* `currExchange.htm` *page.*

When a user submits the `currExchange.htm` page by clicking the OK button, the `currExchangeBean.jsp` page displays the result to the user as shown in Figure 24-4.

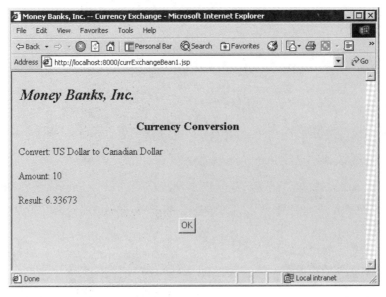

FIGURE 24-4 *The screen displays the* currExchangeBean.jsp *page calculation results.*

Summary

In this chapter, you learned how to create the Currency Exchange page. The currency exchange utility enables a user to determine how much a specified amount of currency would value when converted into another currency. The concepts of JSP and JavaBeans were used to create the utility. JSP was used to call the calculator bean, set the values in bean, obtain the result from the bean class, and display the result to the user. The bean class contains a method that calculates the result and returns it to the JSP page.

Chapter 25

Creating the Account Details Page

In this chapter, you'll learn how to create the Account Details page of the banking application at Money Banks, Inc. You will do this by using the following technologies:

◆ JDBC

◆ JSP

You learned about these technologies in detail in Chapter 19, "Creating the Registration Page for Account Holders."

The Account Details Page

As per the stated design of the application, the Account Details page is displayed when a user logs on to the application after providing logon information in the Login page. The Account Details page will display the transaction details of the account number specified in the Login page. Figure 25-1 depicts the interaction between the Login page and the Account Details page.

You're already aware of JDBC and JSP concepts. Therefore, I'll take you directly to the code of the Account Details page. The code is given in Listing 25-1.

Listing 25-1 acDetails.jsp

```
<html>
<head>
<title>Money Banks, Inc. -- Account Details</title>
</head>
<body bgproperties="fixed" bgcolor="#CCCCFF">
<p></p>
<table border="0" width="100%" height="42">
  <tr>
    <td width="50%" height="36"><b><font size="5" ><i>Money Banks,
Inc.</i></font></b></td>
    <td width="50%" height="36"></td>
  </tr>
```

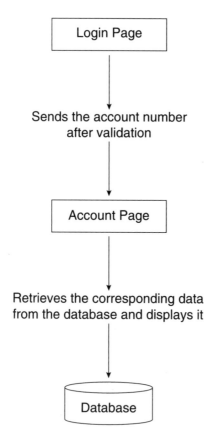

FIGURE 25-1 *The interaction between the Login page and the Account Details page.*

```
</table>
            <%@ page import="java.util.*" %>
            <%@ page import="java.sql.*" %>
            <%@ page import="java.text.*" %>
            <%@ page import="java.sql.Date" %>
            <%@ page language = "java" %>
            <%
            try{
            Class.forName("sun.jdbc.odbc.JdbcOdbcDriver");
            Connection connect;
            connect=DriverManager.getConnection("jdbc:odbc:BankDataSource","","");
            Statement state;
```

```
            String act=request.getParameter("txtActNumber");
            state = connect.createStatement();
            String strQuery1 = "select Register_Info.First_Name from Login_Info,
Register_Info where Login_Info.Register_Id=Register_Info.Register_Id and
Login_Info.Account_No='"+act+"'";
            ResultSet result1 = state.executeQuery(strQuery1);
            int ctr1=0;
    while(result1.next())
        {
                    out.print("<p><font size=\"3\">Account Holder: ");
                    out.print(result1.getString("First_Name"));
                    out.print("<p><font size=\"3\">Account Number: ");
                    out.print(request.getParameter("txtActNumber"));
                    out.println("</font></p>");
        }
        }
        catch(Exception e){
        out.println("done exception" +e);
        }
        %>
<p><font size="3" ><b>Transaction Details: </b></font></p>
<table border="1" width="95%" height="21">
  <tr>
    <td width="17%" valign="top" height="15"><font size="3" >Date</font></td>
    <td width="25%" height="15" valign="top"><font size="3" >Debit Amount
($)</font></td>
    <td width="25%" height="15" valign="top"><font size="3" >Credit Amount
($)</font></td>
    <td width="35%" height="15" valign="top"><font size="3" >Check Number
($)</font></td>
  </tr>
        <%
        try{
        Class.forName("sun.jdbc.odbc.JdbcOdbcDriver");
        Connection connect;
        connect=DriverManager.getConnection("jdbc:odbc:BankDataSource","","");
        Statement state;
        String act=request.getParameter("txtActNumber");
```

```
            state = connect.createStatement();
            String strQuery1 = "select * from TransCounter_Info where
Account_No='"+act+"'";
            ResultSet result1 = state.executeQuery(strQuery1);
            int ctr1=0;
    while(result1.next())
            {
                        out.println("<tr>");
                        out.println("<td width=\"17%\" valign=\"top\"
height=\"15\">");
                        out.println(result1.getDate("Transaction_date"));
                        out.println("<td width=\"25%\" valign=\"top\"
height=\"15\">");
                        out.println(result1.getFloat("Debit_Amount"));
                        out.println("<td width=\"25%\" valign=\"top\"
height=\"15\">");
                        out.println(result1.getFloat("Credit_Amount"));
                        out.println("<td width=\"35%\" valign=\"top\"
height=\"15\">");
                        out.println(result1.getString("Check_No"));
                        out.println("</tr>");
            }
            }
            catch(Exception e){
            out.println("done exception" +e);
            }
            %>
</table>
            <p align="left"><font size="3" >Balance Amount ($): </font>
            <%
            try{
            Class.forName("sun.jdbc.odbc.JdbcOdbcDriver");
            Connection connect;
            connect=DriverManager.getConnection("jdbc:odbc:BankDataSource","","");
            Statement state;
            String act=request.getParameter("txtActNumber");
            state = connect.createStatement();
            String strQuery1 = "select Balance from AcHolder_Info where
```

```
Account_No='"+act+"'";
            ResultSet result1 = state.executeQuery(strQuery1);
            int ctr1=0;
    while(result1.next())
            {
                    out.print("<align=\"right\">");
                    out.print(result1.getFloat("Balance"));
            }
            }
            catch(Exception e){
            out.println("done exception" +e);
            }
            %></p>
<p><font size="3" >In case of any questions, please contact our office at <A
href="mailto:helpdesk@MoneyBanks.com">helpdesk@MoneyBanks.com</a>.</font></p>
  <p align="center"><input type="button" value="OK " name="Ok"
onClick="window.open('Home_page.htm')">  
  </font>
</body>
</html>
```

This JSP code displays account details when a user logs on. I'll now discuss the highlighted code snippets in Listing 25-1.

```
            Class.forName("sun.jdbc.odbc.JdbcOdbcDriver");
            Connection connect;
            connect=DriverManager.getConnection("jdbc:odbc:BankDataSource","","");
            Statement state;
            String act=request.getParameter("txtActNumber");
            state = connect.createStatement();
            String strQuery1 = "select Register_Info.First_Name from Login_Info,
Register_Info where Login_Info.Register_Id=Register_Info.Register_Id and
Login_Info.Account_No='"+act+"'";
            ResultSet result1 = state.executeQuery(strQuery1);
```

The preceding statements establish a connection with the database. The code identifies the account number of the user and extracts the corresponding rows from the Login_Info and Register_Info tables. The result is stored in a Result-Set object.

```
while(result1.next())
        {
                    out.print("<p><font size=\"3\">Account Holder: ");
                    out.print(result1.getString("First_Name"));
                    out.print("<p><font size=\"3\">Account Number: ");
                    out.print(request.getParameter("txtActNumber"));
                    out.println("</font></p>");
        }
```

The preceding code snippet displays the account holder's name and account number.

```
Class.forName("sun.jdbc.odbc.JdbcOdbcDriver");
        Connection connect;
        connect=DriverManager.getConnection("jdbc:odbc:BankDataSource","","");
        Statement state;
        String act=request.getParameter("txtActNumber");
        state = connect.createStatement();
        String strQuery1 = "select * from TransCounter_Info where
Account_No='"+act+"'";
        ResultSet result1 = state.executeQuery(strQuery1);
        int ctr1=0;
    while(result1.next())
        {
                    out.println("<tr>");
                    out.println("<td width=\"17%\" valign=\"top\"
height=\"15\">");
                    out.println(result1.getDate("Transaction_date"));
                    out.println("<td width=\"25%\" valign=\"top\"
height=\"15\">");
                    out.println(result1.getFloat("Debit_Amount"));
                    out.println("<td width=\"25%\" valign=\"top\"
height=\"15\">");
                    out.println(result1.getFloat("Credit_Amount"));
                    out.println("<td width=\"35%\" valign=\"top\"
height=\"15\">");
                    out.println(result1.getString("Check_No"));
                    out.println("</tr>");
        }
```

The above code snippet executes the query to obtain transaction details of a particular account, and displays the transaction details to the user.

```
Class.forName("sun.jdbc.odbc.JdbcOdbcDriver");
    Connection connect;
    connect=DriverManager.getConnection("jdbc:odbc:BankDataSource","","");
    Statement state;
    String act=request.getParameter("txtActNumber");
    state = connect.createStatement();
    String strQuery1 = "select Balance from AcHolder_Info where
Account_No='"+act+"'";
    ResultSet result1 = state.executeQuery(strQuery1);
    int ctr1=0;
while(result1.next())
    {
            out.print("<align=\"right\">");
            out.print(result1.getFloat("Balance"));
    }
```

These statements will execute the query to obtain the balance amount from the `AcHolder_Info` table and display it.

A sample output of the `acDetails.jsp` page is displayed in Figure 25-2.

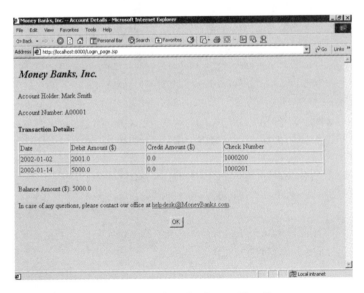

FIGURE 25-2 *The figure displays the Account Details page.*

Summary

In this chapter, you learned how to create the Account Details page of the banking application. The concepts of JDBC and JSP were used to create the page. The JSP interacts with the database by using the JDBC concepts. The transaction details of the particular account number, which is entered by the user in the Login page, are displayed in the JSP page.

Chapter 26

In this chapter, you'll see how to run the entire banking application that you have developed for Money Banks, Inc.

The Steps to Execute the Application

Before you execute the application, you need to follow the steps that are listed as follows:

1. Ensure that the paths for JDK and J2EE are correctly configured.
2. Start J2EE by executing the command given here:

   ```
   c:\>j2ee -verbose
   ```
3. Copy the JSP and HTML files in the `j2skee1.2.1\public_html` folder.
4. Copy the .class files of beans in the `j2skee1.2.1\lib\classes` folder.
5. Deploy the `Counter` servlet.

Now, here's an example to see how the application works.

Mark is an account holder at Money Banks, Inc., and wishes to sign up for the online banking services. He has followed the steps given above and passed the URL of the servlet to the browser. The Welcome Page is displayed to Mark, as seen in Figure 26-1.

Mark clicks the link labeled "Click here to continue" to go to the Home page of the application, as seen in Figure 26-2.

To view his account details, Mark first needs to register with the application, and then log on by supplying his account number and password. To register to use the online banking services, Mark clicks the link labeled "Registered account holders," as seen on the Home page. Next, in the Registration page, Mark needs to provide his personal and account information. See the Registration page in Figure 26-3.

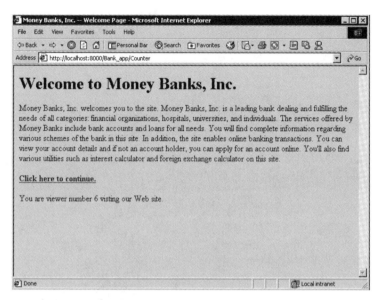

FIGURE 26-1 *The screen shows the Welcome page that Mark sees.*

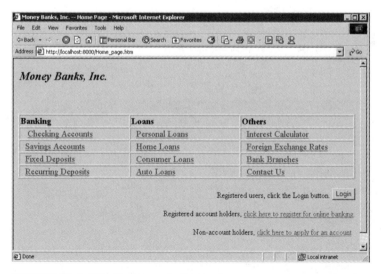

FIGURE 26-2 *The Home page is displayed.*

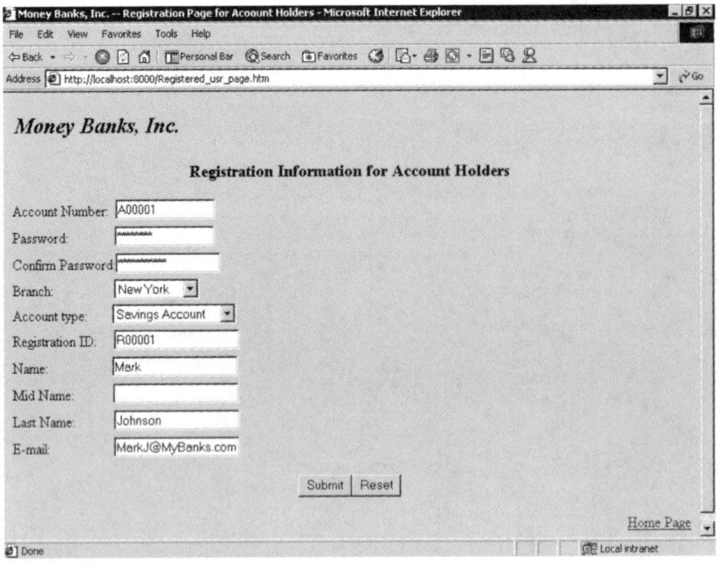

FIGURE 26-3 *The Registration page for account holders is displayed.*

When Mark submits the information on the Registration page, a JSP page receives and validates the information. After a successful validation, a confirmation message is displayed. See Figure 26-4.

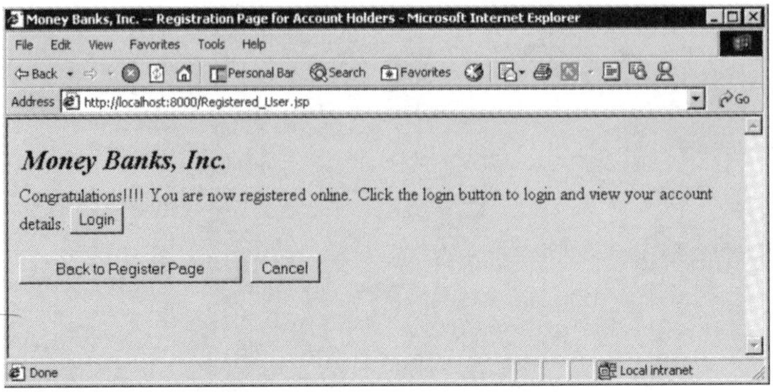

FIGURE 26-4 *This message is displayed after a successful validation.*

If some of the information provided by Mark in the Registration page is not validated, an error message is displayed. See Figure 26-5.

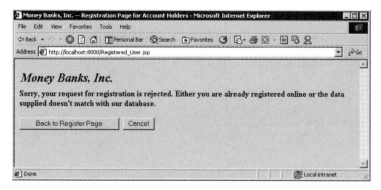

FIGURE 26-5 *The error message displayed after an unsuccessful validation.*

In the example I'm giving here, the information provided by Mark is validated successfully and a "Congratulations!!!" message is displayed. Mark can now log on to the application by providing his account number and password in the Login page. You can see the Login page in Figure 26-6.

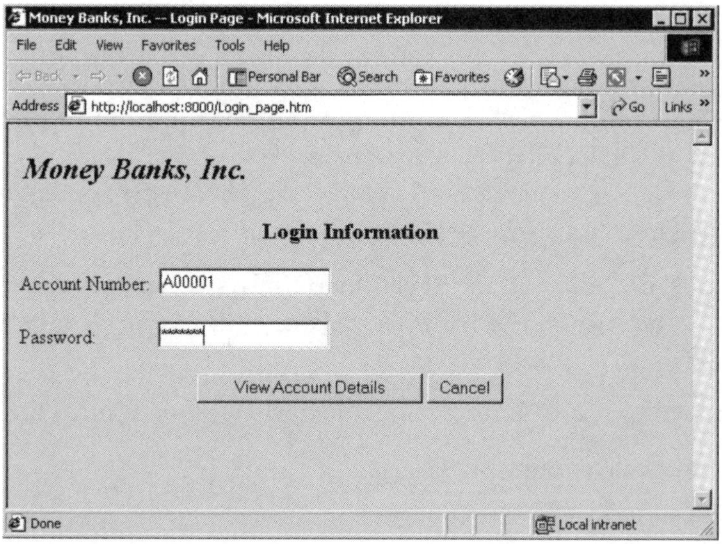

FIGURE 26-6 *The Login page is displayed.*

If the account number and password Mark supplies on the Login page are correct, the transaction details of Mark's account are displayed on the Account Details page. See Figure 26-7.

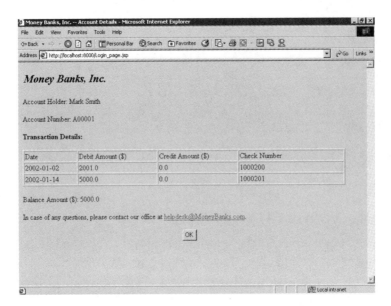

FIGURE 26-7 *The transaction details of Mark's account are displayed.*

Another user, Jim, who doesn't have an account with Money Banks, Inc., visits the Home page. Jim wants to open an account with the bank. Jim can request to do this by clicking the link called "Non-account holders" on the Home page. This will lead him to the Registration page for non-account holders. Jim needs to provide personal information on the Registration page, as seen in Figure 26-8.

After registering Jim's request, the application displays a message to Jim, confirming that the bank's database has been updated with the details necessary to open Jim's new account. See Figure 26-9.

Two utilities are provided with the application at Money Banks, Inc. These are:

◆ Interest calculator utility
◆ Foreign currency calculator utility

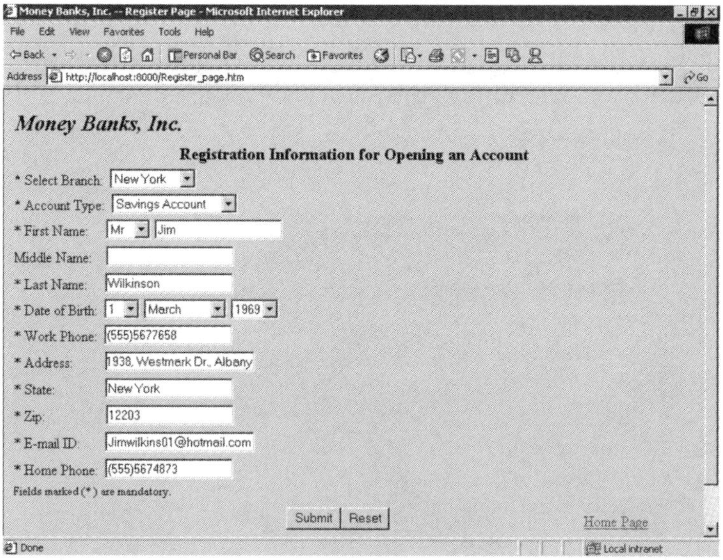

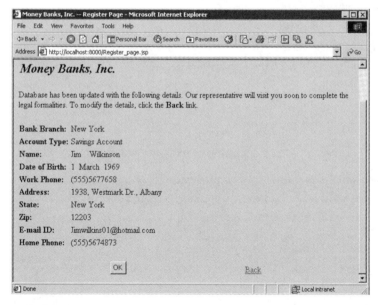

FIGURE 26-8 *The Registration page for non-account holders is shown here.*

FIGURE 26-9 *The Registration page displays an updated message to Jim.*

A third user, Nancy, wants to calculate the interest that she would need to pay based on a fixed interest rate over a specified period of time. To do this, she uses the interest calculator, which can be accessed from the Home page. The Interest Calculator page is illustrated in Figure 26-10.

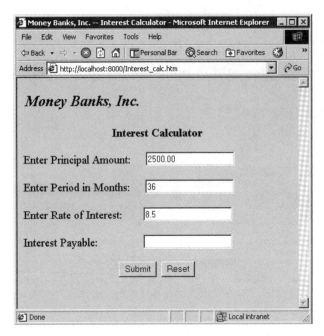

FIGURE 26-10 *The Interest Calculator page is displayed here.*

The result of Nancy's interest calculation is displayed in Figure 26-11.

Another user, Julie, is planning to visit Australia for the holidays. To ascertain the amount of money she should take with her, she uses the currency calculator to figure out the value of American dollars in Australian dollars. She goes to the Currency Calculator page, as seen in Figure 26-12.

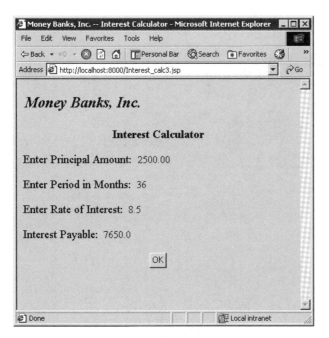

FIGURE 26-11 *This figure shows the results of Nancy's interest calculation.*

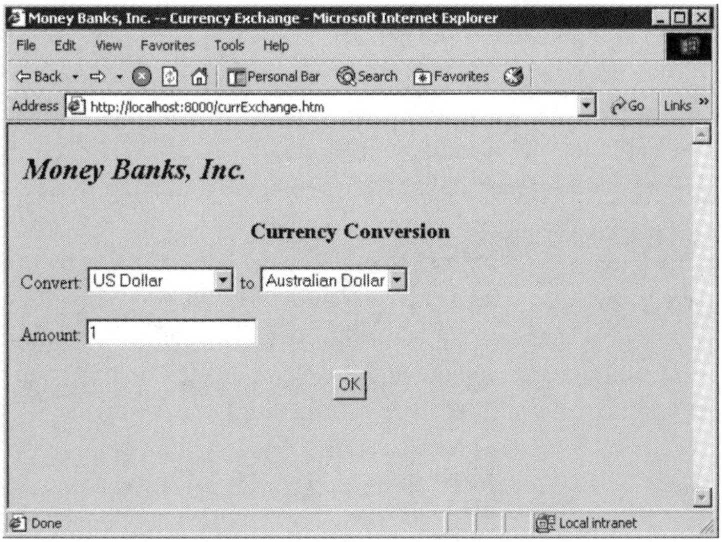

FIGURE 26-12 *The Currency Exchange Calculator page is displayed to Julie.*

The results of Julie's currency calculation are displayed in Figure 26-13.

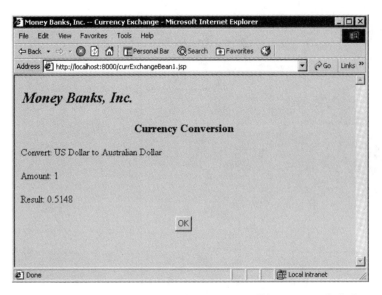

FIGURE 26-13 *This figure shows the answer to Julie's currency calculation query.*

Summary

In this chapter, you saw how to use the banking application at Money Banks, Inc. There are four users in the example shown in this chapter. Each user has a different requirement. In this chapter, you learned how the banking application caters to the needs to each user. Mark, the account holder at Money Banks, Inc., used the Registration page for account holders to register with the application so that he can log on and use the online banking services. Jim, who doesn't hold an account at the bank, registers a request to open a new bank account by using the Registration page for non-account holders. Nancy and Julie used the interest calculator and currency exchange calculator, respectively, to obtain the information they needed. Now all the requirements of the development team's original design for the banking application have been successfully fulfilled.

PART V

Professional Project — 3

Project 3

**Creating an
Online Music
Application**

Project 3 Overview

This music application is an online Web site for a music store. The application is a virtual showcase for everything related to the music store. The site has information regarding the latest songs, albums, and artists.

The music application has the following functionalities:

◆ The application will enable a visitor to register with the application.

◆ The application will enable visitors to perform activities such as search for music items, vote for popular music, and view the latest releases and chart toppers.

◆ The application will enable a registered user to select items such as CDs and cassettes for purchase using the shopping cart.

◆ The application will have an administrator's page, which will enable administrators to maintain user details and manage the music items in the inventory.

◆ The application will allow users to search for music based on multiple keywords such as album name, music category, or singer.

The concepts that I'll use to build the music application are:

◆ Enterprise Java Beans

◆ Java Server Pages (JSP)

◆ JDBC

◆ Java Beans

◆ Deployment of the Application on J2EE

Chapter 27

MusicWorld is a leading music store in New York. Due to aggressive marketing strategies and benefits offered to the customers, the business of MusicWorld has grown manifold in various cities across the United States in recent years. Recently, MusicWorld announced the opening of various new branches across the country. In addition, to keep pace with the Web age, MusicWorld has plans to develop a music application. The application will be known as `eMusicWorld`.

The application will cater to the needs of all visitors to the online application, registered users, and administrators.

A team of developers is appointed to build the application. The members of the team are:

- Larry Peterson, the Project Manager
- John Wallace, a Web Designer
- Henry Forsythe, a Web Developer
- Ken Barrett, a Web Developer
- Katie Frye, a Web Developer

You, as part of the team, need to help develop the music application. Now, I'll discuss the life cycle of the project as identified by the team.

The Project Life Cycle

The development life cycle of a project usually involves three stages:

- Project initiation
- Project execution
- Project completion

In the project initiation stage, the development team prepares the project plans and finalizes the outcome of each phase. In this stage, the team also prepares a comprehensive list of tasks involved in each phase, and the project manager assigns responsibilities to the team members, depending on their skills.

In the project execution stage, the team develops the product. In the case of the music application development team, they will develop the online music application. This stage consists of the following phases:

◆ Requirements analysis

◆ High-level design

◆ Low-level design

◆ Construction

◆ Testing

◆ Acceptance

I'll now discuss each of these phases in detail.

The Requirements Analysis Phase

During the requirements analysis phase, the development team analyzes the requirements to be fulfilled by the online music application and identifies the probable approach for meeting these requirements. To identify the requirements needed of the application, the team decides to study the existing music portals and conduct extensive interviews among MusicWorld's customers and managers. During interviews it is noticed that instead of viewing a comprehensive list of song items available, the customers would prefer to look for the song items in the specific song category and then place the order.

Finally, the team identifies that the music application should:

◆ Enable a visitor to register with the application after validation has been performed on the data provided by the user

◆ Enable visitors to perform activities such as search for music items, vote for popular music, and view latest releases and chart toppers

◆ Enable a registered user to select items for purchase

◆ Enable registered users to provide feedback to the site

◆ Enable registered users to select song items and place them in a shopping cart

◆ Enable administrators to maintain user details and manage music items in the inventory

The High-Level Design Phase

In this phase, the team decides how the application should function. The formats for data input and output are finalized here. The functional specifications documentation of the application is presented in a language that can be understood by all. The finished project design is, however, executed only on the project manager's approval.

The development team identifies three categories in which the interfaces of the music application will be divided. These categories are:

- Visitor Interface
- User Interface
- Administrator Interface

The Visitor Interface category will have the following pages:

- The Home Page
- The Chart Toppers Page
- The Search Page
- The Vote Page
- The New Releases Page
- The Register Page
- The Login Page
- The Help Page

The User Interface category will have the following pages:

- The User Home Page
- The Shopping Cart Page
- The Wishlist Page
- The Feedback Page
- The Buy Page
- The Logout Page

The Administrator Interface category will have the following pages:

- The Delete User Page
- The Add Item Page
- The Modify Item Page

◆ The Reports Page, which includes sales reports for a specified day, previous week, and previous month

◆ The View Wishlist Page

◆ The View Messages Page

During this phase the design of the database is finalized. You'll look at the interfaces and database design in Chapter 28, "Designing Interfaces and Database."

The Low-Level Design Phase

In this phase, a detailed design of software modules, based on the high-level design, is created. In addition, the team also creates specifications for the various software modules of an application.

Figure 27-1 illustrates the functionality of the online music application and the interaction between the various interfaces in the application.

The Construction Phase

In the construction phase, the software components are built. This phase uses the output of the low-level design to produce software items. During the construction phase, the development team divides the responsibilities among its team members. Some team members are assigned the task of designing the interface, whereas others take the job of writing the code to develop the application.

The Testing Phase

Software modules are tested for their functionality as per the requirements identified during the requirements analysis phase. To test the functionality of the music application, a Quality Assurance (QA) team is formed. The requirements identified during the requirements analysis phase are submitted to the QA team. The QA team will, in this phase, test the application for these requirements. The development team also submits a test case report to the QA team so that the application can be tested in various possible scenarios.

The Acceptance Phase

In this phase, based on the predefined acceptance criteria, the marketing team conducts acceptance testing for client projects. In the case of the online music

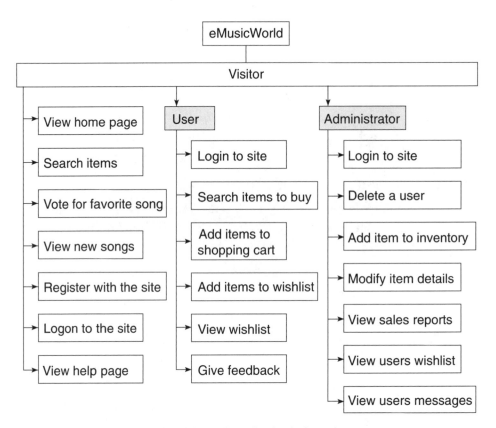

FIGURE 27-1 *The functionality of the music application is shown here.*

application, the acceptance criteria are the fulfillment of all the requirements identified during the requirements analysis phase.

Summary

In this chapter, you learned about the development stage, in the life cycle of the music application. A team was constituted to develop the application. The various interfaces of the application were determined during the design phase. In the next few chapters, you'll look at the creation and development of the interfaces of the music application. You'll also design the database in Chapter 28.

Chapter 28

**Designing
Interfaces and a
Database**

In this chapter, you will look at the design of the various interfaces of the eMu-sicWorld application, as decided upon during the initial design phase. You'll also look at the design of the database.

Designing Interfaces

First I'll discuss the design of the interfaces in detail. To begin, I'll show you the design for pages of the Visitor Interface category.

The Visitor Interface Category

As identified during the design phase, the Visitor Interface category has the following pages:

- The Home Page
- The Chart Toppers Page
- The Search Page
- The Vote Page
- The New Releases Page
- The Register Page
- The Login Page

Now take a look at each of these.

The Home Page

The Home page of the music application will be the first page to be displayed when a person visits the music application. The page will display a welcome message and, in addition, it will display various menus to facilitate navigation through the application.

A sketch of the Home page is depicted in Figure 28-1.

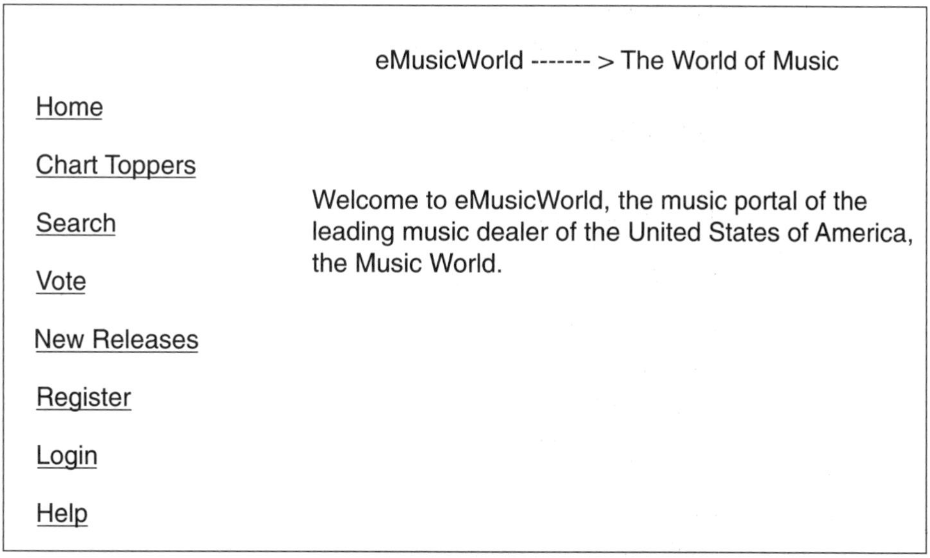

eMusicWorld ------- > The World of Music

Home

Chart Toppers

Search   Welcome to eMusicWorld, the music portal of the
                       leading music dealer of the United States of America,
Vote   the Music World.

New Releases

Register

Login

Help

FIGURE 28-1 *The figure displays the design of the Home page.*

The Chart Toppers Page

The Chart Toppers page will display a list of the most popular songs. The popularity of the song will be decided based on the voting at the Vote page. A sketch of the Chart Toppers page is depicted in Figure 28-2.

The Search Page

The Search page will enable users to perform a search of songs based on the song categories. The sketch of the Search page is displayed in Figure 28-3.

The Vote Page

The Vote page of the music application will enable a user to vote for his favorite songs. A sketch of the Vote page is displayed in Figure 28-4.

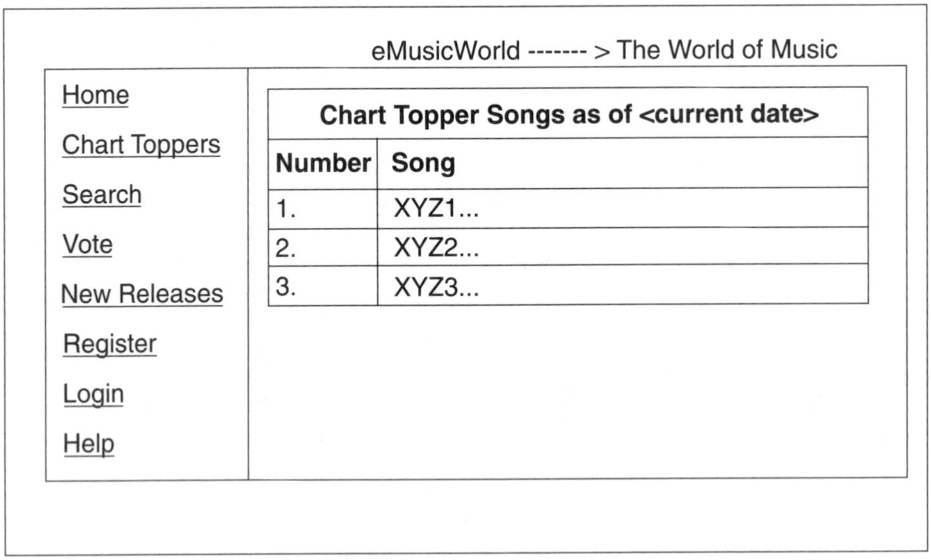

eMusicWorld ------- > The World of Music

Home		
Chart Toppers		
Search		
Vote		
New Releases		
Register		
Login		
Help		

Chart Topper Songs as of <current date>	
Number	**Song**
1.	XYZ1...
2.	XYZ2...
3.	XYZ3...

FIGURE 28-2 *The figure displays the design of the Chart Toppers page.*

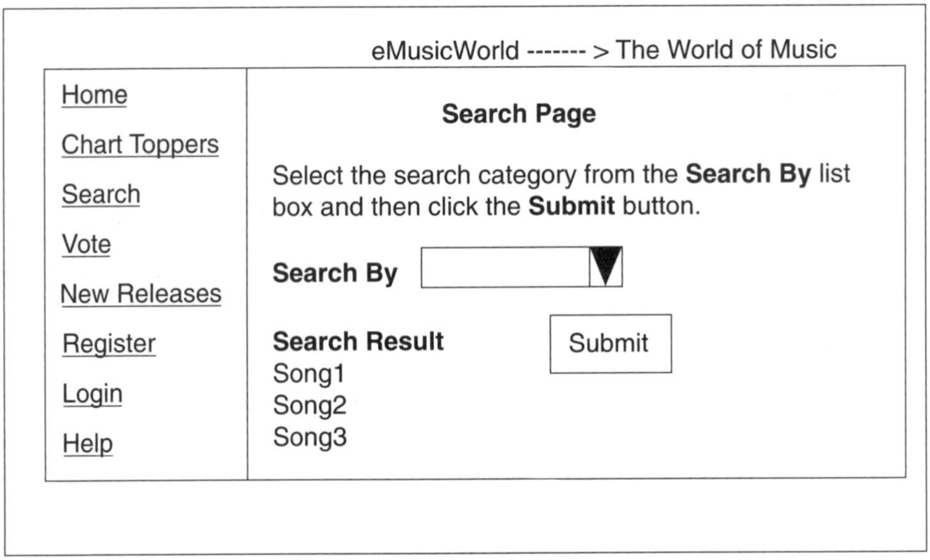

eMusicWorld ------- > The World of Music

Home

Chart Toppers

Search

Vote

New Releases

Register

Login

Help

Search Page

Select the search category from the **Search By** list box and then click the **Submit** button.

Search By [▼]

Search Result   [Submit]
Song1
Song2
Song3

FIGURE 28-3 *The figure displays the design of the Search page.*

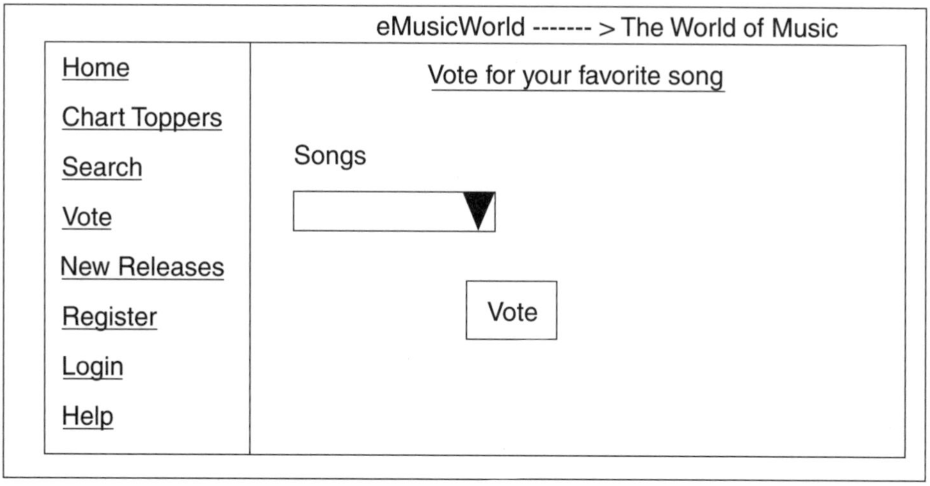

FIGURE 28-4 *The figure displays the design of the Vote page.*

The New Releases Page

The New Releases page of the music application will display a list of the latest songs released during the last month. A sketch of the New Releases page is displayed in Figure 28-5.

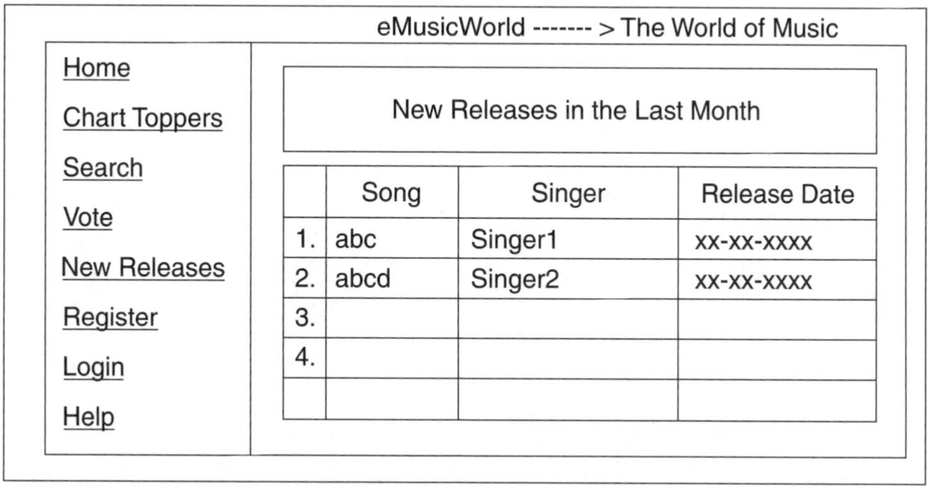

FIGURE 28-5 *The figure displays the design of the New Releases page.*

The Register Page

The Register page will be used by visitors to register with the application. Visitors will need to provide information such as username, password, address, and credit card details during registration. A sketch of the Register page is displayed in Figure 28-6.

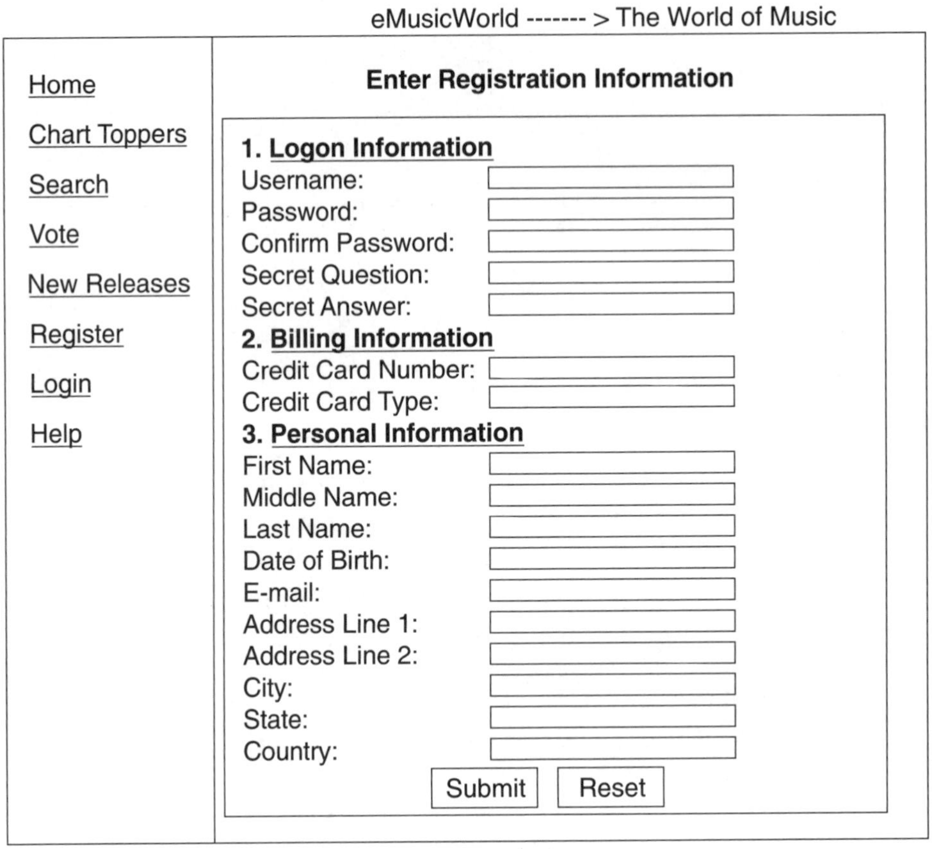

eMusicWorld ------- > The World of Music

Home	**Enter Registration Information**
Chart Toppers	**1. Logon Information**
Search	Username:
	Password:
Vote	Confirm Password:
New Releases	Secret Question:
	Secret Answer:
Register	**2. Billing Information**
Login	Credit Card Number:
	Credit Card Type:
Help	**3. Personal Information**
	First Name:
	Middle Name:
	Last Name:
	Date of Birth:
	E-mail:
	Address Line 1:
	Address Line 2:
	City:
	State:
	Country:
	Submit Reset

FIGURE 28-6 *The figure displays the design of the Register page.*

The Login Page

To log on to the music application, visitors will provide logon information in the Login page. Whether the visitor is a user or administrator is determined based on the username provided by the visitor. Respective home pages for the users and administrators are then displayed. A sketch of the Login page is displayed in Figure 28-7.

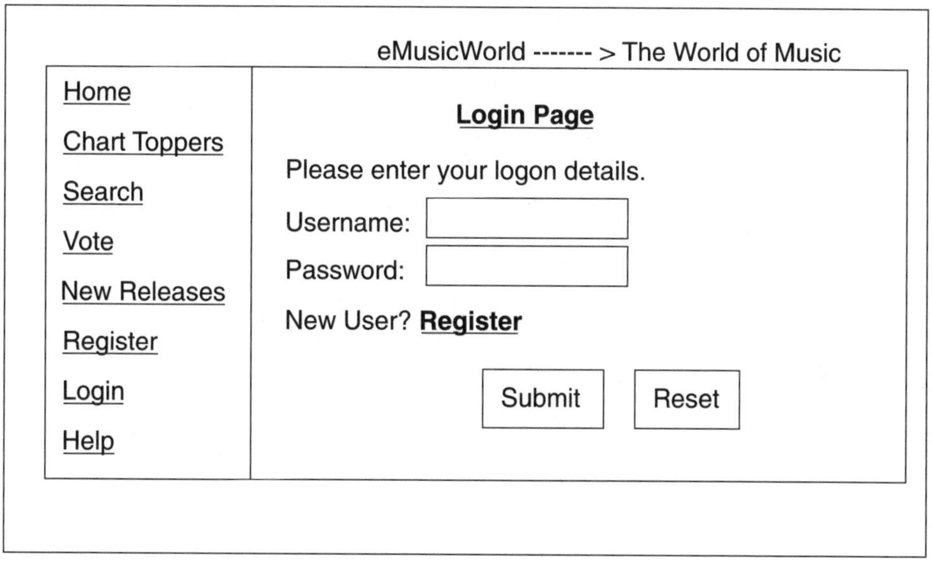

FIGURE 28-7 *The figure displays the design of the Login page.*

Next, I'll show you the design of pages in the User Interface category.

The User Interface Category

The User Interface category, as determined during the design phase, will have the following pages:

- ◆ The User Home Page
- ◆ The Shopping Cart Page
- ◆ The Wishlist Page
- ◆ The Feedback Page
- ◆ The Buy Page

Now take a look at each of these.

The User Home Page

The User Home page is displayed to a user when the user logs on to the music application. A sketch of the User Home page is displayed in Figure 28-8.

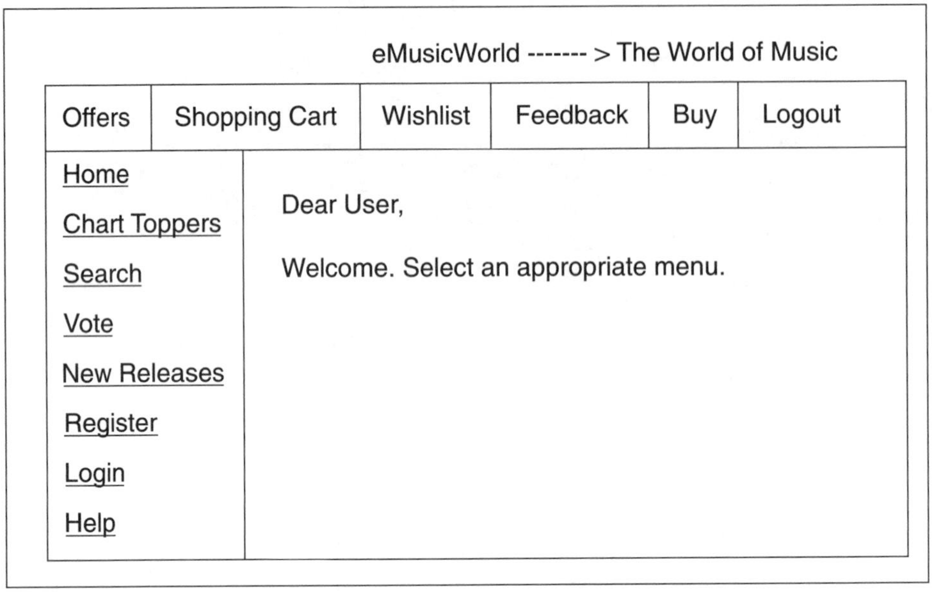

eMusicWorld ------- > The World of Music					
Offers	Shopping Cart	Wishlist	Feedback	Buy	Logout

Home
Chart Toppers
Search
Vote
New Releases
Register
Login
Help

Dear User,

Welcome. Select an appropriate menu.

FIGURE 28-8 *The figure displays the design of the User Home page.*

The Buy Page

To purchase a music item, a user needs to select songs based on a search criterion. A user can search for items based on song categories and select the songs to purchase on the Buy page. The sketch of the Buy page is displayed in Figure 28-9.

The Shopping Cart Page

The shopping cart contains the items that a user has selected for buying. The Shopping Cart page of the music application will display a list of CDs, cassettes, and other music items selected by the user. Users can add the items to their wishlist by clicking the check box next to the items and then clicking on the Add to Wishlist button. They can also specify the quantity of the items. The Shopping Cart page is displayed in Figure 28-10.

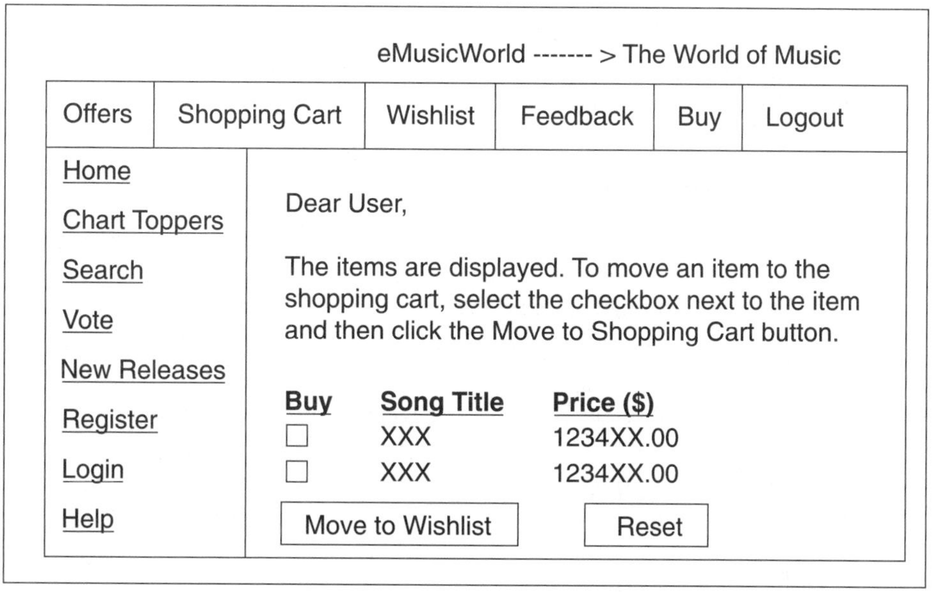

eMusicWorld ------- > The World of Music

| Offers | Shopping Cart | Wishlist | Feedback | Buy | Logout |

Home

Chart Toppers

Search

Vote

New Releases

Register

Login

Help

Dear User,

The items are displayed. To move an item to the shopping cart, select the checkbox next to the item and then click the Move to Shopping Cart button.

Buy	Song Title	Price ($)
☐	XXX	1234XX.00
☐	XXX	1234XX.00

[Move to Wishlist]   [Reset]

FIGURE 28-9 *The design of the Buy page*

eMusicWorld ------- > The World of Music

| Offers | Shopping Cart | Wishlist | Feedback | Buy | Logout |

Home

Chart Toppers

Search

Vote

New Releases

Register

Login

Help

Dear User,

Your shopping cart contains the following items:

Select	Item Code	Item Description	Price($)	Quantity
☐	XXX	XXXXXXX	1234XX.00	[ ]
☐	XXX	XXXXXXX	1234XX.00	[ ]

[Add to Wishlist]   [Reset]

FIGURE 28-10 *The figure displays the design of the Shopping Cart page.*

The Wishlist Page

A user can move the items in the shopping cart to a wishlist for later purchase. For example, if the credit limit of a user is exhausted and the user has an item in the shopping cart that he is inclined to purchase, he can put the item on the wishlist and purchase the item later. The music application enables a user to view his wishlist. The Wishlist page is displayed in Figure 28-11.

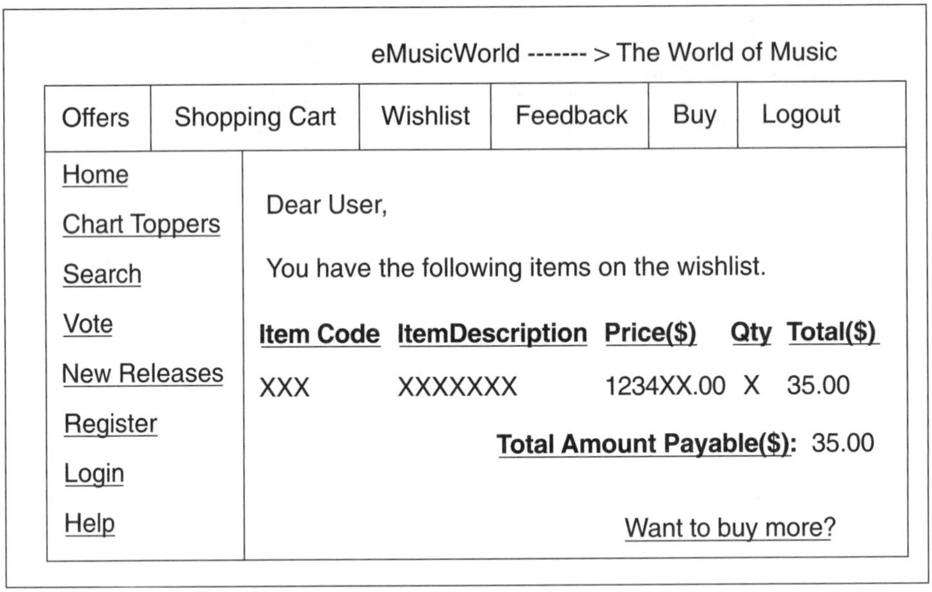

eMusicWorld ------- > The World of Music					
Offers	Shopping Cart	Wishlist	Feedback	Buy	Logout

Home
Chart Toppers
Search
Vote
New Releases
Register
Login
Help

Dear User,

You have the following items on the wishlist.

Item Code	**ItemDescription**	**Price($)**	**Qty**	**Total($)**
XXX	XXXXXXX	1234XX.00	X	35.00

Total Amount Payable($): 35.00

Want to buy more?

FIGURE 28-11 *The figure displays the design of the Wishlist page.*

The Feedback Page

To enable users to send feedback to the eMusicWorld site, the application developers have designed the Feedback page. The sketch of the Feedback page is displayed in Figure 28-12.

The last category of interfaces is the Administrator Interfaces category. The designs of pages in this category are discussed in detail in the following section.

eMusicWorld ------- > The World of Music

Offers	Shopping Cart	Wishlist	Feedback	Buy	Logout

Home

Chart Toppers

Search

Vote

New Releases

Register

Login

Help

Dear User,

Your feedback is valuable to us and it's a guiding factor in providing better service to you.

Your Message*:

(*means mandatory field)

Submit   Clear

FIGURE 28-12 *The figure displays the design of the Feedback page.*

The Administrator Interface Category

The Administrator Interface category will have the following pages as per the design of the music application:

♦ The Delete User Page

♦ The Add Item Page

♦ The Modify Item Page

♦ The Reports Pages, which will include daily, previous week, and previous month's sales reports pages

♦ The View Wishlist Page

♦ The View Messages Page

The Delete User Page

An administrator can delete a user by using the Delete User page. The sketch of the Delete User page is displayed in Figure 28-13.

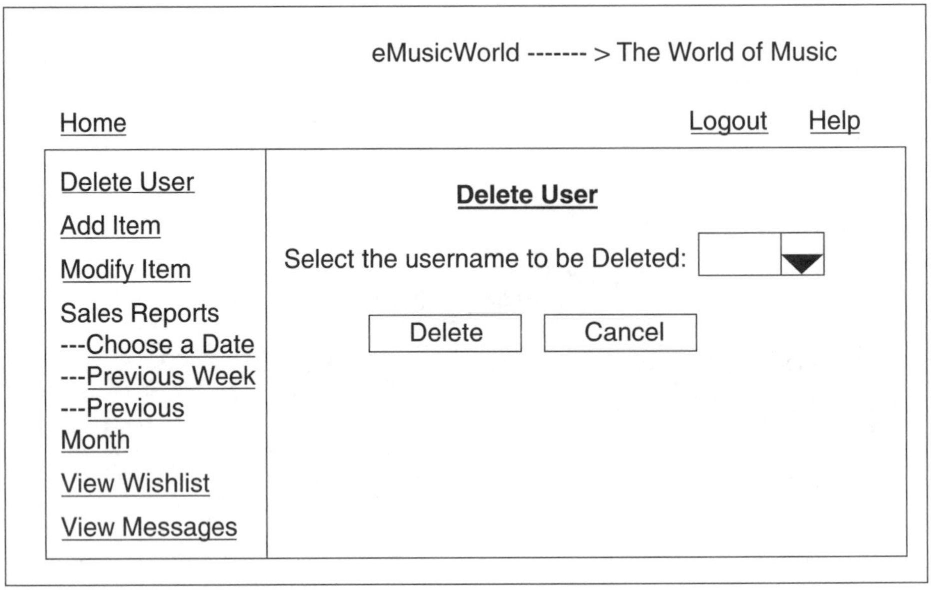

FIGURE 28-13 *The figure displays the design of the Delete User page.*

The Add Item Page

The music application needs to allow the administrator to manage the inventory. To enable administrators to add items to inventory, the application developers need to create the Add Item page as per the sketch given in Figure 28-14.

The Modify Item Page

To enable administrators to manage and modify item details in the inventory, the application developers need to create the Modify Item page. The sketch of the Modify Item page is given in Figure 28-15.

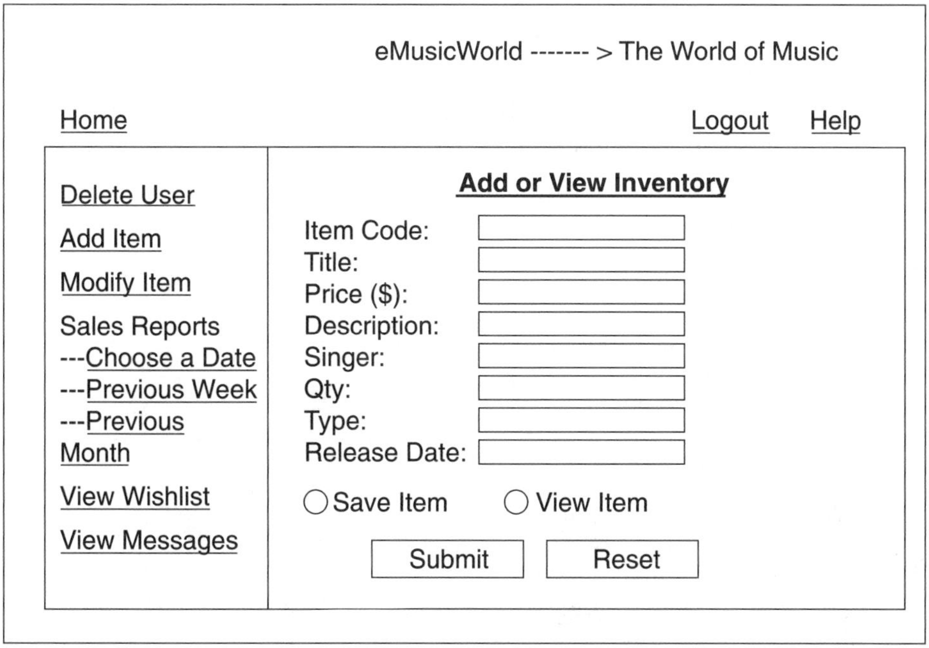

eMusicWorld ------- > The World of Music

Home   Logout   Help

Delete User

Add Item

Modify Item

Sales Reports
---Choose a Date
---Previous Week
---Previous
Month

View Wishlist

View Messages

Add or View Inventory

Item Code:
Title:
Price ($):
Description:
Singer:
Qty:
Type:
Release Date:

◯ Save Item   ◯ View Item

Submit   Reset

FIGURE 28-14 *The figure displays the design of the Add Item page.*

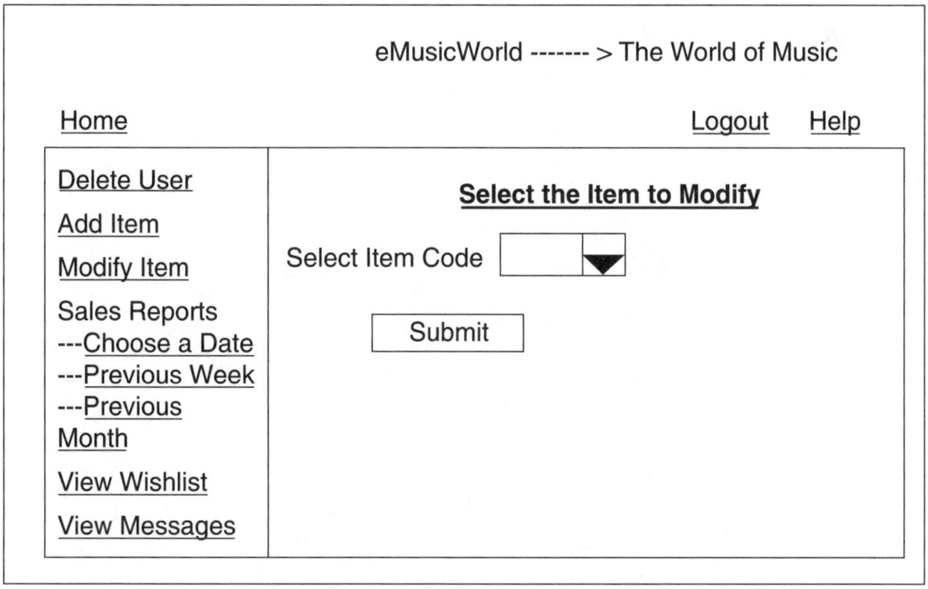

eMusicWorld ------- > The World of Music

Home   Logout   Help

Delete User

Add Item

Modify Item

Sales Reports
---Choose a Date
---Previous Week
---Previous
Month

View Wishlist

View Messages

Select the Item to Modify

Select Item Code

Submit

FIGURE 28-15 *The figure displays the design of the Modify Item page.*

The Reports Pages

The music application will allow administrators to view sales reports. The sales reports can be generated for the previous week, previous month, or for any particular date selected by the administrator. The sketches of the Reports pages are displayed in Figures 28-16, 28-17, and 28-18.

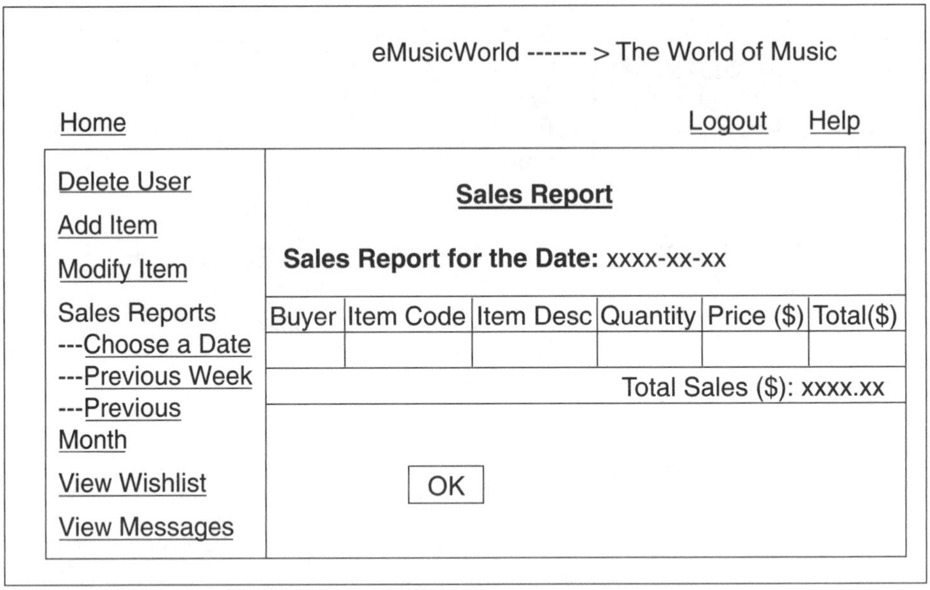

FIGURE 28-16 *The figure displays the design of the Date-wise sales report page.*

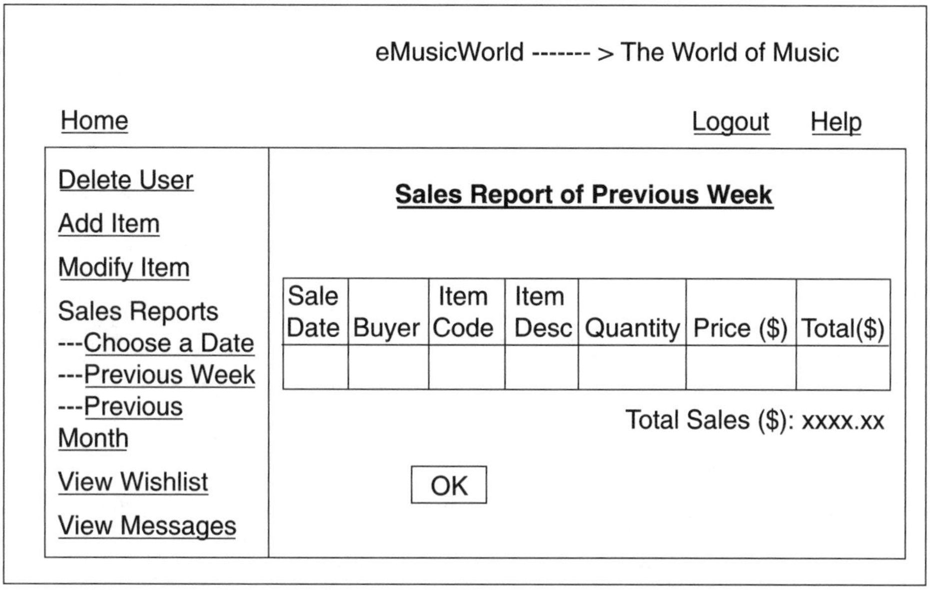

FIGURE 28-17 *The figure displays the design of the Previous Week's sales report page.*

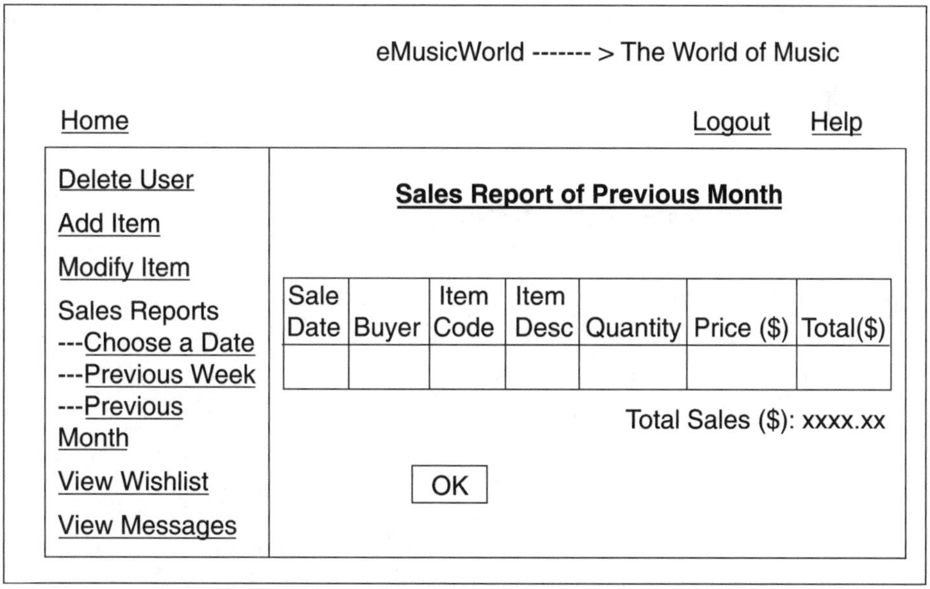

FIGURE 28-18 *The figure displays the design of the Previous Month's sales report page.*

The View Wishlist Page

To enable administrators to view the wishlist of the users, the application developers need to create the View Wishlist page as per the design given in Figure 28-19.

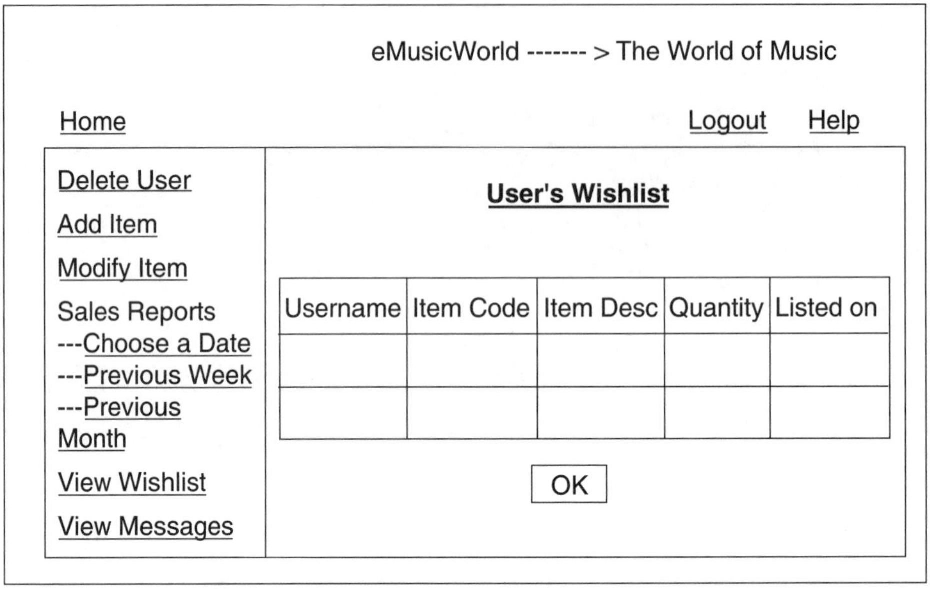

```
                    eMusicWorld ------- > The World of Music

  Home                                            Logout    Help
 ┌─────────────────┬──────────────────────────────────────────┐
 │ Delete User     │              User's Wishlist             │
 │ Add Item        │                                          │
 │ Modify Item     │  ┌────────┬─────────┬────────┬────────┬────────┐ │
 │ Sales Reports   │  │Username│Item Code│Item Desc│Quantity│Listed on│ │
 │ ---Choose a Date│  ├────────┼─────────┼────────┼────────┼────────┤ │
 │ ---Previous Week│  │        │         │        │        │        │ │
 │ ---Previous     │  ├────────┼─────────┼────────┼────────┼────────┤ │
 │ Month           │  │        │         │        │        │        │ │
 │ View Wishlist   │            ┌──────┐               │
 │ View Messages   │            │  OK  │               │
 └─────────────────┴──────────────────────────────────────────┘
```

FIGURE 28-19 *The figure displays the design of the View Wishlist page.*

The View Messages Page

The users can send feedback about the Web site by using the Feedback page. The administrators need be able to view these messages so that they can act on the users' suggestions. Therefore, to enable administrators to view feedback from users, a View Messages page has been designed. The sketch of the View Messages page is displayed in Figure 28-20.

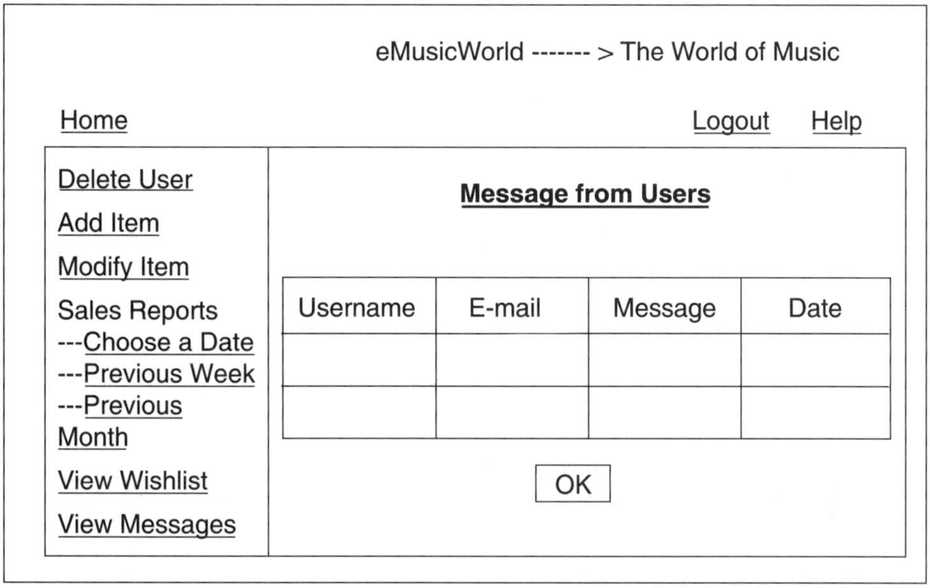

```
                        eMusicWorld ------ > The World of Music

   Home                                              Logout    Help
  ┌─────────────────────────────────────────────────────────────────┐
   Delete User                    Message from Users
   Add Item
   Modify Item
                    ┌──────────┬──────────┬──────────┬──────────┐
   Sales Reports    │ Username │  E-mail  │ Message  │   Date   │
   ---Choose a Date ├──────────┼──────────┼──────────┼──────────┤
   ---Previous Week │          │          │          │          │
   ---Previous      ├──────────┼──────────┼──────────┼──────────┤
   Month            │          │          │          │          │
                    └──────────┴──────────┴──────────┴──────────┘
   View Wishlist
                              ┌──────┐
   View Messages              │  OK  │
                              └──────┘
  └─────────────────────────────────────────────────────────────────┘
```

FIGURE 28-20   *The figure displays the design of the View Messages page.*

I'll now discuss the design of the database.

Designing the Database

The development team designed a database called Music, which will be created by using Microsoft SQL Server 2000.

Designing Tables of the Music Database

The Music database will hold the data of the eMusicWorld application. The tables of the database are explained as follows.

The Item_Master *Table*

The Item_Master table will hold the details of the items in the inventory. The structure of the Item_Master table is given in Table 28-1.

Table 28-1 The *Item_Master* Table

Column Name	Data Type	Size
Item_Code	char	8
Title	varchar	50
Rate	float	50
Item_Desc	varchar	50
Singer	varchar	50
Qty_on_hand	int	4
Type	varchar	50
Release_Date	datetime	8

The User_Info Table

The User_Info table will hold the details of user information. The structure of the User_Info table is given in Table 28-2.

Table 28-2 The *User_Info* Table

Column Name	Data Type	Size
Request_ID	int	4
User_name	varchar	20
First_name	varchar	20
Middle_name	varchar	20
Last_name	varchar	20
Date_of_Birth	datetime	80
E_mail	varchar	50
Address_Line1	varchar	50
Address_Line2	varchar	50
City	varchar	50
State	varchar	50

Column Name	Data Type	Size
Credit_Card	char	16
Credit_Card_Type	char	25

The Login_Info Table

The Login_Info table will hold the logon information of the users. The structure of the Login_Info table is given in Table 28-3.

Table 28-3 The *Login_Info* Table

Column Name	Data Type	Size
User_name	varchar	20
Password	varchar	20
Secret_question	varchar	50
Secret_answer	varchar	20
Role	char	10

The Sales_Master Table

The Sales_Master table will hold the details of the sales transactions. The structure of the Sales_Master table is given in Table 28-4.

Table 28-4 The *Sales_Master* Table

Column Name	Data Type	Size
Sale_Date	datetime	8
Item_code	char	8
Sale_qty	int	4
Rate	money	8
User_name	varchar	20

The Wishlist_Info *Table*

The `Wishlist_Info` table will store the wishlist items of the users. The structure of the `Wishlist_Info` table is given in Table 28-5.

Table 28-5 The *Wishlist_Info* Table

Column Name	Data Type	Size
User_name	varchar	20
Item_code	char	8
Qty	int	4
Wish_Date	datetime	8

The Feedback_Master *Table*

The `Feedback_Master` table will store the feedback of the users. The structure of the `Feedback_Master` table is given in Table 28-6.

Table 28-6 The *Feedback_Master* Table

Column Name	Data Type	Size
User_name	varchar	20
Message	varchar	50
Msg_Date	datetime	8

The Reply_Info *Table*

The `Reply_Info` table will store the replies of the administrators to the users. The structure of the `Reply_Info` table is given in Table 28-7.

Table 28-7 The *Reply_Info* Table

Column Name	Data Type	Size
Reply_date	datetime	8
Reply_msg	varchar	50
Reply_user_name	varchar	20

The Vote_Info *Table*

The Vote_Info table will store the number of votes for a favorite song. The structure of the Vote_Info table is given in Table 28-8.

Table 28-8 The *Vote_Info* Table

Column Name	Data Type	Size
Item_code	char	8
Number_votes	int	4

The relationship between tables of the Music database is displayed in Figure 28-21.

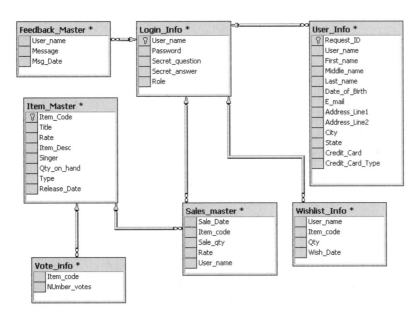

FIGURE 28-21 *The database diagram of the Music database is displayed.*

Summary

In this chapter, you looked at the designs of various interfaces of the music application. You also looked at the database design of the application.

Chapter 29

Creating the Visitor Interface Pages

In this chapter, you'll create the pages of the Visitor Interface category of the music application. The pages in this category are displayed to all the visitors to the site including registered users and the administrators. As identified during the design phase, this category will contain the following pages:

◆ The Home Page
◆ The Chart Toppers Page
◆ The Search Page
◆ The Vote Page
◆ The New Releases Page
◆ The Register Page
◆ The Login Page
◆ The Help Page

In the next section you'll start creating these pages.

Creating the Home Page

The Home page is the first page to be displayed to the visitors of the site. The Home page provides information about the company and the site to the visitor.

The code for the Home page is given in Listing 29-1.

Listing 29-1 Home_page.htm

```
<html>
<head>
<meta http-equiv="Content-Type" content="text/html; charset=windows-1252">
<meta http-equiv="Content-Language" content="en-us">
<title>Home Page</title>
</head>
<body bgcolor="#C0C0C0" topmargin="0"
background="http:\\localhost:8000\music\Background.bmp" >
```

```
<table border="0" width="100%">
  <tr>
    <td width="100%">
      <table border="0" width="97%" height="19">
        <tr>
          <td width="18%" height="13" valign="middle" align="right">
        <font face="Arial" size="5" color="#800000"><b><i>eMusicWorld-----&gt; The
World of Music</i></b></font>
          </td>
        </tr>
      </table>
    </td>
  </tr>
</table>
<table border="0" width="100%" height="353">
  <tr>
    <td width="15%" height="347" valign="top">
<p><font face="Arial" size="2" color="#800000"><b><a
HREF="http://localhost:8000/music/home_page.htm">Home</a></b></font></p>

<p><b><font face="Arial" size="2" color="#800000"><a
HREF="http://localhost:8000/music/chart_toppers.jsp">Chart
Toppers</a></font></b></p>
<p><b><font face="Arial" size="2" color="#800000"><a
HREF="http://localhost:8000/SearchContext/SearchAlias">Search</a></font></b></p>
<p><b><font face="Arial" size="2" color="#800000"><a
HREF="http://localhost:8000/music/vote_page.jsp">Vote</a></font></b></p>
<p><b><font face="Arial" size="2" color="#800000"><a
HREF="http://localhost:8000/music/new_release_page.jsp">New Releases</a></font></b>
<p><font face="Arial" size="2" color="#800000"><b><a
HREF="http://localhost:8000/Register/RegisterPage.htm">Register</a></b></font>
<p><font face="Arial" size="2" color="#800000"><b><a
HREF="http://localhost:8000/music/login_page.htm">Login</a></b></font>
<p><font face="Arial" size="2" color="#800000"><b><a
HREF="http://localhost:8000/music/help_page.htm">Help</a></b></font></p>
                </td>
```

```
<td width="85%" height="347" valign="middle">
<font face="Arial" size="2" color="#800000">Welcome to <b>eMusicWorld</b>,
the music portal of the leading music dealer of United States of America,
the <b>MusicWorld</b>. In our constant endeavor to provide you with better and more
efficient service, here's yet another gift for you. We have brought you this site
for your ultimate comfort and ease in purchasing your favorite music from our
store. Now you can buy music cassettes and CDs from our store, hassle-free. All you
have to do is sit back in the comfort of your own home, place items on order for
delivery, and we'll be at your service on your doorstep.</font>
    </td>
  </tr>
</table>
</body>
</html>
```

The output of Listing 29-1 is displayed in Figure 29-1.

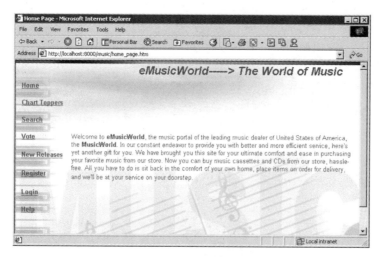

FIGURE 29-1 *The Home page is displayed here.*

The next page in the Visitor Interface category is the Chart Toppers page.

Creating the Chart Toppers Page

The Chart Toppers page displays a list of the most popular songs as voted by the visitors to the site. This page will query the Vote_Info table in the Music database to obtain the result.

The code of the Chart Toppers is displayed in Listing 29-2.

Listing 29-2 Chart_Toppers.jsp

```
<html>
<head>
<meta http-equiv="Content-Type" content="text/html; charset=windows-1252">
<meta http-equiv="Content-Language" content="en-us">
<title>Chart Toppers</title>
</head>
<body bgcolor="#C0C0C0" topmargin="0"
background="http:\\localhost:8000\music\Background.bmp" >
<table border="0" width="100%">
  <tr>
    <td width="100%">
      <table border="0" width="97%" height="19">
        <tr>
          <td width="18%" height="13" valign="middle" align="right">
      <font face="Arial" size="5" color="#800000"><b><i>eMusicWorld-----&gt; The
World of Music</i></b></font>
          </td>
        </tr>
      </table>
    </td>
  </tr>
</table>
<form method="POST" action="http://localhost:8000/music/home_page.htm">
                <%@ page import="java.util.*" %>
                <%@ page import="java.sql.*" %>
                <%@ page import="java.text.*" %>
                <%@ page import="java.sql.Date" %>
                <%@ page language = "java" %>
```

```
<%! String time;%>
<!--Get the current date.-->
<%Calendar cal = Calendar.getInstance(TimeZone.getDefault());
    String DATE_FORMAT = "MMMMM dd, yyyyy";
    java.text.SimpleDateFormat sdf=new java.text.SimpleDateFormat(DATE_FORMAT);
    sdf.setTimeZone(TimeZone.getDefault());
    time=sdf.format(cal.getTime());
%>
<table border="1" width="100%" height="363">
  <tr>
    <td width="18%" height="357">
<p><font face="Arial" size="2" color="#800000"><b><a
HREF="http://localhost:8000/music/user_home_page.jsp">Home</a></b></font></p>
<p><b><font face="Arial" size="2" color="#800000"><a
HREF="http://localhost:8000/music/chart_toppers.jsp">Chart
Toppers</a></font></b></p>
<p><b><font face="Arial" size="2" color="#800000"><a
HREF="http://localhost:8000/SearchContext/SearchAlias">Search</a></font></b></p>
<p><b><font face="Arial" size="2" color="#800000"><a
HREF="http://localhost:8000/music/vote_page.jsp">Vote</a></font></b></p>
<p><b><font face="Arial" size="2" color="#800000"><a
HREF="http://localhost:8000/music/new_release_page.jsp">New Releases</a></font></b>
<p><font face="Arial" size="2" color="#800000"><b><a
HREF="http://localhost:8000/Register/RegisterPage.htm">Register</a></b></font>
<p><font face="Arial" size="2" color="#800000"><b><a
HREF="http://localhost:8000/music/login_page.htm">Login</a></b></font>
<p><font face="Arial" size="2" color="#800000"><b><a
HREF="http://localhost:8000/music/help_page.htm">Help</a></b></font></p>
      <p> </td>
    <td width="82%" valign="top" >
  <table border="1" width="100%" >
    <tr>
      <td width="100%" valign="top" colspan="2" height="19" align="center"><b><font
face="Arial" color="#800000" size="3">Chart
        Topper Songs as on <%=time%></font></b></td>
    </tr>
    <tr>
                <td  valign="top" colspan="1"  align="center"><b><font
```

```
face="Arial" color="#800000" size="2">Number</font></b></td>
<td  valign="top" colspan="1" align="center"><b><font face="Arial" color="#800000"
size="2">Song</font></b></td>
     </tr>
                          <%
                 try{
                 Class.forName("sun.jdbc.odbc.JdbcOdbcDriver");
                 Connection connect;

connect=DriverManager.getConnection("jdbc:odbc:RegisterDataSource","","");
                 Statement state;
                 state = connect.createStatement();
                 String strQuery1 = "SELECT top 10 Vote_info.Item_code,
Item_Master.Item_Desc FROM Vote_info, Item_Master where
Vote_info.Item_code=Item_Master.Item_code ORDER BY Number_votes desc;";
                 String str;
                 int ctr=1;
                 ResultSet result1 = state.executeQuery(strQuery1);
                 while(result1.next())
                 {
                             %><tr>
      <td width="10%" valign="top" height="19" align="top"><font face="Arial"
color="#800000" size="2">
<%out.println(ctr+".");%>
                 </font></td>
 <td   valign="top" height="19" align="top"><font face="Arial" color="#800000"
size="2">
<%out.println(result1.getString("Item_Desc"));%>
                 </font></td>
     </tr>
                 <%
                                  ctr=ctr+1;
                 }
                                  connect.close();
                 }
                 catch(Exception e){
                 out.println("done exception" +e);
                 }
```

```
%>
  </table>
    </td>
  </tr>
</table>
<p>  </p>
<p>  </p>
</form>
</body>
</html>
```

The output of the preceding code is displayed in Figure 29-2.

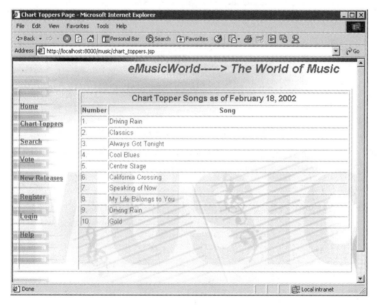

FIGURE 29-2 *The Chart Toppers page is displayed here.*

The next section analyzes the Chart_Toppers.jsp code.

Analyzing the *Chart_Toppers.jsp* Code

```
<%@ page import="java.util.*" %>
<%@ page import="java.sql.*" %>
<%@ page import="java.text.*" %>
<%@ page import="java.sql.Date" %>
```

The preceding statements will import the necessary API classes for activities such as database interactivity.

```
String strQuery1 = "SELECT top 10 Vote_info.Item_code,
Item_Master.Title FROM Vote_info, Item_Master where
Vote_info.Item_code=Item_Master.Item_code ORDER BY Number_votes desc";
```

The above SQL query will return the Top 10 songs. Along with the Item code, the query will return the title of the songs.

```
ResultSet result1 = state.executeQuery(strQuery1);
while(result1.next())
{
            %><tr>
    <td width="50%" valign="top" height="19" align="top"><b><font face="Arial"
color="#800000" size="2">
<%out.println(ctr+". "+result1.getString("Title"));%>
            </font></b></td>

    </tr>
        <%
                ctr=ctr+1;
        }
```

The preceding statements will execute the SQL query and store the result in the `ResultSet` object, `result1`. Next, the while loop will obtain the rows in the `result1` and print the description in a table.

Now, take a look at the next page in the Visitors Interface category, the Search page.

Creating the Search Page

The Search page will enable a visitor to search for a song based on the category. The Search page has been created by using the concepts of Enterprise JavaBeans (EJB). A container-managed entity bean has been used to perform the search operation. The following components are used to create the Search page:

◆ ItemHome.class

◆ ItemEjb.class

◆ Item.class

◆ SearchBean.class

◆ SearchItem.jsp

Now take a look at each of these components in detail.

ItemHome.class

The ItemHome.class is the home interface of the EJB. The home interface defines methods that allow EJB clients to create and find EJB components. The code of the source of the home interface is given in Listing 29-3.

Listing 29-3 ItemHome.java

```
import java.util.Collection;
 import java.rmi.RemoteException;
 import javax.ejb.*;

public interface ItemHome extends EJBHome
      {
               public Item create(int itemCode,String title, String rate,String
itemDescription, String singer, String quantityOnHand, String type,String
releaseDate) throws RemoteException,CreateException;


        public Item findByPrimaryKey(int itemCode) throws
FinderException,RemoteException;


public Collection findByType(String type)throws FinderException,RemoteException;
      }
```

The home interfaces are created by extending the EJBHome interface. The return type of the create() method in the interface is the remote interface of the EJB. The findByType() method is used to search items in the database.

Item.class

The source code for the remote interface is given in Listing 29-4.

Listing 29-4   Item.Java

```
import javax.ejb.EJBObject;
import  java.rmi.RemoteException;

public interface Item extends EJBObject
        {
                public int getitemCode() throws RemoteException;
                public String gettitle() throws RemoteException;
                public String getrate() throws RemoteException;
                public String getitemDescription() throws
RemoteException;
                public String getsinger() throws RemoteException;
                public String getquantityOnHand() throws RemoteException;
                public String gettype() throws RemoteException;
                public String getreleaseDate() throws RemoteException;


        }
```

A remote interface defines all the business methods of the enterprise bean that the EJB client would invoke. The business methods defined in the remote interface are implemented in the EJB class. Notice that the remote interface imports the javax.ejb.EJBObject and java.rmi.RemoteException interfaces. In addition, the access modifier for the remote interface and the methods declared within it are public. The methods must throw RemoteException. The RemoteException is thrown if any problem occurs with distributed object communication, such as network failure or failure in locating the object server.

ItemEJB.class

The methods defined in the `Item.java` code are implemented in `ItemEJB.class`. The source code of the EJB class is given in Listing 29-5.

Listing 29-5　ItemEJB.java

```java
import java.sql.*;
import javax.sql.*;
import java.util.*;
import javax.ejb.*;
import javax.naming.*;
import java.rmi.*;

public class ItemEjb implements EntityBean
{
public int itemCode;
public String title;
public String rate;
public String itemDescription;
public String singer;
public String quantityOnHand;
public String type;
public String releaseDate;
private EntityContext ctx;
Connection con;
public ItemEjb(){}
public int getitemCode()
 {
   return itemCode;
 }
public String gettitle()
 {
   return title;
 }
public String getrate()
   {
     return rate;
```

```
    }
public String getitemDescription()
  {
     return itemDescription;
  }
public String getsinger()
  {
     return singer;
  }
public String getquantityOnHand()
 {
    return quantityOnHand;
 }
public String gettype()
 {
    return type;
 }
public String getreleaseDate()
 {
    return releaseDate;
 }
public String ejbCreate(int itemCode,String title, String rate,String
itemDescription, String singer, String quantityOnHand, String type,String
releaseDate)throws   CreateException {
this.itemCode=itemCode;
this.title=title;
this.rate=rate;
this.itemDescription=itemDescription;
this.singer=singer;
this.quantityOnHand=quantityOnHand;
this.type=type;
this.releaseDate=releaseDate;
return null;
}

public void setEntityContext(EntityContext ctx){
this.ctx=ctx;
}
```

```
public void ejbActivate(){
                    Object obj=ctx.getPrimaryKey();
        String id=obj.toString();
        itemCode=Integer.parseInt(id);
}

public void ejbPassivate(){
itemCode=0;
    }
public void ejbStore(){}
public void ejbLoad(){}

public void ejbRemove(){}
public void unsetEntityContext(){}
public void ejbPostCreate(int itemCode,String title, String rate,String
itemDescription,String singer, String quantityOnHand, String type,String
releaseDate){}
}
```

The EJB class implements all the business methods declared in the remote interface. The EJB class implements the EntityBean interface. The code for the enterprise bean class contains the callback methods and the methods to access the data
in the database. Now I'll show you how to deploy the EJB.

Deploying the EJB

To be able to use the EJB classes, first you need to deploy them on the J2EE
server. The steps to deploy the application are given as follows:

1. Type start j2ee -verbose at the command prompt to start the J2EE
   server.

2. Type deploytool at the command prompt. The Application Deployment
   Tool window is displayed.

3. Select New Application from the File menu. The New Application dialog box is displayed.

4. Click the Browse button and select the folder where you need to deploy the application. Specify the application name as `MusicApp`, as shown in Figure 29-3.

FIGURE 29-3 *The New Application dialog box is shown.*

5. Click on the New Application button to close the dialog box.

6. Notice that the Application File Name box displays the complete path. Application Display Name is displayed as `MusicApp`.

7. Click on OK to close the New Application dialog box. In the Application Deployment Tool window, notice that the `MusicApp` is displayed in the left pane.

8. Next, select New Enterprise Bean command from the File menu. The New Enterprise Bean Wizard — Introduction page is displayed.

9. Click on the Next button. The New Enterprise Bean Wizard — EJB JAR dialog box is displayed.

10. Specify `ItemJar` in the JAR Display Name box. In the Contents group box, click on the Add button. The Add Files to .JAR dialog box appears.

11. Select `Item.class` and click the on the Add button. Similarly, select `ItemEJB.class` and click on the Add button. Also, select `ItemHome.class` and then click on the Add button. The files that you add are displayed in the lower text box of the dialog box, as shown in Figure 29-4.

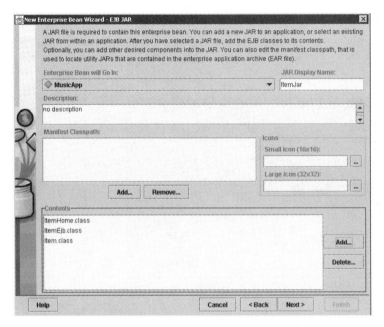

FIGURE 29-4 *The New Enterprise Bean Wizard — EJB JAR dialog box is displayed.*

12. Click on OK. The Add Files to .JAR dialog box closes. Under Contents, verify that the three files that you added appear.

13. Click on the Next button. The New Enterprise Bean Wizard — General dialog box is displayed, as shown in Figure 29-5.

14. From the Enterprise Bean Class drop-down list, select `ItemEJB`. From the `Home Interface` drop-down list, select `ItemHome`. From the Remote Interface drop-down list, select `Item`. In the Enterprise Bean Display Name box, type `ItemBean`.

15. In the Bean Type group box, select the `Entity` option.

16. Click the Next button. The New Enterprise Bean Wizard — Entity Settings dialog box is displayed.

17. In the Persistence Management group box, select Container-Managed Persistence. The various container-managed fields appear.

18. Select the check boxes as displayed in Figure 29-6.

19. From the Primary Key Field Name list, select `ItemCode`.

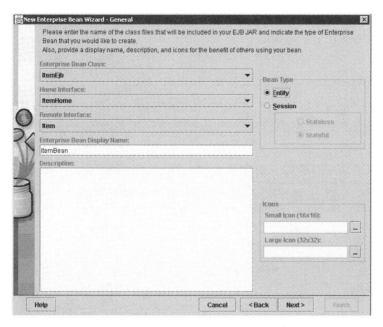

FIGURE 29-5 *The New Enterprise Bean Wizard — General dialog box is shown.*

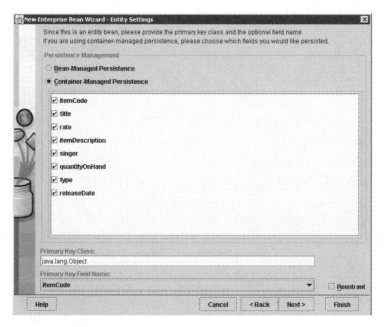

FIGURE 29-6 *The New Enterprise Bean Wizard — Entity Settings dialog box is displayed.*

20. Click the Next button. The New Enterprise Bean Wizard — Environment Entries dialog box appears.

21. Click the Next button. The New Enterprise Bean Wizard — Enterprise Bean References dialog box is displayed.

22. Click the Next button. The New Enterprise Bean Wizard — Resource References dialog box is displayed, as shown in Figure 29-7.

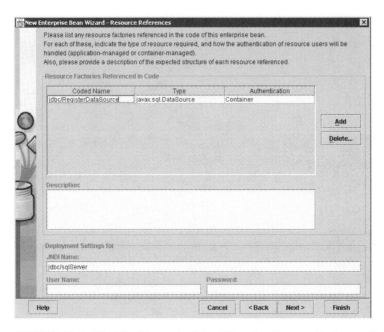

FIGURE 29-7 *The New Enterprise Bean Wizard — Resource References dialog box is shown.*

23. In the New Enterprise Bean Wizard — Resource References dialog box, specify Coded Name as `jdbc/RegisterDataSource`. Specify JNDI Name as `jdbc/sqlServer`.

24. Again, click the Next button. The New Enterprise Bean Wizard — Security dialog box appears.

25. Click the Next button. The New Enterprise Bean Wizard — Transaction Management dialog box is displayed.

26. In the New Enterprise Bean Wizard — Transaction Management dialog box, select `Required` from the drop-down list for the rows as shown in Figure 29-8.

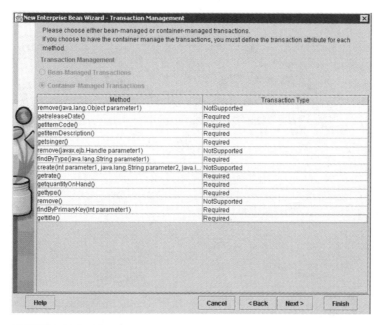

FIGURE 29-8 *The New Enterprise Bean Wizard — Transaction Management dialog box is displayed.*

27. Click the Next button. The New Enterprise Bean Wizard — Review Settings dialog box is displayed.

28. Click the Finish button. The enterprise bean is now packaged. Note that `ItemJar` appears below the `MusicApp` application in the left pane.

29. In the left pane, select `ItemJar` in the tree view.

30. Expand `ItemJar` and select `ItemBean`, as seen in Figure 29-9.

31. Next, click the Entity tab.

32. Click the Deployment Settings button. The Deployment Settings dialog box appears, as seen in Figure 29-10. You need to maximize the dialog box if the Deployment Settings button is not visible.

33. In the Database JNDI Name box, enter `jdbc/sqlServer`.

34. Click the OK button. A message box appears with the Generate SQL Now button.

35. Click the Generate SQL Now button. As seen in Figure 29-11, the SQL Generator message box appears indicating SQL generation for the DBMS: Microsoft SQL Server.

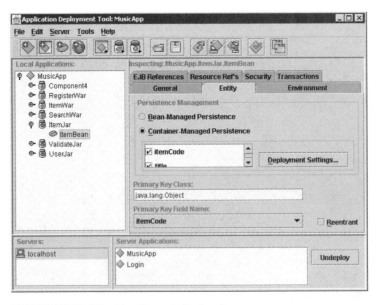

FIGURE 29-9 *The* ItemBean *is displayed.*

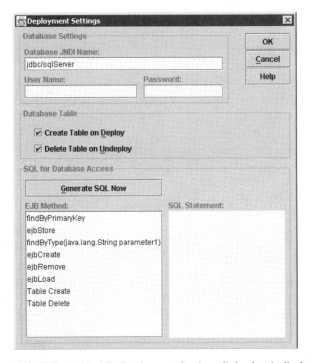

FIGURE 29-10 *The Deployment Settings dialog box is displayed.*

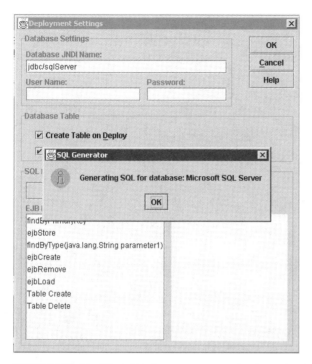

FIGURE 29-11 *The SQL Generator message box is displayed.*

36. Click the OK button. The Provide finder SQL message box appears, as seen in Figure 29-12.

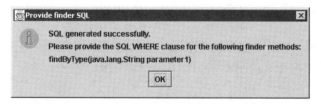

FIGURE 29-12 *The Provide finder SQL message box is displayed.*

37. Click the OK button to close the message box.

38. From the EJB Method list, select findByType(java.lang.String para-meter1). In the SQL Statement area, a partial SQL query appears, as seen in Figure 29-13.

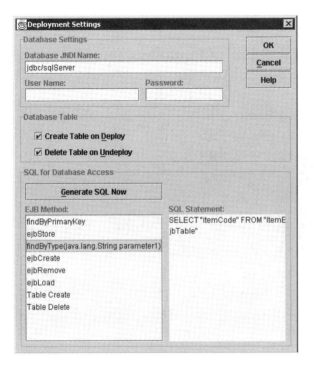

FIGURE 29-13 *A partial SQL query is shown.*

39. Add the following phrase to the SQL statement: WHERE "type" = ?1. See Figure 29-14.

40. Click the OK button to close the Deployment Settings dialog box.

41. Select the New Web Component command from the File menu. The New Web Component Wizard — Introduction dialog box is displayed.

42. Click the Next button. The New Web Component Wizard — .WAR File General Properties dialog box is displayed. Note that MusicApp is displayed in the Web Component will Go In drop-down list.

43. Type SearchWar in the WAR Display Name text field.

44. Click on Add in the Contents group box. The Add Files to .WAR — Add Content Files dialog box is displayed.

45. Click the Browse button and select your working directory. Select SearchItem.jsp in the scroll pane.

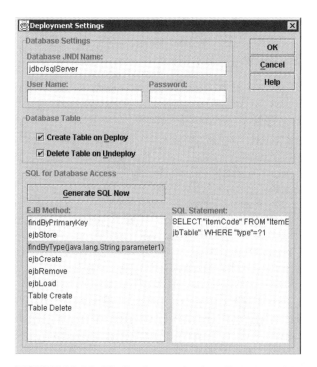

FIGURE 29-14 *The Deployment Settings dialog box with the SQL query is displayed.*

46. Click the Add button. `SearchItem.jsp` gets added in the Files to be Added group box.

47. Click the Next button. The Add Files to .WAR — Add Class Files dialog box is displayed.

48. Click on Browse and select your working directory. Select `SearchBean.class` in the scroll pane.

49. Click the Add button in the Files to be Added group box. `SearchBean.class` gets displayed in the Files to be Added group box.

50. Click the Finish button. The New Web Component Wizard — WAR File General Properties dialog box is displayed, as seen in Figure 29-15. Note that `SearchBean.class` and `SearchItem.jsp` are displayed in the Contents group box.

51. Click the Next button. The New Web Component Wizard — Choose Component Type dialog box is displayed.

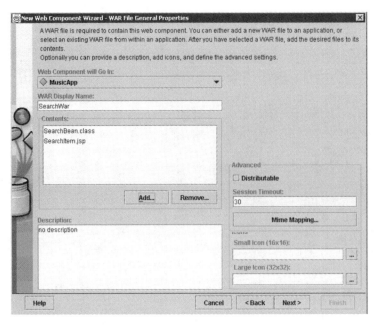

FIGURE 29-15 *The New Web Component Wizard — WAR File General Properties dialog box is shown.*

52. Select JSP as the Web Component Type.

53. Click the Next button. The New Web Component Wizard — Component General Properties dialog box is displayed, as seen in Figure 29-16.

54. Select SearchItem.jsp from the JSP Filename drop-down list. Type Component3 in the Web Component Display Name text field.

55. Click the Next button. The New Web Component Wizard — Component Initialization Parameters dialog box is displayed. Click the Next button.

56. The New Web Component Wizard — Component Aliases dialog box is displayed.

57. Click the Add button. Specify alias name as SearchAlias in the Aliases text box.

58. The New Web Component Wizard — Component Security dialog box is displayed. Click the Next button.

59. The New Web Component Wizard — WAR File Environment dialog box is displayed. Click the Next button.

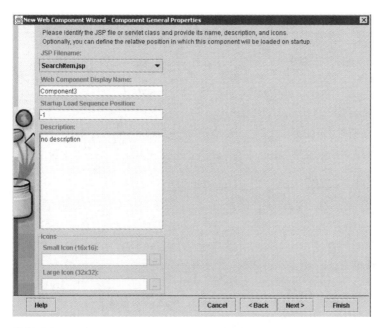

FIGURE 29-16 *The New Web Component Wizard — Component General Properties dialog box is shown.*

60. The New Web Component Wizard — Enterprise Bean References dialog box is displayed, as shown in Figure 29-17.

61. Click the Add button. A new entry appears in the EJB's Referenced in Code group box.

62. Type ejb/Item in the Coded Name column. Select Entity from the Type column list. Type ItemHome in the Home column and Item in the Remote column. Specify JNDI Name as Item.

63. Click the Finish button. The Application Deployment Tool: MusicApp window is displayed. Note that ItemWar is displayed in the left pane below Local Applications.

64. Select the Deploy Application command from the Tools menu. The Deploy MusicApp — Introduction dialog box is displayed.

65. Click the Next button. The Deploy MusicApp — JNDI Names dialog box is displayed. Note that the JNDI names are displayed.

66. Click the Next button. The Deploy MusicApp — .WAR Context Root dialog box is displayed. Note that the entry in the Context Root column is SearchContext.

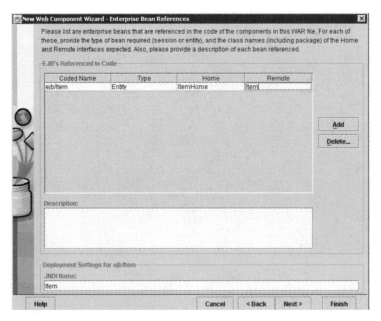

FIGURE 29-17 *The New Web Component Wizard — Enterprise Bean References dialog box is shown.*

67. Click the Next button. The Deploy MusicApp — Review dialog box is displayed.

68. Click the Finish button. The Deployment Progress dialog box is displayed.

69. Click on OK when the deployment of MusicApp is complete.

70. The Application Deployment Tool: MusicApp window appears. Note that MusicApp is displayed below Server Applications.

71. Select the Exit command from the File menu to return to the command prompt.

The next component of the Search page is SearchBean.class.

SearchBean.class

The SearchBean class is a Javabean class. The JSP page will interact with the SearchBean class. The SearchClass, in turn, interacts with the EJB classes to obtain the desired results. The source code of SearchBean.class is given in Listing 29-6.

Listing 29-6 SearchBean.java

```java
import java.util.*;
import java.io.*;
import javax.naming.Context;
import javax.naming.InitialContext;
import javax.rmi.PortableRemoteObject;

public class SearchBean
{
private String searchBy;
ItemHome itemHome;
Item item;
Vector vect;
public SearchBean()
{
vect = new Vector();
try
{
Context ctx=new InitialContext();
Object obj=ctx.lookup("java:comp/env/ejb/Item");
itemHome=(ItemHome)PortableRemoteObject.narrow(obj,ItemHome.class);
}
catch(Exception e)
{
System.out.println("Could not find Item home"+e);
}
}
public void setSearchBy(String str)
{
searchBy=str;
searchBy=searchBy.trim();
}
public String getSearchBy()
{
return searchBy;
}
```

```java
public Vector performSearch()
{
try
{
if(searchBy!=null)
{
 Collection collect=itemHome.findByType(searchBy);
 Iterator itr=collect.iterator();
 while(itr.hasNext()){
    int i=0;
    item=(Item)itr.next();
    String title=item.gettitle();
    vect.add(i,title);
    i++;
}
}
else
{
   vect.add(0,"");
}
}
catch(Exception e)
{
System.out.println("Error in finding by type"+e);
}
return vect;
}
}
```

Now that you have looked at the bean classes that go into the creation of the Search page, take look at the JSP code to create the Search page.

SearchItem.jsp

The JSP code for the Search page is given in Listing 29-7.

Listing 29-7 SearchItem.jsp

```
<html>
<jsp:useBean id="search" scope="session" class="SearchBean" />
<jsp:setProperty name="search" property="*" />
<%! Vector vect; %>
<%! int cap,i;
Object obj;%>
<!--Retrieve the search result from the EJB through JavaBeans-->
<% vect = search.performSearch();%>
<html>
<head>
<meta http-equiv="Content-Type" content="text/html; charset=windows-1252">
<meta http-equiv="Content-Language" content="en-us">
<title>Search Page</title>
</head>
<body bgcolor="#C0C0C0" topmargin="0"
background="http:\\localhost:8000\music\Background.bmp" >
<table border="0" width="100%">
  <tr>
    <td width="100%">
      <table border="0" width="97%" height="19">
        <tr>
          <td width="18%" height="13" valign="middle" align="right">
      <font face="Arial" size="5" color="#800000"><b><i>eMusicWorld-----&gt; The
World of Music</i></b></font>
          </td>
        </tr>
      </table>
    </td>
  </tr>
</table>
<form method="POST" action="SearchItem.jsp">
<table border="1" width="100%">
  <tr>
    <td width="18%">
<p><font face="Arial" size="2" color="#800000"><b><a
HREF="http://localhost:8000/music/home_page.htm">Home</a></b></font></p>
<p><b><font face="Arial" size="2" color="#800000"><a
```

```
HREF="http://localhost:8000/music/chart_toppers.jsp">Chart
Toppers</a></font></b></p>
<p><b><font face="Arial" size="2" color="#800000"><a
HREF="http://localhost:8000/SearchContext/SearchAlias">Search</a></font></b></p>
<p><b><font face="Arial" size="2" color="#800000"><a
HREF="http://localhost:8000/music/vote_page.jsp">Vote</a></font></b></p>
<p><b><font face="Arial" size="2" color="#800000"><a
HREF="http://localhost:8000/music/new_release_page.jsp">New Releases</a></font></b>
<p><font face="Arial" size="2" color="#800000"><b><a
HREF="http://localhost:8000/Register/RegisterPage.htm">Register</a></b></font>
<p><font face="Arial" size="2" color="#800000"><b><a
HREF="http://localhost:8000/music/login_page.htm">Login</a></b></font>
<p><font face="Arial" size="2" color="#800000"><b><a
HREF="http://localhost:8000/music/help_page.htm">Help</a></b></font></p>
        <p> </td>
      <td width="82%" valign="top">
<p align="center"><font face="Arial" size="3" color="#800000"><b><u>Search
Page</u></b></font></p>
   <font face="Arial" size="2" color="#800000">Select the search category from the
<b>Search By</b> list box and then click the <b>Submit</b> button.</font>
   <p><font face="Arial" size="2" color="#800000"><b>Search By </b></font><select
size="1" name="searchBy" style="color: #800000; font-family: Arial; font-size:
10pt">
     <option selected>Classical</option>
     <option>Jazz</option>
     <option>Pop</option>
     <option>Rock</option>
   </select>  </p>
   <p>
   <input type="submit" value="Submit" name="Submit">
<%
out.println("<font face=\"Arial\" size=\"2\" color=\"#800000\">");
cap=vect.size();
out.println("<table><tr><td valign=\"center\">");
out.println("<font face=\"Arial\" size=\"2\" color=\"#800000\"><b><u>Search
Result</u></b></font></td></tr>");
int j=1;
<!--Display the result-->
```

```
for(i=cap-1;i>=0;i--, j++)
{
out.println("<tr><td><b>");
out.println("<font face=\"Arial\" size=\"2\" color=\"#800000\">");
out.println("</font>");
String str=(String)vect.elementAt(i);
out.println("<font face=\"Arial\" size=\"2\" color=\"#800000\">");
out.println((String)vect.elementAt(i));
out.println("</b></td></tr>");
out.println("</font>");
}
<!--Clear the Vector-->
 vect.clear();
%>
     </td>
</tr>
</table>
</form>
</body>
</html>
```

The output of the SearchItem.jsp code is displayed in Figure 29-18.

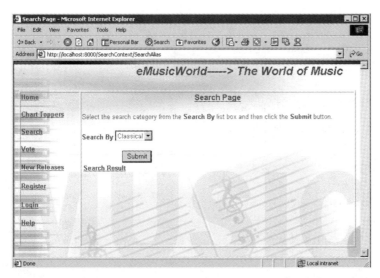

FIGURE 29-18 *The* SearchItem.jsp *page is displayed.*

The next page in the Visitor Interface category of eMusicWorld is the Vote page.

The Vote Page

The Vote page is displayed to a visitor when he clicks on the Vote link in the left menu. The Vote page displays a list of the latest songs, which were released in the last month, to the visitor. The visitor can select a song as his favorite choice and then submit the choice. The number of votes for a song is tracked in the Vote_Info table. The Vote page is made up of two pages:

- ◆ Vote_page.jsp
- ◆ Vote_result_page.jsp

Now I'll show you the code for each of these pages.

Vote_page.jsp

The Vote page displays the list of songs where a visitor can specify his favorite song. The code of Vote_page.jsp is given in Listing 29-8.

Listing 29-8 Vote_page.jsp

```
<html>
<head>
<meta http-equiv="Content-Type" content="text/html; charset=windows-1252">
<meta http-equiv="Content-Language" content="en-us">
<title>Home Page</title>
</head>
<body bgcolor="#C0C0C0" topmargin="0"
background="http:\\localhost:8000\music\Background.bmp" >
<table border="0" width="100%">
  <tr>
    <td width="100%">
      <table border="0" width="97%" height="19">
        <tr>
          <td width="18%" height="13" valign="middle" align="right">
        <font face="Arial" size="5" color="#800000"><b><i>eMusicWorld-----&gt; The
World of Music</i></b></font>
```

```
          </td>
        </tr>
      </table>
    </td>
  </tr>
</table>
                    <%@ page import="java.util.*" %>
                    <%@ page import="java.sql.*" %>
                    <%@ page import="java.text.*" %>
                    <%@ page import="java.sql.Date" %>
                    <%@ page language = "java" %>
<%! int ctr=0;%>
<%! String[] songs=new String[10];%>
<%

                    try{
                    Class.forName("sun.jdbc.odbc.JdbcOdbcDriver");
                    Connection connect;

connect=DriverManager.getConnection("jdbc:odbc:RegisterDataSource","","");
                    Statement state;
                    state = connect.createStatement();
                    String strQuery1 = "SELECT top 10 Item_Master.Title FROM
Vote_info, Item_Master where Vote_info.Item_code=Item_Master.Item_code ORDER BY
Number_votes desc";
                    String str;
                    ResultSet result1 = state.executeQuery(strQuery1);
                    while(result1.next())
                    {
                                    songs[ctr]=result1.getString("Title");
                                    ctr++;
                    }
                                    connect.close();
                    }
                    catch(Exception e)
                    {}
%>
<form method="GET" action="http://localhost:8000/vote_result_page.jsp">
      <table border="1" width="100%">
```

```
<tr>
   <td width="18%">
<p><font face="Arial" size="2" color="#800000"><b><a
HREF="http://localhost:8000/music/home_page.htm">Home</a></b></font></p>
<p><b><font face="Arial" size="2" color="#800000"><a
HREF="http://localhost:8000/music/chart_toppers.jsp">Chart
Toppers</a></font></b></p>
<p><b><font face="Arial" size="2" color="#800000"><a
HREF="http://localhost:8000/SearchContext/SearchAlias">Search</a></font></b></p>
<p><b><font face="Arial" size="2" color="#800000"><a
HREF="http://localhost:8000/music/vote_page.jsp">Vote</a></font></b></p>
<p><b><font face="Arial" size="2" color="#800000"><a
HREF="http://localhost:8000/music/new_release_page.jsp">New Releases</a></font></b>
<p><font face="Arial" size="2" color="#800000"><b><a
HREF="http://localhost:8000/Register/RegisterPage.htm">Register</a></b></font>
<p><font face="Arial" size="2" color="#800000"><b><a
HREF="http://localhost:8000/music/login_page.htm">Login</a></b></font>
<p><font face="Arial" size="2" color="#800000"><b><a
HREF="http://localhost:8000/music/help_page.htm">Help</a></b></font></p>
      <p> </td>
   <td width="82%" valign="top">
  <p align="center"><font face="Arial" size="2" color="#800000"><b><u>Vote for your
favorite song</u></b></font></p>
  <table border="0" width="100%">
     <tr>
        <td width="50%" valign="middle" align="left"><font face="Arial" size="2"
color="#800000"><b>       
        Songs</b></font></td>
     </tr>
     <tr>
        <td width="50%" valign="middle" align="left"><font face="Arial" size="2"
color="#800000"> </font>  
        <select size="1" name="Song1">
<%
                for(ctr=0;ctr<songs.length;ctr++){
%>
                <option><% out.println(songs[ctr]); }
                %></option>
```

```
      </select></td>
    </tr>
  </table>
  <input type="submit" value="Vote" name="submit"></p>
    </td>
  </tr>
</table>
</form>
</body>
</html>
```

The output of `Vote_page.jsp` is displayed in Figure 29-19.

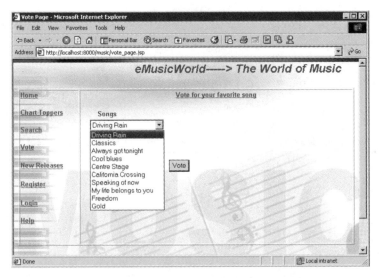

FIGURE 29-19 *The output of* `Vote_page.jsp` *page is shown here.*

The next component of the Vote page is `Vote_result_page.jsp`.

Vote_result_page.jsp

The `Vote_result_page.jsp` displays a message to the user indicating the number of people who have voted for the user's favorite song, which he specified in the `Vote_page.jsp`. The `Vote_result_page.jsp` identified the song selected by the user in the Vote_page.jsp page and then it obtains the number of votes for that particular song from the Vote_info table of the Music database. The code for Vote_result_page.jsp is shown in Listing 29-9.

Listing 29-9 Vote_result_page.jsp

```
<html>
<head>
<meta http-equiv="Content-Type" content="text/html; charset=windows-1252">
<meta http-equiv="Content-Language" content="en-us">
<title>Home Page</title>
</head>
<body bgcolor="#C0C0C0" topmargin="0"
background="http:\\localhost:8000\music\Background.bmp" >
<table border="0" width="100%">
  <tr>
    <td width="100%">
      <table border="0" width="97%" height="19">
        <tr>
          <td width="18%" height="13" valign="middle" align="right">
        <font face="Arial" size="5" color="#800000"><b><i>eMusicWorld-----&gt; The
World of Music</i></b></font>
          </td>
        </tr>
      </table>
    </td>
  </tr>
</table>
                    <%@ page import="java.util.*" %>
                    <%@ page import="java.sql.*" %>
                    <%@ page import="java.text.*" %>
                    <%@ page import="java.sql.Date" %>
                    <%@ page language = "java" %>
<%! int voteNum=0;%>
<%! String selSong=new String();%>
<%
selSong=request.getParameter("Song1");
selSong=selSong.trim();
```

```
                try{
                Class.forName("sun.jdbc.odbc.JdbcOdbcDriver");
                Connection connect;

connect=DriverManager.getConnection("jdbc:odbc:RegisterDataSource","","");
                Statement state,state2;
                ResultSet result1;
                state = connect.createStatement();
                state2 = connect.createStatement();
<!--Increment the vote numbers for the selected song-->
                String strQuery1 = "update Vote_info set
Number_votes=Number_votes+1 where Item_code=(select Item_Code from Item_Master where
Title='"+selSong+"') ";
                state.executeUpdate(strQuery1);
<!--get the number of votes for the selected song-->
                String strQuery2="select Number_votes from Vote_info where
Item_code = (select Item_code from Item_master where Title='"+selSong+"')";
                result1=state2.executeQuery(strQuery2);
                while(result1.next())
                {
                                voteNum=result1.getInt("Number_Votes");
                }
                                connect.close();
                voteNum=voteNum+1;
                }
                catch(Exception e)
                {}
%>
<form method="GET" action="http://localhost:8000/music/home_page.htm">
<table border="1" width="100%">
  <tr>
    <td width="18%">
<p><font face="Arial" size="2" color="#800000"><b><a
HREF="http://localhost:8000/music/home_page.htm">Home</a></b></font></p>
<p><b><font face="Arial" size="2" color="#800000"><a
HREF="http://localhost:8000/music/chart_toppers.jsp">Chart
Toppers</a></font></b></p>
<p><b><font face="Arial" size="2" color="#800000"><a
```

```
HREF="http://localhost:8000/SearchContext/SearchAlias">Search</a></font></b></p>
<p><b><font face="Arial" size="2" color="#800000"><a
HREF="http://localhost:8000/music/vote_page.jsp">Vote</a></font></b></p>
<p><b><font face="Arial" size="2" color="#800000"><a
HREF="http://localhost:8000/music/new_release_page.jsp">New Releases</a></font></b>
<p><font face="Arial" size="2" color="#800000"><b><a
HREF="http://localhost:8000/Register/RegisterPage.htm">Register</a></b></font>
<p><font face="Arial" size="2" color="#800000"><b><a
HREF="http://localhost:8000/music/login_page.htm">Login</a></b></font>
<p><font face="Arial" size="2" color="#800000"><b><a
HREF="http://localhost:8000/music/help_page.htm">Help</a></b></font></p>
        <p> </td>
      <td width="82%" valign="top">
<!--Display the number of people who have voted for the song-->
   <p align="left"><font face="Arial" size="3" color="#800000"><b><u>You voted for
the song:</u></b>
<p align="left"><font face="Arial" size="3"
color="#800000"><b><%=request.getParameter("Song1")%></b></font></p>
<p align="left"><%=voteNum%> <font face="Arial" size="3" color="#800000">people have
voted for this song so far.</font></p>
   <input type="submit" value="OK" name="submit"></p>
    </td>
  </tr>
</table>
</form>
</body>
</html>
```

The output of Vote_result_page.jsp is displayed in Figure 29-20.

Another page in the Visitor Interface category is the New Releases page.

The New Releases Page

The New Releases page of the Visitor Interface category displays songs that have been released in the last month. The code for the New Releases page is shown in Listing 29-10.

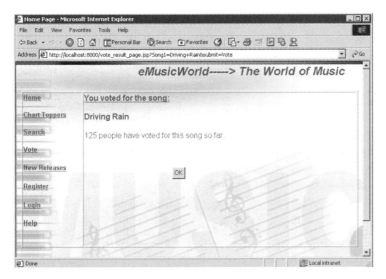

FIGURE 29-20 *The output of* Vote_result_page.jsp *page is shown here.*

Listing 29-10 New_release_page.jsp

```
<html>
<head>
<meta http-equiv="Content-Type" content="text/html; charset=windows-1252">
<meta http-equiv="Content-Language" content="en-us">
<title>New Releases Page</title>
</head>
<body bgcolor="#C0C0C0" topmargin="0"
background="http:\\localhost:8000\music\Background.bmp" >
<table border="0" width="100%">
  <tr>
    <td width="100%">
      <table border="0" width="97%" height="19">
        <tr>
          <td width="18%" height="13" valign="middle" align="right">
      <font face="Arial" size="5" color="#800000"><b><i>eMusicWorld-----&gt; The
World of Music</i></b></font>
          </td>
        </tr>
      </table>
```

```
      </td>
    </tr>
  </table>
<%! String time;%>
<%@ page import="java.util.*" %>
                  <%@ page import="java.sql.*" %>
                  <%@ page import="java.text.*" %>
                  <%@ page import="java.sql.Date" %>
                  <%@ page language = "java" %>
<!--Obtain the current date-->
<%Calendar cal = Calendar.getInstance(TimeZone.getDefault());
    String DATE_FORMAT = "MMMMM dd, yyyyy";
    java.text.SimpleDateFormat sdf=new java.text.SimpleDateFormat(DATE_FORMAT);
    sdf.setTimeZone(TimeZone.getDefault());
    time=sdf.format(cal.getTime());
%>
<form method="POST" action="http://localhost:8000/music/user_home_page.htm">
     <table border="1" width="100%">
  <tr>
    <td width="18%">

<p><font face="Arial" size="2" color="#800000"><b><a
HREF="http://localhost:8000/music/home_page.htm">Home</a></b></font></p>


<p><b><font face="Arial" size="2" color="#800000"><a
HREF="http://localhost:8000/music/chart_toppers.jsp">Chart
Toppers</a></font></b></p>
<p><b><font face="Arial" size="2" color="#800000"><a
HREF="http://localhost:8000/SearchContext/SearchAlias">Search</a></font></b></p>
<p><b><font face="Arial" size="2" color="#800000"><a
HREF="http://localhost:8000/music/vote_page.jsp">Vote</a></font></b></p>
<p><b><font face="Arial" size="2" color="#800000"><a
HREF="http://localhost:8000/music/new_release_page.jsp">New Releases</a></font></b>
<p><font face="Arial" size="2" color="#800000"><b><a
HREF="http://localhost:8000/Register/RegisterPage.htm">Register</a></b></font>
<p><font face="Arial" size="2" color="#800000"><b><a
HREF="http://localhost:8000/music/login_page.htm">Login</a></b></font>
<p><font face="Arial" size="2" color="#800000"><b><a
```

```
HREF="http://localhost:8000/music/help_page.htm">Help</a></b></font></p>
     <p> </td>
   <td width="82%" valign="top">
  <p align="center"><font face="Arial" size="2" color="#800000"><b><u>New Releases
in Last One Month</u></b></font>
<table border="1" width="100%" >
    <tr>
</tr>
<tr>
<font face="Arial" size="2" color="#800000"><b>
<td></td>
<td><font face="Arial" size="2" color="#800000"><b>Song</b></td>
<td><font face="Arial" size="2" color="#800000"><b>Singer</b></td>
<td><font face="Arial" size="2" color="#800000"><b>Release Date</b></td>
</tr>
<%
                try{
                Class.forName("sun.jdbc.odbc.JdbcOdbcDriver");
                Connection connect;

connect=DriverManager.getConnection("jdbc:odbc:RegisterDataSource","","");
                Statement state;
                state = connect.createStatement();
                String strQuery1 = "select Title, Singer, Release_Date from
Item_Master where DATEDIFF(month, Release_Date, GETDATE())<= 1 Order by
Release_Date desc";
                ResultSet result1 = state.executeQuery(strQuery1);
                int ctr=1;
                String title, singer, releasedate;
<!--Display the result-->
                    while(result1.next())
                    {
                            out.println("<tr><td>");
                            out.println("<p><font face=\"Arial\" size=\"2\"
color=\"#800000\">");

                            title=result1.getString("Title");
                            singer=result1.getString("Singer");
                            releasedate=result1.getString("Release_Date");
```

```
                                      releasedate=releasedate.substring(0, release-
date.length()-7);

                                      out.println(ctr+". ");
                                      out.println("</td>");
                                      out.println("<td><font face=\"Arial\" size=\"2\"
color=\"#800000\">");

                                      out.println(title);
                                      out.println("</td>");
                                      ctr=ctr+1;
                                      out.println("<td><font face=\"Arial\" size=\"2\"
color=\"#800000\">");

                                      out.println(singer);
                                      out.println("</td>");
                                      out.println("<td><font face=\"Arial\" size=\"2\"
color=\"#800000\">");

                                      out.println(releasedate);
                                      out.println("</td>");
                                      out.println("</p>");
                                      out.println("</tr>");
                    }
                    connect.close();
                    }
                    catch(Exception e){
                    out.println("done exception" +e);
                    }
%>
</tr>
<font face="Arial" size="1" color="#800000"><p align="center"> (The release date of
the songs is calculated from today. Today's Date: <%=time%>.)
</table>
</td>
</tr>
</table>
<p>  </p>
<p>  </p>
</form>
</body>
</html>
```

The new_release_page.jsp picks up the songs that are released in the last one month from the Item_master table of the Music database. The output is displayed in Figure 29-21.

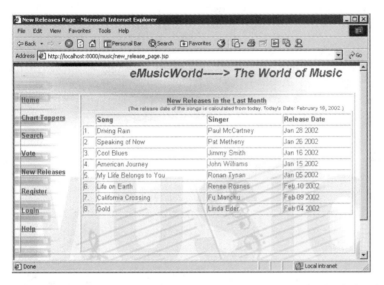

FIGURE 29-21 *The output of* new_release_page.jsp *page is displayed.*

The Register Page

The Register page enables visitors to register with the eMusicWorld application. Registration is mandatory to purchase music items from eMusicWorld. The Register page has been created using the concept of EJB. The registration process is taken care of by two beans; one takes care of inserting user details in the database whereas the other validates the credit card information provided by the user. The components of the Register page are:

- ◆ RegisterPage.htm
- ◆ MiddleRegister.class
- ◆ MyHome.class
- ◆ Register.class
- ◆ Register.jsp
- ◆ RegisterEJB.class

◆ Validate.class

◆ ValidateEJB.class

◆ ValidateHome.class

Now I'll analyze the code of each of these components in detail.

RegisterPage.htm

The RegisterPage.htm is displayed to a user when he clicks the Register link on the left menu. The code for the RegisterPage.htm is given in Listing 29-11.

Listing 29-11   RegisterPage.htm

```
<html>
<head>
<meta http-equiv="Content-Type" content="text/html; charset=windows-1252">
<meta http-equiv="Content-Language" content="en-us">
<title>Registration Page</title>
</head>
<body bgcolor="#C0C0C0" topmargin="0"
background="http:\\localhost:8000\music\Background.bmp" >
<table border="0" width="100%">
  <tr>
    <td width="100%">
      <table border="0" width="97%" height="19">
        <tr>
          <td width="18%" height="13" valign="middle" align="right">
        <font face="Arial" size="5" color="#800000"><b><i>eMusicWorld-----&gt; The
World of Music</i></b></font>
          </td>
        </tr>
      </table>
    </td>
  </tr>
</table>
<script Language="JavaScript">
function verify()
{
```

```
var ctr=0;
var txtT1=form.T1.value;
var txtT2=form.T2.value;
var txtT3=form.T3.value;
var txtT4=form.T4.value;
var txtT5=form.T5.value;
var txtT10=form.T10.value;
var txtT6=form.T6.value;
var txtT11=form.T11.value;
var txtT13=form.T13.value;
var txtT14=form.T14.value;
var txtT7=form.T7.value;
var txtT8=form.T8.value;
var txtT9=form.T9.value;
var txtCountry=form.country.value;
if(!((txtT14.indexOf('@'))>=0))
{
            alert("email not proper");
            ctr=1;
}
<!--Check whether any mandatory field is mandatory-->
if((txtT1.length==0)||(txtT2.length==0)||(txtT3.length==0)||(txtT4.length==0)||(txtT
5.length==0)||(txtT10.length==0)||(txtT6.length==0)||(txtT11.length==0)||(txtT13.len
gth==0)||(txtT14.length==0)||(txtT8.length==0)||(txtT9.length==0)||(txtCountry.lengt
h==0))
            {
                        alert("Please enter all the values. The fields
marked (*) are mandatory.");
                        ctr=1;
            }
<!--Check the length of the password-->
            if(txtT2.length<4)
            {
                        alert("The length of the password should not be
less than four.");
                        ctr=1;
            }
<!--Check whether the Password and Confirm Password fields match-->
```

```
                    if (!(txtT2==txtT3))
                    {
                                    alert("Password and Confirm Password fields do
not match.");
                                    ctr=1;
                    }

                    if(ctr!=1)
                    form.submit();
}
</script>
<form method="POST" name="form" action="http:\\localhost:8000\Register\Register">
        <table border="1" width="100%">
  <tr>
    <td width="18%" valign="top">
<p><font face="Arial" size="2" color="#800000"><b><a
HREF="http://localhost:8000/music/home_page.htm">Home</a></b></font></p>
<p><b><font face="Arial" size="2" color="#800000"><a
HREF="http://localhost:8000/music/chart_toppers.jsp">Chart
Toppers</a></font></b></p>
<p><b><font face="Arial" size="2" color="#800000"><a
HREF="http://localhost:8000/SearchContext/SearchAlias">Search</a></font></b></p>
<p><b><font face="Arial" size="2" color="#800000"><a
HREF="http://localhost:8000/music/vote_page.jsp">Vote</a></font></b></p>
<p><b><font face="Arial" size="2" color="#800000"><a
HREF="http://localhost:8000/music/new_release_page.jsp">New Releases</a></font></b>
<p><font face="Arial" size="2" color="#800000"><b><a
HREF="http://localhost:8000/Register/RegisterPage.htm">Register</a></b></font>
<p><font face="Arial" size="2" color="#800000"><b><a
HREF="http://localhost:8000/music/login_page.htm">Login</a></b></font>
<p><font face="Arial" size="2" color="#800000"><b><a
HREF="http://localhost:8000/music/help_page.htm">Help</a></b></font></p>
        <p> </td>
    <td width="82%" valign="top">
  <p align="center" style="margin-top: 1; margin-bottom: 1"><b><u><font
color="#800000" face="Arial" size="3">Enter Registration
Information</font></u></b></p>
  <p align="left" style="margin-top: 1; margin-bottom: 1"><font face="Arial"
```

```
size="2" color="#800000"><b>1.

<u>

Logon Information</u></b></font></p>

<p align="left" style="margin-left: -2; margin-right: -2; margin-top: 1; margin-
bottom: 1"><font face="Arial" size="2" color="#800000"> User

Name*:           <input
type="text" name="T1" size="20"></font></p>

<p align="left" style="margin-left: -2; margin-right: -2; margin-top: 3; margin-
bottom: 3"><font face="Arial" size="2"
color="#800000"> Password*:        &nbs
p;   

<input type="password" name="T2" size="20"> </font><font face="Arial" size="1"
color="#800000">(Password

should be atleast 4 characters long.)</font></p>

<p align="left" style="margin-left: -2; margin-right: -2; margin-top: 3; margin-
bottom: 3"><font face="Arial" size="2" color="#800000"> Confirm

Password*: <input type="Password" name="T3" size="20"></font></p>

<p align="left" style="margin-left: -2; margin-right: -2; margin-top: 3; margin-
bottom: 3"><font face="Arial" size="2" color="#800000"> Secret

Question*:    <input type="text" name="T4" size="20"></font></p>

<p align="left" style="margin-left: -2; margin-right: -2; margin-top: 3; margin-
bottom: 3"><font face="Arial" size="2" color="#800000"> Secret

Answer*:      <input type="text" name="T5"
size="20"></font></p>

<p align="left" style="margin-top: 1; margin-bottom: 1"> </p>

<p align="left" style="margin-top: 1; margin-bottom: 1"><b><font face="Arial"
size="2" color="#800000">2.

<u>

Billing Information</u></font></b></p>

<p align="left" style="margin-left: -2; margin-right: -2; margin-top: 3; margin-
bottom: 3"><font face="Arial" size="2" color="#800000"> Credit

Card Number*:<input type="text" name="T10" size="20"></font></p>

<p align="left" style="margin-left: -2; margin-right: -2; margin-top: 3; margin-
bottom: 3"><font face="Arial" size="2" color="#800000"> Credit

Card Type:     <select size="1" name="D1">

  <option selected>Visa</option>

  <option>Master</option>

  <option>American Express</option>
```

```
    <option>Diner's Club</option>
    <option>Standard Chartered</option>
  </select></font></p>
  <p align="left" style="margin-left: -2; margin-right: -2; margin-top: 3; margin-
bottom: 3"> 
  <font face="Arial" size="2" color="#800000"></font></p>
  <p align="left" style="margin-top: 1; margin-bottom: 1"><font face="Arial"
size="2" color="#800000"><b>3.
  <u>
  Personal Information</u></b></font></p>
  <p align="left" style="margin-left: -2; margin-right: -2; margin-top: 1; margin-
bottom: 1"><font face="Arial" size="2" color="#800000"> First
  Name*:            <input
type="text" name="T6" size="20"></font></p>
  <p align="left" style="margin-left: -2; margin-right: -2; margin-top: 3; margin-
bottom: 3"><font face="Arial" size="2" color="#800000"> Middle
  Name:          <input type="text"
name="T12" size="20"></font></p>
  <p align="left" style="margin-left: -2; margin-right: -2; margin-top: 3; margin-
bottom: 3"><font face="Arial" size="2" color="#800000"> Last
  Name*:            <input
type="text" name="T11" size="20"></font></p>
  <p align="left" style="margin-left: -2; margin-right: -2; margin-top: 3; margin-
bottom: 3"><font face="Arial" size="2" color="#800000"> Date
  of Birth*:          <input
type="text" name="T13" size="20"></font></p>
  <p align="left" style="margin-left: -2; margin-right: -2; margin-top: 3; margin-
bottom: 3"><font face="Arial" size="2" color="#800000"> E-
mail*:             
     
  <input type="text" name="T14" size="20"></font></p>
  <p align="left" style="margin-left: -2; margin-right: -2; margin-top: 3; margin-
bottom: 3"><font face="Arial" size="2" color="#800000"> Address
  Line1*:       <input type="text" name="T7"
size="20"></font></p>
  <p align="left" style="margin-left: -2; margin-right: -2; margin-top: 3; margin-
bottom: 3"><font face="Arial" size="2" color="#800000"> Address
  Line2*:       <input type="text" name="T7"
```

```
size="20"></font></p>
  <p align="left" style="margin-left: -2; margin-right: -2; margin-top: 3; margin-
bottom: 3"><font face="Arial" size="2"
color="#800000"> City*:        &n
bsp;           
  <input type="text" name="T8" size="20"></font></p>
  <p align="left" style="margin-left: -2; margin-right: -2; margin-top: 3; margin-
bottom: 3"> </p>
  <p align="left" style="margin-left: -2; margin-right: -2; margin-top: 3; margin-
bottom: 3"><font face="Arial" size="2"
color="#800000"> State*:       
              <input
type="text" name="T9" size="20"></font></p>
<p align="left" style="margin-left: -2; margin-right: -2; margin-top: 3; margin-
bottom: 10"><font face="Arial" size="2"
color="#800000"> Country*:     
           <input type="text"
name="country" size="20"></font></p>
  <table border="0" width="100%">
    <tr>
      <td width="50%" valign="middle" align="center"><input type="button"
value="Submit" name="B1" onClick="verify()"><input type="reset" value="Reset"
name="B2"></td>
      <td width="50%" valign="middle" align="center"></td>
    </tr>
  </table>
  <p align="left" style="margin-left: -2; margin-right: -2; margin-top: 3; margin-
bottom: 3"> </p>
    </td>
  </tr>
</table>
</form>
</body>
</html>
```

The output of the RegisterPage.htm is displayed in Figure 29-22.

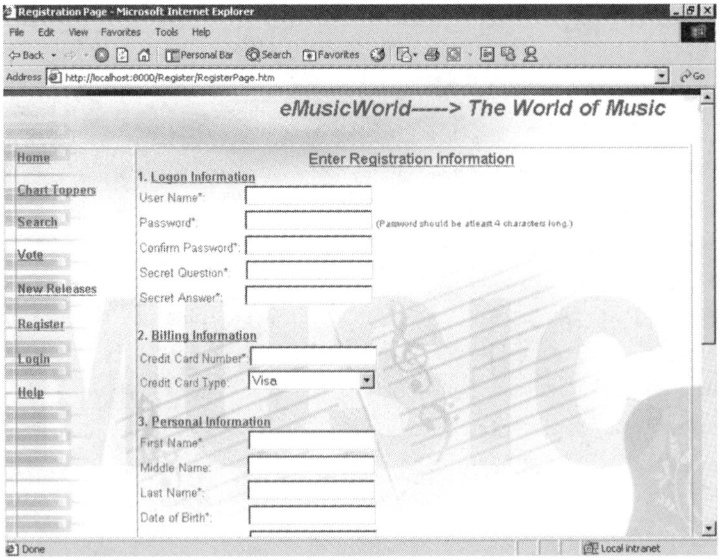

FIGURE 29-22 *The output of the* `RegisterPage.htm` *page is displayed.*

Now take a look at the EJB components of the Register page.

MiddleRegister.java

The code of `MiddleRegister.java` is shown in Listing 29-12.

Listing 29-12 MiddleRegister.java

```java
import java.util.*;
import java.io.*;
import javax.naming.Context;
import javax.naming.InitialContext;
import javax.rmi.PortableRemoteObject;

public class MiddleRegister
{
private String requestId;
private String userName;
private String firstName;
```

```
private String middleName;
private String lastName;
private String dateOfBirth;
private String email;
private String addressLine1;
private String addressLine2;
private String city;
private String state;
private String creditCard;
private String creditCardType;
private String password;
private String secretQuestion;
private String secretAnswer;
private ValidateHome validateHome;
private Validate validate;
private MyHome registerHome;
private Register register;

public MiddleRegister()
{
}
public void   setRequestId(String req)
                {
                                        requestId=req;
                }
public void setUserName(String user)
                {
                                        userName=user;
                }
public void   setFirstName(String first)
                {
                                        firstName=first;
                }
public void   setMiddleName(String middle)
                {
                                        middleName=middle;
                }
public void   setLastName(String last)
```

```
                                {
                                                lastName=last;
                                }
        public void   setDateOfBirth(String date)
                                {
                                                dateOfBirth=date;
                                }
        public void   setEmail(String em)
                                {
                                                email=em;
                }
        public void   setAddressLine1(String address1)
         {
           addressLine1=address1;
         }
        public void   setAddressLine2(String address2)
         {
           addressLine2=address2;
         }
        public void setCity(String cit)
         {
           city= cit;
         }
        public void   setState(String sta)
         {
           state= sta;
         }
        public void setCreditCard(String credit)
         {
        creditCard=credit;

         }
        public void setCreditCardType(String creditType)
         {
        creditCardType=creditType;
         }
        public void setPassword(String pass)
                        {
```

```
                                        password=pass;
                }
public void setSecretQuestion(String secretQ)
                {
                                        secretQuestion=secretQ;
                }
public void setSecretAnswer(String secretA)
                {
                                        secretAnswer=secretA;
                }
public String getRequestId()
                {
                                        return requestId;
                }
public String getUserName()
                {
                                        return userName;
                }
public String getFirstName()
                {
                                        return firstName;
                }
public String getMiddleName()
                {
                                        return middleName;
                }
public String getLastName()
                {
                                        return lastName;
                }
public String getDateOfBirth()
                {
                                        return dateOfBirth;
                }
public String getEmail()
                {
                                        return email;
                }
```

```java
public String getAddressLine1()
                {
                                        return addressLine1;
                }
public String getAddressLine2()
                {
                                        return addressLine2;
                }
public String getCity()
                {
                                        return city;
                }
public String getState()
                {
                                        return state;
                }
public String getCreditCard()
                {
                                        return creditCard;
                }
public String getCreditCardType()
                {
                                        return creditCardType;
                }
public String register(){
        if(validateCard()){
            processRegistration();
            return "You have been successfully registered.";
        }
        else{
            return ("Sorry! Please check your credit card details.");
                }
}
private boolean validateCard()
                {
                                        try
                                        {
                                        Context ctx1=new InitialContext();
```

```
                              Object obj=ctx1.lookup("java:comp/env/ejb/Validate");

validateHome=(ValidateHome)PortableRemoteObject.narrow(obj,ValidateHome.class);
                              validate = validateHome.create(creditCard);
                              int  res =validate.validate(creditCard);
                  if (res==0)
                              {

                              return true;
                              }
                              else
                              {

                              return false;
                  }
                              }
                  catch(Exception ex)
                              {
                              System.out.println("Cannot find Card myHome 1
"+ex);
                  }
                  return false;
                  }
public void processRegistration()
                  {
         try{
                                 Context ctx2=new InitialContext();
                     Object obj=ctx2.lookup("java:comp/env/ejb/Register");
                                 registerHome=(MyHome)PortableRemoteObject.nar-
row(obj,MyHome.class);

                                 register = registerHome.create( userName,
firstName, middleName, lastName,  dateOfBirth, email, addressLine1, addressLine2,
city,   state, creditCard, creditCardType,password, secretQuestion, secretAnswer);
}catch(Exception e){}
         }
public String invalidMessage()
                  {
                  return "Your Credit Card is invalid";
```

```
          }
}
```

MyHome.java

The home interface of the EJB is shown in Listing 29-13.

Listing 29-13 MyHome.java

```java
import java.util.Collection;
import java.rmi.RemoteException;
import javax.ejb.*;

public interface MyHome extends EJBHome
     {
               public Register create(String userName,String firstName, String
middleName,String lastName, String date, String email, String address1,String
address2,String city, String state, String creditcard, String credittype, String
password,String scretq,String secretans) throws RemoteException,CreateException;

          public Register findByPrimaryKey(String st) throws
FinderException,RemoteException;


     }
```

Register.java

The code for the remote interface for the EJB is given Listing 29-14.

Listing 29-14 Register.java

```java
import javax.ejb.EJBObject;
import   java.rmi.RemoteException;

public interface Register extends EJBObject
     {
```

```
        public String getUserName() throws RemoteException;
        public String getFirstName() throws RemoteException;
        public String getMiddleName() throws RemoteException;
        public String getLastName() throws RemoteException;
        public String getDateOfBirth() throws RemoteException;
        public String getEmail() throws RemoteException;
        public String getAddressLine1() throws RemoteException;
        public String getAddressLine2() throws RemoteException;
        public String getCity() throws RemoteException;
        public String getState() throws RemoteException;
        public String getCreditCard() throws RemoteException;
        public String getCreditCardType() throws RemoteException;
}
```

Register.jsp

The Register.jsp displays the success or failure message of the credit card validation. The code for Register.jsp is available in Listing 29-15.

Listing 29-15 Register.jsp

```
<body bgcolor="#c0c0c0">
<jsp:useBean id="registerBean" scope="session" class="MiddleRegister"/>
<%
String cc=request.getParameter("T1");
String cc1=request.getParameter("T2");
String cc3=request.getParameter("T4");
String cc4=request.getParameter("T5");
String cc5=request.getParameter("T10");
String cc6=request.getParameter("D1");
String cc7=request.getParameter("T6");
String cc8=request.getParameter("T12");
String cc9=request.getParameter("T11");
String cc10=request.getParameter("T13");
String cc11=request.getParameter("T14");
String cc12=request.getParameter("T7");
String cc13=request.getParameter("T7");
```

```
String cc14=request.getParameter("T8");
String cc15=request.getParameter("T9");
%>
<jsp:setProperty name="registerBean" property="*"/>
<jsp:setProperty name="registerBean" property="userName" value="<%=cc%>"/>
<jsp:setProperty name="registerBean" property="password" value="<%=cc1%>"/>
<jsp:setProperty name="registerBean" property="secretQuestion" value="<%=cc3%>"/>
<jsp:setProperty name="registerBean" property="secretAnswer" value="<%=cc4%>"/>
<jsp:setProperty name="registerBean" property="creditCard" value="<%=cc5%>"/>
<jsp:setProperty name="registerBean" property="creditCardType" value="<%=cc6%>"/>
<jsp:setProperty name="registerBean" property="firstName" value="<%=cc7%>"/>
<jsp:setProperty name="registerBean" property="middleName" value="<%=cc8%>"/>
<jsp:setProperty name="registerBean" property="lastName" value="<%=cc9%>"/>
<jsp:setProperty name="registerBean" property="dateOfBirth" value="<%=cc10%>"/>
<jsp:setProperty name="registerBean" property="email" value="<%=cc11%>"/>
<jsp:setProperty name="registerBean" property="addressLine1" value="<%=cc12%>"/>
<jsp:setProperty name="registerBean" property="addressLine2" value="<%=cc13%>"/>
<jsp:setProperty name="registerBean" property="city" value="<%=cc14%>"/>
<jsp:setProperty name="registerBean" property="state" value="<%=cc15%>"/>


<%=registerBean.register()%>


<p><a href='RegisterPage.htm'>Back</a>    <a
href='http://localhost:8000/music/home_page.htm'>Home Page</a></p>
</body>
```

RegisterEJB.java

The RegisterEJB class is the implementation class for the register EJB bean. This class will update the User_Info table in the Music database. The code for RegisterEJB.java is shown in Listing 29-16.

Listing 29-16   RegisterEJB.java

```
import java.sql.*;
import javax.sql.*;
import java.util.*;
```

```
import javax.ejb.*;
import javax.naming.*;
import java.rmi.*;

public class RegisterEjb implements EntityBean
{
private String requestId;
private String userName;
private String firstName;
private String middleName;
private String lastName;
private String dateOfBirth;
private String email;
private String addressLine1;
private String addressLine2;
private String city;
private String state;
private String creditCard;
private String creditCardType;
private String password;
private String secretQuestion;
private String secretAnswer;
Connection con;
int id=0;
public RegisterEjb(){}
public void   setRequestId(String req)
                    {
                                        requestId=req;
                    }
public void setUserName(String user)
                  {
                                      userName=user;
                  }
public void   setFirstName(String first)
                    {
                                        firstName=first;
                    }
public void   setMiddleName(String middle)
```

```
                              {
                                          middleName=middle;
                      }
public void   setLastName(String last)
                      {
                                          lastName=last;
                      }
public void   setDateOfBirth(String date)
                      {
                                          dateOfBirth=date;
                      }
public void   setEmail(String em)
                      {
                                          email=em;

          }
public void   setAddressLine1(String address1)
 {
   addressLine1=address1;
 }
public void   setAddressLine2(String address2)
 {
   addressLine2=address2;
 }
public void setCity(String cit)
 {
   city= cit;
 }
public void   setState(String sta)
 {
   state= sta;
 }
public void setCreditCard(String credit)
 {
creditCard=credit;

 }
public void setCreditCardType(String creditType)
```

```
 {
creditCardType=creditType;
 }
public void setPassword(String pass)
                {
                                        password=pass;
                }
public void setSecretQuestion(String secretQ)
                {
                                        secretQuestion=secretQ;
                }
public void setSecretAnswer(String secretA)
                {
                                        secretAnswer=secretA;
                }
public String getRequestId()
                {
                                        return requestId;
                }
public String getUserName()
                {
                                        return userName;
                }
public String getFirstName()
                {
                                        return firstName;
                }
public String getMiddleName()
                {
                                        return middleName;
                }
public String getLastName()
                {
                                        return lastName;
                }
public String getDateOfBirth()
                {
                                        return dateOfBirth;
```

```
                                }
        public String getEmail()
                        {
                                                return email;
                        }
        public String getAddressLine1()
                        {
                                        return addressLine1;
                        }
        public String getAddressLine2()
                        {
                                        return addressLine2;
                        }
        public String getCity()
                        {
                                        return city;
                        }
        public String getState()
                        {
                                        return state;
                        }
        public String getCreditCard()
                        {
                                        return creditCard;
                        }
        public String getCreditCardType()
                        {
                                        return creditCardType;
                        }
        public String ejbFindByPrimaryKey(String id) throws FinderException{

        return new String(new Integer(id).toString());
        }
        public String ejbCreate(String userName,String firstName,String middleName,String
        lastName, String  dateOfBirth,String email,String addressLine1,String
        addressLine2,String city, String state,String  creditCard,String
        creditCardType,String password,String secretQuestion,String secretAnswer)throws
        CreateException {
```

```
try{
                        getConnection();
                        Statement st= con.createStatement();
System.out.println("Afterget1"+st);
ResultSet rst=st.executeQuery("Select max(request_id) from User_Info");
while(rst.next()){
                                                        id=rst.getInt(1);


                                }


System.out.println("Inside setEntityContext");
        }catch(Exception e){
                        System.out.println("In setEntityContext() :"+e);

        }

this.userName=userName;
this.firstName=firstName;
this.middleName=middleName;
this.lastName=lastName;
this.dateOfBirth=dateOfBirth;
this.email=email;
this.addressLine1=addressLine1;
this.addressLine2=addressLine2;
this.city= city;
this.state= state;
this.creditCard=creditCard;
this.creditCardType=creditCardType;
this.password=password;
this.secretQuestion=secretQuestion;
this.secretAnswer=secretAnswer;

try
  {
    insertDetails(userName, firstName, middleName,lastName, dateOfBirth, email,
addressLine1,addressLine2,city,state,
 creditCard,creditCardType,password,secretQuestion,
 secretAnswer);
    }
```

```java
catch(Exception ex)
  {
   System.out.println("Exception in inserting details in database"+ex);
  }
try
  {
   closeConnection();
  }
catch(Exception ex)
  {
   System.out.println("Exception in closing Connection"+ex);
  }
return (new Integer(id).toString());
}


private void getConnection() throws NamingException,SQLException
 {
  InitialContext inc=new InitialContext();
  DataSource datsrc=(DataSource)inc.lookup("java:comp/env/jdbc/RegisterDataSource");

  con=datsrc.getConnection();

 }

private void insertDetails(String userName,String firstName,String middleName,String
lastName,String dateOfBirth,String email, String addressLine1,String
addressLine2,String city,String state,String creditCard,String creditCardType,String
password,
String secretQuestion,String secretAnswer)throws SQLException
{
try
{
Statement st= con.createStatement();
                                ResultSet rst=st.executeQuery("Select
max(request_id) from User_Info");
                                while(rst.next()){
                                            id=rst.getInt(1);
```

```
                                        }
                        }catch(Exception e){
                                        System.out.println("Exception in Activate"+e);
                        }
id++;

 String role="user";
 String insert1="Insert into User_Info values(?,?,?,?,?,?,?,?,?,?,?,?,?)";
 String insert2="Insert into Login_Info values (?,?,?,?,?)";
 PreparedStatement stat1=con.prepareStatement(insert1);
 PreparedStatement stat2=con.prepareStatement(insert2);
 stat1.setInt(1,id);
 stat1.setString(2,userName);
 stat1.setString(3,firstName);
 stat1.setString(4,middleName);
 stat1.setString(5,lastName);
 stat1.setString(6,dateOfBirth);
 stat1.setString(7,email);
 stat1.setString(8,addressLine1);
 stat1.setString(9,addressLine2);
 stat1.setString(10,city);
 stat1.setString(11,state);
 stat1.setString(12,creditCard);
 stat1.setString(13,creditCardType);
 stat2.setString(1,userName);
 stat2.setString(2,password);
 stat2.setString(3,secretQuestion);
 stat2.setString(4,secretAnswer);
stat2.setString(5,role);
 stat1.executeUpdate();
 stat1.close();
 stat2.executeUpdate();
 stat2.close();
 }
private void closeConnection() throws SQLException
 {
    con.close();
```

```
        }
        public String ejbPostCreate(String userName,String firstName,String
        middleName,String lastName, String dateOfBirth,String email,String
        addressLine1,String addressLine2,String city, String state,String creditCard,String
        creditCardType,String password,String secretQuestion,String secretAnswerr){return
        new Integer(id).toString();}
        public void ejbActivate(){
                        try{
                                                getConnection();
                                                Statement st= con.createStatement();
                                                ResultSet rst=st.executeQuery("Select
        max(request_id) from User_Info");
                                                while(rst.next()){
                                                                        id=rst.getInt(1);
                                                }
                                }catch(Exception e){
                                                System.out.println("In Activate() :"+e);
                }
        }
        public void ejbLoad(){}
        public void ejbPassivate(){
        try{
                        closeConnection();
           }catch(Exception e){
                        System.out.println("In setEntityContext() :"+e);
            }
        }
        public void ejbRemove(){}
        public void ejbStore(){}
        public void setEntityContext(EntityContext ctx){
        try{
                                                getConnection();
                                                }
                                catch(Exception e){
                                                System.out.println("In Activate() :"+e);
                }
        }
        public void unsetEntityContext(){
```

```
try{
                    closeConnection();
 }catch(SQLException e){
   }
}
}
```

Validate.java

The remote interface for EJB that validates the credit card information is given in Listing 29-17.

Listing 29-17 Validate.java

```
import java.util.*;
import javax.ejb.EJBObject;
import java.rmi.RemoteException;

public interface Validate extends EJBObject
{
  public int validate(String CardNo) throws RemoteException;
}
```

ValidateEJB.java

The code for ValidateEJB.Java, which implements the methods to validate the credit card information provided by the user, is given in Listing 29-18.

Listing 29-18 ValidateEJB.java

```
import java.util.*;
import javax.ejb.*;

public class ValidateEJB implements SessionBean {
    String cardNo;
    public void ejbCreate(String CardNo) throws CreateException
      {
```

```
              if( CardNo.equals(""))
              {
                 throw new CreateException("Null person or card number not
allowed.");
              }
        else
                              cardNo=CardNo;
      }
public static char leftchar(String CardNo)
{
 return(CardNo.charAt(0));
}
public static char rightchar(String CardNo)
{
return(CardNo.charAt(CardNo.length() - 1));
}
public static int chtoint(char ch)
{
        if (ch == '0') return(0);
        if (ch == '1') return(1);
        if (ch == '2') return(2);
        if (ch == '3') return(3);
        if (ch == '4') return(4);
        if (ch == '5') return(5);
        if (ch == '6') return(6);
        if (ch == '7') return(7);
        if (ch == '8') return(8);
        if (ch == '9') return(9);
        return(0);
    }
   public int validate(String CardNo)
            {
               int i;
                int total = 0;
             String tempMult = "";
   for (i = CardNo.length(); i >= 2; i -= 2)
   {
     total = total + chtoint(CardNo.charAt(i - 1));
```

```
    tempMult = "" + (chtoint(CardNo.charAt(i - 2)) * 2);
    total = total + chtoint(leftchar(tempMult));
    if (tempMult.length() > 1)
    {
    total = total + chtoint(rightchar(tempMult));
    }
    }

  if (CardNo.length() % 2 == 1)
  {
  total = total + chtoint(leftchar(CardNo));
  }
  if (total % 10 == 0)
  {
  return 0;
  }
  else
  {
  // System.out.println("Invalid card number");
   return 1;
  }
}
    public ValidateEJB() {}
    public void ejbRemove() {}
    public void ejbActivate() {}
    public void ejbPassivate() {}
    public void setSessionContext(SessionContext sc) {}
}
```

ValidateHome.java

The home interface of the validate EJB is given in Listing 29-19.

Listing 29-19 ValidateHome.java

```
import java.io.Serializable;
import java.rmi.RemoteException;
```

```
import javax.ejb.CreateException;
import javax.ejb.EJBHome;

public interface ValidateHome extends EJBHome
{
    Validate create(String CardNo) throws RemoteException, CreateException;
}
```

Now that you have looked at the code for creating the EJB classes, you can deploy the EJB.

Deploying the EJB for the *Register* Page

The deployment process can be divided into three steps:

♦ Deploy the `Validate` Bean
♦ Deploy the `Register` Bean
♦ Deploy the Web Component

Now I'll show you each step.

Deploying the Validate Bean

The steps to deploy the `Validate` bean are:

1. Select `MusicApp` from the left pane. You created the `MusicApp` while deploying the EJB for the Search page.

2. In the Application Deployment Tool window, select New Enterprise Bean from the File menu. The New Enterprise Bean Wizard — Introduction screen appears.

3. Click the Next button. The New Enterprise Bean Wizard — EJB JAR dialog box is displayed, as seen in Figure 29-23.

4. Specify `ValidateJar` in the JAR Display Name text box.

5. In the Contents group box, click the Add button. The Add Files to .JAR dialog box is displayed, as seen in Figure 29-24.

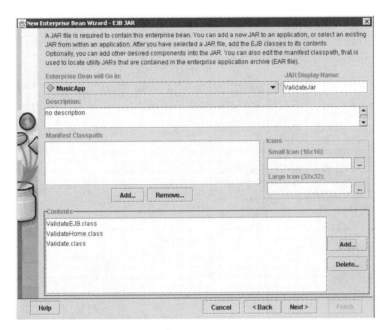

FIGURE 29-23 *The New Enterprise Bean Wizard — EJB JAR dialog box is shown.*

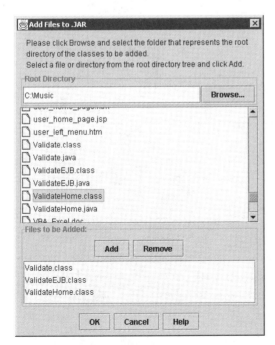

FIGURE 29-24 *The Add Files to .JAR dialog box is shown after clicking the Add button.*

6. Select `Validate.class` and click the Add button. Similarly, select the `ValidateEJB.class` and `ValidateHome.class` files. Verify that the files that you add appear in the lower text box of the dialog box.

7. Click on OK. Verify that all the .class files you added appear in the Contents area of the New Enterprise Bean Wizard — EJB JAR dialog box. See Figure 29-25.

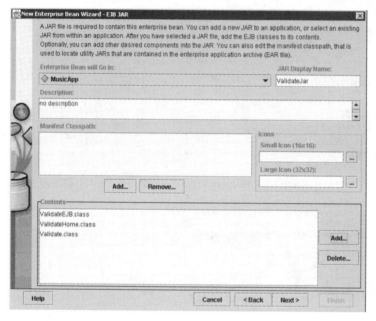

FIGURE 29-25 *The New Enterprise Bean Wizard — EJB JAR dialog box is displayed.*

8. Click the Next button. The New Enterprise Bean Wizard — General dialog box appears.

9. In New Enterprise Bean Wizard — General dialog box, from the Enterprise Bean Class: drop-down list, select `ValidateEJB`. From the `Home Interface` drop-down list, select `ValidateHome`. From the Remote Interface: drop-down list, select `Validate`. In the Enterprise Bean Display Name box, type `ValidateBean`. Under Bean Type, verify that Session and Stateful appear selected. See Figure 29-26.

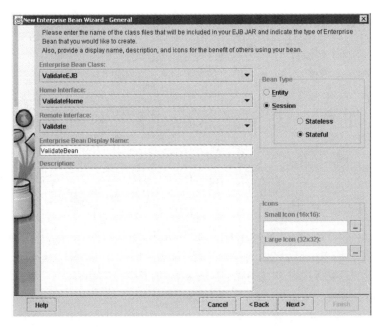

FIGURE 29-26 *The New Enterprise Bean Wizard — General dialog box is displayed.*

10. Notice that the Bean Type is Stateful Session Bean by default. Click on Next. The New Enterprise Bean Wizard — Environment Entries dialog box appears.

11. Click the Next button. The New Enterprise Bean Wizard — Enterprise Bean References dialog box appears.

12. Click the Next button. The New Enterprise Bean Wizard — Resource References dialog box appears.

13. Click the Next button. The New Enterprise Bean Wizard — Security dialog box appears.

14. Click the Next button. The New Enterprise Bean Wizard — Transaction Management dialog box appears.

15. Click the Next button. The New Enterprise Bean Wizard — Review Settings dialog box appears.

16. Click the Finish button. Notice that the `ValidateJar` is displayed in the left pane below `MusicApp`.

Deploying the Register *Bean*

The steps to deploy the Register bean are:

1. Select MusicApp from the left pane.

2. Select New Enterprise Bean from the File menu. The New Enterprise Bean Wizard — Introduction dialog box is displayed.

3. Click the Next button. The New Enterprise Bean Wizard — EJB JAR dialog box is displayed. Specify JAR Display Name as UserJar.

4. Click the Add button in the Contents group box. The Add Files to .JAR dialog box is displayed.

5. Click on Browse and then select the root directory where the files are stored. Select the MyItem.class, Register.class, and RegisterEJB.class files and then click the Add button.

6. Click on OK. The class files are displayed in the Contents group box of the New Enterprise Bean Wizard — EJB JAR dialog box. See Figure 29-27.

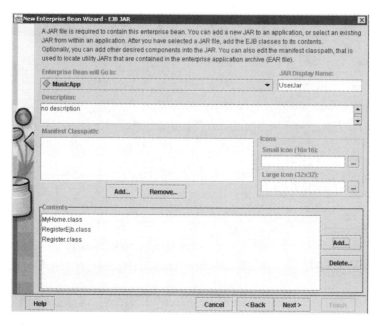

FIGURE 29-27 *The New Enterprise Bean Wizard — EJB JAR dialog box is displayed.*

7. Click the Next button. The New Enterprise Bean Wizard — General dialog box is displayed, as seen in Figure 29-28.

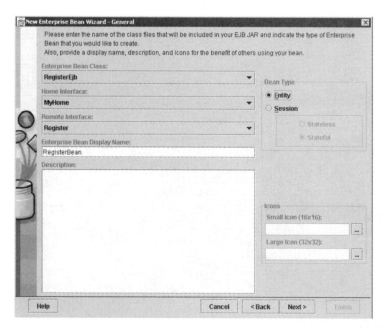

FIGURE 29-28 *After clicking the Next button, the New Enterprise Bean Wizard — General dialog box is shown.*

8. Select Entity as the bean type. Select RegisterEJB from the Enterprise Bean Class drop-down list. Select MyHome from the Home Interface drop-down list. Select Register from the Remote Interface drop-down list. Type RegisterBean in the Enterprise Bean Display Name text field.

9. Click the Next button. The New Enterprise Bean Wizard — Entity Settings dialog box is displayed. Ensure that Bean-Managed Persistence option is selected.

10. Click the Next button. The New Enterprise Bean Wizard — Environment Entries dialog box is displayed.

11. Click the Next button. The New Enterprise Bean Wizard — Enterprise Bean References dialog box is displayed.

12. Click the Next button. The New Enterprise Bean Wizard — Resource References dialog box is displayed. See Figure 29-29.

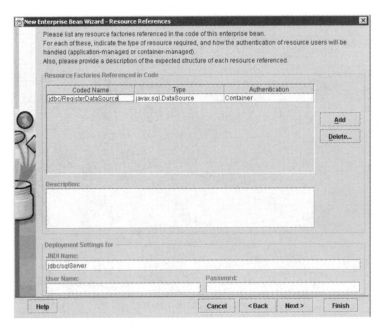

FIGURE 29-29 *The New Enterprise Bean Wizard — Resource References dialog box is shown.*

13. Click the Add button. A row appears in the Resource Factories Referenced in Code group box.

14. Type `jdbc/RegisterDataSource` in the Coded Name column. Specify JNDI Name as `jdbc/sqlServer`.

15. Click the Next button. The New Enterprise Bean Wizard — Security dialog box is displayed.

16. Click the Next button. The New Enterprise Bean Wizard — Transaction Management dialog box is displayed. See Figure 29-30.

17. Select the Transaction Type as `Required` for the business methods as shown in Figure 29-30.

18. Click the Next button. The New Enterprise Bean Wizard — Review Settings dialog box is displayed.

19. Click the Finish button. The Application Deployment Tool: MusicApp window is displayed. Notice that `UserJar` is displayed in the left pane below `MusicApp`.

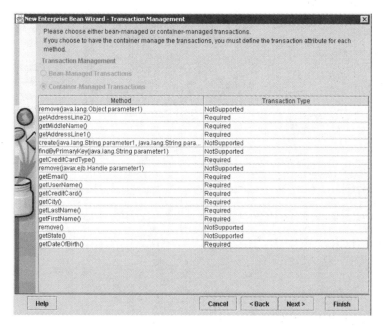

FIGURE 29-30 *The New Enterprise Bean Wizard — Transaction Management dialog box is shown.*

Deploying the Web Component

The steps to deploy the Web component are:

1. Select MusicApp from the left pane.

2. Choose File, New Web Component. The New Web Component Wizard — Introduction dialog box is displayed.

3. Click the Next button. The New Web Component Wizard — .WAR File General Properties dialog box is displayed. Note that MusicApp is displayed in the Web Component will Go In drop-down list.

4. Type RegisterWar in the WAR Display Name text field.

5. Click the Add button in the Contents group box. The Add Files to .WAR — Add Content Files dialog box is displayed. See Figure 29-31.

6. Click on Browse and select your working directory. Select Register-Page.htm and Register.jsp in the scroll pane.

7. Click the Next button. The Add Files to .WAR — Add Class Files dialog box is displayed.

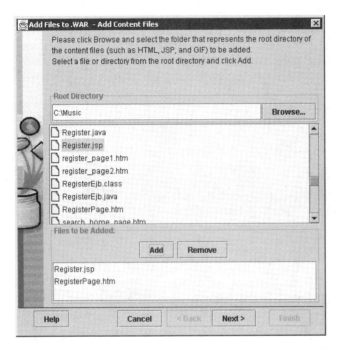

FIGURE 29-31 *The Add Files to .WAR — Add Content Files dialog box is shown.*

8. Click on Browse and select your working directory. Select `MiddleRegister.class` in the scroll pane.

9. Click the Add button in the Files to be Added group box. `MiddleRegister.class` is displayed in the Files to be Added group box.

10. Click the Finish button. The New Web Component Wizard — .WAR File General Properties dialog box is displayed, as seen in Figure 29-32.

11. Click the Next button. The New Web Component Wizard — Choose Component Type dialog box is displayed.

12. Select `JSP` as the Web Component Type.

13. Click the Next button. The New Web Component Wizard — Component General Properties dialog box is displayed.

14. Select `Register.jsp` from the JSP Filename drop-down list. Type `Component1` in the Web Component Display Name text field.

15. Click the Next button. The New Web Component Wizard — Component Initialization Parameters dialog box is displayed. Click the Next button.

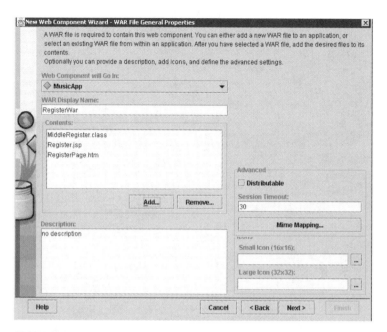

FIGURE 29-32 *The New Web Component Wizard —WAR File General Properties dialog box is shown.*

16. The New Web Component Wizard — Component Aliases dialog box is displayed. Click the Add button.

17. Specify the Alias name as `Register` in the Aliases text box. Click the Next button.

18. The New Web Component Wizard — Component Security dialog box is displayed. Click the Next button.

19. The New Web Component Wizard — WAR File Environment dialog box is displayed. Click the Next button.

20. The New Web Component Wizard —— Enterprise Bean References dialog box is displayed. See Figure 29-33.

21. Click the Add button. A new entry appears in the EJB's Referenced in Code group box.

22. Type `ejb/Validate` in the Coded Name column. Select `Entity` from the Type column list. Type `ValidateHome` in the Home column and `Validate` in the Remote column. Specify JNDI Name as `Validate`.

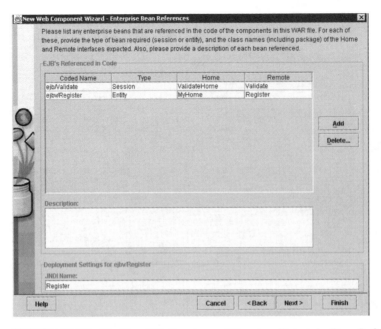

FIGURE 29-33 *The New Web Component Wizard — Enterprise Bean References dialog box is shown.*

23. Again, click the Add button. Specify Type as Entity, Home as MyHome, Remote as Register, and JNDI Name as Register.

24. Click the Finish button. The Application Deployment Tool: MusicApp window is displayed. Note that RegisterWar is displayed in the left pane below Local Applications.

25. Click the Web Context tab in the right pane. Specify Register in the Context Root column.

26. Choose Tools, Deploy Application. The Deploy MusicApp — Introduction dialog box is displayed.

27. Click the Next button. The Deploy MusicApp — JNDI Names dialog box is displayed. Note that the JNDI names are displayed. See Figure 29-34.

28. Click the Next button. The Deploy MusicApp — .WAR Context Root dialog box is displayed. Note that the entry in the Context Root column is Register. See Figure 29-35.

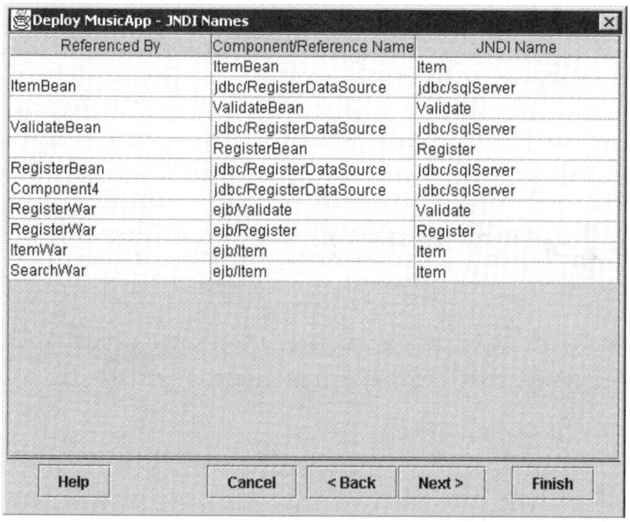

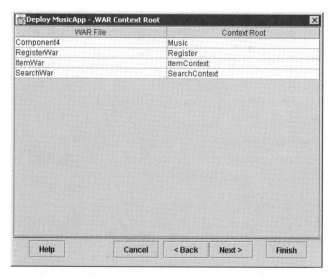

FIGURE 29-34 *The Deploy MusicApp — JNDI Names dialog box is shown.*

WAR File	Context Root
Component4	Music
RegisterWar	Register
ItemWar	ItemContext
SearchWar	SearchContext

FIGURE 29-35 *The Deploy MusicApp — .WAR Context Root dialog box is shown.*

29. Click the Next button. The Deploy MusicApp — Review dialog box is displayed.

30. Click the Finish button. The Deployment Progress dialog box is displayed.

31. Click on OK when the Deployment Progress dialog box indicates that the deployment of MusicApp is complete. You have deployed the Register page and the associated EJB beans. Now create the Login page of the eMusicWorld application.

Creating the Login Page

A user can log on to the music application after providing logon details such as username and password. The Login page will query the Login_Info table in the Music database for the similar combination of username and password.

The Login page consists of two underlying pages:

◆ login_page.htm

◆ login_page.jsp

The code for each of these pages is given in Listing 29-20.

Listing 29-20 login_page.htm

```
<html>
<head>
<title>Login Page</title>
</head>
<body bgcolor="#C0C0C0">
<form method="get" action="login_page.jsp">
      <marquee style="font-family: Arial; font-size: 14pt; color: #800000; font-
style: italic; font-weight: bold">eMusicWorld
      -----&gt; The World of Music</marquee>
<table border="1" width="100%">
  <tr>
    <td width="18%">
<p><font face="Arial" size="2" color="#800000"><b><a
HREF="home_page.htm">Home</a></b></font></p>
<p><b><font face="Arial" size="2" color="#800000"><a HREF="chart_toppers.jsp">Chart
Toppers</a></font></b></p>
<p><b><font face="Arial" size="2" color="#800000"><a
HREF="search_home_page.htm">Search</a></font></b></p>
<p><b><font face="Arial" size="2" color="#800000"><a
```

```
HREF="vote_page.jsp">Vote</a></font></b></p>
<p><b><font face="Arial" size="2" color="#800000"><a
HREF="download_page.htm">Downloads</a></font></b></p>
<p><b><font face="Arial" size="2" color="#800000"><a HREF="new_release_page.jsp">New
Releases</a></font></b>
<p><font face="Arial" size="2" color="#800000"><b><a
HREF="register_page1.htm">Register</a></b></font>
<p><font face="Arial" size="2" color="#800000"><b><a
HREF="help_page.htm">Help</a></b></font></p>
        <p> </td>
    <td width="82%" valign="top">


<p><font face="Arial" size="2" color="#800000">Please enter your logon
details.</font> </p>
<p><font face="Arial" size="2" color="#800000">User Name :</font> <input
type="text" name="username" size="20">
</p>
<p><font face="Arial" size="2" color="#800000">Password :</font>   <input
type="text" name="password" size="20"></p>
<p><font face="Arial" size="2" color="#800000">New User? <a HREF=" http://local-
host:8000/Register/RegisterPage.htm ">Register</a></font></p>


  <p align="center"><input type="submit" value="Submit" name="B1"><input
type="reset" value="Clear" name="B2"></p>
        <p> </td>
  </tr>
</table>
<p>  </p>
<p>  </p>
</form>
</body>
</html>
```

When executed, the code in Listing 29-20 will display the login page to the user, as shown in Figure 29-36. Notice that the page has two text boxes for accepting username and password. Notice the action attribute of the <form> tag. The form will be submitted to the login_page.jsp page since the value assigned to the action attribute is login_page.jsp.

The output of login_page.htm is displayed in Figure 29-36.

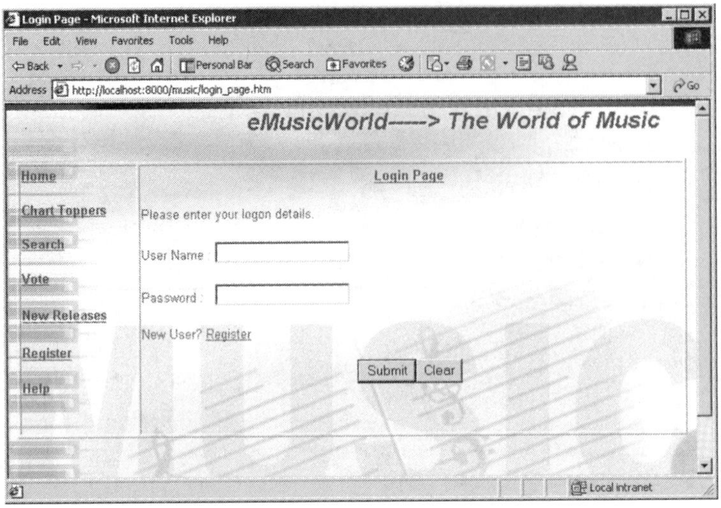

FIGURE 29-36 *The output of* login_page.htm *is shown here.*

Listing 29-21 shows the code for the login_page.jsp page.

Listing 29-21 login_page.jsp

```
<html>
<head>
<title>Login Page</title>
</head>
<body bgcolor="#C0C0C0">
<form method="GET" action="http:\\localhost:8000\login_page.jsp">
     <marquee style="font-family: Arial; font-size: 14pt; color: #800000; font-
style: italic; font-weight: bold">eMusicWorld
     -----&gt; The World of Music</marquee>
<table border="1" width="100%">
  <tr>
    <td width="18%">

<p><font face="Arial" size="2" color="#800000"><b><a
```

```
HREF="home_page.htm">Home</a></b></font></p>

<p><b><font face="Arial" size="2" color="#800000"><a HREF="chart_toppers.jsp">Chart
Toppers</a></font></b></p>
<p><b><font face="Arial" size="2" color="#800000"><a
HREF="search_home_page.htm">Search</a></font></b></p>
<p><b><font face="Arial" size="2" color="#800000"><a
HREF="vote_page.jsp">Vote</a></font></b></p>
<p><b><font face="Arial" size="2" color="#800000"><a
HREF="download_page.htm">Downloads</a></font></b></p>
<p><b><font face="Arial" size="2" color="#800000"><a HREF="new_release_page.jsp">New
Releases</a></font></b>
<p><font face="Arial" size="2" color="#800000"><b><a
HREF="register_page1.htm">Register</a></b></font>
<p><font face="Arial" size="2" color="#800000"><b><a
HREF="help_page.htm">Help</a></b></font></p>
      <p> </td>
    <td width="82%" valign="top">
<%! String username;%>
<%! String password;%>
<%! String role;%>


                    <%@ page import="java.util.*" %>
                    <%@ page import="java.sql.*" %>
                    <%@ page import="java.text.*" %>
                    <%@ page import="java.sql.Date" %>
                    <%@ page language = "java" %>
<%

                    try{
                    Class.forName("sun.jdbc.odbc.JdbcOdbcDriver");
                    Connection connect;

connect=DriverManager.getConnection("jdbc:odbc:MusicDataSource","","");
                    Statement state;
                    state = connect.createStatement();


                    String strQuery1 = "select Password, Role from Login_Info where
User_name='"+username+ "'";
```

```
username=request.getParameter("username");

password=request.getParameter("password");
ResultSet result1 = state.executeQuery(strQuery1);
String pass;
String user="user";
  while(result1.next())
  {
                    pass=result1.getString("Password");
                    role=result1.getString("Role");

                    role=role.trim();

if((pass.equals(password))&&(role.equals("user")))
                            {
                            role="user";
                            session.setAttribute("username", username);
                            }
                            else if
((pass.equals(password))&&(role.equals("admin")))
                            role="admin";
                            else
                            role="no_user";
  }
  }
  catch(Exception e){
  out.println("done exception" +e);
  }

  role=role.trim();
  if(role.equals("user")) {%>
  <jsp:forward page="user_home_page.jsp" />
  Vector vc=new Vector(1,1);
  session.setAttribute("Shopping_List",vc);
  <%}
  else if (role.equals("admin")){
  %>
  <jsp:forward page="admin_home_page.htm"/>
```

```
                    <%}
                    else
                    out.println("<p><font face=\"Arial\" size=\"2\"
color=\"#800000\"><b>You have entered incorrect logon information. Please enter
correct logon details.</b></font> </p>");
     %>
<p><font face="Arial" size="2" color="#800000">Please enter your logon
details.</font> </p>
<p><font face="Arial" size="2" color="#800000">User Name :</font> <input
type="text" name="username" size="20">
</p>


<p><font face="Arial" size="2" color="#800000">Password :</font>   <input
type="text" name="password" size="20"></p>
<p><font face="Arial" size="2" color="#800000">New User? <a HREF=" http://local-
host:8000/Register/RegisterPage.htm ">Register</a></font></p>
   <p align="center"><input type="submit" value="Submit" name="B1"><input
type="reset" value="Clear" name="B2"></p>
        <p> </td>
   </tr>
</table>
<p>  </p>
<p>  </p>
</form>
</body>
</html>
```

Analyzing the Code of *login_page.htm*

Now analyze the code in Listing 29-20.

```
                    try{
                    Class.forName("sun.jdbc.odbc.JdbcOdbcDriver");
                    Connection connect;

connect=DriverManager.getConnection("jdbc:odbc:MusicDataSource","","");
                    Statement state;
                    state = connect.createStatement();
```

```
            String strQuery1 = "select Password, Role from Login_Info where
User_name='"+username+ "'";
                username=request.getParameter("username");
                password=request.getParameter("password");
                ResultSet result1 = state.executeQuery(strQuery1);
```

The above set of statements will connect to the Music database and execute the select query to obtain the Password and Role field values from the database. In addition, the username and the password submitted by the user in the login_page.jsp page are stored in the variables, username, and password by using the getParameter() method of the request object. Next, the database query is executed.

```
            while(result1.next())
        {
                            pass=result1.getString("Password");
                            role=result1.getString("Role");

                            role=role.trim();

if((pass.equals(password))&&(role.equals("user")))
                                {
                                role="user";
                                session.setAttribute("username", username);
                                }
                                else if
((pass.equals(password))&&(role.equals("admin")))role="admin";
                                else
                                role="no_user";
            }
        }
```

In the preceding code, the password and the role fields are being accessed and matched with that provided by the user. If the password matches and the role is user, the value user is assigned to the role variable. Next, the attribute is set for the session object. The session.setAttribute("username", username) statement sets the attribute username in the session object. The session object is an implicit object that is accessible to all the JSP pages. If the role of the user as mentioned in the Login_Info table of the database is administrator, the value admin is assigned to the role variable. If the user is neither administrator nor a user, the value no_user is assigned to the variable, role.

```
if(role.equals("user")) {%>
Vector vc=new Vector(1,1);
session.setAttribute("Shopping_List",vc);
<jsp:forward page="user_home_page.jsp" />
<%}
else if (role.equals("admin")){
%>
<jsp:forward page="admin_home_page.htm"/>
<%}
else
out.println("<p><font face=\"Arial\" size=\"2\"
color=\"#800000\"><b>You have entered incorrect logon information. Please enter
correct logon details.</b></font> </p>");
```

In the preceding statements, the value of the role variable is determined and appropriate action is being taken. If role is user, an attribute is set in the session object. This attribute, Shopping_List, initially contains an empty Vector object. After the attribute is set, the page is forwarded to the user_home_page.jsp page. If the user is admin, the page is forwarded to the admin_home_page.htm. Otherwise, an error message is displayed to the user.

The output of the Login_page.jsp when the user provides incorrect logon information is displayed in Figure 29-37.

The last page in the Visitor Interface category is the Help page.

Creating the Help Page

The Help page can be used by visitors to seek information about the site. Since the Help page of the application is still under construction, a message is displayed to the visitor. The code of the Help page is given in Listing 29-22.

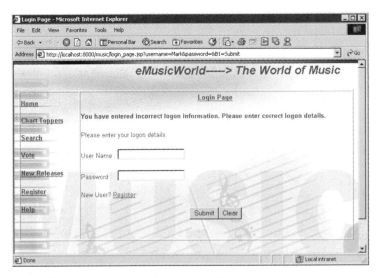

FIGURE 29-37 *The* Login_page.jsp *displays an error message.*

Listing 29-22 Help_page.htm

```html
<html>
<head>
<meta http-equiv="Content-Type" content="text/html; charset=windows-1252">
<meta http-equiv="Content-Language" content="en-us">
<title>Help Page</title>
</head>
<body bgcolor="#C0C0C0" topmargin="0"
background="http:\\localhost:8000\music\Background.bmp" >
<table border="0" width="100%">
  <tr>
    <td width="100%">
      <table border="0" width="97%" height="19">
        <tr>
          <td width="18%" height="13" valign="middle" align="right">
        <font face="Arial" size="5" color="#800000"><b><i>eMusicWorld-----&gt; The
World of Music</i></b></font>
          </td>
        </tr>
      </table>
```

```
          </td>
      </tr>
  </table>
  <form method="POST" action="http://localhost:8000/music/user_home_page.jsp">
          <table border="1" width="100%">
      <tr>
         <td width="18%">
  <p><font face="Arial" size="2" color="#800000"><b><a
  HREF="http://localhost:8000/music/home_page.htm">Home</a></b></font></p>
  <p><b><font face="Arial" size="2" color="#800000"><a
  HREF="http://localhost:8000/music/chart_toppers.jsp">Chart
  Toppers</a></font></b></p>
  <p><b><font face="Arial" size="2" color="#800000"><a
  HREF="http://localhost:8000/SearchContext/SearchAlias">Search</a></font></b></p>
  <p><b><font face="Arial" size="2" color="#800000"><a
  HREF="http://localhost:8000/music/vote_page.jsp">Vote</a></font></b></p>
  <p><b><font face="Arial" size="2" color="#800000"><a
  HREF="http://localhost:8000/music/new_release_page.jsp">New Releases</a></font></b>
  <p><font face="Arial" size="2" color="#800000"><b><a
  HREF="http://localhost:8000/Register/RegisterPage.htm">Register</a></b></font>
  <p><font face="Arial" size="2" color="#800000"><b><a
  HREF="http://localhost:8000/music/login_page.htm">Login</a></b></font>
  <p><font face="Arial" size="2" color="#800000"><b><a
  HREF="http://localhost:8000/music/help_page.htm">Help</a></b></font></p>
          <p> </td>
         <td width="82%">
  <p><b><font face="Arial Black" size="3" color="#800000">This is the help
  page........now under construction....</font></b></p>
          </td>
      </tr>
  </table>
  <p>  </p>
  <p>  </p>
  </form>
  </body>
  </html>
```

Now that you have learned how to create the pages of the eMusicApp application, navigate through these pages and take a look at their functionality.

An Example

Take an example and see the functionality of the pages in the Visitor Interface category. Mark Smith visits the eMusicWorld site. The first page that is displayed to him is the Home page. See Figure 29-38.

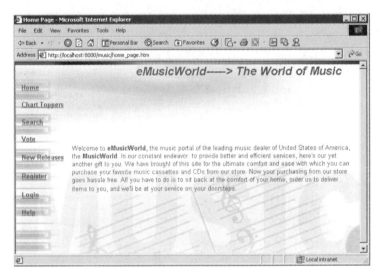

FIGURE 29-38 *The Home page is displayed.*

To vote for his favorite song, Mark opens the Vote page by clicking the Vote link. The Vote page displays the list of songs, as seen in Figure 29-39.

After Mark selects his favorite song and clicks on the link Vote, the Vote result page is displayed, as shown in Figure 29-40.

Mark wants to view whether the song he has voted for is the chart topper. The Chart Toppers page displays the songs that have been most popular with the visitors. See Figure 29-41.

Before logging on and buying a music item, Mark wants to ensure that the music collection is available at eMusicWorld. He searches for songs based on the

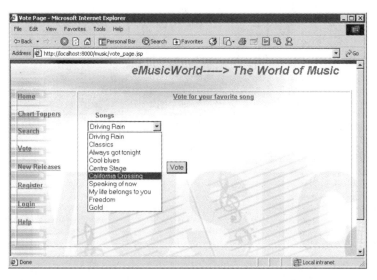

FIGURE 29-39 *The Vote page is displayed.*

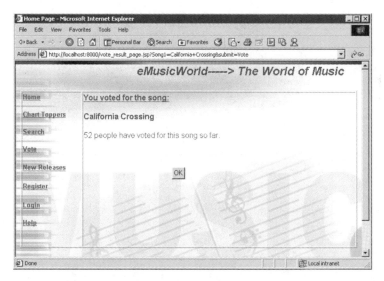

FIGURE 29-40 *The Vote result page is shown.*

category. To search for a song, he selects a category and clicks the Submit button. The Search page is shown in Figure 29-42.

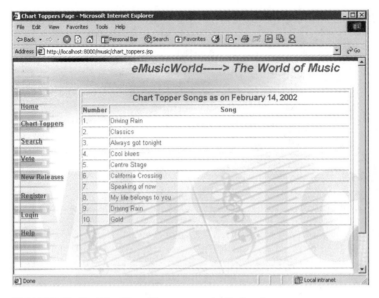

FIGURE 29-41 *The Chart Toppers page is displayed.*

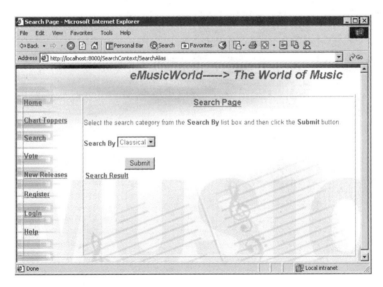

FIGURE 29-42 *The Search page is displayed.*

The results of the search performed by Mark are displayed in Figure 29-43.

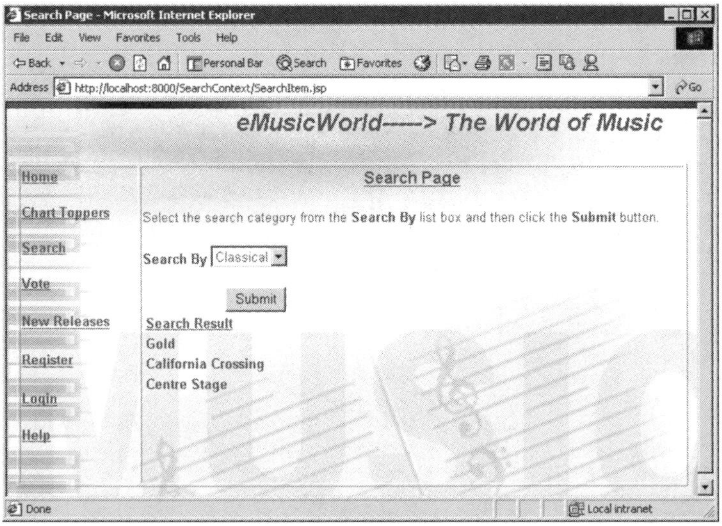

FIGURE 29-43 *The search result is shown.*

Mark finds the song that he was looking for in the search. Before being able to buy the collection, Mark needs to register by using the Register page. Mark opens the Register page and enters his details. Figure 29-44 shows the `Logon Informa-tion` and `Billing Information` sections.

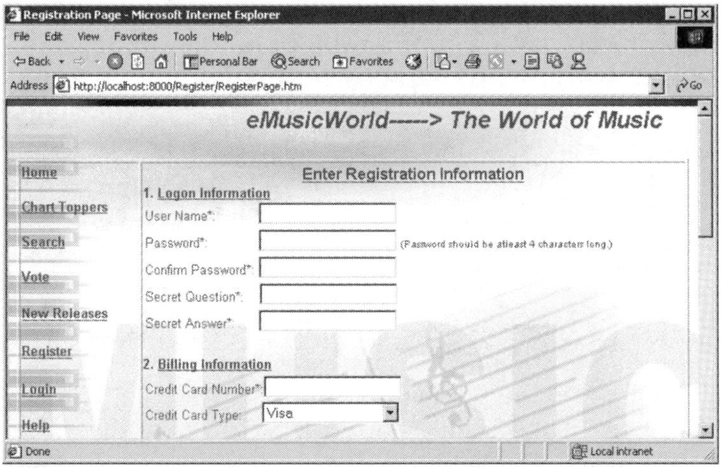

FIGURE 29-44 *The* `Logon Information` *and* `Billing Information` *sections of the Register page are displayed.*

Next, the `Personal Information` section of the Register page is displayed as seen in Figure 29-45.

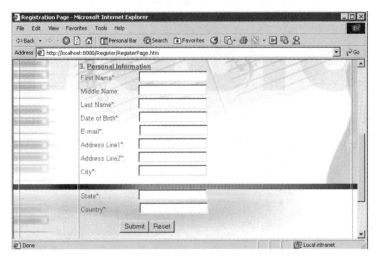

FIGURE 29-45 *The* `Personal Information` *section of the Register page is displayed.*

By mistake, Mark enters incorrect credit card number. The `Validate` bean validates the credit card number and displays an error message. See Figure 29-46.

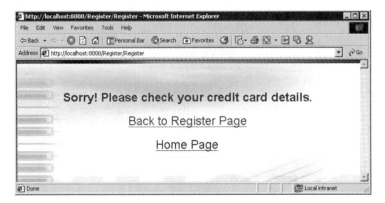

FIGURE 29-46 *The error message is displayed.*

Mark comes back to the Registration page and enters the correct details. The success message is displayed to Mark, as shown in Figure 29-47.

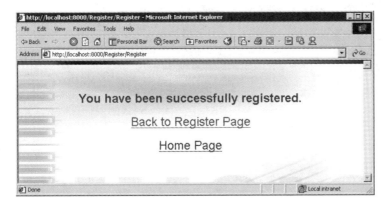

FIGURE 29-47 *The success message is shown.*

After successful registration, Mark can now log on. For logon purposes, he needs to invoke the Login page. See Figure 29-48.

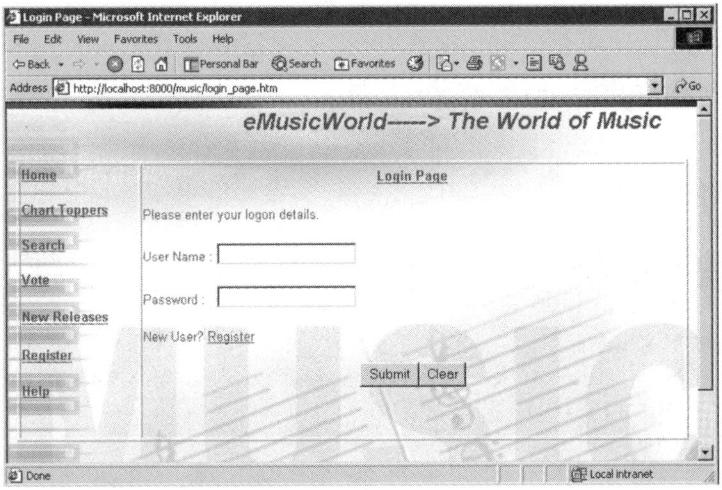

FIGURE 29-48 *The Login page is invoked.*

Again, Mark enters incorrect logon information. The Login page displays an error message, as shown in Figure 29-49.

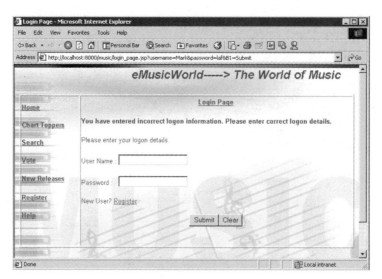

FIGURE 29-49 *The invalid logon message is displayed.*

Finally, Mark provides correct logon details. After validating the logon details, the eMusicWorld application determines that Mark is a user. Therefore, the home page for the users is displayed to Mark.

Summary

In this chapter, you learned how to create the pages for the Visitor Interface category of the music application. You also looked at the functionality of each page. You learned how to create and deploy EJB beans used in the Visitor Interface pages. In addition, the interaction between various pages of the Visitor Interface category was discussed in this chapter.

Chapter 30

In this chapter, you'll create the pages of the User Interface category of the music application. The pages in this category are displayed to the users who are registered with the application. As identified during the design phase, this category will contain the following pages:

- ◆ The Login Page
- ◆ The User Home Page
- ◆ The Shopping Cart Page
- ◆ The Wishlist Page
- ◆ The Feedback Page
- ◆ The Buy Page
- ◆ The Logout Page

Now start creating the pages.

Creating the Login Page

A user can log on to the music application after providing logon details such as username and password. The Login page will query the Login_Info table in the Music database for the similar combination of username and password.

The Login page consists of two underlying pages:

- ◆ login_page.htm
- ◆ login_page.jsp

The code for each of these pages is given in Listing 30-1.

Listing 30-1   login_page.htm

```
<html>
<head>
<title>Login Page</title>
</head>
```

```
<body bgcolor="#C0C0C0">
<form method="get" action="login_page.jsp">
      <marquee style="font-family: Arial; font-size: 14pt; color: #800000; font-
style: italic; font-weight: bold">eMusicWorld
      -----&gt; The World of Music</marquee>
<table border="1" width="100%">
  <tr>
    <td width="18%">
<p><font face="Arial" size="2" color="#800000"><b><a
HREF="home_page.htm">Home</a></b></font></p>
<p><b><font face="Arial" size="2" color="#800000"><a HREF="chart_toppers.jsp">Chart
Toppers</a></font></b></p>
<p><b><font face="Arial" size="2" color="#800000"><a
HREF="search_home_page.htm">Search</a></font></b></p>
<p><b><font face="Arial" size="2" color="#800000"><a
HREF="vote_page.jsp">Vote</a></font></b></p>
<p><b><font face="Arial" size="2" color="#800000"><a
HREF="download_page.htm">Downloads</a></font></b></p>
<p><b><font face="Arial" size="2" color="#800000"><a HREF="new_release_page.jsp">New
Releases</a></font></b>
<p><font face="Arial" size="2" color="#800000"><b><a
HREF="register_page1.htm">Register</a></b></font>
<p><font face="Arial" size="2" color="#800000"><b><a
HREF="help_page.htm">Help</a></b></font></p>
      <p> </td>
    <td width="82%" valign="top">

<p><font face="Arial" size="2" color="#800000">Please enter your logon
details.</font> </p>
<p><font face="Arial" size="2" color="#800000">User Name :</font> <input
type="text" name="username" size="20">
</p>
<p><font face="Arial" size="2" color="#800000">Password :</font>   <input
type="text" name="password" size="20"></p>
<p><font face="Arial" size="2" color="#800000">New User? <a HREF=" http://local-
host:8000/Register/RegisterPage.htm ">Register</a></font></p>

  <p align="center"><input type="submit" value="Submit" name="B1"><input
```

```
type="reset" value="Clear" name="B2"></p>
      <p> </td>
  </tr>
</table>
<p>  </p>
<p>  </p>
</form>
</body>
</html>
```

The code in Listing 30-1 will display the login page to the user as shown in Figure 30-1. Notice that the page has two text boxes for accepting username and password. Notice the action attribute of the <form> tag. The form will be submitted to the login_page.jsp page since the value assigned to the action attribute is login_page.jsp.

The output of the Login_page.htm is displayed in Figure 30-1.

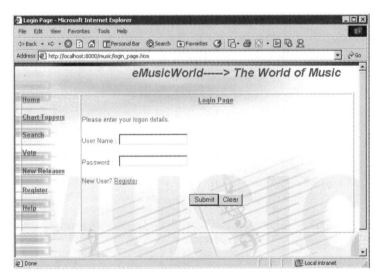

FIGURE 30-1 *The output of* Login_page.htm *is shown here.*

Listing 30-2 lists the code for the login_page.jsp page.

Listing 30-2   login_page.jsp

```
<html>
<head>
<title>Login Page</title>
</head>
<body bgcolor="#C0C0C0">
<form method="GET" action="http:\\localhost:8000\login_page.jsp">
      <marquee style="font-family: Arial; font-size: 14pt; color: #800000; font-
style: italic; font-weight: bold">eMusicWorld
      -----&gt; The World of Music</marquee>
<table border="1" width="100%">
  <tr>
    <td width="18%">

<p><font face="Arial" size="2" color="#800000"><b><a
HREF="home_page.htm">Home</a></b></font></p>

<p><b><font face="Arial" size="2" color="#800000"><a HREF="chart_toppers.jsp">Chart
Toppers</a></font></b></p>
<p><b><font face="Arial" size="2" color="#800000"><a
HREF="search_home_page.htm">Search</a></font></b></p>
<p><b><font face="Arial" size="2" color="#800000"><a
HREF="vote_page.jsp">Vote</a></font></b></p>
<p><b><font face="Arial" size="2" color="#800000"><a
HREF="download_page.htm">Downloads</a></font></b></p>
<p><b><font face="Arial" size="2" color="#800000"><a HREF="new_release_page.jsp">New
Releases</a></font></b>
<p><font face="Arial" size="2" color="#800000"><b><a
HREF="register_page1.htm">Register</a></b></font>
<p><font face="Arial" size="2" color="#800000"><b><a
HREF="help_page.htm">Help</a></b></font></p>
      <p> </td>
    <td width="82%" valign="top">
<%! String username;%>
<%! String password;%>
<%! String role;%>
```

```jsp
<%@ page import="java.util.*" %>
<%@ page import="java.sql.*" %>
<%@ page import="java.text.*" %>
<%@ page import="java.sql.Date" %>
<%@ page language = "java" %>
<%

        try{
        Class.forName("sun.jdbc.odbc.JdbcOdbcDriver");
        Connection connect;

connect=DriverManager.getConnection("jdbc:odbc:MusicDataSource","","");
        Statement state;
        state = connect.createStatement();

        String strQuery1 = "select Password, Role from Login_Info where
User_name='"+username+ "'";
        username=request.getParameter("username");

        password=request.getParameter("password");
        ResultSet result1 = state.executeQuery(strQuery1);
        String pass;
        String user="user";
          while(result1.next())
          {
                        pass=result1.getString("Password");
                        role=result1.getString("Role");

                        role=role.trim();

if((pass.equals(password))&&(role.equals("user")))
                                {
                                role="user";
                                session.setAttribute("username", username);
                                }
                                else if
((pass.equals(password))&&(role.equals("admin")))
                                role="admin";
                                else
```

```
                              role="no_user";
                }
                }
                catch(Exception e){
                out.println("done exception" +e);
                }

                role=role.trim();
                if(role.equals("user")) {%>
                <jsp:forward page="user_home_page.jsp" />
                Vector vc=new Vector(1,1);
                session.setAttribute("Shopping_List",vc);
                <%}
                else if (role.equals("admin")){
                %>
                <jsp:forward page="admin_home_page.htm"/>
                <%}
                else
                out.println("<p><font face=\"Arial\" size=\"2\"
color=\"#800000\"><b>You have entered incorrect logon information. Please enter
correct logon details.</b></font> </p>");
 %>
<p><font face="Arial" size="2" color="#800000">Please enter your logon
details.</font> </p>
<p><font face="Arial" size="2" color="#800000">User Name :</font> <input
type="text" name="username" size="20">
</p>

<p><font face="Arial" size="2" color="#800000">Password :</font>   <input
type="text" name="password" size="20"></p>
<p><font face="Arial" size="2" color="#800000">New User? <a HREF=" http://local-
host:8000/Register/RegisterPage.htm ">Register</a></font></p>
  <p align="center"><input type="submit" value="Submit" name="B1"><input
type="reset" value="Clear" name="B2"></p>
        <p> </td>
  </tr>
</table>
<p>  </p>
```

```
<p>  </p>
</form>
</body>
</html>
```

Analyzing the Code of *login_page.htm*

Now I'll analyze the code in Listing 30-2.

```
try{
Class.forName("sun.jdbc.odbc.JdbcOdbcDriver");
Connection connect;

connect=DriverManager.getConnection("jdbc:odbc:MusicDataSource","","");
Statement state;
state = connect.createStatement();
String strQuery1 = "select Password, Role from Login_Info where
User_name='"+username+ "'";
username=request.getParameter("username");
password=request.getParameter("password");
ResultSet result1 = state.executeQuery(strQuery1);
```

The above set of statements will connect to the Music database and execute the select query to obtain the Password and Role field values from the database. In addition, the username and the password submitted by the user in the login_page.jsp page are stored in the variables, username and password, by using the getParameter() method of the request object. Next, the database query is executed.

```
while(result1.next())
{
                pass=result1.getString("Password");
                role=result1.getString("Role");

                role=role.trim();

if((pass.equals(password))&&(role.equals("user")))
                {
                role="user";
```

```
                                    session.setAttribute("username", username);
                                }
                                else if
((pass.equals(password))&&(role.equals("admin")))
                                    role="admin";
                                else
                                    role="no_user";
                }
                }
```

In the preceding code, the `password` and the `role` fields are being accessed and matched with that provided by the user. If the password matches and the role is user, the value user is assigned to the `role` variable. Next, the attribute is set for the `session` object. The `session.setAttribute("username", username)` statement sets the attribute `username` in the `session` object. The `session` object is an implicit object that is accessible to all the JSP pages. If the role of the user as mentioned in the `Login_Info` table of the database is `administrator`, the value `admin` is assigned to the `role` variable. If the user is neither administrator nor a user, the value `no_user` is assigned to the variable, `role`.

```
            if(role.equals("user")) {%>
            Vector vc=new Vector(1,1);
            session.setAttribute("Shopping_List",vc);
            <jsp:forward page="user_home_page.jsp" />
            <%}
            else if (role.equals("admin")){
            %>
            <jsp:forward page="admin_home_page.htm"/>
            <%}
            else
            out.println("<p><font face=\"Arial\" size=\"2\"
color=\"#800000\"><b>You have entered incorrect logon information. Please enter
correct logon details.</b></font> </p>");
```

In the preceding statements, the value of the `role` variable is determined and appropriate action is being taken. If role is user, an attribute is set in the `session` object. This attribute, `Shopping_List`, initially contains an empty `Vector` object. After the attribute is set, the page is forwarded to the `user_home_page.jsp` page. If the user is admin, the page is forwarded to the `admin_home_page.htm`. Otherwise, an error message is displayed to the user.

The output of the Login_page.jsp when the user provides incorrect logon information is displayed in Figure 30-2.

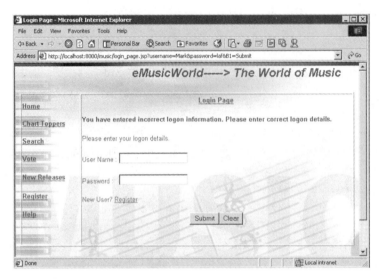

FIGURE 30-2 *The* Login_page.jsp *displays an error message.*

The interaction between the two pages is displayed in Figure 30-3.

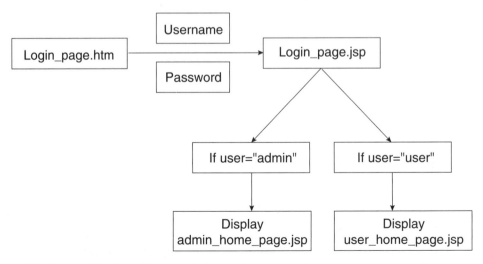

FIGURE 30-3 *The figure illustrates the interaction between the* Login_page.htm *and* Login_page.jsp *pages.*

Creating the Home Page

The Home page displays a welcome message to the user. The Home page is displayed after a user logs on.

The code to create the Home page is displayed in Listing 30-3.

Listing 30-3 user_home_page.jsp

```
<html>
<head>
<meta http-equiv="Content-Type" content="text/html; charset=windows-1252">
<meta http-equiv="Content-Language" content="en-us">
<title>Home Page</title>
</head>
<body bgcolor="#C0C0C0" topmargin="0"
background="http:\\localhost:8000\music\Background.bmp" >
<table border="0" width="100%">
  <tr>
    <td width="100%">
      <table border="0" width="97%" height="19">
        <tr>
          <td width="18%" height="13" valign="middle" align="right">
        <font face="Arial" size="5" color="#800000"><b><i>eMusicWorld-----&gt; The
World of Music</i></b></font>
          </td>
        </tr>
      </table>
    </td>
  </tr>
</table>
                   <%@ page import="java.util.*" %>
<form method="get" action="http://localhost:8000/music/user_home_page.jsp">
<table border="1" width="100%">
  <tr>
          <td width="11%" height="13" valign="middle" align="center"><font
face="Arial" size="2" color="#800000"><b><a
href="Offers.jsp">Offers</a></b></font></td>
```

```
        <td width="20%" height="13" valign="middle" align="center"><font
face="Arial" size="2" color="#800000"><b><a HREF="http://localhost:8000/music/shop-
ping_cart.jsp">Shopping Cart</a></b></font></td>
        <td width="16%" height="13" valign="middle" align="center"><font
face="Arial" size="2" color="#800000"><b><a HREF="http://localhost:8000/music/wish-
list_page.jsp">Wishlist</a></b></font></td>
        <td width="8%" height="13" valign="middle" align="center"><font
face="Arial" size="2" color="#800000"><b><a HREF="http://localhost:8000/music/feed-
back_page.jsp">Feedback</a></b></font></td>
        <td width="13%" height="13" valign="middle" align="center"><font
face="Arial" size="2" color="#800000"><b><a
HREF="http://localhost:8000/music/user_buy_page.htm">Buy</b></font></a></b></font></
td>
        <td width="9%" height="13" valign="middle" align="center"><font
face="Arial" size="2" color="#800000"><b><a
HREF="http://localhost:8000/music/logout_page.jsp">Logout</a></b></font></td>
  </tr>
</table>
<table border="1" width="100%">
  <tr>
    <td width="18%">
<p><font face="Arial" size="2" color="#800000"><b><a
HREF="http://localhost:8000/music/home_page.htm">Home</a></b></font></p>
<p><b><font face="Arial" size="2" color="#800000"><a
HREF="http://localhost:8000/music/chart_toppers.jsp">Chart
Toppers</a></font></b></p>
<p><b><font face="Arial" size="2" color="#800000"><a
HREF="http://localhost:8000/SearchContext/SearchAlias">Search</a></font></b></p>
<p><b><font face="Arial" size="2" color="#800000"><a
HREF="http://localhost:8000/music/vote_page.jsp">Vote</a></font></b></p>
<p><b><font face="Arial" size="2" color="#800000"><a
HREF="http://localhost:8000/music/new_release_page.jsp">New Releases</a></font></b>
<p><font face="Arial" size="2" color="#800000"><b><a
HREF="http://localhost:8000/Register/RegisterPage.htm">Register</a></b></font>
<p><font face="Arial" size="2" color="#800000"><b><a
HREF="http://localhost:8000/music/help_page.htm">Help</a></b></font></p>
      <p> </td>
    <td width="82%" valign="top">
```

```
<%! String name;%>
<%                   try
            {
<!--OBTAIN THE USER NAME FROM THE SESSION OBJECT -->

name=session.getAttribute("username").toString();
            }
            catch(Exception e)
            {
            }
%>
<!-- DISPLAY A CUSTOMIZED MESSAGE TO THE USER -->
  <p><font face="Arial" size="2" color="#800000">Dear  <%=name%>, </font></p>

  <p><font face="Arial" size="2" color="#800000">Welcome. Select an appropriate
  menu.</font></p>
      <p> </td>
  </tr>
</table>
<p>  </p>
<p>  </p>
</form>
</body>
</html>
```

The highlighted code in bold in Listing 30-3 accesses the username attribute from the session object and displays a customized message to the user. The Home page of a user, Mark, is displayed in Figure 30-4.

Creating the Buy Page

The Buy page consists of two pages:

◆ The user_buy_page.htm Page
◆ The user_buy_page.jsp Page

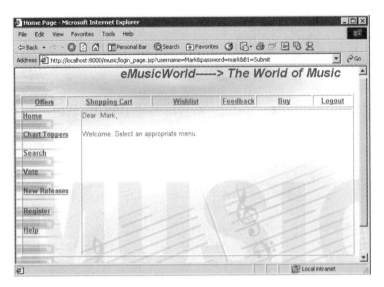

FIGURE 30-4 *The Home page for the user named Mark is displayed.*

The user_buy_page.htm page is displayed before the user_buy_page.jsp page. In the user_buy_page.htm page, the user can select the category in which he or she wants to purchase items such as CDs. The category selected is accessed by the user_buy_page.jsp and then this page executes the query to obtain items of the specified category. The jsp page then displays the output to the user. Now take a look at the code of these pages one-by-one in Listing 30-4.

Listing 30-4 user_buy_page.htm

```
<html>
<head>
<meta http-equiv="Content-Type" content="text/html; charset=windows-1252">
<meta http-equiv="Content-Language" content="en-us">
<title>Buy Page</title>
</head>
<body bgcolor="#C0C0C0" topmargin="0"
background="http:\\localhost:8000\music\Background.bmp" >
<table border="0" width="100%">
  <tr>
    <td width="100%">
```

```
        <table border="0" width="97%" height="19">
          <tr>
            <td width="18%" height="13" valign="middle" align="right">
          <font face="Arial" size="5" color="#800000"><b><i>eMusicWorld-----&gt; The
World of Music</i></b></font>
            </td>
          </tr>
        </table>
      </td>
    </tr>
  </table>
  <form method="POST" action="user_buy_page.jsp">
        <table border="1" width="100%">
    <tr>
          <td width="11%" height="13" valign="middle" align="center"><font
face="Arial" size="2" color="#800000"><b><a
href="Offers.jsp">Offers</a></b></font></td>
          <td width="20%" height="13" valign="middle" align="center"><font
face="Arial" size="2" color="#800000"><b><a HREF="shopping_cart.jsp">Shopping
Cart</a></b></font></td>
          <td width="16%" height="13" valign="middle" align="center"><font
face="Arial" size="2" color="#800000"><b><a
HREF="http://localhost:8000/wishlist_page.jsp">Wishlist</a></b></font></td>
          <td width="8%" height="13" valign="middle" align="center"><font
face="Arial" size="2" color="#800000"><b><a
HREF="feedback_page.jsp">Feedback</a></b></font></td>
          <td width="13%" height="13" valign="middle" align="center"><font
face="Arial" size="2" color="#800000"><b><a
HREF="user_buy_page.htm">Buy</b></font></a></b></font></td>
          <td width="9%" height="13" valign="middle" align="center"><font
face="Arial" size="2" color="#800000"><b><a
HREF="logout_page.jsp">Logout</a></b></font></td>
    </tr>
  </table>
  <table border="1" width="100%">
    <tr>
      <td width="18%">
  <p><font face="Arial" size="2" color="#800000"><b><a
```

```
HREF="home_page.htm">Home</a></b></font></p>
<p><b><font face="Arial" size="2" color="#800000"><a HREF="chart_toppers.jsp">Chart
Toppers</a></font></b></p>
<p><b><font face="Arial" size="2" color="#800000"><a
HREF="search_home_page.htm">Search</a></font></b></p>
<p><b><font face="Arial" size="2" color="#800000"><a
HREF="vote_page.jsp">Vote</a></font></b></p>
<p><b><font face="Arial" size="2" color="#800000"><a HREF="new_release_page.jsp">New
Releases</a></font></b>
<p><font face="Arial" size="2" color="#800000"><b><a
HREF="register_page1.htm">Register</a></b></font>
<p><font face="Arial" size="2" color="#800000"><b><a
HREF="help_page.htm">Help</a></b></font></p>
      <p> </td>
    <td width="82%" valign="top">
<p align="center"><font face="Arial" size="2" color="#800000"><b><u>Buy
Page</u></b></font></p>
  <p><font face="Arial" size="2" color="#800000">Select the search item to buy from
the
  <b>Search By</b> list box and then click the <b>Submit</b> button.</font></p>
  <p><font face="Arial" size="2" color="#800000"><b>Search By </b></font> <select
size="1" name="SearchBy" style="color: #800000; font-family: Arial; font-size:
10pt">
    <option selected>Classical</option>
    <option>Jazz</option>
    <option>Pop</option>
    <option>Rock</option>
  </select>   </p>
    <input type="submit" value="Submit" name="Submit"><input type="reset"
value="Reset" name="Reset"></p>
    </td>
  </tr>
</table>
<p>  </p>
<p>  </p>
</form>
</body>
</html>
```

The *user_buy_page.jsp* Page

The next page to be displayed is the user_buy_page.jsp page. The code for this page is given in Listing 30-5.

Listing 30-5   user_buy_page.jsp

```
<html>
<head>
<meta http-equiv="Content-Type" content="text/html; charset=windows-1252">
<meta http-equiv="Content-Language" content="en-us">
<title>Buy Page</title>
</head>
<body bgcolor="#C0C0C0" topmargin="0"
background="http:\\localhost:8000\music\Background.bmp" >
<table border="0" width="100%">
  <tr>
    <td width="100%">
      <table border="0" width="97%" height="19">
        <tr>
          <td width="18%" height="13" valign="middle" align="right">
          <font face="Arial" size="5" color="#800000"><b><i>eMusicWorld-----&gt; The
World of Music</i></b></font>
          </td>
        </tr>
      </table>
    </td>
  </tr>
</table>
<form method="get" action="http://localhost:8000/music/shopping_cart.jsp">
<table border="1" width="100%">
  <tr>
          <td width="11%" height="13" valign="middle" align="center"><font
face="Arial" size="2" color="#800000"><b><a
href="Offers.jsp">Offers</a></b></font></td>
          <td width="20%" height="13" valign="middle" align="center"><font
face="Arial" size="2" color="#800000"><b><a HREF="http://localhost:8000/music/shop-
ping_cart.jsp">Shopping Cart</a></b></font></td>
```

```
                <td width="16%" height="13" valign="middle" align="center"><font
face="Arial" size="2" color="#800000"><b><a HREF="http://localhost:8000/music/wish-
list_page.jsp">Wishlist</a></b></font></td>
                <td width="8%" height="13" valign="middle" align="center"><font
face="Arial" size="2" color="#800000"><b><a HREF="http://localhost:8000/music/feed-
back_page.jsp">Feedback</a></b></font></td>
                <td width="13%" height="13" valign="middle" align="center"><font
face="Arial" size="2" color="#800000"><b><a
HREF="http://localhost:8000/music/user_buy_page.htm">Buy</b></font></a></b></font></
td>
                <td width="9%" height="13" valign="middle" align="center"><font
face="Arial" size="2" color="#800000"><b><a
HREF="http://localhost:8000/music/logout_page.jsp">Logout</a></b></font></td>
    </tr>
</table>
<table border="1" width="100%">
    <tr>
        <td width="18%">

<p><font face="Arial" size="2" color="#800000"><b><a
HREF="http://localhost:8000/music/home_page.htm">Home</a></b></font></p>

<p><b><font face="Arial" size="2" color="#800000"><a
HREF="http://localhost:8000/music/chart_toppers.jsp">Chart
Toppers</a></font></b></p>
<p><b><font face="Arial" size="2" color="#800000"><a
HREF="http://localhost:8000/SearchContext/SearchAlias">Search</a></font></b></p>
<p><b><font face="Arial" size="2" color="#800000"><a
HREF="http://localhost:8000/music/vote_page.jsp">Vote</a></font></b></p>

<p><b><font face="Arial" size="2" color="#800000"><a
HREF="http://localhost:8000/music/new_release_page.jsp">New Releases</a></font></b>
<p><font face="Arial" size="2" color="#800000"><b><a
HREF="http://localhost:8000/Register/RegisterPage.htm">Register</a></b></font>
<p><font face="Arial" size="2" color="#800000"><b><a
HREF="http://localhost:8000/music/help_page.htm">Help</a></b></font></p>
        <p> </td>
      <td width="82%" valign="top">
```

```
<%! String songtype;%>
<% songtype=request.getParameter("SearchBy");

%>
                <%@ page import="java.util.*" %>
                <%@ page import="java.sql.*" %>
                <%@ page import="java.text.*" %>
                <%@ page import="java.sql.Date" %>
                <%@ page language = "java" %>
```

<p align="center"><font face="Arial" size="2" color="#800000"><b><u>Buy
Page</u></b></font></p>
<p><font face="Arial" size="2" color="#800000">Dear <%=session.getAttribute("user-
name")%>,
The items are displayed. To move an item to the shopping cart, select the checkbox
next to the item and then click the Move to Shopping Cart button.</font></p>
<table>
<tr>
<td width="5%"><font face="Arial" size="2" color="#800000"><b>Buy</b></font></td>
<td width="25%"><font face="Arial" size="2" color="#800000"><b>Item</b></font></td>
<td width="25%"><font face="Arial" size="2" color="#800000"><b>Price
($)</b></font></td>
</tr>

```
<%
                try{
                Class.forName("sun.jdbc.odbc.JdbcOdbcDriver");
                Connection connect;

connect=DriverManager.getConnection("jdbc:odbc:RegisterDataSource","","");
                Statement state;
                state = connect.createStatement();
                String strQuery1 = "select * from Item_Master where Type='"+song-
type+"'";
                ResultSet result = state.executeQuery(strQuery1);
                String username, itemcode, qty, wishdate;
                while(result.next())
                {
                        out.println("<tr>");
```

```
                                        out.println("<td width=\"25%\"><font
face=\"Arial\" size=\"2\" color=\"#800000\">");
                                        out.println("<font face=\"Arial\" size=\"2\"
color=\"#800000\">");
                                        itemcode=result.getString("Item_Code");
                                        out.println("<p><input type=\"checkbox\"
name="+itemcode+" value=\"ON\">");
                                        out.println("</td>");
                                        out.println("<td width=\"25%\"><font
face=\"Arial\" size=\"2\" color=\"#800000\">");
                                        out.println(result.getString("Title"));
out.println("</td>");
out.println("<td width=\"25%\"><font face=\"Arial\" size=\"2\" color=\"#800000\">");
                                        out.println(result.getString("Rate"));
out.println("</td>");

                                        out.println("</font>");
                                        out.println("</tr>");
                        }
                        connect.close();
                        }
                        catch(Exception e)
                        {
                                        out.println("Exception: " + e + " occurred.");
                        }
%>


</table>
  <input type="submit" value="Move to Shopping Cart"
name="Submit">  <input type="reset" value="Reset" name="Reset"></p>
    </td>
  </tr>
</table>
<p>  </p>
<p>  </p>
</form>
</body>
</html>
```

Analyzing the Code of *user_buy_page.jsp*

Now I'll analyze the code in Listing 30-5.

```
<%! String songtype;%>
<% songtype=request.getParameter("SearchBy");
```

The above statements will extract the selection made by the user in the user_buy_page.htm page and store it in a variable, songtype.

```
            String strQuery1 = "select * from Item_Master where Type='"+song-
type+"'";
```

The above query will be used to search for records in the Item_Master table that matches the condition specified.

```
            while(result.next())
            {
                        out.println("<font face=\"Arial\" size=\"2\"
color=\"#800000\">");
                        itemcode=result.getString("Item_Code");
                        out.println("<p><input type=\"checkbox\"
name="+itemcode+" value=\"ON\">");
                        out.println(result.getString("Title"));
                        out.println("</font>");
            }
```

Next, the preceding code snippet displays the records to the user. The title names are displayed. The Item_Code of titles in the resultant rows is stored in the String variable, itemcode. Each row will have a check box associated with it. Notice that the name of the check box is same as the itemcode.

The diagrammatic interaction between the two pages is displayed in Figure 30-5.

The output of the user_buy_page.htm is displayed in Figure 30-6.

The output of the user_buy_page.jsp is displayed in Figure 30-7.

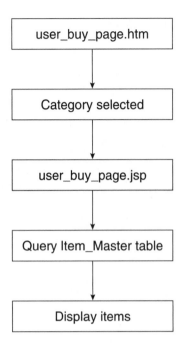

FIGURE 30-5 *The figure displays the interaction between the* user_buy_page.htm *and* user_buy_page.jsp *pages.*

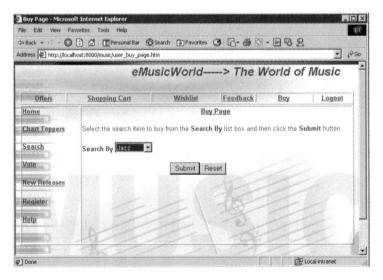

FIGURE 30-6 *The output of the* user_buy_page.htm *page is displayed.*

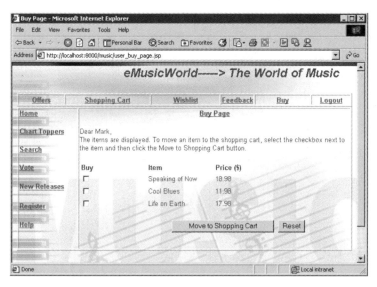

FIGURE 30-7 *The output of the* `user_buy_page.jsp` *page is shown here.*

Creating the Shopping Cart Page

The shopping cart consists of two pages:

◆ `shopping_cart.jsp`

◆ `update_wishlist.jsp`

The `update_wishlist.jsp` identifies the items selected in the `shopping_cart.jsp` page. After obtaining the items selected, the `update_wishlist.jsp` updates the database by executing a simple SQL query. The code for each of these two pages is given in Listing 30-6.

Listing 30-6 shopping_cart.jsp

```
<html>
<head>
<meta http-equiv="Content-Type" content="text/html; charset=windows-1252">
<meta http-equiv="Content-Language" content="en-us">
<title>Shopping Cart Page</title>
</head>
<body bgcolor="#C0C0C0" topmargin="0"
```

```
background="http:\\localhost:8000\music\Background.bmp" >
<table border="0" width="100%">
  <tr>
    <td width="100%">
      <table border="0" width="97%" height="19">
        <tr>
          <td width="18%" height="13" valign="middle" align="right">
          <font face="Arial" size="5" color="#800000"><b><i>eMusicWorld-----&gt; The
World of Music</i></b></font>
          </td>
        </tr>
      </table>
    </td>
  </tr>
</table>
<form method="get" action="http://localhost:8000/music/update_wishlist.jsp">
<table border="1" width="100%">
  <tr>
        <td width="11%" height="13" valign="middle" align="center"><font
face="Arial" size="2" color="#800000"><b><a
href="Offers.jsp">Offers</a></b></font></td>
        <td width="20%" height="13" valign="middle" align="center"><font
face="Arial" size="2" color="#800000"><b><a HREF="http://localhost:8000/music/shop-
ping_cart.jsp">Shopping Cart</a></b></font></td>
        <td width="16%" height="13" valign="middle" align="center"><font
face="Arial" size="2" color="#800000"><b><a HREF="http://localhost:8000/music/wish-
list_page.jsp">Wishlist</a></b></font></td>
        <td width="8%" height="13" valign="middle" align="center"><font
face="Arial" size="2" color="#800000"><b><a HREF="http://localhost:8000/music/feed-
back_page.jsp">Feedback</a></b></font></td>
        <td width="13%" height="13" valign="middle" align="center"><font
face="Arial" size="2" color="#800000"><b><a
HREF="http://localhost:8000/music/user_buy_page.htm">Buy</b></font></a></b></font></
td>
        <td width="9%" height="13" valign="middle" align="center"><font
face="Arial" size="2" color="#800000"><b><a
HREF="http://localhost:8000/music/logout_page.jsp">Logout</a></b></font></td>
  </tr>
```

```
</table>
<table border="1" width="100%">
  <tr>
    <td width="18%">
<p><font face="Arial" size="2" color="#800000"><b><a
HREF="http://localhost:8000/music/user_home_page.jsp">Home</a></b></font></p>

<p><b><font face="Arial" size="2" color="#800000"><a
HREF="http://localhost:8000/music/chart_toppers.jsp">Chart
Toppers</a></font></b></p>
<p><b><font face="Arial" size="2" color="#800000"><a
HREF="http://localhost:8000/SearchContext/SearchAlias">Search</a></font></b></p>
<p><b><font face="Arial" size="2" color="#800000"><a
HREF="http://localhost:8000/music/vote_page.jsp">Vote</a></font></b></p>

<p><b><font face="Arial" size="2" color="#800000"><a
HREF="http://localhost:8000/Register/RegisterPage.htm">New Releases</a></font></b>
<p><font face="Arial" size="2" color="#800000"><b><a
HREF="http://localhost:8000/music/register_page1.htm">Register</a></b></font></p>
<p><font face="Arial" size="2" color="#800000"><b><a
HREF="http://localhost:8000/music/help_page.htm">Help</a></b></font></p>
<p> </p>
    </td>
    <td width="82%" valign="top">

<p><font face="Arial" size="2" color="#800000">Dear <%=session.getAttribute("user-
name")%>,</font></p>
<p><font face="Arial" size="2" color="#800000">Your shopping cart contains
following items:</font></p>
<table border="0" width="105%">
  <tr>
<%! Vector vector=new Vector(1,1);%>
<%@ page import="java.util.*" %>
                <%@ page import="java.sql.*" %>
                <%@ page import="java.text.*" %>
                <%@ page import="java.sql.Date" %>
                <%@ page language = "java" %>
                <%
```

```
<!--OBTAIN THE SHOPPING_LIST ATTRIBUTE OF THE SESSION OBJECT. THIS ATTRIBUTE CON-
TAINS THE LIST OF ITEMS SELECTED BY THE USER IN THE BUY PAGE.-->
Vector shoppingVectors=(Vector)session.getAttribute("Shopping_List");
int ctr=shoppingVectors.capacity();

int i=0;
try{

                for(;i<ctr;i++)
                {
                                String
str=((String)shoppingVectors.elementAt(i));
                }
}
catch(Exception e)
{
                System.out.println("Exception " + e + "occurred.");
}
try{
<!--OBTAIN THE PARAMETERS AND STORE THE PARAMETERS IN A VECTOR-->
                Enumeration paramNames = request.getParameterNames();
Vector existingVector=(Vector)session.getAttribute("Shopping_List");
    while(paramNames.hasMoreElements())
                {
                                        String paramName =
(String)paramNames.nextElement();
                                String str=request.getParameter(paramName);
                                existingVector.addElement((String)paramName);

                }
<!--UPDATE THE SHOPPING_LIST ATTRIBUTE OF THE SESSION OBJECT-->
session.setAttribute("Shopping_List", existingVector);

}
catch(Exception e)
{
                System.out.println("Exception" + e+"occurred");
}
```

```
                try{
                Vector
itemsInVectors=(Vector)session.getAttribute("Shopping_List");
                Class.forName("sun.jdbc.odbc.JdbcOdbcDriver");
                Connection connect;


connect=DriverManager.getConnection("jdbc:odbc:RegisterDataSource","","");
                Statement state;
                state = connect.createStatement();
<!--SQL QUERY TO OBTAIN ALL THE ROWS OF THE ITEM_MASTER TABLE -->
                String strQuery1 = "select * from Item_Master";
                String str, title, itemrate;
                ResultSet result1 = state.executeQuery(strQuery1);
                ResultSet result2;
                String strQuery2;
                int ctr1=0;
                String desc=new String("");
                String itemcode;
                float rate=0;
                int ctr2=0;
                float total=0;
                 out.println("<tr>");
out.println("<td width=\"11%\"><font face=\"Arial\" size=\"2\"
color=\"#800000\"><b>Select</b></font></td>");
    out.println("<td width=\"11%\"><font face=\"Arial\" size=\"2\"
color=\"#800000\"><b>Item Code</b></font></td>");
    out.println("<td width=\"18%\"><font face=\"Arial\" size=\"2\"
color=\"#800000\"><b>Item Description</b></font></td>");
    out.println("<td width=\"10%\"><font face=\"Arial\" size=\"2\"
color=\"#800000\"><b>Price ($)</b></font></td>");
out.println("<td width=\"10%\"><font face=\"Arial\" size=\"2\"
color=\"#800000\"><b>Quantity</b></font></td>");
  out.println("</tr>");
<!--IF THE ITEM CODE IN THE VECTORE AND THE RESULTSET MATCHES, DISPLAY THE ITEM
CODE, TITLE, AND RATE OF THE ITEM -->
                while(result1.next())
                {
```

```
                                    itemcode=result1.getString("Item_Code");
                                    itemcode=itemcode.trim();
                                    if(itemsInVectors.contains(((String)itemcode)))
                                    {
                                    title=result1.getString("Title");
                                    itemrate=result1.getString("Rate");
out.println("<tr>");%>
<td width="11%"><font face="Arial" size="2" color="#800000"><input type="checkbox"
name="+<%=itemcode%>+" value="<%=itemcode%>"></font></td>
<%
    out.println("<td width=\"11%\"><font face=\"Arial\" size=\"2\"
color=\"#800000\">"+itemcode+"</font></td>");
    out.println("<td width=\"18%\"><font face=\"Arial\" size=\"2\"
color=\"#800000\">" +title+"</font></td>");
    out.println("<td width=\"5%\"><font face=\"Arial\" size=\"2\"
color=\"#800000\">"+itemrate+"</font></td>");
%>
<td width="10%"><input type="text" size="5"></td>


<%
out.println("</tr>");
                                                        }
                                                        ctr2++;
                                }
                                }
                                catch(Exception e){
                                                System.out.println("done exception" +e);
                                }



  %>
    </tr>
</table>
<p> </p>
<p>  
<input type="submit" value="Add to Wishlist" name="Submit">  <input
type="reset" value="Reset" name="Reset"></p>
        <p> </td>
```

```
     </tr>
    </table>
    <p>  </p>
    <p>  </p>
    </form>
    </body>
    </html>
```

Now I'll explain the important code snippets in detail.

```
Vector shoppingVectors=(Vector)session.getAttribute("Shopping_List");
```

Here, the `Vector` object from the `Shopping_List` attribute of the session object is extracted and stored in the `Vector` variable, `shoppingVectors`.

```
            Enumeration paramNames = request.getParameterNames();
        Vector existingVector=(Vector)session.getAttribute("Shopping_List");


    while(paramNames.hasMoreElements())
                {
                                String paramName =
(String)paramNames.nextElement();
                        String str=request.getParameter(paramName);
                        existingVector.addElement((String)paramName);


                }
session.setAttribute("Shopping_List", existingVector);
```

Next, the parameters from the previous page, `user_buy_page.jsp`, are obtained and assigned to an `Enumeration` variable, `paramNames`. The `Vector` object from the `Shopping_List` attribute of the `session` object is extracted and stored in the `Vector` variable, `existingVectors`. After this, all the parameters in the `session` object are added to the `existingVectors`. The vector is then assigned to the `Shopping_List` attribute of the `request` object by using the `setAttribute()` method of the `session` object.

```
            String strQuery1 = "select * from Item_Master";
```

The above statement will define a query to return all the rows from the `Item_Master` table.

```
                   while(result1.next())
             {

                                 itemcode=result1.getString("Item_Code");
                                 itemcode=itemcode.trim();
                                 if(itemsInVectors.contains(((String)itemcode)))
                                 {
                                 title=result1.getString("Title");
                                 itemrate=result1.getString("Rate");
out.println("<tr>");%>
<td width="11%"><font face="Arial" size="2" color="#800000"><input type="checkbox"
name="+<%=itemcode%>+" value="<%=itemcode%>"></font></td>
<%
   out.println("<td width=\"11%\"><font face=\"Arial\" size=\"2\"
color=\"#800000\">"+itemcode+"</font></td>");

   out.println("<td width=\"18%\"><font face=\"Arial\" size=\"2\"
color=\"#800000\">" +title+"</font></td>");

   out.println("<td width=\"1%\"><font face=\"Arial\" size=\"2\"
color=\"#800000\">"+itemrate+"</font></td>");
out.println("</tr>");
                                 }
                   }
                   }
```

The preceding statements will navigate through the resultant ResultSet object. If the item code in the ResultSet object, result1, matches with an item code in the itemsInVectors object, the rows are displayed. Similar to the user_buy_page.jsp, a check box is assigned a name the same as the itemcode and it is displayed next to the rows. The user will select the items that he wishes to add to the wishlist. The code for the update_wishlist.jsp is given in Listing 30-7.

Listing 30-7 update_wishlist.jsp

```
<html>
<head>
<title>Update Wishlist Page</title>
</head>
```

```
<body bgcolor="#C0C0C0">
<form method="get">
<%! Vector selectedVector=new Vector(1,1);%>
<%! Vector itemsInVectors=new Vector(1,1);%>
<%! int capacity;%>

<%@ page import="java.util.*" %>
                <%@ page import="java.sql.*" %>
                <%@ page import="java.text.*" %>
                <%@ page import="java.sql.Date" %>
                <%@ page language = "java" %>
<%! int ctr=0;%>
                <%

try{
                Enumeration paramNames = request.getParameterNames();
        selectedVector.removeAllElements();
            while(paramNames.hasMoreElements())
                {
<!--ADD THE PARAMETERS, EXCEPT THE 'ADD TO WISHLIST' PARAMETER, OBTAINED FROM THE
SHOPPING CART PAGE TO A VECTOR-->
                                        String paramName =
(String)paramNames.nextElement();
                                String str=request.getParameter(paramName);
                                str=str.trim();
                                if(!str.equals("Add to Wishlist"))
                                selectedVector.addElement((String)paramName);
                                ctr++;

                }


}
catch(Exception e)
{
                out.println("Exception" + e+"occurred");
}

                try
                {
```

```
                              itemsInVectors=(Vector)session.getAttribute("Shopping_List");
                              String username=(String)session.getAttribute("username");
                              Class.forName("sun.jdbc.odbc.JdbcOdbcDriver");
                              Connection connect;


connect=DriverManager.getConnection("jdbc:odbc:MusicDataSource","","");


                              PreparedStatement stat;

connect=DriverManager.getConnection("jdbc:odbc:MusicDataSource","","");
<!--UPDATE THE WISHLIST TABLE WITH THE USERNAME AND THE ITEMS SELECTED BY THE USER
-->
                                             for(int i=0;i<=ctr;i++)
                                             {
                                                          String
itemcode1=(String)selectedVector.elementAt(i);
                                                          itemcode1=itemcode1.trim();
                                                          itemcode1=itemcode1.sub-
string(1, itemcode1.length()-1);

                                                          out.println("itemcode1 after
substring" +itemcode1);

                                                          out.println("itemcode"+item-
code1);

stat=connect.prepareStatement("Insert into Wishlist_Info values(?,?,?,getdate())");
                                                          stat.setString(1,username);
                                                          stat.setString(2,itemcode1);
                                                          stat.setInt(3,1);
                                                          stat.executeUpdate();
<! --REMOVE THE ITEMS FROM THE VECTOR THAT HAVE BEEN ADDED TO THE WISHLIST_INFO
TABLE-->

selectedVector.remove((String)itemcode1);

itemsInVectors.remove((String)itemcode1);
                                                          connect.close();
                              }//end of for
```

```
<!--UPDATE THE SHOPPING_LIST ATTRIBUTE WITH THE UPDATED VECTOR -->
                                    session.setAttribute("Shopping_List",
itemsInVectors);
                } //end of try
                catch(Exception e)
                {
                                out.println("Exception occurred");
                }
%>
<jsp:forward page="user_home_page.jsp"/>
</form>
</body>
```

Analyzing the Code of the *update_wishlist.jsp* Page

Now I'll discuss the code in Listing 30-7.

```
                Enumeration paramNames = request.getParameterNames();
        selectedVector.removeAllElements();
            while(paramNames.hasMoreElements())
                {
                                String paramName =
(String)paramNames.nextElement();
                            String str=request.getParameter(paramName);
                            out.println("display item"+str);
                            str=str.trim();
                            if(!str.equals("Add to Wishlist"))
                            selectedVector.addElement((String)paramName);
                            ctr++;
                }
```

In the preceding code snippet, the parameters from the shopping_cart.jsp page are stored in the Enumeration variable, paramNames. Next, the parameters are stored in a Vector variable, selectedVector. One of the parameters that the update_wishlist.jsp page receives from the shopping_cart.jsp page is Add to Wishlist. You do not need to store the Add to Wishlist parameter in selected-Vector.

```
                for(int i=0;i<=ctr;i++)
```

```
                                        {
                                                              String
itemcode1=(String)selectedVector.elementAt(i);

                                                      itemcode1=itemcode1.trim();
                                                      itemcode1=itemcode1.sub-
string(1, itemcode1.length()-1);

                                                      out.println("itemcode1 after
substring" +itemcode1);

                                                      out.println("itemcode"+item-
code1);


stat=connect.prepareStatement("Insert into Wishlist_Info values(?,?,?,getdate())");
                                                      stat.setString(1,username);
                                                      stat.setString(2,itemcode1);
                                                      stat.setInt(3,1);
                                                      stat.executeUpdate();

selectedVector.remove((String)itemcode1);

itemsInVectors.remove((String)itemcode1);
                                                      connect.close();
                                        }//end of for
                                        session.setAttribute("Shopping_List",
itemsInVectors);
                        } //end of try
```

Next, a for loop is executed that inserts rows in the Wishlist_Info table. The username, item code, and the current date are inserted in the table.

The interaction between the two pages is displayed in Figure 30-8.

Mark selects two items in the user_buy_page.jsp and clicks on the Add to Shopping Cart button. The output of the shopping_cart.jsp is displayed in Figure 30-9.

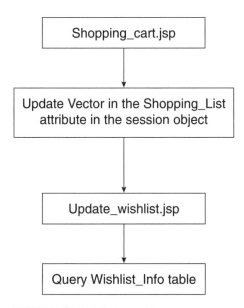

FIGURE 30-8 *The interaction between* `shopping_cart.jsp` *and* `update_wishlist.jsp` *is shown here.*

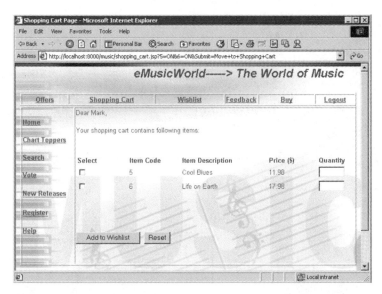

FIGURE 30-9 *The output of the* `shopping_cart.jsp` *is shown here.*

On this page, the user can specify the quantity of items, select the item code, and click on the Add to Wishlist button to add the items to the wishlist.

Creating the Wishlist Page

The Wishlist page queries the database and displays the items that have been selected in the previous sessions. The code for the Wishlist page is given in Listing 30-8.

Listing 30-8 wishlist_page.jsp

```
<html>
<head>
<meta http-equiv="Content-Type" content="text/html; charset=windows-1252">
<meta http-equiv="Content-Language" content="en-us">
<title>Wishlist Page</title>
</head>
<body bgcolor="#C0C0C0" topmargin="0"
background="http:\\localhost:8000\music\Background.bmp" >
<table border="0" width="100%">
  <tr>
    <td width="100%">
      <table border="0" width="97%" height="19">
        <tr>
          <td width="18%" height="13" valign="middle" align="right">
        <font face="Arial" size="5" color="#800000"><b><i>eMusicWorld-----&gt; The
World of Music</i></b></font>
          </td>
        </tr>
      </table>
    </td>
  </tr>
</table>
<%@ page import="java.util.*" %>
                 <%@ page import="java.sql.*" %>
                 <%@ page import="java.text.*" %>
                 <%@ page import="java.sql.Date" %>
                 <%@ page language = "java" %>
```

```
<%! float grandTotal=0;%>
<form method="POST" action="http://localhost:8000/music/user_home_page.jsp">
<table border="1" width="100%">
  <tr>
          <td width="11%" height="13" valign="middle" align="center"><font
face="Arial" size="2" color="#800000"><b><a
href="Offers.jsp">Offers</a></b></font></td>
          <td width="20%" height="13" valign="middle" align="center"><font
face="Arial" size="2" color="#800000"><b><a HREF="http://localhost:8000/music/shop-
ping_cart.jsp">Shopping Cart</a></b></font></td>
          <td width="16%" height="13" valign="middle" align="center"><font
face="Arial" size="2" color="#800000"><b><a HREF="http://localhost:8000/music/wish-
list_page.jsp">Wishlist</a></b></font></td>
          <td width="8%" height="13" valign="middle" align="center"><font
face="Arial" size="2" color="#800000"><b><a HREF="http://localhost:8000/music/feed-
back_page.jsp">Feedback</a></b></font></td>
          <td width="13%" height="13" valign="middle" align="center"><font
face="Arial" size="2" color="#800000"><b><a
HREF="http://localhost:8000/music/user_buy_page.htm">Buy</b></font></a></b></font></
td>
          <td width="9%" height="13" valign="middle" align="center"><font
face="Arial" size="2" color="#800000"><b><a
HREF="http://localhost:8000/music/logout_page.jsp">Logout</a></b></font></td>
  </tr>
</table>
<table border="1" width="100%">
  <tr>
    <td width="18%">
<p><font face="Arial" size="2" color="#800000"><b><a
HREF="http://localhost:8000/music/user_home_page.jsp">Home</a></b></font></p>
<p><b><font face="Arial" size="2" color="#800000"><a
HREF="http://localhost:8000/music/chart_toppers.jsp">Chart
Toppers</a></font></b></p>
<p><b><font face="Arial" size="2" color="#800000"><a
HREF="http://localhost:8000/SearchContext/SearchAlias">Search</a></font></b></p>
<p><b><font face="Arial" size="2" color="#800000"><a
HREF="http://localhost:8000/music/vote_page.htm">Vote</a></font></b></p>
<p><b><font face="Arial" size="2" color="#800000"><a
```

```
HREF="http://localhost:8000/music/new_release_page.jsp">New Releases</a></font></b>
<p><font face="Arial" size="2" color="#800000"><b><a
HREF="http://localhost:8000/Register/RegisterPage.htm">Register</a></b></font>
<p><font face="Arial" size="2" color="#800000"><b><a
HREF="http://localhost:8000/music/help_page.htm">Help</a></b></font></p>
<p> </p>
    </td>
    <td width="82%">
<%! String username;%>
<%
try
{
                username=session.getAttribute("username").toString();
}
catch(Exception e)
{
                out.println("<p><font face=\"Arial\" size=\"2\"
color=\"#800000\"><b>");
                out.println("Please login before viewing the wishlist.");
                out.println("</font></b>");
}

%>
<p><font face="Arial" size="2" color="#800000">Dear <%=session.getAttribute("user-
name")%>, </font></p>
<p><font face="Arial" size="2" color="#800000">You have following items in the
wishlist.</font></p>
<table border="0" width="105%">
  <tr>
    <td width="11%"><font face="Arial" size="2" color="#800000"><b>Item
Code</b></font></td>
    <td width="18%"><font face="Arial" size="2" color="#800000"><b>Item
      Description</b></font></td>
    <td width="10%"><font face="Arial" size="2" color="#800000"><b>Price
($)</b></font></td>
    <td width="7%"><font face="Arial" size="2"
color="#800000"><b>Qty</b></font></td>
    <td width="32%" colspan="3"><font face="Arial" size="2"
```

```
color="#800000"><b>Total ($)
      </b></font></td>
  </tr>
                    <%
                    try{
                    Class.forName("sun.jdbc.odbc.JdbcOdbcDriver");
                    Connection connect;

connect=DriverManager.getConnection("jdbc:odbc:RegisterDataSource","","");
                    Statement state;
                    state = connect.createStatement();
                    String strQuery1 = "select * from Wishlist_Info where
User_name='"+username+ "'";
                    String str;
                    ResultSet result1 = state.executeQuery(strQuery1);
                    ResultSet result2;
                    String strQuery2;
                    int ctr1=0;
                    String desc=new String("");
                    String strRate=new String();
                    float rate=0;
                    int qty;
                    float total=0;
                    grandTotal=0;
                       while(result1.next())
                       {
                                     out.println("<tr>");
                                     out.println("<td width=\"10%\" valign=\"top\"
height=\"15\"><font face=\"Arial\" size=\"2\" color=\"#800000\">");

                                     str=result1.getString("Item_code");
                                     out.println(str);
                                     Statement state1;
                                     Connection connect1;

connect1=DriverManager.getConnection("jdbc:odbc:RegisterDataSource","","");
                                     state1 = connect1.createStatement();
                                     strQuery2 = "select * from Item_Master where
```

```
Item_Code='"+str+ "'";
                                    result2 = state1.executeQuery(strQuery2);
                                    while(result2.next())
                                    {
                                            rate=result2.getInt(3);
                                            desc=result2.getString(4);
                                    }
                                    out.println("<td width=\"13%\" valign=\"top\"
height=\"15\""><font face=\"Arial\" size=\"2\" color=\"#800000\">");
                                    out.println(desc);
                                    out.println("<td width=\"19%\" valign=\"top\"
height=\"15\""><font face=\"Arial\" size=\"2\" color=\"#800000\">");
                                    out.println(rate);
                                    out.println("<td width=\"13%\" valign=\"top\"
height=\"15\""><font face=\"Arial\" size=\"2\" color=\"#800000\">");
                                    qty=result1.getInt("Qty");
                                    out.println(qty);
                                    total=(rate*qty);
                                    out.println("<td width=\"19%\" valign=\"top\"
height=\"15\""><font face=\"Arial\" size=\"2\" color=\"#800000\">");
                                    out.println(total);

                                    out.println("</tr>");
                                    connect1.close();
                                    grandTotal=grandTotal+total;
                        }
                        }
                    catch(Exception e){
                    out.println("done exception" +e);
                    }
    %>
    </table>
    <table border="0" width="75%">
    <tr>
    <td>
    <p align="right"><font face="Arial" size="2" color="#800000"><b>Total Amount
    Payable($):  <%= grandTotal %></b></font>
    </tr>
```

```
</td>
</table>
<p> </p>
<p>  
<font face="Arial" size="2" color="#800000"><a
href="http://localhost:8000/music/user_buy_page.htm">Want to buy
more?</a></font></p>
        <p> </td>
  </tr>
</table>
<p>  </p>
<p>  </p>
</form>
</body>
</html>
```

Let's analyze the preceding code.

```
                String strQuery1 = "select * from Wishlist_Info where
User_name='"+username+ "'";
```

The above statement will declare a SQL query to select records from the Wish-list_Info table based on a condition. After this query is executed, another query is performed to obtain the item details from the Item_Master table. The item details of the items in the wishlist are then displayed to the user.

The output of the Wishlist_page.jsp is displayed in Figure 30-10.

Creating the Feedback Page

The code for the Feedback page is displayed in Listings 30-9 and 30-10. You can send a feedback message to the administrator using this page. The feedback feature also consists of two pages:

◆ feedback_page.jsp

◆ feedback_update.jsp

The code for these pages is given in Listing 30-9.

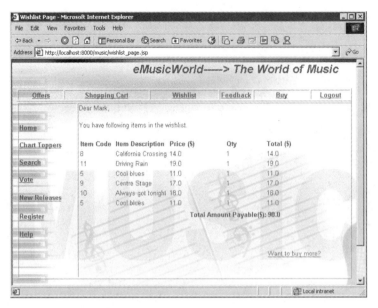

FIGURE 30-10 *The output of the* `Wishlist_page.jsp` *is shown here.*

Listing 30-9 feedback_page.jsp

```
<html>
<head>
<meta http-equiv="Content-Type" content="text/html; charset=windows-1252">
<meta http-equiv="Content-Language" content="en-us">
<title>Feedback Page</title>
</head>
<body bgcolor="#C0C0C0" topmargin="0"
background="http:\\localhost:8000\music\Background.bmp" >
<table border="0" width="100%">
  <tr>
    <td width="100%">
      <table border="0" width="97%" height="19">
        <tr>
          <td width="18%" height="13" valign="middle" align="right">
        <font face="Arial" size="5" color="#800000"><b><i>eMusicWorld-----&gt; The
World of Music</i></b></font>
          </td>
```

```
            </tr>
        </table>
    </td>
  </tr>
</table>
                        <%@ page import="java.util.*" %>
                        <%@ page import="java.sql.*" %>
                        <%@ page import="java.text.*" %>
                        <%@ page import="java.sql.Date" %>
                        <%@ page language = "java" %>
<form name="form1" method="get"
action="http://localhost:8000/music/feedback_update.jsp">
<table border="1" width="100%">
  <tr>
        <td width="11%" height="13" valign="middle" align="center"><font
face="Arial" size="2" color="#800000"><b><a
href="Offers.jsp">Offers</a></b></font></td>
        <td width="20%" height="13" valign="middle" align="center"><font
face="Arial" size="2" color="#800000"><b><a HREF="shopping_cart.jsp">Shopping
Cart</a></b></font></td>
        <td width="16%" height="13" valign="middle" align="center"><font
face="Arial" size="2" color="#800000"><b><a HREF="http://localhost:8000/music/wish-
list_page.jsp">Wishlist</a></b></font></td>
        <td width="8%" height="13" valign="middle" align="center"><font
face="Arial" size="2" color="#800000"><b><a HREF="http://localhost:8000/music/feed-
back_page.jsp">Feedback</a></b></font></td>
        <td width="13%" height="13" valign="middle" align="center"><font
face="Arial" size="2" color="#800000"><b><a
HREF="http://localhost:8000/music/user_buy_page.htm">Buy</b></font></a></b></font></
td>
        <td width="9%" height="13" valign="middle" align="center"><font
face="Arial" size="2" color="#800000"><b><a
HREF="http://localhost:8000/music/logout_page.jsp">Logout</a></b></font></td>
  </tr>
</table>
<table border="1" width="100%">
  <tr>
    <td width="18%">
```

```html
<p><font face="Arial" size="2" color="#800000"><b><a
HREF="http://localhost:8000/music/home_page.htm">Home</a></b></font></p>
<p><b><font face="Arial" size="2" color="#800000"><a
HREF="http://localhost:8000/music/chart_toppers.jsp">Chart
Toppers</a></font></b></p>
<p><b><font face="Arial" size="2" color="#800000"><a
HREF="http://localhost:8000/SearchContext/SearchAlias">Search</a></font></b></p>
<p><b><font face="Arial" size="2" color="#800000"><a
HREF="http://localhost:8000/music/vote_page.jsp">Vote</a></font></b></p>
<p><b><font face="Arial" size="2" color="#800000"><a
HREF="http://localhost:8000/music/new_release_page.jsp">New Releases</a></font></b>
<p><font face="Arial" size="2" color="#800000"><b><a
HREF="http://localhost:8000/Register/RegisterPage.htm">Register</a></b></font>
<p><font face="Arial" size="2" color="#800000"><b><a
HREF="http://localhost:8000/music/help_page.htm">Help</a></b></font></p>
       <p> </td>
     <td width="82%" valign="top">

<%! String username;%>
<%


try
{
                  username=session.getAttribute("username").toString();


}
catch(Exception e)
{
                  out.println("<p><font face=\"Arial\" size=\"2\"
color=\"#800000\"><b>");
                  out.println("Please login before sending us the feedback.");
                  out.println("</b></font></p>");
}
%>


<p><font face="Arial" size="2" color="#800000">Dear
 <%=username%>,</font>   
</p>
```

```
<p><font face="Arial" size="2" color="#800000">Your feedback is valuable to us
and it's a guiding factor in providing better services to you.</font> </p>
<p>
<font face="Arial" size="2" color="#800000">Your Message *:</font><br><textarea
rows="4" name="msg_txt" cols="72" style="font-family: Arial; font-size:
10pt"></textarea><br><font face="Arial" size="1" color="#800000">( * means mandatory
fields)</font></p>
   <p align="center"><input type="button" value="Submit" name="B1"
onClick="check()"><input type="reset" value="Clear" name="B2"></p>
    </td>
   </tr>
</table>
<!--WRITE A JavaScript FUNCTION TO ENSURE THAT THE MESSAGE TEXT BOX IS NOT EMPTY --
>
<script language="JavaScript">
function check()
{
                var txtMsg=form1.msg_txt.value;
                if(txtMsg.length==0)
                                alert("Please enter message.");
                else
                                form1.submit();
}
</script>
<p>  </p>
<p>  </p>
</form>
</body>
</html>
```

Notice that the form in this page is submitted to the feedback_update.jsp page.
The username is obtained from the session and displayed. A text box for entering feedback is also displayed by this page. A check is performed on the feedback
text box to ensure that the text box is not blank while it is submitted. The
JavaScript function written to perform this check is given here:

```
<script language="JavaScript">
function check()
```

```
{
            var txtMsg=form1.msg_txt.value;
            if(txtMsg.length==0)
                        alert("Please enter message.");
            else
                        form1.submit();
}
</script>
```

In the check() method, the length of the text in the text box is identified. If the length is equal to zero, an error message is displayed to the user. Otherwise, the form is submitted to the feedback_update.jsp page. The check() method is called when the user clicks on the Submit button. The code for the feedback_update.jsp page is given in Listing 30-10.

Listing 30-10 feedback_update.jsp

```
<html>
<head>
<meta http-equiv="Content-Type" content="text/html; charset=windows-1252">
<meta http-equiv="Content-Language" content="en-us">
<title>Feedback Page</title>
</head>
            <%@ page import="java.util.*" %>
            <%@ page import="java.sql.*" %>
            <%@ page import="java.text.*" %>
            <%@ page import="java.util.Date" %>

            <%@ page language = "java" %>

<body bgcolor="#C0C0C0" topmargin="0">
<!--OBTAIN THE USERNAME AND THE MESSGAE-->
<% String username=session.getAttribute("username").toString(); %>
<% String message=request.getParameter("msg_txt"); %>
<%! int ctr=0;%>
<!--OBTAIN THE CURRENT DATE AND TIME -->
<% SimpleDateFormat formatter
    = new SimpleDateFormat ("MM.dd.yyyy");
```

```
Date currentTime_1 = new Date();
String dateString = formatter.format(currentTime_1);

try{
                Class.forName("sun.jdbc.odbc.JdbcOdbcDriver");
                Connection connect;



connect=DriverManager.getConnection("jdbc:odbc:MusicDataSource","","");
                Statement state;
                state = connect.createStatement();
<!--INSERT THE FEEDBACK ALONGWITH THE USERNAME AND THE CURRENT DATE IN THE FEED-
BACK_MASTER TABLE-->
                String strQuery1 = "Insert into Feedback_Master values('"+user-
name+ "','"+message+"','"+ dateString +"')";

                state.executeUpdate(strQuery1);
                ctr=ctr+1;
                connect.close();
                }
                catch(Exception e)
                {
                                out.println("done exception" +e);
                }

%>
<jsp:forward page="user_home_page.jsp"/>
</body>
</html>
```

The code in Listing 30-10 will update the Feedback_Master table. The username, feedback, and the date of feedback are inserted in the table. The Feedback_ Update.jsp page is then forwarded to the user_home_page.jsp.

The interaction between the two pages is displayed in Figure 30-11.

FIGURE 30-11 *The interaction between* `feedback_page.jsp` *and* `feedback_update.jsp` *is shown here.*

The output of the `feedback_page.jsp` page is displayed in Figure 30-12.

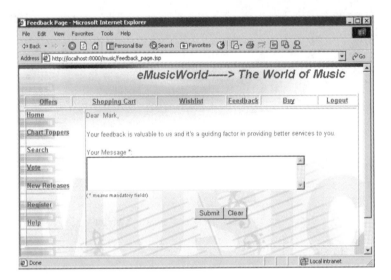

FIGURE 30-12 *The output of the* `feedback_page.jsp` *page is shown here.*

The Logout Page

The Logout page logs out a user from the application. The user session is no longer maintained.

The code for the Logout page is given in Listing 30-11.

Listing 30-11 Logout_page.jsp

```
<html>
<head>
```

```
<meta http-equiv="Content-Type" content="text/html; charset=windows-1252">
<meta http-equiv="Content-Language" content="en-us">
<title>Logout Page</title>
</head>
<body bgcolor="#C0C0C0" topmargin="0"
background="http:\\localhost:8000\music\Background.bmp" >
<table border="0" width="100%">
  <tr>
    <td width="100%">
      <table border="0" width="97%" height="19">
        <tr>
          <td width="18%" height="13" valign="middle" align="right">
      <font face="Arial" size="5" color="#800000"><b><i>eMusicWorld-----&gt; The
World of Music</i></b></font>
          </td>
        </tr>
      </table>
    </td>
  </tr>
</table>
<table border="1" width="100%" height="353">
  <tr>
    <td width="15%" height="347" valign="top">

<p><font face="Arial" size="2" color="#800000"><b><a
HREF="http://localhost:8000/music/home_page.htm">Home</a></b></font></p>
<p><b><font face="Arial" size="2" color="#800000"><a
HREF="http://localhost:8000/music/chart_toppers.jsp">Chart
Toppers</a></font></b></p>
<p><b><font face="Arial" size="2" color="#800000"><a
HREF="http://localhost:8000/SearchContext/SearchAlias">Search</a></font></b></p>
<p><b><font face="Arial" size="2" color="#800000"><a
HREF="http://localhost:8000/music/vote_page.jsp">Vote</a></font></b></p>

<p><b><font face="Arial" size="2" color="#800000"><a
HREF="http://localhost:8000/music/new_release_page.jsp">New Releases</a></font></b>
<p><font face="Arial" size="2" color="#800000"><b><a
HREF="http://localhost:8000/Register/RegisterPage.htm">Register</a></b></font>
```

```
<p><font face="Arial" size="2" color="#800000"><b><a
HREF="http://localhost:8000/music/login_page.htm">Login</a></b></font>
<p><font face="Arial" size="2" color="#800000"><b><a
HREF="http://localhost:8000/music/help_page.htm">Help</a></b></font></p>
                  </td>
      <td width="85%" height="347" valign="top">
          <p><b><font color="#800000" size="3" face="Arial Black">Please wait while you
are being logged out....................</font></b></p>
<!--REMOVE THE USERNAME ATTRIBUTE FROM THE SESSION OBJECT-->
<% session.removeAttribute("username");%>
          </td>
      </tr>
</table>
</body>
</html>
```

The Logout_page.jsp will remove the username attribute from the session object. The session will end. The output of the Logout_page.jsp page is illustrated in Figure 30-13.

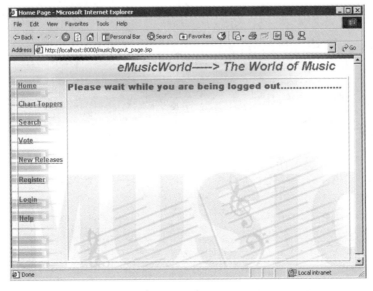

FIGURE 30-13 *The output of the* Logout_page.jsp *page is shown here.*

Interaction Between Pages of User Interfaces

You have now learned how to create various pages of the eMusicWorld application. Now take a look at how the pages interact in the application. The interaction between each of these pages is illustrated in Figure 30-14.

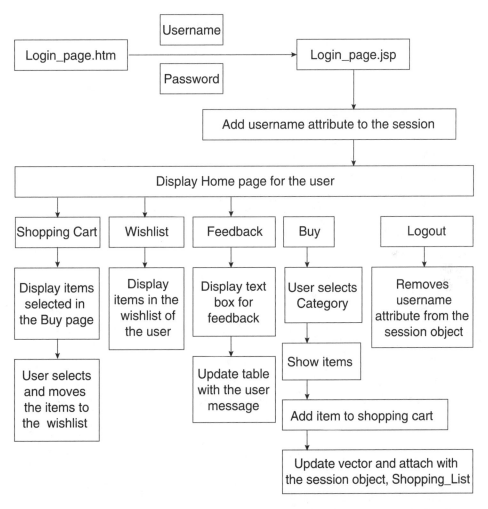

FIGURE 30-14 *The interaction between pages of the* eMusicWorld *application is displayed.*

An Example

Now I'll give you an example to show you the functionality of the pages of the User Interface category. Mark Smith is a user of the music application. He can log on to the application by using the Login_page.htm as depicted in Figure 30-15.

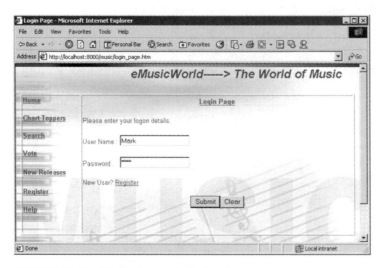

FIGURE 30-15 *The Login page is displayed.*

After Mark has provided the correct user information, the Home page is displayed, as seen in Figure 30-16.

Next, Mark clicks on the link to the Buy page. The Buy page is displayed in Figure 30-17.

Mark selects some items in the Buy page and clicks on the Move to the Shopping Cart button. The Shopping Cart page is then displayed to Mark. See Figure 30-18.

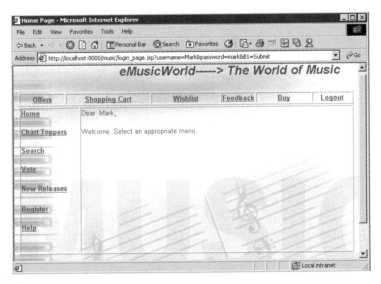

FIGURE 30-16 *The Home page is shown to Mark.*

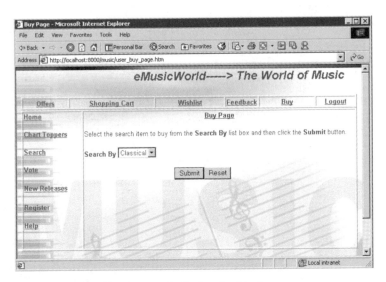

FIGURE 30-17 *The Buy page is displayed to Mark.*

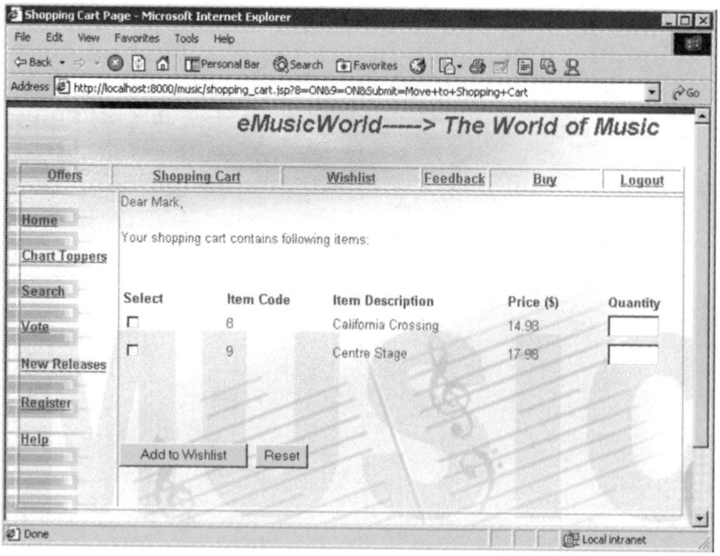

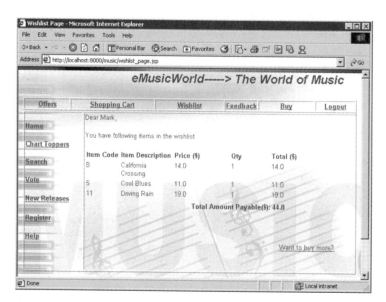

FIGURE 30-18 *Mark selects the Shopping Cart page.*

Mark can now move the items in the shopping cart to the wishlist. He can do this by first selecting the items to be moved to the wishlist and then clicking on the Add to the Wishlist button. Mark can view the items in the wishlist by visiting the Wishlist page, as seen in Figure 30-19.

FIGURE 30-19 *The Wishlist page is displayed.*

After navigating through the application, Mark comes up with an idea for improving the application. He wants to send a suggestion to the administrator. The Feedback page enables him to do so. See Figure 30-20.

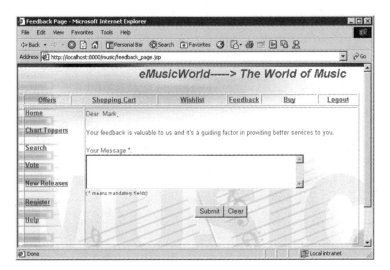

FIGURE 30-20 *Mark accesses the Feedback page.*

Now, Mark wants to logout of the application. He needs to click on the Logout link on the left. The Logout page is displayed, as seen in Figure 30-21. Mark has now successfully navigated the eMusicWorld application.

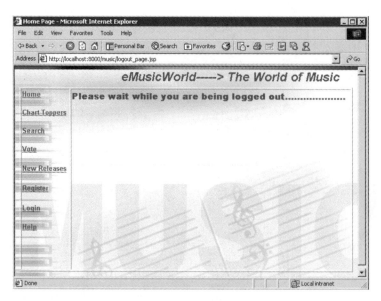

FIGURE 30-21 *The Logout page is displayed to Mark.*

Summary

In this chapter, you learned how to create the pages of the User Interface category of the music application. You also looked at the functionality of each page. In addition, the interaction between various pages of the User Interface category was discussed in this chapter. Finally, an example was given showing how a visitor to the application uses the services of eMusicWorld.

Chapter 31

In this chapter, you'll create the pages of the Administrator Interface category of the music application. The pages in this category are displayed to the administrators of the eMusicWorld application. As identified during the design phase, this category will contain the following pages.

- ◆ The Delete Page
- ◆ The Add Item Page
- ◆ The Modify Item Page
- ◆ The Sales Reports Page
- ◆ The View Messages Page
- ◆ The Logout Page

Now I will start creating the pages.

Creating the Delete Page

At times, administrators of the eMusicWorld application might need to delete a registered user. The Delete page of the Administrator Interface category enables the administrators to do so. The code for each of these pages is given in Listing 31-1.

Listing 31-1 admin_del_user.jsp

```
<html>
<head>
<meta http-equiv="Content-Type" content="text/html; charset=windows-1252">
<meta http-equiv="Content-Language" content="en-us">
<title>Delete User Page</title>
</head>
<body bgcolor="#C0C0C0" topmargin="0"
background="http:\\localhost:8000\music\Background.bmp" >
<table border="0" width="100%">
  <tr>
    <td width="100%">
```

```
    <table border="0" width="97%" height="19">
      <tr>
        <td width="18%" height="13" valign="middle" align="right">
      <font face="Arial" size="5" color="#800000"><b><i>eMusicWorld-----&gt; The
World of Music</i></b></font>
        </td>
      </tr>
    </table>
  </td>
 </tr>
</table>


<table border="0" width="100%">
    <tr>
      <td width="100%"><table border="0" width="100%" height="19">
        <tr>
          <td width="9%" height="13" valign="middle" align="center"><font
face="Arial" size="2" color="#800000"><b><a
HREF="welcome_page.htm">Home</a></b></font></td>
          <td width="10%" height="13" valign="middle" align="center"></td>
          <td width="19%" height="13" valign="middle" align="center"></td>
          <td width="13%" height="13" valign="middle" align="center"></td>
          <td width="13%" height="13" valign="middle" align="center"></td>
                    <td width="11%" height="13" valign="middle" align="cen-
ter"></td>
                                        <td width="10%" height="13"
valign="middle" align="center"></td>
          <td width="9%" height="13" valign="middle" align="center"><font
face="Arial" size="2" color="#800000"><b><a
HREF="home_page.htm">Logout</b></font></td>
          <td width="9%" height="13" valign="middle" align="center"><font
face="Arial" size="2" color="#800000"><b><a
HREF="http://localhost:8000/music/admin_home_page_old.htm">Help</a></b></font></td>
        </tr>
      </table>
    </td>
  </tr>
</table>
```

```
<table border="1" width="100%" height="353">
  <tr>
   <td width="15%" height="347" valign="top">

<p><font face="Arial" size="2" color="#800000"><b><a
HREF="http://localhost:8000/music/admin_del_user.jsp">Delete User</a></b></font></p>
<p><font face="Arial" size="2" color="#800000"><b><a
HREF="http://localhost:8000/ItemContext/ItemAlias">Add Item</a></b></font></p>
<p><font face="Arial" size="2" color="#800000"><b><a
HREF="http://localhost:8000/music/admin_mod_item.jsp">Modify Item</a></b></font></p>
<p><font face="Arial" size="2" color="#800000"><b>Sales Reports<br>---<a
HREF="http://localhost:8000/music/daily_sales_report.jsp">Choose a Date</a><br>---<a
HREF="http://localhost:8000/music/weekly_sales_report.jsp">Previous
Week</a><br>---<a
HREF="http://localhost:8000/music/monthly_sales_report.jsp">Previous
Month</a></b></font></p>
<p><font face="Arial" size="2" color="#800000"><b><a
HREF="http://localhost:8000/music/admin_wishlist.jsp">View
Wishlist</a></b></font></p>
<p><font face="Arial" size="2" color="#800000"><b><a
HREF="http://localhost:8000/music/admin_messages.jsp">View
Messages</a></b></font></p>
                </td>
    <td width="85%" height="347" valign="top">
<p align="center" style="margin-top: 1; margin-bottom: 1"><b><u><font
color="#800000" face="Arial" size="2">Delete
User</font></u></b>
<p align="center" style="margin-top: 1; margin-bottom: 1">
<form method="get" action="http://localhost:8000/music/admin_del.jsp">
  <p align="left" style="margin-left: -2; margin-right: -2; margin-top: 1; margin-
bottom: 1"><font face="Arial" size="2" color="#800000">Select
  the Username to be Deleted:</font> <select size="1" name="delUserName">

                <%@ page import="java.util.*" %>
                <%@ page import="java.sql.*" %>
                <%@ page import="java.text.*" %>
                <%@ page import="java.sql.Date" %>
```

```
<%@ page language = "java" %>
<%
try{
Class.forName("sun.jdbc.odbc.JdbcOdbcDriver");
Connection connect;

connect=DriverManager.getConnection("jdbc:odbc:RegisterDataSource","","");
Statement state;
state = connect.createStatement();
String strQuery1 = "select User_name from User_Info order by
User_name asc" ;
ResultSet result1 = state.executeQuery(strQuery1);
int ctr1=0;
while(result1.next())
{
%>
<option><%=result1.getString("User_name")%></option>
<%
}
connect.close();
}
catch(Exception e)
{
out.println("Exception: "+e);
}
%>
</select></p>
</select></p>
<p align="left" style="margin-left: -2; margin-right: -2; margin-top: 3; margin-
bottom: 10">   <font face="Arial" size="2"
color="#800000"></font></p>
<table border="0" width="100%">
<tr>
<td width="50%" valign="middle" align="right"><font face="Arial" size="2"
color="#800000"> 
  </font><input type="submit" value="Delete" name="B1"><input type="but-
ton" value="Cancel" name="B2"></td>
<td width="50%" valign="middle" align="right"><font face="Arial" size="2"
color="#800000">  </font></td>
```

```
    </tr>
  </table>
</form>
      </td>
    </tr>
  </table>
</body>
</html>
```

The output of the `admin_del_user.jsp` page is displayed in Figure 31-1.

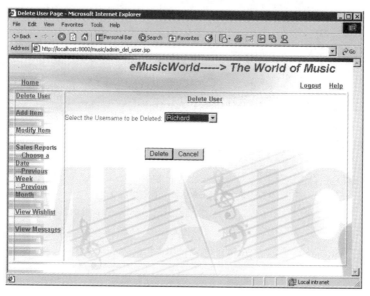

FIGURE 31-1 *The output of the* `admin_del_user.jsp` *page is shown here.*

To delete a user, an administrator needs to select the username from the drop-down list as displayed in Figure 31-1 and then click the Delete button.

Creating the Add Item Page

The Add Item page enables an administrator to add an item to the inventory. The Add Item page uses the concept of EJB. The components that constitute the Add Item page are:

- Item.class
- ItemBean.class
- Item.jsp
- Item.Ejb.class
- ItemHome.class
- SearchBean.class
- SearchItem.jsp

Now take a look at each of these components in detail.

ItemHome.class

The source code for the home interface, ItemHome.class is given in Listing 31-2.

Listing 31-2 ItemHome.java

```
import java.util.Collection;
 import java.rmi.RemoteException;
 import javax.ejb.*;
public interface ItemHome extends EJBHome
        {
                public Item create(int itemCode,String title, String rate,String
itemDescription, String singer, String quantityOnHand, String type,String
releaseDate) throws RemoteException,CreateException;

         public Item findByPrimaryKey(int itemCode) throws
FinderException,RemoteException;

public Collection findByType(String type)throws FinderException,RemoteException;
        }
```

Item.class

The Item.class is the remote interface of the EJB. The source code for the
Item.class is given in Listing 31-3.

Listing 31-3   Item.java

```
import javax.ejb.EJBObject;
import   java.rmi.RemoteException;


public interface Item extends EJBObject
       {
               public int getitemCode() throws RemoteException;
               public String gettitle() throws RemoteException;
               public String getrate() throws RemoteException;
               public String getitemDescription() throws
RemoteException;
               public String getsinger() throws RemoteException;
               public String getquantityOnHand() throws RemoteException;
               public String gettype() throws RemoteException;
               public String getreleaseDate() throws RemoteException;


       }
```

ItemBean.java

The ItemBean.class implements the business methods defined in the home interface. See Listing 31-4.

Listing 31-4   ItemBean.java

```
import java.util.*;
import java.io.*;
import javax.naming.Context;
import javax.naming.InitialContext;
import javax.rmi.PortableRemoteObject;


public class ItemBean
{
private String action;
private int itc;
private String ttl;
```

```java
private String rt;
private String id;
private String sng;
private String qty;
private String typ;
private String rld;
ItemHome itemHome;
Item item;
public ItemBean()
{
try
{
Context ctx=new InitialContext();
System.out.println("Context has been created created");
Object obj=ctx.lookup("java:comp/env/ejb/Item");
itemHome=(ItemHome)PortableRemoteObject.narrow(obj,ItemHome.class);
}
catch(Exception e)
{
System.out.println("Could not find Item home"+e);
}
reset();
}
public String performAction()
{
String msg="";
try
{
if(action.equals("v1"))
{
System.out.println("If action is update");
item=itemHome.create(itc,ttl,rt,id,sng,qty,typ,rld);
System.out.println("create method called");
msg="Item Inserted";

}
else if(action.equals("v2"))
{
```

```
item=itemHome.findByPrimaryKey(itc);

selectItem();
msg="Item displayed";
}
}
catch(Exception e)
{
System.out.println("Cannot find by PK"+e);
}
return msg;
}
public int getItc()
{
return itc;
}
public void setAction(String z)
{
action=z;
}
public String getAction()
{
return action;
}
public void setItc(int i)
{
itc=i;
}
public void setTtl(String t)
{
ttl=t;
}
public void setRt(String r)
{
rt=r;
}
public void setId(String d)
{
```

```
id=d;
}
public void setSng(String s)
{
sng=s;
}
public void setQty(String q)
{
qty=q;
}
public void setTyp(String y)
{
typ=y;
}
public void setRld(String l)
{
rld=l;
}
public String getTtl()
{
return ttl;
}
public String getRt()
{
return rt;
}
public String getId()
{
return id;
}
public String getSng()
{
return sng;
}
public String getQty()
{
return qty;
}
```

```
public String getTyp()
{
return typ;
}
public String getRld()
{
return rld;
}
private void selectItem()
{
try
{
setTtl(item.gettitle());
setRt(item.getrate());
setId(item.getitemDescription() );
setSng(item.getsinger());
setQty(item.getquantityOnHand());
setTyp(item.gettype());
setRld(item.getreleaseDate());
}
catch(Exception e)
{
System.out.println("Cannot call remote method"+e);
}
}
private void reset()
{
int it=0;
setItc(it);
setTtl(" ");
setRt(" ");
setId(" ");
setSng(" ");
setQty(" ");
setTyp(" ");
 setRld(" ");
setAction(" ");
}
```

```
}
```

Item.jsp

The Item.jsp page is displayed to the administrator. In the Item.jsp page, the administrator fills in the details of the new item. This page uses the ItemBean javabean class. Listing 31-4 contains the code for the Item.jsp page.

Listing 31-4 Item.jsp

```
<html>
<jsp:useBean id="item" scope="session" class="ItemBean" />
<jsp:setProperty name="item" property="*" />
<%! String msg; %>
<% msg = item.performAction(); %>
<head>
    <title>Item Display</title>
</head>
<body bgcolor="#C0C0C0" topmargin="0"
background="http:\\localhost:8000\music\Background.bmp" >

<table border="0" width="100%">
  <tr>
    <td width="100%">
      <table border="0" width="97%" height="19">
        <tr>
          <td width="18%" height="13" valign="middle" align="right">
        <font face="Arial" size="5" color="#800000"><b><i>eMusicWorld-----&gt; The
World of Music</i></b></font>
          </td>
        </tr>
      </table>
    </td>
  </tr>
</table>

<form method="POST" action="Item.jsp">
```

```javascript
<script language="javascript">
function year()
{
            document.write("<option value=\"- - - -\">- - - -</option>");
            for (i=1900;i<2000;i++)
            {
                                        document.write("<option
value="+i+">"+i+"</option>");
            }
}
function date()
{
            document.write("<option value=\"- - \">- - </option>");
            for (i=01;i<=31;i++)
            {
                                        document.write("<option
value="+i+">"+i+"</option>");
            }
}
function verify()
{
            var ctr=0;
            var txtTitle=form.txtTitle.value;
            var txtRate=form.txtRate.value;
            var txtDesc=form.txtDesc.value;
            var txtSinger=form.txtSinger.value;
            var txtQty=form.txtQty.value;
            var txtType=form.txtType.value;

if((txtTitle.length==0)||(txtRate.length==0)||(txtDesc.length==0)||(txtSinger.length
==0)||(txtQty.length==0))
            {
                                alert("Please enter all the values.");
                                ctr=1;
            }
            if(ctr!=1)
            form.submit();
}
```

```
</script>
<table border="0" width="100%">

  <tr>
    <td width="100%"><table border="0" width="100%" height="19">
        <tr>
          <td width="9%" height="13" valign="middle" align="center"><font
face="Arial" size="2" color="#800000"><b><a
HREF="welcome_page.htm">Home</a></b></font></td>
          <td width="10%" height="13" valign="middle" align="center"></td>
          <td width="19%" height="13" valign="middle" align="center"></td>
          <td width="13%" height="13" valign="middle" align="center"></td>
          <td width="13%" height="13" valign="middle" align="center"></td>
                    <td width="11%" height="13" valign="middle" align="cen-
ter"></td>
                                        <td width="10%" height="13"
valign="middle" align="center"></td>
          <td width="9%" height="13" valign="middle" align="center"><font
face="Arial" size="2" color="#800000"><b><a
HREF="home_page.htm">Logout</b></font></td>
          <td width="9%" height="13" valign="middle" align="center"><font
face="Arial" size="2" color="#800000"><b><a
HREF="http://localhost:8000/music/admin_home_page_old.htm">Help</a></b></font></td>
        </tr>
      </table>
    </td>
  </tr>
</table>


<table border="1" width="100%" height="6">
  <tr>
    <td width="15%" height="347" valign="top">

<p><font face="Arial" size="2" color="#800000"><b><a
HREF="http://localhost:8000/music/admin_del_user.jsp">Delete User</a></b></font></p>
<p><font face="Arial" size="2" color="#800000"><b><a
HREF="http://localhost:8000/ItemContext/ItemAlias">Add Item</a></b></font></p>
<p><font face="Arial" size="2" color="#800000"><b><a
```

```
HREF="http://localhost:8000/music/admin_mod_item.jsp">Modify Item</a></b></font></p>
<p><font face="Arial" size="2" color="#800000"><b>Sales Reports<br>---<a
HREF="http://localhost:8000/music/daily_sales_report.jsp">Choose a Date</a><br>---<a
HREF="http://localhost:8000/music/weekly_sales_report.jsp">Previous
Week</a><br>---<a
HREF="http://localhost:8000/music/monthly_sales_report.jsp">Previous
Month</a></b></font></p>
<p><font face="Arial" size="2" color="#800000"><b><a
HREF="http://localhost:8000/music/admin_wishlist.jsp">View
Wishlist</a></b></font></p>
<p><font face="Arial" size="2" color="#800000"><b><a
HREF="http://localhost:8000/music/admin_messages.jsp">View
Messages</a></b></font></p>
                </td>
   <td width="85%" height="347" valign="top">
<p align="center">   <b><u><font color="#800000" face="Arial"
size="2">Add
or View Inventory</font></u></b>
</p>
  <p align="left" style="margin-left: -2; margin-right: -2; margin-top: 3; margin-
bottom: 3"><font face="Arial" size="2" color="#800000">Item
  Code :     <input type="text" name="itc" size="20"
value="<jsp:getProperty name="item" property="itc" />"></font></p>
  <p align="left" style="margin-left: -2; margin-right: -2; margin-top: 3; margin-
bottom: 3"><font face="Arial" size="2"
color="#800000">Title:          &n
bsp;
     <input type="text" name="ttl" size="20" value="<jsp:getProperty
name="item" property="ttl" />"></font></p>
  <p align="left" style="margin-left: -2; margin-right: -2; margin-top: 3; margin-
bottom: 3"><font face="Arial" size="2" color="#800000">Price
($):    
      <input type="text" name="rt" size="20" value="<jsp:getProperty
name="item" property="rt" />"></font></p>
  <p align="left" style="margin-left: -2; margin-right: -2; margin-top: 3; margin-
bottom: 3"><font face="Arial" size="2"
color="#800000">Description:   
  <input type="text" name="id" size="20" value="<jsp:getProperty name="item" prop-
```

```
erty="id" />"></font></p>
   <p align="left" style="margin-left: -2; margin-right: -2; margin-top: 3; margin-
bottom: 3"><font face="Arial" size="2"
color="#800000">Singer:          
   <input type="text" name="sng" size="20" value="<jsp:getProperty name="item" prop-
erty="sng" />"></font></p>
   <p align="left" style="margin-left: -2; margin-right: -2; margin-top: 3; margin-
bottom: 3"><font face="Arial" size="2"
color="#800000">Qty:         &nbs
p;   
   <input type="text" name="qty" size="20" value="<jsp:getProperty name="item" prop-
erty="qty" />"></font></p>
   <p align="left" style="margin-left: -2; margin-right: -2; margin-top: 3; margin-
bottom: 3"><font face="Arial" size="2"
color="#800000">Type:          &nb
sp; 
   <input type="text" name="typ" size="20" value="<jsp:getProperty name="item" prop-
erty="typ" />"></font></p>
   <p align="left" style="margin-left: -2; margin-right: -2; margin-top: 3; margin-
bottom: 3"><font face="Arial" size="2" color="#800000">Release
   date: <input type="text" name="rld" size="20" value="<jsp:getProperty name="item"
property="rld" />">
   </font></p>
   <p align="left" style="margin-left: -2; margin-right: -2; margin-top: 3; margin-
bottom: 3"> </p>
   <p align="left" style="margin-left: -2; margin-right: -2; margin-top: 3; margin-
bottom: 3"> </p>
   <p align="left" style="margin-left: -2; margin-right: -2; margin-top: 3; margin-
bottom: 3"><font face="Arial" size="2" color="#800000"><b><input type="radio"
value="v1" name="action" >
Save
Item            <input
type="radio" value="v2" name="action" >
 View Item </b></font></p>
   <p align="left" style="margin-left: -2; margin-right: -2; margin-top: 3; margin-
bottom: 3"> </p>
   <p align="center" style="margin-left: -2; margin-right: -2; margin-top: 3; mar-
gin-bottom: 3"><input type="submit" value="Submit" name="B1"><input type="reset"
```

```
value="Reset" name="B2"></p>
    <%=msg%>
      </td>
    </tr>
</table>
</form>
</body>
</html>
```

The output of the Item.jsp page is displayed in Figure 31-2.

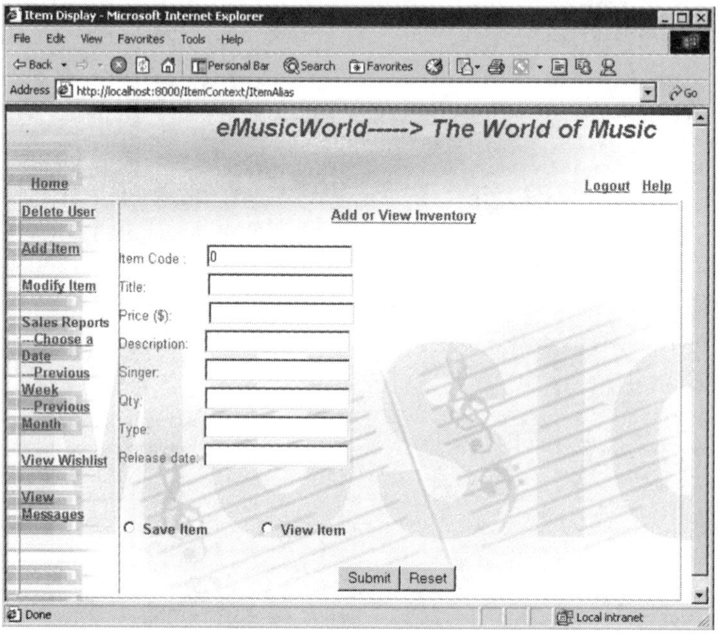

FIGURE 31-2 *The output of the* Item.jsp *page is shown here.*

ItemEJB.class

The ItemEJB.class implements the business methods declared in the home interface. The source code of the ItemEJB class is displayed in Listing 31-5.

Listing 31-5   ItemEJB.java

```java
import java.sql.*;
import javax.sql.*;
import java.util.*;
import javax.ejb.*;
import javax.naming.*;
import java.rmi.*;

public class ItemEjb implements EntityBean
{
public int itemCode;
public String title;
public String rate;
public String itemDescription;
public String singer;
public String quantityOnHand;
public String type;
public String releaseDate;
private EntityContext ctx;
Connection con;
public ItemEjb(){}
public int getitemCode()
 {
   return itemCode;
 }
public String gettitle()
 {
   return title;
 }
public String getrate()
  {
    return rate;
  }
public String getitemDescription()
  {
    return itemDescription;
  }
```

```java
public String getsinger()
  {
    return singer;
  }
public String getquantityOnHand()
 {
    return quantityOnHand;
 }
public String gettype()
  {
    return type;
  }
public String getreleaseDate()
  {
    return releaseDate;
  }
public String ejbCreate(int itemCode,String title, String rate,String
itemDescription, String singer, String quantityOnHand, String type,String
releaseDate)throws  CreateException {
this.itemCode=itemCode;
this.title=title;
this.rate=rate;
this.itemDescription=itemDescription;
this.singer=singer;
this.quantityOnHand=quantityOnHand;
this.type=type;
this.releaseDate=releaseDate;
return null;
}
public void setEntityContext(EntityContext ctx){
this.ctx=ctx;
}
public void ejbActivate(){
            Object obj=ctx.getPrimaryKey();
        String id=obj.toString();
        itemCode=Integer.parseInt(id);
}
public void ejbPassivate(){
```

```
itemCode=0;
    }
public void ejbStore(){}
public void ejbLoad(){}

public void ejbRemove(){}
public void unsetEntityContext(){}
public void ejbPostCreate(int itemCode,String title, String rate,String
itemDescription,String singer, String quantityOnHand, String type,String
releaseDate){}


}
```

SearchBean.class

The SearchBean is a JavaBean class that is used by the SearchItem.jsp page to perform a search for the items in that inventory. The source code of the Search-Bean class is given in Listing 31-6.

Listing 31-6 SearchBean.java

```
import java.util.*;
import java.io.*;
import javax.naming.Context;
import javax.naming.InitialContext;
import javax.rmi.PortableRemoteObject;

public class SearchBean
{
private String searchBy;
ItemHome itemHome;
Item item;
Vector vect;
public SearchBean()
{
vect = new Vector();
try
```

```java
{
Context ctx=new InitialContext();
Object obj=ctx.lookup("java:comp/env/ejb/Item");
itemHome=(ItemHome)PortableRemoteObject.narrow(obj,ItemHome.class);
}
catch(Exception e)
{
System.out.println("Could not find Item home"+e);
}
}
public void setSearchBy(String str)
{
searchBy=str;
searchBy=searchBy.trim();
}
public String getSearchBy()
{
return searchBy;
}
public Vector performSearch()
{
try
{
if(searchBy!=null)
{
Collection collect=itemHome.findByType(searchBy);
Iterator itr=collect.iterator();
 while(itr.hasNext()){
   int i=0;
   item=(Item)itr.next();
   String title=item.gettitle();
   vect.add(i,title);
   i++;
}
}
else
{
   vect.add(0,"");
```

```
    }
    }
    catch(Exception e)
    {
    System.out.println("Error in finding by type"+e);
    }
    return vect;
    }
    }
```

SearchItem.jsp

The `SearchItem.jsp` page uses the `SearchBean` bean to connect to the Search EJB. The code for the `SearchItem.jsp` page is given in Listing 31-7.

Listing 31-7 SearchItem.jsp

```
<html>
<jsp:useBean id="search" scope="session" class="SearchBean" />
<jsp:setProperty name="search" property="*" />
<%! Vector vect; %>
<%! int cap,i;
Object obj;%>
<% vect = search.performSearch();%>
<html>
<head>
<meta http-equiv="Content-Type" content="text/html; charset=windows-1252">
<meta http-equiv="Content-Language" content="en-us">
<title>Search Page</title>
</head>
<body bgcolor="#C0C0C0" topmargin="0"
background="http:\\localhost:8000\music\Background.bmp" >
<table border="0" width="100%">
  <tr>
    <td width="100%">
      <table border="0" width="97%" height="19">
        <tr>
```

```
                    <td width="18%" height="13" valign="middle" align="right">
        <font face="Arial" size="5" color="#800000"><b><i>eMusicWorld-----&gt; The
World of Music</i></b></font>
                </td>
            </tr>
        </table>
    </td>
  </tr>
</table>
<form method="POST" action="SearchItem.jsp">
<table border="1" width="100%">
  <tr>
    <td width="18%">
<p><font face="Arial" size="2" color="#800000"><b><a
HREF="http://localhost:8000/music/home_page.htm">Home</a></b></font></p>
<p><b><font face="Arial" size="2" color="#800000"><a
HREF="http://localhost:8000/music/chart_toppers.jsp">Chart
Toppers</a></font></b></p>
<p><b><font face="Arial" size="2" color="#800000"><a
HREF="http://localhost:8000/SearchContext/SearchAlias">Search</a></font></b></p>
<p><b><font face="Arial" size="2" color="#800000"><a
HREF="http://localhost:8000/music/vote_page.jsp">Vote</a></font></b></p>
<p><b><font face="Arial" size="2" color="#800000"><a
HREF="http://localhost:8000/music/new_release_page.jsp">New Releases</a></font></b>
<p><font face="Arial" size="2" color="#800000"><b><a
HREF="http://localhost:8000/Register/RegisterPage.htm">Register</a></b></font>
<p><font face="Arial" size="2" color="#800000"><b><a
HREF="http://localhost:8000/music/login_page.htm">Login</a></b></font>
<p><font face="Arial" size="2" color="#800000"><b><a
HREF="http://localhost:8000/music/help_page.htm">Help</a></b></font></p>
        <p> </td>
      <td width="82%" valign="top">
    <font face="Arial" size="2" color="#800000">Select the search category from the
<b>Search By</b> list box and then click the <b>Submit</b> button.</font>
    <p><font face="Arial" size="2" color="#800000"><b>Search By </b></font><select
size="1" name="searchBy" style="color: #800000; font-family: Arial; font-size:
10pt">
      <option selected>Classical</option>
```

```
      <option>Jazz</option>
      <option>Pop</option>
      <option>Rock</option>
  </select>  </p>

<p>            &nb
sp;    
   
  <input type="submit" value="Submit" name="Submit"></p>
<p> </p>
<%
cap=vect.size();
for(i=cap-1;i>=0;i--)
{
String str=(String)vect.elementAt(i);
out.println("<font face=\"Arial\" size=\"2\" color=\"#800000\">");
out.println((String)vect.elementAt(i));
out.println("<BR>");
out.println("</font>");
}
%>
    </td>
</tr>
</table>
</form>
</body>
</html>
</html>
```

Now it's time to deploy the bean.

Deploying the Bean for Search

The steps to deploy the Search bean are:

1. Select MusicApp from the left pane.
2. Choose File, New Enterprise Bean. The New Enterprise Bean Wizard — Introduction screen appears.

3. Click the Next button. The New Enterprise Bean Wizard — EJB JAR dialog box appears.

4. Specify "ItemJar" in the JAR Display Name box. In the Contents group box, click the Add button. The Add Files to .JAR dialog box appears.

5. Select Item.class and click the Add button. Similarly, select ItemEJB.class and click the Add button. Also, select ItemHome.class and then click the Add button. The files that you add appear in the lower text box of the dialog box as shown in Figure 31-3.

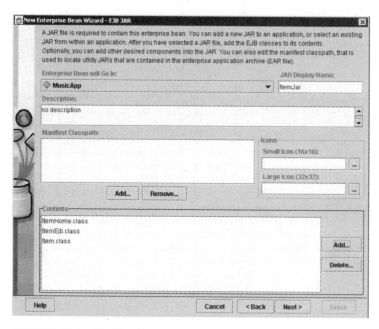

FIGURE 31-3 *The New Enterprise Bean Wizard — EJB JAR dialog box is displayed.*

6. Click the OK button. The Add Files to .JAR dialog box closes. Under Contents, verify that the three files that you added appear.

7. Click the Next button. The New Enterprise Bean Wizard — General dialog box is displayed. See Figure 31-4.

8. From the Enterprise Bean Class drop-down list, select ItemEJB. From the Home Interface drop-down list, select ItemHome. From the Remote Interface drop-down list, select Item. In the Enterprise Bean Display Name box, type ItemBean.

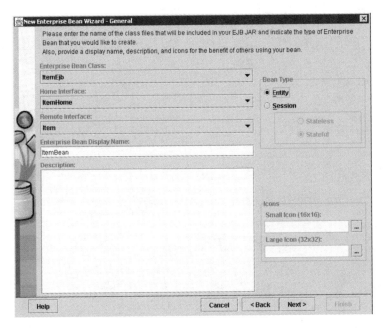

FIGURE 31-4 *The New Enterprise Bean Wizard — General dialog box is displayed.*

9. Under Bean Type, select Entity.

10. Click the Next button. The New Enterprise Bean Wizard — Entity Settings dialog box appears. See Figure 31-5.

11. Under Persistence Management, select Container-Managed Persistence. The various container-managed fields are displayed.

12. Select all the check boxes as displayed.

13. From the Primary Key Field Name list, select ItemCode.

14. Click the Next button. The New Enterprise Bean Wizard — Environment Entries dialog box appears.

15. Click the Next button. The New Enterprise Bean Wizard — Enterprise Bean References dialog box appears.

16. Click the Next button. The New Enterprise Bean Wizard — Resource References dialog box appears. See Figure 31-6.

17. Click the Next button. The New Enterprise Bean Wizard Security dialog box appears.

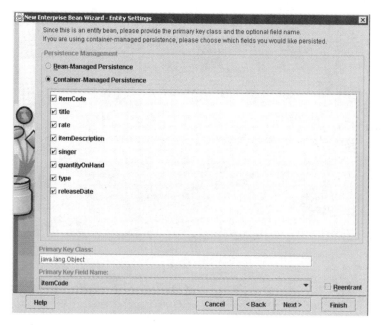

FIGURE 31-5 *The New Enterprise Bean Wizard — Entity Settings dialog box is displayed.*

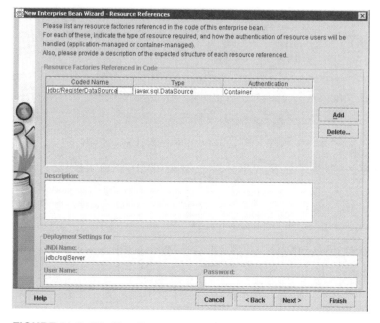

FIGURE 31-6 *The New Enterprise Bean Wizard — Resource References dialog box is displayed.*

18. In the New Enterprise Bean Wizard — Security dialog box, specify Coded Name as `jdbc/RegisterDataSource`. Specify JNDI Name as `jdbc/sqlServer`.

19. Click the Next button. The New Enterprise Bean Wizard — Transaction Management dialog box appears. See Figure 31-7.

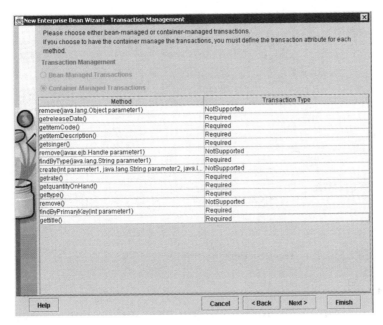

FIGURE 31-7 *The New Enterprise Bean Wizard — Transaction Management dialog box is displayed.*

20. In the New Enterprise Bean Wizard — Transaction Management dialog box, select `Required` from the drop-down list for the rows as shown.

21. Click theNext button. The New Enterprise Bean Wizard — Review Settings dialog box appears.

22. Click the Finish button. The enterprise bean is now packaged. Note that `ItemJar` appears below `MusicApp` in the upper-left pane. Also, verify that Application Deployment Tool: MusicApp appears as the title.

23. In the left pane, select `ItemJar` in the tree view.

24. Expand `ItemJar` and select `ItemBean`.

25. Click the Entity tab. The Entity page for `ItemBean` is displayed as shown in Figure 31-8.

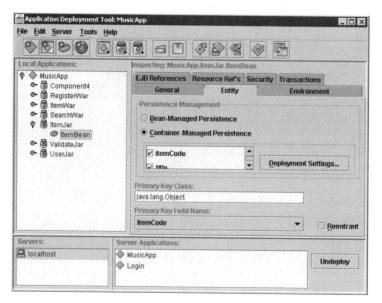

FIGURE 31-8 *The Entity page for* `ItemBean` *is displayed.*

26. Click the Deployment Settings button. The Deployment Settings dialog box appears. See Figure 31-9.

You need to maximize the dialog box if the Deployment Settings button is not visible.

27. In the Database JNDI Name box, enter `jdbc/sqlServer`.

28. Click the OK button. A message box appears with the Generate SQL Now button.

29. Click the Generate SQL Now button. The SQL Generator message box appears indicating SQL generation for the DBMS: Microsoft SQL Server. See Figure 31-10.

30. Click the OK button. The Provide finder SQL message box appears. See Figure 31-11.

31. Click the OK button. The message box closes.

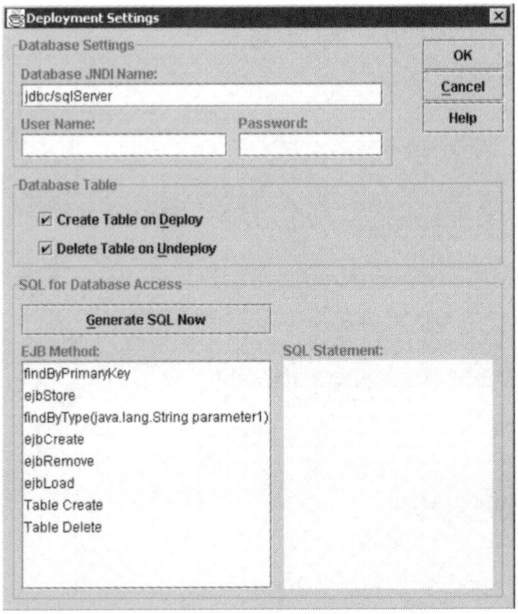

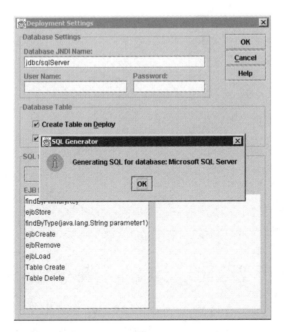

FIGURE 31-9 *The Deployment Settings dialog box is displayed.*

FIGURE 31-10 *The SQL Generator message box is displayed.*

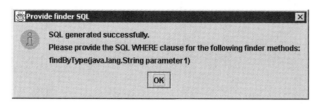

FIGURE 31-11 *The Provide finder SQL message box is displayed.*

32. From the EJB Method list, select `findByType(java.lang.String para-
meter1)`. In the SQL Statement area, a partial SQL query appears. See
Figure 31-12.

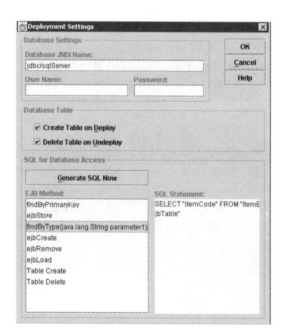

FIGURE 31-12 *The Deployment Settings dialog box is displayed.*

33. Add the following phrase to the SQL statement: `WHERE "type" = ?1.`
See Figure 31-13.

34. Click the OK button. The Deployment Settings dialog box closes.

35. Choose File, New Web Component. The New Web Component Wizard
— Introduction dialog box is displayed.

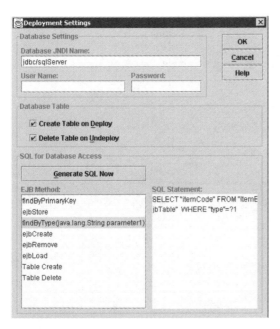

FIGURE 31-13 *The Deployment Settings dialog box is displayed with the updated SQL statement.*

36. Click the Next button. The New Web Component Wizard — WAR File General Properties dialog box is displayed. Note that MusicApp is displayed in the Web Component will Go In drop-down list.

37. Type SearchWar in the WAR Display Name text field.

38. Click the Add button in the Contents group box. The Add Files to .WAR — Add Content Files dialog box is displayed.

39. Click on Browse and select your working directory. Select SearchItem.jsp in the scroll pane. Click the Add button.

40. Click the Next button. The Add Files to .WAR — Add Class Files dialog box is displayed.

41. Click on Browse and select your working directory. Select SearchBean.class in the scroll pane.

42. Click the Add button in the Files to be Added group box. SearchBean.class gets displayed in the Files to be Added group box.

43. Click the Finish button. The New Web Component Wizard — WAR File General Properties dialog box appears, as seen in Figure 31-14.

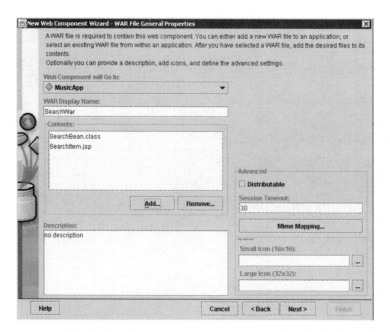

FIGURE 31-14 *The New Web Component Wizard — WAR File General Properties dialog box is displayed.*

Note that SearchBean.class and SearchItem.jsp are displayed in the Contents group box.

44. Click the Next button. The New Web Component Wizard — Choose Component Type dialog box is displayed.

45. Select JSP as the Web Component Type.

46. Click the Next button. The New Web Component Wizard — Component General Properties dialog box is displayed. See Figure 31-15.

47. Select SearchItem.jsp from the JSP Filename drop-down list. Type Component3 in the Web Component Display Name text field.

48. Click the Next button. The New Web Component Wizard — Component Initialization Parameters dialog box is displayed. Click the Next button.

49. The New Web Component Wizard — Component Aliases dialog box is displayed. Click the Add button.

50. Specify alias name as SearchAlias and then click the Next button.

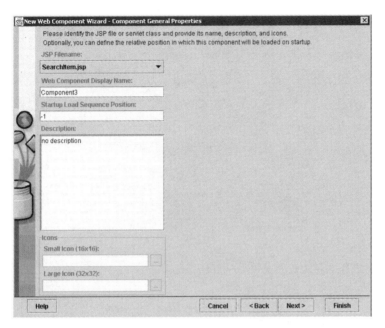

FIGURE 31-15 *The New Web Component Wizard — Component General Properties dialog box is displayed.*

51. The New Web Component Wizard — Component Security dialog box is displayed. You need to click the Next button.

52. The New Web Component Wizard — WAR File Environment dialog box is displayed. You need to click the Next button.

53. The New Web Component Wizard — Enterprise Bean References dialog box is displayed. See Figure 31-16.

54. Click the Add button. A new entry appears in the EJB's Referenced in Code group box.

55. Type `ejb/Item` in the Coded Name column. Select `Entity` from the Type column list. Type `ItemHome` in the Home column and `Item` in the Remote column. Specify JNDI Name as `Item`.

56. You need to click the Finish button. The Application Deployment Tool: MusicApp window is displayed.

57. Click the Web Context tab in the right pane.

58. Next, type `SearchContext` in the Context Root column.

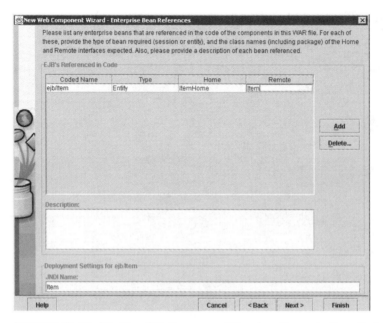

FIGURE 31-16 *The New Web Component Wizard — Enterprise Bean References dialog box appears.*

59. Select the Deploy Application command from the Tools menu. The Deploy MusicApp — Introduction dialog box is displayed.

60. You need to click the Next button. The Deploy MusicApp — JNDI Names dialog box is displayed.

61. Again, click the Next button. The Deploy MusicApp — .WAR Context Root dialog box is displayed.

62. Click the Next button. The Deploy MusicApp — Review dialog box is displayed.

63. Now, click the Finish button. The Deployment Progress dialog box is displayed.

64. Finally, you need to click the OK button when the deployment of MusicApp is complete.

Creating the Modify Item Page

The Modify Item page enables an administrator to modify details of items in the inventory. This consists of three pages:

◆ Admin_mod_item.jsp

◆ Admin_mod_item_update.jsp

◆ Admin_mod.jsp

Now, take a look at each of these pages in detail.

Admin_mod_item.jsp

This page displays a list of available items in the inventory. The administrator needs to select the item code of the item that needs to be identified. The code of the admin_mod_item.jsp is given in Listing 31-8.

Listing 31-8 Admin_mod_item.jsp

```
<html>
<head>
<meta http-equiv="Content-Type" content="text/html; charset=windows-1252">
<meta http-equiv="Content-Language" content="en-us">
<title>Modify Item Page</title>
</head>
<body bgcolor="#C0C0C0" topmargin="0"
background="http:\\localhost:8000\music\Background.bmp" >
<table border="0" width="100%">
  <tr>
    <td width="100%">
      <table border="0" width="97%" height="19">
        <tr>
          <td width="18%" height="13" valign="middle" align="right">
        <font face="Arial" size="5" color="#800000"><b><i>eMusicWorld·····&gt; The
World of Music</i></b></font>
          </td>
        </tr>
      </table>
    </td>
```

```
        </tr>
    </table>
    <form name="form" method="get"
    action="http://localhost:8000/music/admin_mod_item_update.jsp" >
    <table border="0" width="100%">
        <tr>
        <td width="100%"><table border="0" width="100%" height="19">
            <tr>
                <td width="9%" height="13" valign="middle" align="center"><font
    face="Arial" size="2" color="#800000"><b><a
    HREF="home_page.htm">Home</a></b></font></td>
                <td width="10%" height="13" valign="middle" align="center"></td>
                <td width="19%" height="13" valign="middle" align="center"></td>
                <td width="13%" height="13" valign="middle" align="center"></td>
                <td width="13%" height="13" valign="middle" align="center"></td>
                            <td width="11%" height="13" valign="middle" align="cen-
    ter"></td>
                                                    <td width="10%" height="13"
    valign="middle" align="center"></td>
                <td width="9%" height="13" valign="middle" align="center"><font
    face="Arial" size="2" color="#800000"><b><a
    HREF="http://localhost:8000/music/logout_page.jsp">Logout</b></font></td>
                <td width="9%" height="13" valign="middle" align="center"><font
    face="Arial" size="2" color="#800000"><b><a
    HREF="http://localhost:8000/music/admin_home_page_old.htm">Help</a></b></font></td>
            </tr>
        </table>
        </td>
    </tr>
    </table>
    <table border="1" width="100%" height="353">
        <tr>
            <td width="15%" height="347" valign="top">
    <p><font face="Arial" size="2" color="#800000"><b><a
    HREF="http://localhost:8000/music/admin_del_user.jsp">Delete User</a></b></font></p>
    <p><font face="Arial" size="2" color="#800000"><b><a
    HREF="http://localhost:8000/ItemContext/ItemAlias">Add Item</a></b></font></p>
    <p><font face="Arial" size="2" color="#800000"><b><a
```

```
HREF="http://localhost:8000/music/admin_mod_item.jsp">Modify Item</a></b></font></p>
<p><font face="Arial" size="2" color="#800000"><b>Sales Reports<br>---<a
HREF="http://localhost:8000/music/daily_sales_report.jsp">Choose a Date</a><br>---<a
HREF="http://localhost:8000/music/weekly_sales_report.jsp">Previous
Week</a><br>---<a
HREF="http://localhost:8000/music/monthly_sales_report.jsp">Previous
Month</a></b></font></p>
<p><font face="Arial" size="2" color="#800000"><b><a
HREF="http://localhost:8000/music/admin_wishlist.jsp">View
Wishlist</a></b></font></p>
<p><font face="Arial" size="2" color="#800000"><b><a
HREF="http://localhost:8000/music/admin_messages.jsp">View
Messages</a></b></font></p>
                </td>
    <td width="85%" height="347" valign="top">
<p align="center">   <b><u><font color="#800000" face="Arial"
size="2">Select
the Item to Modify</font></u></b>
</p>
  <p align="left" style="margin-left: -2; margin-right: -2; margin-top: 3; margin-
bottom: 3"><font face="Arial" size="2" color="#800000">Select
  Item Code: </font>
<select size="1" name="lstItemCode">
                <%@ page import="java.util.*" %>
                <%@ page import="java.sql.*" %>
                <%@ page import="java.text.*" %>
                <%@ page import="java.sql.Date" %>
                <%@ page language = "java" %>
                <%
                try{
                Class.forName("sun.jdbc.odbc.JdbcOdbcDriver");
                Connection connect;

connect=DriverManager.getConnection("jdbc:odbc:RegisterDataSource","","");
                Statement state;
                state = connect.createStatement();
                String strQuery1 = "select Item_Code from Item_Master order by
  Item_Code asc" ;
```

```
                    ResultSet result1 = state.executeQuery(strQuery1);
                    int ctr1=0;
        while(result1.next())
                    {
                    %>
                    <option><%=result1.getString("Item_Code")%></option>
    <%
                       }
                    connect.close();
                    }
                    catch(Exception e)
                    {
                                out.println("Exception: "+e);
                    }
    %>
    </select></p>
      <p align="left" style="margin-left: -2; margin-right: -2; margin-top: 3; margin-
    bottom: 3"> </p>
      <p align="center" style="margin-left: -2; margin-right: -2; margin-top: 3; mar-
    gin-bottom: 3"><input type="submit" value="Submit" name="submit"></p>
    </form>
      <p align="left" style="margin-left: -2; margin-right: -2; margin-top: 3; margin-
    bottom: 10"> </p>
      <p align="center" style="margin-left: -2; margin-right: -2; margin-top: 3; mar-
    gin-bottom: 10"> </p>
    </form>
    </body>
    </html>
```

Admin_mod_item_update.jsp

The admin_mod_item_update.jsp page displays the details of the item selected by the administrator. It displays the information in text boxes. The administrator can modify the values in the text boxes and then click the Submit button to save the modifications in the Music database. The source code of the admin_mod_item_update.jsp is available in Listing 31-9.

Listing 31-9   Admin_mod_item_update.jsp

```
<html>
<head>
<meta http-equiv="Content-Type" content="text/html; charset=windows-1252">
<meta http-equiv="Content-Language" content="en-us">
<title>Modify Item  Page</title>
</head>
<body bgcolor="#C0C0C0" topmargin="0"
background="http:\\localhost:8000\music\Background.bmp" >
<table border="0" width="100%">
  <tr>
    <td width="100%">
      <table border="0" width="97%" height="19">
        <tr>
          <td width="18%" height="13" valign="middle" align="right">
      <font face="Arial" size="5" color="#800000"><b><i>eMusicWorld-----&gt; The
World of Music</i></b></font>
          </td>
        </tr>
      </table>
    </td>
  </tr>
</table>
<form name="form" method="get" action="http://localhost:8000/music/admin_mod.jsp" >
<script language="javascript">
function year()
{
            document.write("<option value=\"- - - -\">- - - -</option>");
            for (i=1900;i<2000;i++)
            {
                                        document.write("<option
value="+i+">"+i+"</option>");
            }
}
function date()
{
            document.write("<option value=\"- - \">- - </option>");
```

```
                for (i=01;i<=31;i++)
                {
                                                    document.write("<option
value="+i+">"+i+"</option>");
                }
}
function verify()
{
                var ctr=0;

                var txtTitle=form.txtTitle.value;
                var txtRate=form.txtRate.value;
                var txtDesc=form.txtDesc.value;
                var txtSinger=form.txtSinger.value;
                var txtQty=form.txtQty.value;
                var txtType=form.txtType.value;


if((txtTitle.length==0)||(txtRate.length==0)||(txtDesc.length==0)||(txtSinger.length
==0)||(txtQty.length==0))
                {
                                alert("Please enter all the values.");
                                ctr=1;
                }
                if(ctr!=1)
                form.submit();
}
</script>

<table border="0" width="100%">
  <tr>
    <td width="100%"><table border="0" width="100%" height="19">
        <tr>
          <td width="9%" height="13" valign="middle" align="center"><font
face="Arial" size="2" color="#800000"><b><a
HREF="http://localhost:8000/music/home_page.htm">Home</a></b></font></td>
          <td width="10%" height="13" valign="middle" align="center"></td>
          <td width="19%" height="13" valign="middle" align="center"></td>
```

```
        <td width="13%" height="13" valign="middle" align="center"></td>
        <td width="13%" height="13" valign="middle" align="center"></td>
                    <td width="11%" height="13" valign="middle" align="cen-
ter"></td>
                                        <td width="10%" height="13"
valign="middle" align="center"></td>
        <td width="9%" height="13" valign="middle" align="center"><font
face="Arial" size="2" color="#800000"><b><a
HREF="http://localhost:8000/music/logout.jsp">Logout</b></font></td>
        <td width="9%" height="13" valign="middle" align="center"><font
face="Arial" size="2" color="#800000"><b><a
HREF="http://localhost:8000/music/admin_home_page_old.htm">Help</a></b></font></td>
        </tr>
      </table>
    </td>
  </tr>
</table>


<table border="1" width="100%" height="353">
  <tr>
    <td width="15%" height="347" valign="top">
<p><font face="Arial" size="2" color="#800000"><b><a
HREF="http://localhost:8000/music/admin_del_user.jsp">Delete User</a></b></font></p>
<p><font face="Arial" size="2" color="#800000"><b><a
HREF="http://localhost:8000/ItemContext/ItemAlias">Add Item</a></b></font></p>
<p><font face="Arial" size="2" color="#800000"><b><a
HREF="http://localhost:8000/music/admin_mod_item.jsp">Modify Item</a></b></font></p>
<p><font face="Arial" size="2" color="#800000"><b>Sales Reports<br>---<a
HREF="http://localhost:8000/music/daily_sales_report.jsp">Choose a Date</a><br>---<a
HREF="http:\\localhost:8000\weekly_sales_report.jsp">Previous
Week</a><br>---<a
HREF="http://localhost:8000/music/monthly_sales_report.jsp">Previous
Month</a></b></font></p>
<p><font face="Arial" size="2" color="#800000"><b><a
HREF="http://localhost:8000/music/admin_wishlist.jsp">View
Wishlist</a></b></font></p>
<p><font face="Arial" size="2" color="#800000"><b><a
HREF="http://localhost:8000/music/admin_messages.jsp">View
```

```
Messages</a></b></font></p>
            </td>
    <td width="85%" height="347" valign="top">
<p align="center">   <b><u><font color="#800000" face="Arial"
size="2">Modify
Item in the Inventory</font></u></b>
</p>
<%! String title, itemdesc, singer, type;%>
            <%! int qty;%>
            <%! float rate;%>
<%! String itemcode;%>

<%@ page import="java.util.*" %>
            <%@ page import="java.sql.*" %>
            <%@ page import="java.text.*" %>
            <%@ page import="java.sql.Date" %>
            <%@ page language = "java" %>
            <%
            try{
            Class.forName("sun.jdbc.odbc.JdbcOdbcDriver");
            Connection connect;
            itemcode=request.getParameter("lstItemCode");

connect=DriverManager.getConnection("jdbc:odbc:RegisterDataSource","","");
            Statement state;

            state = connect.createStatement();
            String strQuery1 = "select * from Item_Master where Item_Code='" +
itemcode +"'";
            ResultSet result1 = state.executeQuery(strQuery1);
            int ctr1=0;
    while(result1.next())
            {
                    title=result1.getString("Title");
                    rate=result1.getFloat("Rate");
                    itemdesc=result1.getString("Item_Desc");
                    singer=result1.getString("Singer");
                    qty=result1.getInt("Qty_on_hand");
```

```
                              type=result1.getString("Type");
                   }
                   connect.close();
                   }
                   catch(Exception e)
                   {
                              out.println("Exception: "+e);
                   }
%>
```
```html
<p align="left" style="margin-left: -2; margin-right: -2; margin-top: 3; margin-
bottom: 3"><font face="Arial" size="2" color="#800000">Item
Code:    
  <input type="text" name="itemcode" size="20" value=<%=itemcode%>></font></p>
  <p align="left" style="margin-left: -2; margin-right: -2; margin-top: 3; margin-
bottom: 3"><font face="Arial" size="2"
color="#800000">Title:          &n
bsp;  
  <input type="text" name="txtTitle" size="20" value=<%=title%>></font></p>
  <p align="left" style="margin-left: -2; margin-right: -2; margin-top: 3; margin-
bottom: 3"><font face="Arial" size="2" color="#800000">Price
($):       
  <input type="text" name="txtRate" size="20" value=<%=rate%>></font></p>
  <p align="left" style="margin-left: -2; margin-right: -2; margin-top: 3; margin-
bottom: 3"><font face="Arial" size="2"
color="#800000">Description:   
  <input type="text" name="txtDesc" size="20" value=<%=itemdesc%>></font></p>
  <p align="left" style="margin-left: -2; margin-right: -2; margin-top: 3; margin-
bottom: 3"><font face="Arial" size="2"
color="#800000">Singer:          
  <input type="text" name="txtSinger" size="20" value=<%=singer%>></font></p>
  <p align="left" style="margin-left: -2; margin-right: -2; margin-top: 3; margin-
bottom: 3"><font face="Arial" size="2"
color="#800000">Qty:          &nbs
p;   
  <input type="text" name="txtQty" size="20" value=<%=qty%>></font></p>
  <p align="left" style="margin-left: -2; margin-right: -2; margin-top: 3; margin-
bottom: 3"><font face="Arial" size="2"
color="#800000">Type:          &nb
```

```
sp; 
  <input type="text" name="txtType" size="20" value=<%=type%>> </font></p>
   </font></p>
  <p align="left" style="margin-left: -2; margin-right: -2; margin-top: 3; margin-
bottom: 10"> </p>
  <p align="center" style="margin-left: -2; margin-right: -2; margin-top: 3; mar-
gin-bottom: 10"><input type="button" value="Submit" name="Submit" OnClick="veri-
fy()"></p>
</form>
    </td>
  </tr>
  <tr>
    <td width="15%" height="347" valign="top">
            </td>
    <td width="85%" height="347" valign="top">
    </td>
  </tr>
</table>
</form>
</body>
</html>
```

admin_mod.jsp

When administrators enter the details in the admin_mod_item_update.jsp page and click the Submit button, the form is submitted to the admin_mod.jsp page. The admin_mod.jsp page updates the Item_master.jsp table in the Music database. The code for admin_mod.jsp is available in Listing 31-10.

Listing 31-10 admin_mod.jsp

```
<%! int update=0; %>
<%@ page import="java.util.*" %>
<%@ page import="java.sql.*" %>
<%@ page import="java.text.*" %>
<%@ page import="java.sql.Date" %>
<%@ page language = "java" %>
```

```
                <%
                try{
                Class.forName("sun.jdbc.odbc.JdbcOdbcDriver");
                Connection connect;

connect=DriverManager.getConnection("jdbc:odbc:RegisterDataSource","","");
                Statement state;
                state = connect.createStatement();
                Float fRate=new Float(request.getParameter("txtRate"));
                float floatRate=fRate.floatValue();
                Integer iQty=new Integer(request.getParameter("txtQty"));
                int intQty=iQty.intValue();
                out.println(floatRate);
                out.println(intQty);
                String strTitle=request.getParameter("txtTitle");
                String strDesc=request.getParameter("txtDesc");
                String strSinger=request.getParameter("txtSinger");
                String strType=request.getParameter("txtType");
                String strItemcode=request.getParameter("itemcode");
                out.println("strItemcode"+strItemcode);
                String strQuery2 = "Update Item_Master set Title='"+strTitle+"',
Rate='"+floatRate+"', Item_Desc='"+strDesc+"', Singer='"+strSinger+"',
Qty_on_hand='"+intQty+"', Type='"+strType+"' where Item_Code='"+strItemcode+"'";
                state.executeUpdate(strQuery2);
                connect.close();
%>

                <jsp:include page="http://localhost:8000/music/admin_home_page.htm"
flush="true"/>
<%

                }
                catch(Exception e){
                out.println("done exception" +e);
                }
                %>
```

Generating the Sales Reports

In the eMusicWorld, administrators can view three types of reports. These are:

- ◆ Based on a specific date
- ◆ Previous week
- ◆ Previous month

Now take a look at the code used create these reports.

Generating a Sales Report Based on a Selected Date

This report consist of two pages:

- ◆ daily_sales_report.jsp

  Displays the list containing the dates on which sales took place. The administrator needs to select a date from the list and then click the Submit button.

- ◆ view_daily_sales_report.jsp

  Extracts and displays the sales data for the day selected by the administrator in the daily_sales_report.jsp.

Now I'll show you the code of these two pages.

The daily_sales_report.jsp *Page*

The daily_sales_report.jsp page selects and displays in a list box the dates on which sales were made. The administrator needs to select a date and click the View Report button. The code of the daily_sales_report.jsp is given in Listing 31-11.

Listing 31-11 daily_sales_report.jsp

```
<html>
<head>
<meta http-equiv="Content-Type" content="text/html; charset=windows-1252">
<meta http-equiv="Content-Language" content="en-us">
<title>Sales Report Page</title>
</head>
```

```html
<body bgcolor="#C0C0C0" topmargin="0"
background="http:\\localhost:8000\music\Background.bmp" >
<table border="0" width="100%">
  <tr>
    <td width="100%">
      <table border="0" width="97%" height="19">
        <tr>
          <td width="18%" height="13" valign="middle" align="right">
        <font face="Arial" size="5" color="#800000"><b><i>eMusicWorld-----&gt; The
World of Music</i></b></font>
          </td>
        </tr>
      </table>
    </td>
  </tr>
</table>
<table border="0" width="100%">
  <tr>
    <td width="100%"><table border="0" width="100%" height="19">
        <tr>
          <td width="9%" height="13" valign="middle" align="center"><font
face="Arial" size="2" color="#800000"><b><a
HREF="http://localhost:8000/music/admin_home_page.htm">Home</a></b></font></td>
          <td width="10%" height="13" valign="middle" align="center"></td>
          <td width="19%" height="13" valign="middle" align="center"></td>
          <td width="13%" height="13" valign="middle" align="center"></td>
          <td width="13%" height="13" valign="middle" align="center"></td>
                      <td width="11%" height="13" valign="middle" align="cen-
ter"></td>
                                          <td width="10%" height="13"
valign="middle" align="center"></td>
          <td width="9%" height="13" valign="middle" align="center"><font
face="Arial" size="2" color="#800000"><b><a
HREF="http://localhost:8000/music/logout_page.jsp">Logout</b></font></td>
          <td width="9%" height="13" valign="middle" align="center"><font
face="Arial" size="2" color="#800000"><b><a
HREF="http://localhost:8000/music/admin_home_page_old.htm">Help</a></b></font></td>
        </tr>
```

```
      </table>
    </td>
  </tr>
</table>
<table border="1" width="100%" height="353">
  <tr>
   <td width="15%" height="347" valign="top">
<p><font face="Arial" size="2" color="#800000"><b><a
HREF="http://localhost:8000/music/admin_del_user.jsp">Delete User</a></b></font></p>
<p><font face="Arial" size="2" color="#800000"><b><a
HREF="http://localhost:8000/ItemContext/ItemAlias">Add Item</a></b></font></p>
<p><font face="Arial" size="2" color="#800000"><b><a
HREF="admin_mod_item.jsp">Modify Item</a></b></font></p>
<p><font face="Arial" size="2" color="#800000"><b>Sales Reports<br>---<a
HREF="http://localhost:8000/music/daily_sales_report.jsp">Choose a Date</a><br>---<a
HREF="http://localhost:8000/music/weekly_sales_report.jsp">Previous
Week</a><br>---<a
HREF="http://localhost:8000/music/monthly_sales_report.jsp">Previous
Month</a></b></font></p>
<p><font face="Arial" size="2" color="#800000"><b><a
HREF="http://localhost:8000/music/admin_wishlist.jsp">View
Wishlist</a></b></font></p>
<p><font face="Arial" size="2" color="#800000"><b><a
HREF="http://localhost:8000/music/admin_messages.jsp">View
Messages</a></b></font></p>
</td>
    <td width="85%" height="347" valign="top">
<p align="center"><b><u><font face="Arial" color="#800000" size="2">Sales
Report</font></u></b></p>
<form method="POST"
action="http://localhost:8000/music/view_daily_sales_report.jsp">
  <table border="0" width="100%" height="1">
    <tr>
      <td width="100%" valign="top" align="left" height="76">
  <p align="left"><b><u><font face="Arial" color="#800000" size="2">Select the
  date from the list to view the sales report:</font></u></b></p>
<p><select size="1" name="date">
                <%@ page import="java.util.*" %>
```

```
<%@ page import="java.sql.*" %>
<%@ page import="java.text.*" %>
<%@ page import="java.sql.Date" %>
<%@ page language = "java" %>
<%
try{
Class.forName("sun.jdbc.odbc.JdbcOdbcDriver");
Connection connect;

connect=DriverManager.getConnection("jdbc:odbc:RegisterDataSource","","");
Statement state;
state = connect.createStatement();
String saledate;
<!--Display the dates on which sales happened-->
String strQuery1 = "select Sale_Date from Sales_Master group by
Sale_Date order by Sale_Date desc";
ResultSet result = state.executeQuery(strQuery1);
while(result.next())
{
        saledate=result.getString("Sale_Date");
        saledate=saledate.substring(0,10);
        out.println("<option>"+ saledate+"</option>");
}
connect.close();
}
catch(Exception e)
{
        out.println("Exception: " + e + " occurred.");
}
%>
  </select></p>
  <p align="center"><input type="submit" value="View Report"
name="view_report"></td>
    </tr>
  </table>
</form>
    </td>
  </tr>
```

```
</table>
</body>
</html>
```

The view_daily_sales_report.jsp Page

The view_daily_sales_report.jsp page displays the sales details for the date specified by the administrator in the daily_sales_report.jsp page. The code for this page is given in Listing 31-12.

Listing 31-12 view_daily_sales_report.jsp

```
<html>
<head>
<meta http-equiv="Content-Type" content="text/html; charset=windows-1252">
<meta http-equiv="Content-Language" content="en-us">
<title>Sales Report Page</title>
</head>
<body bgcolor="#C0C0C0" topmargin="0"
background="http:\\localhost:8000\music\Background.bmp" >
<table border="0" width="100%">
  <tr>
    <td width="100%">
      <table border="0" width="97%" height="19">
        <tr>
          <td width="18%" height="13" valign="middle" align="right">
        <font face="Arial" size="5" color="#800000"><b><i>eMusicWorld-----&gt; The
World of Music</i></b></font>
          </td>
        </tr>
      </table>
    </td>
  </tr>
</table>

<form method="get" action="http://localhost:8000/music/admin_home_page.htm">
<table border="0" width="100%">
```

```
    <tr>
      <td width="100%"><table border="0" width="100%" height="19">
        <tr>
          <td width="9%" height="13" valign="middle" align="center"><font
face="Arial" size="2" color="#800000"><b><a
HREF="http://localhost:8000/music/home_page.htm">Home</a></b></font></td>
          <td width="10%" height="13" valign="middle" align="center"></td>
          <td width="19%" height="13" valign="middle" align="center"></td>
          <td width="13%" height="13" valign="middle" align="center"></td>
          <td width="13%" height="13" valign="middle" align="center"></td>
                        <td width="11%" height="13" valign="middle" align="cen-
ter"></td>
                                                <td width="10%" height="13"
valign="middle" align="center"></td>
          <td width="9%" height="13" valign="middle" align="center"><font
face="Arial" size="2" color="#800000"><b><a
HREF="http://localhost:8000/music/logout_page.jsp">Logout</b></font></td>
          <td width="9%" height="13" valign="middle" align="center"><font
face="Arial" size="2" color="#800000"><b><a
HREF="http://localhost:8000/music/admin_home_page_old.htm">Help</a></b></font></td>
        </tr>
      </table>
    </td>
  </tr>
</table>
<table border="1" width="100%" height="353">
  <tr>
    <td width="15%" height="347" valign="top">

<p><font face="Arial" size="2" color="#800000"><b><a
HREF="http://localhost:8000/music/admin_del_user.jsp">Delete User</a></b></font></p>
<p><font face="Arial" size="2" color="#800000"><b><a
HREF="http://localhost:8000/ItemContext/ItemAlias">Add Item</a></b></font></p>
<p><font face="Arial" size="2" color="#800000"><b><a
HREF="http://localhost:8000/music/admin_mod_item.jsp">Modify Item</a></b></font></p>
<p><font face="Arial" size="2" color="#800000"><b>Sales Reports<br>---<a
HREF="http://localhost:8000/music/daily_sales_report.jsp">Choose a Date</a><br>---<a
```

```
HREF="http://localhost:8000/music/weekly_sales_report.jsp">Previous
Week</a><br>---<a
HREF="http://localhost:8000/music/monthly_sales_report.jsp">Previous
Month</a></b></font></p>
<p><font face="Arial" size="2" color="#800000"><b><a
HREF="http://localhost:8000/music/admin_wishlist.jsp">View
Wishlist</a></b></font></p>
<p><font face="Arial" size="2" color="#800000"><b><a
HREF="http://localhost:8000/music/admin_messages.jsp">View
Messages</a></b></font></p>
                </td>
    <td width="85%" height="347" valign="top">
<p align="center"><b><u><font face="Arial" color="#800000" size="2">Daily Sales
Report</font></u></b></p>
<!--Get the date selected by the user in the previous page-->
            <%
                        String date;
                        date=request.getParameter("date");
            %>
<p align="left"><b><u><font face="Arial" color="#800000" size="2">Sales Report for
the Date:</u> <%=date%></font></b></p>
<table border="1" width="100%">
  <tr>
<td width="20%"><font face="Arial" size="2" color="#800000"><b>Buyer</b></font></td>
    <td width="15%"><font face="Arial" size="2" color="#800000"><b>Item
Code</b></font></td>
<td width="20%"><font face="Arial" size="2" color="#800000"><b>Item
Desc</b></font></td>
    <td width="10%"><font face="Arial" size="2"
color="#800000"><b>Quantity</b></font></td>
    <td width="15%"><font face="Arial" size="2"
color="#800000"><b>Price($)</b></font></td>
<td width="15%"><font face="Arial" size="2"
color="#800000"><b>Total($)</b></font></td>
  </tr>
            <%! float totalsale;%>
            <%@ page import="java.util.*" %>
            <%@ page import="java.sql.*" %>
```

```
                    <%@ page import="java.text.*" %>
                    <%@ page import="java.sql.Date" %>
                    <%@ page language = "java" %>
                    <%
                    try{
                    Class.forName("sun.jdbc.odbc.JdbcOdbcDriver");
                    Connection connect;

connect=DriverManager.getConnection("jdbc:odbc:RegisterDataSource","","");
                    Statement state;
                    state = connect.createStatement();
                    String saledate;
                    saledate=request.getParameter("date");
                    String strQuery1 = "select Sales_master.*, Item_Master.Item_Desc
from Sales_Master, Item_Master where Sale_date='" + saledate + "' and
Item_Master.Item_Code=Sales_master.Item_code";
                    ResultSet result = state.executeQuery(strQuery1);
                    String username, itemcode, itemdesc;
                    int quantity;
                    float rate;
                    totalsale=0;
<!--Display the result-->
                    while(result.next())
                    {
                                    itemcode=result.getString("Item_code");
                                    quantity=result.getInt("Sale_qty");
                                    rate=result.getFloat("Rate");
                                    username=result.getString("User_name");
                                    itemdesc=result.getString("Item_Desc");
                                    totalsale=totalsale+(rate*quantity);

                                    out.println("<tr>");
    out.println("<td width=\"20%\"><font face=\"Arial\" size=\"2\"
color=\"#800000\">" + username + "</font></td>");
    out.println("<td width=\"20%\"><font face=\"Arial\" size=\"2\" color=\"#800000\">" +
itemcode + "</font></td>");
    out.println("<td width=\"20%\"><font face=\"Arial\" size=\"2\" color=\"#800000\">" +
itemdesc+ "</font></td>");
```

```
out.println("<td width=\"20%\"><font face=\"Arial\" size=\"2\" color=\"#800000\">" +
quantity+ "</font></td>");
out.println("<td width=\"20%\"><font face=\"Arial\" size=\"2\" color=\"#800000\">" +
rate+ "</font></td>");
out.println("<td width=\"20%\"><font face=\"Arial\" size=\"2\" color=\"#800000\">" +
rate*quantity+ "</font></td>");

        out.println("</tr>");
                }
                connect.close();
                }
                catch(Exception e)
                {
                                out.println("Exception: " + e + " occurred.");
                }
%>




   <tr>
     <td> </td>
     <td> </td>
     <td> </td>
     <td> </td>
     <td><font face="Arial" size="2" color="#800000"><b>Total
Sale($)</b></font></td>
     <td><font face="Arial" size="2"
color="#800000"><b><%=totalsale%></b></font></td>
   </tr>
</table>
   <table border="0" width="100%">
     <tr>
       <td width="50%" valign="middle" align="right">
   <input type="submit" value="OK" name="ok"></td>
       <td width="50%" valign="middle" align="right"></td>
     </tr>
   </table>
```

```
</form>
    </td>
  </tr>
</table>
</body>
</html>
```

The output of the `daily_sales_report.jsp` and the `view_daily_sales_report.jsp` pages are displayed in Figures 31-17 and 31-18.

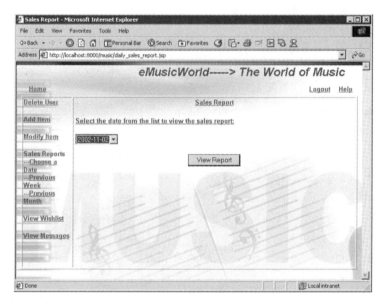

FIGURE 31-17 *The output of the* `daily_sales_report.jsp` *page is shown here.*

Generating a Sales Report for the Previous Week

The `eMusicWorld` application also enables administrators to view the sales data of the past week. The code to do this is given in Listing 31-13.

Listing 31-13 weekly_sales_report.jsp

```
<html>
<head>
```

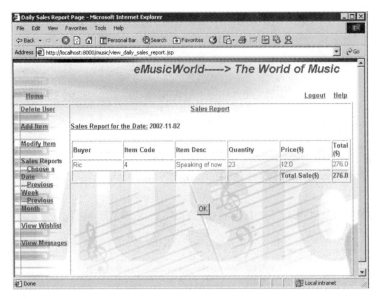

FIGURE 31-18 *The output of the* `view_daily_sales_report.jsp` *page is shown here.*

```
<meta http-equiv="Content-Type" content="text/html; charset=windows-1252">
<meta http-equiv="Content-Language" content="en-us">
<title>Weekly Sales Report</title>
</head>
<body bgcolor="#C0C0C0" topmargin="0"
background="http:\\localhost:8000\music\Background.bmp" >
<table border="0" width="100%">
  <tr>
    <td width="100%">
      <table border="0" width="97%" height="19">
        <tr>
          <td width="18%" height="13" valign="middle" align="right">
      <font face="Arial" size="5" color="#800000"><b><i>eMusicWorld-----&gt; The
World of Music</i></b></font>
          </td>
        </tr>
      </table>
    </td>
  </tr>
</table>
```

```
<form method="get" action="http://localhost:8000/music/admin_home_page.htm">
<table border="0" width="100%">
  <tr>
    <td width="100%"><table border="0" width="100%" height="19">
        <tr>
          <td width="9%" height="13" valign="middle" align="center"><font
face="Arial" size="2" color="#800000"><b><a
HREF="http://localhost:8000/music/home_page.htm">Home</a></b></font></td>
          <td width="10%" height="13" valign="middle" align="center"></td>
          <td width="19%" height="13" valign="middle" align="center"></td>
          <td width="13%" height="13" valign="middle" align="center"></td>
          <td width="13%" height="13" valign="middle" align="center"></td>
                        <td width="11%" height="13" valign="middle" align="cen-
ter"></td>
                                              <td width="10%" height="13"
valign="middle" align="center"></td>
          <td width="9%" height="13" valign="middle" align="center"><font
face="Arial" size="2" color="#800000"><b><a
HREF="http://localhost:8000/music/logout_page.jsp">Logout</b></font></td>
          <td width="9%" height="13" valign="middle" align="center"><font
face="Arial" size="2" color="#800000"><b><a
HREF="http://localhost:8000/music/admin_home_page_old.htm">Help</a></b></font></td>
        </tr>
      </table>
    </td>
  </tr>
</table>
<table border="1" width="100%" height="353">
  <tr>
    <td width="15%" height="347" valign="top">
<p><font face="Arial" size="2" color="#800000"><b><a
HREF="http://localhost:8000/music/admin_del_user.jsp">Delete User</a></b></font></p>
<p><font face="Arial" size="2" color="#800000"><b><a
HREF="http://localhost:8000/ItemContext/ItemAlias">Add Item</a></b></font></p>
<p><font face="Arial" size="2" color="#800000"><b><a
HREF="http://localhost:8000/music/admin_mod_item.jsp">Modify Item</a></b></font></p>
<p><font face="Arial" size="2" color="#800000"><b>Sales Reports<br>···<a
HREF="http://localhost:8000/music/daily_sales_report.jsp">Choose a Date</a><br>···<a
```

```
HREF="http://localhost:8000/music/weekly_sales_report.jsp">Previous
Week</a><br>---<a
HREF="http://localhost:8000/music/monthly_sales_report.jsp">Previous
Month</a></b></font></p>
<p><font face="Arial" size="2" color="#800000"><b><a
HREF="http://localhost:8000/music/admin_wishlist.jsp">View
Wishlist</a></b></font></p>
<p><font face="Arial" size="2" color="#800000"><b><a
HREF="http://localhost:8000/music/admin_messages.jsp">View
Messages</a></b></font></p>
                    </td>
    <td width="85%" height="347" valign="top">
<p align="center"><b><u><font face="Arial" color="#800000" size="2">Sales Report of
Previous Week</font></u></b></p>
<table border="1" width="100%">
  <tr>
<td width="16%"><font face="Arial" size="2" color="#800000"><b>Sale
Date</b></font></td>
<td width="14%"><font face="Arial" size="2" color="#800000"><b>Buyer</b></font></td>
    <td width="13%"><font face="Arial" size="2" color="#800000"><b>Item
Code</b></font></td>
<td width="16%"><font face="Arial" size="2" color="#800000"><b>Item
Desc</b></font></td>
    <td width="13%"><font face="Arial" size="2"
color="#800000"><b>Quantity</b></font></td>
<td width="13%"><font face="Arial" size="2"
color="#800000"><b>Price($)</b></font></td>
    <td width="13%"><font face="Arial" size="2"
color="#800000"><b>Total($)</b></font></td>
  </tr>
                    <%! float totalsale;%>
                    <%@ page import="java.util.*" %>
                    <%@ page import="java.sql.*" %>
                    <%@ page import="java.text.*" %>
                    <%@ page import="java.sql.Date" %>
                    <%@ page language = "java" %>
                    <%
                    try{
```

```
                    Class.forName("sun.jdbc.odbc.JdbcOdbcDriver");
                    Connection connect;

connect=DriverManager.getConnection("jdbc:odbc:RegisterDataSource","","");
                    Statement state;
                    state = connect.createStatement();
                    String strQuery1 = "select Sales_master.*, Item_Master.Item_Desc
from Sales_Master, Item_Master where datediff(wk,Sale_Date, getdate())<=1 and
Item_Master.Item_Code=Sales_master.Item_code";
                    ResultSet result = state.executeQuery(strQuery1);
                    String username, itemcode, itemdesc, saledate;
                    int quantity;
                    float rate;
                    totalsale=0;
<!--Print the report.-->
                    while(result.next())
                    {
                                    saledate=result.getString("Sale_Date");
                                    saledate=saledate.substring(0,10);
                                    itemcode=result.getString("Item_code");
                                    quantity=result.getInt("Sale_qty");
                                    rate=result.getFloat("Rate");
                                    username=result.getString("User_name");
                                    itemdesc=result.getString("Item_Desc");
                                    totalsale=totalsale+(rate*quantity);

                                    out.println("<tr>");
                    out.println("<td ><font face=\"Arial\" size=\"2\"
color=\"#800000\">" + saledate + "</font></td>");
    out.println("<td ><font face=\"Arial\" size=\"2\" color=\"#800000\">" + user-
name + "</font></td>");
out.println("<td ><font face=\"Arial\" size=\"2\" color=\"#800000\">" + itemcode +
"</font></td>");
out.println("<td ><font face=\"Arial\" size=\"2\" color=\"#800000\">" + itemdesc+
"</font></td>");
out.println("<td ><font face=\"Arial\" size=\"2\" color=\"#800000\">" + quantity+
"</font></td>");
out.println("<td ><font face=\"Arial\" size=\"2\" color=\"#800000\">" + rate+
```

```
"</font></td>");
out.println("<td ><font face=\"Arial\" size=\"2\" color=\"#800000\">" + rate*quanti-
ty+ "</font></td>");
       out.println("</tr>");
                    }
                    connect.close();
                    }
                    catch(Exception e)
                    {
                                  out.println("Exception: " + e + " occurred.");
                    }
%>
  <tr>
    <td > </td>
    <td > </td>
    <td > </td>
                  <td > </td>
                  <td > </td>
    <td width="15%"><font face="Arial" size="2" color="#800000"><b>Total
Sale($)</b></font></td>
<!--Display the total sale value-->
    <td><font face="Arial" size="2"
color="#800000"><b><%=totalsale%></b></font></td>
  </tr>
</table>
  <table border="0" width="100%">
    <tr>
      <td width="50%" valign="middle" align="right">
  <input type="submit" value="OK" name="submit_ok"></td>
      <td width="50%" valign="middle" align="right"></td>
    </tr>
  </table>
</form>
    </td>
  </tr>
</table>
</body>
</html>
```

The output of the weekly_sales_report.jsp is displayed in Figure 31-19.

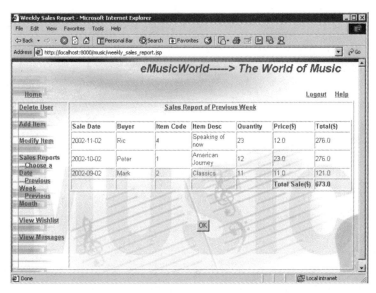

FIGURE 31-19 *The output of the* weekly_sales_report.jsp *page is shown here.*

Generating a Sales Report for the Previous Month

The eMusicWorld application also enables administrators to view the sales data of the past month. The code to do this is given in Listing 31-14.

Listing 31-14   monthly_sales_report.jsp

```
<html>
<head>
<meta http-equiv="Content-Type" content="text/html; charset=windows-1252">
<meta http-equiv="Content-Language" content="en-us">
<title>Monthly Sales Report Page</title>
</head>
<body bgcolor="#C0C0C0" topmargin="0"
background="http:\\localhost:8000\music\Background.bmp" >
<table border="0" width="100%">
  <tr>
    <td width="100%">
```

```
<table border="0" width="97%" height="19">
  <tr>
    <td width="18%" height="13" valign="middle" align="right">
<font face="Arial" size="5" color="#800000"><b><i>eMusicWorld-----&gt; The
World of Music</i></b></font>
      </td>
    </tr>
  </table>
    </td>
  </tr>
</table>

<form method="get" action="http://localhost:8000/music/admin_home_page.htm">
<table border="0" width="100%">
  <tr>
    <td width="100%">
    </td>
  </tr>
  <tr>
    <td width="100%"><table border="0" width="100%" height="19">
      <tr>
        <td width="9%" height="13" valign="middle" align="center"><font
face="Arial" size="2" color="#800000"><b><a
HREF="http://localhost:8000/music/home_page.htm">Home</a></b></font></td>
        <td width="10%" height="13" valign="middle" align="center"></td>
        <td width="19%" height="13" valign="middle" align="center"></td>
        <td width="13%" height="13" valign="middle" align="center"></td>
        <td width="13%" height="13" valign="middle" align="center"></td>
                    <td width="11%" height="13" valign="middle" align="cen-
ter"></td>
                <td width="10%" height="13" valign="middle" align="center"></td>
        <td width="9%" height="13" valign="middle" align="center"><font
face="Arial" size="2" color="#800000"><b><a
HREF="http://localhost:8000/music/home_page.htm">Logout</b></font></td>
        <td width="9%" height="13" valign="middle" align="center"><font
face="Arial" size="2" color="#800000"><b><a
HREF="http://localhost:8000/music/admin_home_page_old.htm">Help</a></b></font></td>
      </tr>
```

```
        </table>
      </td>
    </tr>
</table>
<table border="1" width="100%" height="353">
  <tr>
    <td width="15%" height="347" valign="top">
<p><font face="Arial" size="2" color="#800000"><b><a
HREF="http://localhost:8000/music/admin_del_user.jsp">Delete User</a></b></font></p>
<p><font face="Arial" size="2" color="#800000"><b><a
HREF="http://localhost:8000/ItemContext/ItemAlias">Add Item</a></b></font></p>
<p><font face="Arial" size="2" color="#800000"><b><a
HREF="http://localhost:8000/music/admin_mod_item.jsp">Modify Item</a></b></font></p>
<p><font face="Arial" size="2" color="#800000"><b>Sales Reports<br>---<a
HREF="http://localhost:8000/music/daily_sales_report.jsp">Choose a Date</a><br>---<a
HREF="http:\\localhost:8000\weekly_sales_report.jsp">Previous
Week</a><br>---<a
HREF="http://localhost:8000/music/monthly_sales_report.jsp">Previous
Month</a></b></font></p>
<p><font face="Arial" size="2" color="#800000"><b><a
HREF="http://localhost:8000/music/admin_wishlist.jsp">View
Wishlist</a></b></font></p>
<p><font face="Arial" size="2" color="#800000"><b><a
HREF="http://localhost:8000/music/admin_messages.jsp">View
Messages</a></b></font></p>
                  </td>
      <td width="85%" height="347" valign="top">
<p align="center">
<b><u><font face="Arial" color="#800000" size="2">Sales Report of Previous
Month</font></u></b></p>
<table border="1" width="100%">
  <tr>
<td ><font face="Arial" size="2" color="#800000"><b>Sale Date</b></font></td>
<td ><font face="Arial" size="2" color="#800000"><b>Buyer</b></font></td>
    <td ><font face="Arial" size="2" color="#800000"><b>Item Code</b></font></td>
<td ><font face="Arial" size="2" color="#800000"><b>Item Desc</b></font></td>
    <td ><font face="Arial" size="2" color="#800000"><b>Quantity</b></font></td>
<td ><font face="Arial" size="2" color="#800000"><b>Price($)</b></font></td>
```

```
    <td ><font face="Arial" size="2" color="#800000"><b>Total($)</b></font></td>
</tr>
                <%! float totalsale;%>
                <%@ page import="java.util.*" %>
                <%@ page import="java.sql.*" %>
                <%@ page import="java.text.*" %>
                <%@ page import="java.sql.Date" %>
                <%@ page language = "java" %>
                <%
                try{
                Class.forName("sun.jdbc.odbc.JdbcOdbcDriver");
                Connection connect;

connect=DriverManager.getConnection("jdbc:odbc:RegisterDataSource","","");
                Statement state;
                state = connect.createStatement();
                String strQuery1 = "select Sales_master.*, Item_Master.Item_Desc
from Sales_Master, Item_Master where datediff(mm,Sale_Date, getdate())=1 and
Item_Master.Item_Code=Sales_master.Item_code";
                ResultSet result = state.executeQuery(strQuery1);
                String username, itemcode, itemdesc, saledate;
                int quantity;
                float rate;
                totalsale=0;
<!--Print the Report-->
                while(result.next())
                {
                        saledate=result.getString("Sale_Date");
                        saledate=saledate.substring(0,10);
                        itemcode=result.getString("Item_code");
                        quantity=result.getInt("Sale_qty");
                        rate=result.getFloat("Rate");
                        username=result.getString("User_name");
                        itemdesc=result.getString("Item_Desc");
                        totalsale=totalsale+(rate*quantity);

                        out.println("<tr>");
                out.println("<td ><font face=\"Arial\" size=\"2\"
```

```
color=\"#800000\">" + saledate + "</font></td>");
    out.println("<td ><font face=\"Arial\" size=\"2\" color=\"#800000\">" + user-
name + "</font></td>");
out.println("<td ><font face=\"Arial\" size=\"2\" color=\"#800000\">" + itemcode +
"</font></td>");
out.println("<td ><font face=\"Arial\" size=\"2\" color=\"#800000\">" + itemdesc+
"</font></td>");
out.println("<td ><font face=\"Arial\" size=\"2\" color=\"#800000\">" + quantity+
"</font></td>");
out.println("<td ><font face=\"Arial\" size=\"2\" color=\"#800000\">" + rate+
"</font></td>");
out.println("<td ><font face=\"Arial\" size=\"2\" color=\"#800000\">" + rate*quanti-
ty+ "</font></td>");

        out.println("</tr>");
                }
                connect.close();
                }
                catch(Exception e)
                {
                        out.println("Exception: " + e + " occurred.");
                }
%>
  <tr>
    <td > </td>
    <td > </td>
    <td > </td>
                <td > </td>
<td > </td>
    <td ><font face="Arial" size="2" color="#800000"><b>Total Sale
($)</b></font></td>
    <td ><font face="Arial" size="2"
color="#800000"><b><%=totalsale%></b></font></td>
  </tr>
</table>
  <table border="0" width="100%">
    <tr>
      <td width="50%" valign="middle" align="right">
```

```
<input type="submit" value="OK" name="submit_ok"></td>
    <td width="50%" valign="middle" align="right"></td>
  </tr>
</table>
</form>
    </td>
  </tr>
</table>
</body>
</html>
```

The output of the monthly_sales_report.jsp is displayed in Figure 31-20.

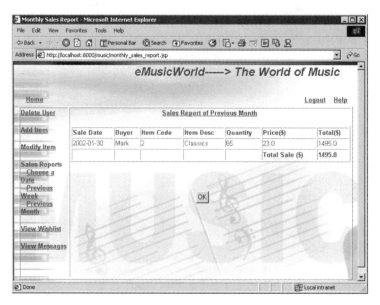

FIGURE 31-20 *The output of the* monthly_sales_report.jsp *page is shown here.*

Creating the View Wishlist Page

The View Wishlist page enables an administrator to view the user's wishlist. The code for this page is given in Listing 31-15.

Listing 31-15   admin_wishlist.jsp

```
<html>
<head>
<meta http-equiv="Content-Type" content="text/html; charset=windows-1252">
<meta http-equiv="Content-Language" content="en-us">
<title>Wishlist Page</title>
</head>
<body bgcolor="#C0C0C0" topmargin="0"
background="http:\\localhost:8000\music\Background.bmp" >
<table border="0" width="100%">
  <tr>
    <td width="100%">
      <table border="0" width="97%" height="19">
        <tr>
          <td width="18%" height="13" valign="middle" align="right">
        <font face="Arial" size="5" color="#800000"><b><i>eMusicWorld-----&gt; The
World of Music</i></b></font>
          </td>
        </tr>
      </table>
    </td>
  </tr>
</table>

<form method="get" action="http://localhost:8000/music/admin_home_page.htm">
<table border="0" width="100%">
  <tr>
    <td width="100%"><table border="0" width="100%" height="19">
        <tr>
          <td width="9%" height="13" valign="middle" align="center"><font
face="Arial" size="2" color="#800000"><b><a
HREF="welcome_page.htm">Home</a></b></font></td>
          <td width="10%" height="13" valign="middle" align="center"></td>
          <td width="19%" height="13" valign="middle" align="center"></td>
          <td width="13%" height="13" valign="middle" align="center"></td>
          <td width="13%" height="13" valign="middle" align="center"></td>
                    <td width="11%" height="13" valign="middle" align="cen-
```

```
ter"></td>
                                                    <td width="10%" height="13"
valign="middle" align="center"></td>
            <td width="9%" height="13" valign="middle" align="center"><font
face="Arial" size="2" color="#800000"><b><a
HREF="http://localhost:8000/music/logout_page.jsp">Logout</b></font></td>
            <td width="9%" height="13" valign="middle" align="center"><font
face="Arial" size="2" color="#800000"><b><a
HREF="http://localhost:8000/music/admin_home_page_old.htm">Help</a></b></font></td>
        </tr>
      </table>
    </td>
  </tr>
</table>
<table border="1" width="100%" height="353">
  <tr>
      <td width="15%" height="347" valign="top">
<p><font face="Arial" size="2" color="#800000"><b><a
HREF="http://localhost:8000/music/admin_del_user.jsp">Delete User</a></b></font></p>
<p><font face="Arial" size="2" color="#800000"><b><a
HREF="http://localhost:8000/ItemContext/ItemAlias">Add Item</a></b></font></p>
<p><font face="Arial" size="2" color="#800000"><b><a
HREF="http://localhost:8000/music/admin_mod_item.jsp">Modify Item</a></b></font></p>
<p><font face="Arial" size="2" color="#800000"><b>Sales Reports<br>---<a
HREF="http://localhost:8000/music/daily_sales_report.jsp">Choose a Date</a><br>---<a
HREF="http:\\localhost:8000\weekly_sales_report.jsp">Previous
Week</a><br>---<a
HREF="http://localhost:8000/music/monthly_sales_report.jsp">Previous
Month</a></b></font></p>
<p><font face="Arial" size="2" color="#800000"><b><a
HREF="http://localhost:8000/music/admin_wishlist.jsp">View
Wishlist</a></b></font></p>
<p><font face="Arial" size="2" color="#800000"><b><a
HREF="http://localhost:8000/music/admin_messages.jsp">View
Messages</a></b></font></p>
                </td>
      <td width="85%" height="347" valign="top">
<p align="center">
```

```
<b><u><font face="Arial" color="#800000" size="2">User's Wishlist</font></u></b></p>
<table border="1" width="86%">
  <tr>
    <td width="20%"><font face="Arial" size="2" color="#800000"><b>User
Name</b></font></td>
    <td width="15%"><font face="Arial" size="2" color="#800000"><b>Item
Code</b></font></td>
    <td width="15%"><font face="Arial" size="2" color="#800000"><b>Item
Desc</b></font></td>
    <td width="10%"><font face="Arial" size="2"
color="#800000"><b>Quantity</b></font></td>
    <td width="20%"><font face="Arial" size="2" color="#800000"><b>Listed
on</b></font></td>
  </tr>
                <%@ page import="java.util.*" %>
                <%@ page import="java.sql.*" %>
                <%@ page import="java.text.*" %>
                <%@ page import="java.sql.Date" %>
                <%@ page language = "java" %>
                <%
                try{
                Class.forName("sun.jdbc.odbc.JdbcOdbcDriver");
                Connection connect, connect1;

connect=DriverManager.getConnection("jdbc:odbc:RegisterDataSource","","");
                Statement state;
                state = connect.createStatement();
                String strQuery1 = "select User_name, Item_code, Qty, Wish_Date from
Wishlist_Info Group by User_name, Item_code, Qty, Wish_Date order by User_name
asc";
                ResultSet result = state.executeQuery(strQuery1);
                String username, itemcode, itemdesc, qty, wishdate;
                while(result.next())
                {
                        username=result.getString("User_name");

                        itemcode=result.getString("Item_code");
```

```
connect1=DriverManager.getConnection("jdbc:odbc:RegisterDataSource","","");
                            itemcode=itemcode.trim();
                            Statement state1;
                            state1 = connect1.createStatement();
                            String strQuery2 = "select Item_Desc from Item_Master
where Item_Code='"+itemcode+"'";
                            ResultSet result1 = state1.executeQuery(strQuery2);
                            itemdesc="";
                            while(result1.next())
                            {

itemdesc=result1.getString("Item_Desc");
                            }
                            qty=result.getString("Qty");
                            wishdate=result.getString("Wish_Date");
                            wishdate=wishdate.substring(0,10);
                            out.println("<tr>");
    out.println("<td width=\"20%\"><font face=\"Arial\" size=\"2\"
color=\"#800000\">" + username + "</font></td>");
    out.println("<td width=\"15%\"><font face=\"Arial\" size=\"2\" color=\"#800000\">"
+ itemcode + "</font></td>");
out.println("<td width=\"15%\"><font face=\"Arial\" size=\"2\" color=\"#800000\">" +
itemdesc + "</font></td>");
out.println("<td width=\"10%\"><font face=\"Arial\" size=\"2\" color=\"#800000\">" +
qty + "</font></td>");
out.println("<td width=\"20%\"><font face=\"Arial\" size=\"2\" color=\"#800000\">" +
wishdate + "</font></td>");
        out.println("</tr>");
                    connect1.close();
                    }
                    connect.close();
                    }
                    catch(Exception e)
                    {
                            out.println("Exception: " + e + " occurred.");
                    }
%>
</table>
```

```
<table border="0" width="100%">
  <tr>
    <td width="50%" valign="middle" align="right">
<input type="submit" value="OK" name="ok_button"></td>
    <td width="50%" valign="middle" align="right"></td>
  </tr>
</table>
</form>
    </td>
  </tr>
</table>
</body>
</html>
```

The output of the `admin_wishlist.jsp` is displayed in Figure 31-21.

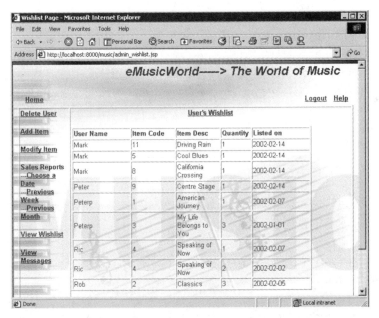

FIGURE 31-21 *The output of the* `admin_wishlist.jsp` *page is shown here.*

Creating the View Messages Page

The View Messages page enables an administrator to view the user's messages. The code for this page is given in Listing 31-16.

Listing 31-16 admin_messages.jsp

```
<html>
<head>
<meta http-equiv="Content-Type" content="text/html; charset=windows-1252">
<meta http-equiv="Content-Language" content="en-us">
<title>Messages Page</title>
</head>
<body bgcolor="#C0C0C0" topmargin="0"
background="http:\\localhost:8000\music\Background.bmp" >
<table border="0" width="100%">
  <tr>
    <td width="100%">
      <table border="0" width="97%" height="19">
        <tr>
          <td width="18%" height="13" valign="middle" align="right">
        <font face="Arial" size="5" color="#800000"><b><i>eMusicWorld-----&gt; The
World of Music</i></b></font>
          </td>
        </tr>
      </table>
    </td>
  </tr>
</table>


<form method="get" action="http://localhost:8000/music/admin_home_page.htm">
<table border="0" width="100%">
    <tr>
    <td width="100%"><table border="0" width="100%" height="19">
        <tr>
          <td width="9%" height="13" valign="middle" align="center"><font
face="Arial" size="2" color="#800000"><b><a
HREF="http://localhost:8000/music/admin_home_page.htm">Home</a></b></font></td>
```

```
            <td width="10%" height="13" valign="middle" align="center"></td>
            <td width="19%" height="13" valign="middle" align="center"></td>
            <td width="13%" height="13" valign="middle" align="center"></td>
            <td width="13%" height="13" valign="middle" align="center"></td>
                    <td width="11%" height="13" valign="middle" align="cen-
ter"></td>

                                            <td width="10%" height="13"
valign="middle" align="center"></td>
        <td width="9%" height="13" valign="middle" align="center"><font
face="Arial" size="2" color="#800000"><b><a
HREF="logout_page.jsp">Logout</b></font></td>
        <td width="9%" height="13" valign="middle" align="center"><font
face="Arial" size="2" color="#800000"><b><a
HREF="http://localhost:8000/music/admin_home_page_old.htm">Help</a></b></font></td>
      </tr>
    </table>
   </td>
  </tr>
</table>

<table border="1" width="100%" height="353">
  <tr>
  <td width="15%" height="347" valign="top">

<p><font face="Arial" size="2" color="#800000"><b><a
HREF="http://localhost:8000/music/admin_del_user.jsp">Delete User</a></b></font></p>
<p><font face="Arial" size="2" color="#800000"><b><a
HREF="http://localhost:8000/ItemContext/ItemAlias">Add Item</a></b></font></p>
<p><font face="Arial" size="2" color="#800000"><b><a
HREF="http://localhost:8000/music/admin_mod_item.jsp">Modify Item</a></b></font></p>
<p><font face="Arial" size="2" color="#800000"><b>Sales Reports<br>---<a
HREF="http://localhost:8000/music/daily_sales_report.jsp">Choose a Date</a><br>---<a
HREF="http://localhost:8000/music/weekly_sales_report.jsp">Previous
Week</a><br>---<a
HREF="http://localhost:8000/music/monthly_sales_report.jsp">Previous
Month</a></b></font></p>
<p><font face="Arial" size="2" color="#800000"><b><a
HREF="http://localhost:8000/music/admin_wishlist.jsp">View
```

```
Wishlist</a></b></font></p>
<p><font face="Arial" size="2" color="#800000"><b><a
HREF="http://localhost:8000/music/admin_messages.jsp">View
Messages</a></b></font></p>
                </td>
    <td width="85%" height="347" valign="top">
<p align="center"><font size="2"><b>
<font face="Arial" color="#800000"><u>Messages from Users</u></font>
</b></font>
</p>
<table border="0" width="100%" height="117">
  <tr>
    <td width="15%" height="19"><b><font face="Arial" color="#800000" size="2">User
      Name</font></b></td>
<td width="15%" height="19"><b><font face="Arial" color="#800000" size="2">E-
mail</font></b></td>
    <td width="30%" height="19"><b><font face="Arial" color="#800000"
size="2">Message</font></b></td>
    <td width="19%" height="19"><b><font face="Arial" color="#800000"
size="2">Date</font></b></td>
  </tr>
                <%@ page import="java.util.*" %>
                <%@ page import="java.sql.*" %>
                <%@ page import="java.text.*" %>
                <%@ page import="java.sql.Date" %>

                <%@ page language = "java" %>
                <%
                try{
                Class.forName("sun.jdbc.odbc.JdbcOdbcDriver");
                Connection connect, connect1;


connect=DriverManager.getConnection("jdbc:odbc:RegisterDataSource","","");

                Statement state;

                state = connect.createStatement();
```

```
                String strQuery1 = "select * from Feedback_Master Order by Msg_Date
desc";

                ResultSet result = state.executeQuery(strQuery1);
                String username, email, message, msgdate;
                while(result.next())
                {
                        username=result.getString("User_name");



connect1=DriverManager.getConnection("jdbc:odbc:RegisterDataSource","","");
                        username=username.trim();
                        Statement state1;
                        state1 = connect1.createStatement();
                        String strQuery2 = "select E_mail from User_Info
where User_Name='"+username+"'";
                        ResultSet result1 = state1.executeQuery(strQuery2);
                        email="";
                        while(result1.next())
                        {
                                email=result1.getString("E_mail");
                        }
                        message=result.getString("Message");
                        msgdate=result.getString("Msg_Date");
                        msgdate=msgdate.substring(0,10);
                        out.println("<tr>");
    out.println("<td width=\"15%\"><font face=\"Arial\" size=\"2\"
color=\"#800000\">" + username + "</font></td>");
out.println("<td width=\"15%\"><font face=\"Arial\" size=\"2\" color=\"#800000\">" +
email + "</font></td>");
out.println("<td width=\"30%\"><font face=\"Arial\" size=\"2\" color=\"#800000\">" +
message + "</font></td>");
out.println("<td width=\"19%\"><font face=\"Arial\" size=\"2\" color=\"#800000\">" +
msgdate+ "</font></td>");
        out.println("</tr>");
                }
                connect.close();
```

```
            }
            catch(Exception e)
            {
                    out.println("Exception: " + e + " occurred.");
            }
%>
</table>

    <table border="0" width="100%">
     <tr>
       <td width="50%" valign="middle" align="right"><input type="submit" value="OK"
name="submit_button"></td>
       <td width="50%" valign="middle" align="right"></td>
     </tr>
   </table>
</form>
     </td>
   </tr>
</table>
</body>
</html>
```

The output of the `admin_messages.jsp` is displayed in Figure 31-22.

Creating the Logout Page

Clicking the Logout link will log out the administrator when he or she is finished using the application. The code for the Logout page is given in Listing 31-17.

Listing 31-17 logout_page.jsp

```
<html>
<head>
<meta http-equiv="Content-Type" content="text/html; charset=windows-1252">
<meta http-equiv="Content-Language" content="en-us">
<title>Logout Page</title>
</head>
```

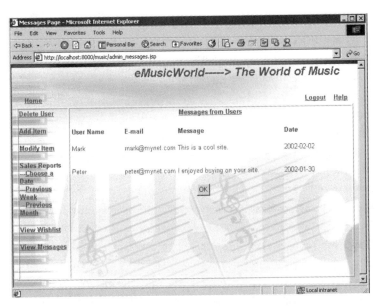

FIGURE 31-22 *The output of the* `admin_messages.jsp` *page is shown here.*

```
<body bgcolor="#C0C0C0" topmargin="0"
background="http:\\localhost:8000\music\Background.bmp" >
<table border="0" width="100%">
  <tr>
    <td width="100%">
      <table border="0" width="97%" height="19">
        <tr>
          <td width="18%" height="13" valign="middle" align="right">
          <font face="Arial" size="5" color="#800000"><b><i>eMusicWorld----->&gt; The
World of Music</i></b></font>
          </td>
        </tr>
      </table>
    </td>
  </tr>
</table>
<table border="1" width="100%" height="353">
  <tr>
    <td width="15%" height="347" valign="top">
```

```
<p><font face="Arial" size="2" color="#800000"><b><a
HREF="http://localhost:8000/music/home_page.htm">Home</a></b></font></p>
<p><b><font face="Arial" size="2" color="#800000"><a
HREF="http://localhost:8000/music/chart_toppers.jsp">Chart
Toppers</a></font></b></p>
<p><b><font face="Arial" size="2" color="#800000"><a
HREF="http://localhost:8000/SearchContext/SearchAlias">Search</a></font></b></p>
<p><b><font face="Arial" size="2" color="#800000"><a
HREF="http://localhost:8000/music/vote_page.jsp">Vote</a></font></b></p>
<p><b><font face="Arial" size="2" color="#800000"><a
HREF="http://localhost:8000/music/new_release_page.jsp">New Releases</a></font></b>
<p><font face="Arial" size="2" color="#800000"><b><a
HREF="http://localhost:8000/Register/RegisterPage.htm">Register</a></b></font>
<p><font face="Arial" size="2" color="#800000"><b><a
HREF="http://localhost:8000/music/login_page.htm">Login</a></b></font>
<p><font face="Arial" size="2" color="#800000"><b><a
HREF="http://localhost:8000/music/help_page.htm">Help</a></b></font></p>
        </td>
    <td width="85%" height="347" valign="top">
      <p><b><font color="#800000" size="3" face="Arial Black">Please wait while you
are being logged out...................</font></b></p>
<% session.removeAttribute("username");%>
      </td>
    </tr>
</table>
</body>
</html>
```

The output of the logout_page.jsp code is shown in Figure 31-23.

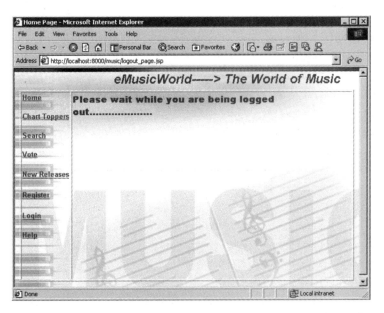

FIGURE 31-23 *The output of the* `logout_page.jsp` *page is displayed.*

Summary

In this chapter, you learned how to create the pages of the Administrator Interface category of the `eMusicWorld` application. You learned how to create the Delete User page, Add Item page, Modify Item page, Reports pages, View Wishlist page, and View Messages page. The concepts of EJB, JSP, and JDBC were used to create these pages.

Chapter 32

You created and deployed various components of the MusicApp in previous chapters. These components are listed here:

♦ UserJar

♦ ItemJar

♦ ValidateJar

♦ ItemWar

♦ SearchWar

♦ RegisterWar

Now you need to add the remaining HTML, JSP, and other files of MusicApp that you created in previous chapters in order to completely deploy the application. In this chapter, I'll discuss the steps to deploy the application on the Web.

Steps to Deploy the MusicApp *Application*

I've listed the steps to deploy MusicApp. Before following these steps, you need to start the J2EE server by executing the J2EE -verbose command at the command prompt. You also need to start the deployment tool by typing deploytool at the command prompt. After you have done this, follow the steps given as follows:

1. Select MusicApp from the left pane.

2. Select the New Web Component command from the File menu. The New Web Component Wizard — Introduction dialog box is displayed.

3. Click on the Next button. The New Web Component Wizard — WAR File General Properties dialog box is displayed. Note that MusicApp is displayed in the Web Component will Go In drop-down list.

4. Type MusicWar in the WAR Display Name text field.

5. Click the Add button in the Contents group box. The Add Files to .WAR — Add Content Files dialog box is displayed.

6. Click on Browse and select your working directory. Select all html pages, jsp pages, and image files that you require in the application from the scroll pane.

7. Click the Add button. The Add Files to .WAR — Add Content Files dialog box is displayed.

8. Click the Next button. The Add Files to .WAR — Add Class Files dialog box is displayed.

9. Click the Finish button. The New Web Component Wizard — WAR File General Properties dialog box is displayed.

10. Click the Next button. The New Web Component Wizard — Choose Component Type dialog box is displayed.

11. Select JSP as the Web Component Type.

12. Click the Next file. The New Web Component Wizard — Component General Properties dialog box is displayed. See Figure 32-1.

13. Select user_home_page.jsp from the JSP Filename drop-down list. Type MusicComponent in the Web Component Display Name text field.

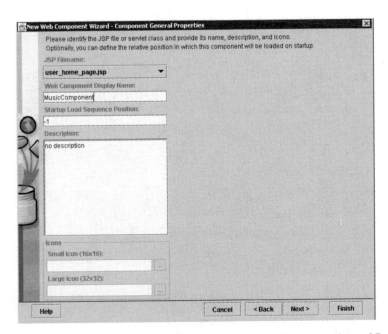

FIGURE 32-1 *The New Web Component Wizard — Component General Properties dialog box appears.*

14. Click the Next button. The New Web Component Wizard — Component Initialization Parameters dialog box is displayed. Again click the Next button.

15. The New Web Component Wizard — Component Aliases dialog box is displayed. Click the Next button.

16. Click the Add button. Specify the alias name as `Music` in the Alias text box.

17. The New Web Component Wizard — Component Security dialog box is displayed. Click the Next button.

18. The New Web Component Wizard — WAR File Environment dialog box is displayed. Click the Next button.

19. The New Web Component Wizard — Resource References dialog box is displayed. Specify the JNDI Name and Coded Name as shown in Figure 32-2.

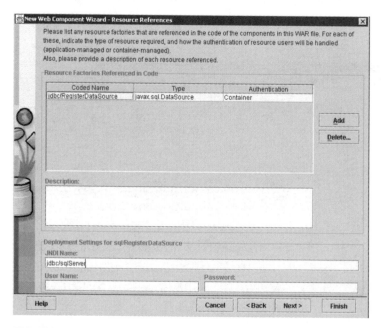

FIGURE 32-2 *The New Web Component Wizard — Resource References dialog box appears.*

20. Click the Finish button. The Application Deployment Tool: MusicApp window is displayed. Note that `MusicWar` is displayed in the left pane below Local Applications.

21. Click on the Web Context tab in the right pane. Type `Music` in the Context Root column of the MusicWar row, as seen in Figure 32-3.

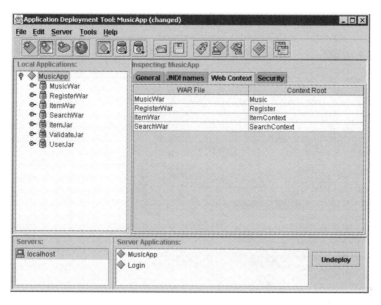

FIGURE 32-3 *Specify the Context Root name in the Web Context tab.*

22. Select the Deploy Application command from the Tools menu. The Deploy MusicApp — Introduction dialog box is displayed.

23. Click the Next button. The Deploy MusicApp — JNDI Names dialog box is displayed. Note that the JNDI names are displayed, as shown in Figure 32-4.

24. Click the Next button. The Deploy MusicApp — .WAR Context Root dialog box is displayed. See Figure 32-5.

25. Click the Next button. The Deploy MusicApp — Review dialog box is displayed.

26. Click the Finish button. The Deployment Progress dialog box is displayed. See Figure 32-6.

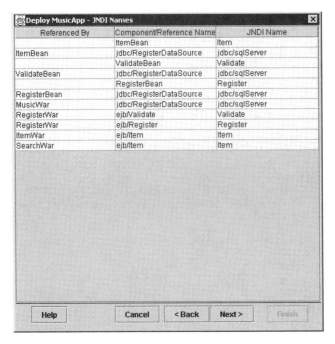

FIGURE 32-4 *The Deploy MusicApp — JNDI Names dialog box appears.*

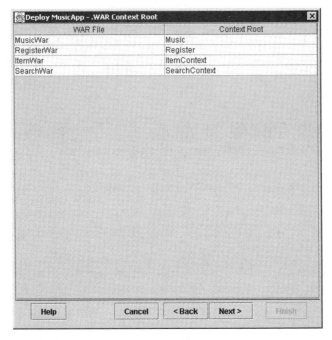

FIGURE 32-5 *The Deploy MusicApp — .WAR Context Root dialog box appears.*

27. Click the OK button when the deployment of MusicApp is complete.

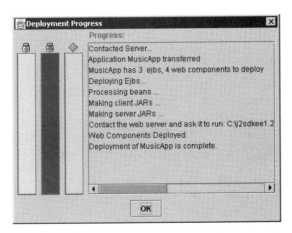

FIGURE 32-6 *The Deployment Progress dialog box appears.*

28. The Application Deployment Tool: MusicApp window is displayed. Note that MusicApp is displayed below Server Applications.

29. Select the Exit command from the File menu to return to the command prompt.

The MusicApp is now fully deployed.

Summary

In this chapter, you learned the complete process to deploy the MusicApp application.

Chapter 33

In this chapter, you'll learn how to run the music application that you developed in previous chapters.

Steps to Execute the Application

Before you execute the application, you need to follow the steps that are listed here:

1. Ensure that the paths for JDK and J2EE are correctly configured.

2. Start J2EE by executing the command given here:

   ```
   c:\>j2ee -verbose
   ```

3. Ensure that the paths are properly configured.

4. Modify the `default.properties` file in the `<drive>\<j2ee folder>\config` folder. The modified text is highlighted in Figure 33-1.

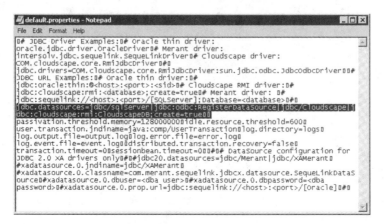

FIGURE 33-1 *The highlight shows the modified text.*

5. Deploy the application and the bean components as explained in the previous chapters.

Now consider an example to see how the music application works. Peter has followed the steps given above and passed the `http://localhost:8000/music/home_page.hm` URL to the browser. The Home page is displayed to Peter. See Figure 33-2.

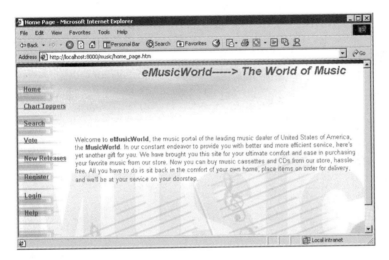

FIGURE 33-2 *The Home page appears.*

To view the songs that are currently at the top of the popularity chart, Peter clicks on the link for the Chart Toppers page, illustrated in Figure 33-3.

To search for the songs that are available in the `Classical` category, Peter opens the Search page and submits the search for the `Classical` category. The search result is displayed to Peter. See Figure 33-4.

Peter votes for his favorite song on the Vote page of the application. The Vote page is shown in Figure 33-5.

Peter views the latest releases by opening the New Releases page. See Figure 33-6.

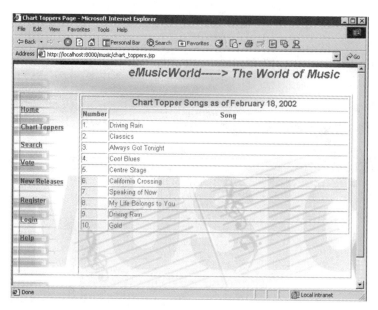

FIGURE 33-3 *The Chart Toppers page is displayed.*

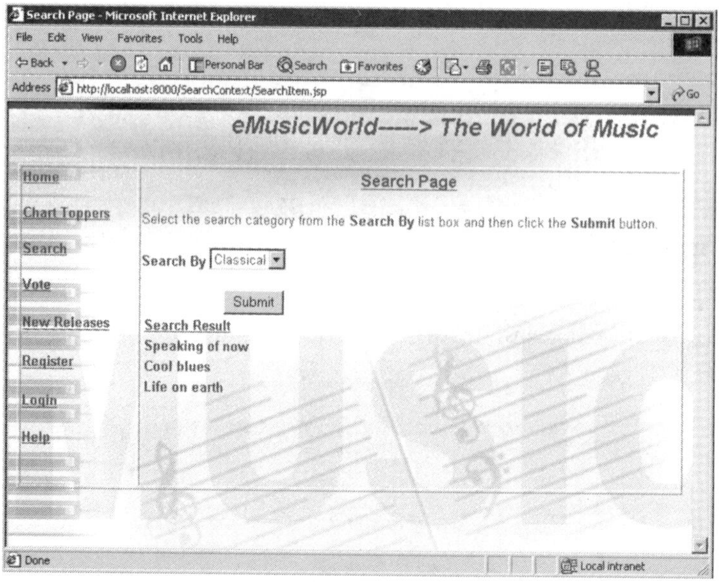

FIGURE 33-4 *The Search result page appears.*

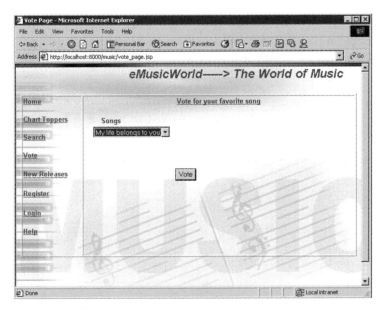

FIGURE 33-5 *The Vote page is displayed.*

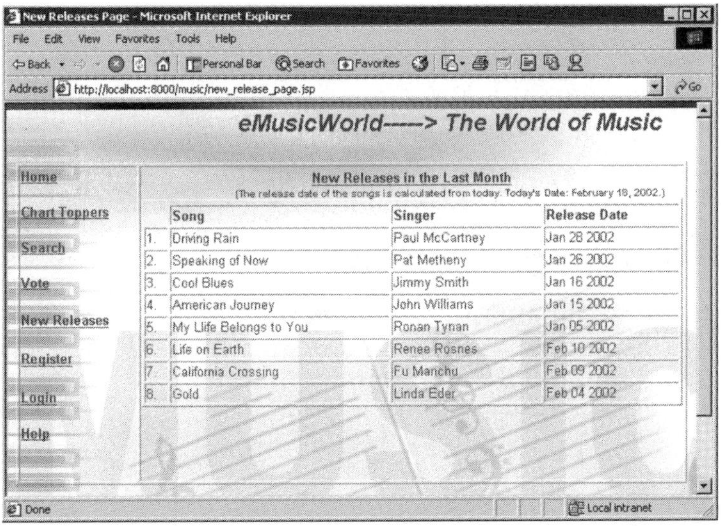

FIGURE 33-6 *The New Releases page is displayed.*

Peter wants to register with the application to become a customer of eMusic-World. To do so, he clicks on the Register link in the left menu. Peter provides the required information in the Registration page, as shown in Figure 33-7.

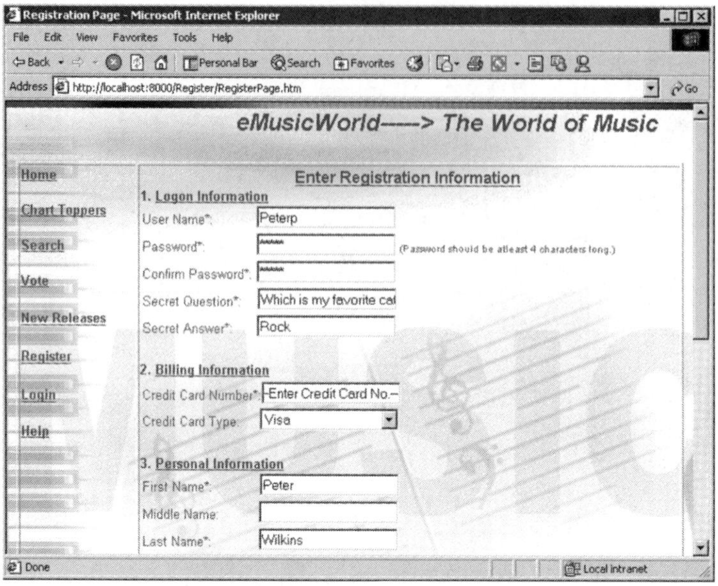

FIGURE 33-7 _The Registration page is displayed._

After successful registration, a message is displayed to Peter. Now he can log on to the site and purchase CDs, cassettes, and DVDs of his favorite songs. To log on, he invokes the Login page. Refer to Figure 33-8.

After successful logon, a message is displayed to Peter. See Figure 33-9.

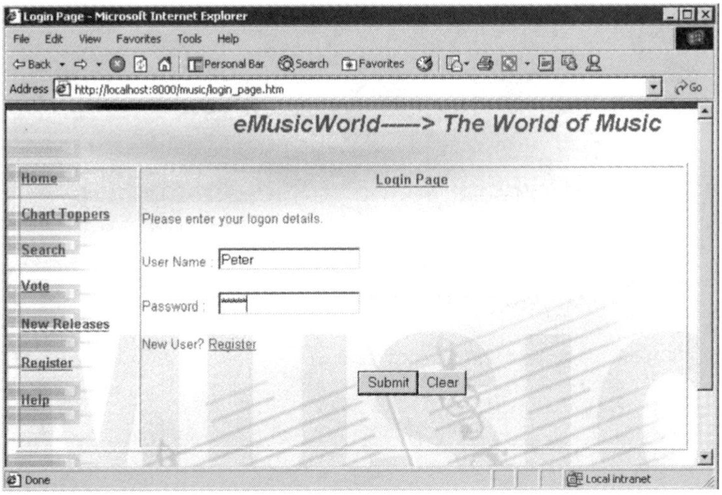

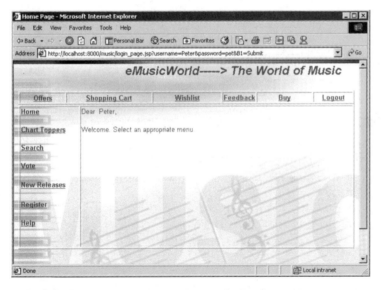

FIGURE 33-8 *The Login page is displayed.*

FIGURE 33-9 *The Home page for Peter is displayed.*

To buy an item, Peter first needs to click on the Buy link. On the Buy page Peter can specify a category for which the application will search for songs. The Buy page is shown in Figure 33-10.

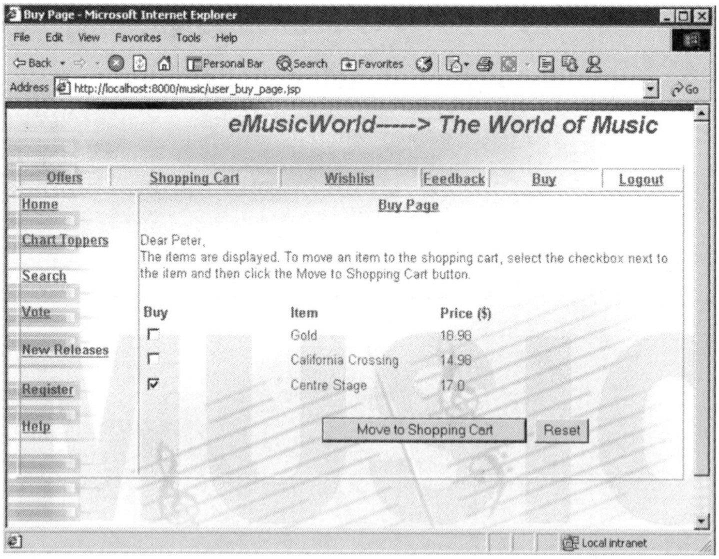

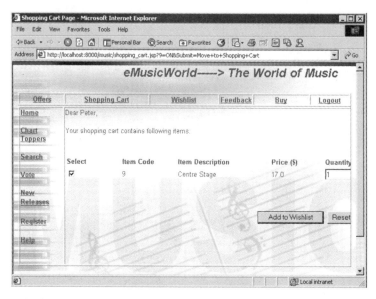

FIGURE 33-10 *The Buy page is displayed.*

Peter selects a song collection and clicks the Move to Shopping Cart button. See Figure 33-11.

FIGURE 33-11 *The Shopping Cart page is displayed.*

From the shopping cart, Peter can select some items and move them to the wishlist for later purchase. Peter can view his wishlist by clicking on the `Wishlist` link in the top horizontal menu of the user home page. The Wishlist is seen in Figure 33-12.

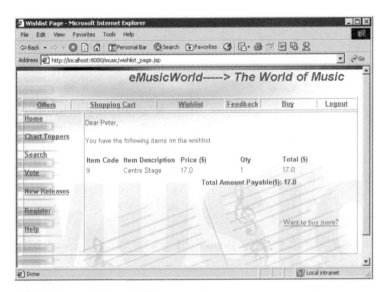

FIGURE 33-12 *The Wishlist page is displayed.*

Peter is looking for a song, but it is not available on the site. So, Peter uses the Feedback page to request that the management of eMusicWorld add the song to the inventory. The Feedback page is illustrated in Figure 33-13.

Now, Peter logs out of the site by clicking on the Logout button.

Meanwhile, Nancy, who is one of the administrators at eMusicWorld, logs on to the site. The Home page for the administrators is displayed to Nancy. See Figure 33-14.

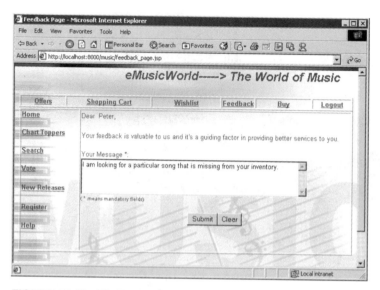

FIGURE 33-13 *The Feedback page is displayed.*

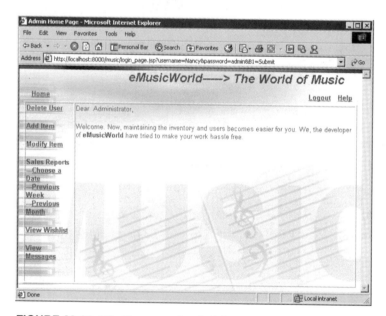

FIGURE 33-14 *The Home page for administrators is displayed.*

One of the registered users, Mark, has requested that Nancy remove him from the list of registered users. To delete Mark, Nancy clicks on the Delete User link on the left menu, as shown in Figure 33-15.

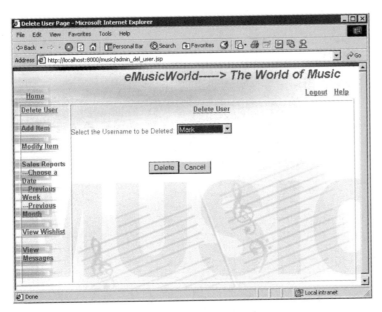

FIGURE 33-15 *The Delete User page is displayed.*

Administrators at eMusicWorld are responsible for inventory management. Nancy can add an item to the inventory by using the Add Item page. Refer to Figure 33-16.

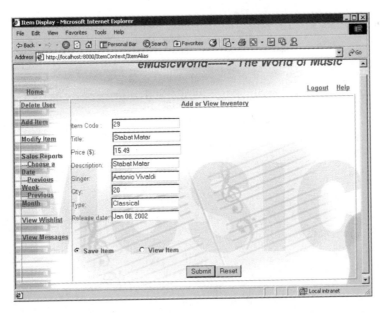

FIGURE 33-16 *The Add Item page is displayed.*

The administrator can modify the details of an item by using the Modify Items page, as seen in Figure 33-17.

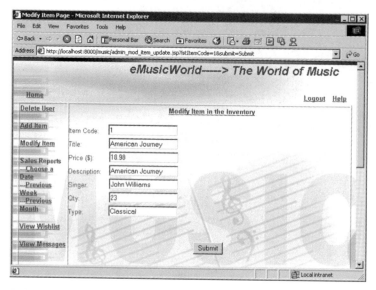

FIGURE 33-17 *The Modify Items page is displayed.*

The three types of sales reports that Nancy can view are:

◆ Sales reports based on a selected date, as seen in Figure 33-18.

◆ Sales report for the previous week, as shown in Figure 33-19.

◆ Sales report for the previous month, illustrated in Figure 33-20.

In addition to these reports, Nancy can view the users' wishlist and the messages sent by the users. The View Wishlist page is shown in Figure 33-21.

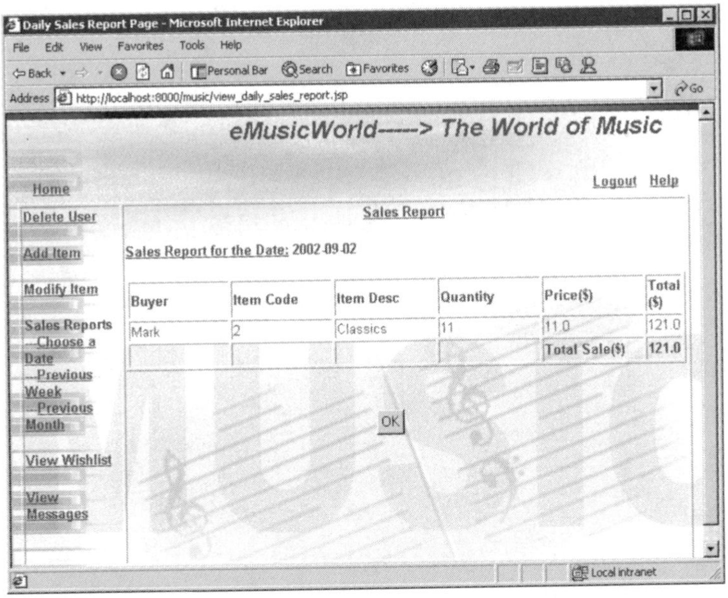

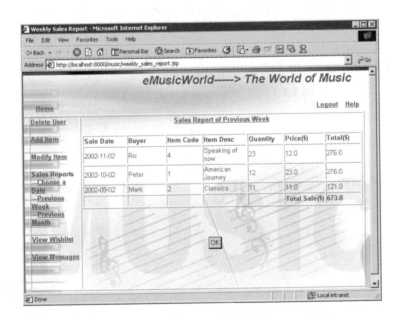

FIGURE 33-18 *The Sales report for a selected date is displayed.*

FIGURE 33-19 *The Sales report for the previous week appears.*

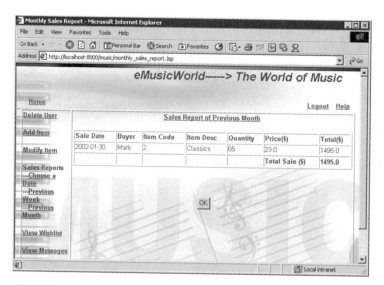

FIGURE 33-20 *The Sales report for the previous month is shown.*

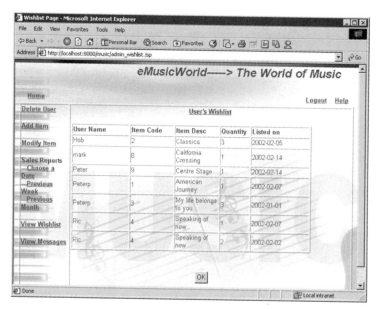

FIGURE 33-21 *The View Wishlist page is displayed.*

The View Messages page is displayed in Figure 33-22.

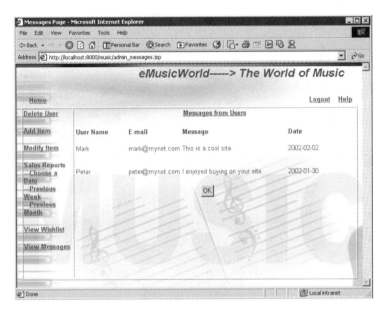

FIGURE 33-22 *The View Messages page is displayed.*

Summary

In this chapter, you learned how to use and navigate through the eMusicWorld site. The example of two users and an administrator was used to explain the functionality of various pages of the application.

PART VI

Beyond The Lab

Chapter 34

An Overview of Jini

In this chapter, I'll introduce you to Jini technology. You will look at the main features and the components of a Jini system. I'll also discuss some of the key concepts of Jini. In addition, you will learn about the benefits of Jini.

An Introduction to Jini

Jini is a software technology created by Sun Microsystems. Jini is written in pure Java and is installed on a JVM (Java Virtual Machine). Jini makes use of RMI (Remote Method Invocation) protocol to handle all low-level communication.

Jini is a set of specifications that provides mechanisms by which a network of electronic devices, services, and applications can be formed. Jini is a system architecture that consists of hardware, software, and network components. It is a distributed computing environment that allows devices to discover each other in the network and provide services that can be used by other devices. These services can be added or removed from the environment seamlessly and without much user intervention. For example, say a new printer is added to a network and announces its presence. A client machine in the network can then directly connect with the printer without the user having to install the printer.

The features of Jini enable computer service networks to be exploited in multiple ways. Some of these features are discussed in the following section.

Features of Jini

Some of the important features of Jini are listed as follows:

- ◆ Jini is platform independent and can be used to connect applications and devices that work on diverse operating systems.
- ◆ Jini helps to reduce the user effort that is required to administer a network of applications and devices.
- ◆ Jini can be incorporated into the existing infrastructure, resulting in low implementation costs.

◆ Jini helps to create a flexible network that is customizable as per the requirements.

◆ Jini is designed to be used with workgroups of 2–1000 nodes or services.

◆ Jini requires the usage of JVM.

◆ In a Jini system, clients can access services irrespective of location.

Now that I've given you a brief overview of the Jini technology and its features, I'll move the discussion to the Jini architecture.

An Overview of the Jini Architecture

As you know, the Jini system is a distributed network. Therefore, all the participants in a Jini network are either clients or servers. A server consists of an interface known as API (Application Programmers Interface). A programmer can use this interface to write services and components. This interface is known as the *service interface* or the service. Therefore, in the context of Jini, a server is essentially an implementation of a service.

The Jini architecture is based on the concepts of object-oriented programming applied to a network. One of the key concepts of object-oriented programming is the separation of interface and implementation. By separating an interface and the implementation, an object can represent a service. This object can be downloaded by the client and executed at the client end. Alternatively, the object can act as a proxy to a remote server.

One of the most important advantages of the Jini architecture is that it allows programs to use services by using any protocol. The underlying protocol used by the service may not even be known to the program that uses the service. For example, a service may be implemented as XML-based and another may be CORBA-based. It is the responsibility of the service to provide the client with the means of communication.

There are three main components of the Jini architecture. These are as follows:

◆ Jini Services

◆ Jini Infrastructure

◆ Jini Programming Model

The Jini architecture with its components is shown in Figure 34-1.

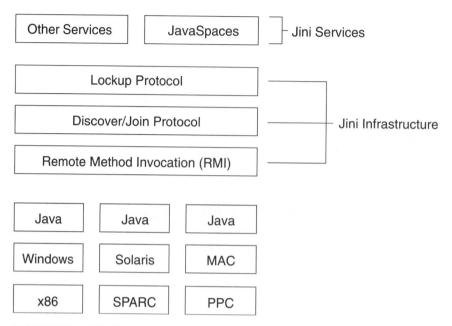

FIGURE 34-1 *The Jini architecture is shown here.*

The Jini services are the basic components of the Jini system. In the Jini architecture, these services are objects that are written in Java programming language. Every service in the Java architecture has an interface. This interface defines the type of operations that can be performed on the service.

The Jini infrastructure is a set of components that builds the Jini system. The infrastructure defines the minimum requirements when implementing Jini. The infrastructure defines the security requirements and the service protocols that enable services to be added and accessed from the Jini network. The infrastructure enables services to discover each other and announce their presence in the network.

In addition, the Jini architecture consists of a programming model that refers to a set of interfaces that allows the development of services. This programming model helps the objects to be moved around in the Jini network. The programming model also controls the allocation and management of services as resources. Additionally, it facilitates event-based communication among the services in a Jini network. The programming model also controls the distributed transactions that occur in the network.

I'll discuss each of these Java architectural components in detail later in the chapter. Now I'll start the discussion with a look at the Jini system.

The Jini System

The Jini *system* or *federation* is a collection of services and clients that communicate with each other using Jini protocols.

As discussed previously, a Jini system consists of the following two parts:

◆ A set of components that provides an infrastructure so that services can be located, accessed, added, and removed from a network.

◆ A programming model that helps to build a distributed system and supports the development of distributed services.

A Jini system is also known as a distributed Jini network or *djinn*. In djinn, there is no central authority that controls and manages the network. Therefore, all the available services form a federation or system. The Jini technology is not embedded in a single computer. Instead it is a system of available services. These services can be both hardware services, such as printers, scanners, digital cameras, and computers, and software services.

In a djinn, when a client accesses a service, a temporary connection is created between the client and the service. The connection between the client and the service is dissolved after the client completes accessing the service. Although Jini is written in pure Java, it does not require the clients and services to be written in pure Java. A Jini system connects devices and software in a way in which a single dynamic architecture is created. A Jini system comprises three main components. These are as follows:

◆ The Jini Service
◆ The Jini Lookup Service
◆ The Jini Client

All three components are connected to each other using TCP/IP as shown in Figure 34-2. Although in Jini specification, any networking protocol can be used to implement networking, currently TCP/IP is being used. The Jini system components are discussed in detail in the following sections.

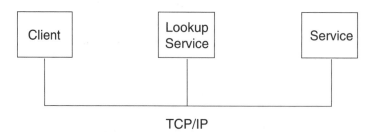

FIGURE 34-2 *The components of a Jini system are shown here.*

The Jini Service

The most important component of the Jini system is a *service*. In djinn, a service can be used by another service, a program, or a person. An example of a service can be a printer, a telephone, or even a user of the system. All members in a djinn collaborate to gain access to services. Services communicate with each other using a *service protocol*. A service protocol is a group of interfaces. These interfaces have been written in Java programming language.

A Jini system enables services and clients to connect to each other by using a *lookup service*.

The Jini Lookup Service

The Jini lookup service acts as a locator for services. The lookup service is the central mechanism for the Jini system. The lookup service acts as a contact point between the users and the system. The lookup service stores each service as a Java object. The client device can then download this object.

A service provider provides service in a Jini system. The service provider not only creates objects that implement the service but also registers these service objects with the lookup service. To add a service to the lookup service, the Jini system includes a pair of protocols. These are the discovery and the join protocols. A service locates an appropriate lookup service using the discovery protocol. It then joins the lookup service by using the join protocol.

To use a service, the user, program, or another service locates the service using the lookup service. The service object is then copied from the lookup service to the device requesting the service. The lookup service is only an intermediary body and therefore is not involved in any transactions between the service and the client device.

One lookup service may include other lookup services to provide a hierarchical lookup. In addition, a lookup service may include objects that form the part of other directory services. This enables clients to gain access to services registered with other forms of lookup services.

The Jini Client

The Jini client is any user, program, or service that asks for other services to accomplish its goal. Jini clients need not include all the code required to gain access to a service. Instead, the code is available within the service that the clients need to connect to. When a client connects with a service, the service object is copied to the client device by the lookup service.

The Working of Jini

In a Jini system, the runtime infrastructure resides on the network. This runtime infrastructure provides a mechanism by which clients can locate, access, add, and remove services. The runtime infrastructure is located on the clients, the service providers, and the lookup services.

As discussed earlier, the clients use the discovery protocol to locate services. In the infrastructure, there are two additional protocols. These are the join and the lookup protocols. Using the join protocol, a service registers itself with the lookup services. The lookup protocol helps clients send a query to look up services to locate an appropriate service.

The working of a Jini system essentially consists of three processes: the discovery process, the join process, and the lookup process. These are explained in the following sections.

The Discovery Process

In the discovery process, the Jini client uses the discovery protocol to locate the lookup services available on the network. Similarly, Jini servers that offer services find a lookup service so that they can register with the lookup service and become available in the Jini system. Discovery is the process in which a service is added to the Jini system. Consider an example where you have a Jini-enabled device, such as a printer. As soon as the printer is connected to the network, it sends a message stating its presence in the network. The message sent by the printer includes its IP address and the port number where the printer can be contacted by the lookup service. The lookup service inspects the message sent by the printer and makes a TCP/IP connection to the printer. The lookup service uses RMI to send a *service registrar* object to the printer. This service registrar object helps the lookup service to communicate with the printer. The printer can then invoke methods on the service registrar object and use the join and lookup processes to continue the communication.

The Join Process

After a service provider obtains a service registrar object, it *joins* the Jini system by using the join protocol. Continuing with the previous example, once the printer receives a service registrar object from the lookup service, it joins the system and becomes a part of the federation of services that are already registered with the lookup service. To join the system, the printer needs to invoke the `register()` method on the service registrar object. Once this method is invoked, information about the service, in this case the printer services, is sent to the lookup service. This service information is stored with the lookup service. The service information is a set of objects that describes the service and is known as a *service item*. The service item contains objects, such as *service object*. Clients use the service object to interact with the service using one or more interfaces implemented by the service object. The interfaces are written in Java and define the methods that can be used to interact with the service.

The Lookup Process

The lookup process is used to locate a specific service and interact with the service. After a service joins the Jini system, the service is available for use by other services, programs, and users. Clients query the lookup service to obtain information about registered services using the lookup process.

To start the lookup process, a client invokes the `lookup()` method on the service registrar object. When using the `lookup()` method, the client provides an object that defines the search criterion for the lookup. This object containing the search criterion is known as a *service template*. After the lookup service receives the service template object from the client, the lookup service sends the matching results to the client, thereby enabling the client to connect to the required service by using the lookup service as an intermediary.

NOTE

A service template is an object that may include a reference to an array of Class objects. These Class objects are used by the lookup service to find the type of service that is required by the client. The service template may include a *service ID*. This service ID identifies the service and defines the attributes of the service. These attributes should be consistent with the attributes contained in the service item.

The working of the Jini system explaining the discovery, join, and lookup processes is shown in Figure 34-3.

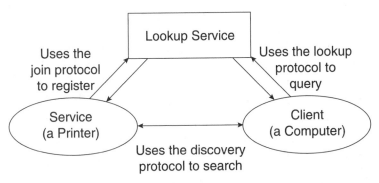

FIGURE 34-3 *This shows the working of the Jini system.*

Having discussed the processes involved in the working of a Jini system, I'll move the discussion to some of the key concepts implemented in the Jini technology.

Important Concepts in Jini

The Jini technology works with some key concepts. These concepts include:

- ◆ Java Remote Method Invocation (RMI)
- ◆ Leasing of Services
- ◆ Transactions in Jini
- ◆ Events in Jini
- ◆ JavaSpaces Services

I'll now discuss these concepts in the following sections.

Java Remote Method Invocation (RMI)

In Java programming, a *remote object* is defined as an object whose methods can be invoked from a Java virtual machine located on a different host. A remote object is defined using one or more *remote interfaces*. These remote interfaces are written in Java and specify the methods that can be invoked on the remote object. In the same context, Remote Method Invocation is the process of invoking methods on a remote object.

Programmers can use Java RMI to create distributed Java-to-Java applications. In these distributed applications, the methods of the remote Java object are invoked using Java virtual machines located on different hosts. Java RMI allows services to communicate with each other by passing objects from one network to another. This movement of objects across the various components of a Jini system is essential to the functioning of a Jini network.

Using Java RMI, distributed applications can locate remote objects, communicate with these objects, load the objects' codes, and transmit data related to the objects.

Leasing of Services

When a Jini client sends a request for a service, it receives a reply from the lookup service regarding the available services. The Jini service requested by the client is implemented using interfaces. These interfaces are obtained from the server. These services that are available to the Jini client are *leased*.

A lease is like a grant of the service for a specific time period. The user of the service makes a request for this lease and, based on the request, access to the service is granted. If required, the client can request a renewal of the lease. If the client does not send a request for renewal or the renewal of service is not granted, the service is leased to other requesting clients and resources in the Jini system.

There are two types of leases:

◆ **Exclusive.** An exclusive lease allows only one client to access the service at any given time. Therefore, no other client can take a lease on the service during the time period of an exclusive lease.

◆ **Nonexclusive.** A nonexclusive lease allows multiple clients to access the service at the same time.

Leasing also checks whether the client requires the service after a stipulated time period. In addition, it helps the lookup service to remove the registered services from the system if the lease is not renewed. Therefore, it is often remarked that that leasing provides Jini with "self-healing" properties.

Transactions in Jini

In a Jini system, *transactions* act as a fundamental mechanism to provide consistency of operations across a Jini network. A transaction consists of a series of operations that are a part of a single service or a group of services. In the Jini distributed network, the use of transactions ensures that a set of operations appears as one operation and therefore either all the operations succeed or all the operations fail. During the implementation of transactions, if one operation fails all the other operations that are a part of that set stop the task to be performed and abort the operation.

To implement transactions, a *two-phase commit* protocol is used. This protocol defines the methods of communication between various objects so that a set of operations can be clubbed together as a transaction.

In the Jini system, the transactions are implemented by the services that use the transaction interfaces. The Jini system merely coordinates the communication between various objects with respect to a transaction and provides minimal protocols and interfaces.

When implementing Jini transactions, there are three entities. These are listed as follows:

- ◆ **Transaction Manager.** A Transaction Manager creates and manages a transaction. The Transaction Manager coordinates the communication so that the transaction is completed. It also keeps track of all the participants and ensures that the participants update the latest information at the end of a transaction.

- ◆ **Transaction Client.** A Transaction Client is responsible for initiating a transaction. To initiate a transaction, a Transaction Client obtains a transaction object from the Transaction Manager. The Transaction Client then invokes a series of methods on the transaction object and commits to the transaction. The Transaction Client and the other participants of a transaction can abort the transaction.

◆ **Transaction Participants.** The Transaction Participants are the services that receive the transaction object from the Transaction Manager. After a Transaction Client commits to a transaction and initiates it, the Transaction Participants enable the use of transactions.

Events in Jini

When the state of an object is modified, an *event* is generated. Events are used to allow asynchronous communication between objects in a Jini system. The concept of events is important in a Jini system because it allows an object in one JVM to be aware of the occurrence of an event in another object stored on another JVM running on a different machine. The Jini system supports distributed events. Therefore an object can register interest in events in another object and receive a notification when that particular event occurs.

The kind of events that occur in an object, as well as the notification of events, is controlled by objects. There are three entities involved in the process of distributed events. These are listed as follows:

◆ The object that registers interest in a specific event

◆ The object in which an event occurs

◆ The object that receives the notification of the occurrence of the event

The object in which an event occurs is also known as the *event generator*. The event generator enables other objects to register interest in the occurrence of a particular event. It also sends out notifications to the *targets* that are interested in the particular event occurrence. These targets are objects that receive the notifications and are also known as *remote event listeners*.

An event generator sends a *remote event* object to the remote event listener as a notification of the occurrence of a specific event. A remote event object contains information, such as a reference to the object in which that event has occurred, the kind of event, and a sequence number. This sequence number defines the instance of the occurrence of the event.

The process of distributed events is shown in Figure 34-4.

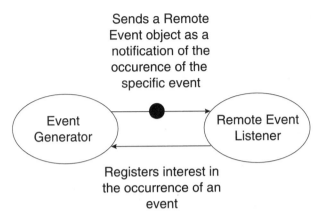

FIGURE 34-4 *The figure shows the working of events in a Jini system.*

JavaSpaces Services

JavaSpaces is a service available in Jini. It is responsible for generating and maintaining a Java objects database. JavaSpaces facilitates the communication process in a Jini system by allowing a lookup for accessing objects. JavaSpaces provides persistent object exchanging mechanisms. The concept of JavaSpaces is highly appreciated in a distributed networking environment such as Jini.

A JavaSpaces service contains *entries*. These entries are a group of objects that are expressed in a class for the Java platform. An entry is *written* into a JavaSpace service. This creates a copy of the entry into the JavaSpaces service.

Basically, two kinds of operations can be performed using the JavaSpaces application-programming interface. These are listed as follows:

◆ A *read* operation that enables programs to obtain a copy of an object using the entry stored in the JavaSpaces service

◆ A *take* operation that combines the operation of reading and deleting an entry from the JavaSpaces service

 NOTE

A *notify* operation can also be performed in the JavaSpaces service. This operation allows programs to keep track of objects that have been written into the JavaSpaces service.

A JavaSpaces service provides a reliable distributed storage system for objects. A JavaSpaces service can also be used in systems to store user preferences, images, and e-mail messages. In addition, JavaSpaces service enable distributed object persistence in the Java programming language.

Security in Jini

The Jini security architecture is largely governed by the Java security model and RMI. Security in Jini is implemented using the security model implemented in Java 2 programs. This Java 2 security model prevents any malicious code from affecting the Java Virtual Machine. However, to implement the Java 2 security model, a security manager needs to be installed in the application. In addition, RMI clients use the security manager to download code from RMI servers. Therefore, a security manager is critical for a Jini system.

Most of the communication in a Jini system occurs using *proxies*. These proxies are objects that are downloaded from the network. Proxies are the components of a service, which are visible to the client. The service objects use RMI to communicate with other objects and are proxies. Proxies act as local objects and implement interfaces on the client. Since most communication involves proxies, security mechanisms involving fixed protocols cannot be implemented in Jini.

As you know, Jini works in a distributed networking environment. Therefore, the need for security is much higher than in a centralized computing environment. Some of the security requirements in Jini are listed as follows:

- There should be a mechanism by which a client can identify whether or not it is communicating with the "right service."
- The security model should allow a client to verify whether it is using the right proxy object. This is because all service objects are downloadable as proxy objects and these objects should represent the service requested by the client.
- Just like authentication of services and proxy objects, the security model should enable a service to identify whether or not the client is authorized to access the service.

Apart from these requirements, some other security features that may need to be incorporated in the Jini security model include securing the attributes of the service such as the security level for a service, defining the access control on the service, and protecting the Jini system from multiple applications that may be executed on JVM. However, the actual security requirements may vary depending on the application.

The Jini technology can be used to develop systems that meet specific requirements and offer services to manage both devices and software. Some of the benefits of the Jini technology are discussed in the following section.

Some Benefits of Jini

The advantages and benefits of the Jini technology allow programmers to build a dynamic and robust network of services in a distributed computing environment. Some of the main advantages of Jini are listed as follows:

♦ The Jini technology is independent of any platform. There are no specific software or hardware requirements for the devices and programs that can be connected using Jini. In addition, the clients are not affected by the underlying networking protocols used by the services. Therefore, device vendors need not use the same network-level protocols. Instead, the vendors use a consistent Java interface, which facilitates the interaction between various devices.

♦ Using the Jini technology, clients can access resources that may be located anywhere on the network. The Jini system is not affected by the location of either the client or the resource.

♦ In a Jini system, devices, users, and services can enter or leave the system without affecting the system. Additionally, there is no manual intervention required for the same. Therefore, the administration effort required to manage the network of services and devices is low. This also facilitates self-management and self-configuration of the devices and services that are a part of the Jini network.

♦ The Jini technology offers networking and service-level protocols that facilitate the integration of heterogeneous networks. Jini offers network plug-and-play capabilities. The devices and services can use the discovery, join, and lookup protocols to communicate with each other.

♦ The Jini technology offers a flexible architecture and therefore it can be customized as per the user's requirements.

The Jini technology can change the way you work in a distributed computing network. Also, the cost of implementing Jini is low because it can be incorporated within the existing infrastructure. A Jini-enabled device needs simply to plug-in and the various resources are made available. This shift towards application development can help to integrate various computer networks containing a range of devices including DVD players, CD players, cell phones, PDAs, computers, printers, and scanners. Every device that joins the Jini system adds value to the existing network.

Summary

Jini is a set of specifications that provides mechanisms by which a network of electronic devices, services, and applications can be formed. It is a system architecture that consists of hardware, software, and network components. It is a distributed computing environment that allows devices to discover each other in the network and provide services that can be used by other devices. These services can be added or removed from the environment seamlessly and without much user intervention.

In this chapter you were introduced to the Jini technology. You learned the main features and the components of a Jini system. You also learned the key concepts of Jini. Finally, you learned about the benefits of implementing the Jini technology.

Chapter 35

**An Introduction
to the Bluetooth
Technology**

In this chapter, I'll discuss the Bluetooth technology. In addition, you will learn about Bluetooth Special Interest Group and Bluetooth features. You will also learn about the Bluetooth architecture and the comparison of Bluetooth with other technologies.

An Introduction to Bluetooth

Simply put, the Bluetooth technology aims to replace all cables and gears that connect computers and other electronic gadgets and devices, such as mobile phones, mobile PCs, and portable devices. Bluetooth is a technology that enables wireless communication between devices. It is a technology standard that uses short-range radio links to connect one device to another. The Bluetooth technology is an open specification for wireless communication of data and voice. For example, the Bluetooth radio technology built into both the cellular telephone and the laptop will replace the cables that are used to connect a laptop to a cellular telephone. The Bluetooth technology provides wireless connectivity for various devices such as printers, PDAs, desktops, fax machines, keyboards, mobile phones, laptops, and other household gadgets, such as microwave ovens and thermostats.

Bluetooth is a wireless protocol used to connect a diverse range of products. The main features of Bluetooth are low cost, low power, low complexity, and robustness. Bluetooth can be used to connect LANs, PSTNs, mobile phone networks, and the Internet.

Bluetooth as a technology has features that can change the way people live and work.

Features of Bluetooth

Some of the key features of Bluetooth are listed as follows:

- ◆ It is a wireless technology.
- ◆ It is an inexpensive technology.

◆ It utilizes the 2.56 GHZ ISM band, which is globally available.

◆ It consumes less power.

◆ It offers 10 meters of transmitting distance.

◆ It offers one Mbps of transmission speed.

To promote and develop the Bluetooth technology, a Special Interest Group (SIG) has been formed. Now I'll talk about the Bluetooth SIG.

The Bluetooth Special Interest Group (SIG)

The Bluetooth *Special Interest Group* (SIG) is an industry group that consists of leaders in the telecommunications, computing, and networking industries. This group is in charge of developing a low-cost, short-range wireless specification to connect mobile devices. Bluetooth SIG was founded by Ericsson, IBM, Intel, Nokia, and Toshiba in February 1998 to develop an open specification for short-range wireless connectivity. Other companies, such as 3COM, Motorola, Microsoft, and Lucent, now promote SIG. The number of members in the Bluetooth SIG has now increased to more than two thousand. These members continuously coordinate among themselves to devise a global standard for wireless connectivity and to develop the standard specification.

The hardware vendors, including Siemens, Intel, and Motorola, have developed a specification for a small radio module. This module can be built into computers, telephones, and entertainment equipment.

Currently, a number of machines communicate using infrared signals. Bluetooth SIG intends to develop a signal that is stronger than infrared signals. This signal will carry one megabyte of data per second, which is 20 times the speed of a dial-up modem. In addition, the signal will be able to carry both data and voice.

Any company that signs the Bluetooth Membership Agreement can join Bluetooth SIG free of cost. The company can later upgrade their membership to avail special benefits, such as access to the Bluetooth specification.

Having briefly introduced the Bluetooth technology and Bluetooth SIG, I'll now move the discussion to how devices are connected using the Bluetooth technology.

Connecting Devices Using Bluetooth

Whenever two or more Bluetooth devices come within a range, they form an ad hoc connection. This collection of Bluetooth devices that connect using the Bluetooth technology is known as a *Piconet*. A Piconet can be started with two connected devices and can incorporate a maximum of eight active Bluetooth devices. After a Piconet is established, one device acts as a *master* and the rest of the devices act as *slaves*. The device that starts the connection becomes the master device. Also, as there is no difference between the hardware and software specification of devices, any master device can become a slave device and vice versa. However, at any given time there can only be one master device. A Piconet between two devices and a Piconet between multiple devices is depicted in Figure 35-1.

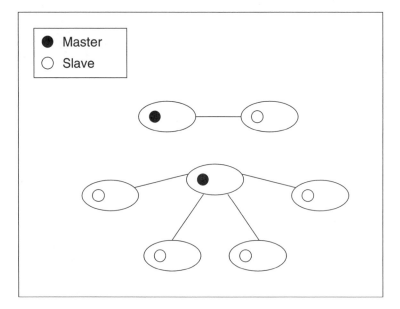

FIGURE 35-1 *Bluetooth devices connected in a Piconet are shown here.*

Several Piconets can exist within the same area. This is known as a *Scatternet*. All devices connected within one Scatternet share the same range of frequency. However, each individual Piconet uses different hop frequencies and transmits on different one-MHz channels. Figure 35-2 displays a Scatternet.

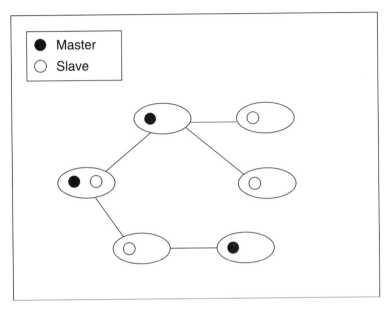

FIGURE 35-2 *Bluetooth devices connected in a Scatternet are shown here.*

All devices, until connected via a Piconet are in the *Standby* mode. In this mode, the unconnected devices pick up messages every 1.28 seconds. The paging messages are transmitted using 32 of the 79 hop frequencies.

In case no data transmission is happening within a Piconet, different powersaving modes can be used for the devices. These modes are the *Hold*, *Sniff*, and *Park* modes.

A master can put a slave device on the Hold mode. The slave device can also demand to be put on the Hold mode. When the slave device is out of the Hold mode, data transfer restarts immediately. The Hold mode is typically used when connecting with multiple Piconets or while managing a low-power device.

Apart from the Standby and the Hold mode, a device can also function in the Sniff mode. In this mode, the slave device picks messages from the Piconet at a reduced rate therefore decreasing the duty cycle. These intervals in the Sniff mode depend on the application and can be modified.

Finally, in the Park mode a Bluetooth device is connected to a Piconet but does not participate actively in the traffic.

The various states of a Bluetooth device are shown in Figure 35-3.

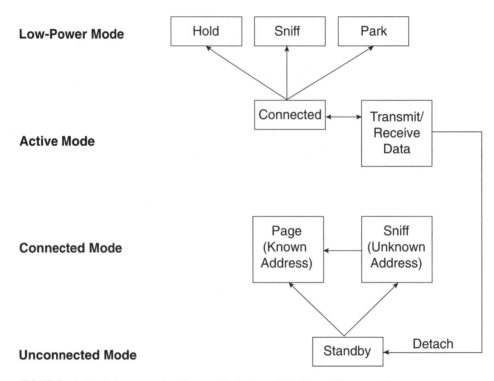

FIGURE 35-3 *Various operational states of a Bluetooth device are illustrated here.*

Now that you are aware of how devices are connected using Bluetooth, I'll discuss the main components of a Bluetooth Wireless Solution.

The Components of a Bluetooth Wireless Solution

To implement the Bluetooth technology, there are four essential components that are required. These are listed as follows:

◆ **Radio unit.** A radio unit is the radio receiver that establishes a link between Bluetooth devices.

◆ **Baseband unit.** A baseband unit is the hardware unit that consists of a CPU and memory. These components interact with the radio unit and the Bluetooth device at the hardware level.

◆ **Software stack.** The software stack is a driver software. It enables the application level software and the Baseband unit to interact with each other.

◆ **Application software.** The application software guides and implements the functionality and the user interface of the Bluetooth device.

Now that I've shown you the main components of a Bluetooth Wireless Solution, I'll discuss the architectural components of the Bluetooth technology.

Bluetooth Architecture

The Bluetooth architecture consists of both Bluetooth-specific protocols and non-Bluetooth-specific protocols. The Bluetooth architecture is divided into different independent layers as is shown in Figure 35-4, and is known as the Protocol Stack.

The following sections briefly discuss the main components of the Bluetooth Protocol Stack.

Bluetooth Radio

The Protocol Stack consists of a Bluetooth radio layer at the bottom. The Bluetooth radio is the wireless device that operates within the 2.4 GHz ISM (Industrial Scientific Medicine) band. The ISM band requires a small antenna. The Bluetooth radio is enabled using a radio transceiver. The Bluetooth radio transmits and receives modulated electronic signals from other Bluetooth devices. The transmitting power of a Bluetooth radio is between one and 100 mW. Therefore, a Bluetooth radio can operate using the power in a battery for many months.

The Bluetooth air interface is based on an antenna power of 0 dBm. To reduce interference and fading, frequency hopping has been incorporated in the Bluetooth technology. Spectrum spreading is also used by frequency hopping in 79 hops displaced by one MHz. This frequency hopping starts at 2.402 GHz and stops at 2.408 GHz. The maximum frequency-hopping rate is 1600 hops/s. However, the bandwidth is reduced in countries such as Japan, France, and Spain. This

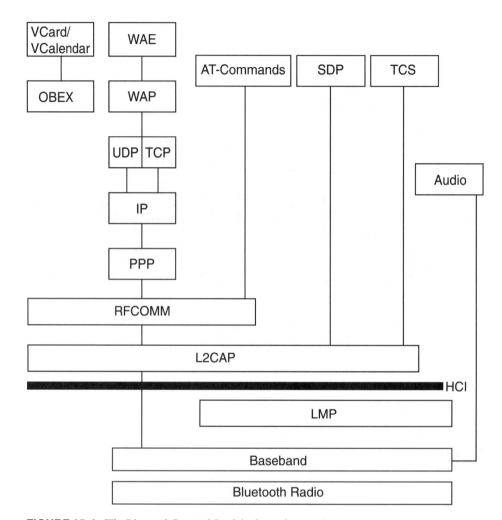

FIGURE 35-4 *The Bluetooth Protocol Stack is shown here.*

is because of local regulations. The normal link range is 10 cm to 10 m. The range can be extended to more than 100 meters by increasing the transmit power.

Depending on the maximum output power of the transmitter, Bluetooth radio devices are classified into the following three classes:

◆ **Power Class 1.** Power Class 1 radios have a maximum output power of 100 mW (20 dBm).

◆ **Power Class 2.** Power Class 2 radios have a maximum output power of 2.5 mW (4 dBm).

◆ **Power Class 3.** Power Class 3 radios have a maximum output power of 1 mW (0 dBm).

The Baseband Layer

The Baseband layer is the most important layer of the Bluetooth Protocol Stack. This layer not only manages the physical channels but also controls links and other services, such as security. The Baseband layer serves as a link controller and manages both ACL (Asynchronous Connectionless) links and SCO (Synchronous Connection-Oriented) links. It supports one asynchronous data link and can support a maximum of three synchronous links for voice.

Synchronous connections ensure timely transmission by reserving time slots. The *master* device can support a maximum of three synchronous connection-oriented links to a single or multiple *slaves*. A slave device, however, can support only two links to different masters. Synchronous connections are typically used for voice transmission.

Asynchronous connectionless links are established as a point-to-multipoint link between the master and all the slaves. Asynchronous connectionless links are typically used for data transmission.

The Link Manager Protocol (LMP)

The Link Manager utilizes the services of the Link Manager Protocol (LMP) to manage security, link set-up, and control. To exchange information, the Link Manager interacts with other Link Managers using LMP.

LMP is a packet-oriented protocol that establishes the link between various Bluetooth radio devices. It is also responsible for power management and the state of a Bluetooth device within a Piconet.

Some of the functions of the Link Manager are listed as follows:

◆ Receives and transmits data

◆ Ensures that a master device establishes connection within specific time slots

◆ Specifies the state of the device within a Piconet

◆ Ensures authentication of master and slave devices

◆ Sets up the connection link between devices

◆ Requests the name of a remote device

◆ Asks for the link address of a remote device

The Host Controller Interface (HCI)

The Host Controller Interface (HCI) provides a uniform method to access the Bluetooth Baseband layer and the hardware capabilities of Bluetooth. HCI offers a command interface to the Baseband layer and the Link Manager. In addition, it enables access to the hardware status and control registers. The host device contains an HCI driver, which acts as an interface between a Bluetooth application and the Bluetooth hardware without any additional implementation details.

The Logical Link Control and Adaptation Protocol (L2CAP)

The Logical Link Control and Adaptation Protocol (L2CAP) layer is a link layer that operates over an asynchronous connectionless link provided by the Baseband layer. The functions of L2CAP include providing both connection-oriented and connectionless data services to the protocols that are present in the upper layers of the Bluetooth Protocol Stack. In addition, L2CAP is responsible for the quality of the service of connection between Bluetooth devices. Sometimes the data packets that need to be transmitted may exceed the MTU (Maximum Transmission Unit). In such cases, L2CAP is responsible for segmenting the data packets before transmitting them. L2CAP also offers protocol multiplexing. This is because multiple protocols, such as SDP and RFCOMM, may operate over L2CAP. I'll discuss these protocols in the following sections.

The RFCOMM Protocol

RFCOMM is a protocol that provides emulation of serial ports. The RFCOMM protocol works above L2CAP. RFCOMM is based on the ETSI standard TS 07.10. This protocol deals with applications that utilize the services of the serial ports of the Bluetooth device.

RFCOMM acts as a transport protocol and can emulate the nine circuits present in RS-232 (EIATIA-232-E) serial ports. The RFCOMM protocol can support a maximum of 60 connections between two Bluetooth devices at a given time.

However, the implementation of Bluetooth within a device defines the number of connections that can be supported in that device.

The RFCOMM protocol supports the following types of devices:

- ◆ **Type 1 Devices.** These are typically communication end points, such as printers and computers.
- ◆ **Type 2 Devices.** These are the devices that are a component of the communication segment, such as modems.

The Service Discovery Protocol (SDP)

The Service Discovery Protocol (SDP), as the name suggests, offers service discovery for the Bluetooth environment. It acts as a means for an application to locate the available services and determine the characteristics of those services. These services can include paging, printing, and sending and receiving faxes. Services can also include information access, such as conferencing and eCommerce facilities. However, SDP does not define the methods that can be used to access available services. In fact, depending on the type of service, there are different ways of accessing it as defined by the Bluetooth technology. SDP can also enable a client to search for a service based on specific criteria.

Security in Bluetooth

As previously discussed, Bluetooth is a wireless solution. In this respect, the need for security and authentication is greater than simply using radio signals. Any Bluetooth device not only needs to have built-in security but should also comply with a system that makes use of security features. Therefore, security in Bluetooth is governed by both authentication and encryption. On one hand, authentication prevents unauthorized access to data. On the other hand, encryption provides a secure transmission, such that the message is delivered in its original form. In addition to these features, the application itself may encrypt the data that is transferred for higher levels of security.

When using the Bluetooth technology, you can define different levels of security for both devices as well as services. Also, different modes of security can be used during connection establishment. The next sections will describe the security levels used for devices and services and security implemented when a connection is established between devices.

Security for Bluetooth Devices

For a Bluetooth device, there are two levels of security. These are as follows:

◆ **Trusted device.** A trusted device can access all services that are available.

◆ **Untrusted device.** An untrusted device does not have a permanent relationship with other devices and has a limited access to services.

Security for Bluetooth Services

For Bluetooth services, three levels of security have been defined. These are as follows:

◆ **Services accessible to all devices.** These services do not require any authentication and the service can be granted openly to all devices without any access approval.

◆ **Services that require only authentication.** These services are granted only after the authentication procedure is completed. However, authorization for these services is not required.

◆ **Services that require both authentication and authorization.** These services are granted automatically to all trusted devices. Other devices need to complete the authentication and authorization procedure.

Security for a Bluetooth Connection

In Bluetooth, three levels of security can be implemented during connection establishment. These levels of security are implemented on the basis of the type of application that is executed. The three levels of security are:

◆ Non-secure

◆ Service-level

◆ Link-level

The following section describes the three levels of security in detail.

The Non-Secure Level

As the name suggests, in the non-secure level, no authentication or encryption is used to transmit data. A non-secure level is also known as *Security Mode 1*. In this mode, a Bluetooth device does not initialize any security procedure. Other devices in the Piconet automatically connect to a device working in this mode.

Service-Level Security

When service-level security is used, the security features are implemented after a connection is established between the Bluetooth devices at the L2CAP layer. This security level is also known as *Security Mode 2*. When working in this mode, it is recommended that a Security Manager be used to limit the access to services and Bluetooth devices. In service-level security, various trust levels can be defined for the availability and accessibility of services and devices.

Link-Level Security

When link-level security is used, the security features are implemented before the connection is established at the LMP layer. This security level is also known as *Security Mode 3*. When working in this mode, the authentication and encryption procedures are enforced at the Baseband level. The link-level security is based on the concept of *link keys*. A link key is a secret 128-bit random number, which is stored individually for each device and is shared by two devices when they communicate with each other.

Implementing Security at the Link-Level

When security is implemented at the link-level, there are four entities that are responsible for setting up and maintaining security. These are as follows:

- ◆ **BD_ADDR.** This is a 48-bit address, which is unique to each Bluetooth device. This address is defined by IEEE (Institute of Electrical and Electronics Engineers). BD_ADDR is a public address and can be obtained from any Bluetooth device automatically using a Bluetooth-protocol enquiry.

- ◆ **Private authentication key.** This is a 128-bit private user key generated using random numbers. This key is used for authentication and is also known as the *link key*.

- ◆ **Private encryption key.** This is an 8- to 128-bit length private user key. This key is used for encryption and is derived from the private authentication key.

- ◆ **RAND.** This is a frequently changing 128-bit random number, which is generated by a Bluetooth device. RAND is regenerated frequently to ensure security during transactions. RAND is generated by using a random or a pseudo-random number generator.

During initialization, before the Bluetooth devices start transferring data, the private authentication and encryption keys are generated. Once the initialization procedure is complete, these keys are not shared among the Bluetooth devices that are trying to establish a connection.

As you may notice, the authentication key is always a 128-bit number. The encryption key, on the other hand may be of a varying length from 8 to 128 bits. This is because different countries have various requirements and regulations. In addition, some scope has been added to allow expansion.

It is important that the key size be determined by the manufacturer. Also, the key should not be generated by the application and software layers. Instead it should be generated by the Bluetooth hardware so that users cannot override the key size.

When implementing security at the link-level, the private authentication key may be regenerated depending on the requirements of the application that is currently running on the Bluetooth device. While the private authentication key is regenerated with every new session, the private encryption key is regenerated only when encryption is enabled.

 NOTE

To ensure that security features are implemented at a higher level, all random numbers that are generated should be non-repeating during the usage of the current authentication key.

Any device can initialize a connection in a Piconet. To implement security for a connection, the mechanism of *key management* is used during the *initialization* procedure. The following section discusses the steps in the initialization procedure.

Key Management During the Initialization Procedure

The initialization procedure consists of the following steps:

1. **Generate Initialization Key.** The first step to initialize and make a connection with other devices is to generate the *initialization* key. This key is generated by using the BD_ADDR value, a random number, and the

PIN code. This PIN (Personal Identification Number) code is entered into both the devices. The PIN code varies from one to 16 octets. Although most applications use the typical four-digit code, some other applications may need longer codes. The PIN code can also be a fixed number that is available with the Bluetooth device.

2. **Generate Authentication Key.** The next step is to generate the authentication key. Each Bluetooth device consists of a *unit* key. This key is only regenerated when the device is switched on and is operational for the first time. This unit key is then used to generate new authentication keys. A device can also use the unit key as a link to connect to other devices in the future. The devices can also derive a *combination* key. At times, a single device may need to send the same information to multiple devices. In such cases, a *master* key is generated that acts as a link key that can be used to connect to all the devices.

3. **Exchange of Authentication Key.** When establishing a connection, the devices exchange the authentication keys. After the authentication keys are exchanged, the initialization key is discarded.

4. **Authentication.** The authentication procedure is done using a challenge-response scheme. In such as scheme, the *challenging* device sends a message that contains a random value. Other devices need to authenticate this message using the current key. In this manner, every device needs to authenticate itself to the other devices to which it is required to make a connection.

5. **Generate Encryption Key.** The final step is to generate the encryption key. This key is generated using the BD_ADDR values, the current authentication keys, and a 128-bit random number. Whenever encryption is required, the encryption key is automatically modified.

Apart from the initialization procedure, there are other steps involved in connection establishment in Bluetooth. The following section discusses the main steps in detail.

Establishing a Connection

The main steps during connection establishment in Bluetooth are as follows:

1. Inquiry

2. Paging

3. Link Establishment

In the following sections, I'll discuss these in detail.

Inquiry

As you already know, all devices, until connected via a Piconet, are in the Standby mode. To establish a connection, these devices discard the Standby mode and move to the *inquiry* mode. In the inquiry mode, the Bluetooth devices initiate an inquiry to gather information about all the access points within the range. After this query is initiated, the device selects from the devices that respond. In addition, the access points available in the range respond with their addresses.

However, it is important to note that a device needs to enter the inquiry mode only if it is unaware of the address of the device that it needs to connect to, or the device needs to communicate with new devices.

 NOTE

During the inquiry mode, the inquiry packet generated by the Bluetooth device is sent either to GIAC (General Inquiry Access Code) or DIAC (Dedicated Inquiry Access Code).

Paging

If a device has previously established connections with other devices, it may not enter the inquiry state and directly enter the *paging* state. To enter into the paging state, a Bluetooth device needs to know only the address of the device that it needs to connect to. During paging, a Bluetooth device synchronizes with the access point. This synchronization is in terms of the *clock* settings and the frequency hopping phase.

Each Bluetooth device has an internal system clock. This clock is responsible for determining the timing of the transceiver unit. The Bluetooth clock is generated from a native clock, which is neither adjusted nor turned off. To synchronize a Bluetooth device with other devices, time offsets are calculated and added to the native clock. This enables the Bluetooth devices to work with clocks that are synchronized with each other and are temporary in nature.

When a Piconet is formed, the information about the master clock is communicated to the slave devices. The required offset is stored by the slave devices to synchronize with the physical link and communicate with that master device.

During paging, the master device utilizes the information about the slave clock and sends a page message. In addition, the master device calculates the Device Access Code (DAC) of the slave device by using the address of that slave device. The page message is sent to the slave device based on the frequency at which the master device calculates that the slave device should be *listening* and be in active mode.

Link Establishment

After the paging procedure is completed, the devices are in the *connected* state. In this state, the link between the devices is established. The LMP layer establishes a link with the access point. The type of link, such as an asynchronous connectionless link or synchronous connection-oriented link will depend on the underlying application.

By using their respective Link Managers, the devices then exchange important information. Even after the link is detached, the device address and device clock information is valid. However, if the link breaks due to other reasons, all the link-related information is reset.

Bluetooth and Other Technologies

In the current market, many standards exist that enable wireless devices to connect to each other. In addition, most of the devices support more than one standard so that the devices are inter-operable with other devices. In the past few years many wireless connection technologies and standards have surfaced. Some of these emerging technologies are Bluetooth, Home RF, SWAP, IrDA, and the IEEE 802.11 standard. Although these technologies offer similar services in some areas, they often complement each other in other areas.

The choice to use which technology depends on the areas of application of each technology. Bluetooth offers a few advantages over other technologies. The following sections compare SWAP and IrDA technologies to Bluetooth.

Bluetooth versus SWAP

SWAP (Shared Wireless Access Protocol) has been developed by Home RF Working Group. SWAP is an industry specification that enables devices, such as cordless telephones, personal computers, and peripherals, to communicate with each other without using any connecting cables.

SWAP technology can be used as an ad hoc network or a managed network controlled by using a connection point. When a SWAP system is used as a peer-to-peer ad hoc network, the network supports only data transfer. All stations act as peers and the control is shared among the stations. When a SWAP system is used as a managed network, a connection point is used to control the system and provide a gateway to a PSTN (Public Switched Telephone Network).

Some of the main features of the SWAP are as follows:

◆ Works in a maximum range of 150 feet with a transmission power of 100 mW.

◆ Utilizes the 2.45 GHz range of an unlicensed ISM band.

◆ Operates using frequency hopping at 50 hops/second.

◆ Allows transfer of interactive voice and high-speed data packets by supporting both TDMA and CSMA/CA service.

◆ Supports a maximum of 120 nodes in the network.

In the current scenario, SWAP has a broader base in comparison to Bluetooth. However, Bluetooth is an emerging technology. On the one hand Bluetooth is used to provide short-range connections between devices, while on the other hand SWAP has been developed to suit the home environment of wireless connectivity.

 NOTE

Home RF Working Group is a subset of ITU (International Telecommunication Union). Home RF is responsible for the development of a standard for inexpensive radio frequency voice and data communication.

Bluetooth versus IrDA

IrDA (Infrared Data Association) is an organization that develops and promotes inexpensive infrared data interconnection standards. These standards support a broad range of communication and computing devices.

IrDA incorporates a set of protocols that cover all data transfer layers. The IrDA DATA protocol is used to deliver data, and the IrDA CONTROL protocol is used to send control information.

Some of the main features of IrDA are as follows:

♦ Provides a point-to-point connection

♦ Allows connection of one meter, which can be extended to a maximum of two meters

♦ Supports bi-directional communication

♦ Offers data transmission at a speed of 9600 bps to 16 Mbps

The choice between Bluetooth and IrDA depends on the application that needs to be implemented. Bluetooth offers omni-directional communication between devices whereas IrDA supports only bi-directional data exchange. Currently, IrDA technology is less expensive than Bluetooth but as the market grows for Bluetooth, the prices for a Bluetooth solution are expected to drop.

The main advantage of Bluetooth with respect to the emerging technologies is that the Bluetooth technology offers connections that consume less power. This enables Bluetooth to be used for a variety of devices at a lower price.

Summary

This chapter gave you an overview of the Bluetooth technology. You learned about the Bluetooth Special Interest Group and Bluetooth features. You also learned about the Bluetooth architecture. Finally, you looked at Bluetooth as compared to other wireless connection technologies and standards.

PART VII

Appendix

Appendix A

Java Messaging
Service (JMS)

JMS

Java Messaging Service (JMS) is a part of the J2EE specification. JMS has been developed by Sun Microsystems. JMS was developed for accessing enterprise-messaging systems. The JMS is used for writing business applications that asynchronously send and receive data. A wide range of enterprise messaging products supports the JMS.

Messaging plays a very important role in enterprise applications. It provides a number of advantages such as scalability and heterogeneity. Messaging also makes an application more modular and reliable. Messaging services use the message server to deliver the messages to the recipients. The main component of the messaging service is the message. Messages contain formatted data. The role of messaging services include:

◆ Delivering messages synchronously or asynchronously

◆ Supporting transactions

◆ Prioritizing messages

The JMS API has all the capabilities of a messaging service. It also minimizes the concepts programmers need to learn to use the messaging service. JMS API specification has the following purposes:

◆ JMS provides a single unified message API

◆ JMS supports messages containing XML pages

◆ JMS supports the development of heterogeneous applications

Messaging systems are classified into the following messaging models:

◆ Publish-Subscribe Messaging

◆ Point-to-Point Messaging

◆ Request-Reply Messaging

Publish-Subscribe Messaging

Publish-Subscribe Messaging is used when many applications need to receive the same message. The central concept in a Publish-Subscribe messaging system is the Topic. In a Publish-Subscribe messaging system, multiple publishers send messages to a Topic, and all the Subscribers to that messaging server receive all the messages sent to that Topic. In a Publish-Subscribe Messaging there may be multiple Senders and multiple Receivers.

The messaging system in a Publish-Subscribe Messaging is diagrammatically depicted in Figure A-1.

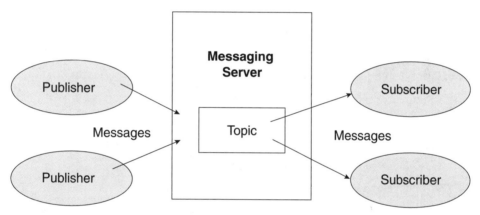

FIGURE A-1 *The figure shows Publish–Subscribe Messaging.*

Point-to-Point Messaging

Point-to-Point Messaging is used when one process needs to send a message to another process. In a Point-to-Point messaging system the client of a messaging system may either send messages and not receive messages, or only receive messages and not send messages, or send and receive messages. Another client can also send and/or receive messages. In Point-to-Point Messaging there may be multiple Senders of messages and a single Receiver for the messages.

The messaging system in Point-to-Point Messaging is diagrammatically depicted in Figure A-2.

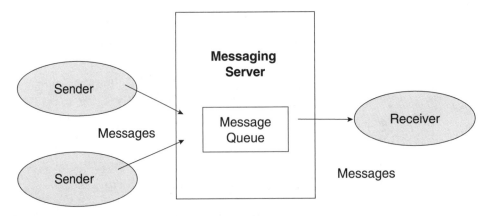

FIGURE A-2 *The figure shows Point-to-Point Messaging.*

Request-Reply Messaging

Request-Reply Messaging can be used when an application sends a message and expects to receive a message back. This messaging model is a subset of one of the other two models discussed in previous sections.

Now I'll discuss the JMS architecture.

The Java Messaging Services (JMS) Architecture

Java Messaging Services implements both Publish-Subscribe Messaging and Point-to-Point messaging systems. However, they are defined by separate interfaces so that a JMS provider does not have to support both. The JMS provider implements JMS for a messaging product. JMS providers are written in Java.

JMS defines Queues and Topics, but it does not require the provider to implement both. JMS thus tries to maximize portability of the solution with as many features as possible. The primary features of JMS are listed as follows:

◆ ConnectionFactories are used in JMS to create connections to a specific JMS provider.

◆ JMS defines the concept of a Topic or a Queue as the target for a Message. Topics are used for Publish-Subscribe Messaging. Queues are used for Point-to-Point Messaging.

◆ The Providers' code is defined by interfaces in JMS, freeing the implementation from the limitations of subclassing.

◆ JMS provides support for distributed transactions.

◆ JMS supports messages containing Java objects.

◆ JMS provides a single, unified message API for creating and working with messages that are independent of the JMS provider.

JMS Interfaces

The JMS messaging systems define the following set of interfaces:

◆ **ConnectionFactory** An administered object used by a client to create a connection

◆ **Connection** An active connection to a JMS provider

◆ **Destination** An administered object that stores the identity of a message destination

◆ **Session** A context for sending and receiving messages

◆ **MessageProducer** An object created by a session that is used for sending messages

◆ **MessageConsumer** An object created by a session that is used for receiving messages sent to a destination

Now I'll discuss the components of a JMS application.

JMS Applications

A JMS application consists of the following parts:

◆ **JMS Clients** Java programs that send and receive messages

◆ **Non-JMS Clients** Use a message system native client API instead of JMS

◆ **Messages** Used to communicate information between the clients

◆ **JMS Provider** A messaging system that implements JMS

◆ **Administered Objects** JMS objects created by an administrator for use by a client. JMS administered objects are of two types:

    ◆ **ConnectionFactory** is an object used by the client to create a connection

    ◆ **Destination** is an object a client uses to specify the destination of messages being sent and the source of message received

Creating a JMS Application

Mainly, a JMS application is made up of JMS clients that exchange messages. However, the JMS application might also involve non-JMS clients. A JMS client executes the following JMS setup steps:

◆ Uses JNDI to locate a `ConnectionFactory` object

◆ Uses JNDI to locate the destination objects

◆ Creates a JMS Connection using the `ConnectionFactory` administered object

◆ Uses the `Connection` administered object to create a JMS session

◆ Uses the `Session` and `Destination` interfaces to create the `MessageProducers` and `MessageConsumers` needed

◆ Notifies the connection to deliver the messages

JMS Messages

JMS messages consist of headers, properties, and body. All messages support a set of header fields. Header fields contain values, which are used by clients and providers to send and receive messages. Some of the JMS message headers are listed as follows:

◆ **JMSDestination** Stores the message destination

◆ **JMSDeliveryMode** Stores the message delivery mode

◆ **JMSMessageID** Stores the value that identifies the message

◆ **JMSTimeStamp** Stores the time the message was handed to a provider to be sent

◆ **JMSCorrelationID** Used by the client to link one message with another

◆ **JMSReplyTo** Stores the message destination

◆ **JMSPriority** Stores the priority of the message

Message properties allow a client to have a JMS provider select messages using criteria specified by the application. Properties have properties names and values. Property names must follow the rules for a message selector identifier. Property values can be boolean, short, byte, int, long, float, String, and double. Properties values are set before sending a message.

JMS provides the following types of message body:

- ◆ **StreamMessage** Contains a stream of Java primitive values
- ◆ **MapMessage** Contains a set of name-value pairs. Names are strings and values are Java primitive types
- ◆ **TextMessage** Contains `java.lang.String`
- ◆ **ObjectMessage** Contains a Serializable Java object
- ◆ **BytesMessage** Contains a stream of uninterrupted bytes

JMS and J2EE

JMS is an integral part of the J2EE platform. The JMS API in the J2EE 1.3 platform has the following features:

- ◆ A message-driven bean, to enable the asynchronous consumption of messages
- ◆ The Message can participate in Java Transaction API (JTA) transactions

The JMS API improves the functionality of the J2EE platform by simplifying enterprise development. The J2EE platform's Enterprise JavaBeansTM (EJBTM) container architecture enhances the JMS API by allowing for the concurrent consumption of messages. It also provides support for distributed transactions.

JMS Security

JMS does not specify APIs for maintaining the security of messages being sent or received. This is handled solely by the JMS provider. The JMS provider is configured by the administrator and not by the JMS clients.

Index

A

GAME DEVELOPMENT.
IT'S SERIOUS BUSINESS.

"Game programming is without a doubt the most intellectually challenging field of Computer Science in the world. However, we would be fooling ourselves if we said that we are 'serious' people! Writing (and reading) a game programming book should be an exciting adventure for both the author and the reader."

—André LaMothe.
Series Editor